PRANCING NOVELIST

BY THE SAME AUTHOR

Novels

Hackenfeller's Ape
The King of a Rainy Country
Flesh
The Finishing Touch
The Snow Ball
In Transit

Drama

The Burglar

Non-Fiction

Black Ship to Hell
Mozart the Dramatist
Don't Never Forget
Black and White, a Portrait of Aubrey Beardsley

Fifty Works of English Literature We Could Do Without
(in collaboration with Michael Levey and Charles Osborne)

PRANCING NOVELIST

A DEFENCE OF FICTION
IN THE FORM OF A
CRITICAL BIOGRAPHY
IN PRAISE OF
RONALD FIRBANK

BY

BRIGID BROPHY

MACMILLAN

© Brigid Brophy 1973

All rights reserved. No part of this publication
may be produced or transmitted, in any form or
by any means, without permission.

SBN 333 13779 5

First published 1973 by
MACMILLAN LONDON LIMITED
London and Basingstoke
Associated companies in New York
Dublin Melbourne Johannesburg and Madras

Printed in Great Britain by
WESTERN PRINTING SERVICES LTD
Bristol

TO
ROBERT COOK

Contents

LIST OF ILLUSTRATIONS

ix

AUTHOR'S NOTE

x

OUTLINE CHRONOLOGY

xi

PREFACE

xiii

PART ONE

Chapters I to V

IN PRAISE OF FICTION

1

PART TWO

Chapters VI to X

IN PURSUIT OF FIRBANK

89

PART THREE

Chapters XI to XV

FIRBANK IN PURSUIT

239

CONTENTS

PART FOUR
Chapters XVI to XX
IN PRAISE OF FIRBANK'S FICTION
391

APPENDIX
Text of Firbank's Preface to *The Flower Beneath the Foot*
569

LIST OF BOOKS CITED
571

INDEX
579

List of Illustrations

Between pages 112 and 113

1. Joseph Firbank's railway lines (from a map in F. McDermott's *The Life and Work of Joseph Firbank*, 1887)
2. Ronald Firbank, circa 1917 (photograph by Bertram Park, hitherto unpublished)
3. Ronald Firbank, Madrid 1905 (photograph by Kaulak; © Thomas Firbank 1962)
4. Ronald Firbank in Egypt (© Thomas Firbank 1962)
5. Ronald Firbank, undated photograph by Lavender of Bromley (© Thomas Firbank 1962)
6. Heather and Ronald Firbank, undated photograph (© Thomas Firbank 1962)

Between pages 272 and 273

7 and 8. Ronald Firbank's rooms in Trinity Hall (© Thomas Firbank 1962)
9. Page from a Firbank notebook (from the notebook in the Henry W. and Albert A. Berg collection, the New York Public Library)
10. Mrs Patrick Campbell and Sarah Bernhardt in *Pelléas et Mélisande* in 1904 (Radio Times Hulton Picture Library)
11. Ronald Firbank, Chamonix, 1904 (from a photograph in the possession of Professor Miriam J. Benkovitz)
12. C. R. W. Nevinson's illustration to *The Flower Beneath the Foot* (1923)
13. The villa in Arcachon (Gironde) where Firbank spent the autumn of 1925 (photographed in 1971)

Author's Note

I AM deeply grateful to Miss Thesa Firbank to whose kindness and courtesy I owe Plate 2 in this volume.

I am also especially grateful to Colonel Thomas Firbank and to Gerald Duckworth Ltd, publishers of *The Complete Ronald Firbank* (1961), for generously allowing me to quote without a fee from copyright material, and to reproduce plates which appeared in *The New Rythum and Other Pieces* (1962).

Professor Miriam J. Benkovitz kindly made available the portrait of Ronald Firbank at Chamonix reproduced as Plate 11.

I thank Mrs Constance Kyrle Fletcher for information I have used in Chapter VI; Sir William Walton for information I publish in Chapters VI and VIII; Mr C. J. White for facts which I publish in Chapter IX, 5; Miss E. A. Shutter for information I record in Chapter IX, 4; the Rev. T. P. O'Beirne for material I use in Chapter X, 5; and Monsieur M. Menard for material I use in Chapter X, 10.

Mr Eric W. White and Mr Michael Levey kindly gave me books. Dame Edith Evans, Mr J. Redfern and Mr Cecil Gould kindly replied to my queries, though their replies were, through no fault of theirs, negative.

I am grateful to Miss Patricia Highsmith for help in getting a catalogue; and to Miss Kay Dick and to Mr Alan Bates for the loan of books.

Miss Maureen Duffy, Mr Robert Cook and Mr Michael Levey discovered things for me and made me the gift of their support and suggestions.

Outline Chronology

JOSEPH FIRBANK (1819–86)
had seven children, including
(JOSEPH) THOMAS FIRBANK (1850–1910)
who, in 1883, married
HARRIETTE JANE (or vice versa – see Chapter VII, 4) GARRETT
(1851–1924)

Their children were:
(1) JOSEPH SYDNEY (1884–1904)
(2) (ARTHUR ANNESLEY) RONALD (Chapter VII, 4)
(1886–1926)
(3) HUBERT SOMERSET (1887–1913), who had a son, THOMAS JOSEPH
(4) HEATHER (1888–1951)

1886 birth of (A. A.) R. F. (17 January)
death (June) of (grandfather) Joseph Firbank
settlement at The Coopers

1895 trials of Oscar Wilde
Thomas Firbank elected (Unionist) M.P.

1900 R. F. at Uppingham

1902 Thomas Firbank knighted

1902–3 or 1903–4 (see Chapter X, 3): R. F. in France

1904 (A. A.) R. F.'s *La Princesse aux Soleils* published in *Les Essais*
death of R. F.'s elder brother

1905 R. F. in Spain
(A. A.) R. F.'s first volume 'published'[1] (*Odette D'Antrevernes*

[1] (Chapter V, 4.) During his life, Firbank's books were published in the legal but (with one and a half exceptions) not in the idiomatic sense of the word.

	A Fairy Tale for Weary People plus *A Study in Temperament*)
1906	R. F. went up to Trinity Hall, Cambridge
1907	(A. A.) R. F.'s *An Early Flemish Painter* published in *The Academy* move from The Coopers (November – see Chapter XII, 3) Vyvyan Holland's 21st birthday R. F. received (by Hugh Benson) into Catholic church
1907–8	(probably) composition of *Lady Appledore's Mésalliance* (published together with *The New Rythum*, 1962)
1909	Moët et Chandon dinner R. F. came down from Cambridge
1910	death of Sir Thomas Firbank *The Artificial Princess* (published 1934) written at least in part
1913	death of R. F.'s younger brother
1915	(15 April – see Chapter VI, 6) *Vainglory* 'published'
1916	*Inclinations* 'published' revised *Odette* 'published'
1917	*Caprice* 'published'
1919	*Valmouth* 'published'
1920	*The Princess Zoubaroff* 'published'
1921	*Santal* 'published'
1923	*The Flower Beneath the Foot* 'published'
1924	(25 March) death of Lady Firbank (March) publication (U.S.) of *Prancing Nigger* (published in Great Britain in November 1924 as *Sorrow in Sunlight*)
1926	(21 May) death (in Rome) of R. F. (29 June) 'publication' of *Concerning the Eccentricities of Cardinal Pirelli*
1930	publication of *Ronald Firbank: A Memoir*, by Ifan Kyrle Fletcher
1934	*The Artificial Princess* published
1951	death of Heather Firbank
1962	*The New Rythum and Other Pieces* published

Preface

THIS is a defence of prose fiction.

It is a *defence* because fiction has been much attacked during much of its history (which is a longer one than many people know) and, in the last 30 or so years, has often been left for dead.

But I am no more 'on the defensive' than Sidney and Shelley were when they wrote their respective defences of poetry (verse fiction). I am claiming not merely that fiction is not-guilty-as-charged but that good fiction is positively and absolutely good.

Arraigned on a capital charge, Socrates put forward the defence not only that he was not-guilty and not only that it would be unjust to cause his death but that, if his fellow-citizens truly wanted to execute justice, they would subsidise his life by voting him pension-rights to free dinners.

His fellow-citizens were not convinced, and humanity has condemned them ever since.

Fiction is frequently tried today on a charge of being already dead – which in the case of an artistic form, as distinct from a person, luckily need mean no more than a temporary interruption. All the same, a literary form needs persons to practise it, and persons need dinners. The most reasonable and practical defence that can be put forward for fiction is to demand justice: in the shape of dinners for its practitioners. If fiction is (temporarily) dead, that is because it has been starved.

The entity so often pronounced dead, something called 'the novel', has no more actual existence than the 2·6 children of the average family. Not every highly individual work of fiction is good fiction; but all good fiction is highly individual. A defence of fiction as a genre can become a positive defence only if it insists how good a good individual work or œuvre can be.

I might have chosen to interleave my generic defence of fiction with an assertion of the individual goodness of Firbank's works of fiction simply because I think Firbank a very good writer. But in fact his connexion with my general theme is more organic.

Fiction seems to me the victim of a prejudice or, more probably, an inhibition (whose causes and manifestations I discuss in Part One of this book). The inhibition has produced false rationalisations and distorted perspectives, including the habit of mistaking the trappings (naturalism) of one particular type of novels (Victorian ones) for the essence of the whole genre.

Firbank, to my mind, is the novelist who freed fiction from naturalism or, to be exact, freed it again in the 20th century. After the death of the naturalistic convention, a convention which had been only an incidental anyway, it was Firbank who saw how fiction could slough off the corpse and proceed, alive and well from the artistic point of view (though its health implies a sharp social appetite for dinners) and also in resumed continuity with such quite non-naturalistic yet traditionally respectable and 'serious' novels as *Don Quixote*.

Consequently it seemed to me that Firbank's was the individual œuvre which I could set, like a solo voice, against the chorus of my general drift, in such a way that each commented on, illustrated and set off the other.

Firbank saw straight, when contemporaries of his, even talented ones, were circling in a fog, thanks to two items in the individual nature of his talent. He had a passion (a critical, connoisseur's passion) for painting; and painting had already lived through a crisis about the death of naturalism; in painting naturalism had been brutally killed by the invention of photography. Firbank was also a militant (defensive in the positive sense) homosexual, which set him free to make rational aesthetic decisions at a time when the arts were still suffering the trauma of the Wilde trials and when heterosexuals and apologetic homosexuals treated the whole subject of aesthetics as taboo.

These considerations created a simple and logical form for my book to inhabit.

Part One, *In Praise of Fiction*, is the opening chorus, which the solo voice penetrates only by way of illustration, as a classic case: it is an anatomy of fiction and an attempt to diagnose the inhibition which obscures fiction's civil rights.

In Part Two, *In Pursuit of Firbank*, the soloist leads and the chorus comments: it is a sketch of Firbank's creative personality.

Part Three, *Firbank in Pursuit*, goes on from the specific inhibition against fiction that was discussed in Part One to the reinforcement of that inhibition by the trauma of 1895. The condemnation of Oscar Wilde by an unjust law damaged people's concept of artistic goodness as deeply as the unjust condemnation of Socrates wounded 'the good' in its moral meaning. So Part

Three considers the effects of the Wilde trials first on literature (and on Firbank's reputation) and then on Firbank. The effect in the second instance was to send him off in slightly ambivalent pursuit of Wilde, a pilgrimage which is the pattern beneath some hitherto inexplicable items in Firbank's history.

Thus Part One is an analysis of fiction; and Parts Two and Three are an analysis of an individual fiction-creating mind and its relation to the figure it adopted as a literary father. Part Four tries to put all this material together: for soloist and chorus. It defends fiction by insisting on the height of one of fiction's individual high peaks. An anatomy of the œuvre Firbank created out of the individuality of his talent plus lessons and counter-lessons he taught himself from Wilde, it is *In Praise of Firbank's Fiction*.

Sidney and Shelley couched their defences of poetry in prose. But I dare say they convinced more people by their poems. On the publication of my most recent novel, *In Transit* (which is as a matter of fact a metaphor of the impulse to fiction), a critic in the United States, Mr Robert Phelps, generously pronounced it 'the best argument I know for claiming that the novel is alive and well in London, S.W.5.' Despite Mr Phelps's generosity, there are few signs of universal conversion by that argument. And I suppose that if you are convinced fiction is dead you won't hear any arguments to the contrary that are put in fiction. So I have (apart from any unintended fictions I've committed by way of errors in fact or logic) written this defence of fiction in the medium of non-fiction – and in the hope of persuading benevolent readers that Firbank's fiction is alive and good.

BRIGID BROPHY
London S.W.5

PART ONE

IN PRAISE OF FICTION

'I will not adopt that ungenerous and impolitic custom so common with novel writers, of degrading by their contemptuous censure the very performances, to the number of which they are themselves adding [. . .] Let us not desert one another; we are an injured body [. . .] our foes are almost as many as our readers [. . .] there seems almost a general wish of decrying the capacity and undervaluing the labour of the novelist, and of slighting the performances which have only genius, wit, and taste to recommend them [. . .] "Oh! it is only a novel!" [. . .] or, in short, only some work in which the greatest powers of the mind are displayed, in which the most thorough knowledge of human nature, the happiest delineation of its varieties, the liveliest effusions of wit and humour are conveyed to the world in the best chosen language.'

Northanger Abbey, I, 5

Contents

OF PART ONE

In Praise of Fiction

Chapter I 'ONLY A NOVEL!'	5
1 Enter Selfconsciousness . . .	5
2 . . . in the Company of Psychology	6
3 Exeunt Readers?	9
4 A Fact about Daydreams	13
5 Confusion about Fiction	16
6 Notes	18
Chapter II 'MOMENTARY SHAME'	19
1 The Furtiveness of Saint Teresa	19
2 The Destruction of a Library	22
3 Cervantes and the Label on the Sauce Bottle	24
4 The Wishful Obituary	26
5 Tricks and Pretexts	28
6 Notes	34
Chapter III 'THE GREATEST POWERS OF THE MIND' ON DISPLAY	36
1 Shakespeare Misapplied and Defied	36
2 A Moral Tale	39
3 Miniature and Minor	40
4 Creation and Analysis	42
5 . . . and Psychoanalysis	45
6 Realism Is Greater than Naturalism	46

7	But It Still Isn't a Social Information Service	48
8	Notes	50

Chapter IV 'A GENERAL WISH OF DECRYING' — 52
1	Freud and the Hero	52
2	Freud Psychoanalysed	60
3	A Further Fact about Daydreams	63
4	Notes	65

Chapter V 'GENIUS, WIT, AND TASTE' — 66
1	Fiction Re-Read	66
2	Firbank and the Isolation of the Image	67
3	Firbank and Psychology	70
4	A Message from Firbank's Career for Socialists	71
5	How Firbank?	76
6	Aesthete and Artist	81
7	Notes	83

I

'Only a Novel!'

1. Enter Selfconsciousness . . .

FIRBANK was not one of the novelists who believe they would be more valuable to mankind (or, simply, more intellectual) if only they could be philosophers, politicians or prophets instead.

Many novelists are of that opinion, and they have included good ones. A fundamental disbelief in the importance of novels need not handicap a novelist too heavily so long as novels wear a naturalistic cloak and canter through extensive plots.

If he is to devise quantities of plot, a novelist must produce quantities of fantasy. His simplest method of doing so is the child's and the daydreamer's: to project himself into the rôles of philosopher, politician and prophet, which attract him by what seems their glamour. In fact the glamour is not theirs. The novelist himself invests them with it, through his belief that they are more important than the rôle which he himself is, by writing, performing in real life.

So long as the daydream mechanism works as unselfconsciously as it does in childhood, the novelist can profitably remain ignorant of how creative, and hence how important, he really is.

Childish daydreams are play. The child truly is unimportant and ineffectual in comparison with the captains and kings he impersonates. But a novel, though it is psychologically evolved from play and continues to resemble it, isn't. Its substance comes out of the writer's life-hours, not his leisure-hours. Even as an economic proposition it would be leisure few writers could afford. Someone, usually the writer himself, has to invest (often without recompense, let alone profit) in his food and shelter while he writes (and thinks). But, in any case, anyone seeking play would pick an activity less painful or less long or both than writing a novel, which, though an exceptionally interesting, is also an exceptionally hard type of hard work, and one that leaves the personality debilitated rather than recruited. Writing novels is creation, not recreation. And the novel which emerges, imagined, formed, analysed, incarnated and achieved, has become a created fact. Its creating is an action, its creator a man of action on a par with the captains and kings or with (the captains and kings of the child's world) the parents whose fantasies or wishes, put into action, resulted in the creation of a real-life child.

A novel is a something in the real world whether or not it is a naturalistic novel. But the naturalistic convention consists of pretending that the novel is a nothing, that it isn't there. Putting the childish mechanism to adult use, the naturalistic novelist pretends to prolong also the insignificance of the child. By the naturalistic convention, the events of the plot succeed one another in the reader's experience as if they were events in real life or in a dream (which, while one is dreaming it, passes for real life) or in a film (which you watch from a darkness that makes you virtually *unable* to see any events except those on the screen). The naturalistic novelist crouches low over his literary film projector, re-assuming the child's inferiority and literal smallness in comparison with the heroes of the daydream, and directing attention away from his own existence and, usually, the existence of the projecting mechanism.

A Victorian novelist might from time to time admit that the mechanism was there – by addressing himself to Gentle Reader. But that only played up the verisimilitude of the events projected. The author admitted to being their purveyor in order to conceal that he was their inventor.

In the 20th century, however, and probably not without relation to the literal invention of film, the lights were switched on and the illusion collapsed.

Selfconsciousness crept upon both novelists and readers. Naturalism died, as any artistic convention must when that happens, because both sides found themselves unable any longer to believe in it. It became the mark of 20th-centuryness in fiction that the rôle of the work or of the author or of both is now a constituent of the work itself.

2. . . . in the Company of Psychology

THE selfconsciousness which impeded naturalism and precipitated 20th-century fiction came into the 20th century along with psychology or, more properly, its adumbrations.

Psychology certainly existed in 1900, which is the date on the title-page of the original edition in German of *The Interpretation of Dreams*. But few people knew it did. That original edition consisted of 600 copies and took eight years to sell out.

However, though so few knew of the thing itself, every literate person expectantly knew the concept, which, together with the name *psychology*, was well established socially and academically. Indeed, seldom has a revolutionary discovery been so extensively bowed into the room: or so spat on when it arrived.

For the time being, the concept of psychology could be bodied out only with already known facts assembled (the novelty was the assembly) from medicine, philosophy, logic and curiosa. But the name was early linked with fiction. In 1832 Benjamin Disraeli published (anonymously) his *Contarini Fleming, A Psychological Romance*. By the end of the century the linkage had achieved a vogue. 'What', Oscar Wilde made Sir Robert Chiltern ask in 1895, 'would those modern psychological novelists, of whom we hear so much, say to such a theory as that?'

Wilde himself did the utmost service to 20th-century fiction – but not through his narrative fictions, which were unmodern, unpsychological and on the whole, at least when they ran to length and elaboration, rather bad. His genius was primarily for axiom and epigram (that is, intellectual analysis) and presently for drama (analysis caught in the operation, a dramatised situation being one whose relationships are analysed by action).

By virtue of his passion for analysis, Wilde in fact anticipated *psychoanalysis*. He condenses the theory of narcissism into a remark and a gesture of Lord Goring's. 'To love oneself is the beginning of a lifelong love affair,' Lord Goring declares – and, before his next line, is stage-directed to look in a mirror. Freud's account of the resolution or non-resolution of the Oedipus Complex by identification with one of the parents was condensed by Wilde into the exchange between Jack Worthing and Algernon Moncrieff in which Algernon formulates: 'All women become like their mothers. That is their tragedy. No man does. That's his.'

Wilde knew the importance of this information, which he probably reached by autobiographical intuition, thanks to his own huge admiration for his remarkable mother. He considered the statement important enough to make Algernon repeat it from an earlier play of Wilde's. (Curiously, both plays have *importance* in their titles.)

At the same time Wilde knew it was information subject, when it appears in the conscious mind of society, to repression. 'Is that clever?' Jack asks about Algernon's formulation. 'It is perfectly phrased!' Algernon replies. 'And quite as true as any observation in civilised life should be.'

Fat himself, Wilde even understood what doctors have only recently noticed, that over-eating may be a signal of misery. Charged by Jack Worthing with heartlessness for eating muffins during an emotional crisis, Algernon replies (in long clauses that mimic onomatopoetically his stuffed, munching mouth) 'When I am in trouble, eating is the only thing that consoles me. Indeed, when I am in really great trouble, as anyone who knows me intimately will tell you, I refuse everything except food and drink.'

Wilde's psychological axioms did not, however, constitute an accessible psychology. The information was implicit, not explicit. Like his perception of the nature of Shakespeare's sonnets (which, though it cannot solve the historical 'problem of the sonnets', is nevertheless a more acute psychological insight than anyone else has produced and which is probably another insight through autobiography, the result of Wilde's likewise being a bisexual dramatist-poet), the psychological statements are attributed by Wilde to fictitious characters – which relieves the world of the obligation to examine their standing as non-fiction truths.

(Wilde himself, however, recognised that they *were* truths. He wrote, retrospectively, from prison: 'I summed up all systems in a phrase, and all existence in an epigram.')

Besides, Wilde's statements are witty; and that prevented people from noticing their truth, even though it is their truth that *makes* them witty. The obscuration was lucky for Wilde personally. (Or perhaps, even, to put his perceptions into fictitious mouths and cast them wittily was an act on Wilde's part, his sole one, of self-preservation.) It is impossible to guess what England, unmodern and unpsychological to its depths, would have said to such a theory as *that* – or what it would have done to Wilde had it realised he was telling it about psychoanalysis as well as about aesthetics, non-authoritarian socialism and the moral harmlessness of homosexuality.

So the content of psychology remained inexplicit or unknown. There was, however, a habit of deliberately thinking about mental actions or, at the least, a fashion for thinking about thinking about them. And that was enough to nudge writers and readers into remarking the childishness of the mental mechanisms through which naturalistic novels were projected and apprehended, even when the novels were themselves works of adult art.

Both sides in the transaction were suddenly embarrassed to notice they were doing something remarkably like sharing a daydream.

The embarrassment this perception gave to novelists can be witnessed in the shiftings of narrative responsibility, the inventions of a narration within the narration and of a narrator-I within the narrator-I, the elaboration of a frame inside the frame to the point of almost blocking out the picture, in the fictions of Joseph Conrad. Robert Louis Stevenson was a potentially great novelist whose greatness could never quite out because he could not discover an alternative convention to naturalism. As a novelist Stevenson died of novelists' embarrassment.

3. Exeunt Readers?

AS for the embarrassment of novel-*readers*, it may have manifested itself in a simple withdrawal of mass readership from novels that are good – as though, having once noticed the childishness of the mechanism, the readers bargained that for the content they would insist on out-and-out childishness, openly tripey wish-fulfilment, and would keep their seriousness for other matters than fiction.

In that case, George Eliot (who died in 1880) was very likely the last writer in history to become rich by writing great novels.

However, the hypothesis may be wrong. It may, indeed, express a hidden wish to slander novels even through the back-handed compliment of implying they have become too intellectually classy to earn their keep in a pop world.

Even the mundane arithmetic of their keep is not easy to compute. Whether a good writer becomes rich in his lifetime may depend on how long his lifetime lasts. Good writers have become rich young, but more have had to starve or be subsidised while giving the world time to get used to their originality. Calculations are not simple even in departments of literature other than fiction. Had Bernard Shaw died at 40, he would have died poor. Had Keats lived to Shaw's last age, he might have been as rich an old man as Shaw.

And in the fiction department itself there have certainly been novelists more recent than George Eliot whose estates have become rich posthumously. Some of them may be great. Not all of them died young.

(Even so: when a writer's estate grows rich, does one account that a mass readership or a minority readership that's had time to be cumulative?)

All the same it is probably true that no good novelist now commands a contemporary readership which, either in numbers or in fidelity, matches the readership of Dickens or George Eliot – and this despite an increased population and a higher rate of literacy in it. But the reason is not necessarily that present-day audiences are embarrassed either by fiction or by goodness in fiction. The mass allegiance of 19th-century fiction-readers was given to tripehounds as well as geniuses. And the Victorian taste for fiction of any kind may imply only that there were few alternatives.

Comparing present-day with Victorian readership is futile, because no one can tell how much of the mid-19th-century readership really liked reading at all. Victorians may have taken fiction as a drug, the best or the only one to be cheaply and respectably available. It would then make small difference to the addict, who might not even notice, whether the narrative was good or bad, provided it *was* narrative and was naturalistic to the point of literary illusionism. Perhaps the greatness of Thackeray, Dickens and George Eliot is a bonus, and the basic social purpose of Victorian narrative was simply to fill in the longueurs of middle-class life and assuage by daydreams the fatigue and the confinement of the life imposed on proletarians.

So it is plausible, though not provable, that there has been no change in the percentage of people who truly like fiction. Those who would all along have preferred bingo or television deserted to it as soon as it became available. The constant core maintained a taste for fiction, though not to the total exclusion of the alternatives; and the existence of the alternatives set going a comparing train of thought which made changes in what likers of fiction demanded or would accept from fiction.

The change is clearest in the people whose liking for novels *is* a drug-addiction and for whom novels are simply their preferred drug. (They are often the same people as those with a serious interest in the art of fiction, but in a different mood.) The arrival of cinema and its subaltern, television, with their even more vivid and more excluding-everything-else illusionism, caused fiction addicts to demand a stronger dosage from what remained their favourite form of the narrative drug. Where Victorian drug-narrative cantered, the 20th-century narrative that performs the same function must gallop through the plot and even fly over its fences. Indeed, the content must be almost all plot, and plot must be convoluted into the form of a maze. The stepping-up of the dosage has, in short, perfected the thriller: a drug which is in fact a purge since, by repeatedly identifying and eliminating the character who is guilty, it repeatedly assures everyone else, including its constant readers, of their innocence.

Then what about the other fiction-readers, the serious ones (or the thriller-readers in their serious mood)? At least they are, especially when they *are* the same people as the thriller-readers, in a position to distinguish between the drug-content and the art in fiction. Victorian readers, for want of alternatives and hence of a standard of comparison, weren't able to. (Many 20th-century critics and academics, especially those who are thriller-*writers*, still aren't.) It's an advance towards, at the least, clarifying a problem in aesthetics. And the situation may in fact be more advanced still.

The 20th-century narrative drug is so strong that it slugs its readers into near-unconsciousness – or certainly into complete unselfconsciousness and something like unconsciousness of all external events except those pell-melling through the story. Perhaps now that the demand for unself-consciousness is so heavily satisfied, the other reading mood will turn towards fictions that expect the reader to retain and exercise more self-consciousness than he could while his head was immersed in a naturalistic narrative.

One mood demanded that fiction catch up with the newly invented alternatives and learn to administer hypnotics or narcotics as well as the cinema can. The other mood, lifting its nose from the magnetic page and becoming thereby capable of selfconsciousness, may use the advantage to look further and make comparisons. It may ask for fiction that does something which, precisely, cinema cannot do. It may even look *all* round and pursue comparisons with more distant arts still, and that might result in its accepting fiction which does not only what cinema cannot but what music *has* been able to do for centuries.

I don't claim readers are shouting for novels that, as well as being written in the temporal 20th century and employing 20th-century props as furniture, will be designed by a 20th-century technique in accordance with a 20th-century aesthetic.

Still less am I implying that such novels would automatically be good. Up-to-dateness is a virtue in itself only in old-fashioned (which is not a vice in itself) capitalist communities like the United States, where it is a virtue necessary to enriching manufacturers and advertisers by persuading the populace to discard this year's goods and buy next year's, which are more up-to-date. To rational consideration, the old-fashioned article remains the better if it *is* better. The artists of the 20th century are, however, 20th-century people. There exist rare artists whose talent is for anachronism. But, for most artists, to use a mode from the past means only to mimic some past artist, which is no more laudable than to mimic a contemporary. The talent for doing that comes close to window-dressing, to a flair for fashion. The talent for antique mimicry comes close to faking, and can quickly lead the artist into emotional faking. It becomes a disguise for the fact that his own emotions aren't concerned in the work.

If, however, readers are not yet demanding these fully creative novels from 20th-century novelists, they may at least be preparing to accept them if the novelists insist. (And novelists with a vocation can't help insisting on writing them though they may, like Firbank, have no notion of how to press their insistence on the public.) It's not a hopeless dream that one day soon there might exist a small troupe of readers as aesthetically literate as the people who listen to music at concerts and on the radio. I would not even be surprised out of my skin if, one day this year or next, the first novelist in English to create a 20th-century aesthetic, idiom and technique (namely Ronald Firbank, wit, ironist and great artist) turned into a pop cult.

A pop cult is an advance on a cult. And by that token, that future year, whichever it turns out to be, will be an advance on 1922.

By 1922 Firbank had been irrecoverably personally hurt by non-notice from critics and public (on whose behalf he had made a larger financial investment in his books than most authors could afford – or than many of them would make even if they could). Besides the hurt, he probably suffered surprise. Osbert Sitwell, one of Firbank's acquaintance who was not in all instances sensitive to Firbank's sensibilities, was probably right in thinking Firbank had been 'simple enough' to expect the popular success of 'Miss Ethel M. Dell or some such book as *Beau Tarzan*' (the latter, I hope it is by now becoming necessary to explain, a fancy title satirically run up by Sitwell out of two of the most widely used drug narratives of the period).

In 1922 Firbank heard by letter across the Atlantic that literary persons in the United States knew nothing of him and that a literary visitor from England had never heard of him either. The visitor was J. C. Squire (Sir John Collings Squire), poet, but more effectively than poet editor, and more effectively even than editor critic; most effectively of all, literary figure: doyen (the dusty word is the word just for him) of the English middlebrow literary establishment. Unlike Firbank's, Squire's reputation was established on both sides of the Atlantic. It was at a dinner given for him by those posh United-States publishers the Knopfs that Squire delivered his declaration of never having heard of Firbank.

Out of his woundedness Firbank replied with a desperate and defiant explanation, a good part of which was fantasy, of why he had never been heard of. His letter said it was because his novels were 'a cult'.

The word (he chose one that was attractive to him perhaps as a Catholic and certainly as an imagist temperament) has damned him. It has been wielded ever since with the implication that his books were private jokes which he didn't *want* enjoyed beyond a clique.

(As a matter of incidental fact, there *was* no Firbank clique. He was incapable of social adherences. I have described Osbert Sitwell as an acquaintance rather than as a friend of Firbank's because Firbank had no friends.)

Of course, the public was just as culpably ignorant as the critic Squire. True, the public expected its Squires to pass information on to it and draw its attention to any great artists that might appear in the world. But then the public was a fool in the first place to let a J. C. Squire appoint himself to such a responsible job and then rely on him to perform it. If pop culture is to be culture as well as pop, it must take care not to be officered by J. C. Squires. But then with luck it will be too egalitarian (each of its citizens will be too responsible to permit it) to be officered at all.

4. A Fact about Daydreams

Why were novelists (and perhaps readers) embarrassed to notice that naturalistic novels resemble shared daydreams?

The answer is a simple fact about daydreams. As soon as its content or its mere existence becomes known outside the head that is doing the daydreaming, a daydream is a source of shame.

As Freud wrote, 'The adult [. . .] is ashamed of his day-dreams and conceals them from other people; [. . .] as a rule he would rather confess all his misdeeds than tell his day-dreams. For this reason he may believe that he is the only person who makes up such phantasies.'

What *makes* daydreaming shameful is probably, in general, its childishness (to do it as an adult confesses to yourself, at the same time as compensating you for the fact, that you are still childishly ineffectual in your relations with the outside world, that you remain smaller than your hero-image of yourself) and, in particular, the associations of its technique. Even daydreams of glory use the same technique as masturbation fantasies (which imply the most shaming of all confessions: either one is *sexually* ineffectual in relation to the outside world and can't attract a partner or one uncharitably and unsociably prefers oneself to anyone else).

Perhaps, therefore, the shame of the daydream is sexual shame, and the entire daydream mechanism has taken the tinge of sexual shame from its use in masturbation. The daydreams of glory which are the only or seemingly the earliest daydreams that some adults permit themselves to remember are probably not so asexual in tone as memory supposes. In any case, the glorious daydreams of childhood are probably worked-over descendants of truly infantile daydreams, in which aggression (the basic material of glory) is probably not much differentiated from the kinetic sensations of an imperfectly visualised sexual breaking and entering. When the infantile fantasy is re-cast as a childish daydream, censorship and ignorance alike oblige the sexual to express itself through the forms of the glorious. A child can furnish his daydreams only with the furniture which he has been permitted to know and which he, schooled already by society into self-censorship, permits himself to know that he knows. And to this day society in its dealings with the child is quite free with the information that the captains and kings *became* captains and kings through the kings' ancestors' killing lots of people and the captains' doing so in person, whereas society is still very chary and scary about imparting to the child the information that his parents became his parents through a sexual act.

My surmise that shame seeped into the whole daydream apparatus from its sexual compartment, which is probably in any case the oldest compartment and the nucleus from which the whole developed, is perhaps corroborated by the behaviour of present society, which does its most active stamping on the relation between daydreams and fiction when the fiction is sexual. Pornography is simply a masturbation fantasy written down, though the commercial pornographer may have pushed his fantasy into corners it wouldn't spontaneously have bothered with, because he wants to cater for all kinds of readers. Individuals may conversationally condemn other sorts of novels as romantic, saccharine or even violent daydreams, and some states censor novels by a political criterion (usually one that betrays ignorance of the relation of fiction to fact), but society has universally mounted a campaign of suppression only against the novels which are pornographic.

States which pride themselves on freedom of political speech legislate against 'obscenity'; totalitarian states, of Left and Right, suppress *both* politically 'subversive' *and* 'obscene' books.

It is probably true that no book has ever been prosecuted in either type of society on the grounds that it corrupted its readers into bad taste, misuse of language or debasement of metaphor. The only literary 'badness' society holds in enough awe to recognise formally concerns politics or sex. And individuals take their turn of thought from the laws. It is unlikely that any citizen has ever made public complaint of being offended by a display of sentimental religious posters, or by a shop window soliciting him to buy postcards depicting goblins under bluebells.

Morally, as libertarians have insisted for decades, society has no more business to interfere with supposed corruption by pornography than it has to interfere with corruption by the tweeness of goblins. Corruption of either kind can attack nobody except the reader, if indeed him, and he is a volunteer. His voluntary corruption or non-corruption is his own responsibility, like his life or suicide.

The libertarians' argument is for the moral *neutrality*, from society's point of view, of pornography. Its point has never been taken by authoritarians whose own internal, self-repressive impulses demand to be acted-out externally, through imposing restrictions on other people's freedom, and who seek to make sexual prohibitions absolute and unquestionable in their own minds by the superstitious, indeed magical, method of enforcing a single, narrow set of rules on the whole diversity of the citizens. The authoritarians' pretext of acting for the public good and for the protection of the citizens is always collapsed by the selectiveness of their behaviour. Their strictness and their paternal concern for their supposedly so vulnerable fellow citizens operates in one area alone. They have no difficulty in accepting the moral neutrality of goblins.

Moral neutrality remains neutral no matter in what quantities it exists. The reactionary movement in Europe and the United States, which in 1970–1 began to pick up some force of law and government but manifests itself chiefly, and quite powerfully, in groups of private vigilantes, demonstrates that it never understood the neutrality argument in the first place by now maintaining that society's neutrality (or 'permissiveness') towards material that is itself neutral has gone 'too far'.

The unspoken meaning of this pronouncement is that an argument which is totally correct can be improved by mixing into it a little incorrectness. It is the application of reason to sexual morals which is held to have gone 'too far', and the reactionary prescription is to mix back into the mores a few anti-reasonable prohibitions whose force rests on the magical style of thinking, according to which a sexual impulse will vanish provided no public mention of it is allowed to be made.

Having failed to understand both themselves and the neutrality argument, the reactionaries can make even less of the argument which goes beyond establishing the neutrality of pornography into suggesting that society stands positively to benefit from a supply of pornography, in a way it probably doesn't from the supply of books about goblins. (In the few states where it has dared to advance from half freedom into complete freedom for pornography, society can shew this positive benefit in action, but the reactionaries in the half-free countries have no difficulty in ignoring the facts which support the positive argument along with the argument itself.)

Freud's second observation about daydreams, that their privacy is so strict that many people don't know that other people have them too, can be transferred to written-down masturbation daydreams, where its importance is even larger because the privacy is even stricter and even more shamefast. Published pornography is the great public informant of the fact that other people have masturbation fantasies too. Society stands to benefit: in general because its citizens are better educated about the human species and better informed about one another; and, in practical particular, by a decrease in the number of its citizens liable to become an expense to it by being driven either mad or to aggress criminally against each other under the stress of their solitary-nightmarish dread that they may be singular and anti-social monsters.

5. Confusion about Fiction

IN an (at least elementarily) educated society, everyone can write (literal sense). This has bred a very common belief that everyone can write (literary sense) or, to be exact, that anyone could write, if he would spare the time from more important activities.

This simple confusion has done an extreme disservice to literature. It has obscured from common knowledge the fact there is such a thing as the technique of writing. And since everyone is taught in childhood not only the literal act of writing but the writing of compositions and exam answers, whereas not everyone is taught musical notation or the perfectly teachable craft of representational drawing, even those few people who know that literary technique exists seldom realise that it is a technique every bit as technical as draughtsmanship or counterpoint.

That disability lies on all literature alike. Fiction has to bear an extra derogatory confusion of its own, which comes to it from the simple fact that daydreaming is shameful.

(Lyric poetry shares a little of the reproach made against fiction – or, rather, lyric poets do, being often called 'dreamy' in a slanderous sense. But poetry is redeemed in the opinion even [or especially] of people who never read it. Poetry is accepted as a more 'spiritual' performance than fictions written in prose.)

Freud undertook his exploration of the similarity between daydreaming and literature in the hope of finding some activity 'in ourselves, or in people like ourselves' which, by being akin to literary activity, would yield 'some insight into the creative powers of imaginative writers'. Freud, however, was exceptionally sensitive, long before he began his investigation, to the creative powers of imaginative artists. His has not been the way most of society has regarded the matter.

When a person reads a novel for the first time, the projection of a sequence of events, which don't claim to be real, as if they were real doesn't strike him as a new experience. To outward appearances the novel is merely doing in print something he himself has been able to do in his head since infancy. (A novel? A child could do it.) He may even suppose, since people keep quiet about their daydreaming and therefore don't know other people do the same, that he himself invented the idea in infancy.

His ready recognition of the narrative idea allows the novice reader to adopt the novel's narrative and enjoy it as if it were one of his own daydreams. But he won't, in the circumstances, be much inclined to credit the novelist or novels in general with creating a new form. And, most detrimentally to the good repute of fiction, the shame which is attached to his enjoyment of his daydreams becomes attached to his enjoyment of the novel.

This confusion obscured and still obscures the creativeness and imaginativeness of fictional literature just as the other confusion (about the two senses of 'writing') obscures the technicalness of literature at large.

The shame of enjoying literature is of old, but not venerable, standing. It made it as socially awkward to be caught reading a novel as to be caught daydreaming or, if one reads through to the elements, masturbating.

The shame (under that word) and the social furtiveness of being surprised reading a novel were dramatised, 174 years ago, in a novel. ' "And what are you reading, Miss ——?" "Oh! it is only a novel!" replies the young lady; while she lays down her book with affected indifference, or momentary shame.'

Jane Austen glozes her figmentary young lady's 'only a novel' (only a daydream, a thing I've been able to make up for myself all my life) with her magnificently baroque pile-up of irony whose climax begins 'or, in short, only some work in which the greatest powers of the mind are displayed'.

There is a counterpart in Jane Austen's private life. Invited, by a Mrs Martin, to join a subscription library, Jane Austen reported (by letter): 'As an inducement to subscribe Mrs. Martin tells us that her Collection is not to consist only of Novels, but of every kind of Literature, &c. &c. – She might have spared this pretension to *our* family, who are great Novel-readers & not ashamed of being so; but it was necessary I suppose to the self-consequence of half her Subscribers.'

Admitting to daydreams is *the* destroyer of self-consequence.

The letter and the passage in the novel both belong to the period of Jane Austen's life when she was working out her own non-naturalistic mode of fiction. This she did by the operation of creating a novel (*Northanger Abbey*); and the creating consisted of destroying, by satire, the gothick romances whose more than illusionistic, whose almost hallucinatory daydream or day-nightmare narratives had obviously (to judge from her betrayingly deep knowledge of them) served her as extensions of her own young fantasy-life.

When she vindicates novels in (as well as by) a novel, Jane Austen's anger at the social injustice done to novels bursts clean through the naturalistic convention, which is in her case never more than a veneer and often only sleight of hand. She was now technically master enough of the convention to play tricks with it, teasing her readers into selfconsciousness of what they are about as they read the novel, without forfeiting their confidence. Unashamed in private life of being a great 'Novel-reader', she is in *Northanger Abbey* a great enough novel-writer to be publicly unashamed of being also that. She admits, she boasts, while the novel is still going on, that it *is* a novel and that there *is* a novelist – one prepared to speak, as 'I', in defence of novels. Through her irony, which is as cutting but also as sensitive as a rapier, she confesses, she indeed claims, that she is the inventor of her characters and ordains their behaviour: 'Alas! if the heroine of one novel be not patronized by the heroine of another, from whom can she expect protection and regard?'

6. Notes to Chapter I

I call 1900 'the date on the title-page' of *The Interpretation of Dreams* because the book was published in November 1899 but 'its title-page was post-dated into the new century' (Freud: *Collected Papers*, Volume V, XXVII). The details I cite of the publication are given in Ernest Jones's *Life* of Freud (Penguin abridgement, p. 306).

The implicit psychologies and the unpsychological psychologies that preceded psychoanalysis are discussed in my *Black Ship to Hell*, III, 14–16 and IV, 2–5.

Sir Robert Chiltern's question is in Act I of *An Ideal Husband* (1895) and Lord Goring's exposé of narcissism in Act III. Algernon elucidates Oedipus in Act I of *The Importance of Being Earnest* (1895). His formulation is repeated from Act III of *A Woman of No Importance* (1893), where the four sentences of Algernon's formulation are split between two speakers. Algernon diagnoses over-eating in Act II of *The Importance*. . . . Wilde's fictionalised truths about Shakespeare's sonnets are in *The Portrait of Mr W. H.* (*Blackwood's Magazine*, July 1889). Wilde's confession that he summed up all existence in an epigram is in *De Profundis* (Epistola: In Carcere et Vinculis), p. 466 in Rupert Hart-Davis's edition of the Wilde *Letters*.

That thrillers have the psychological purpose of acquitting their readers of blood guilt I have argued in an essay on the thriller's ancestor, the detective story, collected in my volume *Don't Never Forget*.

The Osbert Sitwell quotation is from his contribution to Ifan Kyrle Fletcher's Firbank *Memoir*, p. 140. The J. C. Squire incident is related, with quotations from Firbank's transatlantic correspondence (which was with Carl Van Vechten), in Miriam J. Benkovitz's Firbank *Biography*, pp. 217–18.

Freud's observations on daydreams are from his paper 'The Relation of the Poet to Day-Dreaming', whose title Greekly uses *poet* to include *novelist*. (Freud: *Collected Papers*, Volume IV, IX.)

Jane Austen's passage on novels is in *Northanger Abbey*, Part (originally Volume) I, Chapter V. The letter quoted is to Cassandra Austen, from Steventon, 18 December 1798. *Northanger Abbey* was written, according to Cassandra Austen's 'memorandum', in 1798 and 1799. It was published, posthumously, in 1818.

II

'Momentary Shame'

1. The Furtiveness of Saint Teresa

FICTION is still attended by irrational shame. The world has not yet taken the message either of Jane Austen's anger on the subject or of the greatness of her own fiction. To this day a public librarian from time to time emulates her private Mrs Martin by telling the public that its taste is getting better and offering, as grounds for the judgment, that in some libraries fewer citizens are borrowing novels and more are taking out 'serious' books.

The notion that 'serious' and 'fictitious' are opposites was endorsed in 1971 by a famous British publisher who, on the sale of a London bookshop of which he had been one of the owners, told the press: 'Serious bookselling isn't easy in the British Isles and we concentrated on poetry, politics and non-fiction.'

The shame had attached itself to fiction long before Jane Austen protested against it. The furtiveness with which Jane Austen's young lady lays down the novel she is reading was already known to Saint Teresa of Ávila (1515–1577 or 1582).

By the time she wrote her autobiography, Saint Teresa had concurred in the world's (including the church's) condemnation of the taste for novels of chivalry which she records acquiring in childhood from her mother and concealing from her father. 'We', she writes (in the sense of 'we children') 'were always making time for reading, and she let us [. . .] This habit of ours so annoyed my father that we had to take care he never saw us with our books. But I began to become addicted to this reading, and this little fault, which I had observed in my mother, began [. . .] to lead me astray [. . .] It did not seem wicked to me to waste many hours of the day and the night on this vain occupation, even though I had to keep it secret from my father; and I was so enthralled by it that I do not believe I was ever happy if I had not a new book.'

(Saint Teresa is there making the classic declaration of the literary temperament.)

For Saint Teresa the wickedness was that the occupation was vain: like daydreaming, it wouldn't get you the fulfilment of your desires (which meant, in Saint Teresa's case, to heaven) in reality. In less literate circles the reproach was sometimes interpreted as the open accusation that fiction was lies.

The accusation was unjust, of course. Authors of fictions (unlike the anonymous, lost-in-the-past and perhaps collective authors of myths) didn't seek to pass their work off as accounts of events that had truly happened. Language itself, however, made it hard for novelists to make their disclaimer quite clear, because it for a long time denied them a distinctive name for their type of writings.

The term *novel* is comparatively recent (which has deceived some incautious literary historians into thinking the phenomenon itself more recent than it is). The novelty of a novel lies, of course, in its being original to its author. The word is, in fact, the author's boast that his story is *not* historically true: the story is novel inasmuch as its existence began with him.

This plain meaning of the word (which is doubly plain when you bear in mind that the reason why the word was needed was in order to differentiate novels from stories that did profess to be true) is not, however, plain to everyone. A recent academic critic has swallowed (and so have his reviewers after him) the notion that the word *novel* is asserting a claim that that *form* of narrative is new.

The implausibility of that interpretation is disclosed by the extreme historical improbability that any informed person would, at the relevant times, have swallowed a claim so preposterous.

Novel, as a name for a 'fictitious prose narrative of considerable length', is dated, by the *Shorter Oxford English Dictionary*, to 1643. The word became usual in the 18th century. In 1713 William Congreve's *Incognita* not only was but was said on its title-page to be a novel. (The *Shorter Oxford English Dictionary* gives 1757 for the generic use of the word and 1728 for *novelist* in its modern sense.)

It is, of course, possible that ignorant or thoughtless people during the 18th century misunderstood the word, just as ignorant, thoughtless or prejudiced critics do in the 20th. The prejudice of many of the 20th-century critics shews when, having maintained that a novel is claiming by its name to be novel in form, they go on to remark that the form has now lost its novelty. But as a matter of fact the form was far from novel when the name came into use. No informed person in the 18th century (or, for the matter of that, in 1643) could have supposed novelists so stupid as to assert a blatantly false claim to novelty on behalf of a narrative form that had been practised not merely by Madame de La Fayette in 1678, Cervantes in 1604,

Thomas Nashe in 1594 and François Rabelais in 1532–64 but actually in ancient Latin by Apuleius and very extensively in ancient Greek.

The Loeb edition of that charmer of an ancient Greek novel, *Daphnis and Chloe*, contains an 'Appendix on the Greek novel' which demonstrates both how widely the genre was practised in Greek and how widely many of its examples were known in English translation to the Elizabethans.

And the text of *Daphnis and Chloe* itself demonstrates that when Longus wrote it (which was probably in the second or third century A.D.) he lacked nothing in the way of a sophisticated literary tradition of novel-writing to write it in. All that was missing was a special name for novels and novelists. Classical scholars, who can read the Greek novels, have no hesitation in recognising them as novels. But scholars of English literature seem able to persuade themselves that novels can't have existed before they had a special name.

It has, indeed, become a vulgar learned error to hold that novels began in the 18th century. In 1961 Susan Sontag compared 'the fifty years of cinema' to 'the more than two hundred year history of the novel', a genre of which she called Samuel Richardson the pioneer. It is an estimate which in fact chops two hundred years at least off the history of novels in modern civilisation, as well as implying that *Don Quixote* and *La Princesse de Clèves* do not exist.

Until the special name came into use, while a novel often called itself, for want of a differentiating word, a *history*, it was not easy for novelists to dodge the spoken or unspoken accusation that their histories, unlike those by historians, were simply lies. The alternative name, *romance*, which the Romance languages still have to use (in the form of *roman* or *romanzo*) for what modern English calls a novel, came to suggest romancing – that is, lying. (And in modern English *romance* has been debased into meaning exclusively a type of novel which is quite openly like a wish-fulfilment daydream – and which is indeed a sort of lie, since its purpose is to falsify external reality without being true to its author's imagination.)

Even when the term *fiction* came into general adoption in English, it was still a word cognate with *figment* and *feign*; and in fact the word was merely diverted into specialised literary use from general use in which it had meant a lie.

On one memorable occasion (but it was a fictitious occasion), fiction escaped the reproach of being, in contrast to factual history, all deception and triviality – and escaped by dodging behind the ambiguous name it was obliged to use before it was accorded a name proper to itself. 'Once, when Mr. Crawley asked what the young people were reading, the governess replied "Smollett". "Oh, Smollett," said Mr. Crawley, quite satisfied. "His history is more dull, but by no means so dangerous as that of Mr. Hume. It is history you are reading?" "Yes", said Miss Rose; without, however, adding that it was the history of Mr. Humphrey Clinker.' (*Vanity Fair*, Chapter 10).

Very occasionally the same charge of deception has been brought against the visual arts. To extreme literal minds, the painting or tapestry on the wall is a lie because it states that a forest exists where in reality only lath and plaster are or that Mars loves Venus when there are no such beings as pagan deities.

Until the 19th century, painting could parry the reproach by an argument which in fact imported grievous confusion into its own aesthetics but served for the time being to fob off the unimaginative. This was the argument that painting copies the real world and therefore gives information about it. Mars and Venus might not exist, but male and female anatomy did and that was what the painter was said to be copying. That he called his figures Mars and Venus could be claimed as informative because it illustrated classical literature, which was too antiquely respectable to be accused of lying; and in any case the small output of pagan pictures was swallowed into acceptability by the enormous output of pictures depicting persons and events set in the past which it was actually obligatory to believe were historically true, namely Christian ones.

The argument whereby painting escaped both religious and worldly reproach was, however, of no use to fiction. Where literature was concerned, it could always be counter-argued that for information or religious edification one should read history or devotional books, not novels. For some time the best that fiction could put forward on its own behalf was that it gave non-fiction information in more assimilable, because more entertaining, form. This was the defence that, for a very typical example, the Abbé Jean Terrasson prefaced to his historical-didactic novel *The Life of Sethos* in 1731. Two decades later, Henry Fielding wrote another version of the same defence into the Exordium to his novel *Amelia*: novels (still going under the name 'histories') are valued as 'models of HUMAN LIFE'; by reading them we shall be 'instructed' in the art of life. It is a defence which comes deplorably near answering 'A novel? A child could do it' with 'It is *for* children.'

2. The Destruction of a Library

THE vindication of novels in theory remains muddled, but practice achieved it long ago. One of its most notable achievements came a generation after

Saint Teresa reproached herself for fiction-addiction, and its site was again Spain. Spain may have been the inevitable battleground of the first phase of the campaign against fiction, since it can be claimed that it was in Spain that both chivalric fiction and Christianity had bitten deepest. It needed only a touch of misunderstanding of the novelists' disclaimer of foisting their creations on the public as historical truths for Christianity to make war on fiction in the belief that fiction was setting up as a rival to Christianity: a rival hallucinatory system, a rival story which claimed to be true but in which it was nevertheless necessary to have faith (which it isn't in events you are simply and on rational grounds convinced are true).

The accusation that fiction is lies was given a psychological elaboration. The accusation now read that too much reading of fictions made one unable to distinguish fiction from fact. The accusation was made, however, in a fiction – and a great one: the great one in which Cervantes shews Don Quixote driven mad (in the classic sense of confusing fantasy with real life) by sharing into adulthood Saint Teresa's childhood passion for romances of chivalry. Cervantes dramatises the old Spanish custom of censorship by having a priest go through Don Quixote's library picking out the volumes which (for Don Quixote's own good and protection, as censorship invariably claims) his housekeeper is to burn.

Don Quixote's reading is, of course, Cervantes's own. Cervantes betrays himself as Jane Austen does: by knowing too much about it. And Cervantes is indeed engaged in a very Jane-Austen-ish enterprise. As she with the gothick, so he with the chivalric romances.

Like Jane Austen, Cervantes is an intensely *literary* writer. All the material of *Don Quixote* comes out of books. Cervantes reduces the images of chivalry to smithereens, battering them with satire. His satire is, of course, self-satire. It is his own mental library he is putting to the fire. He is destroying his own immersion in the chivalric daydream.

And, like Jane Austen again, Cervantes accomplishes destruction in the course of construction. The novel Cervantes assembles out of the smithereens keeps its head well above the level of immersion-in-a-daydream. It obliges its reader to stand back from it by the same distance that the author has, by satire, put between himself and his hero. Cervantes forces the reader to hold off, and he does it by just such sophisticated literary devices for shuffling the narrative perspective as Jane Austen uses when she admits, during *Northanger Abbey*, to being the creator of *Northanger Abbey*. Cervantes causes his invented characters in *Don Quixote* to mention other works by Cervantes; in one instance the character attributes the work to Cervantes under his real name. In Part II he has another of his inventions refer to the (true at the time he wrote Part II) fact that Part I is already in print; and presently he causes a whole group of his inventions, including Don Quixote himself, to provide by their conversation in Part II a literary critique of *Don Quixote*, Part I.

3. Cervantes and the Label on the Sauce Bottle

IN real life (where not merely very young but quite stupid children shew themselves infallibly capable of distinguishing fantasy from fact), fiction-addiction does not drive people mad. It is more likely, if talent is there too, to turn them into novelists like Cervantes, capable of creating mad, fiction-addicted knights.

Indeed, in real life, the habit of reading fiction is a great sharpener of the faculty for keeping fact and fantasy distinct. If anything is likely to weaken that faculty, it will be (especially if literary talent is there, which will then be denied its proper nourishment) giving up reading fiction.

And that is what in effect happened to Saint Teresa. When she put away novels as vain things, Saint Teresa turned her back on her evident vocation to be a great novelist in favour of the vocation, which was at one time repugnant to her, of nun. Great literary vocations are, however, indestructible so long as the personality in which they are incarnated remains alive. Saint Teresa *is* a great novelist: but in a work of supposed non-fiction, her autobiography. Having no alternative but to express the force of imagination in her, she was obliged to do it at the cost of her ability to tell fact from fiction. As Bernini shewed he (whether consciously or unconsciously) recognised, in his great sculpture of her in an ecstasy indistinguishable from orgasm, her saintly experiences were erotic fantasies or, more exactly, erotic poems of overwhelming power. But, since she would not admit them to be literary images, Saint Teresa had to let herself believe they were the images of a literal visitation; and thereby she succumbed, from the opposite cause, to Don Quixote's madness of hallucination.

Saint Teresa's personality is in strange suspension. It did express itself in art, yet it was, in its capacity as artist's personality, frustrated, because it would not admit its self-expression to *be* art. Its strange state has uniquely attracted other great artists to give it the expression it denied itself. Saint Teresa is incarnated not only in her own masterpiece but in two masterpieces by others: Bernini's sculpture, which is in the literal sense an illustration of Saint Teresa's own writings; and *Middlemarch*, where George Eliot fashioned Dorothea out of the notion that 'Many Theresas have been born who found for themselves no epic life.'

Saint Teresa stands patron saint to artists rationalist (like George Eliot) and Catholic – including an artist highly influential on Firbank (namely Aubrey Beardsley) and Firbank himself.

After an episode of illness in 1923 Firbank wrote in a letter that he was 'already gadding about again à la Sainte Thérèse'.[1] In a letter of 1924 he said that to have a single publisher was 'better than gadding, as Saint Teresa did'.[2]

Firbank lent his own devotion to Saint Teresa to Cardinal Pirelli. The saint appears to the drunken Cardinal, who, addressing her as 'Mother', implores her (in a reference necessarily as much literary as pious) to shew him the way of perfection. The Cardinal sees her at his summer retreat, the monastery of the Desierto, where she 'had composed a part of the *Way of Perfection*'; and now she haunts the garden in the rôle not of saint but of writer – in, indeed, the most bereft state that can befall writers in their literary capacity, for she is 'seeking, it was supposed, a lost sheet of the manuscript of her *Way of Perfection*'.[3]

Great novelists and 'great novel-readers' (the ones who did not desert as soon as alternative drugs came on the market) almost invariably begin as addicted readers, though not systematic or even long-remembering ones. They read whether the reading-matter presented to their eyes is good or bad (which is why I suspect that the people who take fiction seriously are the same people as the drug-takers in a different mood) or merely neutral. The

---

[1] Firbank often (but, as the next quotation from him in my text demonstrates, not always) used the French form of the name. I suspect that to be because, certainly in the Nineties and perhaps right on into the Twenties, Saint Teresa's works were known in England chiefly in French translation. In 1898 Aubrey Beardsley wrote (*Letters*, 1971 edition, p. 438) to his sister 'Hachette or Dulau will easily get the Teresa for you.' And although he speaks of 'Teresa' he goes on to specify 'S. Térèse [. . .] *Vie de S. T écrite par elle-même*', etc. The firm of Dulau plays by coincidence a tiny part in the bibliographical history of Firbank. When Ifan Kyrle Fletcher (on p. 24 of his 1930 *Memoir* of Firbank) mentioned two of Firbank's then totally unpublished early works, *The Mauve Tower* and *True Love* (extracts from both of which are in *The New Rythum and Other Pieces*, 1962), he added a footnote recording his indebtedness 'to Messrs Dulau, of Old Bond Street, for permission to examine the typescripts'.

[2] This remark is a re-casting of one which, in *Vainglory* (1915), is thrown during a literary slanging-match between the writers Miss Valley and Miss Hospice. Its *Vainglory* form is borrowed from another of Firbank's devotions (one which Chapter VII, 3 will document): to butterflies. Miss Hospice, who is evidently published by a firm resembling a monopolistic John Murray, tells Miss Valley: 'My publisher, at any rate, could be found [. . .] I've had the same man always. Byron had him. And Coleridge had him. And Keats. I should be really ashamed to flutter from *firm to firm* like some of those things one sees. . . .' (*Complete* Firbank, p. 167).

[3] In 1916, when Firbank was correcting proofs of *Odette* at Torquay, 'the wind bore off with them seawards' (according to a quotation from a Firbank letter on p. 216 of Miriam J. Benkovitz's *Biography*).

temperament which families, who use it to recognise and tag the literary child among them, describe as 'He'd read the label on the sauce bottle,' existed long before sauce bottles. Cervantes (thereby implicitly confessing the identity between his own and Don Quixote's addiction) described it in himself, in propria persona: 'I have a taste for reading even torn papers lying in the streets.'

4. The Wishful Obituary

NOWADAYS the streets offer mass-scale alternatives to the reading of torn papers as a time-and-consciousness filler. Compulsive reading of torn papers is therefore left to people of compulsive literary temperament.

That doesn't, however, diminish their shame about the habit. Indeed, they now feel the extra reproach, if they apply the irrational criterion by which it *is* a reproach, of being a little old-fashioned in their tastes.

Out of this intensified shame there has been marshalled phase two of the campaign against fiction.

The early accusation that fiction was lies was made chiefly, though not solely, by non-intellectuals (who were unfamiliar with the convention and simply didn't understand that fiction wasn't pretending to be true) or by intellectuals like Saint Teresa turned anti-intellectual on religious grounds. But phase two of the campaign is waged, characteristically, by intellectuals.

In this second phase, the traditional, Victorian shame of the intellectual in a philistine world has come to concentrate on the literary strand in intellectuality. While the British Empire believed its greatest need was to produce athletic, energetic and not too thoughtful District Officers and subalterns, it developed a public school system whose effect on children of an intellectual bent was to convince them of their inferiority. The quintessential literary result of the system is Rudyard Kipling – who, when he fictionalised his own schooling, could justify his literary talent to himself only by using it to exalt the quintessential subaltern, Stalky, and could admit himself as novelist to his novel only under the name of the lowest, scuttlingest form of insect life, as the inky (which means given to writing, which means dirty, which again evokes the masturbation-shame of fantasy) Beetle.

Subalterns of a sort are still a national requirement in the British non-empire, and even more in the United-States neo-empire, but the service required of them is to keep their country (or bring dependent countries) up-to-date in temporal 'progress' rather than push its frontiers wider still and wider in geography. Their power, to some extent restricted in its exercise over 'the natives' and 'the men', can no longer afford to consist solely of brute force and the unthinking conventions of class and race. So the subalterns may and sometimes must be intellectual, provided their intellectuality asserts a tough imperial competence over material where it can be seen to be competent. Intellectuality is no longer shameful, provided it turns towards science (which is so admirably intellectually tough in its dealings with facts and so immorally, thoughtlessly and traditionally [to the point of superstition] callous in many scientists' dealings with the animals the facts are tested on) or towards technology, which is the up-to-date name for applied science, which is science at the intellectually junior-officer level.

But let intellectuality turn itself towards the technique of literature or, worse still, of fictional literature, and the shame is redoubled. For if you single out the fictioneering strand in intellectuality, you are singling out the element closest to daydreams.

True, a scientific hypothesis is also a daydream, in that it spins statements that are not – or are not yet known to be – true. But it is a daydream specialised: in both its making and its final destiny. In its making, the hypothesis adopts its furniture from a single problem or a small group of problems in the outside world. When it is made, it is tested against the outside world and, if it fails to tally, is discarded. Fiction and daydreams pick their material more eclectically; and when they are complete they decline to submit to, they refuse to recognise the jurisdiction of, any test against the outside world. Yet, far from being discarded, they claim to be valuable. The daydream is valuable only to the spinner, who affectionately guards its privacy. But fiction claims to be valuable to the public, whom it brashly invites to buy it.

Evidently it was fiction's connexion with daydreams that provoked the intensity of the first, the 'fiction-is-lies' assault. The same rationalised pretexts existed or could have been twisted for bringing the same accusation against painting. Yet in that case it wasn't, with anything like equal or equally sustained force, brought.

And behind the connexion of novels with daydreams it is possible to discern the ultimate provocation, the connexion of daydreams with masturbation. (Our fury on this point may be an attempt to deny our psychological evolution. It might be that we owe some of the distinguishing elasticity of our species's imagination, both our scientific and artistic imagination, to the sexual pleasure that first drew us into the habit of spinning fantasies.)

The disparagement of fiction was expressed, especially during the 19th century, in minor rules of behaviour: that one shouldn't read fiction in the morning or on Sunday; or perhaps at all, if one was a child. These rules seem to me to belong to a wide group of rules and adages, enforced particularly on children, that includes the prohibition against thumb-sucking (illustrated, in 1847, by the terrifying tale which through symbolism warned children that the penalty for disobeying the rule was castration) and the eerie axiom that Satan finds work for idle hands.

These rules are all insisted on with disproportionate emotional energy. The prohibition is unreasonable even when it is rationalised. It remains an absolute, authoritarian prohibition and won't agree to the compromise it would be bound to allow if the rationalisation were the true reason. I suspect, therefore, that the prohibitions take their extra energy from being, originally, prohibitions against masturbation. Thumb-sucking is oral masturbation; daydreaming is mental masturbation; where idle hands might stray is obvious. The prohibition can't compromise with the person, usually the child, it's being addressed to because it is only distantly concerned with him. The child who was its original recipient is the prohibitor himself.

This represents a considerable repressive force lying in ambush for fiction. I imagine it is this repressive force which creates what Frank Kermode has called 'the puritanism of modern thinking about novels'. This particular puritanism is indeed modern: because, though the ambush had been prepared all along, it did not receive its rationalisation and pretext until technology (the respectable branch of intellectuality) devised alternatives to fiction as a mass-drug.

Phase two, which thereupon began, takes the lethal wishes so long directed against fiction for the lethal deed and pronounces fiction dead.

5. Tricks and Pretexts

THE pronouncement 'The Novel is dead' has never, within my own lifetime as a literary observer, been out of fashion; and it has had, within the same span, three conspicuous vogues.

In 1945–6 it was widely considered so obvious as to be a truism that fiction could not cope with the horrors lately disclosed by the war. That supposition again reflected the discovery of the seeming childishness of the technique of naturalistic narrative; it confused breadth with depth (a non-fiction statistical account can state the extent of the horrors of war, but can't incarnate the depth of horror in one of, let alone all, its statistical items); and it again made the incorrect assumption that all fiction is naturalistic fiction. Fiction was being asked to mirror the results of humanity's destructive instinct, and was inevitably found wanting. But it should have been asked to embody humanity's creative instinct.

In 1965–6 it became fashionable to think that novels had suddenly been made obsolete by a form popularly called 'the non-fiction novel'. That form is a perfectly respectable and useful supplementary department of fiction. It permits writers who possess narrative skill but small invention to exercise their skill – to the benefit of readers, who thereby get better-written and better-constructed accounts of real-life events than they usually do from journalists pasting together a book. Only, however, a very strong wish that fiction *should* be superseded could frame the notion that 'the non-fiction novel', instead of merely supplementing fiction, was positively, in 1964, ousting fiction. For to suppose that entailed re-writing literary history, since it entailed believing that that 'the non-fiction novel' was new in 1964; and *that* entailed forgetting that Daniel Defoe published a non-fiction novel (*A Journal of the Plague Year*) in 1722.

In practice, the vogue neither of 1945–6 nor of 1964–5 for saying it was dead managed to make fiction dead. Accordingly, a third vogue was summoned up, in 1970, in which *publishers* pronounced fiction dead: of financial starvation. Publishers were even better placed than critics to *make* their announcement come true. More than one of them announced they were no longer going to publish fiction. Their decision, besides in its own right killing some fiction, necessarily reduces the competition between publishers to secure works of fiction, with the result that even those publishers who continue to publish novels believe they need not now invest so much money and attention in them; with smaller investment, there will be smaller returns; and within a few years it may become feasible for publishers genuinely to kill fiction as a business.

Already by 1971 the proportion of fiction paperback titles to the totality of paperback titles had been reduced to 17 per cent.[1] And at least one large multiple retailer had decided (or, which in its effects amounts to the same, was believed by publishers to have decided) to stock only a given (and tiny) number of hardback fiction titles a year. That decision will in turn cause publishers to cut down yet further the number of novels they publish. It will, moreover, incline them to publish only those mediocre and middlebrow novelists who at present have an established market among middle-aged and middle-class readers. Younger readers will not be colonised for fiction of any kind; and good or explorative fiction will not be acquiring new readers of any age: with the result that, when the present middlebrow readership has died off, publishers and retailers will have arranged for fiction to have extinguished itself.

However, publishing as a capitalist business has always been run to the disadvantage of authors and of literature. The publisher takes a quick return

---

[1] (*Evening Standard* of 1 February 1971.) It is still, of course, possible (and even probable) that, in the number of *copies* sold, fiction out-sells non-fiction.

and a quick profit while a newly published book is new. At six weeks' old, the book, though still capable of yielding profit, is yielding it more slowly. The publisher withdraws his attention and invests it in a new book – by another author, since the author of the previous book won't yet have a new one ready. As commercial articles, books are grossly under-exploited, because the only person with an interest in thoroughly exploiting them is the author, who does not run the business. Publishers are not prepared to put their time and money into expanding the book-buying market by making more books more available and more attractive to more buyers. There is no financial incentive to them to do so. Though authors can't, publishers can make a quick (and, compared with the authors', easy) living by dividing the existing market between them. Publishing as a business is concerned neither with making available to the public the books the public wants, as distinct from the few the publisher persuades the retailer to stock at a given moment, nor with persuading the public to appreciate the books an author has already created. It puts pressure on only one party in the entire transaction: the authors – whom it presses to create more books. The polite jostling of publisher by publisher is competition seldom for a book, hardly ever for an œuvre, but regularly for an *author*, who is regarded solely as the producer of future books – and who can be squeezed into indeed producing them because his previous books are so under-exploited that he cannot live on the royalties.

However, in buying that productive unit, an author, a publisher acquires only the *right* to publish the author's next product – without any obligation whatever to do so. The option system is a system for binding author to publisher, while leaving the publisher quite free to turn the author down.

An author whose book has been 'freed' from an option clause is not, however, free to increase his income by circulating his book to several publishers and accepting the best offer. The convention among publishers is not to consider a book that is under consideration by another publisher. Publishing as a capitalist business does not include a free market on which authors can sell their products.

When it becomes clear to authors that it is not in publishers' financial interest to exploit any book to its commercial utmost but is, on the contrary, to the publishers' interest to keep the author poor so that he can be pressed into producing constant new articles for the publishers to sell briefly and then abandon, authors will remove their works from publishers and, on their own account, employ commercial technicians whose job will be to exploit authors' works to the authors' benefit. Publishing will cease to be a profession: the authority of expertise will no longer lend credibility to a publisher who announces the death of novels (or poetry or short stories, both of which have at certain times been the victims of publishers who conceived their job to be not to sell books to the public but to force authors' creativeness into the forms most convenient to publishers): and businessmen will no longer wield the power to bring about the demises they have proclaimed.

No doubt there were other vogues for pronouncing fiction dead before I came to literary consciousness – but not so very long before. Until the last decade of the 19th century, the claim (though it may, of course, have been freakishly made) would not have been plausible. However ardently people wished novels dead, novels patently, in a sense patent to the least imaginative, weren't. The Victorians were mass consumers of fairly cheap (in the financial sense) fiction. Jane Austen's upper- and middle-class contemporaries did, no matter how furtively, gobble the stuff up despite its comparative costliness (which they might mitigate by using a subscription library). The irony lay in its being considerable numbers which Jane Austen was tossing about when she remarked that novelists' foes were almost as numerous as their readers. And as early as early in the 17th century Cervantes put into *Don Quixote* dialogue which affirms that there are already more than 12,000 copies of Part I of the novel in print (with a particular appeal, he ironically diagnoses, to gentlemen's pages: 'there is not a gentleman's antechamber in which you will not find a *Don Quixote*').

When the huge readerships withdrew, all that could reasonably, by a person without animus against fiction, be said to have died was the element in novels which had served the purpose of filling in time. (And even that went on to pursue an independent existence in thrillers, which kill time so much more swiftly and mercilessly.)

The death of that element should in justice excite novelists and readers alike to rejoicing. The modern non-naturalistic novelist, so often accused of being a cult writer and an elitist, is in reality in a position to be the opposite. He is able now to treat his readers as equals. He need no longer tell them the naturalistic details they could equally well supply for themselves. He need not talk down to them by filling in every 'he said' and 'she said'. He is no longer required, indeed, to talk for the sake of talking. It has ceased to be part of the novelist's service to his public to fill the hours. His labour can now be valued by piece-work rates. He can offer his readers, on the supposition that they are his grown-up equals, only the things they can *not* supply for themselves because they are things unique to him, the products of his imagination.

The obituarists of fiction don't, however, take this point. They assume that, because long, naturalistic narrative is (happily for people who care for fiction) dead, novels as a genre must be dead – which is happy news for those who cannot forgive the daydream connexion. And indeed the obituarists, like most people who speak of 'the novel' in the singular, as though it were a form as strict as the sonnet instead of an enormous, elastic net that encompasses fish as various as *À la Recherche du Temps Perdu* and *Daphnis and Chloe*, usually mean by 'the novel' the 19th-century novel. More strictly, they mean the Victorian novel. The distinction is important because of the cardinally important instance of Jane Austen. Her short life continued by 17 years into the 19th century. But her novels, like the architecture of the period, continue to develop the style and the aesthetic of the 18th.

Once you have fixed on the Victorian novel as *the* novel, it is fairly easy to prove it dead. Even so, you will find it helpful to use unfair comparisons. You enumerate the giants of Victorian fiction and then hold up this autumn's publishers' lists demanding where the equivalent giants are to be found. The Victorian period *was* exceptionally rich, but it is advisable, if you are to carry your point, to make the comparison with the present look more unfavourable than it is by pretending that all the gigantic Victorian novels appeared in a single publishing season instead of over, say, the span of 32 years that lies between the publication of *Vanity Fair* and the death of George Eliot.

Then there are two accidents of history that seem to corroborate the notion that the great Victorian fruitfulness had become, by the end of the 19th century, exhausted. One is the fin-de-siècle literary fashion for decadence – which, too literally interpreted (as it often, with animus, was, because it included a fashion for homosexuality), suggests sterility. In fact, as one needs only to read the poetry of Charles Baudelaire to remark, decadence in literature is more likely to be artistic fertility. The other was the accident that the next obvious giant to appear in English literature after the death of George Eliot was Bernard Shaw, whose genius happened to be not for novels but for the theatre – a fact he did not discover himself until he had made an energetic effort to become a novelist, writing novels whose narrative has no use for the novelist's privilege of breaking the scenic unities, with the result that his narrative virtually consists of stage directions.[1] Shaw's own description of this as 'a false start in 19th-century fashion as a novelist' indicates how completely the 19th-century novel dominated 19th-century literature – a dominance that has since been mistranslated into the supposed dominance of the 19th-century novel over novels in general.

[1] See the notes at the end of this chapter.

However, it is not ultimately by tricks or by turning historical accidents to their purpose that the obituarists make out their case for the deadness of the (Victorian) novel but by misunderstanding Victorian novels. They mistake the naturalism of the manner for the novel itself.

And often they ignore the patent fact that not all Victorian novels *are* naturalistic. *Vanity Fair* is a design in quite unnaturalistic symmetry in the manner of Jane Austen, executed through a technique Thackeray learned from 18th-century writers: it uses every device of perspective to distance the reader from the characters and from the novelist (who speaks in his own person), with the purpose of forcing the reader to give, in *his* own person, conscious consideration to the book's sad and ironic query whether humans are beings sufficiently free from social and economic circumstance to exercise morality.

But even when a great Victorian novel has a naturalistic surface, it is not the naturalism that makes the greatness. *Middlemarch* mirrors a community but simultaneously analyses it. If you demand of modern novelists that they produce those large panoramic views, those crowd scenes, those towering, quirky, self-consistent 'characters' that make the Victorian giants great, you will not get a successor to George Eliot but merely this year's possibly computer-manufactured bestseller.

But do not be so unfair as to pronounce, in your disappointment, that therefore the novel is dead. The mistake may well have been yours. In another perspective, those elements are not what make the great Victorian novelists great. They are the mere incidentals of the Victorian manner, and sometimes a great Victorian novel has to contrive to be great in spite of them. Perhaps your literary judgment was wrong in picking on 'characters' as an essential: wrong in the same way as Victorian literary criticism (which overspilled well into the 20th century) was wrong when it virtually re-wrote Shakespeare's plays by insisting on treating his poetic-dramatic personages, who exist only as poetic images made manifest in action, as the 'characters' of a Victorian novel, equipped with enumerable, describable, 'characteristics' (which schoolchildren were obliged to learn by rote and then describe and enumerate in exam answers).

And indeed your realistic judgment may be as wrong as your literary. Perhaps you cannot even recognise naturalism, unimportant though that is from the artistic point of view, because you have a mistaken apprehension of human nature. People are not 'characters'. They may pretend to be, perhaps in the hope of becoming as popular as the characters in Victorian fiction. Or they may continue to act out in adult social situations one of the broadly and unsubtly drawn character-rôles which were thrust on boys, as identifying marks, in the depersonalised and philistine social situation of an English public school and which continued for so long to dominate the concept of characterisation in English novels. But the truth about people in real life, if you experience them in relationships where they shew enough of themselves to let you mentally impersonate them, is that they consist hardly at all of bundles of traits or humours or characteristics but very largely of dynamic personalities which are defined in their actions, experiences and relationships as they go along.

6. Notes to Chapter II

The date of Saint Teresa's death is given by some reference books as 1577 and by others as 1582. The quotation from her autobiography is in the translation by J. M. Cohen (whose introduction implies that he favours 1577 as the year of her death) and is from Chapter 2. Saint Teresa must have been under twelve when her mother let her find time for novels because, as she records in Chapter 1, when she was 'a little under twelve', her mother died.

Saint Teresa records (Chapter 1) that as a small child she played at nuns and perhaps wanted to be one, but (Chapter 2) later, when she was being educated in a convent, she was 'bitterly averse to taking the habit'.

Saint Teresa was canonised in 1622. Gian Lorenzo Bernini's sculptural group, *The Ecstasy of Saint Teresa*, executed 1645–52, is in the Cornaro chapel in the church of Santa Maria della Vittoria, Rome.

The George Eliot quotation is from the Prelude to *Middlemarch*.

Beardsley's respect for Saint Teresa is demonstrated ('Her books are wonderful') also on p. 435 of his *Letters*, Cassell, 1971.

Firbank's two letters about gadding like Saint Teresa are quoted on p. 229 and p. 257 of Miriam J. Benkovitz's *Biography* of Firbank. The quotations and citations from *Concerning the Eccentricities of Cardinal Pirelli* are on pp. 675 and 683–4 of *The Complete Ronald Firbank*.

The quotations from *Don Quixote* are in J. M. Cohen's translation. Part I of *Don Quixote* was published in 1604, Part II in 1614. Don Quixote's library is winnowed in I, 6. Characters mention other (real) works by Cervantes in I, 6 and 48, in the former case mentioning Cervantes's name. Part I is discussed in Part II, 2 and 3. It is in II, 3 that the gentlemen's pages and the 12,000 copies are mentioned.

Kipling fictionalised his schooling (at the United Services College, Devon) in *Stalky & Co.*, 1899.

The warning tale against thumb-sucking is (in the English translation) 'The Story of Little Suck-a-Thumb' who, though warned by his mother that 'The great tall tailor always comes To little boys that suck their thumbs', sucks his thumb when his mother leaves him alone; the tailor shears his thumbs off. The story is in Heinrich Hoffman's *Struwwelpeter*, 1847.

The Frank Kermode quotation is from a review by him in *The Listener*, 25 September 1969.

Shaw's stage-directions-type narrative is beautifully exemplified in the opening chapter of his novel *The Irrational Knot* (written in 1880). Paragraph one sets the scene: 'At seven o'clock on a fine evening in April the gas had just been lighted in a room on the first floor of a house in York Road, Lambeth.' Etc. etc. Paragraph two gives practical details of the position of the windows and the furniture in the room. Paragraph three describes a sound in an adjoining room; the narrative disdains the novelist's ability to go through the door to discover what the noise is, but waits in the scene it has set for the entrance of the character responsible for the noise. Shaw's narrative uses the actual verb 'entered' when she arrives. (This observation, the gist of which I published in an article in 1962, was spontaneously made by Colin Wilson and appears on pp. 48–9 of his *Bernard Shaw, A Reassessment*, of 1969.)

The description of Shaw's 'false start' is from the blurb to his plays in their Penguin editions. I have assumed the description to be Shaw's own because I cannot imagine him allowing someone else to write the blurb.

III

'The Greatest Powers of the Mind' on Display

1. Shakespeare Misapplied and Defied

THUS historical coincidence brought about the sad paradox that the fury which fiction had long provoked by its resemblance to daydreams was set free to assault fiction at the very moment when fiction, relieved of its social duty to carry merely time-filling narrative, was coming to bear less and less resemblance to daydreams. Intellectual thought, having cheated in the argument by equating 'the novel' with the Victorian novel, now cheats its own inmost and dearest desire: it has put itself in a position where it exalts Victorian novels, which are often the very ones that most resemble daydreams, in order that the comparison may tell against the post-Victorian fiction which is using intellectual organisation to divorce and distance itself from daydreams.

The habit of forgetting that naturalistic novels are not the only kind of novels has quickly passed from teachers to pupils. In the last year or two I have been repeatedly horrified, in London and Dublin, when I have attended assemblies of undergraduates or students who wished to ask or tell me something about fiction and have found myself the only person present who did not take it for a truism too obvious to argue about that the sole function of a novel is to reflect the society it is written in, and that the novel's sole value to that society is to shew it its own image in the mirror.

The commonness of this view shews what mischief results if you take the phrase 'to hold, as 'twere, a mirror up to nature', which one of Shakespeare's fictional or fictionalised creations, Hamlet, calls the 'purpose' of the interpretative art of acting, and mis-apply it to a creative art, meanwhile ignoring the explicit statement of another of his creations, Duke Theseus, that the creative imagination produces 'things unknown'.

It is ignorance of Theseus's account of poetic creation that shapes a query which is often raised about, and occasionally by, novelists – a query that has once or twice been brought home to me at home by journalists visiting for an interview: whether a novelist, once he becomes known as such, does not cease meeting 'ordinary' people in 'ordinary' relationships, and whether he does not thereby cease to meet subject-matter for his novels.

The first part of the query makes a thoroughly unnaturalistic representation of British society – a society which in practice shews a commendable lack of respect for its novelists (for the uncommendable reason that it feels no respect for novels), with the result that I doubt if there is now a novelist in the country who could not, in everyday social contexts, maintain his anonymity with an ease positively affronting to his vanity.

The second part of the query betrays simple ignorance of how novels are created. Beneath the ignorance there is probably the wish that, if novels as a genre refuse to *quite* dry up, then at least individual novelists may soon be obliged to, for want of material.

This does not prevent the query from being raised by people who are themselves novelists. Novelists may feel the shame of fiction as well as anyone else, and they have to bear it more personally. As Jane Austen knew, and as she says when her great baroque defence of novels accuses novelists of the 'ungenerous and impolitic custom' of speaking ill of fiction, the disparaging 'Only a novel!' may be exclaimed by its writer as well as its reader, if the writer is more ignorant than Jane Austen was of both literature and himself. And many novelists are indeed as ignorant as the public of how novels are created, particularly if they are so afraid of finding the shaming answer 'Like daydreams' that they refuse (as many novelists systematically do refuse, for superstitious fear that to understand their talent would destroy it) to scrutinise their own mental processes.

The correct answer to the query is that the people a novelist meets, whether ordinary or extraordinary, are in no way necessary to the creation of novels, which are not necessarily concerned either with depicting 'ordinary life' or with delineating extraordinary 'characters'.

The notion that success cuts off a novelist from material necessary to his creativeness is one that few novelists become famous enough nowadays to put to the test, but the answer is supplied by the career of Charles Dickens, whose novels are by no means short of naturalistic details about the externals of contemporary life and who belonged to the mass-readership age when a novelist could have the fame of a present-day pop star. And indeed, thanks to his public appearances, Dickens added, to his huge literary fame, the numinous glamour of the performer. Yet Dickens's fame never caused him to suffer the least diminution of his creative fertility and power. His last, unfinished, novel is his best. For, of course, Dickens continued, through the growth of his fame, to use the subject-matter he had used all along, namely the nightmare relationships he had taken part in as a child.

And in fact all the material a novelist absolutely needs is available to him as a child. The same is true of all the experience of life the reader needs to appreciate the novelist's work. Before the age of five novelist and reader alike are personally acquainted with the emotions of, and the relationships sustained by, rapists, romantic lovers, murderers, dethroned kings and exiles. (We were all dethroned and exiled when we were weaned, which made romantic lovers of us, who turned into doomed romantic lovers when we were frustrated of the Oedipal lusts that constituted us, in intention, rapists and murderers.) And these emotions are possibly more starkly experienced at five than ever again, because there is less cultural furniture in the imagination to pad them.

Any of that later-acquired cultural furniture may be used by a novelist to decorate his basic material. But, unless his basic material consists of that first, childhood acquaintance with the facts of imaginative life, he will not be a great novelist, and he will fail to elicit from his readers the deeply imagined recognition of his material that comes from their own first acquaintance with it.

All that a novelist needs to acquire in his post-childhood life is expertise: expertise not in the details of any of the departments of real adult life from which he may want to draw the incidental furniture of his books, but expertise in his own profession, which involves learning both to negotiate his own temperament (so that he can keep open his own routes of access to the childhood material) and to create designs for eliciting from his readers (who include the novelist himself – if, indeed, he is lucky enough not to be his own only reader) a recognition unmuted in its starkness.

Sometimes a great literary creator, if he lives to a more extreme old age than Dickens did, is noticed to have grown 'out of touch with reality'. Often the charge is superficial and means only that the writer has got his draperies a touch awry; summoning up naturalistic bric-à-brac for his people's speech, he may carelessly put into their mouths the slang of 50 years ago. But when the charge is true, it is so not because the writer is out of touch with the social reality round him but because he has outlived his own access to his childhood.

From a psychoanalytic point of view, the childhood of all artists, good or bad (like, indeed, the childhood of all demented scribblers, compulsive doodlers and absent-minded hummers of tunes), is interesting and valuable as a key to the themes they select or invent. But when you consider a great artist, as this book will consider Firbank, his childhood is crucial not only psychoanalytically but critically, as the key not only to the content of his themes but to the content of his talent for disposing them into designs.

As for the naturalistic draperies with which a novelist may clothe his material, novelists take as much or as little as suits them from observation of life or from, which often serve quite as well, reference books. The fallacy that ordinary meetings in ordinary life provide novelists with their material has its corollary in the fallacy that any ordinary meeting that occurs in the novelist's pages must have a counterpart, which it was copied from, in the novelist's real life. Indeed, many people, noticing there is often more feeling in novels than one could expect to be born of cold observation, become uneasy about the false proposition that the naturalistically observed novel is the only possible novel and leap to the yet more blatantly false conclusion that the only possible novel is the directly and in-detail autobiographical novel, a view now so widespread that I guarantee any novelist who sets his next novel in a jam factory that he will presently be asked which years of his life he spent in a jam factory.

Some novelists find naturalistic facts, by whatever means acquired, psychologically indispensable – not to the novel but to the novelist: they help to charm the truly indispensable material up from the depths, perhaps by defending the novelist against self-accusations of daydreaming. For most Victorian novelists, some sort of continuous plausibility was necessary, neither artistically nor psychologically but economically, if the novels were to catch the big public, which, being available, might just as well be caught if that could be done without detriment to the work of art. For a 20th-century novelist, the big public is seldom available, whether or not he dispenses with plausibility, unless he also dispenses with art; and even then he can't be sure of it. So if he is an artist, unless a plausible surface attracts him sensuously or as a talisman, he might just as well concentrate on acquiring the expertise of his own profession rather than dissipate himself on picking up smatterings of others, especially as his own may take a lifetime to master, and on pursuing through his proper expertise the harder and higher achievement of that rightness of design which constitutes artistic plausibility.

2. A Moral Tale

I LAY claim to having exploded the 'novels mirror society' fallacy (at least for the purposes of my own continuing self-education, which is not a small claim) when by chance an editor sent me for review an impressive volume by the United-States author, Mr Maxwell Geismar, called *Henry James and his Cult* (the word, again, that damns Firbank).

James, of course, is not a Victorian but an Edwardian giant – a distinction whose point is not just temporal and stylistic, but, very pointedly, financial.

By the Edwardian era, literary giants no longer commanded the giant incomes. Economically as well as stylistically, James is the first of the modern great novelists, inasmuch as he, like Firbank, could not have got by without a private income.

Since catchpenny naturalism would no longer catch many pennies, there was no very pressing impulse to keep it in being. Indeed, if you are cynical about the human species, you can argue that the surface of plausibility in James's novels is already worn pretty thin by the fact that he requires a large portion of all the personages in them to share his own exact and exacting sensibility to nuances of emotion and expression.

To this superficial charge against James's plausibility in the representation of real life, Mr Geismar's massive work added a whole (and well-aimed) salvo of depth charges. James, he charged, chose to people his novels with American capitalists and European aristocrats and to place them in relationships of sexual love, and yet he had not a three-year-old child's understanding of the workings of either capitalism or feudalism, while of sexuality itself his apprehension actually *was* that of a three-year-old voyeur impotently peeping through his parents' bedroom keyhole.

Of this heavy indictment I wrote a ravingly favourable review – for which Mr Geismar has generously long since forgiven me. For I agreed with every word of Mr Geismar's anatomy of James's fiction. The only mistake I found in his book was his belief that it was an indictment of James, instead of a very thorough explanation of the ways in which James is great.

What the supposed indictment really established was that James, like Jane Austen, wrote not from observation but out of his imagination. In Jane Austen's phrase, they are both 'Writers of Fancy'. To expect or even want James's novels to report the facts of capitalism is to miss the point in the same way as if you consulted the *Oedipus Rex* of Sophocles as a textbook on the problems of prehistoric kings coping with epidemics of the plague. The greatness of James and Sophocles alike consists in their access to (their talent), and their power of deploying in designs (their artistry), the stark emotions of the three-year-old voyeur at the bedroom door.

3. Miniature and Minor

IF the Victorian novel had not been taken for the only possible novel, and if the naturalistic surface manner of many Victorian novels had not been taken for the substance of all novels, the fallacy that fiction reproduces the life of or around its author could never have become current. And that would have had the great advantage that it then could not have hidden, as it still does hide, an important historical fact.

Before the high naturalistic gloss of the Victorian interlude intervened to dazzle everyone's perceptions, there was an established and developing tradition under which novels need not be naturalistic in their essentials at all. They were free to be as unnaturalistic as the novels of Jane Austen, whose patterns pair lovers as formally as the couples in a formal dance. Lovers emerge from her plots sorted as firmly by the designer's hand as they do from a poetic drama like *A Midsummer Night's Dream* or a formal opera like *Così Fan Tutte*.

The essential designingness of Jane Austen is still often obscured; for, of course, if you think you know absolutely that all novels are mere reproductions of life, then of course you know that hers must be, too. This presumed knowledge makes it impossible for many people to hear her own explicit statement on the matter. For she is reliably reported to have told a friend 'that it was her desire to create, not to reproduce'.

It was her power to create which one of her contemporary reviewers recognised as Shakespearean. Nowadays, when it is assumed she must be a mere copyist, since that is what all novelists are assumed to be, Jane Austen is less likely to be called Shakespearean than a miniaturist. For, of course, if you know that a novel merely mirrors society, then you can very easily judge which are major and which are minor novels. You may not be quite so naïve as to make a purely quantitative judgment. Some aesthetic criterion must be used if you are to separate *Gone With the Wind* from *War and Peace*. But, once you have picked your group of good novels, a belief in the mirror theory commits you to hold that the major ones among them are those that reflect a major slice of society. By this standard, many artists are simply blasted with size. Jane Austen is reduced to a miniaturist, and Firbank is kept in his place as 'minor'.

The text for the Jane-Austen-as-miniaturist theory is taken from one of her own letters. In order to serve the theory, however, the text has had to be taken out of context. Indeed, as an episode of literary history, the case makes a beautiful and bizarre demonstration of how proponents of novels-as-naturalism may find themselves obliged to re-interpret plain meanings into their opposites.

In the much-quoted passage, Jane Austen wrote of herself working on a 'little bit (two Inches wide) of Ivory'. This has been widely wielded both as a description of Jane Austen's work and as an account of how she herself thought of it and rated it. The wielders, however, have been gratified by the ivory to the point of missing the irony. Jane Austen, whose talent was so much for the sardonic that her undoubted sweetness of nature expressed itself through the idiom of satire, was writing to her nephew, who had just left school. At the beginning of her letter she congratulates him on being now old enough to be addressed on its outside as Esquire, and she goes on to congratulate him on his aspirations to be a writer. She conjures up her own two inches of ivory solely in order to contrast them with his 'strong, manly spirited sketches'. She seriously believed herself to be the author of two-inch miniatures precisely as much as she believed a schoolboy to be a strong, manly, spirited literary artist.

4. Creation and Analysis

THE moment you drop the social-mirror theory as untenable, you see major and minor fictions according to a quite different scale, and you stop seeing the history of fiction as a scale at all.

The history, it turns out, is not a steady ascent towards the perfection of Victorian representationalism, in the way Giorgio Vasari supposed the history of painting to be an ascent towards Renaissance representationalism (with, of course, in both graphs, a sad falling-off virtually unto death after the peak). When you are no longer dazzled by the gloss of naturalism, the essential tradition of creative design turns out to be continuous; it proceeded, under the gloss, through the Victorian episode, and on till now. The tradition is not, however, a progress. A later author need not be better than an archaic one (though he may be if he is more talented), even in the matter of technical expertise, for the technique of a novel succeeds in the measure that it copes with the material of the book, and that is individual to each individual book.

Anyone who now wants to tell which, of these individual novels, are major and which minor will have bravely to apply aesthetic standards all the way through his act of judgment. Bravery is needed in the form of independence of mind, because standards of this type can't be simply, quantitatively checked against the outside world. A novel will now have to be judged not on its width (which can be easily checked) but on its depth. And that amounts to judging the performance of its powers of analysis.

A novel, in other words, is not just a creation but a formal creation. The novelist is creative not only in respect of the material but in respect of the design that organises the material.

Even the most brazenly daydream-like of romantic novels is more organised than daydreams are. True, daydreams themselves usually make some concessions to plausibility and narrative continuity. If there's a house which is to burn almost to ashes before he heroically rescues the family inside, the daydreamer won't situate it immediately next door to the fire station. Likewise he won't just sprout Mercurial wings on his ankles but will have himself requested by a scientist to swallow the experimental potion that will cause them to sprout. But the daydreamer makes concessions only to his own standards, which may be quirky. The romantic novel, being a commercial article, has its readers' standards of plausibility in mind. And even the serious artist, who may concede nothing to potential readers from among the public, if indeed he expects to have any, must bear at least one reader in mind, namely a distanced version of himself, to whom, imagined as coming fresh and cold-eyed to the book, the book must be made acceptable and comprehensible. Besides, the daydreamer can always whack up his own faith, which is the faith of a willing and interested party, in what is going on in the daydream, by practising a loving and lingering repetition of the images – a mental counterpart of masturbation technique – whereas the novelist who repeats his information will bore his reader and destroy the reader's faith in the fantasy.

Very simple (and very bad) novels are, however, though more organised than daydreams, organised along the same lines as daydreams. The difference is a matter of a stronger and longer narrative thread, a more coherent skin of plausibility, a vivider naturalistic representation of surface appearance. A fully created novel, on the other hand, carries its creativeness into its design by causing the design to analyse the creativeness of the material.

It is the design that demonstrates, in operation, the relationship and proportion of each theme in the material to all the others. A narrative thread, along which you want to hurry in order to find out what happens next or in the end, is only a single, though it may be a strong, line to pull you on through the book. The disclosure, as you proceed through the book, of its design may exert an attraction just as strong, and also subtler and more-dimensioned. And from the artistic point of view it has the great superiority to the narrative thread that it is sweeter. The pleasure given by the uncovering of the design is sensuous pleasure.

Fantasy itself, the basic material of novels and daydreams alike, is rather neutral stuff artistically. Fantasy is also the basic material[1] of scientific hypotheses – and it is in itself scientifically neutral. The good hypothesis is not of its nature more fertile or more ingenious than the bad. It turns out to *be* good only when it turns out to be consistent with external, checkable reality. Likewise artistic hypotheses (that is, fantasies) turn out to be good or bad only when they are proved or when they fail in relation to the internal structure of the work of art as a whole.

[1] Cf. Chapter II, 4.

The difference between tripe and great art is made very largely by technique. The donnée of a work of art – a situation, a skeleton plot, the nucleus of a poem, a melody – is scarcely deep-stained enough to be good or bad in itself. It may, of course, have become stained with banality by having been previously put to banal use. An English novelist might at present hesitate to recount the hesitations, between a blonde and a brunette typist, of a firm-chinned, blue-eyed, 31-year-old architect named Mark. Nonetheless he *could*, even now, battle down données magaziney associations or turn them to satirical use; and I find myself surprised as I write that, before these associations were accreted and while the material was still of cheeseclothly neutrality, Henry James in fact did not bring a Bostonian architect named Mark to some eclectically 'historical' country-house named Seal or Zeal, near Deal or Theale, there to hesitate between a well-born Englishwoman and a titled Frenchwoman, both now obliged, to the distress of their families, to work as typewriters (for in those days the depersonalisation of clerical workers had not yet been taken into language and the typewriter was the operative, not the machine; by a similar history, the secretary, who had long been a person and now is exclusively a person again, became during the 18th century both the person and the desk he worked at). And banality itself, indeed baanality itself, the tune of 'Baa, baa, black sheep', set Mozart's imagination off on a train of inspired variations.

The fantasy, if the novelist is fertile, is billowy stuff, full of air and short on weight, and seemingly, by the easy process of the association of ideas, self-increasing. It behaves, indeed, like a newly landed parachute which the novelist, if it is not to drag him cross-country against his will, must beat vigorously about its billows, applying the utmost intellectual severity until he forces it to serve his design. He must, however, take care not to cudgel it too puritanically with the accusation that it's all airy, vapid daydream, or it will shrivel and leave him with a highly developed fictioneering intellect but no novel to exercise it on. Great art is the perfect match between productive fantasy and reductively analytic design. But it is important to remember that the design, too, is made of the fantasy stuff. Its creation, too, is an act of imagination. Art is a counterpoint between the billowing and the organising fantasy. And probably it is that counterpoint, rather than the associations of whatever subject-matter may be represented (after all, music represents nothing), which incarnates the author's, and arouses the audience's, emotion.

5. ... and Psychoanalysis

BESIDES being an analysis, a novel is a sort of psychoanalysis. It is, however, a highly specialised sort; and writing or reading a novel won't serve writer or reader as a substitute for a psychoanalysis in the usual sense of the word.

The heart of the resemblance lies, of course, in the novelist's charming up infantile themes and emotions from his unconscious and the reader's being charmed to recognise them by their assonance with material in himself, material known to him but perhaps not accessible to him until a novel lends it the fantasy of fiction as a disguise under which it can make its appearance in the reader's consciousness.

Strictly, it is perhaps the novel's analytic design (or, in the reader's case, his apprehension of the design as it is disclosed) which resembles psychoanalysis. The novel as a whole perhaps resembles both the psychoanalysis and the pathological condition it analyses.

Compulsive production of the billowing stuff of novels is very like the compulsive production of hysterical fantasies. (Freud, with his usual appreciative courtesy towards the arts, put the comparison the other way about, firmly in the arts' favour, when he called hysteria 'a caricature of an artistic creation'.) And in the reader addictive reading is very like a persistent neurotic symptom.

'Very like' is not, however, 'the same' (as Freud emphasised by choosing the word 'caricature'). The novelist, unlike the hysteric, is not hallucinated into taking his fantasy for literal truth. Unlike a neurotic, the reader gives his consent to his addiction to reading, though he may consider himself weak-minded for doing so. And the writer cannot carry out *his* compulsion to write without making a positive act of will to concur in it.

All those items, however, which differentiate novels from symptoms, also differentiate daydreams from symptoms. Even the novelist's act of will is carried out on a small scale by the daydreamer when he repeats his images in order to induce himself to believe in them. What differentiates a novel from both symptoms and daydreams is its formal organisation.

And the great analytic effort which goes into that organisation is also differentiated from the analytic effort in psychoanalysis. For the analytic criteria of psychoanalysis are checked against the real, the outside world. Those of a novel's organisation aren't. They are fantasy, too.

A symptom is organised according to the logic of its unseen motivations. A daydream obeys the Ego's wishes. A novel organises its fantasy material according to its own, the material's, thematic logic. In doing so, the novel is, of course, obeying a wish of the novelist's Ego – the desire to enjoy the sensuous pleasure of discovering the novel's design; but that wish is governed by a more highly evolved function of the Ego than the simple fulfilment of direct Ego wishes which happens in daydreams.

6. Realism Is Greater than Naturalism

ONCE you agree that a novel resembles but isn't the same as a psychoanalysis, you leap to a sense in which a non-naturalistic novel may in fact contain more truth to nature than a naturalistic one. The sense is, of course, psychological.

When Mr Maxwell Geismar's indictment of Henry James remarked that James's fictions about capitalism and feudalism were, at bottom, infantile fantasies in which capitalism and feudalism figured not in their real natures but in the eating-and-excreting terms of infancy, I boldly answered that precisely such fantasies might in fact be the inmost, reallest truth about the real natures of capitalism and feudalism.

A similar answer can be made to the 'miniaturist' tag affixed to Jane Austen and to the fact, so often held against her, that she wrote at the period of the Napoleonic Wars and yet makes barely an allusion to them in her work and never so much as begins to attempt a panoramic view of their vast social effects. The same charge might be made against Firbank for publishing *Vainglory* in 1915.

However, these true facts can be interpreted as accusations only by ignoring (as well as the independent importance of art) psychology – a thing which the world is, of course, very prone to do. It is possible to answer that both novelists in fact provide a deeper and rarer insight than any war panorama could do, because, declining to be diverted by the particulars of particular wars, they go to the constant human heart of the matter: their fictions are using, as their actual material, the very emotions that *cause* wars and the very fantasies which, when whole societies act them out, *are* wars.

That answer will make sense only to people who agree that humans are psychological beings. Some people are not prepared to grant that; and among those who are, many are not so struck as I am by psychoanalysis as the psychological hypothesis which, to my experience, is the most consistently and multiply consistent both with itself and with observable reality. Some of these people have in fact denied themselves the *chance* to be struck, because they have never actually *read* the works of Freud – an abstention they often justify by believing, simultaneously, that they can pick up enough knowledge of what he said from its currency in the modern air and that it is so old-hat and non-current as not to be worth picking up.

But if you grant that our being takes place in *some* psychological dimension, not necessarily one interpretable by psychoanalysis, then the large social events are at least partly psychological events. No wise person would deny the force of economic and directly biological causes. (Our psychology is, of course, part of our biology.) But it is very hard to understand how large numbers of people disregard, in a war, their individual economic and biological self-interest (which ceases to exist if one gets killed) unless you allow also for psychological motivations and are prepared to include the fantasy in which Belgium was 'raped', and the myth-fantasy of the hero, among the causes that led young Frenchmen and Englishmen to die in the 1914-18 war and other young Frenchmen to go to their deaths for the sake of Napoleon.

Similarly, capitalism itself, though an economic construction, is one which many of its observers believe they can actually see to be a fantasy. And certainly it is a system which either could not keep going, or has itself succumbed to the fantasy of believing it could not keep going, unless the fantasies incarnated in its advertising are swallowed by its consumers, who are also its producers, its creators at the same time as its slaves and creatures.

These considerations imply only psychology. What, specifically, psychoanalysis adds to them is that the moving fantasies and impulses originate in infancy and are unconscious.

When Emma Woodhouse, in the course of a pleasure party at Box Hill, makes a witticism at the expense of poor old Mrs Bates, Jane Austen contrives an effect of violence more shocking than many melodramatists can manage with a murder.

And, psychologically considered, the aggressive impulse in Emma's personality which Jane Austen is using as part of her literary material is identical with the psychological force that produces real murders. Again, the reader's apprehension of the violence rests, psychologically, on the existence of the same psychological force in him.

However, what brings the effect home to the reader is not psychological knowledge or technique but literary expertise and technique. If it were otherwise, any good psychologist could become a great novelist. Jane Austen is not writing about psychology but about Emma, and she is not conducting a psychoanalysis but creating that type of analysis which is a novel.

It is as a novelist that she digs deeper into her smaller-surfaced material than melodramatic writers can dig into the large and socially important subject of murder. The greater effect she makes on the reader is a greater *literary* effect, achieved by her greater mastery of literary means. Her analysis is deeper because her design, in whose structure the analysis takes place, is a better (a literary judgment) design.

7. But It Still Isn't a Social Information Service

NOT only does fiction resemble psychoanalysis; its material is inherently psychological.

This latter is not only a question of the novelist's being a psychological organism himself, who can't help his creations' shewing it. That is true equally of painters and composers. Neither is it just a matter of novels' usually containing people. I can imagine, if indeed I have not already read, a novel that dispensed with them, and I doubt if it would have dispensed with psychology. The psychologicalness of fiction must, I think, lie ultimately in words – which, though a novel may refuse to arrange them in sentences that convey meaning, are themselves undivorceable from concepts. Even if a novelist breaks words into fragments, the syllables and groups of letters can't be divorced from associations with whole words. A musical note or an intensity of colour, which carries or may carry no concept, may thereby carry a more stark emotional charge. The concepts attached to words may blunt them a little as direct emotional weapons. But it is, I think, the concepts that make words inherently psychological instruments and give literature its specialised potential as the psychological art, the one which can echo the relationships in its design by specific psychological and conceptual relationships in its material.

All the same, it is only the material that is psychological, not the treatment, which must be expertly literary or the psychology will go for nothing. The psychologicalness of literature does not open the side door for the return of the fiction-as-mirror theory. The psychologicalness does not imply that the purpose of fiction is to shew society its own psychological face.

Indeed, since a novel is only like, not identical with, a psychoanalysis, fiction does not even do the state some service (if you will agree with me that that would be a service, and a desperately needed one) by giving the citizenry information about psychoanalysis. Fiction contains such information, but it is all implicit, like the psychoanalytic information in the aphorisms of Wilde's dramatis personae.

As a matter of fact, fiction cannot even give explicit, accessible information about the nature of *fiction* – which is why the nature of fiction is misunderstood even, sometimes, by people who write fiction, and also why I am setting out this anatomy of fiction in these non-fiction terms. I know my Irishly rational tone of voice is infuriating to some readers – or, rather, to some reviewers;[1] and if anyone is irritated by this exposition I shall be

---

[1] Reviewers are not always readers. The review-reading public might be amazed if it knew how often a reviewer, by factually misreporting it, demonstrates he hasn't read the

delighted for him to take the same message from my novel *In Transit*, where he will find this anatomy in its implicit, fictional incarnation. Indeed, he may equally take a good part of my anatomy of Firbank's fiction, which this book is working towards, from my novel in a superficially Firbankian idiom, *The Finishing Touch*.

If fiction is to ask society for support, as I (who am, however, an interested party) think it entitled to do, it must do so on the same grounds as any other art, namely the absolute goodness of good art. It will not get away with pretending it can render society a direct quid pro quo by serving as a short-cut to the production of better-informed (about psychology) citizens or even better citizens.

The naïve theory that enjoying good art makes good citizens or good individual people is discountenanced by a folk villain of our civilisation, the Nazi concentration-camp guard who, after spending his day off playing in Beethoven quartets, returns the more cheerfully to gassing his prisoners.

Documentation may or may not exist to establish the historical existence of this monster either as individual or as significant statistic. I suspect him of being a myth (which need not mean he lacks a nucleus of historical truth) because of his versatility. I often encounter him in my pursuit of one of my non-fiction vocations. If you habitually speak in favour of decent behaviour to animals of other species than our own, you will sooner or later be met by this same concentration-camp guard; but now he spends his day off in being excessively nice to his dogs and feeling squeamish about 'sports' that consist of killing animals for the pleasure of the 'sportsmen'.

As a statistical comment, the myth is void because it doesn't take into account that decency to animals is a fairly, and musicianship a very, conspicuous and established strand in German culture. In England, which is where the myth is most current, killing most kinds of animal for fun is common, setting much value on dogs is rare (unless they are the dogs who retrieve the animals you have just shot) and being skilled enough to participate in a string quartet is extremely rare. When the Englishman hears of

book he is reviewing. Publishers' blurbs, too, fairly often give a factually erroneous account of the book they jacket, and their errors make a test for the reviewers – half of whom usually copy the blurb's example, not the text's. Reviewing is a trade that trades on the probability that neither the public nor the editor of the journal that publishes the review will have read the book before the review of it appears. The only person who has, for a certainty, read it is the author; and he is silenced by the fear that, if a review is against him, complaint would look acrimonious or, worse still, if the review praises him, that it would look ungrateful.

the guard's musicianship and kindness to animals, they seem to him outlandish traits instead of traits that have long been quite widely distributed in the German population. So it doesn't occur to him to ask whether there was a higher incidence of kindness to animals among concentration-camp guards than among the ordinary population or a higher incidence of musicianship under Hitler than in the Weimar Republic.

If it were to be made, the inquiry might well shew that there was actually a lower percentage of musicians among concentration-camp guards than among the population at large. But, even if it did, that would in no way establish Beethoven as even a moderate (for that he wasn't strong enough to prevail history shews) social prophylactic against Nazism.

If the myth is arguing that being musicianly or being kind to animals is a positive hindrance to behaving decently to one's fellow humans, it is nonsense. But, if it is merely stating that there is no significant correlation either way, then it is one of the myths that incarnate a commonsense perception by the implicit method of fictions, which has the advantage that it is vivid, condensed and memorable and the disadvantage that, when you try to draw it out into explicitness, you may misinterpret it.

It is such a misinterpretation if anyone tries to extract from fiction the message that fiction does good. Its claim should be that it *is* good.

8. Notes to Chapter III

Hamlet's account of acting is in Act III, ii of *Hamlet*, Theseus's of poetic creation in *A Midsummer Night's Dream*, V, i.

The review I mention of *Henry James and his Cult* is collected in *Don't Never Forget*.

Jane Austen included herself among Writers of Fancy in her letter of 31 December 1815, to the Countess of Morley.

Jane Austen was compared with Shakespeare (on the point, however, of their common power to create characters) in an unsigned notice in the *Quarterly Review* in 1821 (that is, three to four years after Jane Austen's death). The reviewer was once thought to be Walter Scott (who expressed similar admiration of her) but was in fact, according to J. E. Austen-Leigh's *Memoir* (8), 'Whately, afterwards Archbishop of Dublin'.

It is Austen-Leigh, Jane Austen's nephew, who is the reliable reporter of her wish 'to create, not to reproduce'. He reports it in Chapter 10 of his 1870 *Memoir of Jane Austen*.

Austen-Leigh is also the nephew to whom, in his youth, when he had not yet added the Leigh to the family surname, Jane Austen wrote (on 16 December 1816) the letter satirically postulating her two inches of ivory.

The Mozart variations are his 12 Variations for Piano on 'Ah, vous dirai-je, Maman', K.265.

Freud's description of hysteria is in *Totem and Taboo*, II, 4.

The witticism at Box Hill is in Volume III, Chapter VI of *Emma*.

IV

'A General Wish of Decrying'

1. Freud and the Hero

FREUD, who didn't miss much, didn't in fact miss the capacity of novels to organise themselves in a far more complex *order* of organisation than daydreams.

He did, however, under-emphasise it; and that left him with a significantly sited gap in his theory – a gap he could fill only by labelling it Unknown.

Freud's paper 'The Relation of the Poet to Day-Dreaming' (where 'poet' has its Greek sense and includes 'novelist') traces the evolution of daydreaming into fictioneering. What it fails to emphasise is the point of no return, the point in the evolution where convertibility stops – the point whose equivalent in biological evolution is when the new species is established, and its members can no longer bear children who will belong to the old species.

Psychological evolutions, however, don't demarcate their species by impossibilities. The Super-Ego evolves from the Ego, but the person who has acquired a Super-Ego doesn't cease to have an Ego. No doubt a great novelist can still daydream. Indeed, he probably *could* still write a novel organised on daydream lines.

The evolution Freud describes is an evolution of capacity. This is true of its history in an individual person and also of its history in civilisation. No doubt the human species could daydream before it could create novels. But it is not certain that it could create daydream-type novels before it could create the more highly organised kind. (The bedevilments are that it's hard to disentangle the earliest fictions from myths; that it may or may not be fair to think of an epic or a saga as a novel that happens – like passages in some of Dickens's – to scan; and that history may have lost from the record whole Ouidas and Marie Corellis contemporary with Homer.) And the fact that Jane Austen had created novels of the more complex species before Freud was born did not prevent dozens of the less complex sort from being created circa 1908, which is the date of Freud's paper.

That fact permitted Freud to name a numerical justification for one of the crucial decisions of his paper. It might have been more illuminating had he opted for the evolutionary justification that the less complex species will be more like the original and will therefore disclose more about how the evolution took place and give hints about how it might set out on the next stage. 'Let us', Freud decides, 'not choose for our comparison those writers who are highly esteemed by critics. We will choose the less pretentious writers of romances, novels and stories, who are read all the same by the very widest circles of men and women.'

By this decision the test material is limited to fictions bad, simple or both. I don't doubt that the novels 'highly esteemed by critics' would have included many bad novels, too. But some would have been good, and even the bad might have been complex in at least the sense of being pretentious.

From his deliberately limited material Freud easily and correctly picks out 'one very marked characteristic': 'they all have a hero who is the centre of interest, for whom the author tries to win our sympathy by every possible means, and whom he places under the protection of a special providence'.

Freud's choice of material has, of course, excluded *Vanity Fair*, which is sub-titled *A Novel Without a Hero*.

In the hero of the less complex type of fictions he has chosen to consider, Freud correctly recognises 'His Majesty the Ego'. This gives Freud the point of similarity between the novels he is considering and daydreams. But then Freud stops talking about one type of novels, whose limitations he chose himself, and suddenly speaks of 'all novels'. He goes on to describe 'His Majesty the Ego' as 'the hero of all day-dreams and all novels'.

The step is not an illegitimate one which Freud simply lets himself get away with. He knows he is taking the step; but he doesn't think it an important one. 'We do not in any way fail to recognize', he writes, 'that many imaginative productions have travelled far from the original naïve daydream.' However, it seemed to Freud that the travels of these less naïve productions had been made by way of 'an uninterrupted series of transitions' and that, in even the extreme variations, it was still possible to discern the pattern of the original.

As a matter of fact, the first of those items is what one would expect of *any* evolution, and the second is what one would expect of any psychological evolution. Freud has not allowed for the possibility that daydreaming may travel in such a direction that it eventually evolves into a new psychological species.

When that happens in the evolution of mental processes, the pattern of the original may well remain discernible in the new process, but the new process nevertheless belongs to a different order and can't be simply converted back into the order of the original. Freud picked out the pattern of the aggressive instinct in intellectual judgments of negation: yet thinking that x is not y belongs to a different order of psychological processes from the wish to destroy.

Although he speaks of the travels that may remove a novel far from daydreams, Freud specifically mentions only one, and that is less travel than multiplication. In the 'psychological novel', he says, using the same, now so faded, term as Sir Robert Chiltern,[1] the daydream hero may become several heroes, because the author has by self-observation split his Ego into several 'component-Egos'.

Even this complexity Freud denies to some psychological novels, where 'only one person – again the hero – is described from within; the author dwells in his soul and looks upon the other people from outside'.

The description makes me suppose Freud was thinking of Dostoevsky, whom he admired and later wrote about. The Karamazov brothers perhaps modelled for the component-Egos, and the heroes of *The Idiot* and *Crime and Punishment* for the person in whose soul the author dwells.

Yet for Freud to recognise the Dostoevsky hero as 'again the hero' of daydreams is to ignore every point of comparison except his central place in the book. Freud says of the hero of daydream fictions, 'If at the end of one chapter the hero is left unconscious and bleeding from severe wounds, I am sure to find him at the beginning of the next [. . .] on the way to recovery'; and he remarks that 'all the women' in a daydream novel 'invariably fall in love with the hero'. This daydream hero may have persisted but he certainly has not simply persisted into a Dostoevsky novel. Dostoevsky's singular heroes perform quite as remarkable a feat as those who multiply into several heroes: they reverse the entire process of wish fulfilment. They are not gloriously wounded in battle: they are more likely to commit squalid crimes of violence. If a Dostoevsky novel is a daydream, it is a masochistic daydream – but not one couched in the daydream terms of masochistic pornography. It has travelled a very long way into at least psychological complexity.

If Freud paid little attention to the distance novels may travel, it was probably because he was concentrating on a vital point which truly is common to daydreams and all novels, including complex novels, namely the importance of material from childhood. His account of the genesis of daydreams and fictions is modelled on his account of the genesis of dreams (in their true, night-time manifestation); and in part at least it tallies with

---

[1] Cf. Chapter I, 2.

Henry James's account of the genesis of fictions. Indeed, the first step, in the genesis according to Freud, tallies with the account James himself gave in his prefaces, and the second step with Mr Maxwell Geismar's account of James's fictions.

Freud takes a minor happening in immediate real life to be the nucleus: James's 'the donnée'. This nucleus summons, by patterns of association, material from childhood. In dream, daydream and fiction alike, the childhood material (which in the dream is unconscious and probably repressed) provides the greatest part of the material for the whole construction.

According to Freud, the ultimate purpose of all these constructions is to fulfil (by acting them out in a sort of experienced cinema-play) the wishes of the Ego.

And Freud remarks that the childhood material has its great importance for authors because the habit of daydreaming (and by extension the habit of writing novels) is an extension of the childhood habit of play.

This seems to me to ignore the psychology of authors, for whom writing their books is no more play than his vocation of fantasising hypotheses and then seeing if they would fit the realities was play by Freud. Both mental activities have evolved from daydreaming and play, but they have evolved beyond the point of no return. Perhaps Freud didn't know how difficult[1] it is to write a novel – not merely through not writing novels himself but through not noticing that they are analogous to another difficult activity, psychoanalysis.

It is, of course, the analytic element in novels that Freud overlooks; and that, precisely, is the element which carries good novels into a different species from daydreams, because it is the element that creates the design.

When he sets out to fulfil the logic of the design, the novelist is investing his own wishes in more than the hero and in more than the narrative thread that will express the Ego's wish-fulfilment when it causes the hero to recover from his wounds.

This investment in the design of the novelist's own will-towards-pleasure withdraws some of his investment from the hero. Freud sees only that the hero himself may split into fragments. But there is another possibility: the novelist may distance himself from the hero. Indeed, it is when the novelist *has* distanced himself that the hero, weakened by the withdrawal of the novelist's Ego from him, is most likely to split.

It is the distancing of all the people and events in a novel from the author (a distancing that happens without loss of clarity or detail, as though the author were looking through the wrong end of a very good telescope) that

---

[1] Cf. the epigraph to Part Four of this book.

makes room for irony and for compassion (in distinction from the self-pity of the hero who represents the author's Ego) in the novel; and it is in those qualities that the atmosphere and texture of great novels mark the difference in species from daydreams.

Distancing belongs par excellence to classical fiction, of the kind written by Jane Austen and Ronald Firbank. It takes place because the novelist has withdrawn some of his own wishes from the happiness of the hero and directed them towards the felicity of the design; and it is in classical fictions that the designs are at their most formal.

This is not to say that non-classical fiction must be less designed. Often its designs can claim to be, if that is a virtue, more organic, by being more ad hoc. And certainly there are other methods, such as Dostoevsky's reversal of the premises of wish-fulfilment into those of masochistic nightmare, which can estrange the novelist from the hero to much the same effect as when the novelist deliberately stands distant. However, Dostoevsky's method passed unnoticed by Freud; the organic designs, *through* being organic and, as it were, covered with creeper, are not always noticed *as* designs. Their structure may vanish from view because the reader sees only the (conspicuous) texture. So perhaps it was because he had read more 19th-century romantic than classic novels that Freud failed to notice the design present in all good novels and thus failed to pick it out as what distinguishes good novels from daydreams.

I suspect that the distance between the novel and the novelist, whether it is achieved by classical or by other means, corresponds to the distance between the Ego and the Ego Ideal. (Freud found the Ego Ideal to be evolved from the Ego; after the development has taken place, 'the Ego now appears in the relation of an object to the Ego Ideal'.) This leaves uncontradicted Freud's hypothesis that the hero represents the novelist's Ego or fragments of it, but it places the novelist himself differently and it ultimately recognises a hero beyond the hero.

Because he assumed that the purpose of the whole construction was to fulfil the Ego's wishes in fantasy, Freud did not question that it is the novelist's Ego that invents the book and projects itself directly into the hero. However, if the novelist's strongest wish is to complete the design according to his ideal conception of it, he is doing something larger than magically manipulating events as they occur in order to guard the hero's safety, and he is doing something he has to look at from a distance as he does it: he is, as Freud begins to hint when he writes of the novelist placing the hero under the protection of a special providence, impersonating God. The providence in a novel is the novelist.

It seems more likely, therefore, that the novelist's psychology ought to be elucidated through his relation to the originals of God, that is, his parents, than through the Ego's negotiation of real life, which so regularly frustrates our wishes that we have to invent daydreams in which our hero the Ego magically fulfils his. It is consistent with the observable psychology of many novelists to hypothesise that, while he is writing, a novelist is inhabiting his Ego-ideal and looking from a distance at his Ego and its immediate wishes.

When he writes, the novelist feels not that his hero is invincible but that he, the novelist, is omnipotent. He cannot write at times when he doesn't feel that; and to feel it may be, much or even most of the time, quite untypical of him.[1] But, at the periods when he can create, the novelist (indeed, the artist of any type) experiences an energy and an invulnerability that might well come from his feeling that he is within sight and hope of catching up with that Ego Ideal which the Ego often has to scramble painfully after.

In Freud's account of the evolution of the Ego Ideal out of the Ego, the two agencies, once they are differentiated from each other, become capable of a relationship, whose nature is dictated by the distance between them. When the distance is completely closed up, the two become fused, and they jointly experience the manic emotions of triumph and immunity to criticism. When the distance between them is long, the Ego becomes subject to melancholic emotions produced by the severe criticisms directed at it by the Ego Ideal because it falls short of that Ideal.

Something of the alternation between manic phases and depressive phases is experienced by very many novelists, and the phases correspond to the periods of being able and being unable to write (or the periods of writing and of having just finished writing a book). In creative periods, the Ego Ideal's faculty of criticism exercises itself in the intellectual negations, rejections and disciplines necessary to the creation of the ideal design. But in the non-creative phase, the criticisms are so severe[2] that they frighten the fantasy out of production, with the result that they have no novel to exercise themselves on, or they turn against and threaten to devour the just-finished book.

However, I do not think a novelist is a straightforward manic-depressive, because that would leave out the third factor present in the writer's case, namely the writing. When the novelist is in his manic (that is, his writing)

---

[1] Chapter VI, 6 will mention an item of untypical behaviour by Firbank which may have been partly caused by creator's confidence.

[2] Chapter XIX, 12 will mention this in application to Firbank.

phase, it is not that his Ego and Ego Ideal have become completely fused, but rather as though the fusion, his inhabitation of his Ego Ideal, were a hypothesis, which he has the chance of *making* true – in and through his book. (And a fiction *is*, after all, a hypothesis, though not one destined to be tested directly against the outside world.) The novelist's sense of triumph while he writes is translatable: I *am* as marvellous as I feel, my Ego *is* identified with my Ego Ideal, *if* I am in fact in the course of making this novel into a beautifully designed creation.

The novelist's hypothesis is invested in the novel. If the hero of the novel is the hero of the novelist's Ego, it is the novel as a whole, the object in process of being designed and created, that is a hero to the novelist's Ego Ideal. The novel itself is the other and more important hero whom Freud didn't spot.

The novel is the novelist's child and, like real children, it carries the investment of some of his narcissistic self-love as a projection of himself. It is, however, an ideal child. It carries the narcissism not of the Ego but of the Ego Ideal. The novelist is working the novel out, in order that, when it is completed, it may provide an external real-life incarnation and justification of the idealness of his Ego Ideal.

When he insisted that the fantasy content of all novels simply and directly expresses the novelist's daydream wishes, Freud missed the beautiful complexity whereby the novel as a whole may express a *negative* wish on the part of the novelist. In that case, the novel's hero does indeed represent the novelist's Ego: but the novelist's Ego Ideal is looking from a distance at that Ego and commenting on it, 'There but for the grace of God go I.' The negative wish, 'May I not be like that', is made true in real life by the writing of the novel.

This might have struck Freud had he asked himself in what sense Gustave Flaubert affirmed 'Madame Bovary, c'est moi!' For Madame Bovary is a Flaubert who doesn't write novels such as *Madame Bovary*. She is the sweet-toothed compulsive daydreamer and addicted consumer of daydream fictions who is the basic stuff of novelists' personalities. But Flaubert is the Ego Ideal who looks from an ironic and compassionate distance by carrying her fantasy material into the new dimension of design.

The Ego Ideal is one of the most fertile of Freud's hypotheses. (It is expounded in, classically, his monograph *Group Psychology and the Analysis of the Ego*.) By understanding that a person's own Ego Ideal might become identified with a person or object in the outside world, Freud was able to elucidate the structure of social groups, in which all the members of the group identify their Ego Ideals with the same leader, and also to illuminate two phenomena not dissimilar to each other, being hypnotised and being in love.

In hypnotism, according to Freud's account, the hypnotist is the leader, the incarnation of the Ego Ideal, and his subject is an Ego so subservient to him as to have temporarily handed over to him even the Ego's functions of consciousness and will. In the state of being in love, the person whom the Ego sexually desires has become identified with the Ego's Ideal, with the result that the lover values the loved not only for the gratification to be had from him but as something ideal, splendid and beyond criticism in his own right.

Both these insights of Freud's seem to me adaptable to the psychology of fiction and, indeed, of art in general. They confirm that the artist projects his Ego Ideal into the work of art, and they suggest that the reader (or the audience) may identify a work of art with his. Audiences in the theatre and concert hall make a group surrender (as the social group does to its leader), and the reader of a novel makes an individual surrender, to the work of art. What is given up consists of all other conscious preoccupations, plus the will that might make it possible to break away – a surrender that resembles, in everything but the yielding up of the last layer of consciousness, the surrender made to the hypnotist who plays the rôle of the Ego Ideal.

As for falling in love, the artist does that with his own work, while he is working on it, with precautions: he is in love with it *on condition that* he is making it ideal and beautiful enough to be worthy. The audience needs make no such conditions, because it has no power to make the work better or worse. When a person makes a cult of a work of art, he has identified it with his Ego Ideal. He makes the cult object immune to criticism from him, and that makes him resentful of other people's criticisms of it. He is to all intents and purposes in love with it.

The only difference from being in love with a person is that sexual gratification cannot be had from the same object that gives so much ideal pleasure. (The pornographic books and pictures which can, at one remove, give sexual pleasure don't become objects of cult; after use, they become cast-offs, sometimes shameful cast-offs.) Even the sexual disability can be more or less overcome, in the case of works of visual art, by collectors, who can revert to infantile modes of sexuality and take possession of the object they have fallen in love with.

The psychology of appreciating works of art is the psychology of falling in love. And the absolute importance and self-justfyingness which lovers attribute to those they are in love with are what aesthetes attribute to art.

In his comparison of fictions to daydreams, Freud did not fail to notice that fictions give their readers 'a purely formal, that is, aesthetic pleasure'. But he failed to emphasise it and therefore to pay it much attention himself. So he did not locate the chief part of the pleasure in the fiction's design, and he did not notice the distancing that makes designing possible.

It is these negligences that cause the gap I mentioned in his theory. For, when Freud asks how a writer can give pleasure to others by recounting what Freud takes to be merely the writer's own personal and egocentric daydreams, he has to confess that the answer is the writer's 'innermost secret; the essential *ars poetica* lies in the technique by which our feelings of repulsion are overcome'.

Freud would not have had to postulate the existence of this inner technique or mystique, which he makes sound more like a confidence trick, if he had not, in common with most of the world, overlooked the existence of the genuine literary technique of fiction – whose great achievement is to make works of fiction into designs, which exist in dimensions the daydream content of the book does not reach.

2. Freud Psychoanalysed

THOUGH I doubt if it ever happens as directly as he supposed, I make no difficulty about agreeing with Freud that the 'less pretentious' novels his paper begins by considering (the ones, that is, which don't claim to be art) consist in essence of daydreams.

As a matter of fact, the daydream is most nearly direct in a type of fictions Freud *didn't* consider, pornography. But the next most direct daydreams are, yes, romantic novels (in the modern sense of that category). It is interesting that they are often also historical novels. I imagine that setting the fantasy in civilisation's past is a direct metaphor of the fact that the daydream originates in the author's own, and appeals to similar material from the reader's own, past – that is, his childhood. Books of this kind are often more historically accurate than naïve intellectuals would expect, which argues that they are already more adapted to plausibility than the average daydream. But it is true that accuracy of historical detail is an adaptation merely along the same lines as the organisation of daydreams, because it echoes and enlarges the daydream's dwelling on detail in order to make it convincing.

There is, however, a conspicuous oddity in what Freud says about the daydreams which he takes novels to be. He assumes that a novelist's personal, egocentric daydream would in the ordinary course of events provoke 'feelings of repulsion' in other people when they read it set out in a novel, and he has therefore to postulate that inmost and utmost 'ars poetica' whereby the novelist overcomes the expected repulsion.

It seems to me that Freud must be on the wrong lines: because in fact it is precisely those novels which are most directly like daydreams that have the smallest quantity of ars poetica expended on them by their authors; but those are *not* the ones that repel the largest quantity of readers.

And, indeed, was Freud correct in assuming that a daydream itself, quite apart from its possible incarnation in a novel, is automatically repulsive to other people if it is disclosed to them?

True, I imagine the reason why most people keep their daydreams private is that they fear the daydream would be unattractive to others or would, which is a slightly different point, make them, the daydreamers, unattractive to others. But their fears are not necessarily justified. There are many things about us that we fear will be unattractive if we disclose them, and many of them luckily aren't.

Besides, repulsion may be the wrong quality to name as what the daydreamer is afraid he will provoke. Perhaps it should rather be ridicule: I will contrive only to emphasise the smallness of my real self, the one other people meet, if I disclose the toweringness of my daydream self. Indeed, a fictioneer who is classically distanced from the incarnation of his Ego in his heroes can make classic fun from the discrepancy. Jane Austen, James Thurber and Mrs Elizabeth Taylor are all expert at it.

Other people's egocentric ambitions may indeed be repulsive, because they make us fear they will be gratified at our expense. But other people's egocentric fantasies reassure us by *being* fantasies. They may warn us, correctly, how little the fantasist would care if our wishes or our very selves were excluded from the world. But the contrast between the tiny fantasist and his hugely ambitious fantasies assures us we will not have to meet the threat of his ambitions in our own real life. On the energy saved, we laugh at him. We have nothing to fear from the fantasist – so long as he remains a fantasist and does not begin either to make his ambitious fantasies come true or to believe, by way of hallucination, that they already are true.

This reassurance fiction blazons on its title-page, by proclaiming that it *is* fiction, that it is *not* true. No matter how egocentric and ambitious the hero, he is now cut off from the author whose egocentricity may have originally animated him, and is contained within the covers of the book, where his ambitions can do no harm to us.

More important still, by his containment in the book the hero becomes a free-floating Ego, which can be snapped up and swallowed into identification by the Egos of readers. To allay its readers' fear or envy of its hero, the romantic novel needs call on no literary expertise in its author. It can rely on its readers. Bribed by the pleasures of acquiring new furniture for their fantasy lives, they adopt the novelist's daydream as their own. This they do by identifying themselves with the hero, whose egocentricity thereupon becomes harmless to them because it has become their own.

That Freud, of all astute people, overlooked this simple point is odd in the extreme: so odd that it demands a search for a cause, which must lie in something peculiar to Freud, of his unusual blindness. And the something is, I think, Freud's profession – which in 1908 still was, numerically, almost exclusive to him and which was all along peculiar to him in the sense that he invented it.

One of the hazards of his profession was that Freud had to listen to his patients narrating their dreams. I call this a hazard because, in common experience, other people's dreams, unless you are in love with the dreamer and prepared to accord all his experiences an importance in their own right, make tedious listening: so actively tedious that to have to hear them from patient after patient in the course of your professional days might well provoke 'feelings of repulsion'.

There is another exception, besides when you are in love, to this experience of tedium. The moment you catch an insight into someone else's dream and begin to interpret it psychoanalytically, the dream ceases to bore you and becomes almost as fascinating to you as matter for objective consideration as it subjectively is to its dreamer.

That intellectual pleasure of interpreting dreams was, of course, known to – indeed, discovered by – Freud. But each time, before arriving at that pleasure, he had to listen to the manifest content of the dream as the patient recounted it. Quite how offensively boring such listening was I suspect Freud would not admit to himself, as a matter of professional pride: because if his ears were not paternally open to his patients he would feel the less a therapist, and because he would not want an admission of tedium to dull the fascinatingness of the discovery he was developing.

But, though he *would* not admit the tedium, he did admit it: unconsciously. When Freud compared dreams with daydreams and found both to be expressions, generated in the mind by a similar process, of an egocentric wish, he unconsciously admitted the tedium of dreams by assuming that the same tedium must apply to daydreams.

Because he had not admitted that narrated dreams *are* tedious, Freud could not observe that it is bending on them the process of psychoanalysis that relieves the listener of their tedium. And that blindness is perhaps the blindness which made him overlook that, in good novels, the reader is relieved of the daydream quality by the author's having bent on the novel the analogous process of literary analysis.

3. A Further Fact about Daydreams

IF Freud did indeed find narrated dreams boring, he was in fact passing a *literary* judgment: on the character of dream narrative.

When he incorrectly assumed that daydreams are repulsive, which he did by analogy with dreams, Freud took it that the repulsiveness lay in the egocentricity of the wish expressed. But that can't be what, in reality, makes dreams repulsive to listen to. For, in the dream as it is related, the distortions, symbolisations and disguises completely hide from the listener, as from the dreamer himself, the fact that the dream *is* a wish and an egocentric one. It is the interpretation that makes the wish and the egocentricity apparent. But it is the interpretation that makes the dream *stop* being tedious to the listener.

Indeed, it is ultimately the concealment of the wish in dreams that makes dream narrative the most boring of literary forms. The dream distortion hides the logic of the dream's events. When there is no evident logic of events, there can be no expectation of what may happen next. Events in dreams follow each other with the freedom of total surprise, because there are no impossibilities in dreams: in dreams anything may happen.

For the dreamer, as he experiences the dream or as he recalls and partly re-experiences it in order to narrate it, the dream is nevertheless absorbing, because the vividness of its events fills his awareness. And, in any case, the hidden thread of logic connecting the events is the thread of *his* wishes. Neither that nor the vividness of experience holds the listener he narrates his dream to.

That is why literary surrealism has been less successful than surrealist painting. A painting can present a group of images in a coup d'œil. But, if literature tries to present unconscious images directly, it has to make itself into an artificial dream, with images strung out along the illogical thread of dream events: and this, when presented to other people's consciousness, is liable to be as tedious as a narrated dream.

Fictions that resemble narrated *day*dreams are better organised to hold readers' attention. Far from the wish in them making them repulsive, it is the wish that is the magnet. Because they have made some concessions to a concept of plausibility common to all their readers, daydream-type novels limit the possibilities of what may happen next. The craft of this kind of narrative consists of adumbrating to the reader's mind two or three possible forms for the next event, in distinction from the limitless possibilities in a dream. Between the two or three possibilities the reader will speculate and hope. By disclosing the general direction of the wish-line in the novel, while holding back its specific course, the daydream-novelist persuades the reader to invest some of his own wishes in the outcome, thereby adopting the daydream.

There is, however, a curious fact about these adoptions. Our own daydreams can never totally and objectively surprise us even in the first place, because it is we who are making them up. Yet the same fantasy or nucleus of fantasy will serve us time and again for daydreaming over, and some people daydream as adults fantasies they invented in childhood. But from our daydream reading we make a rule of requiring objective surprise every time.

Occasionally a daydream-type narrative that is read early in childhood enters truly under the adopter's guard and he may re-read the narrative as often as he takes out and plays over one of his daydreams. But as a rule the more a novel depends on its narrative thread to attract the reader through the book, the more openly it represents a wish, the more it invites the reader to invest his own wishes in the limited expectancy of limited surprises – the more, in short, it resembles a daydream, the less is the reader prepared to treat it as he treats his own daydreams and the smaller tolerance he shews of going through it again.

It is not even a matter of remembering the surprises of the narrative. You can pick up a novel which depends strongly on its narrative, a thriller for instance, and read a third of it without remembering you have read it before. But then a stir in the memory, rather like the experience of déjà vu, and amounting to nothing so definite as being able to predict from memory any of the incidents or even the final result, will be enough to make you discard the book with feelings that could correctly be called repulsion.

It is as if, by its very effort to get itself adopted as one's own, daydream fiction provokes a kind of mental tissue rejection.

Because of this reaction, the popular notion among educated people that all novels are naturalistic narratives – that is, extended and plausible daydreams – has damaged the finances of fiction. For who *would* spend money on buying and housing a book which he may read once with pleasure but which, if he tries a second time, will excite him to 'feelings of repulsion'?

The ars poetica which Freud thought the novelist must exercise in order to overcome the initial repulsiveness of daydreams must in fact be exercised in order to overcome their initial attraction and subsequent repulsiveness.

And that can be done only by making novels into designs which belong to a different psychological species from daydreams.

4. Notes to Chapter IV

Freud's paper about fiction and daydreams is the one I mentioned in Chapter I, 4–5: number IX of Volume IV of his *Collected Papers*.

His papers 'Negation' (1925) and 'Dostoevsky and Parricide' (1928) are numbers XVI and XXI of *Collected Papers*, Volume V.

The Freud quotation about the Ego and the Ego Ideal is from *Group Psychology and the Analysis of the Ego*, XI.

Flaubert's affirmation is recorded in Part III of, and his relation with his fiction discussed throughout, *Flaubert and Madame Bovary*, by Francis Steegmuller.

V

'Genius, Wit, and Taste'

1. Fiction Re-Read

THE fact that adopted daydreams are subject to tissue rejection dictates some of the development of 20th-century fiction.

If fiction is to cast off not just the unfair reproaches that are brought against daydreams but also the genuine disability that goes with the daydream form, then it must rid itself of the Victorian novel's subservience to narrative.

That need not mean it must rid itself of narrative. But the narrative, if there's to be one, together with its demands on continuity and naturalistic plausibility, must be subordinated to the design – in which narrative is welcome to be one of the elements, as it is in the novels of Jane Austen.

This process may bring 20th-century fiction fewer readers, but it will bring it more readings.

At the same time, it will give fiction the means of restoring itself to parity with the other arts. A collector desires to possess a painting precisely because he would like to look at it more than once. A music-lover would think it absurd to hear a symphony or an opera once with enjoyment and then never dream of hearing it again. Yet fiction, during the period when it was tied to the importance narrative has in daydreams, was tied to exactly that absurdity.

While narrative dominated it, fiction, though it might be great art as well, was consumer-goods – and perishable consumer-goods. The best claim it could make on society was that it did the state a generalised version of the service done by pornography:[1] a generalised but thereby less urgent version, since the private existence of daydreams in general produces less anxiety, and therefore less danger to the state, than the private existence of masturbation fantasies.

Now, however, fiction need not make claims on society at all. It can, if its practitioners design well enough, assert the autonomous importance of an art.

Towards their designing well enough, novelists have a new freedom to exploit – which, naturally, terrifies many of them. A novelist is no longer

[1] Cf. Chapter I, 4.

tied to the Victorian and daydream habit of designing in terms of hero and events. He can design thematically, in units that consist of emotional or linguistic (or both) motifs, which he may distribute over the events, and over the people and their dialogue, according to the logic of the design rather than the logic of narrative and characterisation.

In this he wields a new method of making his images important. A good lyric poem or a good operatic aria has always been infinitely re-readable or re-hearable because the image, in its sensuously attractive verbal or vocal incarnation, makes itself important enough to command its auditors to fall in love with it and turn it into an object of their personal cult, to which they seek repeated recourse.

In producing this result, prose lacks the regular and repetitive rhythms of music and verse, which work on the auditor like incantatory charms – though prose may gain, by its subtler rhythms, a greater flexibility in making effects of intellectual onomatopoeia. A novelist cannot wholly rely on rhythm and the sensuous sound of his words to seal his images into their own importance. He must either invest them, by his language, with such emotional intensity that each image is surrounded by its own nimbus; or, which is Firbank's method, he must design his book in terms not only of material but of space, so that by disposing his spaces he can give his images their full intensity of importance by displaying them in isolation.

2. Firbank and the Isolation of the Image

FIRBANK'S images[1] leave a strong and composed impression on the retina of the reading mind. He inks in the elements of the thing, relation or scene he is presenting. This nexus is already delimited by the shapes and omissions of its own content, and Firbank often isolates it further still, frames it and sets it in perspective, by placing it inside the dialogue of one of his personages.

Between the spoken image and the speech Firbank sets up a reflective relation, of irony or contrast. A paragraph of *The Flower beneath the Foot* frames an impression of what it is, visually, like to be royalty inside the disclosure that King William of Pisuerga is the sort of person to notice and make complaint of his condition: ' "Whenever I go out," the King

[1] Complaint has lately been made (by a phonetic namesake of Firbank) against the use, in writing about writing, of the word *image* in the way I am using it now. I will explain in a note in sub-section 7 of this chapter why I think the complaint has no force. *Image* seems to me a useful word in writing about fiction in general, because it is cognate with (and therefore reminds you of) *imagination*, and in writing about Firbank's fiction in particular, because his methods resemble (and perhaps have the same chinoiserie/japonaiserie inspiration as) the methods of Ezra Pound's Imagist poetry.

complained, "I get an impression of raised hats." ' A paragraph of *Vainglory* exposes a little of the speaker's nature and all of the nature of the forthcoming marriage she is discussing, at the same time compiling a complete and ineradicable visual image of comic-grotesque horror, like a floral chamberpot enshrined: ' "The cake", Mrs. Henedge said, beginning to purr, "is to be an exact replica of the Victoria Memorial." '

The technique of isolating a single image in space Firbank learned from his cult of the black-and-white drawings of Aubrey Beardsley – round so many of which Beardsley drew frames, either elaborately decorative or of the most exactly sited ruled lines. It is a technique which Beardsley in turn had learnt largely from the Japanese,[1] who practise it both in the visual arts and in poetry.

The isolation an image holds in Japanese poetry is achieved also in the ancient Greek poetry of Sappho which, brief to begin with, has often been lopped into sharp fragments by the accidents of history. Firbank's first-published fully Firbankian novel, *Vainglory*, concerns the fictitious recovery of a hitherto unknown fragment of Sappho – and thereby gave notice that Firbankianness consists of recovering the japonaiserie method practised by Sappho in collaboration with historical accident, and putting it to use in 20th-century novels.

(Well before he adopted and adapted the literary method of the Greek originator, Firbank made a cult object[2] of the name Sappho: in its French and 19th-century form as the Sapho of Alphonse Daudet's novel of 1884. At the age of 15, Firbank went with his brother to see Réjane [an actress much depicted by Beardsley] play in the dramatised version. The brothers named a dog Sapho in celebration of the performance.)

In literal fact, there is quite a lot of white space in a Firbank novel, because he composes in shortish sections. His is a lyric brevity. But there are even more spaces to be mentally heard than to be seen. The continuity of Firbank's prose changes direction with almost each of his shortish paragraphs or lines of dialogue. The small hiatus, the moment's glottal stop, which this makes in the reader's attention as he finds the new path, constitutes the space which is as important in Firbank's designs, and in Beardsley's, as the images themselves.

This is the only material whereby a writer can create the equivalent of the draughtsman's white space. Firbank is a writer of dandified fastidiousness

---

[1] 'I struck out a new style and method of work which was founded on Japanese art but quite original in the main.' (Beardsley in 1892 to his former headmaster; pp. 33–4 in the 1971 edition of his *Letters*.)

[2] There will be more about this cult of Firbank's in Chapter XV, 13–14.

and extreme condensation. 'I think nothing', he wrote in a letter, 'of fileing fifty pages down to make a brief, crisp paragraph, or even a row of dots!' He said while he was writing it that *Concerning the Eccentricities of Cardinal Pirelli* was to be very 'short & very elaborate & condensed'. He described his own writing as Jane Austen might have described hers: 'aggressive, witty, & unrelenting'.

Unrelentingly indeed Firbank discards superfluities and selects only those images that bear a highly condensed metaphorical weight. These he does not dispose as if they were building-blocks, squarely one on top of the other, in the expected continuities of narrative, argument or exposition, where so much is put in merely for the sake of the narrative's, argument's or exposition's thread and an impression of solidity is built up by the cheat of the writer's telling the reader a great many things the reader could supply for himself.

Instead, Firbank disposes his images in zig-zag relations to each other. The isolation of the images, which continuous prose cannot achieve by Japanese poetry's method of simply stopping at the end of the image, is achieved by the jagged juxtaposition of one image to another. The image is displayed in its importance during the pause the reader is forced to make as he negotiates its unpredictable relation to the image before it.

Firbank is a mosaicist, and one who designs with the shapes of the gaps as well as the shapes of the pieces. While he was working out the method, Firbank echoed the mosaic nature of his compositions in his literal procedure for composing. By the time the method was mature, he had resorted to notebooks, but his acquaintance Sir Coleridge Kennard[1] recorded his earlier habit of writing phrases on long strips of paper, which he hoarded until he was ready to compose by placing each of them 'here and there like a piece of velvet or brocade'. No doubt Firbank changed his method because he feared the fate which (as I mentioned in Chapter II, 3) he afterwards, when he felt safe to do so, attributed to the ghostly Saint Teresa, that of losing one of the pieces.

The changes of direction between Firbank paragraphs, which throw the images of both paragraphs into isolated conspicuousness and importance, follow the method of that moving 16th-century love song:

> O Western wind, when wilt thou blow
> That the small rain down can rain?
> Christ, that my love were in my arms,
> And I in my bed again!

[1] Of whom Chapter XII, 5 and 6 will give some account.

3. Firbank and Psychology

FIRBANK'S method of composing in bits and gaps has the advantage of making the surface of his books exceptionally flexible. For the surface consists of a sort of (glittering) chain mail.

This allowed Firbank to respond before other writers to the 20th century's awareness of psychology. The flexible chain mail can flex with, and thus disclose, the coilings and uncoilings of the unconscious motifs beneath the book's surface. Firbank wielded not only the traditional power of the novelist to express unconscious images in metaphors but a new power to disclose the directions of concealed motivations in his design by the shapes of the gaps in his texture.

The changes of direction in his surface continuity are dictated by the logic of the unconscious structure of the book. By the book's superficial logic, they appear arbitrary. But at the same time they help to make the book's surface attractive, because their arbitrariness has the quality of being perverse and bizarre. Their unconscious logic is like the truth in a witticism that makes it witty. They are arbitrary not because they discount logic but because they are obeying the invisible and more powerful logic beneath; and that makes their perversity not wilful but Baudelairean.

Thus, by developing an artistic method for the sake of art, Firbank solved a problem which baffled many 20th-century writers who went after a solution for the sake of psychology.

Surrealist writers ran into the tedium of dream-narrative – which is tedious because one can plunge totally into the logic of the unconscious only by becoming unconscious, when one invents one's own dreams. Where no logic except the unconscious kind is visible, the conscious is given no material in which to construct an interpretation of the unconscious logic. The content of the unconscious can be revealed to the conscious mind of a reader only by glimpses: through, for example, Firbank's gaps.

Other writers went a longer way round in pursuit of the unconscious, a way round that was predestined never to arrive. How extensively Freud was misunderstood, how the misunderstanding was dictated by resistance to what he had disclosed, and how the most resistance-provocative item among his disclosures was not, as it is commonly considered to be, the sexual content of the unconscious but the unconsciousness of the unconscious: all that is nicely demonstrated by the fact that the first and most numerous literary responses to Freud's discovery of the unconscious consisted of more and more detailed and extensive representations of consciousness. Undisciplined by the muscled paragraphing and parenthesising of Proust's intellectual talent, the streams of literary consciousness flowed ever more profuse and ever more diffuse, as though the introduction of psychoanalysis to the world had added to it nothing except the technique of free association.

4. A Message from Firbank's Career for Socialists

WITH one important exception,[1] Firbank's fictions contain no message whatsoever to society. But his career as an author of fictions contains a message for socialists – in the Edwardian-onwards sense whereby 'we are all socialists nowadays'.

Works of art have and need no justification but themselves. Art is a self-justifying activity in the same way that (probably) life is, asserting its own importance instinctually, and vindicating its importance not by where it is going but by the intensity with which it *is*.

Life is a growth, perhaps ultimately a pathological growth, on matter. It rearranges the patterns of matter into a new *order* of organisation, so that particles of matter, quite recognisable as themselves, become, in the new organisation, alive instead of inert. Art can claim in its turn to be a growth on life (chiefly but probably not quite exclusively human life), though it might admit that it, too, is ultimately a pathological growth.

However, though art is a superstructure that claims to be self-vindicating, it is not self-supporting. Art can come into existence only while artists' lives continue in existence. The creation and appreciation of works of art will stop if society, which is the distributive organisation of human life, stops arranging some particles of matter into bread-and-butter and stops distributing some slices of that in the direction of artists' mouths.

During the Victorian interlude, it was occasionally not necessary for society to arrange to distribute a subsidy to its fictioneers in advance of their producing the fictions. It was just possible for a novelist to make a beginning by subsidising himself, while he did it, by his work at some other trade.

However, doing two jobs is always an exhausting scramble, likely to lead to scamping both. A few timid literary temperaments prefer two jobs, because they fear to invest all their self-esteem as well as all their financial prospects in their literary talent. But most novelists, when they can become full-time professionals, do. And a Victorian novelist, if he could once float himself, stood a goodish chance of being swept up by mass readerships.

However, the Victorian interlude was an exception, brought about by the coincidence of cheap print, newly widened literacy, a mass demand for drugs and the absence of alternative types of drug. And a Victorian novelist

[1] Which Chapters XV, 14 and XIX, 18 will discuss.

could supply the drug-demand only by developing to its utmost the daydreamer's skill of filling in time – which might, though it doesn't necessarily, mean that while he was forming himself as a novelist he scamped on the development of more exhausting fictional skills.

Before the Victorian episode, European society was quite in the habit of directly subsiding some of its fictioneers. However, its own social prejudices, which were often also those of the fictioneers, sometimes prevented both parties from seeing that that was what society was doing.

In 1813, when she had published two novels, Jane Austen wrote to her brother: 'every copy of S. & S. is sold & [. . .] it has brought me £140 besides the Copyright, if that shd ever be of any value. – I have now therefore written myself into £250 – which only makes me long for more.'

And in 1870 her nephew, Austen-Leigh, computed that 'the profits of the four' novels 'which had been printed before her death had not at that time amounted to seven hundred pounds'.

Austen-Leigh rightly thought the less than £700 little enough. But as a matter of fact it was even littler than he thought, because he was mistaken in describing it as 'profits'. That is how many outsiders, many publishers and even a few naïve authors compute an author's profits. A publisher deducts from his own profits the 'overheads' of running and housing his secretariat, but it is frequently forgotten that an author also makes a running investment, by the way of keeping himself and his imagination alive, which has to be deducted from any possible profit you may compute as coming from his imaginative works.

In the case of Jane Austen, the investment that kept her (just) alive while she taught herself how to write consisted of the extremely straitened family income. This didn't seem to Austen-Leigh a subsidy, invested in her writing, because she would have had the benefit of it in any case, whether or not she wrote. To him, and most probably to her, it seemed a private income, to which she had a right.

To socialist eyes, she had no more right to it than anyone else. She could exert a right only by claiming it as a literary subsidy, in the name not of her birth but of her vocation. But even in non-socialist, in merely social eyes, it is clearly a social income, derived from somebody's work, which society accidentally, through its system of private 'rights' to property, directed to Jane Austen.

This method of subsiding some fictioneers western society maintained through the Victorian interlude; and after the Victorian readerships seceded it became virtually the only financial system on which fiction could be produced. Marcel Proust, Henry James and James Joyce were subsidised by society via their own or someone else's private income. In 1904, E. M. Forster inherited £8,000, which alone, he declared later, made his career 'as a writer possible'. Neither were novelists the only literary artists to need subsidy. The socialist pamphleteer-dramatist Bernard Shaw married a private income. And in poetry the need for one was taken for granted. In 1915, Firbank's Cambridge acquaintance Rupert Brooke touchingly left not only his royalties but the capital from his private allowance to three fellow poets.

Firbank himself was one of the novelists society subsidised through a private income. The Firbank family income was created in the first place by the bodily labour of the men who, during the 19th century, built the English railways. The novelist's grandfather, Joseph Firbank, after starting work at the age of seven as a miner in County Durham and getting himself a schooling (for which he had to pay) at evening classes, turned labourer on a railway construction scheme. The secondary source of the family income was the shrewdness and energy with which this labouring Firbank organised his fellow labourers, securing continued work for them and for himself continued work and profit – some of which he had the further shrewdness to invest in land about to be bought by the railways. He began by getting a sub-contract. He became a free-lance contractor, who (witness Plate 1) built a great many lines for the then numerous, privately owned and quickly expanding railway companies of Britain.

Out of the income derived from those sources, Ronald Firbank made the investment in himself that most novelists make, though some of them have to be their own labourers. That is to say, he kept himself alive while he learned to write and wrote. But Firbank also made a further and unusual investment: not merely in the writing but in the peddling of his works.

The publishers of the first eight of Firbank's ten completed books were the publishers only in name. It was not they but Firbank who put up the capital for the enterprise.

Six months after that eighth book appeared, Firbank complained to his 'publisher': 'I find since 1914 I have spent not far short of £1000 on the production of my books & it is not unreasonable in 1923 to be expecting some return.'

No return ever came. However, in Firbank's next and ninth book, a publisher, not in Great Britain but in the United States, was prepared to make the investment that publishers normally make. In 1924 *Prancing Nigger* was published under that name, which Carl Van Vechten gave it by extrapolation from Firbank's text, in the United States, and then in Britain under Firbank's own title for it, *Sorrow in Sunlight*: in both countries by the United-States publisher Brentano's.

(In the next year Brentano's went back virtually to the beginning of Firbank's œuvre and gave commercial publication in the United States to *Vainglory*, whose publication in Britain Firbank had financed himself a decade before.[1])

In July 1924, Firbank received a cheque from his publishers: 'this reward for my work – the first indeed after so long!' he called it. There was another cheque, for $695, in October.

But Firbank's next, tenth and, as it turned out, last complete book, *Concerning the Eccentricities of Cardinal Pirelli*, was refused by Brentano's on 'religious and moral grounds'. Firbank reverted to self-subsidy. He put up the money for ... *Cardinal Pirelli* to be published and died, aged 40, five and a bit weeks before it came out, leaving £1,000 in trust on which the Society of Authors was to pay for someone to publish a posthumous collected edition of all his work.

Throughout his life Firbank did what the Society of Authors strongly counsels all writers not to do, for the sake alike of their purses and of their professional standing. The argument runs that, if a book is of professional standard, a professional publisher will sooner or later publish it, and for an author to subsidise the publication is merely to gratify his vanity (whence author-subsidised publishing is sometimes called 'vanity publishing').

But the argument holds true only if you can be sure that at least one of your publishers will be professional enough to spot a good, let alone a Firbankianly great, artist, despite the fact that the artist may be using an original, and therefore disconcerting, idiom. Even then it holds good only if you can, further, be sure that the public contains enough professional readers to back the publisher financially in his insight. For a publisher who invests in his private taste, without the expectation of public support, is being an unprofessional publisher.

As it happens, paying for his own works to be published *didn't* gratify Firbank's vanity. That he had to do it wounded him. But, even if it had gratified him, his vanity would still have been the least of the things to benefit from being subsidised out of the hard work of railway construction labourers. The other beneficiary is the art of fiction, which benefited chiefly by Firbank's own masterpieces but also by several good books and many good public entertainments written under the inspiration of Firbank. If all writers who owe an artistic debt to Firbank were to pay back to him a tithe of their royalties, tiny though those royalties are in many of our cases, the total would accumulate well beyond the 'return' Firbank hoped to see. But

---

[1] This is the half in the one and a half exceptions I footnoted in the Outline Chronology at the beginning of the book.

then the total wouldn't have accumulated until long after Firbank's death. For Firbank's disability as a financial investment was that he wrote what one of his 'publishers' described as 'advanced modern work' – an investment that takes time to mature.

Firbank's is the crucial case on which the apparent empirical commonsense of our western system of publishing as a small-scale capitalist investment breaks down. And so does the even older system in which society subsidises authors through private incomes.

That older system was always unjust (a socialist comment) and wasteful (a social one). A talented artist might be born outside sniffing distance of a private income. And at the same time quantities of cash were squandered on the private incomes of people who were neither artists nor socially useful or decorative. Nowadays, whether by the designs of social justice or by the accidents of a more fluid capitalism, private (inherited) incomes are drying up in many western countries. This possibly cuts down the waste of society's money but it increases the chances of wasting great artists. The less randomly society distributes its private incomes, the smaller chance it has of hitting an artistic talent with one of them.

The social message to be read in Firbank's career is that it is highly unlikely that a present-day Firbank would be in a position to subsidise English literature as Firbank did. This puts to present-day society the problem of how it is going to subsidise literature from now on.

Lending Right (equivalent to the performing fees paid to composers) might enable some established writers to finance their future books on the proceeds of their past ones. But this act of simple justice would still not finance a writer while he *becomes* established. Public subsidy is often suspect, thanks to public fear of being conned. And, indeed, all plans for public subsidy yet devised are liable to result in some money going to self-deceiving frauds (genuine bad artists) or to candidates whose talent is not for literature but for impressing committees.

The remedy, however, is not smaller but greater generosity. Only by spreading the money more widely can we increase the chances of getting some of it to the new Firbank. Ultimately society will solve this and many other of its problems by introducing equality of income for everyone. But as an interim solution, designed to keep literature alive meanwhile, there is no more practical instrument than large subsidies. It is a random method, in which waste is virtually inevitable. But the waste is much smaller and the chances of success much higher than under the old system of random private incomes, and the alternative is the closing-down of literature.

5. How Firbank?

FICTION, when Firbank began writing it, had suffered the sudden loss of the public support it had once commanded through its dependence on narrative; and at the same time it had reached a point where it could artistically save itself only by throwing what was left of the prop away.

There was an aesthetic crisis. Not only had readers lost faith in novelists: novelists had lost faith in novels.

Firbank answered to the crisis both before and better than contemporary talented writers. What put him in a way to doing so was simply, I suspect, that he was better acquainted than most writers with the visual arts.

His acquaintanceship with them went, historically, both forward and back.

He was a collector and the son of collectors, who became also a patron and a bohemian.

His childhood and adolescence were spent in an 18th-century house, surrounded by often 18th-century objects collected by the taste, probably, of both his parents and by his father's inherited money – this at a time when Edwardian fashion made a taste for the 18th century permissible but by no means so de rigueur as it has since become.

Thus Firbank's earliest stylistic pioneering was into the past. To submit yourself to an idiom unfamiliar through disuse is as pioneering an act as to submit yourself to one unfamiliar because it has never been used before. And the elasticity you develop in the one will serve you in the other. When I was an adolescent in London in the 1940s and acquainting myself with the orchestral repertory, concert audiences could scarcely be scraped together to heed music composed in their own lifetimes unless it was in a very old-fashioned idiom or very patriotic. But then the standard concert repertory scarcely went back beyond J. S. Bach either. In the 70s ordinary concert audiences will accept a 'modern' idiom – and also the idioms of Monteverdi and the Elizabethans.

When he became a collector in his own right, Firbank at first collected almost anything collectable and then suffered his concentrated attention to fix on the 18th century and, as it crept towards the less distant past, the Nineties – from whose artists he picked out, however, Aubrey Beardsley and Oscar Wilde, both of whom were pioneers of the future partly by virtue of reviving the methods of the 18th century.[1]

---

[1] Beardsley was surprised, in 1895, to learn that Goethe's collection included a drawing by Watteau, because 'The cult for him is so entirely modern' (p. 89 in the 1971 Cassell edition of Beardsley's *Letters*). Beardsley's belief is significant though it may not be

By the time he became a patron of Percy Wyndham Lewis and was conversant with all the -isms of modernism in the visual arts, Firbank was himself pioneering modernism in fiction. But his modernity, like most of the great modernities in art, consisted partly and importantly, though not mainly, of revivalism.

In this development, the visual arts were bound to be the crucial precipitator and Firbank's chief educator. The crisis Firbank was negotiating in fiction, the loss of confidence in the aesthetic self-sufficiency of naturalism, had happened before: in the visual arts.

There it was provoked by a technological invention: photography. The eventually extremely fertile nervous breakdown which photography caused the art of painting to suffer remains emotionally *the* aesthetic crisis, just as the French Revolution remains *the* revolution.

As a matter of fact, the aesthetics of painting never *had* depended on naturalism. And no sooner did Renaissance painting perfect the craft of representing scenes in naturalistic perspective than painters and inlayers of wood (such as those who worked in the Ducal Palace at Urbino) began playing with it the equivalent of Cervantes's narrative tricks, which forced the spectator to become conscious of the illusion and thus alienated him from his immersion in it.

But Vasari, with his vision (itself a false perspective) of the history of painting as a progress towards the Renaissance mastery of naturalistic representation, and with his almost ritual anecdotes of how this or that painter's goodness was proved when some animal, child or peasant unsophisticatedly mistook the painter's depiction for the actual object depicted, made it *seem* as if goodness in painting was the same thing as success in representationalism.

The painters themselves had at least half swallowed the error. Then a machine was invented which could be worked by comparatively unskilled and untrained hands and yet produce representations as true-to-appearances as paintings but cheaper, quicker and capable of being replica'd ad infinitum – which last point virtually abolished an entire métier, which had been useful to temporarily hard-up or permanently uninspired painters, that of copyist of paintings that copied appearances.

Inevitably painters suffered loss of livelihood or dread of losing it. No Sir Peter Lely was now needed to paint series of royal mistresses and classy courtesans. The series now consisted of picture (which now meant photographic) postcards. Firbank collected them when he was a boy.

correct. (A *Harlequin à la Watteau*, for instance, was staged in 1857 [A. E. Wilson: *Christmas Pantomime*].)

Royalty itself need no longer sit to Goya. It had itself photographed and handed out copies signed not (or not only) by the taker of the likeness but by the sitter. Firbank as a young man, during a visit to Spain on which he admired the Goyas, acquired (in exchange for a copy of his first volume) a royal photograph inscribed to him and signed by Isabel de Bourbon.

In 1908 royalty finally closed even the gap in skill which had made Goya obviously the superior of his socially supreme patrons. Queen Alexandra published her 'Christmas Gift Book' consisting of 'Photographs from my Camera'. Acknowledgement was made at the front to 'Kodak Limited (whose Kodaks were used by Her Majesty)'. Royalty stopped short only of taking royalties. The book was 'To be Sold for Charity'.

The loss of livelihood to painters entailed the loss of subject-matter to painting. It was not only royal faces and figures that were withdrawn as potential content for great paintings. Patrons, who in the past had sometimes laid down the thematic scheme a painter or decorator was to follow, now became unreceptive even to the painters' own schemes. History painting, a term in which the 'history' comprises fiction and mythology as well as history, fell out of favour, and the literary content, consisting of people and objects in illustration of or allusion to narratives true or imagined, fell out of painting.

Even ecclesiastical patronage turned lukewarm towards subject matter – in obedience to fashion rather than rationalised pretext, since photographs of Jesus Christ could not be supplied by machine. However, when canonisation had had time to catch up with photography, photographs of saints could. The standard icon in the cult of Saint Thérèse of Lisieux is her photograph. Even when the labour of painting by hand seems more pious, the paintings are usually copied from photographs.

Photography put painting in the position which fiction had been in since it ceased to rest on mythology, and which music had always been in (unless you exempt the theme-and-variations form): that of having to think up its own subject-matter.

Some painters adopted a type of subject-matter more appropriate to literature, and painted anecdotes. Painting is so unsuited to making a story clear to the spectator, unless he knows it in advance from a literary text, that some anecdotal pictures turned into the 'problem pictures' that gave scandal and pleasure to spectators at the Royal Academy. (So fashionable did the genre become that Sir Edward Elgar invented a problem picture in music, his Enigma Variations.)

Painters of greater independence of mind began, however, to move clean away from subject-matter. Some tried to outdo the camera by capturing more precise and fleeting truths-to-nature than cameras could, in which case the subject-matter began to vanish behind an impressionist or pointillist haze. Expressionist painters subordinated the subject to the emotions it provoked; presently the subject became only the incarnation of the emotions. And eventually abstract painting removed subject-matter totally.

These developments contained a lesson for fiction, which Firbank read: the subordinate importance of subject-matter. Indeed, a work's design can be its own subject-matter. That is not to say that subject-matter may not be a theme in a fiction's design. But a fictioneer does not need to take large or important subject-matter in order to write a great and important fiction.

In painting, the need for painters to think up their own subject-matter had the advantage of forcing them to think out their own aesthetic – by forcing them to analyse their relation to their subject-matter. The panic in painting consisted of painters' belief, though it wasn't true, that they had lost their aesthetic, the direst loss an artist can suffer.

Before the 19th century, a school of painting represented fashions in taste among patrons and, among the painters, reflected who had been apprenticed to whom or travelled where to become subject to what influences. After photography precipitated modern painting, a school meant an ideological movement, an -ism: a militant group united by having communally thought out its own aesthetic.

It was photography that accidentally created the avant-garde situation.

And because photography was a technological device and one that had seemed to disrupt an aesthetic, artists in the avant-garde situation were deceived into trying to borrow back for themselves the prestige of technology. 'Experimental art' was a catchphrase (one that Firbank used in adaptation) which was often a false attempt to give an art the kudos of a science.

The catchphrase implied that the result of a successful experiment would be not just the artistic success of the individual work of art concerned but, as it is in science, the formulation of a general rule, by knowing which other artists in the -ism group, and indeed art in general, would progress in the sense that science progresses.

This brought aesthetics back to its condition under Vasari, but now it wore a laboratory overall.

At the same time there was opened up the gap between artists and public which gave Firbank so much grief.

For, in the avante-garde situation, the patron, who commissions the work and agrees to or even lays down its subject-matter and its aesthetic, has almost entirely turned into (by a transformation which happened earlier in literature than in painting, because of the invention of print) a public, which selects or rejects the works after the artist has devised everything about them himself.

Instead of resting on the absolute importance of the artistic solutions a work of art makes when it analyses its own individual fantasy content, the militant avant-garde -isms implied that they could, by experiment, discover universal artistic solutions to artistic problems, in the way science does to scientific problems. Their militancy provoked the public to suspicion. For if one -ism were to be absolutely right, the others would be absolutely wrong. If art were indeed a progress like science, you, the public, might get caught in the ridiculous position of having invested your money and affection in a side-channel instead of the mainstream. And as it is *not* in fact a progress like science, there are none of the rational criteria that there are in science by which, if you are informed and intelligent, you can make your choice.

Public suspicion of the modern in the arts consists of that deepest dread experienced by anyone who has his own approval and his own or the public's money to disburse, the fear of being conned.

Firbank was both a member of the public with some of his family income to spend and also a patron in the old sense that he decreed that the subject-matter of the drawings he commissioned was to be his face.

He knew that the portrait of himself he had Wyndham Lewis draw would seem to public taste puzzlingly modern: he agreed with his 'publisher' that it was 'wildly obscure' but insisted on reproducing it in one of his books all the same.

Simultaneously, Firbank was a modern practitioner: in a small way, of pencil and watercolour drawing, and in a major way of fiction.

Thus he was perfectly placed to take the great lesson modern painting held for all the arts, namely that it is the design that matters. 'I am all design – once I get going,' Firbank wrote of himself as literary artist.

Yet at the same time Firbank's practice as an artist gives the lie to the modernist fallacy that art is a progression in which the most advanced art must be among the most recent art, because his practice consists of pioneering backwards.

Firbank demonstrated that the most advanced art to be produced in England in 1915 – so far advanced, indeed, ahead of the public that the gap between the public and the art was painful to the artist – was a novel which applied the aesthetic theory of Oscar Wilde, constructed its design in the manner of Jane Austen[1] and put together its fabric by the more-than-two-millennia-old imagist method of Sappho.

---

[1] As Chapters XVIII and XIX in general (and XIX, 3 in particular) will elaborate.

6. Aesthete and Artist

FIRBANK, as I shall presently relate,[1] bound himself in tacit apprenticeship to Oscar Wilde: in the subjects of aestheticism and homosexuality.

The conviction of the autonomous importance of arts, which Jane Austen put into practice, Wilde made into an explicit aesthetic. Firbank adopted the faith from Wilde and on the courage of it managed to go on writing his own works of art despite the reluctance of critics and public to agree with him that they were important or, even, that they *were* art.

Wilde himself, in the Irish manner shared by Bernard Shaw (a manner probably imposed on the nation by its not being allowed to *be* a nation and by the resultant lack of practical power in its citizens), began by theorising better than he could practise.

Firbank, who was only half Irish, theorised less and also much less well. He kept his theorising down to a single, early essay in art-historical criticism[2] and his preface to the United-States edition of *The Flower Beneath the Foot*, plus those conversations early in his life which his first and better memorialist, Ifan Kyrle Fletcher,[3] reported as full of 'attractive theories – the affinity between prose narrative and Impressionist painting and the ineluctable brightness[4] of *le mot juste*'.

Wilde was not given time to vindicate his theory in practice by producing more than one perfect work of art[5] before he was caught by the outlandish persecution of homosexuals then promoted by English law.

At the time of Wilde's trials, Firbank (who never lost sight of the message they held about what society might do to *him*) was nine and Wilde himself 40, though giving 39 in cross-examination.

Wilde's lie set a camp precedent for Firbank's ritually camp answer (when at the age of 36 he was asked by letter for details about himself) that he was in fact older but never admitted to more than 19.

However, Firbank's honesty soon amended the tease by supplying the literal answer. Three months later, he wrote again to the same correspondent (who was the United-States novelist, Carl Van Vechten,[6] who began writing

---

[1] in Part Three (Chapters XI–XV).
[2] which will be discussed in Chapter IX, 6, 7 and 9.
[3] whose *Memoir* will be discussed in Chapter VI, 2.
[4] I suspect this word (which is on p. 43 in the *Memoir*) of being a misprint for 'rightness'.
[5] the one whose dialogue he described as 'sheer comedy, and the best I have ever written' (p. 369 in Rupert Hart-Davis's edition of the Wilde *Letters*).
[6] of whom in the following year (1923) Gertrude Stein wrote *Van or Twenty Years After, A Second Portrait of Carl Van Vechten* (included in *Look at Me Now and Here I Am*).

to Firbank when he discovered Firbank's work and, simultaneously, J. C. Squire's ignorance of it[1]) and said that, on the strength of some for once applauding newspaper cuttings, he felt 'quite like a bottle of prohibition whiskey' instead of like what he really was, a '*Veuve Cliquot* (1886), special cavee'. (The last word is presumably either Firbank's or the transcriber's mistake for *cuvée*.) This Firbank's more recent biographer quotes without noticing that in it Firbank makes amends for the 'coyness' she reproves in his previous letter. The vintage year he assigns to the champagne is the true year of Firbank's birth, and he answers the request for information about himself very fully and fairly – by also throwing in the truth about his sexual disposition encoded in the gender of the veuve.

(There will be more about this champagne in Chapter IX, 3.)

Later still, and still in his correspondence with Van Vechten, Firbank de-widowed himself, while preserving the gender: 'I am a *spinster* sir, & by God's grace, intend to stay so.'

Even in his one perfected creative work, *The Importance of Being Earnest*, Wilde demonstrated how deeply his true as well as brilliant aesthetic theory had been developed from his adoration of Jane Austen's aesthetic practice. This he did by lifting Lady Bracknell's interview technique with Jack Worthing directly from Lady Catherine de Bourgh's in the interview where she tries to intimidate Elizabeth Bennet out of similar marital pretensions; by lifting Algernon Moncrieff's flirtation technique, in his passage with Cecily Cardew on the subject of her keeping a journal, directly from Henry Tilney's with Catherine Morland on the identical subject; and by causing the Hon. Gwendolen Fairfax to couch her suggestion that she and Cecily should escape from the young men in the words 'Let us go into the house. They will scarcely venture to follow us there' – words that echo the 'Let us go and look at the new arrivals. They will hardly follow us there', which is Isabella Thorpe's suggestion to Catherine Morland for *their* escape from young men in the Pump-Room at Bath.

Thus it was Wilde who took Firbank back to the 18th-century tone in which Firbank wrote 'wildly obscure' works of 20th-century fiction.

E. J. Dent, a musicologist who had been an acquaintance of Firbank's at Cambridge, recorded afterwards his reaction to *Vainglory* when it was first published in 1915: 'You can imagine how puzzled I was by its style.'

Something must be subtracted from E. J. Dent's account to allow for how easy it was to puzzle E. J. Dent – which can be judged from his book on Mozart's operas. To be fair to Dent, the very things that puzzled him also

---

[1] Cf. Chapter I, 3.

pleased him. He went on to record that he enjoyed *Vainglory* 'hugely', and presumably he also enjoyed Mozart's operas. Indeed, his was one of the influences that procured their revival in England. But he so misconceived the artist he was promoting that he could not even recount Mozart's plots without blunders, and he practised so many inadvertent insensibilities and condescensions towards Mozart that he might have contributed more to his appreciation by leaving him alone.

What attracted and yet puzzled E. J. Dent was in fact the same quality in both Mozart and Firbank:[1] an 18th-century quality (which, however, by no means all 18th-century artists possess).

Vainglory declared itself emancipated, in 1915, from the long Victorian tyranny of plot. Its story is no more to be taken literally than that of *Die Zauberflöte*, no more to be taken seriously as a thing in itself than that of *Die Entführung aus dem Serail*. Yet the emotions provoked in its toils are as serious as Constanze's and Belmonte's courage and love unto death. Mrs Asp, in *Vainglory*, discloses that in her new novel 'There's no plot [. . .] no plot exactly.' And Mrs Thumbler, like E. J. Dent, is 'unable to imagine a novel without a plot'.

Newly emancipated, *Vainglory* exploits its freedom by achieving a new tone. What made it so modern, in 1915, as to be puzzling was that it did something that had scarcely been achieved in English fiction since the death of Jane Austen and, when it was attempted, had not been much appreciated: it sets the author (and the reader) at a distance from his material, without making him emotionally remote from it.

Firbank is in no way an archaiser. His methods are governed by a 20th-century aesthetic. His wit is more fragmented than Jane Austen's, his irony more terrified, less resigned, in its tragicness. He is the 20th century's, and entirely the 20th century's, Jane Austen: one of the great artists whose greatness consists in their being, intensively, *artists*.

7. Notes to Chapter V

The chief objection raised (in *Reflections on the Word 'Image'*, by P. N. Furbank, 1970) against *image* as a counter in literary discussion is the literal-minded one that in its ordinary meaning an image is 'a likeness, a picture, or a simulacrum', which can be seen, whereas a literary image can't be seen and, according to the objector, often can't be visualised. 'If you read Milton's phrase, "a Forest huge of

---

[1] The similarity was recognised, though apologetically, by Cyril Connolly in 1936: 'That doesn't mean I think he is as good as Mozart, I hasten to say, but that in him more than in any contemporary writer I find that taste.'

Spears", the final result of your reading can't be a picture, since you cannot permanently present something to your mind's eye as being both a forest and spears.'

This seems a sad underestimation of the mind's eye. Goodness knows why *permanence* should be a criterion: I can't present *anything* permanently to my mind's eye; but momentarily *my* mind's eye, for one, can't help, when I read Milton's phrase, superimposing a quick mental allusion to the abstract, skeletal shape of a forest on a similarly brief and abstract mental allusion to spears (about which the forest has given me the information that they are standing up, not lying down or sloped).

But even where (if there are such instances) a literary image truly can't be visualised, there is still nothing against calling it an image. Language (and par excellence the English language) is metaphorical. If I may say 'I see' when I mean 'I understand', I need not hesitate to use the word *image* of something I perceive (another word which basically means *see*) by senses other than sight.

And even when I look at the most palpably visible type of image, a picture, and even when it is a representational picture, it is still not by my eyes alone that I 'see' it. My dog sees the same object merely as a square of canvas. If I see it as a landscape, that is because my mind, schooled to the conventions of western art, 'reads' what my eyes shew me. In order to *be* an image, a picture has to be readable. Not only may literature consist of images; images in their most literal sense are also reading-matter. Word-sounds are only slightly more formalised symbols than the flicks of pen or paint we agree and learn to read as light, shade and outline. Some alphabets even merge the two types of symbolisation.

The objections to *image* are, at heart, objections that can be made only by forgetting the fact of fiction: not only in fictional literature but in painting. Even a representational painting is not merely or simply a transcription of something the painter has before his eyes. A painting may *represent* a mother and child whom the painter has seen and yet be an *image* of the madonna and child whom he hasn't seen and whom he may not believe to objectively exist. The painter (or mythology) has invented the imagist content of that picture. And in all representational painted pictures the painter has invented the relation of the representation to the shape of the whole: he has invented the composition which holds the subject-matter together and emphasises part of it; and he has invented the *style* of his representationalism. Only a camera transcribes appearances by fixed formula (though even then the formula as a whole can be slightly varied by photographer and developer). The representationalism of late Titian is quite different from that of early Titian, which is quite different from that of Ingres or of Giotto.

All this is forgotten in the objector's remark that 'the most obvious difference between literature and painting is that a writer has only to use a word like "beech-tree" or "pagoda" for the reader to run up a complete imaginary model of a beechtree or a pagoda unaided. Thus in so far as a writer is thought of as using "images", he has no need of a medium – he need not toil over paint and canvas.'

But, although representing a beechtree can supply the painter with enough subject-matter to cover his canvas, the representation that can be read as 'beechtree' will be the least important (the least individual to the painter, the least pleasure-giving to the spectator, the least capable of incarnating the painter's emotion) of the many things to be discerned in his canvas. The symbols which can be deciphered to read 'tree' are no more than the raw material of the image. The essence of the image is in the composition and the style which are the painter's inventions. A tree by Claude and a tree in a Japanese print are not two versions of the same image. They are two images.

For a writer, 'beechtree', because it is recognisable in itself as a symbol of a beechtree, can't even *seem*, incorrectly, to provide the material of his composition. The non-fiction writer employs that quick and efficient symbol 'beechtree' in order to make a statement (true or false, useful or pointless) about the beechtree. The fictioneer, however, has to *invent* the subject-matter through which to make his beechtree important to the reader. He can't claim a real-life relevance of beech-trees to readers. The importance he gives the beechtree is a strictly literary importance. By the sensuous content of the words (their sound, their onomato-poetic effect, the sensuous values of what they signify), and by the internal tensions, the design, of the image he builds with the words, he impresses the literary image on the attention, the memory and the affection of his readers.

'I love you', in real life a statement deeply important to X if made by Y, is not a love poem. It may have the urgency of real-life truth and sincerity but it has no literary urgency. The fictioneering imagination has to re-conceive and re-create it, inventing a language of conceits (a word that could be used as an alternative to *images*, were it not that *conceit* is a doublet of *concept* and *concept* has been sullied by metaphysicians). That language is needed not to express but to incarnate the thought; for the thought without its literary substance *has* no literary being, but only a real-life being. A writer of fiction doesn't look for images to clothe 'what he wants to say'. If what he wants to say doesn't present itself to him in the form of images, he is not and should not try to be a writer of fiction.

An image in fiction is simply a small literary invention (on the scale whereby the whole design of a novel or a dramatis persona plus his life-history is a large one). Though small, the image may be very condensed. Each item in it may be a hook which links it into the design of the work as a whole. By the same token, each item in it is related to the other internal items, which gives the image its unity, con-stituting it a single image – which impresses itself on the reader's imagination and memory in a single coup d'œil (or a coup of other sense organs).

The objection to using the name image for 'Milton's phrase "a Forest huge of Spears" ' rests ultimately on the elementary mistake of supposing that Milton was making a descriptive and non-fiction statement – that he was pointing out 'There are certain elements in common between a forest and a quantity of spears.' In reality, Milton's phrase (which is in line 447 of Book I of *Paradise Lost*) is about neither forests nor spears, but about the recruitment of morale (hence the importance of the uprightness of the spears) among the infernal host after their defeat by God.

The objections made by the same critic against a certain use of the word *world* have not prevented me from using the word, in my sub-sections and their titles *A Single World* and *A World Lost and Re-Created*, in just that way. The usage seems to me not vague but rich, and not a recent aberrant piece of jargon but a legitimate extension of an old and respectable tradition.

Indeed, the supposed vagueness of *world* is all present in the Latin *saeculum*; and the use that I and other writers of English make of *world* was implicit from the moment that the English church translated the creed's 'vitam venturi saeculi' as 'the life of the world to come'.

The impression of raised hats is on p. 503 in the *Complete* Firbank, the Victoria Memorial on p. 76.

The visit to the *Sapho* performance and the naming of the dog are recorded in Miriam J. Benkovitz's Firbank *Biography*, p. 29, which cites a Firbank letter of 1901.

Firbank's letter about 'fileing' down is of 17 May 1924 and is quoted in Miriam J. Benkovitz's *Biography*, p. 116. The same book quotes, on p. 262, Firbank's advance description of . . . *Cardinal Pirelli* and, on p. 191, his description of his work at large.

Sir Coleridge Kennard recorded Firbank's early procedure in composition in his Introduction (p. viii) to Firbank's *The Artificial Princess* (posthumously published in 1934).

Edward VII's 'We are all socialists nowadays' is quoted from his Mansion House speech of 1895 in *The Penguin Dictionary of Quotations*.

Jane Austen's financial letter was written to her brother Francis on 3 July 1813. Austen-Leigh's computation is in his *Memoir* of her, Chapter 6.

E. M. Forster's remark is quoted under 1904 in *The Literary Life* by Robert Phelps and Peter Deane.

Rupert Brooke's bequest to the three poets (Lascelles Abercrombie, Walter de la Mare and Wilfred Gibson) was expressed in a letter to his mother which is quoted in Section VII of Edward Marsh's *Memoir* of Rupert Brooke.

My account of Firbank's grandfather is founded on the 1887 biography of him by Frederick McDermott. The details and quotations about Firbank's publishing arrangements are in Miriam J. Benkovitz's *Bibliography* of Firbank's œuvre. Part of the quotation from his complaint to his 'publisher' is published in the 1961 catalogue of the Firbank sale at Sotheby's and re-published in an Appendix to *The New Rythum*.

Firbank's tastes as a collector are described in the Kyrle Fletcher *Memoir* and the Miriam J. Benkovitz *Biography*. Chapter V of the latter relates his acquisition of the Spanish royal photograph in 1905, citing information Firbank gave by letter to Carl Van Vechten in 1922.

Firbank's allusion to the theory of experiment in art is in his 1907 essay in art history, 'An Early Flemish Painter'.

Firbank's description of the Wyndham Lewis portrait is quoted in Miriam J. Benkovitz's *Biography*, p. 223. The same book (p. 155) quotes his 'I am all design' from his July 1924 letter to Stuart Rose.

Ifan Kyrle Fletcher's account of Firbank's conversational theorising is on pp. 43–4 of his *Memoir*.

Oscar Wilde lied about his age when he was cross-examined in the first trial, which was his own action for libel against the Marquess of Queensberry in April 1895. The lie is recorded on p. 120 of *The Trials of Oscar Wilde*, edited by H. Montgomery Hyde.

Firbank's letter about not admitting to more than 19 was to Carl Van Vechten and is quoted on pp. 218–19 of Miriam J. Benkovitz's Firbank *Biography*. The same book quotes the *Veuve Clicquot* letter on p. 223 and the spinster letter (which is of 1925) on p. 290.

Lady Bracknell interviews in Act I, and Algernon flirts and Gwendolen suggests retreat in Act II, of *The Importance of Being Earnest*. Lady Catherine interviews in *Pride and Prejudice*, Volume III, Chapter XIV. Henry Tilney flirts in Chapter III, and Isabella Thorpe suggests retreat in Chapter VI, of Volume I of *Northanger Abbey*.

E. J. Dent's remarks on *Vainglory* are quoted in Ifan Kyrle Fletcher's Firbank *Memoir*, p. 98.

The Cyril Connolly essay quoted in the footnote is called 'The Novel-Addict's Cupboard' and is collected in his *The Condemned Playground*.

The *Vainglory* quotations about the 'novel without a plot' are from p. 89 of *The Complete Ronald Firbank*.

PART TWO

IN PURSUIT OF FIRBANK

' "The King met us at the Railway station with his Crown on, and at the sight of him, poor Mamma lost all control of herself and laughed till she wept: 'He looks like a piece off a chess-board!' she gasped. 'How totally sweet!' " '

The Artificial Princess

Contents

OF PART TWO

In Pursuit of Firbank

Chapter VI	FIRBANK'S DEATH; LIVES OF FIRBANK; THE PRESENT STATE OF FIRBANK STUDIES	93
1	21 May 1926	93
2	The Memoir, 1930	95
3	Recognition, 1929	97
4	Further Critics	101
5	Further, however, Editions	104
6	Further Biographers – 1	106
7	Further Biographers – 2	115
8	Notes	117
Chapter VII	THE PORTRAIT BEGUN	120
1	The Wriggler and Giggler	120
2	The Drop-out with a Private Income	123
3	The Incipient Paranoiac	129
4	The Unnamed	136
5	The Flower Child – 1	145
6	Notes	147
Chapter VIII	THE PORTRAIT PURSUED	151
1	The Fully Dressed	151
2	The Minion	155
3	The Phobic	155

4	The Abstainer	157
5	The Gypsy	160
6	The Devil's Disciple	164
7	The Haunted	168
8	The Campist	171
9	The Inventor If Need Be	173
10	Notes	176

Chapter IX THE PORTRAIT RE-TOUCHED — 181

1	The Flower Child (?) – 2	181
2	Firbank and Sir Thomas	182
3	Firbank and Sir Thomas's Cellar	185
4	Firbank's Foot in his Father's World	187
5	A Further Meanness Uncovered	189
6	The Most Possible Profession	192
7	Portrait as Self-Portrait	196
8	Self-Portrait as Minion	197
9	Art History as Autobiography	199
10	Self-Portrait through an Incurable Feature	201
11	Self-Portrait as a Black	202
12	Notes	204

Chapter X PRINCESS ARTIE — 207

1	An Escort of fantastic Demons	207
2	A Single World	207
3	A World Lost and Re-Created	209
4	Home . . .	210
5	. . . and Church	211
6	The Church and Lady Appledore	212
7	A Cult Photograph	216
8	A Coronation	218
9	Imperial Chislehurst	219
10	Firbank and Tours	223
11	Firbank and French	225
12	Firbank and the Rules	228
13	Notes	234

VI

Firbank's Death; Lives of Firbank; the Present State of Firbank Studies

1. 21 May 1926

IN May 1926, when he was 40, Firbank was staying at the Quirinale hotel in Rome.

Apart from a necessary interruption during the 1914–18 war, it was the habit of his adult life to spend a good part of the year (a winter in one place, a spring in another) outside England.

The habit was to the benefit of his health and perhaps of his imagination (though he thought that living, as his nomadism often obliged him to, in clubs when he was in England and in hotels when he was abroad was an impediment to his writing).

Probably, being abroad also relieved him of the claustrophobic feelings which the legal persecution in England then induced in men who were homosexual. And – an argument he wielded explicitly – living abroad was cheaper. When his sister, Heather Firbank, found it hard to live on her portion of the family income, Firbank suggested she copy his example: for someone whose income came in English currency, the favourable exchange rates made the money stretch further abroad.

In May Firbank was planning a visit to England, which would be warming up for the summer. And from his hotel in Rome he was looking round for a flat in Rome, which he intended to rent at once and return to after his English visit.

Only one of Firbank's English acquaintance was in Rome at the time: Lord Berners, composer[1] (as well as dedicatee of William Walton's grand monument of musical Art Deco, *Belshazzar's Feast*) and painter, and, in the exercise of both those métiers, eccentric.

---

[1] 'the maître d'orchestre had struck up a capricious concert waltz, an enigmatic *au delà* laden air: Lord Berners? Scriabin? Tschaikovski?' (*Valmouth*; p. 452 in *The Complete Ronald Firbank*).

In England, Lord Berners would sometimes entertain a horse in the drawing-room of his country house while he painted its portrait.[1] And he had installed in his car a keyboard instrument (exactly what sort of keyboard instrument is discrepantly described), in order that he might compose on it while having himself inspiringly driven about the countryside.

So, at least, some of his friends believed and recorded. But another of them, Sir William Walton, besides authoritatively categorising the instrument in the car as a clavichord, says 'it was not there permanently – he was transporting it to Rome'.

At Rome Lord Berners kept up the habit of motoring, though evidently without the clavichord in the car. One day that May he took Firbank on a trip to Lake Nemi.

For the next four or five days there was no communication between Firbank and Lord Berners. Then, on the evening of 21 May, Firbank was seriously ill. He asked the manager of his hotel to telephone for Lord Berners to come.

Lord Berners spoke by phone not only to the manager but to the doctor who had been called in to attend Firbank. The doctor reported Firbank much better: so much better that he had sent away a nurse engaged for the night. Lord Berners therefore promised to come the next morning. But Firbank died that evening.

Like most people who knew Firbank, Lord Berners knew little about him. He knew he had a sister alive, but not where. He didn't know Firbank was a Catholic. So he and the British consulate had Firbank buried in the Protestant Cemetery in Rome.

The name of Firbank's solicitors turned up by chance 'on a crumpled piece of paper'. News of his death was, therefore, sent to England, though it was delayed. After a further delay, Heather Firbank recognised the mistake about the denomination of the cemetery. Eventually she managed, from England, to put through the arrangements whereby, in September, Firbank's body was shifted to the Catholic municipal cemetery at Verano.[2]

---

[1] Perhaps it was Lord Berners's sitter that Firbank, in pursuit of his passion for plants (cf. Chapter XV), transformed into the nectarines which sit to the painter Sir Victor Vatt in *Valmouth* (p. 431 in the *Complete* Firbank).

[2] In his account of the burial (which he contributed to Ifan Kyrle Fletcher's 1930 *Memoir* volume) Lord Berners knows of the mistake but not that Heather Firbank afterwards put it right. The same is true of Osbert Sitwell in *his* contribution to the *Memoir* (p. 143). Sotheby's catalogue (most of which is published as an Appendix in *The New Rythum*) of the sale of Firbank papers in 1961 includes (under 'Miscellaneous') 'copies of correspondence with Heather Firbank relating to his burial in Rome, showing that (contrary to Lord Berners's account) his remains were removed to the Catholic cemetery at Verano'.

2. The Memoir, 1930

THE difficulty, for Lord Berners and the British consulate, of knowing whom to communicate Firbank's death *to* was increased by the fact that the passport Firbank had with him in Rome gave his address as Saint Julian's, Newport, Monmouthshire.

It was not an address Firbank had ever actually lived at. However, it was the fixed point in his vagrant life, though its fixity there was not domestic but financial. And by curious chance it was the point that brought Firbank his first and most perceptive memorialist.

Firbank's ex-labourer grandfather, Joseph Firbank, went to Newport in 1854 in pursuit of his contracting business. It was in land there that he invested his profits from the business. He settled at Saint Julian's House, Newport, shocked his neighbours by being a freethinker and died there (five months after Firbank's birth) in 1886.

Of Joseph's seven children, it was Joseph Thomas (who became Sir Thomas) Firbank who carried on the business and inherited the estate at Newport. Sir Thomas was Ronald Firbank's father. The estate at Newport was, therefore, one source of Firbank's income. After Sir Thomas's death, it was Ronald Firbank who was responsible for the estate, which was entailed on him as the eldest surviving son.

The businesslike way Firbank managed his financial affairs surprised Osbert Sitwell in a personality seeming so wilting and impractical. Firbank was, Sitwell wrote, 'always coming to me to request that I would witness wills, deeds, sales of land and the like, so that there must have been a quite extensive business undercurrent to his life. One document I recall concerned his sale of a cemetery to a Welsh town, and seemed all that it could be of a morbid bargain.'

Though she gives him no credit, Miss Miriam J. Benkovitz in fact confirms Osbert Sitwell's memory in a detail she records, from Firbank family letters, in her 1969 *Biography* of Firbank: it was from the Newport estate that Firbank sold some land that was wanted for enlarging a cemetery.

In his adolescence Firbank involuntarily made a family pilgrimage to his grandfather's Newport house. His intention was to make a literary pilgrimage, to the old Saint Julian's House at Newport, where Lord Herbert of Cherbury wrote *De Veritate*, which Firbank was at the time reading. But on hearing the address the local cab-driver took him to the locally much more famous Saint Julian's House, the 'Victorian neo-classic mansion' which Firbank's grandfather had named after Lord Herbert's house.

The story is told, together with the history of Joseph Firbank and his

Newport estate, by Firbank's first memorialist, Ifan Kyrle Fletcher. His *Ronald Firbank, A Memoir* was published in 1930 by Duckworth's. Duckworth's (which was owned by a half-brother of Virginia Woolf) was the firm with which the Society of Authors arranged to spend the money (or rather, as it turned out, half the money) which Firbank left in trust:[1] their collected edition of Firbank's works, limited to 235 copies of each of the five volumes, had appeared in 1929.

Duckworth's also published, in 1929-30, a public collected edition which they called, from the various colours of the volumes' binding, the Rainbow Edition. Ifan Kyrle Fletcher's *Memoir* was issued in the same format and constituted the black-bound (in mourning, presumably) volume.

In addition to Kyrle Fletcher's *Memoir* itself, the 1930 volume included, probably at the suggestion of Duckworth's, essays in reminiscence by Vyvyan Holland (who came his nearest to knowing Firbank well while they were both up at Cambridge but who didn't wholly lose touch with him afterwards), Lord Berners (whose contribution included his account of Firbank's death), Osbert Sitwell (whose contribution was an expansion of a 'biographical memoir' he had already contributed to the first volume of the Duckworth collected edition of Firbank's works) and Augustus John (whose contribution was brief and thin, because he had already allowed Osbert Sitwell to quote his best reminiscences in Sitwell's piece in the collected edition).

The *Memoir*, with these appendages, is the nucleus of everything that is known about Firbank. But until now Firbank studies have not inquired how it came to be written. I owe my information, gratefully, to its author's widow, Mrs Constance Kyrle Fletcher.

Ifan Kyrle Fletcher (1905-69) never met Firbank in person. His *Memoir* contains (quite apart from the separate essays) information, and often verbatim quotations, collected from people who did. Probably Kyrle Fletcher did most of his information-seeking by letter. At the time he wrote the *Memoir*, he was living in Newport.

And in fact his interest in Firbank began by being an antiquarian's interest in the Firbank family and its Newport estate, an interest Kyrle Fletcher was well placed to pursue because he happened to be a friend of the agent for the Firbank estate at Newport. Both the father, John Kyrle Fletcher, and the son Ifan, who in 1923 began a bookselling business in the basement of his father's shop, were students of the history, celebrities and old houses of Monmouthshire.

Ifan Kyrle Fletcher was a bookseller who liked books and even liked

[1] Cf. Chapter V, 4.

writing: his catalogues were prefaced by essays by himself. Chiefly, however, his literary interests went towards the theatre. He founded and consolidated the Newport Playgoers Society before he, in 1935, moved his bookselling branch of his father's business to London. In 1938 he and his wife set up in independent business there, specialising in theatrical books. Ifan Kyrle Fletcher became a friend, and eventually one of the bibliographers, of Edward Gordon Craig; founder and presently editor of the periodical *Theatre Notebook*; and founder (in 1955) of the International Federation for Theatre Research.

Perhaps one of the qualities that attracted him to Firbank's novels was their concentration on and in dialogue. And indeed Firbank was also a playwright, and a far from inconsiderable one – as Ifan Kyrle Fletcher recognised, discerning in *The Princess Zoubaroff* the tone of Congreve.

As a result of its author's sympathy, the *Memoir* is not only an invaluable collection of biographical facts, carefully followed up while the trail was still visible, but a clear and sustained appreciation of Firbank's art. Ifan Kyrle Fletcher knew what *sort* of artist Firbank was: 'baroque'. He understood Firbank's evolution from Impressionism to 'the disciplined rigours of Post-Impressionism'. He understood Firbank's Baudelairean dandyism of the soul: 'Never did he pose; never was he deliberately eccentric.'

Osbert Sitwell recognised, with astonishment, the business man – and also the practical solitary traveller – inside the wilting personality he was acquainted with. Ifan Kyrle Fletcher recognised the even tougher and braver artist's personality inside Firbank. 'The urge of creation', he wrote in the *Memoir*, 'must have been strong in him to force so nervous and sensitive a man to subject himself repeatedly to neglect or disdain'.

Kyrle Fletcher granted: 'One cannot blame the critics that they did not recognise in' Firbank's first, pre-Firbankian novel, *Odette D'Antrevernes*, 'the first work of a potential genius. One cannot blame his present admirers if they find it tiresomely precious.' But, for the bad notices and sheer lack of notice which met the truly Firbankian novels, Ifan Kyrle Fletcher did blame the critics. He called the response to Firbank 'a pathetic example of the obtuseness of the professional critics'. And his savage, aesthetically righteous indignation sounds, unshrill, convinced and generous, throughout the *Memoir*.

3. Recognition, 1929

As a matter of fact, Firbank had been recognised as baroque even before the *Memoir*.

The recogniser was not a critic by profession but (at that time not much more than incipiently) a novelist: Evelyn Waugh, who did Firbank condensed justice in six pages of the periodical *Life & Letters* in the issue of March 1929.

Firmly Waugh put in Firbank as 'a figure of essential artistic integrity and importance' in his own right, and went on to define, with great precision, Firbank's further importance as a *modern* writer.

To condemn Firbank, Waugh argued, was to shew 'distaste for a wide and vigorous tendency in modern fiction'. The width of the tendency he exemplified by listing contemporary writers who were 'developing the technical discoveries upon which Ronald Firbank so negligently stumbled'. (As the *Memoir* had not yet been published, Waugh had no biographical source-book to correct the impression Firbank gave of negligence.) Waugh's list names Osbert Sitwell, Carl Van Vechten, Harold Acton, William Gerhardi and (to my eye a touch surprisingly) Ernest Hemingway.

Waugh did not neglect to notice that Firbank pioneered initially by going back to the Nineties. He mentions Firbank's debt to, in particular, Baron Corvo and Beardsley's *Under the Hill*. But he perceives that 'the more attentively' Firbank 'is studied, the more superficial does the debt appear', and it is on Firbank the modernist that he insists.

And in Firbank's modernity it is his technique that Waugh picks out. He remarks that Firbank re-established distance between author and material: 'Other solutions are offered [. . .] but in them the author has been forced into a subjective attitude to his material; Firbank remained objective.'

He remarks that Firbank resolved the crisis of naturalism by applying himself to design: Firbank 'is the first quite modern writer to solve for himself [. . .] the aesthetic problem of representation in fiction; to achieve, that is to say, a new, balanced interrelation of subject and form'.

He remarks that Firbank emancipated novels from slavery to narrative, and hints that it was from the visual arts that Firbank learned how to do it. That insight Waugh probably owed to the fact that he shared Firbank's bi-artistry. (At the time he wrote the article, Waugh was a fairly recent former art-student; in 1934 he was to publish his novel *A Handful of Dust* with illustrations by himself.)

'Nineteenth-century novelists', Waugh's article said, 'achieved a balance' (between subject and form) 'only by complete submission to the idea of the succession of events in an arbitrarily limited period of time. Just as in painting until the last generation the aesthetically significant activity of the artist had always to be occasioned by anecdote and representation, so the novelist was fettered by the chain of cause and effect.' But Firbank's 'later novels are almost wholly devoid of any attributions of cause to effect'.

Waugh remarks even the orientalism of Firbank's images: 'But by its nature Firbank's humour defies quotation. Perhaps it is a shade nearer to the abiding and inscrutable wit of the Chinese.'

In the whole article Evelyn Waugh utters only one reproach against Firbank, but it is a grave one: 'Some silliness, a certain ineradicable fatuity, seems to have been inherent in him.'

In early Firbank, Waugh diagnoses, what comes out as silliness does so through a technical failure. In the later books, he says, where the same impulse is given better expression, the seeming silliness turns out to be 'exquisitely significant'. Yet even in the late books, to Waugh's mind, there remains that irreducible, 'ineradicable' small quantity of dross.

Perhaps, however, Waugh's mind was wrong. Or, more exactly, perhaps it was right when it likened Firbank's humour to the 'inscrutable wit of the Chinese': and perhaps Firbank's inscrutability was acting as a mirror and shewing Waugh his own face, in default of recognising which he mis-saw silliness in Firbank.

I hypothesise this (with deep literary admiration for Evelyn Waugh) from the nature of the examples he picked of Firbank's supposed silliness. There are only three of them, and in each case it is as easy to believe that Waugh's own personality was putting forward a defence as that Firbank's artistry was defective.

One of Waugh's examples is Firbank's coy 'naughtiness about birches and pretty boys', which Waugh maintains 'will bore most people with its repetition'.

Another is 'a certain intemperance in portraiture', by which I assume Waugh meant (speaking through a reticence designed to avoid calling Firbank libellous) Firbank's caricaturing of his personal acquaintances in his novels. Waugh must have noticed that Winsome Brookes in *Vainglory* was named after Rupert Brooke, though he can hardly have known that for the United-States edition Firbank planned[1] (but he repented before his plan got into print) to caricature Sacheverell Sitwell in the same stroke by renaming the character Sacheverell Brookes. And certainly Waugh will have noticed the whole caricature gallery which Firbank worked into *The Flower Beneath the Foot*. About Firbank's 'silliness' in portraiture, however, Waugh virtually admits he is squashing a temptation to the same 'intemperance' in himself. He writes that Firbank indulged 'too gluttonously an appetite other novelists, even his most zealous admirers, struggle to repress'.

---

[1] There will be more about this plan in Chapter VII, 4.

The third supposed silliness is Firbank's 'introduction of his own name in *The Flower Beneath the Foot* and *Prancing Nigger*'. This Waugh finds 'intolerable *vieux jeu*'.

Vieux it indeed is, and there's the curiosity of Waugh's judgment. Why should Waugh, a traditionalist, find silliness in one of the most long-lineaged of literary jeux – and one which (as well as serving a technical purpose by distancing narrator, narrative and reader from one another) might be expected to look sanctioned, if not indeed positively sanctified, in Waugh's eyes by its occurrence in Cervantes?

The answer that comes to my mind comes by way of autobiographical insight. I wondered, before I began writing this book about Firbank, if it would be in bold Bad Taste or merely silly of me to mention my own Firbankian novel. I boldly have mentioned it. But in doing so I had a safety net under me. If I didn't want to take the responsibility of my own Bad Taste, I had only to quote John Anthony Kiechler's 1969 monograph on Firbank: 'But probably the most concentrated single example of Firbank's influence, really a posthumous monument to him, is Brigid Brophy's novel *The Finishing Touch* (1963) [. . .] it is not only' an 'open allusion to Firbank that establishes a direct line of descent. The style and mental approach contain all those symptoms of Firbank's technique of satire discussed in' Mr Kiechler's 'foregoing pages. Its significance lies in the fact that it establishes Firbank beyond all doubt as an active influence on contemporary writing [. . .] the spirit and intention of his work is very much alive and appreciated by creative writers today.'

Evelyn Waugh, in the year in which I was born and his literary career was only just begun, possessed no such safety net to give him the courage of what might turn out to be poor taste – about committing which he would suffer one worry more than I would, by adding the social to the aesthetic sense of poor taste.

The 'other novelists', who are 'zealous admirers' of Firbank and yet repress the intemperance which therefore has to become a 'silliness' in Firbank when he doesn't repress it, are simply and obviously Waugh himself, with his name left out. And his name is left out again from his list of contemporary writers who are disciples of Firbank in technique. As his œuvre afterwards demonstrated in extenso, Waugh was in fact tackling problems far more conspicuously Firbankian, by a technique Firbankian to a far more conscious and deliberate extent, than any of the novelists he does name. But in 1929 he can't have felt himself in a position to say so. He had published only his life of Dante Gabriel Rossetti and his first novel, *Decline and Fall*. As a matter of fact, *Decline and Fall* was sufficient credentials, but

Waugh couldn't count on the literary world's seeing that it was. At the time he wrote his article on Firbank, Evelyn Waugh was compelled to read 'silliness' in Firbank's mention of his own name in his novels because Evelyn Waugh had not yet written the novels that would justify his mentioning his own name in his article.

4. Further Critics

EVELYN WAUGH was bolder in Firbank's behalf than in his own. Unfortunately (not for Waugh but for Firbank's reputation and the respectability of the literary world), Evelyn Waugh was crediting the literary world with a perceptiveness that was in reality almost exclusively his own. 'It is no longer necessary to be even mildly defiant in one's appreciation of Ronald Firbank,' his article begins – and is thereby more than mildly defiant itself.

In the same year,[1] 1929, that Waugh recognised and analysed Firbank's modernity, E. M. Forster published an article about Firbank in which he asserted that 'there is nothing up to date in him'. It is perhaps possible to praise E. M. Forster for drawing attention to Firbank three years after his death and at the same time as Evelyn Waugh was doing so, but not for drawing it to anything important, or even perhaps anything actually to be found, in Firbank.

How short of favourable notice Firbank was during his life can be judged from the first edition of *The Princess Zoubaroff*, which appeared in 1920. At the back of the volume Firbank and his 'publisher' advertised Firbank's five previous books with quotations from the reviews. Mostly, they have to make do with very brief snippets of very mild praise. 'The result is amusing,' said the *New Statesman* of *Inclinations*. *Vainglory* produced a couple of 'sparkle's (from *The Times* and the *Observer*) and a pair of 'clever's (from the *Pall Mall Gazette* and the *Belfast Whig*).

Sometimes the juxtaposition of mild brevities is tragically telling. Perhaps it was Firbank's own hand[2] turned against himself in irony that arranged:

---

[1] It was the year of the collected edition of Firbank. Perhaps therefore that publication was the occasion of both articles. Evelyn Waugh's doesn't take the form of a review. Neither does E. M. Forster's – in, at least, the version he re-published. But, since the collected Firbank was a limited edition, editors might have preferred a general article to a specific review.

[2] Certainly by 1923 Firbank (who paid for the advertising of his books) was himself selecting the review quotations to be used and deciding their arrangement (according to Miriam J. Benkovitz's *Ronald Firbank*, p. 231, which cites a Firbank letter).

> TIMES:
> 'There is humour.'
>
> HARROGATE HERALD:
> 'A quiet vein of humour.'

The sole perceptive remark, though it may not have been meant as praise, comes from the *Glasgow Herald*: 'Mr Ronald Firbank's fiction bears a strong resemblance to the work of the Futurists in painting.' Presumably the *Scotsman* meant neither to praise nor to be perceptive (though it achieved both) when it remarked, of *Valmouth*, 'There is no particular plot.' And sometimes the advertisements are driven to that desperate advertiser's recourse of quoting adverse notices which might at least make the work sound interesting. 'This is the real decadence,' a journal called *Land and Water* is quoted as saying of *Valmouth*: 'Huysmans and his friends were muscular giants, playing at bizarre senility, compared with Mr Firbank.' The *Liverpool Post* went one bitchier: 'Had Shelley written nothing but *Julian and Maddalo* and *The Cenci*, we might have called Mr Firbank a prose Shelley.'

But in the end the praise is even sadder than the blame. *Caprice* can muster only one quotation, of two words. The entire advertisement reads:

> TOWN TOPICS
> 'Intensely amusing.'

It is an object lesson in the reception literary circles can be counted on to give to innovating and perfected works of literature.

Only by dying did Firbank achieve safety, and even that turned out to be temporary. The Rainbow Edition[1] of 1929–30 marshalled splendid quotations. Arnold Bennett in the *Evening Standard* described Firbank's work as 'strange, odd, clear, queer, humorous, unlike anything else'. But it was a description written after Firbank's death. So, obviously, was S. P. B. Mais's 'In losing Ronald Firbank we lose the Mercutio of our time.'

Appreciation then began to lapse. The dust jacket of the *Complete* Firbank of 1961 wielded more praise than Firbank saw in his lifetime but less than the Rainbow Edition had done. Perhaps only two of its five quotations are without tinge of condenscension. Edmund Wilson recognised that Firbank had overcome the read-once-and-throw-away quality of consumer fiction, in saying that Firbank's works 'are extremely intellectual and composed with the closest attention: dense textures of indirection that always disguise point. They have to be read with care, and they can be read again and again.' And

---

[1] Cf. sub-section 2 of this chapter.

an unnamed writer in *The Listener* is quoted as writing 'Firbank is one of the few writers of this century who is certain to survive it, if anything does.'

Yet, despite those exceptions, literary fashion about Firbank has been a rapid slide down from Waugh's defiant 'figure of essential artistic integrity and importance'.

In 1936, when Firbank was a decade dead, Cyril Connolly published an article about collecting contemporary first editions which included a paragraph on Firbank. In its conclusion, Mr Connolly found that Firbank 'can be extremely aggravating and silly' but also that 'he was a true innovator, and his air of ephemerality is treacherous in the extreme.'

It is unfortunate that, through no fault of Mr Connolly's, that part of his concluding sentence about Firbank has been less often quoted than its beginning: 'Of course, it is quite useless to write about Firbank – nobody who doesn't like him is going to like him.'

That proposition, if it is true at all (and it well may be), is true of all writers. Pinning it to Firbank in particular seems to have dissuaded many of his admirers from even *trying* to proselytise on his behalf. It has probably contributed to the false myth that Firbank wrote for an élite and neither wanted to nor can ever command a large public (from which it follows, to quantitative minds, that he can't be an important artist). And by suggesting there is nothing 'universal' about him it has probably helped fix to him the label 'minor'. (One of the notices quoted on the back of the *Complete* Firbank calls Firbank a 'classic' but prefixes the word with 'minor'.)

By 1969 Mr Connolly seemed to have agreed with the slide of literary fashion and to have gone back on his 1936 judgment that Firbank is not ephemeral. He included Firbank in a 'host of happy entertainers' of the Twenties, along with Carl Van Vechten,[1] Jean Cocteau, Noël Coward and Michael Arlen.[2]

The slide down of literary fashion has scarcely been arrested even by writers who evidently thought they were praising Firbank, like Jocelyn Brooke in his brief *Ronald Firbank* of 1951 in 'The English Novelists Series' and his yet briefer British Council booklet of 1962, which consists of essays on Firbank and on John Betjeman. In 1964 a history of recent literature by another critic found Firbank 'child-like' (and meant it as praise); shewed itself as ignorant of Firbank's life as if Lord Berners had never published his account of his own some-time ignorance of Firbank's Catholicism (Firbank 'seems never to have become a Catholic', this history says); and, of course, labelled Firbank 'minor'.

[1] There will be more about this inclusion in Chapter VIII, 9.
[2] Firbank's relation to whom will be mentioned in Chapter VII, 1 and 4.

As a matter of fact, the 1964 history's 'child-like' can be traced back to Jocelyn Brooke's little book of 1951, which in turn gets it, though here with acknowledgements, from W. H. Auden – who, it says, 'confessed' that he would have wished to write like 'Firbank, Potter, Carroll, Lear'. Jocelyn Brooke noted that three of the four are writers for children and developed that perception into a concept of Firbank's 'quality of innocence', which by 1964 had been extended by other hands into Firbank's child-like-ness.

The adhesiveness of critical judgments is further exemplified in Jocelyn Brooke's 1951 volume: the adhesiveness, in particular, of Cyril Connolly's discouraging remark, in his 1936 essay (which Jocelyn Brooke's volume elsewhere cites), that 'it is quite useless to write about Firbank – nobody who doesn't like him is going to like him'. This remark of Cyril Connolly's turns up, paraphrased and unacknowledged, on the opening page of Jocelyn Brooke's attempt to write about Firbank. This time it runs: 'For one may as well say it right away: you either like Firbank or you don't, and no amount of criticism, however sympathetic, will ever create a taste for him in those who find him uncongenial.'

Ten years later, the same judgment turns up yet again. It is now in Anthony Powell's Preface to *The Complete Ronald Firbank* (published in 1961), where it takes the form 'Ronald Firbank is not a writer to be critically imposed by argument [. . .] Either you find entertainment – even food for thought – in the Firbankian Universe, or you do not.'

These remarks (including the earliest version of them) seem to rate the powers of criticism too low. Perhaps criticism cannot persuade anyone to Firbank: but what about dissuading people from reading him with a spontaneous eye?

Certainly the evidence is that criticism is highly influential – on, at least, critics.

By such processes are literary reputations made or held down to drown.

On Firbank literary fashion has so stickily affixed the label 'minor' that an essay of perceptive praise by Ernest Jones, which was published in the United States in 1949, had to begin: 'Ronald Firbank is a better and more important writer than it has ever been fashionable to suppose'.

5. Further, however, Editions

ERNEST JONES's essay was, however, a review: of a newly published volume consisting of five Firbank novels re-issued.

Critics might accept from one another's beaks the parrot-judgment 'minor'; might assume, without trying, that proselytising could never make converts for Firbank; and might actually feel pleased at that thought. ('His works will never, certainly, be an obligatory subject for "Eng. Lit."; nor, thank goodness, will they ever be "popular",' wrote Jocelyn Brooke.) Yet, with small help from critics, Firbank's works began to seep out to the wider public.

(Thank goodness. It is possible that people's pleasure in Firbank might be blurred if they had to read him as part of Eng. Lit. – though equally possible that his inclusion in the syllabus might make Eng. Lit. a livelier subject. But I can't follow the logic of an admirer of Firbank who hopes Firbank won't become popular, because I can imagine no method by which popularity could posthumously diminish his excellence.)

The editions of his books which Firbank himself financed were, by financial necessity, always tiny and often limited in the number of copies they amounted to. Taste took hardly more than a couple of decades after his death to begin catching up with him. His books began to be re-published, in larger editions, in the ordinary way of commerce.

In 1961 and 1962 he turned paperback in, respectively, Britain and the United States. In Britain three of his novels made a paperback volume under the taste-fixing series title 'Penguin Modern Classics'. *The Princess Zoubaroff* was presented on the London stage in 1951. Sandy Wilson's musical of *Valmouth*, with Fenella Fielding in its cast, was produced in 1958–9. (In 1924–5 Firbank agreed to a New York plan, which came to nothing, for a George Gershwin musical of *Prancing Nigger*.)

There were also additions to the canon of Firbank's novels. The five 1929 volumes of the Duckworth's collected edition were joined, in 1934, by a sixth, which contained *The Artificial Princess*, a fully Firbankian but very early work (of 1906 or 1910 according to Firbank's own discrepant later accounts) originally called (in some form[1]) *Salome, Or 'Tis A Pity That She Would*. Firbank at some time re-titled it, and towards the end of his life he completed the text and half-intended[2] to publish it. He hesitated so long that he didn't,

---

[1] The original title (which appears, crossed out, on one of the typescripts) is given without an accent on the *Salome* and with a comma after the name in Miriam J. Benkovitz's Firkbank *Bibliography* (p. 88). But the same author's Firbank *Biography* (p. 77) gives the title with an accented *Salomé* and no comma. Firbank was not always self-consistent, but that the title should include the accent is perhaps supported by the text (in the 1934 edition), which (on p. 19) spells the name 'Salomé'.

[2] Miriam J. Benkovitz's *Bibliography* (p. 62) concludes that Firbank had 'definite plans' to publish because he wrote to Carl Van Vechten promising him a copy of the book when it should be published. (The *Bibliography* gives the date of the letter to Van Vechten as 11 September 1925 but it may well be wrong. As I shall have to detail in Chapter XIII, 3, the *Bibliography*'s entry for *The Artificial Princess* has inextricably muddled 1925 and 1924.) The Introduction which Sir Coleridge Kennard wrote to *The Artificial Princess* makes it

in the event, have time. Sir Coleridge Kennard brought it out posthumously.

In 1961 Duckworth's published all the completed and previously published novels, and the play, in their single hardback volume *The Complete Ronald Firbank*.

In 1962 they demonstrated that the *Complete* Firbank was not totally complete: by publishing *The New Rythum*, a sizeable chunk of a mature Firbank novel in writing which he was interrupted by death. The volume included selections of and from immature works Firbank had not intended to publish.

In 1963, a United-States scholar, Professor Miriam J. Benkovitz, brought out her *A Bibliography of Ronald Firbank*, to which I owe some of the chronology of my last few paragraphs. A comparison with the *Bibliography* or, better still, with the first editions themselves, shews that the contents page of the *Complete* Firbank gives incorrect publication dates for three of Firbank's books.

6. Further Biographers – 1

A BIOGRAPHICAL sketch of Firbank appeared even before the *Memoir*, but it was a caricature.

Harold Nicolson was in Spain (where his father was British Ambassador) in 1905. That was the year in which Firbank turned 19 (in January), went (in February) to stay in Madrid in order to learn Spanish, and became (in June) a precociously published (at his own expense) novelist (or at least novella-ist).

In Madrid Firbank had himself photographed [Plate 3] holding a copy of his book in its special large-paper edition. According to the Firbank *Bibliography* by Miriam J. Benkovitz, the large-paper edition consisted of only ten copies, and they contained only Firbank's story *Odette D'Antrevernes*. The copies of the edition that was for sale, whose price (one florin) is marked on the cover, contain both *Odette D'Antrevernes* and another Firbank story, *A Study in Temperament*.[1]

---

clear that Firbank's plans to publish were far from 'definite'. When Firbank died, the manuscript was with Lord Berners because Firbank was seeking his advice about whether or not to publish it. Lord Berners later passed the manuscript to Kennard. I shall discuss Firbank's acquaintance with Sir Coleridge Kennard in Chapter XII, 6; the question of *when* Firbank renamed and finished the book in Chapter XIII, 3; and the causes of his hesitation to publish it in Chapter XIII, 3, 4, 6 and 8.

[1] In (according to Miriam J. Benkovitz's *Bibliography*) 1916 Firbank republished the first of these stories in a volume on its own. His declared (in 1922) motive for the republication was (again according to the *Bibliography*) to please his mother, to whom he

A copy of the large-paper edition (conceivably the very copy in the photograph) is the book I mentioned in Chapter V, 5: before he left Spain Firbank presented it to Spanish royalty and received in exchange a copy of her photograph.[1]

Two of Firbank's other (than being photographed) activities in Madrid he on occasion did in the company of Harold Nicolson: horse-riding; and visiting the Prado.[2]

(' "When we all go to Spain to visit Velasquez –" ', an altercation in the Café Royal begins, in *Caprice*; and continues:

' "Goya – !"

' "Velasquez!"

' "Goya! Goya! Goya!" ')

In 1927, the year after that of Firbank's death, Harold Nicolson published his book of semi-fiction, *Some People*, which consisted of a gallery of word-portraits. One of the portraits caricatured Firbank under the name Lambert Orme. The Orme I will try to explicate in a moment; the Lambert I take to be from Lambert Simnel, because he was a pretender (to the throne of Henry VII; he was defeated in 1487 and made into a domestic servant in the royal kitchens). Harold Nicolson may have been satirising Firbank's social pretensions, pointing out that, three generations back, the Firbanks had been of the domestic-servant class. Or perhaps he was hitting at what seemed to him Firbank's literary pretensions, explaining that Firbank's novels were mere confections, simnel cakes.

In his Lambert Orme piece, Harold Nicolson recorded his real-life surprise at discovering, in Spain, that Firbank was an efficient horseman – a parallel to Osbert Sitwell's surprise at the efficiency of the traveller and the business man.

In caricaturing Firbank, Harold Nicolson was only practising a Firbank habit. *The Flower Beneath the Foot* is full of caricatures, to which Firbank gave his mother, privately, an explicit key. One of the caricatures is of Harold

---

dedicated the new edition. (The *Complete* Firbank, p. 766, gives the dedication as 'In all the world to the dearest of mothers'.) Firbank revised the text for the 1916 edition, where the story has the title *Odette*. In the 1905 edition the title is *Odette D'Antrevernes*; the surname is spelt with a *D* in the title but a *d* in the text. The *Complete Ronald Firbank* of 1961 prints a text which does not agree with that of the 1905 edition and is presumably the revised text of 1916 – as the contents page suggests by giving the title as *Odette* without the surname; however, the contents page gives the date as 1915, and the spine of the jacket lists the story as *Odette d'Antrevernes*, with a small *d* that would not be correct for the title even of the 1905 text. As a footnote to Chapter XIII, 2 will detail, Miriam J. Benkovitz has added, to this muddle, a muddle about the sub-title of the two editions.

[1] The royal photograph will recur in Chapter X, 7.
[2] I shall tentatively identify a souvenir of Firbank's Prado-going in Chapter X, 7.

Nicolson's wife, the writer Victoria Sackville-West, under the superb name Mrs Chilleywater.

To that portrait a key was scarcely needed. 'Mrs. Harold Chilleywater', Firbank had the gossip-columnist in his novel note, '[. . .] a daughter of the fortieth Lord Seafairer of Sevenelms Park (so famous for its treasures) [. . .] very artistic and literary, having written several novels of English life under her maiden name of Victoria Gellybore-Frinton.'

By 'Sevenelms Park' Firbank intended Victoria Sackville-West's family stately home, Knole, which is at Sevenoaks.[1] Firbank transmuted the geographical oaks into elms, and I think it may have been the elms that Harold Nicolson brandished at him in return – by further translating 'elm', this time into French, and thus arriving at Orme for the surname of his Firbank caricature.

(Perhaps one of the troubles between Firbank and Victoria Sackville-West was that they had in common a passion for horticulture and were both rather *exact* about the species of plants. Theirs might have been the sardonic dialogue in *Vainglory* between Winsome Brookes and the rhyme that accompanies Mrs Henedge's gift to him of breakfast-time flowers. The rhyme ends 'These *orchids dear* as well.' 'These opening pinks as well,' Winsome corrects.)

Even after publishing his Mrs Chilleywater (which he did in 1923), Firbank possibly gave and certainly took further offence in a tiff[2] with a group that included both Nicolsons. Osbert Sitwell, however, was convinced that the trouble between Firbank and Harold Nicolson dated back to their early acquaintance in Spain – where it might, I think, be a matter of Firbank's already being an author, which Harold Nicolson wanted to be, and Firbank's wondering if he wanted to and could become a diplomat. (That was why Firbank was learning Spanish. He had already made a stay in Tours to learn French.)

But Osbert Sitwell located the trouble in the Spanish horse-riding. (It is amusing that Sitwell, although he had evidence of other practicalities in Firbank, obviously believed Firbank was inventing when he claimed to be good at riding.) Sitwell's essay in the *Memoir* volume records that Firbank 'always accused a then promising young diplomat (and now a promising young author) of having stolen his charger; an unlikely, indeed mythical theft [. . .] It accounts for the rather unflattering portraits of young diplomats

---

[1] Evidently Firbank early had his eye on this house, which is not far from Chislehurst. The hero of *A Study in Temperament*, the story included in Firbank's first published volume, is named Lord Sevenoaks.

[2] which I will describe in Chapter VII, 4.

in *The Flower Beneath the Foot*, just as it accounts, also, for the rather unflattering portraits of eccentric writers in a certain book by a young diplomat.'

(That was not the only mythical theft Firbank suffered. Chapter VII, 3 will discuss his susceptibility to such myths of his own making.)

Although Harold Nicolson took the background of Lambert Orme from his real-life acquaintance with Firbank, he ascribed to Firbank-as-Lambert-Orme a wholly fictitious death: a death, in the brave, upper-class English officer manner, in the 1914–18 war.

The fictitious death must, I think, be modelled on the real death of Rupert Brooke; and, as I reconstruct his motives, Harold Nicolson must have meant simultaneously to pay Firbank out in his own coin and to compensate him (in Harold Nicolson's).

No doubt Harold Nicolson was embarrassed to be publishing his answer to Firbank's caricatures in the year immediately after that of Firbank's death. But I imagine he set against that scruple the fact that Firbank himself had published his knock at Rupert Brooke, the Winsome Brookes of *Vainglory*, in the very year of Rupert Brooke's death.

In reality *Vainglory* appeared eight days *before* Brooke died. But, unless Harold Nicolson paid strict attention to, and recorded, the sequence of events at the time and then consulted his record a decade later, he is unlikely to have held the sequence exactly in mind when he wrote *Some People*. (Of course, Harold Nicolson *was* a diarist. But his published diaries, at least, do not begin so early. And, if he consulted only the first edition of *Vainglory*, it would inform him only of the year; the publisher's catalogue that was included in the volume would refine on that only as far as 'Spring, 1915'.)

If Harold Nicolson's object was, in patriotic chivalry, to avenge Firbank's caricature of Brooke, he achieved it by making Firbank die, in fiction, Brooke's premature death. But, by the time Harold Nicolson was writing, Firbank himself was in reality newly, and also prematurely, dead. So Harold Nicolson compensated Firbank for any malice that might be suspected in Harold Nicolson by crediting Firbank with Brooke's heroism.

The compensation came, however, in currency valued by Harold Nicolson, not Firbank, who was convulsively anti-military. Firbank managed, which was not surprising given his ill-health, to limit his own army service to a single day of 1917. And he thundered in a silence of 'malicious purpose', the *Memoir* records, throughout his first meeting, in the Café Royal in 1915, with C. R. W. Nevinson, because Nevinson was in khaki, though he later 'discovered that Nevinson's opinions about the war coincided with his own'. Indeed, the *Memoir* says, Firbank 'was frequently very rude to men in uniform'. So Firbank might have preferred, to Harold Nicolson's fictitious portrait of him as a brave regimental officer, recognition of his true courage, which was as an artist.

I surmise that Harold Nicolson was aroused to avenge Rupert Brooke partly by a story told by Edward Marsh (Sir Edward Howard Marsh 1872–1953), the author of the memoir of Rupert Brooke prefaced to Brooke's collected poems. Marsh was a person who knew 'everyone' (with 'who was anyone' understood) and was known to 'everyone' (in the same sense) by his chummy nickname Eddie. His biographer calls him 'one born with a talent for gossip'. Eddie Marsh probably told his Firbank story (which, the story itself makes plain, was his only one) extensively. It was probably repeated extensively. It probably did Firbank extensive social damage.

One of the people Marsh's story reached was Ifan Kyrle Fletcher, who in the *Memoir* quotes verbatim Marsh's account of how Firbank, whom he didn't know, accosted him during an interval in a performance by the Russian Ballet at Drury Lane.

Ifan Kyrle Fletcher puts the incident in 1914 and, though that is not one of the bits he gives in direct quotation, the implication of his text is that he had the date, as well as the setting, from Marsh. Yet the significant part of Marsh's story begins with Firbank asking him abruptly 'You knew Rupert Brooke, didn't you?' – a form of words that must imply that Brooke was already dead.

The account Marsh gave Ifan Kyrle Fletcher thus contains a self-contradiction. And to put the date 1914 on a story that implies Brooke was by then dead was a curious error to be made, in giving the story to Fletcher, by Marsh, who had published (in 1918) his memoir of Brooke and could be expected to have it clearly in his mind, as Brooke's biographer, even if as Brooke's close friend he was vague about dates, that Brooke died in 1915.

Marsh might, however, have been forced into that strange error if, in an attempt to avoid the contradiction, he had tried shifting the date of his exchange with Firbank to 1915.

Marsh would then have discovered that the shift was impossible if he wanted to keep the plausibly Firbankian (and no doubt true) setting at the Russian Ballet, and to imply (as I think Marsh did want to imply) that such a setting was the only place where he would be likely to encounter Firbank. For the 1914 season was the last one the Russian Ballet gave in London before the company was shattered and scattered by the outbreak of the war.

Marsh couldn't have claimed to have spoken to Firbank at the Russian Ballet in London in 1915 or, indeed, in 1916 or 1917, because the Russian Ballet was not in London then. Neither would it have been plausible for

Marsh to claim that he and Firbank travelled abroad in war-time and saw the Russian Ballet elsewhere.

The earliest date at which Firbank and Marsh could have met at the Russian Ballet in London after Rupert Brooke's death is 1918. But that was so long after Rupert Brooke's death that, if Marsh claimed 1918 as the date of Firbank's derogation of Rupert Brooke, he would lose the anti-Firbank point of Rupert Brooke's being *recently* dead. Marsh obviously preferred to keep that point, which was, indeed, his story's only point, even though it cost him the contradiction of putting a date on his story which made nonsense of the past tense he attributed to Firbank's words.

Marsh was thus caught with 1914 as the latest plausible date. I surmise that this conversation with Firbank did in fact take place in 1914 or earlier. But by sticking to the date and the setting Marsh had trapped himself into having to edit (perhaps unconsciously) Firbank's words in order to make them imply that Rupert Brooke was already dead (although the implication he was attributing to Firbank was in fact contradicted by the date Marsh was giving the story).

Whatever Firbank really said must have been said in the present tense. But Marsh, in indignation against Firbank, altered it to the past tense, so that Firbank should seem to be vaunting himself over a Rupert Brooke recently dead. For Marsh, in his indignation with Firbank, wanted Firbank's opinion of Brooke to tell as blackly as possibly against Firbank.

Indignant Marsh confessedly was. By his account, the conversation continued with Firbank asking:

' "Did you admire him very much?"

' "Yes," I said.

' "You're wrong – I'm better than he." '

Marsh, by his own account, then 'executed the manœuvre known as turning on one's heel'.

And certainly Marsh's intention in telling the story was that it should tell against Firbank. 'Later in the evening', his account in the *Memoir* ends, 'someone told me the man was Ronald Firbank. And so if in my old age I am asked, "And did you once see Firbank plain?" that is what I shall have to tell.' And tell it Marsh did.

(Marsh's is a thunderously ambiguous 'have to'. I suspect him of meaning Gwendolen Fairfax's 'On an occasion of this kind it becomes more than a moral duty to speak one's mind. It becomes a pleasure.')

Since the external probability is that the conversation (or whatever in real life corresponded to Marsh's account of it) took place in or before 1914, I think it permissible to go on to guess that Firbank's remarks came so abruptly because they came directly out of what his creative mind was playing on at the time, namely *Vainglory*. That would make 1913 a more probable date for the conversation with Marsh than 1914, because Firbank began writing *Vainglory* at the end of 1912 and certainly finished it by Christmas 1914 (when his 'publisher' read it).

If Firbank truly accosted Marsh without knowing him, that was highly unusual behaviour on Firbank's part. But possibly Marsh was mistaken about not knowing Firbank. Marsh became a friend of Rupert Brooke's at Cambridge in 1906, and they were close friends by 1909. It is highly probable that Marsh *had* met Firbank, probably at Cambridge, but had forgotten him.

Even so, it would be moderately unusual behaviour in Firbank to accost Marsh without making sure of being remembered. Firbank had, I think, a specific motive (which I shall mention in Chapter XII, 6) and he allowed himself to act on it on grounds, I suppose, of internal, not external, familiarity. He saw Marsh and associated him with Rupert Brooke – and then spoke to Marsh because his own private thoughts were dwelling on Rupert Brooke as one of the textural strands for *Vainglory*.[1]

Firbank and Brooke were amicable enough at Cambridge: but Firbank must have felt, at Cambridge and afterwards, outshone by Brooke on themes particularly Firbankian. Brooke, too, had from his schooldays made a '*culte*' (Marsh's word) of the Nineties. At Cambridge Brooke even 'had Aubrey Beardsleys in his room'. Indeed, he even bought two drawings by Augustus John – and before Firbank had bought any. By 1913 Brooke was, like Firbank, devoted to the Russian Ballet. And, with all these resemblances, Brooke was *so* much the better-looking – in that pastel mode for which Firbank found the bitchily perfect adjective when he named his caricature Winsome.

No doubt Firbank's emotions towards Rupert Brooke were those of *Vainglory*'s Mrs Shamefoot towards Winsome Brookes: 'Without any positive reason for disliking him, she found him, perhaps, too similar in temperament to herself to be altogether pleased.'

(And perhaps another person who was not 'altogether pleased' by the pointed resemblances between Brooke and Firbank was Edward Marsh – who must have early on known *of* Firbank, from Brooke himself and by Cambridge repute, even if he was correct in thinking he hadn't met Firbank until the fatal 1913–14 conversation. By 1909 Marsh had invested his own self-esteem in Rupert Brooke's literary talent. He did his utmost, with his Brooke memoir, to canonise that talent posthumously. He probably achieved

---

[1] If Firbank was indeed creating *Vainglory* at the time, creation (cf. Chapter IV, 1), helped perhaps by drink, might have lent him the untypical confidence with which he approached Marsh.

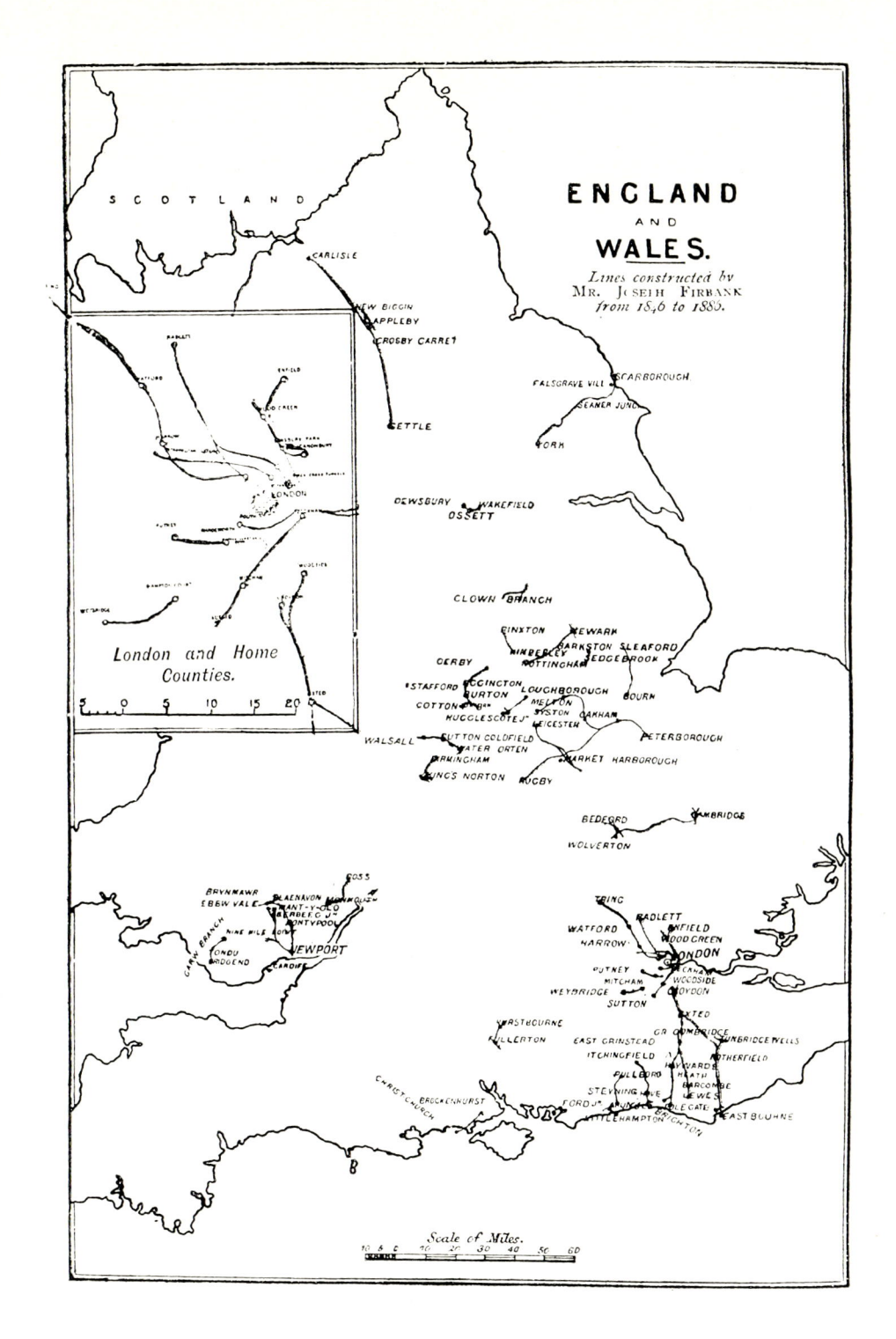

1 Joseph Firbank's railway lines (from a map in F. McDermott's
The Life and Work of Joseph Firbank, 1887)

2 Ronald Firbank, *circa* 1917 (photograph by Bertram Park, hitherto unpublished)

3 Ronald Firbank, Madrid 1905

4 Ronald Firbank in Egypt

5 Ronald Firbank, undated photograph by Lavender of Bromley

6 Heather and Ronald Firbank, undated photograph

as much towards damning Firbank's talent: by telling his anti-Firbank story to influential people. But sometimes, as he told his anti-Firbank story, Marsh may have wondered if Firbank was in fact right in judging himself the better writer. Surely it crossed Marsh's mind that in Rupert Brooke's case he might have mistaken good looks for good books – and that, between two Cambridge undergraduates of remarkably similar tastes, he, Marsh, had picked the wrong one to put his emotional money on. If he had such thoughts, Marsh certainly countered them: by blackening Firbank. The thoughts would be provoked by the resemblances between Brooke and Firbank, which would invite Marsh to a comparison between Brooke and Firbank: and in his anti-Firbank story, which consisted of Firbank's making a comparison between himself and Brooke, and which Marsh no doubt used to put down his own doubts about the result of the comparison, Marsh insisted on a setting which was a focusing point of the similarity between Brooke's taste and Firbank's. No doubt that is the cause of Marsh's emotional obstinacy in sticking to the Russian Ballet as the locale of his story, even though doing so involved him in intellectual self-contradiction.)

In *Vainglory*, Firbank makes Winsome Brookes a pianist and composer with 'the most bewitching hair' (which he spends 'whole hours together grooming fitfully' – with his patron's permission: ' "Don't mind me", his gracious lady often said to him, "if you care to calm your hair. I know that with you it takes the place of a cigarette" '). Winsome Brookes's musical compositions are knowledgeably modelled on Rupert Brooke's literary compositions during his Nineties *'culte'* (which Edward Marsh said lasted from 1905 until 'well into his second year at Cambridge'). Brooke began writing a novel in which 'One of the chief characters is a dropsical leper'. Brookes's opera *Justinian* contains 'the folk-song of the Paralytics', who are 'grouped invalidishly about the great doorway of Santa Sophia'.

Even Rupert Brooke's friends were in Firbank's knowledgeable thoughts when he wrote *Vainglory*. 'Read to me,' demands Mrs Henedge. 'What shall I read?' asks Winsome, and the answer is 'Get the Lascelles Abercrombie' (one of the poets[1] to whom Rupert Brooke left money).

However, good literature is not pressed from sour grapes. In *Vainglory* Firbank is not expressing his envy of Rupert Brooke but overcoming it. He is using the similarity of their temperaments to form an identification with Brooke.

In token of the identification, Winsome Brookes is given one of Firbank's own most particular and most comic characteristics,[2] a concern for his diet

---

[1] Cf. Chapter V, 4.
[2] There will be more on this theme in Chapters VIII, 4 and XIV, 10.

through concern for his figure: 'In her cooking, he found his landlady scarcely solicitous enough about his figure . . .' The send-up is of Rupert Brooke *and* Ronald Firbank. Affectionately, Firbank even allowed Winsome Brookes to consider undertaking his own favourite flower (and female) impersonation:[1] Brookes thinks of using, 'for musical purposes', the name Rose de Tivoli.

Firbank's judgment that he was a better writer than Rupert Brooke was sober (and just). It erupted in his conversation with Marsh with abrupt (and perhaps drunken) belligerence because Firbank was in the process of creating the book that should *make* him the better writer. *Vainglory* was to justify as well as contain his caricature of Rupert Brooke. If Firbank could shape his novel as he was intending, it would establish his right to send up Brooke and, at the same time, to stop envying Brooke, by sending himself up in identification with Brooke.

And I think there is evidence that the encounter between Firbank and Marsh took place while *Vainglory* was still being formed – and, therefore, before Rupert Brooke died. I think, that is, that the encounter is commemorated in the actual text of *Vainglory*, where Firbank's imagination has associated Rupert Brooke with Brooke's friend and, as he proved in the encounter with Firbank, Brooke's champion, Edward Marsh. Well before the Firbank encounter (in 1905, to be exact), Edward Marsh had become private secretary to Winston Churchill. And 'Winsome' is, surely, Firbank's inspired mutilation of 'Winston'?

If Winsome represented Winston,[2] then it was by an inevitable train of associations that Firbank picked Winsome, when any masculine proper name in the book might have served, to consider altering to Sacheverell.[3] Winston and Sacheverell are alike in being aristocratic idiosyncrasies of name, their owners recognisable, and caricaturable, by first name alone.

Firbank, I expect, envied their owners. As I shall mention again in Chapter VII, 4, he suffered from the lack, in his writing name, of a distinctive (and perhaps of an aristocratic) first name.

It is by an irony or perhaps by a further act of unconscious compensation that Harold Nicolson's caricature gave him one.

---

[1] There will be more about this theme in Chapter XV, 4–5.

[2] I shall mention in Chapter IX, 5 a couple of instances where Firbank's thoughts, provoked perhaps by Marsh, played on the Churchill family in general.

[3] Cf. sub-section 3 of this chapter.

7. Further Biographers – 2

GLANCES at Firbank are taken by several autobiographies and memoirs. Vyvyan Holland's autobiography adds to his contribution to the Firbank *Memoir*; and Osbert Sitwell, a copious autobiographer, proved not to have exhausted the subject with *his* contribution to the *Memoir* and the collected edition. But Firbank did not receive a full-length biography (the *Memoir* runs to pith, not length) until 1969, when his 1963 bibliographer turned biographer.

The 1969 *Biography* is a work of such conventionality of mind that it produces, when the conventionality is trained on the subject of Firbank, a riot of Firbankian irony. The only conventional quality the *Biography* lacks is scholarly accuracy.[1] Between them (and sometimes by means of a conflict between them) the *Biography* and the *Bibliography* manage to muddle a considerable deal of the documentary evidence about Firbank – of which they are often the only published sources. It is a significant (and comic) symptom that the first sentence of the *Biography* mentions the *Bibliography* – and gives its title incorrectly.[2]

The blurb to the original (United-States) edition labels the *Biography* 'not a "critical biography" ', but the blurb has not restrained the text from crass and often cliché comments on Firbank's writings. In *The New Rythum* the *Biography* finds a 'decline in power' to be 'sadly apparent'. It asserts that Firbank 'could make little of' *The Artificial Princess*. Destiny has allotted him a biographer for whom it isn't enough that he came near to making a masterpiece of it.

---

[1] Incorrect statements in *Ronald Firbank, A Biography*, by Miriam J. Benkovitz will be corrected in Chapter VII, 4 (about where Firbank's mother died); Chapter IX, 5 (about the name of a painter whose work Firbank bought and the terms of the transaction); Chapter X, 12 (about the date of a letter written by Firbank's sister); Chapter XII, 3 (about a recipient of a presentation copy from Firbank); Chapter XII, 6 (about the chronology of Sir Coleridge Kennard's career and acquaintance with Firbank); Chapter XIII, 2 (about the sub-title of one of Firbank's works).

Misleading or insufficient statements in the *Biography* will be corrected in Chapter VII, 4 (about the priest who received Firbank into the Catholic church); Chapter VII, 4 (about Firbank's mother's name); Chapter XIV, 4 (about internal evidence for dating a story by Firbank).

Inaccuracies in the same scholar's *A Bibliography of Ronald Firbank* will be mentioned in Chapters VII, 4 and XIII, 2 (about the 1905 edition of Firbank's first volume); Chapter XII, 6 (about the name of an acquaintance and dedicatee of Firbank's); Chapter XIII, 3 (about when Firbank retrieved and finished *The Artificial Princess*) and Chapter XIII, 3 (about his ending to that novel).

A discrepancy between the *Biography* and the *Bibliography* has been mentioned in Chapter VI, 5. Others will be mentioned in Chapter XII, 3, Chapter XII, 6, and Chapter XIX, 17.

[2] p. vii.

The *Biography* is, if that is conceivable, even more crass about Firbank's psychology than about his œuvre. It states its suspicion that Firbank turned Catholic for the sake of the aesthetic value of 'the mass, the music and candles and incense'; and although it concludes that 'a religion dependent on the aesthetic was too limited' for Firbank, it maintains en route that the aestheticism theory 'gains credence' from the elegant manner of Firbank's life as an undergraduate.

In that finding, the *Biography* ignores both Firbank's psychology and the very facts of his life which it itself provides. (What did, in general and in particular, precipitate Firbank into Catholicism I shall discuss in Chapter VIII, 8 and in Chapter X, 5.) At the same time, the *Biography* ignores the fact that Ifan Kyrle Fletcher took the trouble to inquire – and discovered that 'The explanation afforded by the aesthetic satisfaction of the Church ritual is not upheld by the testimony of a friend who met him in Paris in 1910' (when Firbank had only by a year ceased to be an undergraduate) 'and found that the service made no appeal to him, but that he was still profoundly moved by the mystic element in religion.'

The *Biography* makes few of the obvious links between the biographical facts and Firbank's works, and it speculates after none of the less obvious ones. However, it does contain biographical facts – and facts inaccessible in any other book, because they are taken, in quotation or digest (and occasionally in mis-transcription or plain mistake[1]) from the Firbank family letters.

From those, the *Biography* can record, for example, the existence of two further Firbank siblings, who were virtually unknown to the *Memoir*. (The *Memoir* does record that Firbank was a second son.) Firbank's elder brother died at the age of 20, his younger brother (whose place in the family was between Firbank and Heather Firbank) at the age of 25.

In the light of those deaths (though the light is not shed by the *Biography*), the conviction of Firbank's adult life that he might die at any moment, which is recorded by Osbert Sitwell and which seemed to Sitwell merely part of Firbank's superstitiousness, begins to look more like a rational calculation of medical probability, even if Firbank disguised its rationality from himself under a hopeful cloak of magic.

Indeed, I think Firbank must have been one of the artists whose economy of artistic means was dictated by their not expecting to live long enough to go the long way round about perfecting their art. In that, Firbank resembled Aubrey Beardsley, and I imagine it was the resemblance that gave Firbank his autobiographically intuitive sympathy with Beardsley and his under-

[1] Cf. Chapter IX, 5.

standing that it was from Beardsley's practice that he could learn the essentials of his own.

Similarly, to the *Memoir* Firbank's mother was simply the former 'Miss Jane Garret [. . .] By birth she was Irish, being the daughter of the Reverend James Perkins Garret, of Kilgarron, County Carlow.' The *Biography*, besides supplying her with an Irish lineage and another *t* on the end of her maiden name, can disclose from the family correspondence that her children spoke to and of her as 'Baba'. But unfortunately the *Biography* is of so unspeculative a turn of mind that it never notices certain queries raised by her name in general[1] and doesn't seem to have wondered how her nickname Baba came about, with the result that it doesn't think of telling you whether or not the correspondence could, if scrutinised, reveal the answer. My own irrepressible speculativeness (which, I may incidentally explain, expresses itself with constant 'I surmise' and 'I imagine' less through egoism than through the obligation to label a hypothesis as hypothesis) makes the obvious guess that 'Baba' was a babyish mangling, by one of the children, of 'Mama' (and, if so, was 'Baba' stressed on the second syllable?), but I have no means of knowing whether or not anything exists in the correspondence that would confirm or contradict the guess.

And Firbank's mother might equally owe her nickname to a fondness for baba au rhum, to telling her children the story of Ali Baba or to singing them 'Baa baa black sheep'.

However, until the total letters and postcards of Ronald Firbank and his family are published (a group of family papers, sold at Sotheby's in 1961, is now dispersed and often the property of private collectors), the *Biography* remains the only, if perilous, route to their contents. It is a route I have made much use of in this book, with frequently infuriated gratitude.

8. Notes to Chapter VI

FIRBANK'S (1925) letter to Heather Firbank about the ill effect of clubs and hotels is quoted on pp. 271–2 of Miriam J. Benkovitz's Firbank *Biography*. His repeated advice that Heather, too, should live outside England is cited on pp. 270 and 289 of that book. P. 289 quotes his mention of the favourable exchange rates.

The main source for the history of Firbank's death and burial is Lord Berners's contribution to the *Memoir* by Ifan Kyrle Fletcher. It is from that that I have quoted. Details are added by the sale catalogue I have quoted and by Miriam J. Benkovitz's *Biography*.

[1] Chapter VII, 4.

How a horse would 'sometimes' sit for its portrait to Lord Berners at Faringdon is reported by Osbert Sitwell in *Laughter in the Next Room*, p. 181.

The keyboard instrument in Lord Berners's car is called 'a small harmonium' by Consuelo (Vanderbilt) Balsan, who reports its once being in the South of France. (This is cited in Miriam J. Benkovitz's Firbank *Biography*, pp. 166–7.) But Leonard Woolf, himself in doubt about the species of the instrument, calls it (in *Beginning Again*, p. 199) 'a piano or harpsichord'. Sir William Walton sent me his solution by letter.

The address Firbank gave in his passport is recorded in Miriam J. Benkovitz's *Biography*, p. 294.

The *De Veritate* of Edward Herbert, first Baron Herbert of Cherbury (1583–1648), was published in 1624 and is, according to the Concise D.N.B., 'the first purely metaphysical work by an Englishman'. (His peerage, however, was Irish.)

The ownership of Duckworth's is given in Leonard Woolf's *Beginning Again*, p. 87.

Ifan Kyrle Fletcher's life and work are described in a booklet printed in 1970 as 'a memorial tribute' by the Society for Theatre Research.

Evelyn Waugh's article on Firbank is in *Life & Letters*, March 1929, pp. 191–6 (not 191–2 as given in the Firbank *Biography*).

Firbank's plan to change the name Winsome is related in Miriam J. Benkovitz's *Bibliography*.

E. M. Forster's article on Firbank is collected in his *Abinger Harvest*.

Cyril Connolly's 1936 article is the one I have already quoted (in a footnote to Chapter V, 6). It is collected in his *The Condemned Playground*. The 1969 quotation is from Cyril Connolly's piece on the Twenties in the *Sunday Times* of 28 December.

The Ernest Jones article (a review of *Five Novels of Firbank*, New Directions) is in *The Nation* of 26 November 1949.

The contents page of the 1961 *Complete* Firbank is incorrect in giving 1915 as the year of *Odette* (instead of 1905 for first publication and, according to Miriam J. Benkovitz's *Bibliography*, 1916 for revised and separate publication). It incorrectly gives 1915 for *The Artificial Princess* (first published 1934) and 1918 (instead of 1919) for *Valmouth*.

The first editions shew that the list of Firbank's dedications at the end of the *Complete* volume is deficient.

In addition, the Preface (by Anthony Powell) to *The Complete Ronald Firbank* is incorrect in calling *Vainglory* Firbank's first published novel and in stating that *The Flower Beneath the Foot* was written, though not published, before *Valmouth*.

Alan Harris's Introduction to *The New Rythum and Other Pieces* records that an 'invitation in Nicolson's hand [. . .] shows that the episode of the ride' in Harold Nicholson's *Some People* 'is at least broadly historical'.

The art-historical altercation from *Caprice* comes on p. 335 of the *Complete* Firbank.

The key Firbank sent his mother to the portraits in *The Flower Beneath the Foot* is quoted in the *Bibliography*, p. 39.

The Mrs Chilleywater quotation from *The Flower Beneath the Foot* is on p. 543 of the *Complete* Firbank. The flowers quotation from *Vainglory* is on p. 107 of the *Complete* Firbank.

The Osbert Sitwell quotation about, but not naming, Harold Nicolson is from p. 129 of the *Memoir*.

Rupert Brooke died on 23 April 1915. *Vainglory* was published on 15 April (according to Miriam J. Benkovitz's Firbank *Bibliography*, which also gives the date when the 'publisher' read the typescript). The date when Firbank began *Vainglory* is from p. 117 of Miriam J. Benkovitz's Firbank *Biography*.

Firbank's certificate of discharge from the army is listed in the Sotheby's catalogue partly republished in *The New Rythum* (p. 134). The information and quotations about his reaction to khaki are from the *Memoir*, p. 54.

Edward Marsh's 'talent for gossip' is thus named on p. 122 of *Edward Marsh*, by Christopher Hassall.

That the Russian Ballet was absent from London 1915–17 is stated in Serge Lifar's *A History of The Russian Ballet* (III, III) and confirmed by Romola Nijinsky's *Nijinsky*. What could be assembled of the company gave a gala charity performance in Geneva in 1915 and took part in a charity performance in Paris in December 1915. The company spent 1916 in the United States and Spain (with tours in Italy) and 1917 in the United States, Italy, Paris, Spain and South America. Firbank was in none of those places at those times.

Edward Marsh recorded the dates of his meeting and becoming close friends with Rupert Brooke in his Brooke memoir, which is also the source of the information and quotations about Brooke's taste. The words about the dropsical leper are Brooke's own, quoted by Marsh.

The Winsome Brookes quotations from *Vainglory* are (in order) on pp. 83, 105, 95, 106 and 107 of the *Complete* Firbank.

Edward Marsh became Private Secretary to Winston Churchill at the end of 1905; he and Winston Churchill remained, in Churchill's words, 'the closest friends' until Marsh's death in 1953 (Christopher Hassall: *Edward Marsh*, p. 119 and p. 680).

The *Biography* comments on *The Artificial Princess* and *The New Rythum* on p. 117 and p. 276.

The *Memoir* quotation about Firbank's Catholicism is from p. 31.

I have discussed the force exerted on Beardsley's style by his expectation of dying young in my *Black and White, A Portrait of Aubrey Beardsley*.

VII
The Portrait Begun

1. The Wriggler and Giggler

WHEN the mind's eye sets out to synthesise a portrait of Firbank from the biographical sources, of which the *Memoir* is much the chief, it is first struck by what struck everyone who met him: Firbank suffered from a social shyness quite exceptionally agonising – to himself and to the people who associated with him.

He was incapable of intimacy and, when he was writing, kept himself secluded. Sometimes he stayed for longish stretches with his mother, but he lived, all his adult life, alone. He never set up a ménage with anyone. His personal and domestic loneliness drove him, especially when he was in England, into society – where he suffered.

Often he put himself in places where he was lonely in society. He frequented the Café Royal, which had the extra advantage, for Firbank's homosexual temperament as it had once had for Oscar Wilde's, that in the snobbishly segregated London of before 1914 it was one of the rare places (like the music halls) whose clientele included both the smart rich and young, butch members of the working class. But he also frequented the Eiffel Tower restaurant in Soho, whose clientele included intellectual bohemians, Wyndham Lewis the Vorticist (and portraitist of Firbank) among them, and where Firbank once declined to sit with some of his acquaintance at table but sat on the floor.

Both places remained Firbank places all his life. To both he often went alone – and often sat getting drunk alone while he awaited (or dreaded) the arrival of someone he might know. When Firbank had become dead drunk the proprietor of the Eiffel Tower would send him home: 'Fritz'[1] (Robert

---

[1] I surmise it was the Eiffel Tower waiter named Fritz to whom Firbank gave a baroque immortality in the thunderstorm in *Valmouth* (p. 425 in the *Complete* Firbank). Mrs Hurstpierpoint seeks comfort from her collection of sacred relics. Bidden to hand her mistress a relic, the maid enquires 'Any one in particular, 'm?' and goes on to offer: 'You used to say the toe, 'm, of the married sister of the Madonna, the one that was a restaurant proprietress (Look alive there with those devilled kidneys, and what is keeping Fritz with that sweet-omelette?), in any fracas was particularly potent.'

(McAlmon quoted him), 'you ged de taxi vor Meester Firbank. He is a goot man und a goot gustomer, put he is trunk.'

To ease Firbank's being bundled off, however, the proprietor would pretend to him that the rest of the customers were leaving too. It was a courtesy quite in Firbank's own charming style. Even Forrest Reid, whose literary opinion, delivered in 1940, was that Firbank had 'not a glimmer of' genius, conceded that 'at least he had excellent manners', adducing in evidence that, when he arrived in casual clothes at Firbank's undergraduate rooms, and found that Firbank had dressed for dinner, Firbank at once put on a blazer.

Yet, though Firbank was concerned to restore his guest to ease, he himself was, Forrest Reid recorded, 'intensely nervous'.

I imagine, however, that Firbank was slightly less shy with (in the social terminology of the time) his social inferiors than with his equals.

His first visit to Augustus John, to have his portrait drawn, is a classic instance of his shyness. (This is one of the stories that Augustus John allowed Osbert Sitwell to quote in his collected-edition–plus-*Memoir*-essay.[1]) Firbank took a cab to John's studio but felt too shy to go in and face John. So he arranged for his cab-driver to go in and prepare the way, while Firbank waited 'in the taxi with averted face, the very picture of exquisite confusion'.

It occurs to me that those of us who are only to a normal extent agonisingly shy would probably have preferred to face John rather than face explaining to the cab-driver that we could not face John.

I read the same significance in Osbert Sitwell's story of how, during the time (war time) when Firbank was living in Oxford he regularly travelled back to Oxford from London on the milk train. Firbank could not face the embarrassments of buying and handling railway tickets. (And as a matter of practical fact, which Osbert Sitwell didn't consider, it may have been difficult to find someone to sell you a ticket in the small hours of the morning.) Again Firbank circumvented the small embarrassment by rushing into what most people would think a graver one. He arranged to run an account with the guard on the train, and settled it every two months.

This facility in getting his own, sometimes eccentric way in workaday negotiations must have contributed to Firbank's surprising[2] efficiency as a traveller. His mode of travel, too, was sometimes sturdier or more

[1] Cf. Chapter VI, 2.   [2] Cf. Chapter VI, 2.

enterprising than people might predict from his droopy legend. During his war-time Oxford sojourn, he bicycled. And in the first half of the Twenties, when it was still a tolerably pioneering thing to do, he travelled between London and both Rome and Constantinople by air.[1]

Firbank's comparative ease with members of the working class is perhaps connected with his homosexuality. But I doubt if that can be its whole source. Heather Firbank, who had heterosexual love affairs and may not have been shy, was also capable of an ease in working-class company that transgressed the conventional class barriers of the time. One of her heterosexual love affairs[2] was with her chauffeur.

In the company of what society considered his equals, Firbank almost disqualified himself from conversability by his seeming irrelevancies, his habit of wriggling and writhing with shyness, and his famous giggle. Augustus John (in his own contribution to the *Memoir*) said Firbank unnerved him 'with his way of emitting a long, hollow laugh about nothing in particular, a laugh like a clock suddenly "running down", accompanied by a fluttering of the hands (not the clock's), hands which he would then proceed to wash with the furtive precipitation of a murderer evading pursuit'.

Firbank's drinking was probably a social defence against social shyness. He was so often seen drunk that it is hard to think he could have got his books written if he had often been drunk in private as well. And in fact drunkenness sometimes did him its social service, by overcoming his diffidence to the point of allowing him to speak publicly of himself as a good writer. Perhaps he was drunk when he accosted[3] Eddie Marsh. And Sewell Stokes has reported occasions about 1922 when Firbank, definitely drunk, proclaimed his own excellence. On one of them Firbank and the best-selling novelist Michael Arlen agreed that Firbank was a better writer than Michael Arlen.

Perhaps they would both have been shocked by Mr Cyril Connolly's 1969 lumping[4] of them together.

Firbank's giggle, on the other hand, was not a social act, though it worked as a social impediment. Lord Berners reported having learnt, from a friend who once had rooms on the opposite side of an Italian courtyard to rooms occupied by Firbank, that Firbank laughed also when he was alone. As Lord

---

[1] In 1915, in *Vainglory* (on p. 216 in the *Complete* Firbank), Mrs Henedge 'would have preferred to fly. "I adore an aeroplane," she breathed; "it gives one such a tint –" '

[2] This will be mentioned further in Chapter IX, 3. Mrs Henedge's wish (in the previous footnote) for an aeroplane follows on the recommendation to her of the services of a chauffeur.

[3] Cf. Chapter VI, 6.

[4] Cf. Chapter VI, 4.

Berners remarked, it was a habit Firbank shared with his invented pope in
... *Cardinal Pirelli*.[1]

No doubt the giggle was an expression of Firbank's sense of tragedy.

2. The Drop-out with a Private Income

A CAUSE, though not the basic one, of Firbank's shyness with his social 'equals' is, surely, the history of his education. He was a drop-out from the entire educational system which in those days regularly *made* social equals (to the upper class) out of third-generation nouveaux riches like Firbank.

At his public school, Uppingham, the *Memoir* records, Firbank lasted only a year. The *Biography* (besides giving corrected dates for the year) can add that his two brothers made similarly short stays at, respectively, Wellington and Eton.

There seems to have been no scandal in any of the droppings-out (unless it was expunged from the family records). Firbank's seems to have been just a quiet (his brothers' was perhaps a noisier) failure to abide by the rules of the system – especially the unspoken, but hearty, rules.

Besides, he was always ill – or, more exactly, poorly; drizzling with perpetuated colds in the head. So there was always a pretext for his parents to move him to another educational establishment.

His ill-health made a pretext also for much childhood travel. 'Frequently', says the *Memoir* about his childhood, 'he was taken to warm climates to repel the advances of the throat affection which, even then, was troubling him.' His childhood set the pattern for the non-pattern, the international nomadism, of his adult life – and, I imagine, for his social uncertainty.

His schooling became an improvisation: the periods en pension in France and Spain while he learned the languages; and a series of crammers – from the last of which he went on to Cambridge.

In *Who's Who* Firbank delicately described his education as 'abroad; Trinity Hall, Cambridge'.

At Cambridge, Vyvyan Holland recorded, Firbank 'never sat for any examination, even the Little-go' (that is, the Cambridge 'Previous'). The *Biography* can supply that, at his crammer's intercession, Firbank was allowed to postpone that supposedly preliminary exam until after he went into residence.

And even so he never took it. But his getting stuck at the point of preparing

---

[1] Pope Tertius II addressed his squirrel.
' "Little slyboots", he said, "I often laugh when I'm alone." ' (*Complete* Firbank, p. 659).

for it stuck in his memory and, I therefore surmise, his gullet.[1] Almost 20 years afterwards, he dated his first writing of *The Artificial Princess* to 'while preparing for the Cambridge "Littlego": (A.D. 1906)'.

At Cambridge Firbank lasted three years (1906–9). But he went down without a degree – and with only a very remote connexion with a literary scandal over a supposed libel in a university paper.[2]

In what subject Firbank *would have* taken a degree I don't know and the *Biography* doesn't say. A remark[3] by Firbank's fellow-undergraduate Vyvyan Holland seems to imply with tolerable certainty that Firbank was not reading law. (Vyvyan Holland was.) According to the *Biography*, the subjects in which Firbank attended, or was supposed to attend, lectures or classes included English, French, German, Italian and 'Euclid'. So perhaps he was reading for some sort of general degree.

As he came down from Cambridge unqualified for any job, the improvisations of Firbank's schooling continued after his schooling was officially ended – and did not stop until in 1912 he fully entered on his true métier, that of Firbankian novelist, by beginning to write *Vainglory* (though he had invented Firbankianism earlier, in the book he eventually named *The Artificial Princess*).

Even so, in 1914, when he feared the war might reduce his private income, the uncertainty had a brief resurrection while Firbank thought he might have to take a job and wondered what job it could be. He fixed on publishing as the least of the potential evils, and asked Wilfred Meynell for help, though he didn't pursue his request.

Between Cambridge (where he had already rejected the diplomatic idea) and beginning *Vainglory*, Firbank seems to have considered and either rejected or been rejected by several possibilities. What one of them was I shall surmise in Chapter IX, 6. Another was some species of job connected with the church he had been converted to while he was an undergraduate.

Although, at the time of Firbank's death, Lord Berners 'had never for a moment imagined that Firbank was a Roman Catholic', he recorded that Firbank 'more than once' said to him, 'The Church of Rome wouldn't have me and so I laugh at her.'

Lord Berners also wrote, in his contribution to the *Memoir*, 'I believe that in his early youth he had thought of taking Holy Orders.' That belief might be the construction Lord Berners came afterwards to put on Firbank's

---

[1] I surmise (and will explain in Chapter XIV, 1) that a particular dread associated with it made Firbank unable to swallow the idea of the examination.
[2] This will be mentioned in more detail in Chapter XII, 2.
[3] The remark will be cited in Chapters IX, 8 and XIV, 10.

remark that the church wouldn't have him. Or it might be information Lord Berners acquired, probably after Firbank's death, from another of Firbank's acquaintance.

Perhaps, therefore, Firbank once thought of becoming a priest: or perhaps Lord Berners's belief that he did was by confusion with another ambition, which the *Memoir* mentions Firbank entertaining just before he came down from Cambridge, namely to apply 'for a post at the Vatican'.

The *Memoir* continues: 'In preparation for this Papal preferment, he talked of going into retreat, adding, as the spirit of absurdity asserted itself, "As much for my looks as for the welfare of my soul".'

The *Biography*, which *has* no spirit of absurdity, takes Firbank's Vatican ambition gravely, accepts from Sir Shane Leslie that the 'post' Firbank had in mind was in the Papal Guard, and specifies that the only branch of the Papal Guard that Firbank could have applied for, because it was the only one he was qualified for, was the Guardia Nobile – though it adds that, as a matter of fact, he was not qualified for that, either, but 'according to report' offered a letter from the Duke of Norfolk in place of qualification. The *Biography* finally remarks 'The Guardia Nobile has neither confirmed nor denied Firbank's application for membership' – which I take to mean it didn't answer a letter of inquiry.

Conceivably Firbank would have liked to be in the Guardia Nobile: it paraded in fancy dress. Perhaps his fantasy swished about in it a little – though, to judge from the papal passage in ... *Cardinal Pirelli*, Firbank's best fantasies took him a good deal closer to the throne of Saint Peter. And from that height, as an incident[1] in the papal passage makes plain, Firbank thought of the (undifferentiated) Papal Guard as, simply, manservants. However, the *Biography*'s long hypothesis that Firbank invested time and emotional energy in trying to join the Guardia Nobile, and was perhaps seriously cast down by being refused, is absurd. Joining would have in no way solved Firbank's problem. Members were unpaid.[2]

(Indeed, mention is made in the dialogue of *The Princess Zoubaroff* of a woman who has to sell her pictures in order to support her lover, 'a tall, dark man in the Pope's body-guard!')

Uncertainty about what one is going to *be*, which is the great misery of

---

[1] The Pope is (*Complete* Firbank, p. 659) visited by Count Cuenca, who 'had been unstrung all day, "just a mass of foolish nerves", owing to a woman, an American, it seemed, coming for her Audience in a hat edged with white and yellow' (the papal colours) 'water-lilies. She had been repulsed successfully by the Papal Guard, but it had left an unpleasant impression.'

[2] – according to *The Times* of 16 September 1970, which was reporting the dissolution of 'the 400-strong Palatine Guard and the 45-man Noble Guard'.

adolescence, was prolonged for Firbank well into adulthood. The educational conditioning which, by the ordinary course of social events at the time, ought to have made him a gentleman and simultaneously qualified him for a gentlemanly job, didn't take. Inevitably, he became and remained socially unsure. All he had to put between himself and membership of the working class to which his grandfather had once belonged was the money he had inherited from his grandfather.

However, Firbank was by no means in the simple situation, commonplace in a snobbish society, of being ashamed of a working-class ancestry. The self-made grandfather was in fact the family's man of distinction.

Joseph Firbank's individualism was sufficiently rough-hewn to hide any appearance of truckling, but objectively considered he was an Uncle Tom of the white proletariat. He wasn't a jumped-up but a painstakingly self-hauled-up proletarian. The methods of his rise, because they consisted of hard work, sobriety, honesty and not scamping the job, earned the approval of the bourgeoisie. So did his behaviour when he was up. He displayed his success in no nouveau riche extravagance, but kept, which was considered laudably unpretentious of him, his north-country accent, his habit of going early to bed and rising at five, and his absorption in his work.

To a capitalist society Joseph Firbank became an exemplar of how a proletarian could and, it was implied, should make his way up. Moreover, his railway contracting was done when the railway system was still being built and when building it was still physically dangerous for the workers and financially risky for the companies and the investors. As soon as it was over, this pioneering capitalism came to look glamorously adventurous. The early railway days were sanctified by late-19th-century British capitalism much as United-States capitalism still sanctifies the pioneers of 'The West'. Joseph Firbank, exemplar of 'self-improvement' in a socially unpolished but also socially undangerous manner, became on a small scale one of the heroes of pioneer capitalism. He achieved an entry in *The Dictionary of National Biography*. And in the year after his death he was accorded, by a barrister named Frederick McDermott, a full-length biography, which praised his character, illustrated several of the beautiful mid-19th-century viaducts and tunnels built by men for whose labour he was contractor, listed his contracts and works (which included the goods depot at Saint Pancras), mapped his railway lines [Plate 1], and was dedicated to the Duke of Beaufort 'who has taken a keen interest in [. . .] the railway system of the country, and notably in those undertaken by the late Mr Firbank'. The epigraph on the title-page, quoted from a speech made in his praise on the day of his death, sums up Joseph Firbank's mana as a capitalist hero: 'He was an excellent specimen of the Englishmen who rise up not so much by any transcendent talents, as by intelligence and energy, and above all by honesty and inspiring confidence in those for whom he had to work.'

Of that ancestry Firbank was certainly not simply ashamed. But neither could he be simply proud by identification with it. He and his grandfather shared a single-mindedness about work. But they would have been in dispute about the values of their respective works. Firbank's social uncertainty was exacerbated not by his proletarian ancestry as such but by his nonconformity to the standards both of his grandfather and of the world to which his grandfather's money bought him entrance.

No doubt it was because Firbank's grandfather began work (at seven) as a miner[1] that Mrs Shamefoot, in *Vainglory*, shamed indeed to find herself afraid of the dark, reflects: 'A collier [...] would laugh at me.' But Firbank's ambiguity takes it revenge. The narrative proceeds to carry Mrs Shamefoot's thoughts to Italy: thence the narrative states (in a paragraph to itself) 'Marble quarries!' and then (in another independent paragraph) 'Dirty, disgusting coal!'

His grandfather having been awarded so many capitalist pats on the head for becoming rich without behaving like a nouveau riche, Firbank seems to have particularly feared the accusation of nouveau-richesse against himself. From the *Biography*'s account of it, one of his early stories, *Mr White-Morgan the Diamond King*, is a satire against a nouveau riche. Firbank's satirical imagination was probably fending the accusation off from himself. In real life, his fender was to anticipate the accusation by acting it out in satire. When he sent himself up, it was often in the character of a nouveau riche. To someone who touched this jumpy nerve by asking if he was lonely, Firbank replied 'I can buy companionship.' Ifan Kyrle Fletcher, who reported it, correctly called that a melodramatic reply. But Firbank was only melodramatising the truth. He was observed at the Café Royal 'always paying for drinks'. Again at the Café Royal, he asked an acquaintance to buy him luncheon and, on hearing that the acquaintance had no money, gave him a pound before sitting down to luncheon with the words 'How wonderful to be a guest!' And to his sister Firbank wrote lovingly of the 'consideration & politeness money brings'.

But when someone else threatened to send Firbank up as nouveau riche, Firbank's gestures turned aristocrat. He shewed Vyvyan Holland a crystal cup he owned and told him it had cost £400. Holland replied that he was not impressed. Firbank smashed the cup on the fender.

In the way of people whose money is inherited, not earned, and who

---

[1] Cf. Chapter V, 4.

therefore can't see where more could come from if they spent what they have, Firbank was stingy. He refused a loan to Vyvyan Holland and was angry that Holland had asked. In his business-man capacity, he scrutinised expenses. The Sotheby's catalogue of the 1961 sale lists and quotes the draft of a business letter Firbank wrote from Bordighera in 1922 'disputing an account: "no authorization was given to take speculators to Newport at my expense" '. He briefly quarrelled with Heather Firbank (the quarrel was mended with tears) because she was partly dependent on him for money and he thought her extravagant. Heather Firbank herself eventually[1] became a hoarder of banknotes between the pages of magazines.

Firbank's prime fidelity was to his money – even when it was sex that tempted him away. The *Biography* recounts his relation with Hunter Stagg, a young literary journalist from the United States who, bearing an introduction from Carl Van Vechten, accosted Firbank in the Café Royal in 1923. Later that year, in Firbank's hotel in Paris, Hunter Stagg (by his own account) 'allowed Firbank's love making to go a great way'. But the love-making stopped short and the relationship lapsed into coolness: Hunter Stagg was seeking to borrow money from Firbank.

Firbank's attitude to disbursement[2] (and, indeed, to pages) was like that of his Mrs Van Cotton (in *The New Rythum*) who, finding 'no ready coin in her pochette [...] rewarded the page who procured the car with a condescending slap on the cheek with her cheque-book'.

For Firbank to have lost his money would have removed the sole socially solid barrier between him and reversion to the working class. As a matter of fact, he was as much a worker, and as hard a worker, as his grandfather Joseph. Society, however, understood its own need of, and was therefore willing to pay for, the network of railways Joseph created across the United Kingdom. It felt the opposite about the fictional kingdom created by the grandson. Firbank had to stick to the money he inherited from Joseph, because only with it could he exercise his vocation. Only on a private income could he pick up the dropped stitches of his protracted schooling and solve his uncertainties by *being* something by way of métier. He was mean with his money because only while he possessed it could he be a social benefactor: he was subsidising (as well as adding to) English literature.

He never did lose his income, but twice it turned out to be smaller than he had thought. At his father's death in 1910 (which happened soon after Firbank had been staying in Italy, perhaps being rejected by the Catholic

---

[1] According to Alan Harris's Introduction to *The New Rythum*, Heather Firbank died in 1951.

[2] – a new instance of which is given in Chapter IX, 5.

church), the inheritance proved to be much less than everyone had been counting on. Earlier still, while Firbank was at Cambridge, the family had to reduce its expenses and leave the house where Firbank had been brought up – an exile of the utmost consequence to his imagination.

3. The Incipient Paranoiac

ONCE or twice, the fluent and engaging material of Firbank's fantasy, much of which he put into his conversation for the amusement of his acquaintance (who did not always understand), seems to me to shape itself into a small thundercloud, a minor but genuine and paranoid delusion.

The tiny delusions that he was the victim of a persecuting conspiracy are the dark, real-life side of one of the great comic mechanisms of his novels: the brief, mistaken or inexplicit hints of the sinister or of the socially inconceivable – that there may be fleas at the Ritz or that one has been followed, persecuted, by a butterfly.

If Firbank had minor delusions that he was persecuted, some of his behaviour was unconsciously designed to make such delusions come true. If his books failed to sell, he had given the people he caricatured in them reason to hope their circulation would remain small.

Not that they or other people he unconsciously tried to turn into enemies were always ungenerous enough to act towards fulfilling such a hope. The Sitwell brothers in particular seem to have kept a sweet-natured serenity towards Firbank. In February 1919 Firbank became convinced (perhaps by delusion) that Sacheverell Sitwell had told a friend that he was interested in Firbank only as a curiosity. Osbert Sitwell nevertheless published, in the spring of 1919, an advance chunk of *Valmouth* (under the title[1] 'Fantasia for Orchestra in F Sharp Minor') in *Art and Letters*, of which Osbert Sitwell was one of the editors; and Sacheverell Sitwell, while denying the remark attributed to him, tried to reconcile Firbank to him.

The people Firbank distorted in fiction or in his delusions might remain generous on their own behalf. Edward Marsh, however, could persuade himself that he was behaving altruistically on behalf of Rupert Brooke. and Marsh's anti-Firbank story perhaps provoked Harold Nicolson to a chivalry in Brooke's cause which he could hardly, though well provoked by Firbank, have put forward in his own. Indirectly, therefore, Firbank did, with his Winsome Brookes caricature, bring about something resembling a persecution of himself.

---

[1] The significance of that title will be discussed in Chapter XVIII, 2, together with a lapse it occasioned in Osbert Sitwell's memory.

The themes on which Firbank's unconscious fantasy shaped his quasi-delusions are, not surprisingly, the priesthood, social class and the theft of possessions from Firbank.

Firbank told more than one witness the story of a sinister, surreal episode which he interpreted as an ecclesiastical kidnap attempt on him. The comic, bat-black visual images have great literary force. (Indeed, they turned up again in Frank Marcus's *The Killing of Sister George*, with the kidnappee still homosexual but transmuted into a female, and the priests transmuted into nuns.) But Firbank seems to have intended his story to be, as well as enjoyed, believed.

In Osbert Sitwell's account of Firbank's account, Firbank, one evening in Rome, asked his hotel to call him a cab and stepped into a black brougham that drew up at the hotel. 'The door was closed at once, and it drove off at a quick trot, before he had time even to tread on the toes of its occupants, for he found, to his bewilderment, that it was occupied by two priests, who quickly pulled him down between them, saying "You are one of us, aren't you?" Eventually, however, Ronald managed to escape.'

The episode may well have had an original in real life, but Firbank worked it up into something halfway between fantasy and delusion. And its content puts it beautifully between the camp and conscious fantasies which accompanied his conscious homosexuality and the paranoid delusions which regularly counter unacknowledged homosexuality.

The classic process that forms such delusions starts, in Freud's analysis, from the proposition 'I (a man) love him.' That unacceptable proposition is denied by the proposition 'I do not *love* him – I *hate* him.' This in its turn has to be translated, so that the perception may seem to come from observation of the outside world: it becomes (again in Freud's formulation) 'I do not *love* him – I *hate* him, because HE PERSECUTES ME.'

The pair of priests in Firbank's fantasy is a pair of homosexual lovers, men in skirts. They assume Firbank is one of *them*: one of the Catholics? or the priests? or the homosexuals? (By another witness's account of Firbank's account, Firbank, after relating the story, fluttered his hands at his throat and asked 'What did they mean, what did they *mean*?')

The priests co-opt Firbank into their own conspiracy, whatever it is a conspiracy *of*, but at the same time they are a conspiracy against him. They persecute him to the point of kidnapping him – and, the story hints, even further. For it is, of course, a ghost story. The priests in the brougham, which in Osbert Sitwell's account is 'smart' and 'black-painted', are spiriting Firbank away to his own funeral – which, since Firbank was indeed one of the Catholics, the two priests will themselves conduct. Lord Berners might not have given Firbank a funeral of the wrong denomination had he known and heeded the story of Firbank's being kidnapped.

Firbank's fantasy-delusion on the theme of social class involved Osbert Sitwell personally.

As a matter of fact, the Firbanks claimed, in Burke's *Landed Gentry*, to be a branch of the 'old border family' Fairbank and to trace their lineage back to 1788. But that was evidently not impressive enough to outweigh a labourer-turned-railway-magnate grandfather. Firbank's fantasy played on the contrast between his own three-generations-up (from the mine and the railway embankment) lineage and Osbert Sitwell's baronetcy and family history.

Firbank, Osbert Sitwell wrote, 'suddenly announced to everyone that I had said the Firbank fortune had been founded on boot-buttons – a remark of which I had never been guilty'.

Round the non-existent remark Firbank spun a fantasy that was evidently compulsive with him, but which was perfectly consciously a fantasy. Indeed, he gave it literary shape and an ironic point in satire of himself (in his usual satirised rôle of nouveau riche). But its ultimate tendency was, all the same, towards Firbank's self-destruction.

Osbert Sitwell reported that Firbank, 'enraged' by the remark his delusion attributed to Sitwell, 'would sit in the Café Royal for hours, practising what he was going to say in court, in the course of the libel action which he intended to bring against me. The great moment in it, he had determined, was to be when he lifted up his hands, which were beautifully shaped, and of which he was very proud, and would say to the Judge, "Look at my hands, my lord! How could my father have made boot-buttons? No, never! He made the most wonderful railways." '

(Thomas Firbank did build railway lines – the Oxted and Groombridge line, begun in Joseph Firbank's lifetime, was 'practically left in the hands of' Thomas – and he did carry on the business, to which he had been introduced when he was 17. Even so, Osbert Sitwell's memory probably confounded Firbank's father with his more famous [though probably not famous in Osbert Sitwell's mental world] grandfather. The story is evidence that Firbank was indeed not simply ashamed of Joseph – or Thomas – Firbank. Perhaps he knew of the wonderfulness of the railways his grandfather built from looking, when he was a child, at the engaging pictures of them in McDermott's biography of Joseph Firbank.)

The fantasy ambition of suing Sitwell for libel is as much a ghost story as the fantasy-delusional episode with the priests.

Firbank plans to spend money on litigation. He will, that is to say, set his inherited money against Sitwell's inherited title and breeding, and he will cause the contest between the two to be settled by a judge.

The judge, as the fantasy's phrasing emphasises, is an ex officio aristocrat. He must be addressed by plaintiffs as 'my lord' – just as hereditary aristocrats must be addressed by the boot-boy. Firbank, in the remark his delusion has attributed to Sitwell, is the boot-button-boy, the buttons who cleans the boots.[1]

In Firbank's fantasy, my lord the judge deputises also for the yet greater lord to whose (last) judgment plaintiffs do not submit until they are dead.

Firbank is, in a sense, already dead in his fantasy. He has destroyed himself in the fantasy, and the fantasy itself explains how: by taking a libel action.

The ghost the fantasy invokes is the ghost of Oscar Wilde – who destroyed himself by taking a libel action, which was against a lord.

(No doubt Firbank knew Wilde's dictum, which is another of Wilde's psychoanalytic anticipations: 'All trials are trials for one's life, just as all sentences are sentences of death.')

Wilde's libel action, by disclosing his homosexuality, exposed him to criminal prosecution and thence, via prison and public spite, to destruction.

Wilde even (as Firbank must have known, if not from written sources then certainly from homosexual mythology) betrayed, and thus ultimately destroyed, himself as a witness in his own behalf in his libel action. Asked if he had ever kissed a certain boy, Wilde replied, 'Oh, dear no. He was a peculiarly plain boy.'

Perhaps it was on that model that Firbank, taken to meet an American in London, 'paused in the doorway, looked once, muttered, "He is much too ugly," and walked away'.

And certainly it is on the Wilde model that Firbank, as fantasist, plans to betray and destroy himself. He will win *his* libel action by displaying, to the ultimate aristocrat and judge, his beautiful hands – and by the same token he will disclose his homosexuality by fluttering them.

Indeed, I think that the butterfly which briefly follows Mrs Calvally in *Vainglory* and which, in various manifestations, is so persistent in the imagery of Firbank's novels[2] that it could be accused of persecuting his

---

[1] The Mouth family in *Prancing Nigger* signal their new social standing with (*Complete Firbank*, p. 616) 'An' since we go into S'ciety, we keep a boy in buttons!'

[2] The monograph by John Anthony Kiechler which I mentioned in Chapter VI, 3 and which is actually called *The Butterfly's Freckled Wings* lists (p. 79) several of the butterflies in Firbank's work – and in other people's when they wrote about Firbank. Its mention of Osbert Sitwell's comparison of Firbank to a butterfly in *Noble Essences* can be supplemented by an elaborate Firbank–butterfly simile in Sitwell's contribution to the *Memoir* (pp. 120–1).

imagination can be identified as Firbank's homosexuality or Firbank's homosexual self.

Perhaps that was why, soon after telling Carl Van Vechten in 1922 that he would not come to New York because he doubted if he had the 'chastity requisite for America', Firbank added that he preferred to stay in Cuba 'butterflying about'.

Had anyone tried to marry Firbank, the result would have been like the ending of *Valmouth*, which builds up to a grand social set-piece as the guests arrive for the wedding; but the bride, says the last sentence of the book, has run 'into the garden, where, with her bride's bouquet of malmaisons and vanessa-violets, she was waywardly in pursuit of – a butterfly'.

The butterfly was an obvious self for Firbank: it shares his passion for flowers.

So, as her name indicates, does Mrs Rosemerchant, in Firbank's last (and unfinished) novel. It is not surprising that, when she is obliged to 'come to a decision on her gown for a forth-coming fancy-ball, everyone to go as animals',[1] Mrs Rosemerchant's immediate thought is to dress as a butterfly. Indeed, that is very nearly, after she has flitted butterfly-fashion through a bestiary of other possibilities, her last thought on the matter, too: it is defeated only in a postscript of soliloquy by the fear that she would not be the only butterfly at the ball. (She settles finally on a flying fox.)

Since it is an image fixed in Firbank's mind from his infancy, the butterfly is sometimes mentally pronounced in the infantile fashion: flutterby. Making ritually homosexual play with his beautiful hands, Firbank was a flutter-boy.

In his fantasy libel suit Firbank makes an indignant denial: I am *not* the boot-button-boy. But that is also an involuntary confession: I am the flutter-boy.

Firbank re-arranged his imagery but kept the point by rendering himself female when he told Siegfried Sassoon: 'I am Pavlova, chasing butterflies.' (The other half of the antithesis was that Siegfried Sassoon was Tolstoy digging worms.)

And in *Prancing Nigger* another chaser after butterflies, Charlie Mouth, undergoes a lesser form of the trial Firbank underwent in fantasy: by going through the customs. Firbank's fiction-making imagination again adopts a model from the mythology of Oscar Wilde – who, when he entered the United

---

[1] In keeping with his habit of borrowing from himself (a habit to be discussed in Chapter XIII, 3), Firbank put this fancy dress ball into both *The New Rythum* and the revised (in 1925) version of the fourth chapter of Part II of *Inclinations* (*Complete* Firbank, p. 304).

States, told the customs he had nothing to declare except his genius.[1] But Charlie Mouth's declaration, at *his* trial-by-customs, makes the same involuntary confession which Wilde in real life and Firbank in fantasy made at the trial of their libel actions. Charlie Mouth's confession is made, however, in Firbankian imagery:

' "Have you nothing, young man, to declare?"

' " . . . Butterflies!" '

Had Firbank ever been involved in a real-life libel suit, it would undoubtedly have been a suit the other way about, with Firbank the sued. In the libellousness[2] of *The Flower Beneath the Foot*, Firbank's behaviour nearly achieved his unconscious purpose: it almost made his delusion of a conspiracy against him come true. Having given the people he caricatured cause to wish his work a limited circulation, he nearly gave them the means to limit it forcibly. There could be no better way of pulling the walls down on himself than by provoking a libel action. Firbank's 'publisher', Grant Richards, was indeed, and justifiably, afraid of just that. Firbank was prudent enough to make changes in the text of *The Flower Beneath the Foot* in order to avoid the libel risk. But had the book run to a larger edition (it was of 1,000 copies) the precautions might not have been enough. As it was, Firbank's victims no doubt felt brought into ridicule and contempt, but not very *wide* ridicule and contempt.

Neither was Firbank in the least unaware of the libel risk he was running with *The Flower Beneath the Foot*: he wrote it into the book. The English Ambassadress, having acquired by imperfect overhearing the misinformation that there are fleas at the Ritz, repeats it; the rumour empties the hotel; and the Ambassadress goes, for the rest of the book, in danger of being sued.

Firbank's financial meanness was probably a rationalised face of his sense of being persecuted. No doubt he conceived of a conspiracy seeking to filch away his income. No doubt that was why he was *angry* when he was asked to lend money.

His sense of persecution shaped itself into definite delusions when he believed something had been stolen from him. Like the libel fantasy, where it is really Firbank who is on trial for being a jumped-up proletarian, the theft delusions are fashioned from social material. What is stolen from Firbank is, though it's disguised, his income. And what is so particularly persecuting about the thievish conspiracy is that the theft implies the accusation

---

[1] As Chapter XX, 24 will detail, Firbank's imagination later re-arranged that declaration in a yet more nakedly Wildean form.

[2] Cf. Chapter VI, 6 (to which Chapter VIII, 5 will make an addition).

that Firbank, not being an hereditary aristocrat, has no right to his hereditary income – or to the collector's pieces it has bought him. The objects are lost to him because they are not his by right.

What is stolen in the delusions is a thing, not necessarily a costly thing, rather than money in its naked manifestation: because Firbank was a collector, and a treasurer of possessions that had personal value and significance for him – as well as a writer in occupational dread of losing a bit of his manuscript.[1]

The conspiracy against him is private. (And his was a *private* income.) The conspiracy aims to filch his most personal treasures. It is not professional burglars he suspects, but personal acquaintances, whose crime is betrayal as well as theft. (And, *were* there to be fleas at the Ritz, that too would be – within a limited group – social betrayal.)

And indeed the dread of social loss in Firbank's delusions only, I think, provides material for the expression of his castration dread. The delusion must have a thing, rather than money, stolen because that makes a more kinaesthetic representation of bodily loss. The conspiracy in the delusion is out to steal the most treasured and most personal possession of all.

Again Firbank's delusion of being persecuted is an attempt to counter his homosexuality, this time by threatening Firbank directly with punishment: persist, the delusion warns, in the wish to be a man in skirts, and you will end up truly castrated.

By that mechanism Firbank, when he was that young man in Spain I discussed in Chapter VI, 6, fantasised the 'mythical' theft from him of that most mythically phallic of possessions, a charger.

But, when the theft delusion recurred later in Firbank's life, it did so in a context that reveals that it, too, is ultimately a ghost story.

On an evening in 1925, Firbank was given a lift by the painter C. R. W. Nevinson (the designer of the dust jacket for *The Flower Beneath the Foot*) and his wife. They drove him from his favourite café, the Café Royal, to his favourite restaurant, the Eiffel Tower. The next morning Firbank arrived at the Nevinsons' studio and demanded his scarf, which he believed he had left in the Nevinsons' car.

There was a search, but no scarf. Firbank, according to the *Memoir*, became 'agitated' and 'hinted pointedly' that the Nevinsons 'knew more about it than they admitted'. The Nevinsons laughed at the accusation but Firbank, Ifan Kyrle Fletcher says, 'was convinced' – seriously enough convinced to refuse to speak to the Nevinsons again until he was about to leave England. When he did leave, it was for the last time.

[1] Cf. Chapter V, 2.

The context in the Café Royal from which the Nevinsons removed Firbank, in order to hand him over to the friendly proprietor of the Eiffel Tower, was of drunken misery. Firbank had that day seen his doctor and been told of the condition of his lungs. Drunk in the Café Royal, he cried out aloud 'I don't want to die!'

That time it was nakedly his life which the in effect no longer delusional conspiracy was filching from him.

4. The Unnamed

FIRBANK signalled his social uncertainty, I think, by his uncertainty about – in his literary capacity, and perhaps in his private life – his name.

His first names were Arthur Annesley Ronald. To his family and for business purposes he was, and remained, Arthur or A. A. R. His first published book says 'by Arthur Firbank' on its title-page and has, lettered across the top of its dusty-rose floppy paper cover,[1] 'Arthur Annesley Ronald Firbank'. A decade later he published his second book, *Vainglory*, as by Ronald Firbank.

But, although Ronald Firbank appeared on the title-page of *Vainglory*, the author was named on the dust jacket as A. A. R. Firbank, and that was at Firbank's own insistence; he explained – or put forward the pretext – that 'I feel sure that copies will sell better that way as one's acquaintances will recognise them sooner.'

Yet, according to the *Memoir*, Firbank had made a satirically solemn 'announcement' to his acquaintance of his resolve to become called Ronald – and, to one of his acquaintance who sent him a letter as Arthur Firbank, wrote an answer or reproof, saying he thought Arthur a horrid name.

Perhaps he hadn't always thought so. Arthur might have had Beardsley connotations to his mind, through Beardsley's illustrations to Malory's *Le Morte Darthur*.

And perhaps it was those connotations which inspired Firbank to compose, probably while he was staying at Tours at the age of 16 or 17, what his biographer describes an 'unnamed French exercise having to do with a "*Guinevere, mignonne*" '.

Perhaps that darling Guinevere was the female self of Arthur Firbank.

---

[1] This is the cover of the edition that was put on sale, at a florin (cf. Chapter VI, 6). The *Bibliography* (p. 15) says this edition was 'issued simultaneously in sea-green stiff paper covers lettered in gilt or in rose stiff paper covers lettered in blue'. The paper cover of my rose copy is not, however, stiff. It is thinner and floppier than the paper of the text. The volume is as much like a pamphlet as like a book. The *Bibliography* also fails to record the sub-title of *Odette D'Antrevernes* – which is on (unnumbered) p. 7 in the 1905 edition.

Indeed, that he chose the name because it was the counterpart to his own seems to me the only explanation of how Firbank came to pick so markedly non-French a name to put into an exercise in French. As the quotation from it is transcribed by the *Biography*, Firbank didn't translate the name into its French form Guenièvre or even try to make Guinevere look plausible in French by putting a grave on the penultimate *e*.

With acquaintance made after or because he became a Firbankian novelist, Firbank succeeded in imposing his change of first name. They spoke of and to him as Ronald.

All the same, he remained touchy about the general subject of how he was addressed. The horridness he on one occasion found in Arthur he on another occasion, which the *Memoir* describes, found in the English public-school habit of man-to-manly address by surnames alone. An acquaintance who put him, when he was drunk one night after supping at the Eiffel Tower, into a taxi and bade him 'Good night, Firbank' was startled that Firbank halted the cab, lowered the window and said 'I wish you wouldn't call me Firbank; it gives me a sense of goloshes' before driving on and away – a drunken brilliance shaped, surely, out of Firbank's public-school or pre-paratory-boarding-school experience of a rainy atmosphere of goloshes assigned to their owners by surnames.

(I don't think he would have minded the thought that someone might write of him after his death, as I am doing, as Firbank. The damp goloshes are long since dry as dust. I am neither a man nor calling on Firbank to be one. I write of him simply as one does of the dead – and of great writers.)

Writers often ring changes and even play tricks with their names, especially at the beginning of their careers. (It usually becomes impractical later.) The game symbolises the quest for a literary identity, and it glories in the creative power of fiction, which it extends beyond the people in the books to the personality of the writer. Round about the time Firbank was changing his first name, Katherine Mansfield was experimenting her way through a gamut of literary pseudonyms. She finally fixed on the one she is recognisable by – but not before she had (as a letter-writer if not a fiction-writer) gone so far as to translate the surname she was born to, Beauchamp, into German and sign herself Kath Schönfeld.

For a woman, as Firbank probably noted with envy, there may be the extra possibility of introducing a married name into the material to be mélanged. Colette, during her marriage to Willy, excelled even Mansfield. She published as Willette Collie.

For Colette and for Katherine Mansfield, the uncertainty about name reflected an uncertainty not only about literary but also about sexual identity.

Not so for Firbank. Perhaps the one uncertainty he never suffered was that which goes with bisexuality. His capacity for sustaining relationships with women was, in his life, wholly absorbed by his mother and his sister and, in his fantasy, wholly expressed in terms of his identifying himself with women and as a woman. In consequence, his emotional relationships were in effect those of an exclusive homosexual, a being as rare as an exclusive heterosexual.

Unlike those bisexuals Colette and Katherine Mansfield, Firbank's exercise on himself of his fiction-creating powers was confined to the *inside* of his fictions, where his self-portraits bear (as I'll discuss in Chapters IX, 7–8, XIV 11 and XV, 6) significant names. About the author's name on the *outside* of the books, which is an author's social front, Firbank's was a social anxiety.

It is true that his transformation from Arthur Firbank to Ronald Firbank did indeed signal that in *Vainglory* he had found and fixed on his literary identity. But in arriving at a new name for his new literary identity, he seems to have entertained no question of inventing a pseudonym. Firbank was anxious about his rightful place in society. So he would exploit the combinations only of those names he had a social right to. And even then he remained anxious that his acquaintance should recognise the Firbank who wrote the book as the Firbank they knew socially.

Perhaps what (besides drink) liberated Firbank to be so bold as I mentioned his being in section 1 of this chapter with Michael Arlen was the fact that Michael Arlen was so little *placed* in English society, and had a right only to a name so unpronounceably Armenian, that he had to publish under a pseudonym.

Among the names available for his juggling, Firbank settled on Ronald for, I suspect, a multiplicity of reasons. And I further suspect that the very multiplicity shews it to be a weak choice. It needed several arguments to sustain it, because it was not in fact the choice Firbank would most have liked to make.

Ronald didn't fulfil a wish Firbank might well have entertained after his conversion, namely to be known by a name that was a saint's name. The utmost Ronald could do for him in that line was slightly and verbally assimilate him to Saint Romuald.

Neither do I think Firbank much wanted to assert Scottishness through the Scottishness of Ronald, though he may have been quite happy to align himself with the Scottish overtones of his sister's name. If the Scottishness of Ronald meant anything definite to him, he probably apprehended it as the best counter to the true fact of his half-Irishness.

Ronald had a more positive attraction, I surmise, from its position in

Firbank's names. I think that to be called by the last of a string of first names struck Firbank as *French*.

That attraction was probably reinforced by a couple of (non-French) examples. One was that of Hugh Benson, the priest who received Firbank into the Catholic church[1] and who exercised a brief influence on his undergraduate life and a lasting one (which I'll describe in Chapters VIII, 6 and X, 6) on his imagination. Benson was known as Hugh, but in full fact his first names were Robert Hugh.

A probably more impressive example came to Firbank from his own immediate family. Short on pedigree, he probably set what store he could on family tradition; and by chance the tradition of making a change in which of one's christian names one was called by seems to have been established by both Firbank's parents.

Firbank's father was known and, indeed, knighted as Thomas. In full, however, he was Joseph Thomas. The obvious guess would be that he used his second name in order to distinguish himself from *his* father, Joseph. But the facts seem, rather, to indicate the opposite. Frederick McDermott's *Life and Work* of Joseph Firbank, which was published in the year following Joseph's death, speaks of Joseph's eldest son as 'Mr Joseph T. Firbank'.

It looks, therefore, as if Joseph Thomas was originally known as Joseph and kept to that name, at least for business purposes, during his father's lifetime. Evidently he wanted not to differentiate himself from his father but to imply the contracting firm's continuity with its founder. Two years before Joseph Firbank died, Joseph Thomas sketched a further continuity for the future by naming his eldest child Joseph, thereby making three generations of Joseph Firbanks.

However, between his father's death, soon after which his father's biographer could still write of him, no doubt with his consent, as 'Joseph T.', and his knighthood, Firbank's father must have decided to change himself from a Joseph into a Thomas. Curiously, the evidence shews that his wife undertook a comparable metamorphosis. Perhaps the double parental example was what finally moved Firbank to change his own christian name. But of the two it was probably his mother's metamorphosis that more influenced him, because it was the more emotionally alive and the less straightforward.

Lady Firbank's christian names present, in fact, a very pretty puzzle – and one which cast her family into a rare confusion.

---

[1] The *Biography* is misleading when it says that in 1907 'Firbank was received into the Catholic Church by Monsignor Hugh Benson.' Benson did not become a papal chamberlain, entitled to be called Monsignore, until 1911.

The *Memoir* gives her maiden name as, simply, Miss Jane Garret. The *Biography* gives it as Harriette Jane Garrett and throughout speaks of Mrs/Lady Firbank as Harriette Jane. However, in speaking of her thus, the *Biography* is ignoring a great deal of evidence and has thereby missed the existence, let alone the significance, of the puzzle.

In several places Lady Firbank appears not as Harriette Jane but as Jane Harriette. In Burke's *Landed Gentry* for 1898, for example, Thomas Firbank entered his wife's name as Jane Harriette. In Burke for 1914, after Sir Thomas's death, she again appears as Jane Harriette. Likewise, in his *Who's Who* entry, Ronald Firbank gave his mother's name as Jane Harriette.

But when he registered his mother's death[1] in 1924, Firbank gave her name as Harriette Jane.

Obviously, the family – and perhaps Harriette Jane or Jane Harriette herself – was muddled about what order her names should take. And neither is it at first sight easy to guess by which of them she was actually known.

The fact that the *Memoir* hadn't heard of the Harriette at all might imply she was known as Jane. But in other cases it is the Jane that goes unmentioned. Thomas Firbank's entries in *Who's Who* and in Kelly's *Handbook* for 1900 name his wife simply as Harriette. Even more significantly, her own entry in Kelly's for 1924 gives, tout court, Harriette.

Although I can't solve the puzzle of the true order of the names, I think I know how the muddle came into being. And I think I can determine by which of her names Miss Garrett/Lady Firbank was called.

The clue is the fact that the *Memoir* is stating her *maiden* name. The *Memoir*'s informant, it is reasonable to suppose, was someone who knew her before her marriage and knew her, evidently, as Jane.

But her own preference was (possibly because of its French form) for Harriette. It was Harriette, on its own, which she wrote into her own Kelly's entry when she was a widow.

However, if you put Harriette together with Garrett, you get a jangle. So long, therefore, as she was Miss Garrett, she had to be called Jane. But when

---

[1] The *Biography* is incorrect in stating (on p. 253) that she died at Denbigh Cottage, Richmond. That, her home during her widowhood, was indeed her address at the time of her death, but her death certificate gives the place of her death as 9 Carlton Road, which I guess to have been a nursing-home. Firbank (who had returned from Rome) registered her death, which was from carcinoma of the cervix, in Wandsworth (Putney) on the day it happened, 25 March 1924. He had her described as 'Widow of Joseph Thomas Firbank a Railway Contractor Knight' and himself as 'R. Firbank Son', giving as his own residence 'Grosvenor Hotel Victoria'. (These particulars are from a copy of the certificate from Somerset House.)

she became Mrs Firbank, she took the opportunity to change her christian as well as her surname and become, which she preferred, Harriette.

Perhaps his wife's change of first name suggested to Joseph Thomas Firbank that he might himself change from Joseph to Thomas. Even so, it must have been confusing for him, who had wooed Jane, to be married to Harriette; and clearly the knowledge that there had been such a change muddled the whole family for ever after on the subject of Lady Firbank's name.

Perhaps, indeed, the precise knowledge that his mother changed her first name on the occasion of her marriage put it into Firbank's mind to make a similar change among his own first names on the occasion, which was *Vainglory*, of his finding and marrying his own Firbankian vocation.

Unlike his parents, Firbank had three first names to play with. The only one he never published under was the middle one, Annesley. Yet as a matter of fact that was the only one that could have been to him what I suspected (in Chapter VI, 6) he envied about Winston and Sacheverell: a distinctive and aristocratic first name.

The aristocraticness of Annesley was literal. According to the *Biography*, Firbank was so named because his mother's aunt was Countess Annesley.[1]

It is possible that Firbank rejected his only aristocratic name in pique because it came to him through his mother and thus lent no social support to his possession of his income. Or, which I think more likely, his pique might have been attached to the fact that, since it came through his mother, the Annesley was an Irish connexion. The younger Miss Mant in *Caprice* discloses that her sister 'hates the stage. She's only *on it* of course to make a match ... she could have been an Irish countess had she pleased, only she said it wasn't smart enough, and it sounded too Sicilian.'

Firbank was quite Irish enough to feel the Irish reaction of rejecting his Irishness. Perhaps that pique drove him to the Scottish Ronald by way of counter-demonstration.

I guess, however, that he wanted to use the name Annesley but didn't, in 1915, when he changed his writing name, dare. He was just up to taking on, by forestalling it with self-satire, the ridicule that always follows, among people who already know one, from changing one's name, but not the ridicule that would have followed changing his name to one with aristocratic pretensions.

---

[1] Evidently the name *was* used as a first name in Lady Firbank's family. Presumably it is a relation-by-marriage of his mother's whom Firbank included in his handwritten list (which the *Bibliography* reproduces) of recipients of *Inclinations* (1916): 'Mrs Annesley Garrett, Ford Cottage, Lingfield, Surrey'. The *Biography* (p. 192) records that in 1920–1 Firbank objected to his kinsmen's treatment of 'his uncle Annesley Garrett, who was in a state of senility'.

And perhaps it was his knowledge that, when the book was finished, he wouldn't dare market it as by Annesley Firbank that made him, in the content of *Vainglory*, so savagely mutilant of Winston/Winsome.

Once a writer is established under one name, it becomes impractical to change it, because[1] publishers buy not books as autonomous articles but authors as going, productive concerns, in which the author's name is a saleable commodity. Firbank, however, *wasn't* established; his publishers didn't pay him and his books didn't sell. His career was so little started that it was possible for him to conceive of re-starting it.

The hope of re-starting or, rather, properly starting it came to Firbank in the spring of 1922 by letter: from the United-States novelist Carl Van Vechten. This was the letter which asked for information about Firbank personally (some of which Firbank eventually supplied by assigning himself a vintage year as a champagne) and which told Firbank that (which Van Vechten was wise enough to see was a matter of congratulation) J. C. Squire had never heard of him.[2]

Now that *he* (Van Vechten) had heard of Firbank, he set honourably about creating Firbank's literary reputation in the United States, writing articles in Firbank's praise and eventually, in 1924, bringing about, in the United States, the first commercial publication of a Firbank novel, that of *Prancing Nigger*, which appeared with a preface by Carl Van Vechten.

Meanwhile Firbank co-operated in getting the whole of his œuvre to Van Vechten, both so that Van Vechten could write informedly about Firbank and in the hope that Firbank's previous, as well as his future, novels could appear in the United States.

In the summer of 1922, Firbank rewarded Van Vechten, for the surprising fact that *Odette* was known of in the United States, by giving him a copy of the first edition – one of the large-paper copies he made play with in Spain and I made play with in Chapter VI, 6. Ten special copies, Firbank wrote to Van Vechten, had been given away; 'Queen Alexandra & the Infanta Isabella', he explained in a name-dropping bracket, 'account for two'; so Firbank sent Van Vechten his own battered copy.

This he inscribed 'Presentation copy from Arthur Annesley Ronald Firbank to Carl Van Vechten Summer 1922—.'

Firbank had to sign the name Arthur in order to make the presentation copy a signed copy, since the book was published as by Arthur Firbank. He had to sign Ronald in explanation to Van Vechten, who knew him as Ronald Firbank. It is only the tiniest anomaly that he signed also the not, from a practical point of view, necessitated Annesley.

[1] Cf. Chapter II, 5.   [2] Cf. Chapter V, 6 and Chapter I, 3.

Perhaps it was just a matter of habit. Firbank might have felt his name would look strange to him written out but with its middle component omitted. Yet he could have signed in a form that would have come very familiarly to his own hand and eye: A. A. R. Firbank – which he signed in 1917 on the photograph of himself by Bertram Park that makes the frontispiece of the *Memoir*. A. A. R. would have rendered the presentation copy signed, and at the same time would have been explanatory enough to Carl Van Vechten.

Perhaps, however, Firbank feared initials would look unfriendly. He hadn't feared so, presumably, in 1917 when he signed the photograph. But in the eased-up world of after the war first names were more insisted on as marks of friendliness – though Firbank could hardly have been suspect, had he signed his initials, of coldness towards Van Vechten, because he had never met him.

The signed Annesley is, therefore, thin grounds for a surmise, and I make it knowing it is a remote one. I think Firbank hoped that Van Vechten, since he was seeking personal information about Firbank, would question him about the Annesley. At the least that would allow Firbank to drop another titled name by explaining how he came to be called Annesley. At the best, I think Firbank hoped, it would lead to an invitation that would give him an opportunity, and the courage, to go back on his timid and second-best decision in 1915 to become Ronald.

Since Van Vechten was proposing to make him a career in the United States, Firbank hoped, I think, that Van Vechten would suggest it be made under the name Annesley Firbank. Firbank was flirting: waiting in a ladylike way for Van Vechten to invite him to change his name.

Van Vechten didn't. *Prancing Nigger* appeared in 1924 as by Ronald Firbank.

There are, I think, two tiny symptoms that, after the publication of *Prancing Nigger* in the United States, Firbank felt bitter that Van Vechten had not pressed him to become Annesley – and that he himself had for the second time been too timid to do it on his own initiative.

(His bitterness must have been ironic. The more he believed the United-States publication was going to bring him success, the more he must have seen it as closing the Annesley opportunity for ever.)

The first symptom concerns a name, though not a personal one, and a name in relation to Carl Van Vechten. Brentano's published *Prancing Nigger* in the United States under that title, which Carl Van Vechten had given the book by way of allusion to its text. Ten months later Brentano's published the book in Great Britain. But that time Firbank insisted it revert to his own title for it, *Sorrow in Sunlight*.[1] He wrote Carl Van Vechten a charmingly apologetic explanation ('In England people love the sun since they so seldom see it'), but his obstinacy in standing by the name of his own devising was perhaps in unconscious reply to Van Vechten's obstinacy in *not* proposing a change in Firbank's own name.

The second symptom concerns the proposed change,[2] which Firbank repented in time, in the name of a dramatis persona in *Vainglory*.

Carl Van Vechten's promotion of Firbank managed to fulfil part of Firbank's wish for his earlier books to appear in the United States. After publishing *Prancing Nigger* in March 1924, Brentano's issued, in October 1924, a United-States edition of Firbank's most recent novel, *The Flower Beneath the Foot*, and then went back to the beginning of his Firbankian œuvre and gave *Vainglory* a United-States edition in 1925.

While (in the early spring of 1925) he prepared the United-States *Vainglory*, Firbank took the chance to avenge the slight he had suffered in October 1923 in his tiff[3] with a group that included the Nicolsons. The gang-leader in the affair was Lord Berners. Firbank (as the *Bibliography* relates the episode on the strength of Firbank's letters) lunched with Lord Berners, one October day of 1923, at Lord Berners's Roman home, where host and guest agreed on the hideousness of a plaster cast of a Psyche which Lord Berners owned. On the next day, Lord Berners gave another luncheon party and wondered aloud how to rid himself of the turbulent cast. One of the Sitwells suggested sending it to Firbank. Accordingly the cast was delivered in a cab by Lord Berners's butler, Psyche's broken crown having been inscribed, in 'Homage to Ronald Firbank', by the entire personnel of the luncheon party: Lord Berners, Edith Sitwell, Sacheverell Sitwell, Geoffrey Lovelace, Aldous and Maria Huxley, Evan Morgan, both Nicolsons and William Walton.[4]

Firbank, who had evidently left behind the autograph collecting of his adolescence, was amused but hurt.

There were ten contributors to his hurt. For immediate punishment, however, Firbank picked neither the ring-leader, Lord Berners, nor the Nicolsons (whom he perhaps felt he'd punished enough *before* the tiff, in *The Flower Beneath the Foot*) but one of the two persons concerned who bore distinctive first names of the type Firbank had recently failed to secure for

[1] A yet earlier version of Firbank's title will be mentioned in Chapter XIX, 17.
[2] Cf. Chapter VI, 3.
[3] Cf. Chapter VI, 6.
[4] Thus (given the corroborating presence of the Sitwells) I expand the 'W. T. Walton' which the *Bibliography* (p. 20) lists deadpan from Firbank's account (although by 1970 Sir William Walton had, as he told me by letter, 'only the haziest remembrance' of the episode).

himself when he failed to arrange to make his first United-States appearance under the name of Annesley. Firbank might, I think, have punished Aldous Huxley for being Aldous, but his preference for a victim went to Sacheverell Sitwell because he believed it to be a Sitwell who first proposed sending the Psyche to Firbank. It was after the Psyche incident that Firbank prepared his second United-States publication, the edition of *Vainglory* in which he proposed to alter Winsome to Sacheverell.

My surmise amounts in total to this. In the *Vainglory* of 1915, Firbank expressed his envy of the name Winston because, though he was already resolved to publish his book under a new first name, he could tell in advance that he was not going to dare to pick, for his new name, the only one of his names that was as distinctive as Winston. In 1924, with *Prancing Nigger*, he had a further chance to take a new name. He let the chance go again – and again experienced the emotions he had expressed by Winsomeing Winston.

It was because he was re-experiencing the same emotions as he had during the writing of *Vainglory* that, after his tiff, he picked, from ten potential enemies, Sacheverell Sitwell to punish in print. It was the name Sacheverell that angered the author who could not edge Carl Van Vechten into inviting him to call himself Annesley.

And, because Firbank was re-experiencing the emotions which had originally created the name Winsome, it was Winsome that he picked, of all the first names in the book, to suppress from the 1925 edition (and it would have been the suppression of a very comic stroke – which is probably why Firbank in the end decided against it) in the cause of punishing Sacheverell Sitwell for possessing a first name Firbank had twice not dared emulate.

5. The Flower Child – 1

FIRBANK was mean about spending money on almost everything except plants.

It was by their extensive and elaborate decoration with cut flowers, a decoration that sometimes stretched to a dinner table 'strewn with orchids', that Firbank's rooms at Cambridge astonished his fellow undergraduates and his rooms at Oxford (where in January 1919 he was still maintaining his war-time retreat[1]) astonished Siegfried Sassoon.

His very conversational irrelevancies, on the occasion of Sassoon's Oxford visit (which Sassoon made in the company of the Sitwell brothers), came in flower terms. When Sacheverell Sitwell praised Firbank's writing, Firbank's shyness permitted him to reply only 'I can't bear calceolarias! Can you?'

[1] Cf. sub-section 1 of this chapter.

Indeed Firbank even marked the passing of time in terms of the blooming of flowers. His next publication day, he wrote to Carl Van Vechten, would 'race the first white lilac'.

His cult of flowers must often have resembled a religious cult indeed. Sassoon recorded that at Oxford, and E. J. Dent that at Cambridge, there were candles as well as flowers.

Firbank kept up his flower cult all his life and from the start extended it into his writing. And his passion was not confined to cut flowers. After listing the 'small collection of *objets d'art* from which' Firbank 'was never parted', Osbert Sitwell, who first saw the collection in Firbank's Oxford rooms, adds: 'There was always, too, a palm-tree near him.'

It was to water the current palm-tree that Firbank arranged for a gardener with a green-baize apron and what Osbert Sitwell called a 'rustic way of speaking' to be sent twice a day to Firbank's nearby flat from a flower-shop in Sloane Square. Even when Firbank moved to Piccadilly, the arrangement held good, Firbank stipulating that the gardener walk the whole distance except when it rained.[1] Sitwell comments that the gardener found Firbank 'very nice-spoken' (no doubt he was more fluent-spoken with the gardener than with the upper classes) and that the proprietor of the flower-shop made no objection because from so good a customer as Firbank 'money rained in on him for orchids'.

Inevitably it was an assistant in a flower-shop who gratifyingly recognised Firbank in Rome when he hadn't been back for years.

No doubt one of the comparative cheapnesses Firbank praised[2] about living abroad was the comparative cheapness of flowers. The Sitwells used to see him in Via Tornabuoni in Florence (a city whose name must have pleased Firbank) 'staggering' under the flowers he had bought and looking 'in a wild and helpless way' for a cab to carry them home in.

Evidently the Via Tornabuoni contained the best Florentine flower-shop. For it was in that street that Firbank embarrassed Reggie Turner by rushing at him and covering him with a gift of lilies.

In Constantinople, *Some People* records, Firbank even sent lilies to Harold Nicolson.

---

[1] It is difficult (for reasons I give in the note on the subject in sub-section 6 of this chapter) to be sure of the date or even the site of the Sloane Square palm-tree watering. But I think *Vainglory* (1915) may commemorate both the Sloane Square gardener's rustic speech and Firbank's waiver about rainy days: in the person of Mrs Shamefoot's 'boy', Jordan, who delivers plants from the flower-shop Mrs Shamefoot keeps 'just at the beginning of Sloane Street'. 'Jordan lately had been imported from the country, only to explain the first time it rained: "It's too-wet-for-to-go-far!"' (*Complete* Firbank, p. 102).

[2] Cf. Chapter VI, 1.

His flower gifts were sometimes embarrassing even in England and even to women. The wife of one of his early acquaintances[1] was embarrassed into poetic prose in her thank-you note: 'I thought that Autumn herself had passed down the street and left them for me.' A woman guest of Augustus John's, whom Firbank met when he lunched with John at the Eiffel Tower, was simply dumped by Firbank, after the luncheon, at Claridge's. Too shy to give her his company, Firbank absented himself in quest of 'highly exotic lilies' to give her instead.

And, for himself, Firbank evidently did not consider himself dressed unless his rooms were dressed in flowers. In June 1924 Philip Moeller sent to Carl Van Vechten, who had still not met Firbank (indeed, he never did), an account of Moeller's unexpected call on Firbank in Rome. Firbank invited his visitor in (he was living at Palazzo Orsini), was, of course, shy – 'And then' (says Moeller's account, which is quoted in the *Memoir*) 'with a glance of despair about him, he suddenly ejaculated: "But there aren't any flowers! None! None!"'

6. Notes to Chapter VII

FIRBANK'S sitting on the floor at and being sent home from the Eiffel Tower restaurant are recorded by Robert McAlmon in *Being Geniuses Together 1920–1930*, pp. 79–80. Forrest Reid's account of Firbank as an undergraduate is in his *Private Road* (1940), pp. 54–8.

Firbank's visit to Augustus John is described by Osbert Sitwell in the *Memoir*, pp. 131–2. The words about Firbank's 'exquisite confusion' are John's, quoted by Sitwell.

Osbert Sitwell tells the story of Firbank and the milk train in the *Memoir*, p. 133.

Firbank's cycling is recorded in the *Memoir*, p. 62 and the *Biography*, p. 163. Osbert Sitwell wrote of Firbank's flying in the *Memoir*, pp. 135 and 136.

Heather Firbank's love affairs are mentioned in the *Biography*, pp. 128–9.

The Augustus John quotation about the laugh is from the *Memoir*, p. 113. Sewell Stokes is reported in the *Biography*, pp. 235–6. Lord Berners's report on Firbank's solitary laughter is in the *Memoir*, pp. 147–8.

The *Memoir* quotation about Firbank's childhood travels is from p. 20.

Firbank's account of his education is quoted from *Who Was Who*.

The Vyvyan Holland quotation about exams is in the *Memoir*, p. 106. Firbank's dating of *The Artificial Princess* is quoted in the *Bibliography*, p. 62. Details of Firbank's Cambridge studies are given in the *Biography*, pp. 83–4.

The *Memoir* records Firbank's notion of working for a publisher on p. 52.

---

[1] There will be more on this subject in Chapter XII, 2.

Lord Berners quotes Firbank on the Catholic church in the *Memoir*, p. 149. The *Memoir* records his Vatican ambition on p. 35.

The lover in the Pope's body-guard is on p. 747 and Mrs Shamefoot's reflexions on mining on p. 213 in the *Complete* Firbank.

The melodramatic reply is in the *Memoir*, p. 79, and the record of Firbank paying for drinks is in the same book, p. 68. The story of Firbank as a paying guest is in Osbert Sitwell's contribution to it, p. 139. Firbank's praise of money to Heather Firbank (in 1915) is quoted in the *Biography*, p. 108.

Vyvyan Holland's account of the smashed crystal cup is quoted in the *Biography*, p. 109. The same page of the same book recounts the loan request. The Sotheby's catalogue information is published in *The New Rythum*, p. 133.

The *Biography* documents Firbank's relation with Hunter Stagg (and with Stagg's friend Montgomery Evans) on pp. 242–4 and p. 274.

Fleas are rumoured in the Ritz (as the result of an incomplete overhear) in *The Flower Beneath the Foot* (*Complete* Firbank, p. 508). Mrs Calvally is followed by a butterfly in *Vainglory* (*Complete*, p. 84).

The Sacheverell Sitwell–Firbank episode is described in the *Biography*, pp. 171–3.

Osbert Sitwell described publishing 'Fantasia in A Sharp Minor' in the fourth volume of his autobiography, *Laughter in the Next Room*, p. 29, and in the *Memoir* p. 127.

Osbert Sitwell related the priestly kidnapping in the *Memoir*, p. 135. The *Biography* (p. 106), without mentioning Sitwell's version, quotes an account (from which I have quoted Firbank's final question) recorded by Nancy Cunard, which differs from Sitwell's version in detail and by omitting the kidnap motif, since the priests offer Firbank a lift home from a restaurant.

Freud's account of the mechanism of paranoia is quoted from his *Collected Papers*, Volume III, IV, III.

The kinship of the Firbanks to the Fairbanks is in Sir Thomas Firbank's entry in *The Landed Gentry* of 1898.

Osbert Sitwell describes Firbank's libel fantasy in his essay in the *Memoir*, p. 129.

The quotation about the building of the Oxted and Groombridge section and the information about Thomas Firbank's introduction to the business are from McDermott's *The Life and Work of Joseph Firbank* . . .

Oscar Wilde's 'All trials are trials for one's life' is from his *De Profundis* letter (pp. 509–10 in Rupert Hart-Davis's edition of his *Letters*). His self-betraying answer is recorded in *The Trials of Oscar Wilde*, edited by H. Montgomery Hyde, p. 150.

The 'too ugly' Firbank anecdote is from the *Memoir*, p. 47.

Firbank's 'butterflying' correspondence is quoted in the *Biography*, pp. 224–5.

Mrs Rosemerchant flits through possible fancy dresses in *The New Rythum*, p. 77.

Firbank's Tolstoy–Pavlova antithesis is recorded by Siegfried Sassoon in *Siegfried's Journey 1916–1920*, p. 137.

VII/6   THE PORTRAIT BEGUN

Oscar Wilde's customs declaration is reported in Hesketh Pearson's *Life* of him, Chapter 6. Charlie Mouth goes through the customs on p. 614 of the *Complete Firbank*.

Grant Richards's libel fears are recorded in the *Bibliography*, p. 39.

The *Memoir* relates the Nevinsons' story on pp. 85–6, and puts it in 'late autumn' 1925. This should probably read 'early autumn'; according to the *Biography* (p. 285), Firbank left England for the last time in early August 1925.

The forms of Firbank's name on *Vainglory*, and Firbank's comment, are from the *Bibliography*.

The *Memoir* describes Firbank's change of first name on p. 53.

The *Biography* describes the Guinevere piece on p. 42.

The *Memoir* records the goloshes on p. 79.

Firbank's prep school was the Mortimer Vicarage School (information in the Appendix to *The New Rythum*, p. 134).

Katherine Mansfield's temporary German pseudonym is recorded in Antony Alpers's *Biography* of her, Chapter 3. I have discussed her and Colette's changes of name in essays on both writers collected in my *Don't Never Forget*.

Michael Arlen was the pseudonym of Dikran Kouyoumdjian.

An Irish countess-ship is rejected on pp. 369–70 of the *Complete* Firbank.

The inscription to Van Vechten and the bibliographical facts are from the *Bibliography*.

Firbank's letter to Van Vechten explaining *Prancing Nigger*'s revision in title is of 27 June 1924 and is quoted in the *Biography*, p. 258.

The account of the Psyche episode given on pp. 72–3 of the *Memoir* names the signatories as 'Gerald Tyrwhitt, Evan Morgan, Aldous Huxley, and some others'. Gerald Tyrwhitt was the family name of Lord Berners.

The Cambridge flowers are described in the *Memoir*. The dinner-table orchids are recorded by Forrest Reid, in *Private Road*, p. 56. The Oxford flowers, including the irrelevant calceolaries, are recorded by Siegfried Sassoon on pp. 135–6 of *Siegfried's Journey 1916–1920*.

Firbank's white lilac letter (of 1922) is quoted in the *Biography*, p. 226.

The palm-tree is recorded by Osbert Sitwell in the *Memoir*, pp. 125 and 139–40. According to Sitwell, the visits of the 'gardener' began when Firbank was renting 'a small flat in Sloane Square'. According to the *Biography* (p. 123 and p. 182), Lady Firbank had a flat at 44 Sloane Street from 1913 to 1918. (In the list, which is reproduced in the *Bibliography*, of people to whom Firbank wanted copies sent of *Inclinations* [published in 1916], another hand has noted at the top that 6 copies each were to be sent to Lady Firbank and to Mr Firbank. The address the note gives for Lady Firbank is 44 Sloane Street. That for Firbank is 28 Pall Mall [a fact on whose significance I will speculate in a footnote to Chapter IX, 5].) The 'gardener' from the Sloane Square shop might well have tended Firbank's palm-tree at his mother's flat in Sloane Street during 1913 or 1914, and thus could easily have made his way into *Vainglory* by spring 1915. But in that case Osbert Sitwell's account must be taken from hearsay, not experience. Osbert Sitwell's contribution to the *Memoir* makes it clear that, although he knew Firbank by sight from 1912 on, he didn't meet Firbank personally until after he had read the published *Vainglory*.

Firbank's being recognised in Rome is recorded, from his letters to his mother, in the *Biography*, p. 127.

Firbank in Florence is recorded by Osbert Sitwell in the *Memoir*, p. 127, and by Harold Acton, who is quoted in the *Biography*, p. 215. The *Biography* quotes the embarrassed thank-you note on p. 74.

The dumping of Augustus John's guest is recorded in the *Memoir*, p. 137. The Memoir quotes Philip Moeller on pp. 82–3.

VIII

The Portrait Pursued

1. The Fully Dressed

ONE of the many objects Firbank made a cult of was himself.

His personality he largely could and did render exquisite. He couldn't cure his shyness. But even that he often turned to wit and charm.

He was no less at pains about his appearance. And having taken care with it he took care to have it recorded in the portraits he commissioned and often reproduced in his books – in one instance, two to a single volume.

In his appearance, too, there were items he couldn't cure. (Chapter IX, 10 will discuss an important one.) He was not confident even of his capacity to control his figure. But he could and did control or at least monitor the representations of his appearance.

It was probably because he had or believed he had more control over them that (anyway for public purposes) he preferred drawings of himself to photographs.[1] The photograph by Bertram Park which, bearing Firbank's family signature[2] (as A. A. R. Firbank) and the date 1917, appeared as the frontispiece to the *Memoir*, is said to be the only photograph of himself that Firbank would permit to be published.

Firbank's control over representations of himself was exercised largely to the avoidance of his profile.[3]

The permitted Bertram Park photograph shews him front-face. Another, taken at the same session (Firbank, wearing the same clothes, sits in the same chair) but not passed for publication, shifts the head slightly towards a profile position. (That photograph is reproduced in the *New Rythum* volume.) Yet a third, which has remained unpublished till now (when it is Plate 2 in this book), is an almost pure profile.

Among draughtsmen, Wyndham Lewis seems to have been exempted from the veto on portraying Firbank's profile. Wyndham Lewis made (in 1922) two drawings of Firbank: one a front-face, one a profile; one for

---

[1] Chapter IX, 9 will mention a passage where the preference is expressed through fiction.
[2] Cf. Chapter VII, 4.
[3] Chapter XII, 2 will mention a possible influence on Firbank's choice.

Wyndham Lewis's private satisfaction (Firbank's biographer doubts whether Firbank ever saw this drawing) and one for Firbank, who reproduced it in *The Flower Beneath the Foot*.[1]

Robert McAlmon recorded that Firbank infuriated Wyndham Lewis by passing the drawing to his publisher without paying Wyndham Lewis for it. Firbank then made himself inaccessible. But, when Firbank and Wyndham Lewis were both at the Eiffel Tower restaurant, Robert McAlmon mediated between them and – 'to my surprise', Robert McAlmon's narrative comments – Firbank made out a cheque.

Paradoxically, by the norm of Firbank's usual preference, it is[2] the profile drawing which was done for Firbank and which he chose to reproduce, and the front-face drawing which remained private to the draughtsmen.

Perhaps Firbank was for once reconciled to his profile because Wyndham Lewis geometricalised and angularised it.

Literary description makes good what Firbank suppressed, and perhaps corrects what Wyndham Lewis angularised. Osbert Sitwell said that Alban Berg had, besides many other facial resemblences, 'the same profile' as Firbank, and described that profile as 'waving in and out with something of the line of a sea-coast'.

Perhaps Firbank feared his coast-line profile might merge with its surroundings to the point of vanishing. It was probably one of the dreads of his own life that he attributed, in *Vainglory*, to Miss Thumbler, who enquires

' "[. . .] Have I changed since yesterday? Sunday in town leaves such scars. . . . Have I my profile still?"

' "You've got it. Just!" he assured her.

'For the dread of Miss Thumbler's life was that one day she would find herself without it.'

(It was a yet franker and bleaker self-portrait in profile that Firbank wrote into *A Study in Temperament*, one of the two stories in his first published volume – where, typically,[3] he appears as a girl and a girl with a floral name: 'Lobelia had no profile; she knew it, and did her best not to show hers. But it is almost impossible to go through life without showing one's profile – at

---

[1] Firbank's description of the drawing was quoted in Chapter V, 5.

[2] Although the *Biography* reproduces both Wyndham Lewis drawings, it doesn't say which is the public and which the private: or, to be exact, it *does*, but only in the indecipherably subjective terms of saying that the private drawing is the one that 'emphasises every aspect of decadence and sickness in Firbank's face'. To discover which drawing Firbank himself commissioned, you have to consult the first edition (1923) of *The Flower Beneath the Foot*, where Firbank reproduced it as a vignette on the title-page: and it is the profile. (The drawing is also used, in vignette form, on the title-page of Ifan Kyrle Fletcher's *Memoir*, 1930.)

[3] as Chapter XV will insist.

dinner-parties, for instance.' Yet in *Vainglory* again he was able to soften his own want of profile at least with a hint of mystery: through the person of Mrs Shamefoot, who carries many[1] of Firbank's own hopes and fears. Mrs Shamefoot is described, by an enemy, as 'With a profile like the shadow of a doubt'.)

Again it is written descriptions, chiefly those assembled in the *Memoir*, which have to supply Firbank's tallness, the tone of his voice ('high-pitched') and the 'feminine' impression made by his figure, gait and gestures. A. C. Landsberg, a friend of Osbert Sitwell and a Cambridge acquaintance of Firbank, said Firbank reminded him in appearance of portraits of 'society' women by Boldini.

With the exception of the 1919 painting in oils by Alvaro Guevara, where Firbank, 'huddled up' (by his own description) and angularised this time by his own shyness, has retreated to the back of the pictures and is almost drowned in the possessions, patterns and 'Orchids' he has surrounded himself with, Firbank usually had himself depicted uncoloured. (Although he ran to reproducing in colour the frontispiece and title-page illustration which, for example, he commissioned for *The Princess Zoubaroff*, he perhaps had it in mind that portraits of himself would be easier to reproduce satisfactorily in his books if they were drawn rather than painted.)

Accordingly it is, yet again, written descriptions that supply his high complexion – and ought to supply the colour of his eyes. The bookseller C. W. Beaumont, quoted by his fellow bookseller Ifan Kyrle Fletcher, calls Firbank's eyes 'blue or bluish-grey'. Augustus John, who made frequent study of Firbank in order to draw him (but in black and white), calls them brown. But Hunter Stagg's[2] friend Montgomery Evans made in his diary (perhaps the most reliable type of document since diaries are usually written up pretty soon after observation) mention of Firbank's 'soft deep blue eyes'.

Firbank was a dandy. C. W. Beaumont's account specifies gloves and cane; Sir William Walton remembers 'a beautifully rolled umbrella and his hat at a rakish angle' – and adds: 'he must I imagine have had an assiduous manservant'.

Firbank's was, however, the 'sober dandyism' of Baudelaire. Osbert Sitwell even found 'something of the ecclesiastic in his appearance'.

Despite the deep and many drag impersonations of his fantasy, Firbank never hinted at drag in his clothes. The ecclesiastic touch in them was of subfusc, not vestments. The *Memoir* records that his suits were 'made by the best tailors' but nevertheless 'always looked a little foreign'.

[1] They will be mentioned in Chapter XV, 17.
[2] Cf. Chapter VII, 2.

Firbank allowed himself only one external mark of his imagination's transvestism. He used cosmetics. Simon Harcourt-Smith has borne witness to 'discreet dabs of rouge' highlighting Firbank's cheekbones. But Firbank's high complexion seems to have needed keeping down more than touching up. He powdered. Once at least he was seen (by Sir William Walton) with his hair powdered at the temples. But as a rule it was his face which he covered with rice powder – a habit his fiction more than once attributes to the sky.[1]

'Overhead', says a sentence buried (by Firbankian standards) in a paragraph of *The Artificial Princess*, 'the sky was so pale that it appeared to have been powdered all over with poudre-de-riz.' The same sentence, with 'all over' changed to 'completely' in order to avoid the assonance between 'all over' and 'overhead', recurs in *Vainglory*, but there it is accorded virtually a paragraph on its own. (Chapter X, 6 will add another item to the poudre-de-riz collection.)

Perhaps the ultimate, furthest-gone baroque extension (an extension with a masochist's erotic wriggle in its whiplash tail) of Firbank's habit of self-portraiture in his fictions is his appearance as an Arabian mare (mate, perhaps, of the stolen Spanish charger) which is ridden by a '*screen artiste*' on the Promenade (Rotten Row with touches of the Bois de Boulogne and of the Prater[2]) in *The Flower Beneath the Foot*. The mare's eyes are 'made up with kohl' and her withers are powdered. Every time the rider 'used her whip the powder rose in clouds'.

And the poudre-de-riz skies are in their turn, I imagine, the mirrors of Firbank's toilet. Since the sky is powered 'all over' or 'completely', I take it Firbank was in the habit of powdering his face all over or completely. Indeed, just as he thought his rooms undressed if they were not flowered, so, I suspect, he thought his face undressed if it was not floured. When he was met unawares by Augustus John in Bond Street, Firbank 'turned in alarm, screening his face with that beautiful hand, and, protesting that he wasn't "fit to be seen", writhed confusedly into the nearest shop'.

That beautiful hand (whose beauty Firbank celebrated in public – 'They are too beautiful. Don't you love my hands?' Robert McAlmon quoted from his conversation) often had its long finger nails 'stained a deep carmine'.

---

[1] – and once, in an application more curious, to a saint. An exhibition of paintings by pupils of a girls' school in . . . *Cardinal Pirelli* (p. 674 in the *Complete* Firbank) includes 'an evasive "nude", showing the posterior poudrederizé of a Saint'.

[2] '[. . .] the scene is some imaginary Vienna' (Firbank's preface to the United-States edition of *The Flower Beneath the Foot*).

2. The Minion

FIRBANK'S finger nails were incarnadined, the *Memoir* makes clear, before 1914. It occurs to me that at that time the habit would have been thought ungenteel – or perhaps actually whorish – even for a woman.

And for the matter of that, even for a woman, even *after* the 1914–18 war, it was not wholly acceptable as well bred to powder one's face in public. Yet that was what Firbank did, some time about 1922, in the Café Royal – though it's true he did it 'apologetically as though to make himself invisible'. But he *didn't* make himself invisible. What I've quoted is his biographer's digest of what Sewell Stokes reported he saw.

I take it, therefore, that the woman Firbank was in his imagination was not a woman of his own class and private means but a woman of the class I think Firbank felt more at ease with: an assistant, very likely, in a flower-shop.

I suspect, too, that the Firbank woman was a woman bought: not up for sale to any bidder, but on the lookout for a particular protector (a métier at last?).

Perhaps the word Firbank attached to what he made himself in his personal fantasy life[1] is *minion*.

It is that word which he makes Mrs Henedge, in *Vainglory*, apply to Winsome Brookes's companion, Andrew: 'I consider your friend to be half a minion, and half an intellectual.'

Mrs Thoroughfare expresses similar thoughts in *Valmouth*, when she describes a pair of 'wisps of boys' as 'Like the minions of Henry the Third'.

Minion is also a word cognate with *mignon*. The ex-chorister boyfriend of Count Cabinet in *The Flower Beneath the Foot* is an unmistakable minion, and he is described as a 'mignon youth'. The taste for (as it were) doublets which *Valmouth* ascribes to Henry the Third has shaped the name (in the novel) of Cardinal Doppio-Mignoni. And *mignonne* is the adjective accompanying that early Guinevere who (I speculated in Chapter VII, 4) was one of the selves of Arthur Firbank.

And that 'Guinevere, mignonne', it is clear even from the half sentence the *Biography* accords her, was a financial realist. She is said to be 'not so stupid as to think lovers can live on "*des mots, des regards et de la sympathie*"'.

3. The Phobic

THOUGH in adult life he never (as least so far as anyone seems to have been permitted to know) wore them in reality, Firbank's skirts, whether whorish

[1] – whose manifestations I shall discuss in Chapter IX, 8 and Chapter XIV, 10.

flounces or ecclesiastical frills, were vivid enough to his imagination to give him, I think, a terror lest a mouse should run up beneath them.

That Firbank had a phobia of mice (which like his theft delusions probably reflected his castration anxiety) I deduce from two episodes in his life which the *Biography* reports in digest from his letters and notebooks.

The first concerns the miserable winter he spent, in 1921, in a rented châlet, ill-named Bon Port, at Montreux. Firbank suffered first from noisy neighbours, then from illness. What the *Biography*, reporting Firbank's letters to his mother, calls the crowning blow was that there turned out to be mice in the châlet.

The other episode was at Firbank's sittings for the drawings by Wyndham Lewis.[1] Wyndham Lewis found Firbank a fidgety sitter, continually leaping off the modelling throne to inspect Wyndham Lewis's work (in which case it seems unlikely that Wyndham Lewis managed to conceal from Firbank the existence of one of the drawings). But, by Firbank's account, the reason he ran about the studio was that there were also mice running about the studio.

That Firbank associated the terror of mice with ecclesiastical skirts I deduce from the last hours of Cardinal Pirelli (whose eccentricities include the habit of prowling the city by night in disguise – his disguise often female, because he doesn't want 'to forgo altogether the militant bravoura of a skirt'). On the last night of his life, the Cardinal repents having imposed too severe a punishment on his favourite ('yet, Thou knowest, I adore the boy!') choirboy, the Chiclet: 'It must have been love that made me do it.' The Chiclet's crime has been to miss the responses during service because he 'had rushed about the cathedral after mice'. The Cardinal's over-severe punishment is to shut the boy in the cathedral 'alone with them after dark'.

Going to rescue his victim, the Cardinal goes to his death – hearing, on his way through the cathedral, a symbol of castration and mortality: 'the determined sound of a tenacious mouse gnawing at a taper-box'. (Firbank has by design insisted, in the previous chapter, on the phallicness of ecclesiastical candles: a woman who is arranging to have a mass said for her lover's safety is asked by the cathedral secretary if she wants the candles 'long and, I dare say, gross'.) By Firbankian irony the Cardinal takes the gnawing mouse for an 'admirable example in perseverance', and his own perseverance in pursuit of the boy kills him.

As a matter of fact, Firbank's account of the mice in Wyndham Lewis's studio consists of a note in one of his notebooks for *Concerning the Eccentricities of Cardinal Pirelli*.

The mice in Firbank's fears are met by traps for mice (or rats) in Firbank's

[1] Cf. sub-section 1 of this chapter.

fictions. In his early unperformed and unpublished[1] one-act play, *A Disciple from the Country*, Mrs Creamway has the line: '(*In a tone of voice she would use to an invalid not expected to recover*) Rats! My poor friend!... (*then with forced cheerfulness*) I can tell you of some wonderful traps that only require half the usual amount of cheese.' And in *The Artificial Princess* the party conversation between the King and the English Ambassadress is described: 'The Ambassadress was complaining, in French, of the mice at the Embassy whilst the King was telling her of some quite wonderful mouse-traps, intermixed with the history of the house.'

Eventually, however, Firbank closed the circle which phobias tend to pursue – by making the antidote as terrifying as the dread it counters. At the end of *Caprice* Firbank told himself the ultimate (to a phobic) horror story. The heroine of *Caprice* is killed through falling victim to a mousetrap.

4. The Abstainer

FIRBANK drank.[2] But he scarcely ate.

He was a great orderer of exotic fruit and fruit out of season; and often (though with much champagne) fruit was all that, in public at least, he ate.

The quantities he ate were sometimes, but not always, tiny. He is recorded to have taken a single grape (for tea) and a single pea (for dinner). But, when Philip Moeller dined with him in Rome, Firbank's meal consisted not only of 'a bottle or two of champagne' but of 'innumerable' peaches.

On an earlier occasion, when Firbank was living in Oxford (which he did from 1915 to 1919), it was Firbank's guest who, embarrassed by Firbank's embarrassment, ate innumerable peaches. Sir William Walton, who 'knew Firbank comparatively well', remembers 'an amusing episode now seen in retrospect, of my going to call on him one summer evening in the lodgings he had opposite Magdalen. When he opened the door I was slightly put out by his having powdered his hair over both temples, but he very nervously asked me upstairs and I even more nervously followed him. Neither of us spoke – he giggled a good deal now and then. There was a bowl of delicious looking peaches on the table to which he barely whispered for me to help myself. After taking one I got so nervous and hysterical that I went through

---

[1] apart from the extracts (one of which I am quoting) published in 1962 in the same volume as *The New Rythum*.

[2] And (according to the *Memoir*, p. 66) 'drugged a great deal'. Forrest Reid recorded that, after dinner in Firbank's Cambridge rooms at a table 'strewn with orchids' (cf. Chapter VII, 5), 'Firbank sat on the hearthrug and smoked "drugged cigarettes"' (*Private Road*, p. 56).

the lot and at the end feeling even more shy and awkward I just fled. He however by the ripples of laughter seemed to be delighted.'[1]

Firbank's passion for fruit reads to me (even when I deliberately put aside the partisanship of my own vegetarianism) as a symptom of his being a crypto-vegetarian. Mrs Cresswell (in *Vainglory*), the uncanonised saint of Ashringford, 'was [. . .] one of our original vegetarians'. ('Her adoration for apricots[2] is well known.') Firbank himself is said to have – besides avoiding Covent Garden because of the 'massacre of the flowers' – held a handkerchief in front of his eyes while he passed a butcher's shop.

That contrast between flower markets and butchery tones the opening sentence of *The Artificial Princess*: ' "You take the white omnibus on the Platz," murmured the Princess, "but do not forget to change into an ultramarine on reaching the Flower Market, or you will find yourself in the 'Abattoirs' ".'

And in *Santal* Firbank has positively lent his own averted eyes to his North African hero Cherif. Crossing the Souk, Cherif passes a butcher's shop in front of which 'a half-naked negro was dragging a reluctant ram by the horns. Cherif turned his head aside to avoid witnessing its writhings: the sight of suffering to him was intensely terrible. "Allah will make amends some day to all sad animals", he reflected passing quickly on.'

Cherif finally leaves home because his aunt slaughters the family pet lamb.

At 19, when he attended bullfights in Spain, Firbank was evidently either unaware of or inconsistent in his emotional responses. Perhaps he never worked out the reasonable necessity behind his emotional inclination, and perhaps he never became consistent in his practice. The *Biography* speaks of his eating chicken livers at the Eiffel Tower restaurant. But more often the records speak of his eating 'asparagus and a bottle of wine' or caviare and champagne.

(Caviare was no offence to any vegetarianism he may have professed. The sturgeon lays her eggs and swims unharmed away before they are collected. Firbank's favourite diet of caviare and champagne should give the lie to the rumour that vegetarians must be ascetics.)

It looks to me as though Firbank was certainly moving towards a reasoned rejection of the conventionally taken-for-granted idea that the other species of animals are merely things for humans to kill and use. In his war-time rooms at Oxford, the *Memoir* says, Firbank took much pleasure in 'the

---

[1] Sir William Walton kindly told me this by letter (8 June 1970).
[2] a taste perhaps borrowed from the Duchess of Malfi (whom, as Chapter XIV, 7 will remark, Firbank quoted in *The Artificial Princess*).

typography and binding' of the books he collected, though he kept them in closed cupboards, because he could not fit their colours into his décor. The *Biography* adds the detail that he had his purchases bound in sky-blue morocco. However, *Inclinations*, which Firbank published in 1916, contains this line spoken about Gerald(ine) O'Brookomore: 'Gerald isn't really hard . . . You wouldn't say so if you knew her well . . . Once she bought a little calf for some special binding, but let it grow up . . . and now it's a cow!' And in 1919, when he left Oxford, Firbank sold his books.

Observers of Firbank's small appetite associated it with his ill health. In general, people seem to have assumed Firbank was consumptive (and therefore non-consuming) perhaps even before he was.

Although the *Memoir* records that by 1925 his cough had become 'monotonously insistent' and some of his acquaintance were urging him to a doctor, others seem to have read the cough as a Firbank characteristic, almost an extension of his laugh. When Lord Berners took Firbank by car to Lake Nemi a few days before Firbank died, he thought Firbank 'coughed a good deal, but not more alarmingly than on other occasions'.

The proprietor of the Eiffel Tower, though he lamented how little Firbank ate, was reconciled (no doubt by how much Firbank drank) to Firbank's habit and teased him about it. A minuscule increase in Firbank's appetite which he once satirically remarked on evidently seemed to him an improvement in Firbank's health. Osbert Sitwell quotes him as saying 'Mr Firbank is much better [. . .] Yesterday for dinner he ate a whole slice of toast with his caviare.'

Firbank's last day in England was typically Firbankian. It was spent at the Eiffel Tower. He arrived in the morning and began drinking cocktails. He refused to eat, lest he spoil his appetite for dinner. His dinner consisted of a bottle of champagne and a caviare sandwich.

Osbert Sitwell believed that Firbank's abstention from food was caused by a bodily malady. 'He suffered, I believe, from a nervous affection of the throat, which prevented him swallowing food easily. To this misfortune was due the fact that he drank so much more than the little he ate.'

Presumably it was, though he was too polite to say so, that theory of Osbert Sitwell's (which he probably read when Sitwell's contribution to the *Memoir* appeared, earlier, in the collected edition) which Ifan Kyrle Fletcher contradicted: 'Observers [. . .] have presumed from his weakly health that his ailment prevented mastication. There is no evidence to support this theory'.

Indeed, rather than Firbank's illness causing him to eat little, it seems likely that his eating little contributed to his illness.

Ifan Kyrle Fletcher countered Osbert Sitwell's theory with an obviously correct one of his own. He believed that Firbank's habitual dieting 'engendered a dislike of food by suggestion'.

Indeed, Firbank, who shewed such solicitude about the threat to Winsome Brookes's figure of his landlady's cooking,[1] was regarded by Vyvyan Holland, who sought his advice, as an expert on slimming.

Firbank, in this, as in literature, in advance of his period, was one of the (historically considered[2]) earliest of those girls, whose number increases as the 20th century proceeds, who are from time to time reported to have slimmed themselves into ill health or even to death.

5. The Gypsy

WHAT Ifan Kyrle Fletcher considered Firbank's 'narcissistic habit' of having his portrait done achieved self-canonisation with the publication of *The Flower Beneath the Foot*, in which Firbank insisted on reproducing *two* portrait drawings of himself. One was the Wyndham Lewis I discussed in the first sub-section of this chapter, the other an Augustus John.

The John drawing Firbank described as 'rather "gypsy" '.

The phrase is a comment on the prevalence of gypsies in Augustus John's subject-matter[3] and at the same time a glimpse into another of Firbank's impersonations.

Of course Firbank was a gypsy. He was a nomad (though a fashionable one who caused 'advertisements of his arrivals from abroad [. . .] to appear in *The Times* and the *Morning Post*'). And he was also a heeder of gypsy's warnings and a seeker after fortune-tellings.

Firbank was much concerned to pick astrologically propitious dates for his publications. (The results should encourage scepticism.) For the appearance of *The Princess Zoubaroff*, for instance, he offered his 'publisher' a choice of the three dates he believed lucky in November 1920.

Osbert Sitwell thought Firbank's superstition possibly satirical but more probably genuine, and he described its multifariousness: 'he was much given to fortune-tellers, crystal-gazers, and givers of Egyptian amulets.'

Indeed, Firbank took 'gypsy' also in its radical sense of Egyptian. Ifan

---

[1] Cf. Chapter VI, 6.

[2] There is a note on this subject in sub-section 10 of this chapter.

[3] 'Mrs Sixsmith placed a hand to her hip in the style of an early John' (*Caprice*; p. 354 in the *Complete* Firbank).

Kyrle Fletcher described his mind as 'entangled by the mystery of the Sphinx' and said Firbank believed that the esoteric significance of things Egyptian would be revealed to him supernaturally.

Firbank was taken to Egypt in the course of his childhood travels (Osbert Sitwell believed sunstroke in Egypt to be the cause of his childhood ill health) and he visited it again (in 1911 and in 1925) as a solitary adult traveller. In Egypt he had himself photographed on a houseboat named (if I have correctly separated the words) Ter el Nil, where he stands in a negligently stylish pose that is almost lost to sight in the patterns of rigging, fretwork and ironwork boat-architecture and palms on the bank behind [Plate 4]; in Egypt, according to Lord Berners, 'in the course of an expedition down the Nile on a dahabeah', Firbank 'succeeded, single-handed, in quelling a mutiny'.

He also collected and admired Egyptian antiquities.

It was probably Firbank's own experience that shaped Mrs Shamefoot's in *Vainglory*. 'In the railway carriage, Mrs. Shamefoot was sufficiently fortunate, too, to secure the seat opposite to herself for a magnificent image of the god Ptah. The terrific immobility of Egyptian things enchanted her, particularly in the train.'

Osbert Sitwell mentions, among the objects from which Firbank 'was never parted', a 'little green-bronze Egyptian figure of some bearded god or pharaoh'. It might be that or another which, as Ifan Kyrle Fletcher recorded, Firbank treated superstitiously. Firbank took a 'whim' to have an opal set in an 'Egyptian bronze statuette' which he owned. When his acquaintance protested that to do so 'would mar the dull green surface', Firbank replied 'It must be done, as a propitiatory offering!'

One, however, of his acquaintance was more superstitious even than Firbank. Helen Carew[1] detested what she believed to be the ill-omened scarab Firbank bought during, and treasured long after, his 1911 visit to Egypt. (In *Vainglory* Mrs Asp [Nilotic name[2]] remarks, of the writer who is one of Firbank's self-portraits: 'He scoured Cairo for me once years ago, to find me a lotus'.)

Firbank may have taken the ancient Egyptian notion of reincarnation seriously – or perhaps only good looks in the ancient Egyptian style. The first time he met a young man named the Honourable Evan Morgan,[3] Firbank perceived a resemblance in his face to the mummy of Rameses and

---

[1] Her rôle in Firbank's life will be described in Chapter XII, 5–6, where I will mention a possible cause of her superstitious dread.

[2] Its associations will be discussed in Chapter XIV, 2.

[3] who will recur in Chapters IX, 4 and XIX, 19.

rushed Morgan to the British Museum 'to see', according to the *Memoir*, ' "his original" '.

Perhaps it was the one time Firbank fell in love at first sight. Perhaps it was the one time he fell in love.

His infatuation with Evan Morgan (and with reincarnation) led Firbank in 1920 to dedicate *The Princess Zoubaroff* 'To the Hon. Evan Morgan in Souvenir Amicale of a "Previous Incarnation" '. However, either Morgan or his family objected to his being associated either with Firbank or with Firbank's play – 'having regard' (as the objection was expressed in a solicitors' letter to Firbank's 'publisher') 'to its general tone towards the Catholic Church of which' Morgan 'is a member'.[1] (Perhaps that solicitors' letter was in Firbank's mind when he told Lord Berners he laughed at the church.)

The dedication had to be literally cut out of the already printed book[2] – which postponed publication to the latest of Firbank's three lucky days.

Three years later, Firbank demonstrated that he was a gypsy also in his habit of putting the evil eye, by way of literary fantasy, on those who offended him. In *The Flower Beneath the Foot*, as Firbank's private key to the cast records, the Honourable Evan Morgan appears as the Honourable 'Eddy' Monteith.

Again it was the enemy's social standing that excited Firbank's anger, as he signalled by perpetuating the 'Honourable' from life into literature. But the 'Eddy', which Firbank put into inverted commas, was perhaps a swipe by the way at an older enemy, 'Eddie' Marsh.

That he held Evan Morgan's family guilty of interference in the affair of the dedication Firbank demonstrated by the clever assonance which transforms the real-life Morgan's real-life father, Lord Tredegar, into the fictitious Monteith's fictitious father, Lord Intriguer.

Not that that lets Morgan himself off. The gypsy's vengeance ushers him into the book and its imaginary kingdom of Pisuerga with an insulting mistake. The Honourable 'Eddy' Monteith has temporarily put aside his ambition of turning Jesuit monk (the Honourable Evan Morgan's 'considering' whether to turn Catholic) and has come to Pisuerga in pursuit of an archaeological expedition. Arriving at the British Embassy, he is mistaken for one of the temporarily hired domestic staff. 'The cloak-room will be in the smoking-room!' the Ambassadress informs him. 'What' (Firbank,

---

[1] (By Evan Morgan's own account, written long after the episode, he was at the time of the dedication only 'considering' becoming a member.) At some point later in his life Evan Morgan combined his literary interests with his Catholicism by founding the Catholic Poetry Society. (I learned this from an incidental mention in a review by William Tonks on p. 56 of the Summer 1966 issue of *The Aylesford Review*.)

[2] with results which Chapter XIX, 19 will describe.

with a memory of how the real Morgan was ushered into his own life,[1] causes the fictitious Monteith to muse) 'was there in his appearance that could conceivably recall a cloakroom attendant –? *He* who had been assured he had the profile of a "Rameses"!'

Firbank despatched Evan Morgan in fiction in the most offhand manner open to an author: in a footnote. 'Alas', the three lines relating Eddy Monteith's death conclude, 'for the *triste* obscurity of his end!'

Firbank's literary revenge was his attempt to overcome the tristesse he suffered when Evan Morgan rejected his book.

In this feud, too, Firbank's sense of a conspiracy against him worked towards, though it didn't reach, the result of producing one. This time Firbank's sense that Morgan's family was intriguing against him provoked the counter-accusation that Firbank himself was the centre of a pro-Firbank conspiracy. Evan Morgan's account of the withdrawal of the *Zoubaroff* dedication, written (according to Firbank's bibliographer, who quotes it) 20 years after the event, claims that Morgan found himself 'the victim of a good deal of adverse criticism on the part of the Firbank cult which had already started'.

As a matter of fact,[2] at the time (1920) of *The Princess Zoubaroff* there was scarcely anything that could, with the worst will in the world, be called a Firbank cult – apart, perhaps, from Firbank's acquaintance with the Sitwells, which was then no more than a year old.[3] Evan Morgan's later belief that there had been such a thing is probably just an extra flight of the Firbank as cult-writer myth. It is, perhaps, a myth that seeks to justify the world's unjust neglect of Firbank by pretending that Firbank and some unnamed admirers of his work constituted a conspiracy to promote him by somehow unfair means. But the myth adds that the conspirators, though villainous in intention, were not clever enough to succeed; for a cult is not recognition.

The myth might be tempted to try a new flight now on the strength of the privacy of some of the matters, like the *Zoubaroff* dedication, that inspired Firbank to fiction. But anyone who makes such a judgment must in logic dismiss the sonnets of Shakespeare as minor works by a cult-writer, since their allusions and inspirations were private at the time and have since

---

[1] Jocelyn Brooke had evidently forgotten the *Memoir*'s account of Firbank's comparison of Morgan to the Rameses mummy when he incorrectly wrote (on p. 33 of his 1951 volume): 'Eddie (sic) Monteith, in *The Flower Beneath the Foot*, is compared to a statue of Rameses'.

[2] a fact which Chapter XV, 16 will explore further.

[3] '[. . .] and when, in the February after the war, I went' to Oxford 'to see my brother, we decided to call on' Firbank. (Osbert Sitwell, *Memoir*, p. 123).

become indecipherable. In reality, pearls of literature are not to be judged by the privacy or even triviality of the grits that irk them into being. Firbank's wound at the hands of Evan Morgan was not, in fact, trivial. Even the seeming pique with which he contemplated a literary revenge (which, however, he withdrew before it reached print) against Sacheverell Sitwell[1] (his supposed fellow-conspirator) was a response to matters that probably looked far from trivial to Firbank's incipiently paranoid vision. And in any case what matters to literature is not the private Evan Morgan but the public and accessible-to-all pearl that Firbank made of Eddy Monteith.

6. The Devil's Disciple

IN *Vainglory* (a novel in which Mrs Shamefoot and Lady Castleyard try, with remarkable results or coincidence, to raise the devil) Jocelyn Brooke correctly heard 'several echoes of Firbank's interest in Black Magic'. That interest (as well as much besides) Firbank probably felt to be sanctioned by the example of the priest who received him into the Catholic church, Hugh Benson.[2]

The influence of Benson on Firbank deserves more exploration than Firbank scholars have allowed. For it was, involuntarily, an influence towards satire. Benson was an almost purely Firbankian personage.

It is true that Benson's Christianity was tinged with the muscular. He was, after all, a convert to Catholicism: one of three novelist sons[3] of an Archbishop of Canterbury. What his Jesuit biographer calls his 'masculine yet slightly feverish energy' produced from him, during the *Confiteor*, thumps on the chest described as 'tremendous'. Yet, even at his heartiest, Benson shewed tinges of camp. In moments of religious exaltation he 'would, literally, break into a laugh, and hug himself, and cry out to friends – "Oh, my dear; isn't it all tremendous? Isn't it sport? Isn't it all huge fun?" '

Robert Hichens found Benson in ordinary life 'unaffected' and 'straightforward' but judged his 'performance in the pulpit' to be 'melodramatic' and 'startlingly sensational'.

When Firbank knew him at Cambridge Benson was displaying largish

---

[1] Cf. Chapter VII, 4.
[2] Cf. Chapter VII, 4.
[3] They were: Arthur Christopher (1862–1925), Edward Frederic (1867–1940) and (Robert) Hugh (1871–1914). E. F. Benson was (from his novel *Dodo, a Detail of the Day*, 1893) known to his contemporaries as Dodo Benson. (Witness Aubrey Beardsley's *Letters*, 1971 edition, p. 254, Robert Hichens's Introduction to the 1949 reissue of *The Green Carnation* and p. 63 of Robert Hichens's autobiography, *Yesterday*.)

quantities of quite high camp; and several of Firbank's ironic teeth shew signs of having been sharpened on Benson.

Benson was, aptly, a literary collaborator of Frederick Rolfe, Baron Corvo – whom he had accosted by fan letter after reading *Hadrian the Seventh*.

Benson's rooms were rumoured 'unsacerdotal'. Besides filling them with flowers that must have pleased Firbank, he had decorated them very carefully, chiefly with green hangings. (Corvo commented by letter that they must look like a salad.)

Benson was a prolific and detailed designer of vestments and vessels for his own sacerdotal use. He specified moonstones and turquoise for chalice and ciborium. He designed an 'ivory-tinted' Christ, which was to be appliqué on a purple chasuble. For other vestments he designed seraphs whose wings were to begin 'with pure blue, and shade to tips through peacock to green'.

Snatches of his conversation have the entire turn of Firbankian dialogue: 'he said he could not pray before a self-coloured statue. He wanted "plenty of paint".'

He is surely present in Cardinal Pirelli. 'I should like to form a small choir – a quartette, perhaps,' Benson wrote. 'My ideal would be to have a boy who could sing, as my servant.'

Camp and fiction-writing did not use up all Benson's 'masculine yet slightly feverish energy' or exhaust the example he set Firbank. Benson was also, according to his biographer, 'from his childhood till his death, preoccupied with the uncanny and the occult'.

Indeed, one of Benson's novels is called *The Necromancers*. And one of his distinctions was to have had his horoscope drawn by Baron Corvo.

It is perhaps Benson's mixture of orthodox with heterodox supernaturalism which Firbank elevated to its apotheosis in *Vainglory*, where Mrs Shamefoot achieves (virtually) sainthood with the incongruous help of the devil. And it was surely in Benson's honour that Firbank invented a book by 'Miss Missingham':[1] *Sacerdotalism and Satanism*.

In what was virtually a fashion among English visitors at the period, Benson found Versailles, as he put it, '*crammed* with apparitions'. A person whom his biographer, Father C. C. Martindale, calls one of Benson's 'entourage' (thereby incidentally sketching the almost prelatical state Benson kept) heard ghostly music at the Trianon. That, too, was in keeping with fashion. The Versailles experiences of Miss Moberly and Miss Jourdain likewise included music heard (and later written down) by one of them. (It

---

[1] Perhaps Firbank extrapolated this finely missish name from Henry Harland's novel of 1893, *Mademoiselle Miss*.

was in – or, at least, she wrote it down in – A flat.) Miss Moberly and Miss Jourdain made their visit in 1901, though they did not publish their claims (which they did under the pseudonyms of Elizabeth Morison and Frances Lamont) until 1911. To their own account they were 'allowed to add an account of the experiences of three persons in 1908'. 1908 was evidently (second only to 1901) a good year for apparitions: it was the year of Benson's visit, too. Benson, however, must have merely sensed the apparitions. For after a lifetime of haunting haunted places he confessed he had never managed to see a ghost.

Firbank, though he shared so much of Benson's occultism, doesn't seem to have gone ghost-hunting. He had psychological reason not to. And when (according to the *Memoir*) he returned to England from his 1911 Egyptian trip he found an apter master than Benson for his superstitious interests: 'the great beast' himself, Aleister Crowley.

This discipleship of Firbank's brought on him, in 1920 (so his discipleship was evidently fairly enduring), the private disapprobation of Katherine Mansfield. Writing home from San Remo to John Middleton Murry about Murry's periodical *The Athenaeum*, she said: 'I note Grant Richards has picked out the Firbank. At the risk of your shouting me down – *please* don't praise Firbank. He's of the family of Aleister Crowley – an "Otter" bird – a sniggering, long-nailed, pretentious and very dirty fellow. As to *honesty* – the fellow would swoon at the sight of such a turnip. Huxley is very silly and young sometimes – and watery-headed.'

Grant Richards (Firbank's 'publisher') had presumably 'picked out' the Firbank in a publisher's advertisement in *The Athenaeum* (or, just possibly, in a note to the literary editor, which Murry might have enclosed when he sent a copy of the paper to Katherine Mansfield). Aldous Huxley had a slight acquaintance with Firbank, who once[1] greeted him with 'Aldous – always my *torture*'. (Perhaps the ultimate rack was Huxley's distinctive first name.[2]) In 1920 Aldous Huxley was working for *The Athenaeum*. From the sequence of Katherine Mansfield's thoughts it looks as though Aldous Huxley admired Firbank's work and was liable to write him a favourable notice.

The Firbank in question must, I think, be *Valmouth*. *Valmouth* was published in November 1919. Katherine Mansfield wrote her letter in January 1920. It seems highly probable that *The Athenaeum* would be a little behind-hand with reviews. Certainly Katherine Mansfield can't have been meaning Firbank's next book, which was *The Princess Zoubaroff*, because that was not published until the November of 1920.

[1] I emphasise that it was once: in contradiction of a mis-representation mentioned in the note on the subject in sub-section 10 of this chapter.   [2] Cf. Chapter VII, 4.

When *The Princess Zoubaroff* did appear, it contained evidence of the partial success (though she might not have accounted it such) of Katherine Mansfield's campaign to prevent *The Athenaeum* from giving *Valmouth* a good notice. The advertisements for Firbank's previous books at the back of *The Princess Zoubaroff* include a quotation from *The Athenaeum*'s notice of *Valmouth* – and, although Firbank and Grant Richards were wielding it as an enticement as near as they could find to praise, it is, as its opening 'But' indicates, one of those condescending reviews which pick out talents only to suggest a better use for them than the author has made: 'But Mr Firbank has talents – a gift of style, a capacity to write dialogue, an appreciation of the beautiful and the absurd. With such gifts he might produce a real comedy of manners. It is to be hoped that he will.'

The ' "Otter" bird' which Katherine Mansfield's letter calls Firbank I can only guess to be a reference to Gwen Otter, who has been described as 'a most generous Chelsea literary hostess' with 'a taste for the bizarre but no vices of her own'. Her taste for the bizarre certainly admitted Katherine Mansfield to her salon, and Mansfield seems to imply that Firbank frequented it, too (though the *Biography* makes no mention of Gwen Otter – or, indeed, of Katherine Mansfield). Indeed, Katherine Mansfield seems to associate the salon, Firbank and Crowley together.

Katherine Mansfield's anti-Firbank fit was probably provoked by one of her frequent revulsions against her own actions. She may have been not so much attacking Firbank as washing herself clean of Aleister Crowley. For Katherine Mansfield herself had (having, perhaps, met him through Gwen Otter?) visited Aleister Crowley and smoked hashish[1] with him.

As for Firbank's relation to Crowley: Firbank put him, I think, into *The Artificial Princess* (a book as deeply black-magical as *Vainglory*, since the devil positively appears in it as one of the dramatis personae).

In Firbank's case it wasn't an act of revulsion: not even (for once) revulsion from the person portrayed.

The portrait is highly flattering (in Crowley's terms) to Crowley.

Indeed, it makes a point of pronouncing the first syllable of his name with an *oh* sound – which I have noticed is to this day one of the methods by which disciples of Crowley signal their discipleship. Sceptics, unless they happen to know the correct pronunciation from another source, are liable to pronounce it with the vowel of *howl*.

The Artificial Princess, though it may have been begun earlier and continued later, was certainly[2] being written in 1910. Crowley's influence on

---

[1] Cf. the *Memoir*'s statement (which I mentioned in sub-section 4 of this chapter) that Firbank, too, 'drugged'.   [2] – as Chapter XIII, 6 will establish.

Firbank therefore probably began a shade earlier than the *Memoir* (in dating it to after Firbank's Egyptian trip of 1911) supposed, though the first influence might have been exerted through, and the portrait done on the strength of, hearsay.

Black magic supplies the structure and the basic substance of *The Artificial Princess*. The Princess remarks (in a form of words that perhaps came to Firbank through a verbal memory of Mozart's *Don Giovanni*[1]): 'it would be cruel of you to spoil any trifling amusement the dear Devil sends my way. Charming Man! He neglects our Court ever since Fräulein Anna Schweidler giggled so disrespectfully at a Black Mass.'

(Maureen Duffy has suggested to me that Fräulein Anna Schweidler is Katherine Mansfield. Not that Firbank is likely to have known of Katherine Mansfield's propensity for Germanising her name.[2] But while he was writing *The Artificial Princess* Firbank would have known of her as the author of the sketches set in Germany which she was publishing in 1909 and 1910 in *The New Age*.[3])

To the last section of *The Artificial Princess* Firbank gave the explicitly black-magical title 'Walpurgis – Polite'; and Section II (which contains what I take to be the portrait of Crowley) is called 'In which the Devil Himself Intervenes'. The Baroness is travelling on a love errand for the Princess. She neglects it and the love goes wrong, because, during the journey, 'the Devil, who had felt wounded, slighted, pained, at the Princess's complaints that afternoon, was hurrying incognito towards the Palace disguised as a sleek black Crow.' His interest is caught by the Baroness beneath. 'Wheeling several times above her, he plucked a feather from his breast and willed . . .'

There might be a tiny side-allusion, by translating his name, to Baron Corvo. But I take the diabolic, high-will-powered Crow to be mainly Crowley.

7. The Haunted

LIKE his delusions (of which indeed it was only a communal version), Firbank's superstition is ultimately a ghost story.

His irrational searching of fate was a response to, and a hopeful attempt

---

[1] – by a reversal of Don Giovanni's Act I recitative pronouncement 'Mi par ch'oggi il demonio si diverta d'opporsi a' miei piacevoli progressi'.

[2] Cf. Chapter VII, 4.

[3] These are the sketches which were in 1911 collected into the volume *In a German Pension*. (The publication dates are given in the Introductory Note by John Middleton Murry in the Penguin edition.)

to dodge, his rational expectation of not living long. Far from hunting, his superstitiousness was concerned to avoid ghosts.

At the end of every summer, when he prepared to leave England, Firbank would 'drive round in state to say good-bye' to the Sitwell brothers; 'each time, he would tell us that he knew there were but a few months more for him to live. These doleful tidings had invariably been conveyed to him either by a Syrian magician or by some wretched drunkard at the Café Royal.'

While Firbank said goodbye to the Sitwells he kept his cab ticking outside so that he could drive on and say goodbye to others.

Naturally, on that night at the Eiffel Tower,[1] Firbank made 'final farewells' to everyone, because 'his fortune-teller had warned him that he was making his last journey'. Naturally everyone, having seen the ritual before, 'had' (in Ifan Kyrle Fletcher's words) 'no premonition that at last superstition had chanced upon the truth'.

Indeed, Firbank's social uncertainty probably has the same ultimate base as his superstition. He was socially unsure because he suffered an insecurity of tenure in life itself.

The basic theme borrowed material from his experience as it proceeded. His social insecurity was complicated by the miserable uncertainties of his education, by his nouveau riche position in a snobbish world, by his for once far from deluded sense that, in England at that time, homosexual men were persecuted, and by his scarcely deluded sense that so were aesthetes.

And he joined, from the English social point of view, yet a third minority (though not this time a persecuted one) when he turned Catholic.

Likewise, Firbank's superstition borrowed from Benson and Crowley. But there was also material to which Firbank was born: for he was born half Irish. It is not surprising that anyone whose mother was born and brought up in Ireland should be extensively and multifariously superstitious.

Only an Irish imagination could have devised the wedding present sent, in *Vainglory*, by Mrs Henedge. Contrasting herself with Mrs Shamefoot, who has sent a rubied crucifix, Mrs Henedge declares: '*I* ran only to a pack of cards; supposed to have once belonged to Deirdre. I got them in Chelsea.'

An Irishman whom Firbank never met but who had much more influence[2] on him than either Benson or Crowley, namely Oscar Wilde, shared precisely Firbank's susceptibility to fortune-tellers. (So Mrs Henedge got her pack of cards in the part of London where Oscar Wilde lived.)

[1] Cf. sub-section 4 of this chapter.
[2] How much influence I shall discuss in Part Three.

Indeed I suspect[1] that Firbank was more Irish than his English observers were in a position to notice. (He may even, as I'll discuss in Chapter IX, 1, have been brought up to be more markedly Irish than observers of his photograph have noticed.) It was, I think, the Irishman who named one of his inventions Mrs Orangeman; and the Catholic-convert son of an Irish protestant parson's daughter who made Miss Sinquier speculate on how people would say, were *she* to be converted, 'Canon Sinquier's only daughter has gone over to Rome'.

(There is a delicate difference of hierarchical grade between the scandal of *Caprice* and that of *Vainglory*. The Romanisation of Canon Sinquier's daughter equals that of Firbank himself, an Irish clergyman's grandson. But the more explosive scandal, which in *Vainglory* resounds through the cathedral city of Ashringford, of the conversion of Mrs Henedge equals the conversion of the priest who converted Firbank: for Mrs Henedge is the widow of the previous Bishop of Ashringford, just as Hugh Benson was the son of an Archbishop of Canterbury.)

Certainly his mixed Irish and English parentage must have been one of the contributors to Firbank's social unease: by making him feel that he was not deep-rooted in either country.

And the mixture of his parentage was written-in to his father's politics. As a Unionist M.P., Thomas Firbank was concerned with preserving the English–Irish union exemplified in his own marriage.

Firbank himself adopted the majority religion of Ireland, but practised it in the minority manner of England. *Valmouth* contrasts the esoteric cults and the aristocratic proselytising of the English Mrs Hurstpierpoint with a drunken Irish rendering of *Lilli burlero* ('Now de heretics all go down [. . .] By Chrish' and Shaint Patrick, de nation's our own –'). When Mrs Hurstpierpoint's stately English home is about to acquire an unorthodox (a black) mistress, it is suggested: 'Oh, she'd better be presented in Ireland, Eulalia. Dublin Castle to *begin* with – afterwards we'll see –!!' (Did Firbank ever wonder if his own unorthodox books would do better were *they* presented in Ireland? But he must have at once realised what the majority religion of Ireland would do to the habit of Firbank's which he described to Lord Berners as laughing at the church of Rome.)

Firbank's considered judgment on Ireland is probably expressed, in his favourite[2] figure-concerned metaphor, in a flash of dialogue in *Inclinations* (so many of whose personages bear Irish names):

' "Tell me, Contessa – have I changed since Greece?"

[1] as I've already implied in Chapter VII, 4.
[2] Cf. Chapter VI, 4 and sub-section 4 of this chapter.

' "I should say you're a little stouter."
' "Ireland makes one sloppy." '

Firbank's nomadism and his internationalism (the *foreign* look of his clothes[1]) were results classically made possible by his being an English–Irish mixture, a child without a native country. By means of his talent Firbank was able to improve on the classic result. His own unrootedness was the material he made into the – in another sense – classic distance he set between himself and his literary subject matter.

8. The Campist

JUST as he put into modern practice Oscar Wilde's aesthetic theory, so Firbank modernised Oscar Wilde's camp.

Firbank is perhaps the inventor, certainly the fixer, of modern camp. Popes, cardinals, choirboys, nuns, flagellants, queens (both senses[2]): all the classic camp dramatis personae are his.

He borrowed even Wilde's engaging camp habit of sending up the Queen (regnant sense).

(*Their* queen – Wilde's and the one set firm in the imagination of Firbank, who was 15 when she died – was of course Queen Victoria.)

'The dear *santissima* woman', the Pope in . . . *Cardinal Pirelli* sighs over the memory of Queen Victoria; 'for he entertained a sincere, if brackish, enthusiasm for the lady who for so many years had corresponded with the Holy See under the signature of *the Countess of Lostwaters*.'[3]

It was in the same sighing breath that Oscar Wilde declared he would happily have married Queen Victoria and that he maintained the fantasy that the Queen kept ardent track of his literary career. (But when he was editor of *The Woman's World* it was Wilde who inquired into hers – by writing to ask her if she had any early verses he might publish.)

The ecclesiastical (and essential) portion of the classic camp personnel was derived (via Beardsley and, perhaps, 19th-century 'cardinal pictures') from 18th-century Gothick: from the disturbing assemblies of monks in the paintings of Alessandro Magnasco, the monks' cells and hermitages that decorate 18th-century architecture and landscaping, and *The* (quintessential) *Monk* of 'Monk' Lewis himself.

[1] Cf. sub-section 1 of this chapter.
[2] Asked (in *Vainglory* – p. 185 in the *Complete* Firbank) what book she is working on now, Mrs Asp discloses: 'I'm preparing a *Women Queens of England*'. And to the objection 'Isn't it idle – to insist?', she replies: 'Not as euphony. *The Queens* of England, somehow, sound bleak. And, really, rather a brigade . . .'
[3] – a title that will be mentioned again in Chapter X, 2 and 9.

Gothick (from which a good part of the pornographic tradition is evolved) makes the flesh that creeps in response to a supernatural visitation a metaphor of erection. Numinous awe is in Gothick a transcription of erotic frisson. A ghost is essentially a dead parent returned to avenge his child's suppressed lethal wishes against him: a Gothick ghost has returned to claim also his child's (equally suppressed) incestuous yearnings towards him. The monastic vow of chastity excitingly represents, in the Gothick tradition, the taboo barrier (an invitation in itself to transgress it) against all unconscious, anti-social and 'unnatural' (incestuous and/or homosexual) wishes.

To this metaphor, the mental furniture of protestantism, which possessed neither monastic orders vowed to chastity nor a celibate priesthood, was inadequate. To the rational temper of the Enlightenment, Catholicism itself came to represent what was tempting but forbidden by taboo. Edward Gibbon's gesture of young rebellion was to become, briefly, a Catholic. In the anti-rational (post-Revolutionary) climate of the following century, John Henry Newman took and took to Catholicism au sérieux – and admitted that the furnishings of Catholicism (a crucifix and a rosary, which Newman drew when he was nine, before he had any knowledge of real-life Catholicism) came into his head from the Gothick: 'from some romance, Mrs Radcliffe's or Miss Porter's'.

The Gothick-erotic strain, a frisson for fun during the Enlightenment, a programme of serious anti-rationalism for Newman and for the architects of the Gothic Revival, was by the end of the 19th century turning back into camp. Through its transmutations it kept the original necessity of Catholicism: hence the conversion to Catholicism of the 'decadents' who influenced Firbank (Henry Harland, Aubrey Beardsley and Oscar Wilde) and of Firbank himself. Like Newman, Beardsley drew (his *Hail Mary*, for instance, when he was about 19) and Firbank wrote (*Odette D'Antrevernes*) in the terms of Catholic talismans, long before they turned Catholic themselves. Cardinal Pirelli belongs to[1] the same imaginative tradition as Cardinal Newman: but the imagination which beheld Pirelli was ironic, comic, distanced, sceptical and tragic.

Perhaps it was because he was personally haunted (by his own ghost) that Firbank was able to re-animate the Gothick dramatis personae with his own tragic camp giggle.

Firbank made a perhaps tidier and neater effort than Oscar Wilde managed (Firbank was tidier with his money, too, than the extravagant and generous Wilde) towards schooling his personality, and the immediate

---

[1] And, as Chapter XX, 24 will detail, it is in Cardinal Pirelli that Firbank brought his camp idiom most fully back to its gothick source.

objects in which he expressed it, into the dandyism and exquisiteness of camp.

Firbank wrote 'usually', he told Carl Van Vechten (perhaps he found it difficult to get, as my secretary did in getting enough for me to write the manuscript of this book), in purple ink. The Sotheby's sale of his notebooks confirms the 'usually'. The earlier notebooks are mainly in black ink and pencil, though the 15 notebooks for *Vainglory* have parts in red and purple ink. By the time of *The Flower Beneath the Foot* the last four of the five notebooks are in purple ink, and it is purple ink from then on.

It was in purple that Firbank made, in his own printed copy of the book, the alterations for the United-States edition of *Vainglory*, including the later withdrawn alteration of Winsome to Sacheverell;[1] and it was 'in violet ink' (the variation in shade is probably in the eye of the beholder rather than in the bottle) and 'his bold, feminine handwriting' that (according to Siegfried Sassoon) Firbank 'wittily inscribed' copies of his books to Sassoon.

What Firbank usually wrote *on* Osbert Sitwell described in his list of Firbank's constant possessions: 'cubes of those large, blue, rectangular postcards upon which it was his habit to write'.

The blue postcards, which (so I interpret the 'cubes') Firbank evidently ordered specially and kept a big stock of, were used for communications – when, that is, Firbank wasn't abroad; when he was, he sent letters (to his mother, and on business) and picture postcards. (Sotheby's sold a batch of 456 he sent to Heather Firbank.) The blue postcards Firbank sent through the post in envelopes.

Osbert Sitwell believed Firbank also wrote his novels on the blue postcards. Perhaps he deduced it from the quantity Firbank always had in hand. Perhaps he muddled the postcards with the strips of paper.[2] Or perhaps he was right and the postcards replaced the strips of paper.

It was on a postcard used for communication, not, however a blue one but an ordinary one, sent through the post (to the Sitwells) without an envelope, that Firbank achieved his masterpiece of private camp. Firbank's message read: 'To-morrow I go to Hayti. They say the President is a *Perfect Dear*.'

9. The Inventor If Need Be

FIRBANK's biographer is cool, in a footnote, about the postcard of Firbank's intention to visit Haiti. 'Firbank may have made that statement,' she writes. 'I have not seen it.'

[1] Cf. Chapter VII, 4.   [2] Cf. Chapter V, 2.

She is cooler still about the idea that Firbank (who, she rightly points out, often announced travel plans he didn't fulfil) ever actually went to Haiti, a country his critics have always taken to have afforded him some of the background for *The Flower Beneath the Foot* and *Prancing Nigger*. Certainly *Prancing Nigger* seems to have deluded (if it is indeed a matter of delusion) John Anthony Kiechler, for example, into accepting its local colour as being realistically Haitian.[1]

However, Firbank, who invented New York (which he never saw) for *The New Rythum*, was quite up to inventing Haiti if need be. Whether or not he actually got there, or whether or not he made serious but frustrated plans to get there (as he did in the case of New York), the masterly message of his postcard was a witticism created by his serious imagination.

The black republic of Haiti, still unshadowed by a President who was to be the opposite of a perfect dear, was ground even more native to Firbank's nomadism than a New York he conceived in the (mis-spelt) rhythms of Negro jazz. Firbank was a violently racially prejudiced man: in favour of the black races – perhaps partly because he saw the surface of their blackness as brushed by mauve, a colour dear[2] to him (*The Mauve Tower* is the title of his early 'dream play'[3]) because it was the colour of the 'decadence'.

The tenor song in *Prancing Nigger* is Firbank's own love song:

> Little mauve nigger boy
> I t'ink you break my heart!

The message is the same, with the sexes transposed, in Miss Sinquier's recitation in *Caprice*:

> Since I first beheld you, Adèle, [. . .]
> I care no longer for all other negresses.

Firbank signalled his passion for the exotic when he revised *Odette D'Antrevernes* of 1905 into *Odette* of 1916. Odette's 'old nurse' became her 'Creole nurse'.

The *Memoir* records that the number of Firbank's 'visits to coloured entertainments, such as "The Blackbirds", was a source of amusement to his friends and of discreet suspicion to his acquaintance'. However, Firbank's pro-Negroism does not consist solely of erotic pursuit. It is equally[4] self-identification.

[1] The blue postcard legend has also deceived him into supposing it was on a *blue* postcard that the Haiti message was written.
[2] – a subject that will recur (Chapter XIII, 9 and Chapter XV, 5 and 9).
[3] some extracts from which are included in *The New Rythum and Other Pieces*, pp. 117–18.   [4] as I'll demonstrate in Chapter IX, 11.

Indeed for Firbank those two were never quite separate. Not that he was a simple narcissist, convinced by his self-love from the start that his self was wonderful. His was sophisticated, masochist's narcissism. He set out to *make* his self worthy of his own cult of it – and chiefly because he strongly doubted if anyone else would consider it so.

And, even then, he could justify his cult of himself only because that self was the producer of the true cult-objects, those imaginative projections of himself, his books.

The Negroes in his books are so deeply created from Firbank's self that his pro-Negroism is without taint of condescension or paternalism. Of all things, Firbank was no empire-builder.

For the novel Firbank called *Sorrow in Sunlight*, Carl Van Vechten picked, from Firbank's text, *Prancing Nigger* for the title of the book in the United States.[1] And, yes, *nigger* is marked in dictionaries as a term usually contemptuous. But the catchphrase Van Vechten picked from the novel is an efflorescence of the patois, the almost a language on its own, which Firbank so marvellously invents for his Negro world; and the catchphrase is spoken by wife to husband, Negro to Negro.

Two years after making *Prancing Nigger* the United-States title of Firbank's novel, Carl Van Vechten published a novel of his own under the title *Nigger Heaven* (a phrase by which one of his characters describes Harlem) in which he footnoted the word *Nigger*, when it occurred in his Negroes' dialogue, with: 'While this informal epithet is freely used by Negroes among themselves, not only as a term of opprobrium, but also actually as a term of endearment, its employment by a white person is always fiercely resented.' (The footnote adds an embargo which Firbank *didn't* observe: 'The word Negress is forbidden under all circumstances.')

Nigger Heaven, as a matter of fact, scarcely bears out Carl Van Vechten's inclusion, any more than *Prancing Nigger* bears out Firbank's, in Cyril Connolly's list (which I mentioned in Chapter VI, 4) of 'happy entertainers' of the Twenties. Carl Van Vechten's novel has, so to speak, a decorative border of local Harlem colour, done in a slightly proto-Damon Runyon style, but the body of the book is a pursuit in terms of sociological sympathy of the Negroism-of-the-mind which Firbank attained by imaginative identification. The manner and mannerisms of *Nigger Heaven* ('psychological' – that is, reporting the psychology of the conscious – narrative, and dialogue without quotation marks) belong to the serious conventions of the Twenties. The story is told wholly from within Negro society and analyses the situation

[1] Cf. Chapter VII, 4.

of 'young coloured intellectuals'. How to respond to the irks of discrimination; whether to take the opportunity to 'pass'; how, without betraying either Negro culture or the common universal culture, to develop an idiom of speech (Van Vechten includes a glossary of Negro dialect) and an idiom of thinking and writing; whether to become a writer tout court or a professionally Negro writer in danger of being displayed in the white cultural circus as a freak: these themes, which United-States culture has persuaded itself to think peculiar to the Sixties and Seventies, are all discussed by Carl Van Vechten's characters of 1926. *Nigger Heaven* is like a thoughtful unravelling and extension of the condensed metaphor of *Prancing Nigger*.

It was unjust to Firbank, of all mauve white people who ever made themselves by imagination mauve blacks, that a project in the Thirties (which like so many projects to popularise Firbank came only to frustration) to make a film musical of *Prancing Nigger* ran into objections from, according to Firbank's bibliographer, 'the American Negro press'. But, though unjust to Firbank, the objections may well at that period have done no less than justice to the film company, and may have prevented it from doing an injustice alike to Firbank as artist and to Negroes.

Exoticism was one of the methods whereby Firbank achieved his classic literary distance. And he understood its mechanism in himself. He told Aldous Huxley he intended 'to go to the West Indies' (a journey he certainly did genuinely make) 'to live among the Negroes so as to collect material for a novel about Mayfair'.

Whether or not he ever truly went or ever truly meant to go to Haiti, it was one of his imagination's dearest wishes that he disclosed to the Sitwells in that illumination of pure camp genius.

10. Notes to Chapter VIII

ALAN HARRIS writes of the Bertram Park photograph in his Introduction to *The New Rythum*, p. 15.

The *Biography* discusses the Wyndham Lewis drawings on p. 222.

Robert McAlmon's account of Firbank's delayed payment is in *Being Geniuses Together 1920–1930*, pp. 76–9.

Osbert Sitwell described Firbank's profile in *Laughter in the Next Room*, p. 182. Miss Thumbler's profile remains to her on p. 151 of the *Complete* Firbank, and Mrs Shamefoot's is described on p. 160. *A Study in Temperament* is reprinted in the *New Rythum* volume; Lobelia's lack of profile is on p. 27.

The Alvaro Guevara painting is reproduced in the *Memoir*. Firbank's description of himself in it is quoted, from a letter of his, in the *Biography*, p. 177. It is from

Firbank's description that I know that the flowers in the painting are 'Orchids' (his respectful capital letter).

C. W. Beaumont's account of the colour of Firbank's eyes is quoted in the *Memoir*, p. 48. Augustus John gave his account in the *Memoir*, p. 113. Montgomery Evans's diary is quoted in the *Biography*, p. 243.

Sir William Walton's Firbank memories are quoted from a letter he sent me in 1970 – a larger passage from which I quote in section 4 of this chapter.

'Ce dandysme sobre' was the phrase that Théophile Gautier used (in 1868) of Baudelaire (in 1849).

Osbert Sitwell mentioned Firbank's 'ecclesiastic' appearance in the *Memoir*, p. 135. Ifan Kyrle Fletcher wrote of the foreign look of his clothes on p. 30.

Simon Harcourt-Smith's description of Firbank (with a 'navy-blue face') as Firbank appeared when Simon Harcourt-Smith visited him (in 'a large, darkened room, over-looking Pall Mall, and richly scented by lilies') in the company of Osbert Sitwell is in his review of Miriam J. Benkovitz's Firbank *Biography* in the *Evening Standard* of 7 April 1970.

The poudre-de-riz quotations appear on p. 30 and p. 151 respectively of the *Complete* Firbank.

Augustus John's account of Firbank fleeing in Bond Street is on p. 115 of the *Memoir*.

The screen artiste's mare comes on p. 526 of the *Complete* Firbank.

Firbank's carmined nails are reported on p. 45 and p. 49 of the *Memoir*. The *Biography* (p. 112) reports a denial by Nancy Cunard, but that can presumably cover only occasions when Firbank was with Nancy Cunard. Robert McAlmon's quotation from Firbank's conversation about the beauty of his hands is in *Being Geniuses Together 1920–1930*, p. 80. Robert McAlmon is mentioned as one of the 'Eiffel Tower group' in a letter of Hunter Stagg's, of 1925, quoted in the *Biography* p. 274.

The *Biography* reports on p. 178 Sewell Stokes's description of Firbank powdering, saying the rice powder was applied from a pink papier-rouge.

The *Vainglory* minion quotation occurs on p. 105 of the *Complete* Firbank, the mignon youth in *The Flower Beneath the Foot* on p. 549. Mrs Thoroughfare's description and the Cardinal are on p. 429 and p. 463 in the *Complete* Firbank.

The quotation from and about the Guinevere piece is from the *Biography*, p. 42.

The châlet episode is reported in the *Biography*, p. 213 and the studio episode on. p. 222.

Cardinal Pirelli's lay skirt is on p. 650 in the *Complete* Firbank, his repentance and the boy's crime on pp. 690–1, the gnawing mouse on p. 693 and the gross candles on p. 685.

The rat-traps are on p. 125 of *The New Rythum and Other Pieces* and the mousetraps reported by the King on p. 71 of the *Complete* Firbank.

The single grape was 'slowly absorbed' by Firbank when he went to tea with Siegfried Sassoon, who recorded the incident on p. 137 of *Siegfried's Journey*

1916–1920. The single pea was reported by Osbert Sitwell in the *Memoir*, pp. 125–6.

Firbank's reaction to butchers' shops is reported in the *Biography*, p. 111. Cherif's similar reaction is on p. 11 in the first edition (1921) of *Santal* (p. 481 in the *Complete* Firbank). Mrs Cresswell's vegetarianism is on p. 210 of the *Complete* Firbank. The *Biography* mentions bullfighting on p. 64 and chicken livers on p. 180. It quotes Augustus John on asparagus on p. 125.

The quotation about the Oxford books is from p. 61 of the *Memoir*. The morocco bindings are recorded on p. 112 of the *Biography*. The calf in *Inclinations* comes on p. 258 in the *Complete* Firbank.

The *Memoir* reports Firbank's cough on p. 85. The Lord Berners quotation is from the *Memoir*, p. 148.

Osbert Sitwell quoted the proprietor (M. Stulik) in the *Memoir*, p. 136.

The *Memoir* records Firbank's last day in England on p. 86.

Osbert Sitwell recorded or hypothesised Firbank's nervous throat in the *Memoir*, p. 125. Ifan Kyrle Fletcher's counter-theory is on p. 36.

Vyvyan Holland's consultation of Firbank is reported in the *Biography*, p. 113.

From a letter in *The Times* of 21 August 1970, from Ivor H. Mills, Professor of Medicine, Addenbrooke's Hospital, Cambridge: 'in the past few years in one clinic alone we have seen over a hundred girls and young women who have purposely starved themselves beyond any reasonable weight. The incidence now is about ten times what it was ten years ago.'

The comment on Firbank's narcissism is from p. 36 of the *Memoir*.

The gypsy comment is quoted in the *Biography*, p. 223.

The quotation about Firbank's advertised arrivals is from p. 53 of the *Memoir*. Osbert Sitwell's contribution to that *Memoir* gives the same information (pp. 135 and 139).

The lucky publication days are recorded in the *Bibliography*, pp. 32–3.

Osbert Sitwell's account of Firbank's superstitions is on p. 141 of the *Memoir* and his account of Firbank's Egyptian sunstroke on p. 121.

The houseboat photograph is reproduced in *The New Rythum*. The Berners quotation about the mutiny is from p. 147 of the *Memoir*.

Mrs Shamefoot and the image of Ptah are on p. 118 in the *Complete* Firbank. In quoting I have run two paragraphs together.

Osbert Sitwell mentions an Egyptian statuette on p. 125, and Kyrle Fletcher on p. 29, of the *Memoir*.

The scarab is reported, from a letter to Firbank, in the *Biography*, p. 110. The lotus quotation comes on p. 89 of the *Complete* Firbank. The Rameses story is from the *Memoir*, p. 47. The withdrawn dedication is described in the *Bibliography*, pp. 32–3. The arrival at the Embassy comes on p. 536 and the footnoted death on p. 581 of the *Complete* Firbank, where the devil-conjuring is on p. 153.

The 'Black Magic' quotation from Jocelyn Brooke is from p. 58 of his 1951 Firbank volume.

Robert Hichens's account of Benson's pulpit manner is in *Yesterday*, pp. 164-5. The other information and quotations from and about Hugh Benson come from Volume II of the two-volume Benson biography (1916) by C. C. Martindale, S.J.

Miss Missingham's work is on p. 124 in the *Complete* Firbank.

The music in A flat is mentioned on p. 71 of the third edition of *An Adventure* (by, pseudonymously, Morison and Lamont). I quote the permission to add the 1908 experiences from p. 8 of that edition.

The *Memoir* dates Firbank's interest in Crowley on p. 41.

The Katherine Mansfield letter (of 7 January 1920) is on p. 451 of the *Letters*, edited by J. Middleton Murry. The Fräulein who giggles at Black Mass is on p. 36 in the *Complete* Firbank.

Firbank's greeting to Aldous Huxley is quoted, from Aldous Huxley, in the *Memoir* (p. 67). Huxley's account sets the episode at the celebration of Robert Nichols's wedding in the Café Royal and makes it clear that Firbank said the remark once – not habitually as Jocelyn Brooke states in his 1951 *Ronald Firbank* (p. 42: ' "Aldous – always my *torture*", Ronald would exclaim, as the author of *Limbo* and *Crome Yellow* took his seat at the café table').

The description of Gwen Otter is from a footnote by Anne Estelle Rice to a letter to her from Katherine Mansfield, one of a group published in *Adam* (no. 300, 1965). The accompanying essay by Anne Estelle Rice records Katherine Mansfield's visiting and smoking with Crowley. The essay puts no date to the visit but recounts it next to an incident of 1915. A brief involvement of Katherine Mansfield's with Crowley's circle and hashish is briefly mentioned on p. 86 of *Katherine Mansfield, The Memories of LM*, which is, however, vague about the date.

The Crow quotations from *The Artificial Princess* come on pp. 47 and 48 of the *Complete* Firbank.

The farewell visits quotation is from Osbert Sitwell (*Memoir*, p. 141); that about farewells at the Eiffel Tower from the *Memoir*, p. 86.

Deirdre's cards are on p. 101 in the *Complete* Firbank.

Oscar Wilde's fortune teller was Mrs Robinson, 'the Sibyl of Mortimer Street'. His susceptibility is witnessed by, for example, his 1894 letter to Lord Alfred Douglas and his letter refusing to be the guest of an anti-superstitions society (on p. 357 and p. 349 respectively of the *Letters*, edited by Rupert Hart-Davis).

Mrs Orangeman is in *Inclinations*, Miss Sinquier's speculations in *Caprice* (*Complete* Firbank p. 229 and p. 319).

The Dublin Castle quotation from *Valmouth* is on p. 472 of the *Complete* Firbank, *Lilli burlero* on p. 452, the Ireland quotation from *Inclinations* on p. 298 and the Lostwaters quotation from . . . *Cardinal Pirelli* on p. 658.

Oscar Wilde's relations with Queen Victoria are recorded in Hesketh Pearson's *Life*, p. 210 and the Wilde *Letters* (edited by Rupert Hart-Davis), p. 65 and p. 215.

Newman's account of his childhood drawings is in *Apologia Pro Vita Sua*, I. Beardsley's *Hail Mary* is dated circa 1891 by Brian Reade (*Beardsley*, p. 312). I have discussed the psychology of Gothick in my *Black Ship to Hell*, III, 12.

The purple ink information to Van Vechten is reported on p. 45 and the purple ink corrections on p. 20 of the *Bibliography*.

Siegfried Sassoon recorded the 'violet' ink inscriptions in *Siegfried's Journey 1916–1920*, p. 137.

Firbank had been 15 for five days when Queen Victoria died (in 1901).

Osbert Sitwell's accounts of the blue postcards and of the Haiti postcard are on p. 125 and p. 134 of the *Memoir*.

The *Prancing Nigger* mauve song comes on p. 613 of the *Complete* Firbank, Miss Sinquier's recitation in *Caprice* on pp. 322–3.

The *Memoir* records Firbank's passion for Negro entertainments, and the reaction of his acquaintance to it, on pp. 73–4.

What Firbank told Aldous Huxley about the West Indies is reported on p. 73 of the *Memoir*.

IX

The Portrait Re-touched

1. The Flower Child (?) – 2

FIRBANK'S biographer remarks that it was from the family home of his childhood, at Chislehurst, with its large and cared-for grounds, that Firbank 'acquired his love for natural beauty'.

Natural beauty in this context evidently means flowers. 'That he was aware of it quite young', the biographer continues, 'is apparent from a photograph, made when he was a small boy of perhaps six, showing him with a large nosegay on his lapel.'

The photograph the biographer (presumably) means is reproduced in *The New Rythum* (and here as Plate 5). As a matter of felicitous incidental and accidental fact, the very name of the photographer is Lavender (of Bromley).

And I think there may be more to be had from scrutinising the nosegay worn by this fair, brushed, rather plump-faced small Firbank.

The flower at the centre of the nosegay, which comes out white in the photograph and probably *is* white, just might be a carnation whose serrations are lost in the print, but I think it is much more like a rose.

As for the background greenery: perhaps it is just some florists' staple or some creeping plant from one of the borders at Chislehurst. The shape of the tiny leaves is hard to make out for certain. But in the *set* of the tuft, the way it is both low and springy, and the way it seems to be united into a single clump and yet puts out straggles, there is something very familiar to me. I cannot assert that it is so, but I think there is a probability that the background section of Firbank's nosegay consists of shamrocks.

In that case, to the 'no date' of the picture's caption in *The New Rythum*, it is possible to supply, though still not a year, a day: 17 March. On Saint Patrick's Day Firbank wore on his lapel an emblem of his mixed ancestry, the Irish shamrocks with the rose of England (no doubt from – in March – a Chislehurst greenhouse).

It is also, of course, an emblem of his father's Unionist politics. Perhaps the little boy was sprigged out in this way, and photographed, in the service of his father's political cause.

The nosegay can't, I think, be an act of direct electioneering. The *Biography* doesn't suggest that Thomas Firbank ever stood unsuccessfully for Parliament; and he wasn't elected (as Unionist M.P. for East Hull) until July 1895. Presumably he didn't begin his election campaign until the June of 1895, which is when the Government fell. By then, Saint Patrick's Day was three months past and Firbank was nearly nine-and-a-half, which is a little older, I think, than he plausibly can be in the photograph.

However, in order to get himself adopted as a Unionist candidate, Thomas Firbank must surely have shewn his Unionist colours some time in advance: and, in some March in one of the years closely before the election, perhaps the colours were pinned to his son's lapel.

As a matter of fact, it was the Unionists' support of the Conservatives in the Government of July 1895 which caused the word Unionist, which had once denoted a Liberal, to come to mean a Conservative.

Indeed, during the very year in which Thomas Firbank was elected (though the play was withdrawn in May because its author had become the object of prosecution and persecution) Lady Bracknell was asking Jack Worthing on the stage of the Saint James's Theatre 'What are your politics?'

'Well, I am afraid I really have none. I am a Liberal Unionist.'

'Oh, they count as Tories. They dine with us. Or come in the evening, at any rate.'

According to the *Biography*, Thomas Firbank stood for Parliament at the insistence of his wife. It might be expected of her, as a protestant Irishwoman, that she would be less concerned with whether Unionist implied Tory or Liberal than with its significance for Ireland.

And very probably Thomas Firbank needed his wife's prompting before he would take an interest in the state of the Union or pay much attention to Ireland at all. Evidently no Irish thoughts crossed his upbringing. *His* father, Joseph Firbank, refused (the *Memoir* says) to make investments in foreign countries because he didn't trust foreign currencies; and he considered (the *Memoir* continues, in a remark so specific that it must surely be derived from detailed information) that 'even Ireland was a foreign country'.

2. Firbank and Sir Thomas

PERHAPS Thomas Firbank himself was not greatly bothered to begin with about the difference between Liberal and Tory. Although *Who Was Who* lists only Conservative or conservative clubs for him, his entry in Burke's *Landed Gentry* for 1898 lists, as well as Tory clubs, the Union, a Liberal club.

From counting, in Lady Bracknellish eyes, as a Tory, Thomas Firbank (who kept his parliamentary seat until 1906) evidently became a solid Tory. And as a reward he further became, in 1902, Sir Thomas.

(His arms are described, posthumously, in Burke's *Landed Gentry* of 1914: '*Arms* Arg a fess nebuly plain cotised sa. between in chief two robins ppr. and in base a martlet sa. *Crest* On a mount vert a sun in splendour ppr. between two ostrich feathers sa.' The motto was 'Coelitus mihi vires' – from heaven my strength.)

The *Memoir* hints he was pompous and implies that he was not only a pillar of established society but a hollow pillar. Even his china collection it credits to the influence of his wife. Beneath his picture it prints the pillar's credentials: 'M.P., D.L., J.P.' (The D.L. I take to be for Deputy Lieutenant. Both Sir Thomas and his father Joseph held the Deputy Lieutenantship of Monmouthshire.)

Perhaps Sir Thomas has been a touch ill-used. He wasn't, given the customs of the time, pompous with his children, who called him Daddy. And, even if it was his wife's taste that formed his collections, it was presumably he who took a markedly (for a Tory knight of the period) pro-aesthetic stand in *Who's Who* by filling the space for his recreations with the note that he was 'very keen on' not only athletics and outdoor sports but 'music, and objects of art'.

The *Memoir*'s slight bias against Sir Thomas is probably taken from reports of the tone of Firbank's own conversation. But the *Memoir*'s controlled indications were later exaggerated into misrepresentation. Jocelyn Brooke's statement that Sir Thomas had a habit of trying to assert his parental authority seems to rest on no evidence except Jocelyn Brooke's own conjecture that it was Sir Thomas who, for fear of the influence of aestheticism, sent Firbank to Cambridge rather than to Oxford. In fact it was at Cambridge that Rupert Brooke was reviving aestheticism. Perhaps Sir Thomas couldn't know that. But then it is improbable that the choice of university was in fact Sir Thomas's at all. (If the *Biography* has correctly unearthed the Cambridge tradition in Lady Firbank's family, then the *Biography* is more likely to be right when it says that it was Lady Firbank who picked Cambridge. My own belief, which I shall argue in Chapter XII, 3 and 4, is that neither parent did the picking: Firbank, with a very pointed purpose, picked his own university and, indeed, his own college in it.) Jocelyn Brooke goes on to mis-apply a Firbank witticism to Sir Thomas. Sir Thomas, he asserts, 'was, moreover, like Mrs Calvally in *Vainglory*, "one of those destined to get mixed over Monet and Manet all their life" ' – which makes a particularly inept slander on Sir Thomas, who, whatever else he wasn't, was a collector.

However, to deny that Sir Thomas was an ogre or a philistine is not to deny the patent truth that Firbank felt himself much less the child of his father than of his mother. Towards his mother, the *Memoir* says, he 'maintained a steady and affectionate regard'. It was to her that he wrote those constant letters (310 of them were sold at Sotheby's).

It was to his mother, as 'Darling Baba', that he dedicated, when he was 18, the manuscript of his 'Romance Parlée', *La Princesse aux Soleils*, of which he wrote both an English and a French text – and illustrated the whole with his own watercolours. (But he demonstrated the secondary dedication of his family life by producing a 'deuxième édition', this time of the French text alone, inscribed 'A ma soeur adorée'.)

It was his mother who responded to his early literariness with the practical flatteries of having one of his childhood poems printed on card and, later, having the manuscript of *Odette D'Antrevernes* typed.

And it was she who worried about his loneliness. 'Lady Firbank', wrote Augustus John, 'was quite sure Ronald was *clever*, but she did wish he would have somebody to look after him.'

That report by Augustus John reappears, in a fuller and more interesting form, in the passages by John which Osbert Sitwell quoted in *his* contribution to the *Memoir*, where it goes: 'His mother once called and lamented the solitary life he led – a dear old lady to whom Ronald was, I think, quite attached. Upon her death he for a moment, in my presence, hesitated on the brink of some almost Dickensian sentiment, but corrected himself just in time. . . . It's amazing how sometimes he struck, amidst his excellent persiflage, a chord of deep and heart-rending sentiment.'

Augustus John was struggling, I think, to convey through the literary medium the predominant impression made by Firbank's personality, his elegance. So he doesn't go beyond the cool 'quite attached' in describing what was certainly the strongest and longest love in Firbank's life. But evidently he did discern, behind the elegance, what, again, the *Biography* can establish from letters: the distress amounting almost to psychological destruction which Firbank experienced when his mother died.

About his father's death, which happened 14 years earlier (that is, in 1910), the *Memoir* observes: 'It is idle to suppose that Ronald can have felt very deeply the death of one who had little sympathy with the ideas and desires which actuated his life.'

No doubt that is a correct account of what could be observed or surmised from Firbank's social behaviour – perhaps even a correct account of his conscious psychology. Firbank's unconscious response to his father's death is discernible only in his fiction (and chiefly in *The Artificial Princess*, which was not accessible when the *Memoir* was written). As I mean to shew (in Chapter XIII, 6), Sir Thomas's death was in fact the crisis in the forming of Firbank's creative personality.

3. Firbank and Sir Thomas's Cellar

CERTAINLY Firbank was sardonic about his father's world. (But one is not sardonic where one is indifferent.) 'He suffered – very bravely I think –' (wrote Augustus John, trying again to sketch Firbank's sophistication of manner through an assumed literary tone) 'under more than one serious disability; his health, of course, was not of the best; the dreadful fact that his father had been an M.P., and then his profile – was it *quite* perfect?'

(Perhaps Firbank had had actually to *tell* John he didn't want to be drawn in profile.[1])

That Firbank was no respecter of his father's knighthood he hinted in an episode of back-stage chatter in *Caprice*. Arriving at a charity performance, the king has, impromptu, knighted an actor. On hearing of it, ' "It's extraordinary I've never seen a man knighted," a show-girl twittered, "and I've seen a good deal . . ." ' (One of her colleagues demonstrates, with a brush; and the comment – on the demonstration? or on the original? – is 'Of all the common –!') And a moment of nonsensical prettiness in *The Princess Zoubaroff* half-confirms Augustus John's estimate of Firbank's estimate of M.P.s. Enid owns herself mortified by her husband's lack of ambition: 'When I consider that one of Caligula's horses was a Member of Parliament'. (Nadine presently drifts into the inspired comment, 'Horrid to be outdone by animals.')

All the same, Firbank was in fact re-scrambling an old House of Commons joke.[2] He didn't think too ill of M.P.s to adapt their witticisms into darts against M.P.s.

If his wish to throw darts at M.P.s began in criticism of his father, it was perhaps reinforced by the fact (according to the *Biography*) that, in 1911–12, his sister was in love with an M.P. (It seems justifiable to guess that the love was her Oedipal reaction to her father's death in 1910.) Heather's sweetheart was married, and in 1914 his wife refused him a divorce, thereby cutting off Heather's hope of marrying him.

According to the *Biography* Heather Firbank's love affair with her

[1] Cf. Chapter VIII, 1.
[2] The joke has been adapted to many House of Commons occasions but according to Robert Blake (*Disraeli*, p. 715) it originated in Gladstone's comment (that there had been nothing like it since Caligula made his horse a consul) when Disraeli had his secretary made a peer.

chauffeur did not begin until after Lady Firbank's death (which was in 1924). Either, however, Heather's inclination towards *some* chauffeur (not necessarily the one who later became her lover, and not necessarily one employed by herself or her family) shewed itself a decade before the *Biography* supposes: or Firbank's imagination was prescient. Within a year of the collapse of Heather's hope of marrying an M.P., Firbank published, in *Vainglory*, the conversation where Mrs Wookie maintains that the best way of finding husbands for girls is to send the girls out sketching. 'That always works. . . . Alice, Grace, Pamela and Teresa, my nieces, all went that way.' 'Oh, Tatty,' Mrs Wookie's daughter interrupts, 'Teresa married a menial. She went away with a chauffeur.' And the conversation proceeds:

' "How very disgraceful!" Aurelia remarked.

' "I suppose it was. Particularly as he wasn't their own." '

Willing to draw on his father's world for a joke against that world, Firbank was more extensively willing to draw on his father's finances: and indeed on his father's cellar.

In 1909, when they were both undergraduates, Firbank and Vyvyan Holland gave a dinner party at Cambridge. Vyvyan Holland provided the food; and Firbank, appropriately to his predilection, the drink.

'The chief advantage of this arrangement', Vyvyan Holland wrote in the *Memoir*, 'was that Firbank possessed some 1884 Moët, originating, I think, from his father's cellar. There was quite a quantity of this, and it was just as well, as two bottles out of every three had departed this life apparently some years before, but when a bottle was good it was indeed good.'

By 1954, when he published his autobiography, Vyvyan Holland had slightly revised his opinion of the champagne – or, rather, he had drawn the logical conclusion from his earlier observation about it.

'It was arranged', he wrote in his 1954 account of this same dinner party, '[. . .] that Ronald would try to get the wine from his father, who had a considerable cellar. The wine in question was Moët et Chandon 1884, which was really far too old to drink in 1909, unless it had been kept with extraordinary care. However, at that time we knew very little about wine and were rather proud of its age.'

In both his accounts Vyvyan Holland makes it clear that he was writing with a copy of the dinner party's menu in front of him. It was from the menu, not memory, that he took the champagne's vintage year, and so he can be counted on to have got it right.

That makes it possible to restore a small, sad fragment of the seemingly irrecoverable past. I can conjecture why the champagne at the Cambridge dinner had gone undrunk beyond its proper term – and also why, when

Firbank repented of his coyness and decided to reveal to Carl Van Vechten how old he in fact was, the material that came to his mind in which to wrap up the information was a champagne whose vintage year was the year of his own birth.[1]

Part of Sir Thomas Firbank's 'considerable cellar' was formed, I think, by his laying down champagne at the birth of each of his children. (Perhaps he really did, by a happy accident, pick a *Veuve Clicquot* for the birth of his second child in 1886.) The Moët et Chandon 1884 which was drunk at the Cambridge dinner party had been laid down for his eldest son, Joseph, who was born in 1884. It was obviously destined to be opened for Joseph's 21st birthday, which would have been in 1905. But Joseph died in 1904. The wine was too sad for the parents to drink at the proper time. By 1909 it was too old for anything except impressing undergraduates with its age.

4. Firbank's Foot in his Father's World

ON Armistice Night 1918 (the *Memoir* records), Firbank took one of 'his Bohemian friends to a very sedate political club'. By the time they left, it was an 'atmosphere of outraged decorum' they were leaving.

Two of Firbank's more or less bohemian acquaintance evidently believed that Firbank eventually opted for bohemianism to the exclusion of sedate political clubs. So Lord Berners seems to imply when he recounts meeting Firbank 'inappropriately enough' outside the Naval and Military Club; the inappropriateness seems to cover both Firbank's real pacificness and his seeming unclubbability in the established manner. And Osbert Sitwell explicitly says that after the war Firbank took to the Eiffel Tower 'though formerly he had frequented one of the "Junior" political clubs'.

However, Lord Berners and Osbert Sitwell had a firm social position from which to adventure into their own bohemianism. They seem not to have reckoned with Firbank's social uncertainty.

As someone who often had no fixed residence in London, Firbank for practical reasons perhaps needed *a* club. But it needn't have been a 'sedate political club'. Yet as a matter of fact he kept that foothold in his father's world all his adult life.

The *Biography* names Firbank's club as the Junior Constitutional. However, that was not 'his club' in the sense of being his only or even his favourite club, though he did for a time belong to it.

The Junior Constitutional Club ceased to exist when it was bombed in the winter of 1940–1. Its records are not in the possession of the parent

---

[1] Cf. Chapter V, 6.

club,¹ so it is impossible to check Firbank's membership through those. However, in Kelly's *Handbook* of 1921, the Junior Constitutional is named as one of Firbank's two clubs. But by 1924 the Junior Constitutional had dropped out of his Kelly's entry, and the Junior Carlton stands alone as his club. The Junior Carlton is also the only club mentioned in his entry in *Who Was Who*.

I conclude, therefore, that it was the Junior Carlton which was Firbank's preferred club.² And that is confirmed by his paying it, in *Vainglory*, the delicate compliment of suggesting in a line of dialogue that it *could* be mixed with bohemianism: '. . . Belongs to the Junior Carlton, the Arts, and to several night *cabarets*'.

Impossible to tell whom the floating line is spoken by, of or to: but perhaps, given the evident *louche*ness, in the final italicised French, of those cabarets, it's an account of Claud Harvester, the writer who is Firbank's self-portrait in the book.

It was not until Sir Thomas Firbank was dead that Firbank consolidated his foothold in his father's world by joining the Junior Carlton Club, which had been one of Sir Thomas's many clubs. Perhaps during his father's lifetime Firbank counted on being his father's guest.

Miss E. A. Shutter, at the Junior Carlton Club, has kindly searched me out the information that Firbank remained a member of the club until his death; he was elected to the club on 11 April 1911, having been recommended by Sir James Heath, Bart., and the Marquess of Abergavenny, K.G.

The *Biography* says nothing of Firbank's two recommenders, but from the information about them in *Who Was Who* it seems safe to guess that they were, in the one case political and in the other neighbourly, friends of Sir Thomas Firbank.

Sir James Heath (1852–1942), who was created a baronet in 1904, was a Conservative M.P. from 1892 to 1906.

The Marquess of Abergavenny perhaps knew Sir Thomas (and, conceivably, Joseph) Firbank through the Monmouthshire connexion. Abergavenny itself is in Monmouthshire.

The other Abergavenny seat, at Eridge Green, may even be the attraction which drew Sir Thomas to Chislehurst. It is 30 or so miles from Chislehurst – and only four from Tunbridge Wells, which is where the Firbank family moved after Chislehurst.

And perhaps Firbank's social anxieties were slightly calmed in the

---

¹ I gratefully owe this information to the Constitutional Club.
² What may be a further reason for thinking so will be mentioned in a footnote to subsection 5 of this chapter.

company of people who had neighbourly connexions with the Firbank estates at Newport. It would not surprise me if the unaccustomed boldness with which, at their first meeting, Firbank swept Evan Morgan away to the British Museum[1] was inspired by the facts that Morgan was the son of Lord Tredegar and that Tredegar, too, is in Monmouthshire.[2]

5. A Further Meanness Uncovered

POLITICAL clubs were not, of course, Sir Thomas's only world. His collection was, the *Memoir* says, 'famous among connoisseurs, who visited him at Petworth[3] and Tunbridge Wells in order to admire his treasures'. Objects he sold at Christie's in 1904 fetched between eight and nine thousand pounds.

Probably it was by following his father that Firbank first entered the world of fine-arts dealers and sale rooms. But his conduct there, on one occasion at least, was pointedly his own.

One of his transactions with Colnaghi's, the dealer's in Bond Street, is mentioned in the *Biography*. But 'the English painter John Downing' who occurs in the *Biography*'s text and index is a figment: a mistake (perhaps by way of a misreading of Firbank's handwriting) for the English portrait and subject painter John Downman (circa 1750–1824).

And the context needs more scrutiny than the *Biography* gives it.

The *Biography* is reporting, from Firbank's letters of 1924 to his sister, on his financial state after their mother's death. Lady Firbank, it records, 'had told him she had set aside £200 to take care of her bequests and had even offered to lend it to him so that he could pay the art dealer Colnaghi for a canvas by the English painter John Downing in 1922 or 1923'.

It isn't clear whether the belief that Firbank bought the John Downman from Colnaghi's in 1922 or 1923 is the biographer's or Firbank's own, but in any case the date is out by seven or so years.

Mr C. J. White, a former director of P. & D. Colnaghi, kindly discovered for me the record of Firbank's dealings with the firm. It is a more complex story than the *Biography* suggests, and in its every item revelatory of Firbank.

Firbank bought his first John Downman from Colnaghi's in November 1914.

[1] Cf. Chapter VIII, 5.
[2] Firbank insisted on the Welsh connexion when he introduced Morgan-Monteith into *The Flower Beneath the Foot* as (*Complete* Firbank, p. 535) an 'eccentric Englishman from Wales'.
[3] The *Biography*, with its access to family papers, does not associate the Firbanks with Petworth, so I imagine this to be a slip for Chislehurst.

The artist probably pleased one of the quieter strands in Firbank's taste for the 18th century. The subject suggests to me that Firbank's thoughts were indeed dwelling on that family one of whose traditional and distinctive first names went (I conjectured in Chapter VI, 6) to the naming of Winsome in *Vainglory* (which Firbank must have just about finished writing at the time he bought the John Downman). It was a picture of 'Major General George Churchill when young'.

Firbank's mind certainly played on the whole Churchill family, with its many distinctive first names. Witness the Greek dance in *Inclinations*: 'I know this dance well. It's *Lady Randolph and the Old Shepherd*!'

Inclinations was written and (in 1916) published when Firbank was living at Oxford, where Lady Randolph Churchill was no doubt thrust continually into his thoughts by the obtrusive augustness of the Randolph Hotel.

Firbank's next purchase from Colnaghi's was made in January 1915. It was a watercolour by Félicien Rops, with the title 'Souvenir de New York'.

Just about the time he bought it, Firbank had another Rops in his possession. At least, I must assume it was a different picture. The *Bibliography* calls it both a 'crayon-drawing' and a 'coloured sketch'. In so far as it was a crayon drawing it can scarcely have been the Colnaghi watercolour. (But Osbert Sitwell mentioned only one Rops in Firbank's possession.)

It was probably (by the *Bibliography*'s dating) in the January of his purchase from Colnaghi's that Firbank made the decision to use his other (his non-Colnaghi) Rops as frontispiece to *Vainglory* (which was published in the April).

So perhaps when he bought the Colnaghi Rops he did so with an idea that he might presently use that for another novel. In its title at least (the subject might have been remote), the Colnaghi Rops makes a reference to New York. It looks as if Firbank's thoughts were already, in 1915, adumbrating the New York novel which, in the event, he didn't begin till near the end of his life and never finished.

Both those purchases from Colnaghi's, the Rops watercolour and the first John Downman, Firbank paid for at the time.

It was in November 1915, not 'in 1922 or 1923', that Firbank bought his second John Downman from Colnaghi's: a Portrait of a young Naval Officer. The price was £180.

To be more exact: he didn't buy it. He took the picture on account. Between 1915 and his death, he neither borrowed the £200 Lady Firbank offered him to cover its price nor devoted £180 of his own to paying Colnaghi's. The bill was repeatedly presented. Firbank never paid it.

(Seven months before taking the picture on account, he published, in *Vainglory*, the dialogue consequent on an accidental meeting in the street:
  ' "Are you going anywhere, dear?"
  ' "I was in the act", she said, shivering, and growing strangely spiritual, "of paying a little bill." ')

When he acquired the picture, Firbank was at his war-time address, 66 High Street, Oxford.[1] It was in the Oxford rooms that Osbert Sitwell first saw Firbank's permanent collection of cult objects, and Sitwell's list (which could have spared the *Biography* its error) includes 'a Félicien Rops drawing' and 'two drawings by Downman'. I imagine Firbank bilked Colnaghi's from the grips of the financial panic which the *Memoir* records seizing the Firbanks when the war began and causing Firbank to wonder if he would be obliged to go to work for a publisher's. So nearly was he paranoid on the theme of money that he would very easily feel unable to bring himself to pay for a picture which had been touched, in his thoughts, by his panic. And perhaps the picture's subject became associated by contrast with another of his dreads, his loathing of the unpretty khaki and unpretty wholesale deaths of young officers in the modern war that was going on when he acquired the picture – the war which he apprehended as a conspiracy to deprive young officers of their lives and himself of his income and of all his pleasure in looking at young officers.

Perhaps Firbank celebrated the peace by putting his unpaid-for Portrait of a young Naval Officer into *Valmouth*, which he published in 1919. Mrs Hurstpierpoint averts 'her eyes towards the young naval officer in the carved Renaissance frame' – a portrait, in fact, of her heir, an officer who fulfils Firbank's hopes of officers by failing (while his exotic bride pursues a butterfly[2]) to turn up for his wedding, because he prefers the affections of a junior-brother-officer.

---

[1] 'He took rooms at 71 High Street; later he moved to No. 66 in the same street' (*Memoir*, p. 53). However, it looks as though, at least in 1916, Firbank maintained an address in London. His list (some of whose contents will be mentioned in a footnote to Chapter XII, 5) of the names and addresses of people who were to receive copies of *Inclinations*, which was published in 1916, bears at the top, in another hand (that of an employee of the 'publisher', presumably), the notes '6 to Lady Firbank, 44 Sloane Street' and '6 to Mr Firbank, 28 Pall Mall' (cf. Chapter VII, 6). Although it is the *Bibliography* which, by reproducing the list, provides the evidence, neither it nor the *Biography* mentions Firbank's being at 28 Pall Mall in 1916 (though the *Biography*, p. 221, says he 'took up residence at 49a Pall Mall' in 1922). While he was in Oxford, Firbank probably kept no more than a room at 28 Pall Mall – a building next door but one to the Junior Carlton Club (which is now at numbers 30–4 and was formerly at 30–5). The proximity to the club of his 1916 London address is another reason for supposing it his favourite club (cf. sub-section 4 of this chapter).

[2] Cf. Chapter VII, 3.

6. The Most Possible Profession

BY bilking Colnaghi's Firbank put an important dealer's out of bounds to himself. However, Colnaghi's, though it sold him the Rops, specialised more towards Old Masters; and Firbank's taste was turning more contemporary at the same time as he was being gripped by the conviction that his income wouldn't, in any case, stretch to Old Master prices.

All the same, I don't think Firbank would have offended a fine-arts dealer until the war had obliged him to the decision, reported by the *Memoir*, 'that if he had to work he would prefer it to be in a publishing house to anywhere else'.

Until then, Firbank had it in mind, I think, that if he had to go to work he would prefer it to be in a fine-arts dealer's.

Quite certainly, to be an art-historian of some sort was the most serious notion Firbank ever entertained of a profession other than that of imaginative writer.

In fact, art history was the only profession other than that of imaginative writer which he ever actually practised.

He practised it when he was at Cambridge, which was his first period of intense art history.

His second was soon after he had come down from Cambridge. Coming down without qualifications no doubt made him brush up his art-historical ambition and, in preparation for fulfilling it, his art-historical knowledge. Perhaps his post-Cambridge stay in Rome was passed in looking at the Vatican pictures as well as in possibly besieging the Vatican for a Papal job.[1]

Firbank possessed considerable art-historical knowledge to brush up – as well as the ultimately even more important asset of a pioneering taste.

In *Vainglory*, he lent his own taste and explorations to Lady Georgia Blueharnis, whose 'investigations of art' have caused her to be known 'as the Isabella d'Este of her day'. Firbank hung Lady Georgia's 18th-century house in Hill Street with the 'blotches of rose and celestial blue' of 'a sumptuous *Stations of the Cross*, by Tiepolo'.

That was in 1915. Tiepolo was known to, though not necessarily admired by, connoisseurs. Indeed he was known 20 years earlier to that sometime critic of painting, Bernard Shaw – who in 1895, in the exercise of another of his métiers (dramatic critic, this time), made passing and not necessarily approving mention of Tiepolo by saying that Sarah Bernhardt's stage make-

---

[1] Cf. Chapter VII, 2.

up caused her characterisations to look 'impossibly like goddesses in a Tiepolesque ceiling'.

But in 1915, when Firbank made his certainly admiring invention of a Stations of the Cross series, Tiepolo was by no means an established great name. Indeed, he still wasn't in 1941, when a popular history of painting rated him of smaller account than Ford Madox Brown.

(It is even more recently that appreciation has caught up with Mozart as a Racine-style music-dramatist of classical themes: exactly how recently I have documented elsewhere. But in 1917, in *Caprice*, Firbank invented an advertisement on an omnibus of a performance of *La Clemenza di Tito*.)

However, as well as having it, Firbank managed (as he did about few subjects[1]) to be tolerably *accurate* about his taste.

'They had hoped it was Tiepolo – but it's only Sebastian Ricci,' runs a line in Firbank's play *The Princess Zoubaroff*, whose publication date is 1920, a date when it was by no means everyday knowledge that Sebastiano Ricci is one of the painters most likely to be confused with Tiepolo.

All Firbank's fictions use art-historical allusions as part of the texture of their imagery.

Indeed, *The Princess Zoubaroff* is so steeped in art history that its allusions have penetrated to the very stage directions: '*Enter* ANGELO, *a boy of sixteen, fair, sleek, languishing, a "Benozzo Gozzoli"* '.[2]

In *The Flower Beneath the Foot* Firbank has reached the point of sending up his own allusiveness. 'It was as if Venus Anadyomene herself, standing on a shell [. . .]', runs the text; and Firbank comments in a footnote: '*Vide* Botticelli'.

The allusions come thickest and carry the greatest imaginative weight in *The Artificial Princess*, Firbank's first-written though last-published complete work of complete Firbankianness.

The Artificial Princess is the only one of Firbank's Firbankian fictions to be composed (at least, most of it was composed) while he still entertained an active notion of becoming an art historian by profession. Evidently he afterwards connected it with his art-historical period. When, towards the end of his life, he finished the manuscript and tried to set a date on its original composition, the two dates that proposed themselves to his memory

---

[1] as section 12 of the next chapter (X) will detail.

[2] Angelo is perhaps the same person, now a touch older, as the page in *The Artificial Princess* who (p. 66 in the *Complete* Firbank) 'wore the dainty trappings of a page in a Benozzo Gozzoli, and was paid a large wage to look wilful, and to stand about the corridors and pout'.

were of his two intensely art-historical periods: 1910, when he had just come down from Cambridge; and 1906, when he was just going or had just gone up.

(His gloze on 1906, 'while preparing for the Cambridge "Littlego"', would, as a matter of fact, in his peculiar non-exam-taking circumstances,[1] cover both before and after his going into residence, which he did in October 1906.)

The Artificial Princess is, as well as a brilliant and sad novel, a documentary of a consciousness playing over the whole repertory of art history.

Its often witty allusions run: Largillière, El Greco, Nattier, a 'landscape painted delicately upon a porcelain cup or saucer, or upon the silken panel of a fan', a 'barocco ceiling', a 'Crucifixion by a pupil of Félicien Rops'[2] (did Firbank, before he bought his own two works by Rops, have to fob himself off with some imitator?), the Flemish Primitives, the elder Brueghel, Verrocchio, Carlo Dolci, Turner, Vermeer, Goya, Dürer, Rubens, Jordaens (this last pair united in a very art-historically turned cattiness: 'Clearly she was a Rubens, with her ample figure, florid colouring and faintly pencilled moustache, a Rubens on the verge of becoming a Jordaens from a too ardent admiration of French cooking, and a preference for sleep'), a Conder fan, Gerard Dow (more usually nowadays spelt Dou), Carpaccio, Donatello, Gozzoli (in relation to the pouting page I have just mentioned in a footnote), Greuze (this in a very delicate item of art criticism: the pastry shop is named 'Maison Greuze'), Limoges enamel 'decorated by Jean Limousine'. . . .

Even the shadows on the grass 'suggested Early Abyssinian Art – "persons returning from a lion-hunt"'. (I can't decide whether Firbank has or hasn't conflated Abyssinia with Assyria.)

It was while he was an undergraduate that Firbank practised as a (non-fiction) art historian. His art-historical essay, 'An Early Flemish Painter', was published in *The Academy* in 1907. It concerns Jan Gossaert, whose date of death (which is all that is, even roughly, known) is circa 1533. Firbank discusses whether Gossaert is identical with the painter called Mabuse, and allots a portrait of the Emperor Charles V to the italianising period in Gossaert's œuvre.

Firbank also published fiction while he was an undergraduate. A story called 'The Wavering Disciple' appeared in the university paper *Granta* during his first term, in 1906. The *Biography*, in reporting on it, discloses that its heroine's name is Lady Eastlake.

As a matter of fact, the name runs true to Firbank's Cambridge pre-

---

[1] Cf. Chapter VII, 2.
[2] There will be more about this invention in Chapter XV, 18.

occupation. It is an art-historical joke. Lady Eastlake (1809–93), wife and presently widow of the National Gallery director Sir Charles Eastlake, is the author of (for example) *Five Great Painters*.

Firbank might, of course, have been equipping himself with art-histotical quips and expertise in preparation for trying to get a job in a museum.

But most museum jobs at that time were too ill paid to tempt Firbank into going to daily work – though the jobs' excuse for being so ill paid would probably have been that they were designed for people with, like Firbank, a private income. Probably Firbank had in mind the much more lucrative world of fine-arts dealing – which was also a world where, through his father's and his own collecting, he would have acquaintances.

An item among the Firbank papers sold at Sotheby's gives that probability a touch of corroboration: 'an autograph draft letter of Lady Firbank to Sir Joseph Duveen' – a knighthood being the grade of dignity reached by that time by the highest-gloss fine-arts dealer in history, who became Lord Duveen of Millbank before he died in 1939.

The *Biography*, whose author has read it, is able to disclose the contents of the letter. Lady Firbank was seeking, in 1921, to raise £1,000 from Duveen for a production of *The Princess Zoubaroff*. Firbank presently met Duveen in Paris, but didn't get the money[1] – or a production.

Perhaps Firbank hoped Duveen would feel sympathetically towards a play containing art-historical expertise. But it seems unlikely that Duveen was the dealer to be struck by a finesse exercised between the not at that time established as great (and therefore not saleable at great prices) names of Tiepolo and Sebastiano Ricci.

The *Biography* doesn't say whether Duveen was a friend or whether Lady Firbank was trying to raise an investment from him out of the blue or whether evidence exists or doesn't exist to shew which.

Some previous connexion seems likely or Duveen would scarcely have agreed to see Firbank. Perhaps Sir Thomas had bought from or sold to Duveen.

Whatever her connexion with him, it came to Lady Firbank to think of Duveen as a possible benefactor for her son turned playwright. Perhaps that was because she had earlier counted on Duveen – or perhaps Duveen had even agreed – to help Firbank turn dealer.

[1] Firbank bore no resentment. At a posh art-historical occasion in *The New Rythum* (an occasion I will mention further in Chapter XV, 13), he causes one of his personages to be about to – before interruption – 'exchange a polite word with Sir Joseph Duveen'.

7. Portrait as Self-Portrait

FIRBANK'S essay in art history sets off from an exhibition he saw in Bruges in 1907, an exhibition which I assume from its title, 'Exposition de la Toison d'Or', to have been concerned with the Burgundian-Flemish order of chivalry, the Golden Fleece.

The portrait of the Emperor Charles V which interested Firbank was attributed in the exhibition, Firbank's essay says, to Gossaert. Firbank's text was reprinted in 1969 as a Christmas card booklet with a reproduction of the only portrait to be thus attributed in the exhibition, though Professor Benkovitz, in a preliminary note to the Christmas card, convicts Firbank of having muddled the picture, in his description of it, with another exhibited at the same time but not attributed to Gossaert.

With that exception, Firbank's art history is accurate and cautious. But his expression of it is idiosyncratic: in fascinatingly proto-Firbankian ways.

As late as 1920 by which time it must have begun to be an affectation kept up through his affection for the Nineties, Firbank used the Victorian-English habit of anglicising the names of Italian painters, the habit by which Bernard Shaw and Oscar Wilde wrote of John Bellini, and John Ruskin wrote of Tintoret and Nicholas the Pisan. In *The Princess Zoubaroff* Firbank himself (or, strictly, his dialogue itself) uses Tintoret – as well as Sebastian, rather than Sebastiano, Ricci.

For Firbank, Tintoret was perhaps a tribute not only to Ruskin but to the French language, which frenchifies almost everyone. (In his art-historical piece, Firbank uses the French Jean Gossart instead of the Flemish Jan Gossaert.) But even Firbank didn't go so far as to translate the French (or the Italian) literally and call Tintoretto 'the Dyer' or even, in modification, 'the Tintoret'.

In his art-historical essay, however, Firbank does something which to a current-English reader's eye looks scarcely less strange, though another instance[1] I have come across shews it to be an acceptable 19th-century English idiom, at least among people who moved in French circles. He calls his Emperor neither Charles V in English nor (though that wasn't, as I'll shew in a moment, far from his mind) Carolus Quintus in Latin. Instead, he takes the French form of the Emperor's name, Charles-Quint,[2] and anglicises it as though it were first name and surname. At the exhibition, his essay begins, 'there is a wonderful portrait of Charles Quint'.

No doubt Quint seemed to him quaint.

---

[1] It is an instance with Firbankian associations, and I will mention it in Chapter X, 9.
[2] 'Charles V, dit Charles-Quint', says the *Larousse de Poche*.

Probably he also liked giving the Emperor the surname of the delinquent valet in *The Turn of the Screw*. (When he was 15 or so, Firbank bought a signature of Henry James's for his collection of autographs.[1])

Most of all, Firbank probably felt confined by the limitation of art history to facts. In form though not substance he invented a personage for his non-fiction essay.

The invention which was half-frustrated in the essay was in fact fulfilled in *The Princess Zoubaroff*. The play's Florentine setting conjured up Firbank the art historian – who arrived dripping the Sebastian and the Tintoret of his probably already old-fashioned art-historical vocabulary of 13 years earlier.

The vocabulary came accompanied by the memory of the Charles Quint half-invented in the essay in art history. In *The Princess Zoubaroff*, the Emperor's name reappears, this time as a regular surname. And the surname consists of the Emperor's numeral – but translated back, this time, into full Latin.

In his new clothes, the Emperor has become a more than slightly Wildean young man named Reggie Quintus.

In Reggie Quintus I recognise (among other important things[2]) another of Firbank's self-portraits. Probably, therefore, Firbank had it in mind that Ronald is the Scottish form of Reginald. I think he can be counted on to have thoroughly looked up the associations of Ronald when he adopted it for his writing name.

But Reggie's first name (which appears in the nickname form even in the list of dramatis personae) was also reached through a direct association with the Emperor whose portrait Firbank had art-historically discussed. Charles V was a king (of Spain) as well as an emperor. And Firbank had already, in projecting Quintus, latinised him. The Reggie he put in front of the Quintus came to Firbank from the Latin for king: *rex – regis*.[3]

It came all the more fluently because Firbank would certainly make a point of pronouncing *regis* in the English Catholic manner: with a soft *g*.

8. Self-Portrait as a Minion

REGGIE Quintus, as described by stage directions in *The Princess Zoubaroff*, is 'incredibly young' and 'incredibly good-looking'; and his voice can on

---

[1] Two months after his art-historical essay was published, Firbank met Henry James (at a dinner party which will be discussed in Chapter XII, 5).
[2] I will expound the others in Chapter XIV, 10.
[3] This type of process will be mentioned again in Chapter XV, 12.

occasion be 'rather like cheap scent' (a description repeated from that of an actorish young man in *Caprice*).

Reggie is the companion of Lord Orkish. 'Lord Orkish has asked me', Reggie says, 'to make his house temporarily my home.' To this the Princess, 'after an instant', returns: 'Is *Lady* Orkish coming out this year?'

The unspoken answer, that whether or not Lady Orkish comes to Florence this year will make small difference, is supplied by Lord Orkish's actions, which include watching young men bathe naked and 'without false modesty of *any* kind' in the Arno (though 'I'm sure if I looked it was quite involuntary,' he maintains) and flirting with the Benozzo Gozzoli footman (whom Lord Orkish has encountered in a previous métier – that of, inevitably, flower-vendor).

In relation to Lord Orkish, Reggie Quintus is Firbank's self-portrait in his minion impersonation.

Evidently, however, Reggie can't quite rely on Lord Orkish for a livelihood, any more than Firbank could *quite* rely on his private income. Reggie is certainly *trying* to make a financial success of minionship. 'He has the manners', says the Princess, 'of one who has nothing to lose and perhaps something to gain.'

But Reggie has to try to gain by other métiers than that of minion. And Firbank attributes to Reggie, in practice or ambition, two of the métiers which Firbank sketched out as possibilities for himself.

No doubt it is by reflexion of that papal possibility of some kind which I discussed in Chapter VII, 2 that Reggie Quintus announces 'I'm hoping to be a Cardinal's secretary soon'.

(Perhaps the Princess's reply explains that Firbank, instead of being merely rejected, desisted from trying: 'You'll get awfully bored, shan't you, going to conversaziones in the religious world?')

And in the meantime, since his Cardinal's secretaryship is not yet definitely fixed up, Reggie goes in for unofficial picture-dealing. 'If the Princess should want a Pinturicchio for her chapel, by the way, I know where there's one to be found,' he offers; and he follows that up with (it is of course the self-portrait who is allotted Firbank's art-historical vocabulary) 'Or, I know of a topping Tintoret.'

I think it is even possible to trace in Reggie Quintus a remark Vyvyan Holland made about Firbank. (What else can be traced in Reggie, and why a remark particularly of Holland's should lodge in this context in Firbank's imagination, I shall explore in Chapter XIV, 10.)

Vyvyan Holland's remark was made in print after Firbank's death. But I think it extremely likely, since Vyvyan Holland was an honourable person and the remark apposite and lively, that he also made it to Firbank in person, probably when they were both at Cambridge, when the remark was at its most apposite.

It is in writing about Cambridge, in his contribution to the *Memoir*, that Vyvyan Holland records that his and Firbank's college, Trinity Hall,[1] consisted mainly at that period of undergraduates reading Law. 'One could not imagine Firbank as a lawyer,' he goes on; 'there was something singularly un-law-like, almost illegal, about him.'

I think Vyvyan Holland told Firbank his bon mot about him, because I think it reappears as a bon mot which the Princess Zoubaroff makes about Firbank's self-portrait as Reggie: 'I hear Reggie Quintus is in the town – looking quite lawless'.

9. Art History as Autobiography

WHEN he extended his art-historical subject Charles Quint into his self-portrait as Reggie Quintus, Firbank was drawing out only one of the autobiographical strands in his art-historical essay.

His chosen painter, whom he chose to name in his French form as Gossart, perhaps represented to Firbank's French-attuned[2] mind the art of that rather cheeky young man, that gosse who dared to practise art history, Arthur Firbank.

And certainly, through tracing the development of Gossaert's art, Firbank predicts the development of his own.

Gossaert's travels become Firbank's own childhood-onwards nomadism. Gossaert journeys, in the essay, through Flanders and also visits Italy; and as a result of the Italian influence on his northern background Gossaert's work 'becomes', Firbank says, 'an experiment' – an autobiographical declaration by Firbank, who had either just invented or was soon to invent Firbankianness in that deeply art-historical work *The Artificial Princess*.

Gossaert's experiment, by Firbank's account, 'wavers continually between the influences of the Flemish School and the Italian Renaissance'; Gossaert 'tries to make a compromise, a blending of both'.

In so far as it concerns art, that is a statement about the painter, not about Firbank, whose art was no compromise. But in 1907, the year before his conversion, Firbank might be describing, through Gossaert's North–South hestitation, his own hesitation between protestantism and Catholicism.

And perhaps Firbank did the same through the title of his story, *The*

---

[1] Vyvyan Holland names (*Memoir*, p. 102) Firbank's rooms in college: F.2 – on the ground floor in the Main Court.   [2] as Chapter X, 10–11 will elaborate.

Wavering Disciple, which he published a year before his account of the wavering of Jan Gossaert.

When he sums up the result of Gossaert's wavering, however, Firbank reverts to writing about his own writing. He does it with a Firbankian oddity and abruptness that are metaphors of the oddity and abruptness of Firbankian images. To his account of Gossaert's 'blending of both' he simply tacks on, as the final sentence of his essay: 'The effect is curious.'

Besides writing a programme for his own artistic development through the history of Gossaert's, Firbank identifies himself (as his later projection of the Emperor as the Firbankian Reggie Quintus shews in extenso) with Gossaert's sitter; and again Firbank makes an autobiographical prediction.

The Emperor, Firbank points out, commissioned Gossaert to paint his (the Emperor's) sister; 'what more likely, then', Firbank art-historically enquires, seeking a firm attribution, than 'that Charles himself should sit to Gossaert for a portrait?'

Firbank's inquiry is asked also of himself. Within a few years of asking it in art history, he was answering it in real life by commissioning a series of portraits of himself from painters and draughtsmen and by writing into his fictions a series of self-portraits which includes one whose name is borrowed from the Emperor's.

(It would be amusing if the Firbank family had recently, when Firbank wrote the essay, commissioned a portrait of *his* sister.)

Firbank's wish to be depicted he eventually expressed through Mira Thumbler (in *Vainglory*) – who, asked to dance for the company, at first declines, lest she seem too like Salome, but agrees when the painter George Calvally promises she may have anything she requests in exchange. What she requests is to sit to Calvally for her portrait.

The pun on the Salome story is never verbally declared. By one of the typical devices of Firbankian fiction, it is swallowed into and expressed by the narrative. The suppressed premiss states that Salome requested a prophet's head on a salver. All that appears in the fiction is the other half of the antithesis: Mira requests her own on a canvas.

Firbank, who adopted Salome[1] as one of his selves, is expressing one of his own wishes through Mira's Salomesque request. As a messianic artist, Firbank wants no John the Baptist to fore-run him: he can play his own forerunner by predicting his future in the disguise of art history. As a princess,[2] he requires no one's head on a salver[3] to bear witness to his

---

[1] Chapter XIV, 1–8 will elaborate this statement.
[2] in how precise an imaginative sense Chapter X will detail.
[3] Firbank's fantasy was careful to avoid requiring both a forerunner and a head on a

attractiveness. His own on canvas or drawing-paper is witness enough: provided, of course, he monitors what the portraitist sets down of his features (which is more susceptible to control than what a camera may pick up of them).[1]

Firbank wholly agreed with the sentiment he attributed to Calvally's wife: 'To be painted once and for all by my husband is much better than to be always getting photographed!'

10. Self-Portrait through an Incurable Feature

ONE of Firbank's reasons for preferring being drawn to being photographed becomes clear if you look through the photographs of him published in *The New Rythum*.

Evidently Firbank had better luck in disguising from his pencil or paint portraitists than from his photographers one of those items in his appearance he could not cure. He had a difficulty in keeping his mouth closed.

There are eight photographs in *The New Rythum* sufficiently in close-up for the observer to tell: and in only three of the eight is Firbank's mouth shut.

One of the three is the Bertram Park photograph which Firbank passed for publication (and which was published after his death in the *Memoir*);[2] and another, perhaps by a special effort for Saint Patrick's Day, is the possibly-shamrocks picture.[3]

But in a photograph [Plate 6[4]] of an even younger Firbank than the putative-shamrocks wearer, his mouth is already open. Perhaps it went with his bad colds.

salver. For reasons Chapter XIII, 6 will make explicit, he was afraid that the person who would be suppressed into a subordinate rôle, and whose head might be delivered up, must be Oscar Wilde, object of Firbank's reverence and author of *Salome*.

[1] Cf. Chapter VIII, 1.
[2] Cf. Chapter VIII, 1.
[3] Cf. sub-section 1 of this chapter.
[4] This photograph is published in *The New Rythum and Other Pieces* with the caption 'HEATHER AND RONALD FIRBANK a nursery photograph, date unknown'. The *Biography* makes no mention of the photograph but it does (p. 13) remark '[. . .] the elegant lace-trimmed clothes – Bertie's and Heather's were sometimes indistinguishable – belong to a Victorian dream'. The *Biography* may be alluding to other family photographs (but then why omit allusion to a photograph which shews the person of whom it is a biography?) or it may have Plate 6 in mind, in which case it takes the elder of the children in the picture to be not Artie (Ronald) but Bertie (Hubert Somerset) Firbank. However, the little boy in Plate 6 seems to me to bear a more than brotherly resemblance to the slightly older shamrocks(?)-wearer of Plate 5. If the boy in Plate 6 is Bertie, he is only a year and three months older than his toddler sister. I think it more convincing that he is Ronald, who was two years and seven months older than Heather.

In a newspaper photograph of the Trinity Hall sports of 1908, Firbank, desperate in knee-length running-shorts, is open-mouthed again – which would not be strange in the context were it not that the starter's pistol has only just, and still visibly in the background, gone off and the other runners lined up with Firbank still hold *their* mouths folded in determination.

And in both the photographs Firbank had taken in Madrid his mouth is lapsing elegantly open.

Harold Nicolson, who knew him in Madrid, did not neglect to note the disability. He wrote of Firbank–Lambert Orme that his underlip 'would come to rest below his upper teeth'. (I think this must be what Augustus John, too, meant when he wrote that Firbank wore his teeth '*à l'anglaise*'.)

Firbank himself bravely, while trying at the same time to pass off the disability as one very common among the upper classes, turned a lament he must often have heard spoken over himself in his childhood into a firework of fantasy in a conversation in *Vainglory*:

> 'We've such trouble', his mother said, 'to get him to close his mouth. He gapes. But at Eton, probably, there are instructors who will attend to *that.*'
> 'There are certain to be classes –'
> 'Perhaps even oftener than any other!'

But a yet more distinctive way of implying that his disability was yet more upper-class had come to Firbank even before *Vainglory*. It wasn't simply imperial longings, though I have reason to think (as I'll explain in Chapter X, 8 and 9) there was indeed a touch of those, which caused Firbank to project himself into the Emperor Charles V. In Jan Gossaert's portrait of him, the Emperor shares (in his case perhaps because his lower lip is dragged down by his sheer Habsburg quantity of chin) Firbank's tendency to gape.

Or, as Firbank the art historian (on this occasion a rather Walter-Paternal art historian) fragrantly puts it, in his description of the Emperor's portrait: 'the lips, parted, inhale, one would say, some sweet perfume.'

11. Self-Portrait as a Black

FIRBANK'S lips, though usually parted, were not fat. But I think he must have felt they became gross through the conspicuousness his disability gave them. And I think it was on the point of a conspicuous mouth that Firbank formed his sense of identity (which I described in Chapter VIII, 9) with Negroes.

It was a sweetener that turned nightmare into wish-fulfilling dream. The very conspicuousness Firbank thought ugly in himself was in Negroes a beauty.

For Firbank, 'little mauve nigger' boys had a further beauty by contrast to himself: they had none of his own need of poudre-de-riz.

It is said of the Negro bride in *Valmouth* 'A book is anathema to her,' to which the return is 'Even a *papier poudre* one': and that is presently elucidated with 'A negress never powders.'

With some help, I suspect, from the always potent[1] example of Oscar Wilde[2] (whose lips, unlike Firbank's, *were* fat), Firbank accomplished the transformation of ugliness (in himself) into beauty (in Negroes) by way of the aesthetic of Paul Gauguin in his paintings of Negroesque islanders.

In 1916 (the year in which he revised Odette's 'old nurse' into a 'Creole nurse'[3]) Firbank published *Inclinations*, where Miss Collins, on shipboard en route for Greece, begs Miss O'Brookomore to visit the lower deck 'and look through the cabin windows [. . .] There's the Negress you called a Gauguin. . . .'

In 1925 Firbank revised a chapter[4] of *Inclinations* itself, perhaps with the (unfulfilled) intention of republishing *that*. The changes he made were, multifariously, towards enrichment, and they include a couple of scintillant Negroisms: a painting ('of the school of Sir Thomas Lawrence') one[5] of whose sitters is 'Mary Marchioness of Jamaica'; and 'a bespangled negro doll' (the property of Mabel's baby daughter) whose name is 'Topolobampa, Queen of the Sunset Isles'.

Meanwhile, the 1916 allusion to Gauguin developed in Firbank's imagination independently. By 1919, for the frontispiece of *Valmouth*, which contains Negro personages of Firbank's own inventing, Firbank wanted (but couldn't find in a form suitable for reproducing in the book) a 'Gauguin negress'.

By 1923 Firbank was adumbrating the final tragedy in *The Flower Beneath the Foot* by inventing 'a sombre study of a strangled negress in a ditch by Gauguin'.

His own Negroism Firbank pursued into . . . *Cardinal Pirelli* (where the Cardinal reads 'The Lives of Five Negro Saints') and through *The Princess*

---

[1] *How* potent it was in Firbank's life is the subject of Part Three.

[2] Horace Wyndham's biography of Wilde's mother, *Speranza*, records (p. 122) that immediately after his marriage Wilde wore his hair in tight curls, and quotes an eye-witness: 'He looked, with his thick lips, like a negro painted white.'

[3] Cf. Chapter VIII, 9.

[4] It is the fourth of Part II. The *Complete* Firbank prints both the 1916 and the 1925 version, one after the other.

[5] It is a double portrait, expressive of another of Firbank's obsessions (which Chapter XV, 13 and 14 will remark) besides Negroism. The Marchioness's companion is 'Miss Elizabeth Cockduck'.

Zoubaroff: through Mrs Mangrove, whose swampy name already hints at the warm Negro republic of Firbank's dream; and through a female homosexual writer,[1] whose name makes her what Firbank was in fantasy, a white Negro – Mrs Blanche Negress. (Firbank verbally inverted the image in a creation jotted in the notes of his unfinished novel *The New Rythum*: 'Mrs White the Negress'.)

Four years after Mrs Blanche Negress, Firbank achieved his black republic – and his Gauguin. About *Prancing Nigger* Firbank wrote to an English publisher 'I bring you the book. It is . . . rather like a Gauguin.'

And in *Prancing Nigger* the Negro family bears the inspired name (inspired by genius and the very point on which Firbank identified himself both with the Emperor and as a Negro) of Mouth.

No wonder that when Reggie Quintus, Firbank's further projection of himself through the Emperor Charles-Quint, goes (it is another of his characteristics borrowed from the personal Firbankian life[2]) crystal-gazing, what, prophetically indeed, he sees in the crystal and proclaims is 'A nigger!'

12. Notes to Chapter IX

THE date of Thomas Firbank's election to Parliament is recorded in the *Biography*, pp. 14–15.

Joseph Firbank's view of Ireland I have quoted from the *Memoir*, p. 16.

The Deputy Lieutenantships of Joseph and Thomas Firbank are recorded in *Who Was Who*.

Jocelyn Brooke's statement that 'Sir Thomas preferred the idea of Cambridge' is on p. 29 of his 1951 *Ronald Firbank*. It is contradicted by the *Biography*, p. 73: 'Baba had chosen Trinity Hall at Cambridge because her grandfather matriculated there.'

Jocelyn Brooke's assertions that Sir Thomas asserted his authority and was as ignorant as Mrs Calvally of connoisseurship are on p. 37 of his 1951 volume. The Firbank remark he quotes is on p. 186 in the *Complete* Firbank.

The *Memoir* quotation about Firbank's love for his mother is from p. 19.

The information about *La Princesse aux Soleils* is from the Sotheby's catalogue (*The New Rythum*) and the *Biography*. Lady Firbank's printing and typing are recorded in the *Biography*, p. 22 and p. 52.

Augustus John's reports about Lady Firbank are from p. 113 and p. 132 of the *Memoir*. The *Memoir* quotation about Sir Thomas's death is from p. 39.

The Augustus John quotation about Firbank's disabilities is from the *Memoir*, p. 114.

[1] – author, of course, of *Lesbia, or Would He Understand?*
[2] Cf. Chapter VIII, 5.

The theatrical-knighting in *Caprice* is on p. 359 in the *Complete* Firbank. The Caligula quotation from *The Princess Zoubaroff* comes on p. 712 of the *Complete* Firbank, and the conversation about Mrs Wookie's nieces on p. 136.

The *Biography*'s account of Heather Firbank's love affairs is on pp. 128-9.

Vyvyan Holland's accounts of the wine at the 1909 dinner-party are in the *Memoir*, p. 109 and *Son of Oscar Wilde* (Penguin, p. 172).

The Armistice Night quotation is from the *Memoir*, p. 67. The Sitwell quotation about clubs is from the *Memoir*, p. 136 and the Lord Berners quotation from p. 146.

The *Vainglory* clubs quotation comes on p. 205 of the *Complete* Firbank.

The *Memoir* quotation about Sir Thomas's collection is from p. 19. The 1904 sale is mentioned in the *Biography*, p. 11, footnote.

The Lady Randolph dance in *Inclinations* comes on p. 258 of the *Complete* Firbank, and the spiritual bill-paying in *Vainglory* on p. 151.

Osbert Sitwell's list is on pp. 124-5 of the *Memoir*.

The *Memoir*'s account of the Firbanks' financial fears is on p. 52.

Mrs Hurstpierpoint looks at the portrait of a naval officer on p. 424 in the *Complete* Firbank.

The Lady Georgia Blueharnis quotations from *Vainglory* come on pp. 75 and 76 of the *Complete* Firbank.

The Shaw–Bernhardt–Tiepolo references and quotations are on pp. 149 and 159 of Volume I of Shaw's *Our Theatres in the Nineties*.

My article *Pro 'Tito'* is in *The Musical Times* of June 1969.

The *Tito* reference in *Caprice* comes on p. 330 of the *Complete* Firbank.

The art-historical quotations from *The Princess Zoubaroff* come on p. 722 and p. 720 of the *Complete* Firbank, and the Botticelli *Flower Beneath the Foot*-note on p. 562.

According to the *Biography* (p. 95 and p. 86), Firbank's art-historical essay was in *The Academy* of 28 September 1907 and his *The Wavering Disciple* in the 24 November and 5 December 1906 issues of *The* (sic) *Granta*.

The *Biography*'s account of the Duveen matter is on pp. 204-5.

The *Biography* mentions Firbank's purchase of Henry James's signature on p. 28 and seems to imply a date of circa 1901.

I took the Ronald–Reginald information from E. G. Withycombe's *The Oxford Dictionary of English Christian Names*.

The 'young man with a voice like cheap scent' in *Caprice* speaks on p. 371 in the *Complete* Firbank.

The Quintus–Orkish quotations from *The Princess Zoubaroff* come, in the *Complete* Firbank, on pp. 716, 717, 738, 724, 739, 708, 737 and 754-5.

Vyvyan Holland's 'almost illegal' is on p. 107 of the *Memoir* and the Princess's 'lawless' on p. 708 of the *Complete* Firbank.

The 'than' which I have supplied between the two bits of the quotation from Firbank's art-historical essay that begins 'what more likely' is in fact left out, by a misprint, from the Christmas card reprinting of Firbank's text.

The portrait-painting quotations from *Vainglory* are on p. 98 and p. 90 in the *Complete* Firbank.

Augustus John on Firbank's teeth is in the *Memoir*, p. 113.

The Eton quotation from *Vainglory* comes on p. 207 and the powdering quotations from *Valmouth* on pp. 467–8 in the *Complete* Firbank.

The Gauguin on the ship to Greece is on p. 238 in the *Complete* Firbank, the later-added Negroisms on p. 305 and p. 306.

Firbank's original wish for the *Valmouth* frontispiece is recorded in the *Bibliography*,p. 29.

The strangled Gauguin is on p. 582 in the *Complete* Firbank and the Cardinal's reading on p. 676.

Mrs Negress's works are named on p. 723 in the *Complete* Firbank. Mrs White is in the extracts from Firbank's notebooks published in *The New Rythum and Other Pieces*, p. 110.

Firbank's Gauguin letter is quoted in the *Memoir*, p. 81.

Reggie Quintus crystal-gazes on p. 743 of the *Complete* Firbank.

X

Princess Artie

1. An Escort of fantastic Demons

FACTUAL chance has endorsed with poetries of its own the poetry of Firbank's imagination.

It is by a poetically apt accidental pun that Arthur Firbank, aesthete, artist, antithesis of the hearty, was from the beginning called (as the *Biography* discloses from the family letters) Artie.

Another, this time posthumous accident of purely Firbankian poetry I discovered by visiting Chislehurst. The Firbank family home there, though it has now become a co-educational one, was, until September 1969, a girls' school.

'A girls'-school passed with its escort of Nuns, and fantastic Demons flying above them (invisible) criss-cross through the air' ... (*The Artificial Princess*).

2. A Single World

THAT family home at Chislehurst (which Firbank's imagination had already, in advance of factual accident, rendered remarkably like a girls' school[1]) was what (after he'd had to quit it) he creatively transmuted into the world of his fiction.

Firbank's is a single fictional world, of which each of his fictions is a fragment. In the œuvre of many novelists there *is* a thematic unity, but it often has to be sought out beneath the varied disguises of naturalism, and naturalism may dictate the shape of each book. Firbank's imaginative world is strong enough to be self-cohesive without borrowing fabric from outside. He chips each of his fictions off the main block, in shapes seemingly haphazard but in fact calculated to give each whole the same exposed isolation as he sets round each of the images that compose it.

Firbank signalled that he was not a naturalist and that the most real world

---

[1] I set my Firbankian novel in a girls' school in advance of the factual accident, too. I took mine direct from the girls' school world of Firbank's imagination.

in his work is the world of his imagination by wrapping all his fictions in a common atmosphere and idiom – and even by tying his work together by threads of common material that run from book to book.

It is not just that he – perhaps unintentionally – repeats lines from one book to another. He quite deliberately perpetuates personages from one book to another.

He can even engineer a meeting between a fresh personage and a revenant. Mrs Asp, in *Vainglory* (1915), is a biographer. So is Miss O'Brookomore in *Inclinations* (1916). In the second chapter of *Inclinations* Miss O'Brookomore, on her way to Harrods, runs into Mrs Asp. 'The veteran Biographer held out a hand.'

Sometimes the perpetuations seem less coherent, perpetuations merely of names too attractive to Firbank to be relinquished. 'And here is Ex-Princess Thleeanouhee,' runs a line of *Inclinations*. By 1923 the ex-princess had been restored and was bodied forth as Queen Thleeanouhee of the Land of Dates (who in *The Flower Beneath the Foot* state-visits the royal family of Pisuerga).

There were cross-perpetuations enough between the books Firbank published in his lifetime for his habit of cross-perpetuation to be noticed and adopted by Evelyn Waugh (and from Waugh it has been picked up by untalented writers). And the cross-perpetuations are redoubled when you add in works Firbank didn't publish but which appeared after his death (and after Evelyn Waugh had contracted the habit).

Lady Appledore, who is mentioned in *Vainglory*, is the eponymous heroine of an earlier story, *Lady Appledore's Mésalliance*,[1] which went unpublished in Firbank's lifetime but appeared as one of the 'other pieces' in *The New Rythum and Other Pieces* in 1962. *The New Rythum* itself, which Firbank did not live to finish, contains Mrs Mandarin Dove, who is also in the last novel he *did* finish, *Concerning the Eccentricities of Cardinal Pirelli*. And the Countess of Lostwaters herself, the inspired pseudonym under which (in . . . *Cardinal Pirelli*) Queen Victoria corresponds with the Pope,[2] has an only slightly less inspired earlier incarnation in *The Artificial Princess* as the 'English Ambassadress, Melissa, Lady Lostwaters'.

An early Firbank story contains Mrs van Cotton, 'a stout little American dressed in yellow and gold. She reminded one vaguely of a restaurant ceiling. She had her portrait in the Academy, which was mistaken by the public for a sunset.' More than 20 years later, in Firbank's all-American novel *The New*

---

[1] – which will be discussed in sub-section 6 of this chapter and in Chapters XIV, 11 and XV, 7.

[2] Cf. Chapter VIII, 8. There will be more about this pseudonym in sub-section 9 of this chapter.

Rythum, she has become Mrs Otto van Cotton,[1] a 'benefactress, arbitress, patroness' and 'a striking example of a well-ordered mind in a well-ordered body, the four orbs of her figure being proportioned equally – before and behind'.

Even Lord Seafairer, through whom Firbank hit in 1923 at Victoria Sackville-West[2] ('daughter of the fortieth Lord Seafairer of Sevenelms Park') was a resurrection of and extrapolation from a one-act play of Firbank's youth. A chunk of that play, *A Disciple from the Country*, is published along with *The New Rythum*. It turns out to contain a Lady Seafairer – and also a Lord Blueharnis, who recurs in *Vainglory*, together with Lady Georgia Blueharnis who there owns the fictitious Tiepolo Stations of the Cross.[3]

And the Lady Georgia Blueharnis who occurs in *Vainglory* in 1915 is herself a perpetuation. She occurs also in Firbank's story (extracts from which are published in *The New Rythum*) *A Tragedy in Green*, which may have been written as early as (though no earlier than[4]) 1907.

3. A World Lost and Re-Created

FIRBANK'S unified fictional world is his childhood's Chislehurst re-created. It is a society swayed by representatives of Lady Firbank, worldly and secular madonna-figures, and moved – in wayward, ironic and usually erotic directions – by the caprices of Princess Artie Firbank.

In *The Artificial Princess* and *The Flower Beneath the Foot* the Chislehurst of Firbank's childhood has been transmuted – for which there were determinants in Chislehurst – into a royal court.

Firbank's fictions are, passim, landscaped by Chislehurst gardens, decorated (and sometimes peopled) by Chislehurst flowers, and tended by Chislehurst gardeners – these last promoted when need be into royal gardeners. (The Duchess of Varna, in *The Flower Beneath the Foot*, recollects that 'she wished to question one of the royal gardeners on a little matter of

---

[1] In *The New Rythum* she appears variously (p. 78 and p. 79) capitalised, as van Cotton and Van Cotton. I expect the double capitals were Firbank's homage to Carl Van Vechten.
[2] Cf. Chapter VI, 6.
[3] Cf. Chapter IX, 6.
[4] The story is dedicated to Sir Coleridge Kennard as 'the Inspirer of the Tragedy', a form of words which conveniently makes it clear that Firbank didn't write a story and then, having met Kennard, dedicate it to him but took the inspiration of the story from Kennard. It must therefore have been written after Firbank's first encounter with Kennard, which was in 1907. Chapter XII, 5 and 6 will give an account of Sir Coleridge Kennard and his and his mother's acquaintance with Firbank (incidentally correcting errors on the subject in the *Biography* and the *Bibliography*).

mixing manure', and it is on that errand that she is lucky enough to meet 'the charming silhouette of the Countess of Tolga'.)

Firbank was uprooted (a metaphor of violence felt more than vegetably by that flower-child) from his many-gardened Chislehurst world when he was 21. It was the most painful of the many exclusions he suffered. It made a beginning of his financial paranoia. For it was shortage of money that enforced the move, which Firbank must have read as a sign that the conspiracy eroding the family income had done its worst at the very beginning of his life as an adult, by expelling him from the garden paradise. And the expulsion confirmed his nomadism as the pattern for his adult life: if he could not have his home at The Coopers, Chislehurst, then he had no home.

But the expulsion from home was also the decisive impetus that made him both a Catholic and, in the urgency of his nomad's, nostalgic wish to re-create his lost home, a Firbankianly imaginative novelist.

4. Home . . .

WHEN Firbank was born (on 17 January 1886), his parents were living at the posh London address of 40 Clarges Street.

But within six months of his birth his grandfather, Joseph Firbank, died. On the money which as a result became his, Firbank's father set up as country gentleman at The Coopers, Chislehurst – which became, therefore, the world on which Firbank's awareness opened its eyes.

From The Coopers Firbank took, as his biographer says, his love of flowers. But The Coopers and, in particular, its environment had to give, and Firbank took, very much more besides.

The house itself probably taught him, through his eye, his ease with the idiom of classical composition. It is of domestic, provincial, haphazard brick, but assembled with the 18th-century felicity of getting the relation of item to item right.

That felicity Firbank adopted as all-but-native to himself. It allowed him, as impresario to the design of the books whose publication he financed himself, to practise Beardsley's art, which Beardsley in turn learned from the 18th century, of placing a drawing exactly aright on the page. When he reproduced his Rops drawing (which he was concerned shouldn't be mistaken for a Beardsley[1]) in *Vainglory*, Firbank negotiated with the production staff about 'hitting an effective position' for the drawing on the page. And it was

---

[1] Beardsley to Leonard Smithers in 1896: 'It will be nice to get [. . .] a Rops' (Beardsley *Letters*, 1971, p. 223).

by virtue of his second-natural understanding of classicism that Firbank pioneered backwards in his taste for Tiepolo and forwards in his own writing, where he set between himself and his sharp fragments of imagery the classical distance which makes it possible to get the images' relation to one another right.

The comely house at Chislehurst turns its back, across a dark strip of coniferous garden, on a high brick wall. The wall runs on your left, if you are arriving from the centre of Chislehurst, along a rustic road.[1]

The old wall is now interrupted by a stretch of recently built low wall and a modern gate which gives access directly to the back of the house. But it is easy to reconstruct that Firbank's family home was grandly entered between a pair of brick gateposts (the gate now across them is modern) which are set in the wall before you reach the house. From the gateposts a drive curved round to the front of the house, which looked away from the road and over the very extensive grounds.

5. ... and Church

ON the other side of the road, almost directly opposite the original grand entrance to Firbank's home, there stands a major clue to Firbank's life and fiction: a Roman Catholic church.

When I first noticed it, I read in the clue no more than the probability, though that is interesting enough, that Catholic ritual was more accessible from the start to Firbank than to most protestant children living in well-off suburbs of English country towns. Hints and murmurs of, comings and goings to and from, the ritual conducted opposite his home must have combined with the Catholic imagery of Firbank's Nineties reading to induce the pious-picture manner of *Odette D'Antrevernes*, which Firbank published before he was converted and which is less Catholic than Catholicesque and quite lacks the adult Firbank's habit of laughing at the Church of Rome – or, indeed, at anything.

It turns out, however, that the Chislehurst Firbank was brought up in was unique among English country towns in that its upper class was, by a tradition whose influence on Firbank I shall discuss in a moment, Catholic. When the Firbanks arrived at The Coopers, the tradition was a little in decay, though quite likely all the more attractive for that to the child Firbank. But in 1900, when Firbank was 14, the tradition was renewed, to the benefit

---

[1] The road, Hawkwood Lane, was, says the *Biography*, 'known in Firbank's time as Botany Bay Lane'. As a matter of fact, if you go half-way along it, you can discover that its continuation still is.

of the church opposite the Firbank house, by the arrival in Chislehurst of a rich and fashionable English Catholic family.

These general associations between Catholicism and the world of Firbank's youth only reinforced the particular connexion between his home and the Catholic church opposite it. For in fact (a fact which Firbank could very easily know and perhaps, even, could not easily avoid knowing, and which I know from a booklet by the parish priest, the Rev. T. P. O'Beirne, which he very kindly sent me by way of answer to my inquiry about the church's history) the church (Saint Mary's, Chislehurst) stands on land that originally belonged to The Coopers.[1]

The church (which is unpretentious – indeed, rather cottagey – neo-gothic) was built in 1853 on an endowment by Captain Henry Bowden, himself a convert to Catholicism, who was at that time living at The Coopers and gave one of his fields to be the site of the church.

Firbank, so ambiguously pained by his lack of pedigree, took the 18th-century house's pedigree for his own, and its owners' history for his family tradition.

When he was excluded from his childhood world at The Coopers, he responded by having himself included in the family of an alternative, communal mother and home, the Catholic church.

The garden of The Coopers was to Firbank what he later made the Princess Zoubaroff call a Florentine garden: 'a Paradise'. Expulsion was the Fall (precisely, a financial fall), after which Firbank enrolled himself on the traditional route towards regaining Paradise.

It was in 1907 that financial losses forced Sir Thomas Firbank to let The Coopers and move his family to Tunbridge Wells. And in December 1907 Firbank was received into the Catholic church.

6. The Church and Lady Appledore

EXPELLED from his home, Firbank began at once to make himself another home by an act of his imagination.

For the time being, while he was perfecting his invention of Firbankian fiction, he had to rely chiefly on a communal work of imagination, a religion.

---

[1] I have followed the *Biography* and the *Bibliography* in calling the house 'The Coopers', which I take to have been its formal name. (I am taking it that the *Bibliography* is accurate when it lists, for example, a Firbank manuscript as consisting of four leaves of 'The Coopers, Chislehurst, letter paper'.) However, the *Biography* (p. 264) quotes (but doesn't comment on) a letter from Firbank to his sister in which he speaks of the house as 'Coopers'. So I suspect that the house was known as 'Coopers' in the Firbank family and in the neighbourhood.

Which one he should formally entertain (though he kept up an eclectic relation with the beliefs of ancient Egypt and several types of superstition, picking himself in Benson a Catholic priest who would raise no objections to his catholicity) was clearly pointed out for him by the traditions and the very site of the home he was replacing by his new religion.

However, he did also at once make a move towards reconstituting his lost world by an act of his individual imagination. His story *Lady Appledore's Mésalliance*, written presumably when he was at Cambridge (since its typescript is stamped by a Cambridge typing bureau), is, as even the *Biography* sees, a response to his having to leave The Coopers.

But the story is *also*: a link between the royal court of Firbank's childhood imagination and those of his later fictions (as I'll shew in sub-sections 7 and 8 of this chapter); a statement of his relation to that deathbed convert Oscar Wilde (a statement I'll make explicit in Chapter XIV, 11); an exercise in the charming narrative manner of another Catholic, Henry Harland[1] (who had an extra claim on Firbank's heart because he was the literary editor of *The Yellow Book* when Beardsley was art editor); and thematic evidence of the necessary connexion in Firbank's psychology between his expulsion (from The Coopers) and his reception (into the Catholic church).

The story, whose sub-title is 'An Artificial Pastoral', concerns a well-bred young man who has suddenly lost all his money (which is evidently inherited: 'until everything was settled, which might take another six months, he had no income at all').

Forced to earn a living, he gets his cousin, Sir George Liss, to recommend him, without saying who he is, to the widowed Lady Appledore for the job of under-gardener. He travels, by third-class train and then cart, to Lady Appledore's country house, which is named (perhaps by the earliest of Firbank's tributes or anti-tributes to the Churchills[2]) Wiston.

On his journey the young man passes a signpost which either already had landscaped or soon would landscape *The Artificial Princess*.[3] 'A signpost,

---

[1] I mentioned in a footnote to Chapter VIII, 6 a more particularised instance where Firbank was probably influenced by Henry Harland.

[2] Cf. Chapter VI, 6 and Chapter IX, 5. The thoughts of the undergraduate (1906-9) Firbank might well seek a posh name for a fictitious country house via the posh reputation at Cambridge of Edward Marsh (who had become associated with Winston Churchill in 1905).

[3] *Lady Appledore's Mésalliance* was certainly (as I'll shew in a moment) written after 1906 and it probably records Firbank's expulsion in 1907 from The Coopers. *The Artificial Princess* was certainly (as I'll shew in Chapter XIII, 6) being written in 1910; but though Firbank was certainly right when he named 1910 as its date he may have been right *also* when he named 1906. It is possible that *The Artificial Princess* was begun, but not finished, before *Lady Appledore's Mésalliance* was written at all.

looking like a very thin Pierrot, pointed a white arm towards Wiston.' Or (in the version in *The Artificial Princess*) 'They pulled up before a signpost, looking like a very thin Pierrot, as it pointed a white arm backwards, towards the Capital.'

Perhaps Firbank was already bribing himself to preserve his own thinness[1] by promising himself it lent him the pathos of a pierrot by Beardsley. And I don't doubt that *wistful*, as well as Winston, went to the forming of Wiston.

The Wiston signpost has a paragraph to itself. The signpost in *The Artificial Princess* begins a longish paragraph. It is one of the paradoxes of Firbank's œuvre that the staccato paragraphing of his mature Firbankian manner is already present in the quite pre-Firbankian *Odette D'Antrevernes* and the no more than proto-Firbankian *Lady Appledore's Mésalliance* but vanishes from *The Artificial Princess*, his first-written work of total Firbankianness.

(That might be because the typist of *The Artificial Princess* simply could not believe the brevity of Firbank's paragraphs. But it seems unjust thus to accuse a typist who evidently[2] obeyed Firbank's instruction 'Keep punc. & cap. letters' to the point of preserving his joke of spelling the capital of his Artificial country with a capital.[3])

Perhaps Firbank associated his brief paragraphs with the false naïveté of *Odette D'Antrevernes* and discarded them while he invented the far from naïf or false tone of Firbankianism. Not till *Vainglory* did he issue his Firbankian tone in the short bursts of his earlier manner.

At Wiston the good looks and the unexpected cultivation of Lady Appledore's new under-gardener astound mistress-class and servant-class alike. But his proletarian disguise is shattered when his aunt comes to stay as Lady Appledore's guest and finds him digging cabbages.

('He turned round, and to his horror beheld the Duchess of St Andrews.

' "Aunt Queenie!" he gasped [. . .]

' "You do not seem quite yourself," she remarked, "but why these Tolstoi habits?" and she pointed to the spade.')

(Aunt Queenie was not to know that Tolstoy was only a front for Pavlova chasing butterflies.[4])

Wistfully indeed, the gardener feels obliged to leave Wiston. But, as he waits on the platform for the train back to London, not only is the sky above

---

[1] Cf. Chapter VI, 6 and Chapter VIII, 4 and 7.

[2] – since Firbank's joke persisted into print (p. 48 in the first edition).

[3] Firbank repeated his capital joke about the capital of Pisuerga in *The Flower Beneath the Foot* (p. 563 in the *Complete* Firbank).

[4] Cf. Chapter VII, 3.

'of such a delicate shade of blue, that it looked as if it had been powdered all over with poudre de riz'[1] but Lady Appledore comes dashing after him, unable to support losing him. They are soon afterwards married, but nouveau riche society refuses to believe he is really well connected; it scandal-mongers that Lady Appledore (whose first husband, it observes with shock, was 'such a staunch Protestant!') has contracted a mésalliance with her gardener.

Thus, with an irony whose gentleness is borrowed from Henry Harland, Firbank's imagination turns the tables on the aristocratic world that believed all too readily that Firbank was a nouveau riche, hints comfortingly to himself that his newly undertaken Catholicism won't make him socially unacceptable (for Lady Appledore does marry her gardener, though the local vicar refuses to perform the ceremony – it is left unsaid whether because the bridegroom is a gardener or because, unlike Lady Appledore's first husband, he is *not* a 'staunch Protestant'), and recovers the lost gardens of Chislehurst: the gardener will, after the story finishes, return to the Wiston gardens, where he once laboured, as master.

The date Firbank himself put (in 1925) on *Lady Appledore's Mésalliance* is, as his biographer says, 'patently mistaken': 1896 – when Firbank was ten.

Perhaps he was unconsciously putting a date on the lost childhood world instead of on his attempt to regain it in fiction.

In reality, Firbank was not a Mozart. He wasn't capable at ten of so polished a performance – and least of all of a polished performance in the Harland manner which Harland himself didn't perfect until four years later. The novel of Harland's which is the most obvious influence on the manner of *Lady Appledore's Mésalliance* (and I think the influence lingered to become, albeit in attenuation, an influence also on the material of . . . *Cardinal Pirelli*) is *The Cardinal's Snuff-Box*, which wasn't published till 1900.

Obviously, if its material is indeed compiled from Firbank's expulsion from The Coopers plus (as the 'staunch Protestant' bit urges me to think) his conversion or impending conversion to Catholicism, *Lady Appledore's Mésalliance* was written in or after 1907. And, as I promised in a footnote, it is possible to shew it can't date from before 1906.

The idea of earning his living as a gardener crossed Firbank's mind (if an anecdote in the *Biography* is correctly dated) even before the expulsion from the Chislehurst gardens made it more probable than ever that a living would by some means have to be earned. According to the *Biography*, when Firbank was in Spain in 1905 he told his partner at a dinner party that 'should he

[1] Cf. Chapter VIII, 1.

ever be obliged to earn his living he would become a gardener' – a 'circumstance', the *Biography* adds, 'later chronicled in' *Lady Appledore's Mésalliance*.

However, the particular form the chronicle takes in Firbank's story could not have been devised before 1906. For, besides incarnating Firbank's imaginative life, *Lady Appledore's Mésalliance* is a literary send-up. It travesties the story, and answers by satire the argument, of a novel called *The Sentimentalists* published in 1906.

The theme of *The Sentimentalists* is, according to its author, 'the reformation of a *poseur* (Chris Dell) by brutality'. The 'brutality' imposed on Chris Dell consists of his being obliged to take a job as an under-gardener. In his 'new life', where he is, like the hero of *Lady Appledore's Mésalliance*, supervised by the head gardener, the young 'poseur' comes near to losing his mind.

Firbank answered the 'brutality' of this back-to-nature fable with his 'artificial pastoral'. Firbank's hero retains the artificiality of a 'poseur' and gets Lady Appledore and the Wiston gardens into the bargain.

What establishes that the expulsion from Chislehurst was inevitably connected for Firbank with his reception into the Catholic church is that the novel he is parodying, *The Sentimentalists*, is by Hugh Benson, the priest who received him.[1]

7. A Cult Photograph

AT the beginning of *Lady Appledore's Mésalliance*, the newly impoverished hero looks sadly round 'the dainty white and gold room' (I imagine the Firbanks restored the 18th-century rooms of The Coopers to 18th-century-style decoration), decides there is unlikely to be a piano at Wiston for the use of the under-gardener and sets about stowing his 'favourite books and music'[2] in an ugly and unsympathetic packing case destined, presumably, to go into store.

Some clothes, however, even an under-gardener must take with him. On this subject the hero soliloquises: ' "And I must just take my simplest clothes, these silk pyjamas are far too smart, but then I can't afford to buy woollen ones, so here goes!" and he rolled them up round a family photograph of a lady in Court dress.'

The photograph is an item of autobiography. It is among the objects with which, Osbert Sitwell wrote, Firbank 'standardised each place wherein he dwelt' and which 'provided for him a sufficiently personal setting': 'a photograph of his mother in Court dress, mounted in a large silver frame'.

[1] Cf. Chapter VIII, 6.   [2] – which will be discussed in Chapter XV, 2.

The *Biography*, whose digest of *Lady Appledore's Mésalliance* doesn't remark the autobiographical photograph, does all the same mention Firbank's picture of Lady Firbank in court dress. It lists it among the framed photographs visible in Firbank's Cambridge room as that appears in a pair of photographs published in *The New Rythum* (and here as Plates 7 and 8).

According to the *Biography*, the room also contains a photograph 'of Heather appearing demure, and, looming large, a picture taken from' Firbank's 'album and framed, the one signed "Isabel de Bourbon" '.

It isn't easy to tell which of the framed photographs *is* the one of Lady Firbank in court dress. I would have guessed it to be the largest of the pictures on the draped occasional table in Plate 8;[1] but in that case where does Isabel de Bourbon 'loom large'?

All the same it is possible to pick out, even from reproductions, one or two interesting items in Firbank's room which the *Biography* doesn't.

One of the pictures crowded on the top of the piano is a framed reproduction of the *Primavera*. Vide, as Firbank later put it,[2] Botticelli.

On the top of the cabinet, which appears in both photographs (which shew partly over-lapping sections of the room), the central object seems to be a relief of naked figures, perhaps a copy of a bit of a Greek frieze or stele. (As the conversation in *Vainglory* remarks of the author who is a self-portrait of Firbank, 'His work calls to mind a frieze with figures of varying heights trotting all the same way.')

The picture on the wall above that cabinet may, I think, though I can't be sure, be a photograph of the outside of the Prado. Among the pictures on the wall behind the sofa [Plate 8], the *Biography* has correctly identified the reproductions of Leonardo and Whistler, but what it calls 'a Madonna possibly by Raphael or Perugino' is[3] a Luini.

What's more, by comparing the overlap, one can deduce that the two photographs were not taken at the same session. The piano stool has a magazine on it in one photograph and not in the other – a change that could easily have been made during a session. But Plate 7, which shews the whole of the piano from the front, gives no sign of the bust (which might be a copy, reproduction or imitation of a Florentine renaissance work) that stands either on or just beside the end of the piano in Plate 8.

[1] Ifan Kyrle Fletcher (*Memoir*, p. 29) records that 'a photograph of his mother in Court dress' held 'a place of honour' in Firbank's Cambridge rooms.
[2] Cf. Chapter IX, 6.
[3] as I'm grateful to Michael Levey for telling me.

8. A Coronation

FOR Firbank – and for the hero of *Lady Appledore's Mésalliance* – the court-dress photograph was a talisman. Turned out of The Coopers, Firbank turned nomad; and the photograph was one of the objects with which he, as Osbert Sitwell remarked, constituted a portable home.

His own adulthood-long nomadism is what Firbank attributed to the hero of *Santal*, who voluntarily exiles[1] himself from home and carries *his* home-in-the-form-of-talismans with him in a knotted kerchief.

In other fictions Firbank re-created his lost home in permanent but often exotic[2] locations: that is, in exile.

After (probably) *Lady Appledore's Mésalliance*, where the court-dress photograph appears in its own shape and serves as portable home, Firbank began serious Firbankian work with a novel set in an artificial exotic country, *The Artificial Princess* – which, though it probably didn't yet bear that explicitly royal title, was in reality already in court-dress itself, since it is a version of the story of Salome and therefore takes place at court.

Human fantasy in general makes parents interchangeable with royalty; and it inclines to experience growing-up as exile or deposition from the royal state enjoyed, among the courtiers and attendants of home, by the most majestical of all incarnations of 'His Majesty the Ego',[3] the infant Ego. When the growing-up coincides with a sliding-down of the family's social or financial rank, there may even be (as I think there was behind Jane Austen's affection for the exiled royal family of the Stuarts) a fantasy in which the throne that the infant had a right to inherit has been usurped.

Those universal promptings towards feelings and fantasies in which one's lost childhood is a kingdom lost were, in Firbank, specifically pointed and reinforced.

It was indeed a family loss of money, whose repetition he ever afterwards dreaded to the verge of paranoia, that caused him, in the very year he (hollowly, he must have felt) came of age, to be expelled from the kingdom of The Coopers. And one of the specific reasons why it was as a kingdom that The Coopers figured to his imagination was summed up in the court-dress photograph which he made into a talisman of what he lost.

Mrs Firbank was translated into Lady Firbank when Firbank was 16. He had undergone the uncertainties of Uppingham and was undergoing those of being tutored. To his social anxiety, the social promotion must have seemed at last to confirm that he was, after all, the princess of his fantasies – and that his mother, by the same token, was queen.

[1] Cf. Chapter VIII, 4.   [2] Cf. Chapters VIII, 9 and IX, 11.   [3] Cf. Chapter IV, 1.

Lady Firbank's titling must have figured in his imaginative world as a coronation ('Six months later', the Artificial Princess narrates, 'the Crown jewels had been all re-set and Mamma was Queen') – almost a Coronation of the Virgin at the hands of her loving son (the Artificial Princess has a Coronation of the Virgin on her ceiling).

And, as a matter of fact, the change of Mrs into Lady Firbank (which is no doubt how she came to attend court and be photographed in court dress) was occasioned by a coronation: Edward VII's in 1902. Sir Thomas Firbank's knighthood was part of the coronation honours list.

9. Imperial Chislehurst

HIS mother's quasi-coronation can only have confirmed what Firbank's imagination had no doubt fixed long before, that the setting of his childhood was a royal court.

Besides re-creating the setting in the royal courts in *The Artificial Princess* and *The Flower Beneath the Foot*, Firbank reflected its (and his own by adoption) royalty in his many princesses: the Artificial Princess herself, the Princess Zoubaroff, the princess heroine of his early play *The Mauve Tower*, and the eponymous heroine of his early 'romance parlée', *La Princesse aux Soleils*.

For Firbank's imaginative conviction that his home was a court there was, besides the universal determinants, another specific determinant – and one which also brought it about that the earliest of Firbank's surviving works on the theme of a princess, *La Princesse aux Soleils*, of 1904, had both an English and a French text.

For the court which first set its pattern on Firbank's childhood was French. And he found its trace in the associations of the Catholic church that stood opposite his home and was built on his home's land.

The very lane which flanks the church and enters Hawkwood Lane almost opposite the Firbank gates is called Crown Lane.

The reason that the upper class in Chislehurst was by tradition a Catholic upper class was that, two decades before the Firbanks came to Chislehurst, Napoleon III did.

The arrival of the exiled emperor in 1871 was responsible for an influx of both French and rich English Catholics (as well as for the shifting and enlarging of the Chislehurst railway).

Indeed, had not the Emperor and, more to the point, the Empress come to Chislehurst, The Coopers would not have been available for the Firbanks to occupy. The Empress Eugénie, as soon as she arrived, set about benefacting her local Catholic church – which was the one opposite The Coopers. She built (but, which later gave the church some trouble, didn't endow) a small chapel attached to the church. In doing so, she blocked the entrance to the family vault of the Bowdens, the family who owned and lived at The Coopers. The Bowden who had built the church was by then buried in the vault. The rest of his family were so angry with the Empress that they sold The Coopers and its estate and left the town.

Napoleon III died at Chislehurst in 1873. His granite sarcophagus, a gift from Queen Victoria, was placed in the Empress Eugénie's chapel in the church opposite The Coopers. The Prince Imperial, too, was buried in the church after his death in British service against the Zulus. (Chislehurst still contains a Prince Imperial Road.)

However, neither father nor son is buried there now. After the Prince Imperial's death in 1879, the Empress Eugénie tried to buy some land, adjoining that which she rented, in Chislehurst. Her intention was to buy the house (Camden Place) which she was living in and, on the extra land, to build a mausoleum for her husband and son. The owner of Camden Place was willing to sell, but the owner of the adjoining land, a German toy-manufacturer, wasn't. So the Empress moved to Farnborough and built her mausoleum there.

Evidently, however, it took some time to complete. On the seventh anniversary of his death, the Prince Imperial's tomb was still at Chislehurst. On the eve of the anniversary the Empress 'went privately and quietly to Chislehurst to pray at her son's tomb, as she said she did not care to show her sorrow to the curious, who would probably be there in crowds the next day' (when a requiem was held at the church opposite The Coopers). The Empress's visit was on 31 May 1886: Firbank was four months old.

It seems absolutely safe to guess that, in growing up in Chislehurst, Firbank grew up into a society ardently mindful of its imperial tradition and of the Empress's mourning fairy-godmother visits. It was a tradition which Firbank adopted into his imaginative world. The exiled Empress of the French was herself Spanish: she incarnated the two European nationalities that stamped Firbank's fiction. Agnes Carey, whose account it is that I quote in the preceding paragraph of the Empress's anniversary return to Chislehurst, and who was governess to the Empress's nieces at Farnborough, records a miniature scene at Farnborough which perhaps had an earlier equivalent at Chislehurst, passed into Chislehurst tradition and re-emerged in the background imagery of ... *Cardinal Pirelli*: 'In the sacristy the Empress one day showed me some wonderful old Spanish vestments'. ... Perhaps also someone at Chislehurst was told, as Agnes Carey was at

Farnborough, the history of a reliquary in the Empress's possession, which she had saved from the Commune and which had been taken from the tomb of Charlemagne by (in Agnes Carey's words, and in Firbank's art-historical words,[1] which were perhaps borrowed from a parallel tradition at Chislehurst) the Emperor Charles Quint.

Perhaps the fact that it was a departed grandeur (departed alike from Chislehurst and from its throne) which made the first grand impressions on his consciousness helped to turn Firbank's gaze historically backwards. 'Tell me', says Mrs Steeple in *Vainglory*, 'who is the Victorian man [. . .]?' And the Victorian man is in fact one of Firbank's self-portraits: 'an elaborate young man, who, in some bewildering way of his own, seemed to find charming the fashions of 1860'.

It was royalty down on its luck that took Firbank's imagination. It is a Chislehurst image which, merged with his favourite mauve (of the decadence),[2] Firbank tosses into the dinner conversation of Mrs Hurstpierpoint and Lady Parvula in *Valmouth*: 'The Baroness Elsassar[3] – I can see her now on her great mauve mount with her profile of royalty in misfortune.'

(The name Elsassar is borrowed and slightly altered [or perhaps Firbank simply slightly misread it] from the 14th chapter of *Genesis*, which mentions 'Arioch king of Ellasar'.[4] The chapter is one which Firbank certainly did read,[5] and which he would in any case be likely to read, with particular attention. It is about Sodom and Gomorrah.)

And perhaps the fact that Chislehurst's departed grandeur was that of an Emperor in exile nudged Firbank into interpreting his own departure from Chislehurst in the emotional terms of a royal exile – as well as making him so readily turn his art-historical curiosity, and his self-identification, towards that (voluntarily, however) abdicated Emperor, Charles V or Charles Quint.

Even the convention whereby correspondence between sovereigns is conducted under slightly absurd aristocratic pseudonyms, a convention which Firbank marvellously expanded into Queen Victoria's writing as the Countess of Lostwaters to the sovereign pontiff,[6] was very likely proposed to Firbank's imagination by factual knowledge of the customs of the Empress Eugénie. The governess Agnes Carey records an evidently customary

---

[1] Cf. Chapter IX, 7.   [2] Chapter XIII, 9 will elaborate the point.
[3] With the title of Countess, this personage appears also (cf. sub-section 2 of this chapter) in *The Artificial Princess* (p. 70 in the *Complete* Firbank).
[4] Firbank borrowed from the Authorised Version, not the Douai (where Ellasar appears under its classical name of Pontus).
[5] Chapter XX, 13 will justify the certainty.
[6] Cf. Chapter VIII, 8 and sub-section 2 of this chapter; there will be another reference to the Isle of Wight holiday in Chapter XIX, 18.

incident in 1886, when it was Queen Victoria who was the recipient of the pseudonymous communication. Queen Victoria was in the habit of lending one of the cottages subsidiary to Osborne House on the Isle of Wight to the Empress and her entourage for their summer holiday. Agnes Carey, who was part of the entourage in July 1886, recorded: 'On our arrival we telegraphed our absent hostess: "To the Queen, Windsor. Just arrived, splendid passage. Osborne looks quite beautiful.–Comtesse de Pierrefonds." '

The imperial grandeur of Chislehurst must have been kept up, during Firbank's infancy, as a recent memory. But the French-speaking tradition that arrived with the imperial family was actively prolonged opposite the Firbank gates. And ultimately it was because it held for him the charm of a lost and past home that French idiom so fixed itself in Firbank's writing that he described himself, in the French order of words, as a young man who 'seemed to find charming the fashions of 1860' rather than by English idiom as one who found the fashions of 1860 charming.

The priest at Saint Mary's, Chislehurst during the time of the Prince Imperial, with whom he was friends, was a French-speaker who had lived in the Channel Islands. He was succeeded, when Firbank was six, by Father A. M. Boone – who was, despite his name, Belgian.

During Father Boone's incumbency (which went on till 1914) five stained-glass windows were added to the church – an event taking place opposite his home which perhaps influenced Firbank's imagination towards Mrs Shamefoot's 'momentary caprice' which 'was to erect with Lady Castleyard, to whom she was devoted, a window in some cathedral to their memory'.

And activities even more Firbankian went on in the church built on The Coopers' land. The priest who had been a friend of the Prince Imperial took with him, when he left Chislehurst, the vestments that were part of the Empress Eugénie's benefactions to the church. While Firbank was between six and ten, the Belgian Father Boone was engaged, from the church opposite, in the entirely Firbankian enterprise of trying to recover exiled royalty's gift from his priestly predecessor's family – an enterprise in which he involved his bishop and the Empress herself, but in which he failed. Perhaps it is Chislehurst Catholic gossip that re-emerges in *The Flower Beneath the Foot*, where a 'former chorister' had 'followed the fallen statesman into exile at a moment when the Authorities of Pisuerga were making minute enquiries for sundry missing articles,[1] from the *Trésor* of the Cathedral'.

[1] The footnote is Firbank's. It reads:
'The missing articles were:
   5 chasubles.
   A relic-casket in lapis and diamonds, containing the Tongue of St. Thelma.
   $4\frac{3}{4}$ yards of black lace, said to have "belonged to" the Madonna.'

10. Firbank and Tours

IMPERIAL Chislehurst made French seem to Firbank a glamorously desirable acquisition. But that did not mean he at once acquired it.

At Uppingham he came 15th out of 16 in French – and picked up so little that, when he went on to stay at Tours, his landlady was convinced that it was with her that he made his first acquaintance with the language.

Exactly when and where Firbank made his sojourn in Tours and learned French is a mystery, except that it came, in his educational career, somewhere between Uppingham and Cambridge.

The *Biography* maintains, on the strength of family letters, that in Tours he stayed '*chez* Madame Bricogne, Le Mortier de St. Symphorien', for about a year – a year that began in October 1902. From Tours he went on for a further stay in the Basses Alpes: in, the *Biography* conjectures, 1903.

However, Firbank's own slap-happiness about dates (as well as several other subjects) seems to have infected both his French hosts. Three or four years after his French sojourn, Lady Firbank (with, I conjecture, a notion of fitting him into some profession or apprenticeship) collected testimonials on his behalf from his hosts at both Tours and the Basses Alpes: and both hosts made, according to the *Biography*, quite hopelessly mistaken statements about when Firbank had been with them.

(The *Biography* thinks Firbank was chez Madame Bricogne at Tours in 1902–3, but Madame Bricogne thought it was in 1903–4. M. A. Escanglon thought Firbank was with him in the Basses Alpes from September to Christmas 1902, but the *Biography* finds that 'impossible' and conjectures 1903.)

To me it seems worth querying, though I have nothing much more than a query to offer, whether it is a very likely coincidence that *both* Lady Firbank's correspondents, writing not so very long after the event, should have made similar errors.

I suppose it is possible that it was Lady Firbank who made the errors and put the wrong dates into her correspondents' heads by her original letters of inquiry. Presumably her letters of inquiry are no longer extant, or the *Biography* would surely have mentioned them, so it isn't possible to check that guess.

But in any case the guess may be too simple a solution. The puzzle contains a further complication, unmentioned by the *Biography*. The *Memoir* states: 'In the summer of 1904 he was sent to a château at Tours to learn French.'

The date seems perhaps to vindicate Madame Bricogne. 1904 is when she *thought* Firbank stayed with her. But then what of the letters in which, according to the *Biography*, both Lady Firbank and Firbank's tutor imply Firbank was in Tours in 1902 and 1903? Perhaps Firbank made *two* stays at Tours.

Even so, there is the oddity that the *Memoir* says he stayed at a château at Tours.

It might be that the *Memoir*'s informant had remembered as 'a château' some reference of Firbank's to the château country of the Loire or had assumed that the Loire château which is the home of the child-heroine in *Odette* was taken by Firbank from residential experience instead of from tourism plus the imaginative conviction that his own childhood had been passed in a sort of château.

But the *Memoir* goes on to report what looks like a detailed and definite memory of Firbank's conversation. 'In after years, he often talked about the château and its inhabitants. His conversation never attempted to recapture the solemn mystery, but always dwelt on some hilariously funny episode of his stay.'

If Firbank was snobbishly romancing when he claimed to have stayed in a château, it is the only time I have caught him doing any such thing. (Robert McAlmon's remark 'as Mary Beerbohm commented, no greater cruelty had ever happened than his being sent to Eton and made to indulge in "games" ' seems to me evidence not that Firbank pretended to be an Etonian but that Robert McAlmon, who was from the United States, couldn't tell one English public school from another.) Everywhere else, even in his libel-fantasy,[1] Firbank was frank about both his nouveau riche position and the social anxiety it gave him. And, with the exception of the paranoid fantasies by which he was himself convinced, he made it plain that his fantasies *were* fantasies – having, like most people of strong invention, a clear sense of what was fact and what fiction and even a tendency (witness his Veuve Clicquot disclosure to Carl Van Vechten[2]) to reveal literal truth through avowed fantasy.

All the same, it is not easy to reconcile the 'château at Tours' (and the notion of a château actually *at* Tours is a touch implausible in itself) with the pension suggestions of 'chez Madame Bricogne' – suggestions underlined by the *Biography*'s implication that 'Le Mortier de St. Symphorien' was sufficient postal address for Madame Bricogne.

As a matter of fact, St Symphorien is one of several quartiers on the opposite side of the Loire to the main and old city of Tours. Le Mortier is one of several sub-sections within the quartier of St Symphorien. And, to

---

[1] Cf. Chapter VII, 3.   [2] Cf. Chapter V, 6.

the defeat of detection, there is not now a building left standing in Le Mortier that could have been there in 1902 or 1904 or whenever it truly was that Firbank made his stay. For 'the simple reason' (as Monsieur M. Menard kindly answered the question which I sent to the Mairie) 'that there were numerous vacant sites near Tours', the whole district has been rebuilt. When I was there in 1969 houses and roads were still being constructed.

The office of the mayor of Tours has, however, been able to trace 'a Monsieur Bricogne, who used to live in St Symphorien, in the rue Piguet Guindon, and who was a lawyer at the Tours bar'. Presumably the Madame Bricogne Firbank stayed with was his wife or widow.

It seems impossible to reconcile that with the château improbably *at* Tours – except by a desperate surmise, which the re-building of the district has rendered uncheckable. It is just conceivable that 'chez Madame Bricogne' and the suppositional château might be one and the same. In what was then a roomy suburb beyond the river, a private house might be a 'château' – in the sense of a Victorian or Edwardian folly, a bourgeois exercise in the Touraine–medieval manner.

11. Firbank and French

WHENEVER and wherever it was done, Firbank did learn French.

The unexpected cultivation whereby Lady Appledore's under-gardener nearly betrays that he is not by upbringing an under-gardener shews when he automatically replies in French to a French remark of Lady Appledore's French maid.

Firbank himself might well have spoken – or at least written – in French automatically. His 456 picture postcards to Heather Firbank, sold at Sotheby's, are described in the catalogue: '[. . .] the majority with no text but some with short text, usually in French before 1914'.

In fact, Firbank not so much learned as steeped himself in French. *The Princess Zoubaroff*, besides quoting Racine to the witty purposes of its stage directions ('LADY ROCKTOWER [*toute entière à sa proie attachée*]: Heartless man; and so you're going to leave us?'), obeys not the English but the French convention of scene-division: a new scene begins and gets a number with each entrance or exit of a dramatis persona.

And Firbank's first publication was, like Edward Gibbon's, actually *in* French. Indeed, so was his second.

The French text of the bilingual, home-decorated book he gave his mother, *La Princesse aux Soleils*, was published in a French periodical, *Les Essais*, in 1904, when Firbank was 18. In the next year the same periodical published his *Harmonie*. Both pieces were labelled 'Trad. de l'anglais par l'auteur' (and both preceded Firbank's first publication in English, which was his first book).

Indeed, in certain ways Firbank learned French *rather than* English. That had, besides the obvious effect of leaving a certain Frenchness in his English, an effect more remote. In November 1925 Firbank told his United-States publishers by letter that (perhaps in their honour, since they had undertaken, as no English publisher had, to publish him in the ordinary meaning of the action[1]) he was proposing to set his new novel in New York ('and as I never was there you may be sure it'll be the new Jerusalem[2] before I've done with it'). Seven weeks later he was writing: 'Is there such a thing as a dictionary of American slang and colloquialisms? I expect to be soon in sore need of a few really racy words – expressions of the *soil*.'[3]

'A copy of Mencken's *The American Language* was', the *Memoir* records, 'sent to him.' In some ways, however, it must have been superfluous. As though his steeping in French truly had made him a foreigner, Firbank in some instances took, like a foreigner, more easily to United-States than to English idiom.

He had, moreover, been doing so all along (or at least since well before his acquisition of a United-States publisher to whom to write 'as I never was there' instead of the modern English for it, 'as I have never been there'). The text of *Vainglory* (1915) remarks: 'she really did enjoy to snub the Bishop's sisters.' 'He anticipated to reach by noon the Oasis', says *Santal* (1921), combining the United-States idiom with an adverbial position entirely French.

It is in such adverbial positions that Firbank's English is most clearly tinged with French. Perhaps the French language's habit of keeping the adverb or adverbial phrase as near as possible to its preceding verb gave him, when he first took up French, difficulty. Having, however, once acquired the French habit, he remained for ever after unwilling to put it aside even when he was writing English.

Firbank's art-historical essay of 1907 places an English adverb in the French position: 'these two journeyed through Flanders, entertaining magnificently all the artists of the towns at which they stopped'.

But that is only one of the essay's verbal oddities. And the quaint anglicisation of the French Charles-Quint into Charles Quint[4] is only one of the

---

[1] Cf. Chapter V, 4.
[2] The *New York–New Jerusalem* play on words extends to the title of Firbank's New York book, *The New Rythum* (which he did not live to finish).
[3] There will be more on this subject in Chapter XIX, 20.   [4] Cf. Chapter IX, 7.

others. Firbank seems to have been at that time so immersed in French, and particularly no doubt the French of the Toison d'Or exhibition catalogue, as to have lost the power to pick the correct English word for what he meant. Michelangelo's frescoes seem more than verbally misplaced on 'the roof of the Sistine Chapel' – whence they would surely have long since been washed away.

However, the art-historical essay would probably have been a touch stiff in any case, since it was Firbank's first (and virtually last) excursion into non-fiction prose. The prose of his fictions makes no literary errors. The French placing of his adverbs is a very deliberate – and very expressive – mannerism, which pervades his œuvre from early till late. *Vainglory* remarks (for one among hundreds of instances) 'it was unlikely that Lady Castleyard would yield immediately to Mrs. Rienzi her chair'. More than a decade later, Cardinal Pirelli 'refilled reflectively his glass' and sat 'considering dreamfully a cornucopia heaped with fruit'.

(Mrs Rienzi's name [which in full is Rienzi-Smith[1]] is an incidental memorial to the fact that Firbank was, as befitted a Beardsleyan, a Wagnerite. Firbank's utmost tribute to Wagner is in a beautifully self-sufficient line of party conversation in *The Artificial Princess*: 'Those "Isolde" cocktails make one very amorous!'[2])

What he called the 'eccentric' (but it is, after all, only French) 'placing of words, particularly adverbs' was named by Jocelyn Brooke as the chief among the mechanisms that produced 'a "syncopated" quality' in Firbank's prose 'which faintly suggests the influence of jazz music, whose beginnings were more or less contemporaneous with Firbank's début as a novelist'.

Firbank's relation to jazz was, however, much more than the accident of contemporaneity. Jazz became to Firbank what Negro masks became to Picasso: a source of his idiom. At the same time, because he included jazz in his Negro cult, Firbank included the idea of jazz in his imagery. For a line in *The New Rythum*, whose title does homage to jazz, he even jazzed up Wagner and his Wagner joke: 'I just love the Isolde cocktail music from *Tristan*, when it's jazzed, don't you?'

Firbank's Negro cult was itself merged with his cult of French. One of John Anthony Kiechler's reasons for finding the patois Firbank invented for his Negro personages so convincingly Haitian is that the patois is French-based and so is the culture of the real-life Haiti. But the underlying

---

[1] An elaboration (not by Firbank) of the name will be mentioned in Chapter XVIII, 2.
[2] In *Lady Appledore's Mésalliance* (*The New Rythum and Other Pieces*, p. 35) the hero and his cousin 'arrived at Covent Garden just as Isolde was swallowing the Love-potion' – whereby the story presages that the hero is going to fall in love with Lady Appledore.

fact is that *Firbank* was French-based. If he invented one French-based patois for his Negroes, his own English prose could be described as another.

The syncopation Firbank achieved by his Frenchly placed adverbs is a highly efficient device. By breaking up the expected rhythm of his sentences, it tumbles his images, on the crest of the held-back beat, into the isolation and conspicuity which are essential to his poetry.

At the same time, the mechanism itself contributes to the material. The syncopation is exotic and bizarre, like jazz. And, because the position of the adverbs is an un-English position, that too makes in itself a delicate effect of exoticism and bizarrerie. Firbank's English prose is, like his suits,[1] faintly, not quite placeably, *foreign*.

12. Firbank and the Rules

NOTHING of smaller potency to his imagination than the imperial past of Chislehurst could have persuaded Firbank to master the formalities of French. For in relation to the formal rules of every other language, including his native one, Firbank time and again demonstrated in every department how rightly Vyvyan Holland called him 'almost illegal' and how rightly the Princess Zoubaroff called a Firbank self-portrait 'lawless'.[2]

Firbank's Spanish, according to his biographer, 'was never as idiomatic or as correct as his French'. I am in no position to offer either praise or blame to the large quantity of Spanish in ... *Cardinal Pirelli*, but I will take the responsibility of asserting that the Italian in *The Princess Zoubaroff* varies between the outré, like his coining of a first name Paolao, and the execrable – like the application of the masculine form *bambino* to what seems (though perhaps Firbank is owed the benefit of the doubt which, in Firbank, always attends such cases) to be a female child.

Firbank's biographer records that at Cambridge Firbank 'had some instruction in Italian'. Evidently it didn't take – any more than his German lessons. The *Biography* quotes a letter of 1906 from Firbank's tutor to Lady Firbank, reporting 'quite satisfactory progress in German'. In 1920 Firbank wrote to his sister that he wished he could read German 'but unfortunately that is a language I have never learnt –'.[3]

---

[1] Cf. Chapter VIII, 1.
[2] Cf. Chapter IX, 8.
[3] Presumably Firbank failed to learn German also from the 'Fräulein' who (according to the *Biography*, p. 24 and p. 29) was part of the Chislehurst household during his childhood. (Heather Firbank was perhaps more successful at learning from 'Fräulein'. In 1920 Heather was translating *Odette* into German [*Biography*, p. 192] – which I imagine was the occasion of Firbank's telling her he wished he could read German.) Compare *Vainglory*

As a matter of fact, not even Firbank's *French* was secure against disintegration. '*Une grande mariage*', says Lady Rocktower on page 99 of the first edition of *The Princess Zoubaroff*; '*un grand mariage*', the *Complete Firbank* tactfully prints.

Firbank was not well placed (though the history of wit must be glad he took the liberty) to sneer at Eddy Monteith in *The Flower Beneath the Foot* who says 'Basta!' (and thus terminates his conversation with the Italian valet who is drying him after his bath) 'with all the brilliant glibness of the Berlitz-school'.

Firbank's own Italian ran rather to gibberish than to glibness. Neither can his printers be blamed. His first editions were meticulously supervised by himself, and he sometimes let through gibberish from which subsequent printers or editors have rescued him.[1] An Italian line in *The Princess Zoubaroff* which in the *Complete Firbank* of 1961 appears respectably as 'Bene, grazie; e lei?' is in the first edition complete nonsense: 'Bene; grazie-é lé?'

When he wasn't rendering it as nonsense, Firbank failed to notice that Italian isn't French. He spells *teatro* with a *th* and writes *representazione* for *rappresentazione*.

The rappresentazione in question takes place, as an advertising circular read aloud in *The Princess Zoubaroff* announces, at a Florentine cinema – named, inevitably in a play about a princess by that dispossessed princess, Artie Firbank, Cinema Reale. The announcement is a beautiful little nexus: of Firbank's obsessive[2] fantasy and invention; and, at the same time, accidentally, of his disregard of the Italian language. He has not thought to italianise a Greek *pph* into *ff* or an Anglo-Greek *y* into an *i*. But he has wantonly transformed an Italian *i* into a *y* justified by neither Italian, Greek nor English. As a result the advertisement reads, inevitably, illiterately and irresistibly: 'Oggi: Cynema (sic) Reale: grande (sic) representazione (sic)! ... Sappho (sic) – Gli Amanti di Mytelene (sic)'.[3]

The attractive slap-happiness about dates in his own life which allowed

(*Complete* Firbank, p. 78): 'They were returning from the large heart of Bloomsbury, where the children were frequently taken to learn deportment from the Tanagras in the British Museum. [. . .] "This afternoon they were uncontrollable!" Fräulein murmured, attempting to hurry them away.' (According to the *Biography*, p. 263, there was in 1924 an unfulfilled project for Heather Firbank to rejoin the Fräulein who had attended her childhood and who was by then in Russia.)

[1] Firbank could mistake even a name art-historically numinous. The first edition of *The Princess Zoubaroff* has (on p. 112) 'Verrocheo'.
[2] Chapter XV, 13 will discuss this obsession.
[3] (*The Princess Zoubaroff*, 1920, p. 111.) The *Complete* Firbank corrects the spelling of *cinema* but not the other mistakes.

Firbank to claim to have written *Lady Appledore's Mésalliance* at the age of ten extended to history. At least I think he stretches the concept of the medieval when he writes in his art-historical essay, of a painter who probably died in 1533, that the last section of his career is 'lost amidst the shadows of the Middle Ages'.

And perhaps Firbank was negligent of geographical distinctions, too. He spent the high summer of 1922 in Cuba, and then went on to Jamaica. He told his mother by post that from Cuba he had taken matter for a new novel (presumably the one that became *Prancing Nigger*). And on the envelope of a letter he received, while he was in Cuba, from Carl Van Vechten, he jotted: '*In Preparation* A novel of The East Indies'. The *Biography*, which quotes the jotting, makes no comment. But surely Firbank had muddled the East with the West Indies?

It is the same princessly hauteur towards detail that inspires Firbank's relation to the language of which he was a literary master but whose syntax, grammar and plain meanings he never concentrated on enough to grasp. He remained in the situation of Mabel Collins's (in *Inclinations*) hoyden sister Daisy. When it is proposed to send her to school, Daisy replies: 'If I studied anywhere it would be abroad'. ('Abroad', Firbank entered in *Who's Who* as an account of his education.[1]) Daisy's father counters: 'Master your native tongue at any rate to begin with.'

The advice was taken neither by Daisy nor by Firbank. There are beautiful occasions when Firbank deliberately strains the elasticity of English syntax and emerges at the end triumphant, logical and having made his deliberate effect. But there are also occasions where he simply hasn't considered how to hitch one part of his sentence to another. 'Like some of Rubens' women, you felt at once her affinity to pearls,' he writes, caring not at all whether he has likened an unknown you to a Rubens woman or implied that Rubens women are themselves sensible of their own affinity to pearls.

When the syntax is right, the grammar is liable to be wrong. The hero of *Santal* is said to get up 'before the last star had scarcely faded from the sky'.

At the age of ten, Firbank committed, in a novel called *Lila* (only a fragment of which survives), the illiterate mistake of writing 'laying' for *lying*: 'Lila's retrever who was laying peaceably on the mat' – a mistake he repeated when he was twelve in a letter to Heather Firbank, where he asked her to take '2^d laying on top of some letters' and buy him some paper. As a young man he committed (in *The Legend of Saint Gabrielle*, a piece that seems, from quotation and description, to be in his pre-Catholic, Catholicesque manner) the grammatical howler of 'memories of Home and she who had

---

[1] Cf. Chapter VII, 2.

made it home'. At 34 he could muddle *either* with *both* ('I fear we shall be without either Adrian or Eric,' says Nadine in *The Princess Zoubaroff*, when she means they will in fact be without both). At 37 he failed (unless printers have failed him) to keep the literate person's customary watch against the intrusion of an *h* into Mark Antony.

Firbank was, indeed, grossly and gloriously ignorant not just of the forms of grammar but of its very terminology. When King William of Pisuerga, in *The Flower Beneath the Foot*, speaks for once as 'I' instead of 'We', Firbank's narrative remarks that it is rare for him to speak in the singular *tense*.

Although his ignorances were disdainful carelessnesses, Firbank was obstinate when they were challenged. His 'publisher' Grant Richards thought that, by a 'depreciated' in *The Flower Beneath the Foot*, Firbank really meant 'deprecated'. Firbank held out. But the context ('For the aggrandisement of the country's trade, an alliance with Dateland is by no means to be depreciated') shews Grant Richards right and Firbank wrong.

And I wonder whether, when Firbank wrote ' "Have I not de satisfaction?" she ubiquitously began, "ob addressing Milady Panzoust?" ', he was implying that the speaker, Mrs Yajñavalkya, is a person so ubiquitous about Valmouth that she knows the name of every visitor to the town: or whether he meant 'obsequiously'.

That Italian differs from French, the East from the West Indies, a tense from a number and the meaning of 'depreciated' from that of 'deprecated' were all, to Firbank, details beneath notice though not beneath obstinacy. But his spelling and punctuation display a lawlessness quite different in kind. Indeed he is not so much ignoring the orthodox laws as practising laws of his own.

Firbank needed no Grant Richards to tell him his spelling was odd, and neither would he have denied, as he did over 'depreciated', his divergence from the standard. About the writer (author of *Vaindreams*) who is his self-portrait in *Vainglory*, he causes this exchange to pass between other dramatis personae:

' "He's too cold. Too classic, I suppose." '

' "Classic! In the *Encyclopaedia Britannica* his style is described as *odd spelling, brilliant and vicious*." '

By 'classic' Firbank meant, in that context, orthodox. For when his printers regularised his punctuation in *Inclinations* he complained: 'By changing punctuation all "goes". Since one never attempted to be classic – ... I feel like "a waiter" in evening-dress!'

In his punctuation, Firbank was attempting not classicism but expression.

Profuse exclamation marks were a family habit. The *Biography* quotes (and grievously misdates[1]) a letter to Firbank from Heather Firbank, predicting the family's mode of arrival at an hotel: 'to the woman who shows us to the rooms!', Heather predicts, her mother will say ' "Sir Thomas M.P.!! can have this room" ', and the scene at dinner will include 'Baba criticising all the poor people! & then call the waiter to tell him to complain of the ½ *raw* peas & meat!!!'

Firbank's fiction has developed multiple exclamation marks and dots of suspension into a tolerably consistent and very forceful system of notation. Firbank's exclamation marks are as meaningful as those by which Bernard Shaw indicates reaction in dramatic dialogue. Indeed, if Firbank did not borrow directly from Shaw,[2] Shaw and Firbank probably evolved their exclamation-mark systems by analogy with the same source, namely musical expression marks.

Firbank's 'odd spelling' often has a Shavian intention, too – when, that is, its oddity is simply that it is phonetic. Obviously Firbank (at an age somewhere between 14 and 19[3]) spelled Old Compton Street 'Old Cumpton Street' because it is pronounced Old Cumpton Street.[4] The spluttered *t* whereby the upper classes insist they are treating 'at all' as a single word Firbank caught by spelling the words 'atall'. (I don't know whether he spelled the upper-class 'at home' as 'attome'. But he shewed his ear for a county slurred vowel by remarking in brackets that his invention, the 'radiant Lady Castleyard' is 'pronounced Castleyud'.)

Perhaps it was a rather Irish pronunciation of his own that Firbank phoneticised as 'rythum' (Irish, I mean, by analogy with the Irish inability to pronounce 'film' except as 'fillum').

[1] The *Biography* states that this letter was 'written a year or two later' than 1896 (*Biography*, pp. 16 and 18). It has failed to notice that in the letter Sir Thomas is already Sir. The letter must date from after his knighting in 1902.

[2] That it is quite likely that he did I shall argue in Chapter XIX, 18.

[3] The date of the story where this spelling occurs will be discussed in a footnote to Chapter XV, 6.

[4] There is probably a similar case in Firbank's story *A Study in Temperament*, which was included in his first published volume. According to the *Biography* (pp. 43–4) Firbank's literary mentor, R. St C. Talboys (whom I shall say more about in Chapter XIII, 5), rendered the name of the woman in the story as Lady Agnes Charteris and Firbank 'changed his heroine's name to Charters'. However, as Charteris is pronounced Charters, Firbank was probably merely spelling her phonetically. That the heroine bears a variant of a name usually spelt in one way and pronounced in another is perhaps a compliment by Firbank to Talboys – whose own middle name was spelt St Clair and, presumably, pronounced Sinclair. Firbank paid a more direct compliment to Talboys in his early, unpublished story *True Love* (extracts from which appear on p. 119 of the *New Rythum* volume) which contains a poet named Alwyn St Claire. (Chapter XV, 17 will mention a probable further influence of Talboys's middle name.)

Firbank was, however, much less programmatic about his phonetic spelling than he was about his expressive punctuation. Indeed he was obviously driven to phonetic spelling by his inability to learn the ordinary sort.

When otherwise literate people are unable to spell, they are usually (I, as one of them, suspect) bearing unconscious witness to some rebellion against the larger rules of society. Jane Austen, who could not conform to the much milder spelling rules of a period when orthography was still fluid, and could not even be self-consistent in her mis-spellings from one day to the next, was in rebellion against the social decline of her once-aristocratic family – a decline which threatened to leave her without a dowry as the entrance-fee to marriage and with, since she was a woman, a very small choice of professions as an alternative to marriage. Indeed, had she not been a novelist, there would have been no alternative for her, had the family dried up, except to turn governess. What she thought of that she shewed, in her capacity as novelist, by impending it like a gothic doom over Jane Fairfax in *Emma*. So, when Jane Austen refused to learn to spell, she had picked her disability with a very practical eye. It perfectly disqualified her from governessing.

For Firbank the equivalent of governessing would have been to become a master in some not very demanding or rewarding (since he had no degree) prep school. For his shyness that would have been a gothic doom indeed. Perhaps his inability to spell began as a precaution against it.

But Firbank's inability had none of the beautifully two-edged (one edge practical) economy of Jane Austen's. Firbank's protest against the rules of spelling was mainly, I think, a wild if expressive protest against the sexual rules of English society.[1] Any practical edge there ever was to his protest was quickly blunted. For, from the moment he mastered French, there *was* a subject in which he *could* have school-mastered.

Evidently, however, he had no need of such chancy precautions as taking care not to know the facts he might be required to teach. It is curious that among the multiple hints and adumbrations of jobs he might take up no one seems ever to have suggested school-mastering. I suspect that Firbank had made himself quite secure against any such idea by letting it be known that he was not a person to whom it would be, in society's view, safe to entrust boys, particularly if society put a birch into his hand. (The scandal would have been the inverse of society's expectation. Between Firbank and a pretty prefect there might well have passed the dialogue between nuns in *The Flower Beneath the Foot*: ' "Now you're here, I shall ask you, I think, to whip me." "Oh, no . . ." ')

---

[1] I will elaborate and, I hope, substantiate this point in Chapter XX, 8.

Programmatically, Firbank wanted his idiosyncratic punctuation to persist into print, and complained when it didn't. But his phonetic or simply aberrant spelling he was happy to see corrected on its route to print. His note to the typist of *The Artificial Princess* reads: 'Keep punc. & cap. letters. Correct spell only.'

Not all his typists can have been as much to be relied on to 'correct spell' as a bureau in an English university town. By an exoticism that is among the poetries with which life endorsed Firbank, the manuscript of *Santal* was typed in Rome by a Russian princess.

Still, she can hardly have been less of an authority on English spelling than Firbank himself.

13. Notes to Chapter X

THE 'girls'-school' quotation from *The Artificial Princess* comes in the *Complete Firbank* on pp. 45–6, the biographers of two novels meet on p. 230, the Ex-Princess of *Inclinations* is on p. 251, the first Lady Lostwaters on p. 68, Lady Appledore's *Vainglory* occurrence on p. 88 and Lord Blueharnis's on p. 199.

Mrs Mandarin-Dove is on p. 72 of *The New Rythum* and, in . . . *Cardinal Pirelli*, on p. 681 of the *Complete* Firbank.

The Mrs van Cotton quotation from *The New Rythum* is from p. 79. The Mrs van Cotton quotation from the early story is from the extracts published in the same volume, p. 117. According to that volume, and also according to the Sotheby's Sale catalogue it reprints as an appendix, the story is called *The Widow's Love* and its heroine's name is Mrs Fawley. Miriam J. Benkovitz's Firbank *Biography* (p. 43), which dates the story probably to 1903, gives the title as *When Widows Love* and the heroine's name as Mrs Franley. The *Bibliography* (p. 91) lists *When Widows Love* and records 'Excerpt published as "The Widow's Love" in *The New Rythum and Other Pieces*'.

The royal gardener questioned by the Duchess of Varna is on pp. 525–6 of the *Complete* Firbank.

The Clarges Street address is taken from the *Biography*, p. 11.

Firbank's negotiations about the placing of the Rops are quoted in the *Bibliography*, p. 19.

The *Memoir* (p. 32) dates Firbank's reception into the Catholic church 1908. The *Biography* (p. 93) dates it 6 December 1907. I have taken the date of the move from The Coopers from p. 96 of the *Biography*, which does not connect move and reception.

The typing bureau's stamp on *Lady Appledore's Mésalliance* is recorded in the Sotheby's catalogue appended to *The New Rythum*, p. 130. Firbank's abbreviated note to the typist of *The Artificial Princess* is quoted in the *Biography*, p. 35, footnote.

Oscar Wilde was received literally on his deathbed and unable to speak in November 1900.

Lady Appledore's signpost is on p. 37 in *The New Rythum*, that in *The Artificial Princess* on p. 50 of the *Complete* Firbank.

Firbank's dating for *Lady Appledore's Mésalliance* and his biographer's comment on it are on p. 34 of the *Biography*.

The Madrid gardening remark is reported on p. 63 of the *Biography*.

The information about *The Sentimentalists* and the quotation from Benson's own account of its theme are from Volume II of C. C. Martindale's Benson biography, pp. 48–53.

The quotations from Osbert Sitwell about Firbank's collection and his photograph of his mother are from pp. 124–5 of the *Memoir*.

The trotting frieze quotation from *Vainglory* is on p. 199 in the *Complete* Firbank.

The knotted kerchief in *Santal* is on p. 33 in the first edition (p. 494 in the *Complete* Firbank).

My reasons for my Stuart–Jane Austen hypothesis are in an essay of mine in a volume edited by B. C. Southam, *Critical Essays on Jane Austen*.

The crown jewels quotation comes on p. 35 and the coronation ceiling on p. 27 of the *Complete* Firbank.

The date and occasion of the knighthood are reported in the *Biography*, p. 37.

The Empress's frustrated attempt to buy extra land at Chislehurst is described on pp. 9–10 of Agnes Carey's *The Empress Eugénie in Exile*. The quotation about her anniversary visit is from p. 162. The sacristy scene is quoted from p. 34. The history of the reliquary is related on pp. 32–4 and the pseudonymous telegram quoted on p. 184.

The Victorian and 1860 quotations are on p. 85 and p. 82 in the *Complete* Firbank, the Baroness Elsassar on p. 406 and Mrs Shamefoot's momentary caprice on p. 81.

The details of the Imperial relation to Saint Mary's Chislehurst I again owe to Father O'Beirne's booklet.

The missing ecclesiastical articles and the footnote itemising them come on p. 565 in the *Complete* Firbank.

Firbank's French at Uppingham is reported on p. 23 of the *Biography* and his Tours landlady's assumption in a footnote on p. 38.

The *Biography*'s dates for Firbank's French sojourns are on p. 38 and pp. 42–3. The *Memoir*'s remarks about the château are on pp. 22–4.

Robert McAlmon's Eton attribution is on p. 79 of *Being Geniuses Together 1920–1930*.

I owe the information about the rebuilding of le Mortier and about Monsieur Bricogne to a letter kindly sent me in 1970 by Monsieur M. Menard, l'Attaché Culturel, Comité des Fêtes Musicales en Touraine, Mairie de Tours, saying: 'nous avons trouvé trace d'un Monsieur Bricogne qui habitait St. Symphorien, rue Piguet Guindon et qui était avocat au barreau de Tours' and 'Le quartier s'est beaucoup reconstruit pour la simple raison que dans cette zone il existait de nombreux terrains de libre à la proximité de Tours.'

The French publication details are from the *Bibliography*, p. 79.

Firbank's letters to his United-States publishers, Brentano's, are quoted and the dispatch of the Mencken volume recorded in the *Memoir*, pp. 87–8.

The snubbing of the Bishop's sisters is on p. 74 of the Rainbow *Vainglory* (p. 125 in the *Complete* Firbank); the anticipated oasis is on p. 32 in the first edition of *Santal* (*Complete* Firbank, p. 493).

The quotation from Jocelyn Brooke about the resemblance between Firbank's prose and jazz is from his 1962 British Council booklet. The same point is made in Jocelyn Brooke's 1951 volume on Firbank, which speaks (on pp. 14–15) of 'inversions which give to his prose a kind of syncopated quality which suggests jazz-music', and in this case Jocelyn Brooke perhaps hints that the resemblance is more than coincidence because he adds: '– an effect which, indeed, was probably intentional'.

The Isolde cocktails are on p. 71 in the *Complete* Firbank and the jazzed Isolde cocktail music on p. 84 of *The New Rythum*.

Paolao and the bambino occur on p. 741 of the *Complete* Firbank and on p. 72 of the first edition of *The Princess Zoubaroff*.

The *Biography* mentions Firbank's Cambridge lessons in German and Italian on pp. 83–4 and quotes Firbank's letter (about German) to Heather Firbank in a note on p. 79.

Eddy Monteith is dried on p. 537 of the *Complete* Firbank.

Firbank's gibberish Italian is on p. 84 of the first edition of *The Princess Zoubaroff* and, corrected, on p. 748 of the *Complete* Firbank.

The mis-spelling of *teatro* is on p. 717 and the advertising circular on p. 764 in the *Complete* Firbank (p. 34 and p. 111 of the first edition of *The Princess Zoubaroff*).

The East Indies jotting is quoted in the *Biography*, p. 225.

Daisy Collins's education is on p. 312 in the *Complete* Firbank.

The Rubens women quotation is from *Vainglory* (p. 19 in the Rainbow edition; *Complete* Firbank, pp. 83–4). *Santal's* misused 'scarcely' is on p. 24 in the first edition (p. 489 in the *Complete* Firbank).

The surviving fragment of *Lila* belongs to Miriam J. Benkovitz, who publishes it on pp. 16–17 of her Firbank *Biography*. The 'laying' letter is quoted in the *Biography*, p. 21 and *The Legend of Saint Gabrielle* on p. 56.

Nadine's 'either' comes on p. 713 in the *Complete* Firbank, 'Anthony' for 'Antony' on p. 518 and 'the singular tense' on p. 503.

Grant Richards's objection is recorded in the *Bibliography*, p. 38. Firbank's 'depreciated' comes on p. 501 in the *Complete* Firbank, and his questionable 'ubiquitously' on p. 414.

The Encyclopaedia Britannica description from *Vainglory* is on p. 199 in the *Complete* Firbank.

Firbank's punctuation complaint is quoted in the *Bibliography*, p. 24.

Heather Firbank's exclamatory childhood letter is quoted in the *Biography*, p. 19.

'Old Cumpton Street' is quoted from a Firbank manuscript in the *Biography*, p. 70.

Letters (to Carl Van Vechten and to Heather Firbank) containing Firbank's 'atall' are quoted in the *Biography*, p. 223, p. 256 and p. 264.

Lady Castleyard's pronunciation is noted (in *Vainglory*) on p. 81 of the *Complete Firbank*.

I have discussed Jane Austen's spelling in my essay in *Critical Essays on Jane Austen* edited by B. C. Southam.

The Russian princess in Rome is recorded in the *Bibliography*, p. 35.

PART THREE

FIRBANK IN PURSUIT

'Français de sympathie, je suis Irlandais de race, et les Anglais m'ont condamné à parler le langage de Shakespeare.'

Oscar Wilde, *1891*

Contents

OF PART THREE

Firbank in Pursuit

Chapter XI	THE IMPORTANCE OF OSCAR WILDE	243
1	Hero and Martyr	243
2	The Trauma of 1895	244
3	How Firbank Was Mistaken for Minor	248
4	Notes	253
Chapter XII	THE WILDE COLLECTION	256
1	Publications – and Publishers	256
2	A Collector's Piece	259
3	Collector's Luck?	261
4	. . . Or Cunning?	264
5	A Birthday Dinner	267
6	The Collection Expands	270
7	Notes	275
Chapter XIII	THE CRISIS IN THE WILDE COLLECTION	279
1	'The Infamous St Oscar of Oxford, Poet and Martyr'	279
2	A Hagiographical Imagination	280
3	Firbank, Wilde and Sphinxes – 1	283
4	Firbank, Wilde and Sphinxes – 2	289
5	A Minor Pupillage	291
6	Creative Parricide	293
7	Firbank, Wilde and Sphinxes – 3	298
8	Firbank and the Sphinx in Person	298
9	From the Sphinx's Point of View	299
10	Notes	301

Chapter XIV   THE WILDE COLLECTION CONCLUDED   304

  1 A Princess of Scandal . . .   304
  2 . . . and of Domesticity   306
  3 Creature and Creation   308
  4 An Engaging Theme   310
  5 Emergence   317
  6 Talismans   319
  7 What's in a Title – 1   320
  8 What's in a Title – 2   322
  9 A Flick at a Passing Bat   325
 10 Double Portrait: A Rakish Pair   326
 11 A Wilde Flower   334
 12 The Ultimate Knot in the Pattern   337
 13 Notes   338

Chapter XV   PRINCESS ARTIE EN FLEUR   341

  1 How Does Your Garden Grow?   341
  2 A Population of Flowers   341
  3 Flower People   345
  4 A Language of Flower Names   346
  5 Portrait of the Artist as a Flower . . .   349
  6 . . . and as an Agriculturalist   350
  7 Arcady Beyond a Wall   352
  8 Strawberry Harvest   353
  9 Princess Artie, Trading as Ronald Firbank   355
 10 Il Faut Souffrir . . .   359
 11 . . . et Maigrir   360
 12 The Namer in the Garden   361
 13 The Sapphic Obsession – 1   363
 14 The Sapphic Obsession – 2   366
 15 Flowers at Shrines   369
 16 Cultus   371
 17 Premature Canonisation   373
 18 Portrait of the Artist as the Messiah ('She Will Provide')   376
 19 Fladge   378
 20 Miracle-Working Icons   384
 21 Notes   386

XI

The Importance of Oscar Wilde

1. Hero and Martyr

IN several important respects, the crucial event in Firbank's life was the prosecution of Oscar Wilde.

Firbank was nine when it happened. Perhaps he caught word of it, spoken or newsprinted, at the time. Or perhaps he came on Wilde only during his adolescent reading. In either circumstance, Wilde must have first presented himself to Firbank as a mystery.

Evidently Firbank incorporated the specific mystery of the Wilde scandal into the general puzzle about sex which preoccupies children and adolescents. A strand not of imitation of Wilde but of homage to him runs consistently and conspicuously through Firbank's fiction. And, if the world of Firbank's fiction is a reconstitution of his childhood world, the actual texture of his fiction, with its incompletenesses and obliquenesses, re-creates the texture of a child's intellectual experience when he sets out to decipher sex. Momentous information, in Firbank's novels, has to be received by inference, by piecing together fragments of statements and by filling in the gaps between snatches of dialogue – snatches which are often, in the strictest interpretation of the metaphor, *overheard*. One of Firbank's regular technical devices is, in fact, to put the reader in the situation of the eavesdropping child, where he can't be sure who is talking, of what and in what context.

Indeed that cardinal Firbankian device occurs in Firbank's first (and pre-Firbankian) volume. Odette d'Antrevernes lies awake 'in her great four-posted bed' and overhears her nurse talking to one of the servants. 'She caught her aunt's name, and then her own, and without realizing that she was doing wrong, she listened.' Odette 'did not really understand what she heard' – and indeed the whole story turns on her sexual 'innocence'. (Odette doesn't recognise a prostitute when she comes across one.)

In his mature Firbankian novels, instead of *narrating* the eavesdropping device and ascribing it to a character, Firbank employs it.

His novels reconstruct the conditions in which the Wilde scandal had been an intellectual mystery to him. In Firbank's life, Wilde ceased to be an intellectual mystery as soon as Firbank became tolerably acquainted with his own temperament; but the solution of the intellectual puzzle was such that it instantly made Wilde, for Firbank, a mystery in the (psychologically) religious sense. Scrutinised, much of Firbank's life and work turns out to have been given to a deliberate pursuit, cult and celebration of the personality of Oscar Wilde, hero and martyr: a way of thinking about Wilde which originated with Wilde,[1] with the result that to adopt it was the utmost of Firbank's acts of reverence towards him.

2. The Trauma of 1895

THE prosecution and conviction of Wilde would have been enormously influential on Firbank even if Firbank had never heard of Wilde. For Wilde, as he wrote himself after the event, 'was a man who stood in symbolic relations to the art and culture of my age'.

The prosecution uniquely united two prevailing British passions, puritanism and philistinism. A public which kept itself ignorant of aesthetics and was kept ignorant of homosexuality (or, indeed, *any* sexuality) was able to mistake the single notorious 'case' obtruded on its notice for a universal pattern. Through the incidental fact that Wilde was the public personification of the aesthetic movement, two prejudices with not a rational leg to stand on between them were able to prop each other up. From 1895 on, an anti-homosexual challenged by the difficult question what exactly was *wrong* about homosexuality could reply that it tended towards the soppily arty, the morbidly affected and the frivolous (that is, the witty); and a philistine challenged to say what was wrong with art could reply that it was tinged with homosexuality.[2]

The trials of Oscar Wilde swallowed up, as well as Wilde's life, the distinction he had pointed to between aesthetics and morals. After the magazine publication of *The Picture of Dorian Gray*, Wilde defended himself against 'pseudo-ethical criticism' masquerading as aesthetic criticism in the reviews; and he equipped the volume publication of *Dorian Gray* with a preface that draws the distinction aphoristically: 'There is no such thing as a moral or an immoral book. Books are well written, or badly written. That is all.'

However, before Wilde could quite clarify the distinction it was totally obfuscated by his trials, where he had to defend himself, more desperately

[1] The point will be taken up in Chapter XIII, 1.
[2] E.g. Flora Thompson's account of village reaction: 'A little later, the trial of Oscar Wilde brought some measure of awareness, for was it not said that he was "one of these new poets"? and it just showed what a rotten lot they were. Thank God, the speaker had always disliked poetry.' (*Lark Rise to Candleford*, World's Classics edition, p. 569).

yet, against a pseudo-aesthetic prejudice against homosexual men which was masquerading as ethics. The obfuscation is not wholly removed to this day. The British law on obscenity, for instance, is still grievously muddled on that very point; and it discourages critics from getting the matter straight in their own minds because, whenever the law prosecutes a book, critics are called to defend the book and their own aesthetics not in aesthetic terms but within the confused terms and concepts of the law.

The prosecution of Wilde was, therefore, a gross setback to aesthetics – which, unlike art, can progress and lately had been progressing, thanks largely to Wilde. Moreover, since in reality there *was* nothing morally wrong about homosexuality, there was not even the compensation that morality was advancing at the cost of aesthetics. The Wilde trials, by sanctioning spite, were a setback equally to the progress of morals. Not till seven decades after it wantonly tortured Wilde did British law cease to practise the immorality of endorsing some people's irrational and intolerant dislike of homosexual men.

Firbank grew up an artist and an (unlike Wilde) exclusive homosexual into an air still electric after the storm about Wilde. Personally, Firbank belonged to the overlap of the two minorities which had been threatened by that act of terrorisation; and he issued his books into a climate from which the reaction sanctioned by the Wilde trials had swept away the aesthetic habit of mind and structure of thought in their entirety.

Firbank's work entered a society that possessed no aesthetic nervous system through which to respond to it. The Wilde trials did more than substitute one aesthetic for another. It was not just that the taste of Baudelaire, Beardsley and Wilde was ousted by the taste of J. C. Squire. It was that the taste of J. C. Squire was non-taste, and the public which allowed him to be appointed the arbiter of non-taste was exercising not a bad aesthetic judgment but a non-aesthetic judgment. The Wilde catastrophe discredited not a system of aesthetics but aesthetics at large.

As a result, philistinism, nothing new in itself, went newly unopposed by any structure of argument. The lack, not wholly remedied yet, was bitterest in the post-Wilde generation of the Twenties and Thirties. The repercussive circle swept by the Wilde affair probably extended throughout western Europe. (An echo of the Wilde scandal was perhaps a small ingredient in the Nazi notion of the decadence of modern art.) But the waves were, of course, most violent in the English-speaking world and in that French-speaking world which was Firbank's adopted world, as it had been, and partly *because* it had been, Wilde's.

In success, Wilde made himself a literary personage in Paris as well as in London. He 'knew French admirably' (the testimonialist is André Gide) and 'had almost no accent'. He had, as he boasted, 'become a French author' through publishing *Salomé* in French (though his French in it was subjected to a few grammatical corrections). The *Echo de Paris* described him in 1891 as 'le "great event" des salons littéraires parisiens'. He was a friend of and (but for the intervention of the Lord Chamberlain) playwright to Sarah Bernhardt – who responded with such unWildean prudence and lack of generosity to his disaster.

And his disaster, because his success had been Anglo-French, traumatised the next French literary generation equally with the English. Between Wilde and that French generation there were threads not only literary but of personal continuity. Wilde had been personally acquainted with two of its giant or gigantesque figures, Marcel Proust and André Gide. (And Jean Cocteau said his life had been ruined by *The Picture of Dorian Gray*.)

In the English-speaking world, the civilising and aestheticising mission of Wilde's lecture tour of the United States in 1882 bore in the next century a golden harvest of irony, when 'Art for Art's Sake', translated into international Latin, re-toured the United States and returned to colonise Europe, its meaning so devalued that it was cynically hung about the neck of that blatantly and imperialisingly commercial emblem, the Metro-Goldwyn-Mayer lion.

During the period when Firbank was publishing his books, the one grounds on which a book could hardly take its stand was that it was beautiful as an autonomous work of art, because that would have implied it rested on the aesthetic premiss which the Wilde débâcle had cut from under literature's feet. Books were promoted as experimental (in ways that implied an unjustifiable claim to share the prestige of science) or avant-garde (with the fallacious implication that art is an evolutionary progress). They were defended as harmless, wholesome or healthy – not, that was to say, 'morbid' or 'decadent' like the literature of the Nineties. It was a defence openly moralistic, which makes no sense as an aesthetic judgment. (As Oscar Wilde had pointed out, 'No artist is ever morbid. The artist can express everying.') Or, of course, books could be forced on to the limp defensive from which they claimed to be 'true to life' – an apology still forced on them by political pseudo-moralisers, whether of the social-realist Left or the obscenity-prosecuting Right. Both wings conspired to ignore Wilde's great imaginative act, the replacement of realism by imagination – in both art and socialism. 'I treated Art as the supreme reality', he said, summing up from prison, 'and life as a mere mode of fiction.'

The disaster the Wilde 'case' brought on the arts, and on writing in particular, is condensed in the fact that the clichés of diction, the banalities of thought and the stereotypes of story-telling technique which Somerset Maugham wove round the little kernel of void at the heart of his work were accepted by public and 'highbrow' critics alike as great literature. Maugham was not the first author of pulp whose pulp could have been manufactured by a computer, but he was the first to be on that account accepted as an intellectual by intellectuals. The treason of the intellectuals in the shadow of the Wilde terror is signified by the fact that Maugham did not even need to be pretentious in order to take them in.

Several of the moralistic judgments which, in the wake of the Wilde trials, replaced aesthetic judgments boiled down to the pseudo-moral question: hetero/homosexual? 'Healthy' (like 'robust', when it passes itself off as a literary judgment) usually means 'heterosexual, but not *too* sexual even so'.

The strongest movement (and one adored by Firbank) to appear within vivid memory of the Wilde trials and make towards re-converting western Europe to aestheticism came from outside western Europe – that is, from outside the immediate repercussive circle of the trials – and was also comparatively frank and un-hangdog about the homosexuality of its leaders: the Russian Ballet.

When Firbank re-introduced into English literature fictions that defied judgment by any criterion except aesthetics, he did it by way of a novel (*Vainglory*) one of whose major motifs is a metaphor of the autonomy and near-immortality of art: Mrs Shamefoot achieves an ever-living memorial to herself while she is yet living; and the memorial, installed in an English cathedral, takes the form of 'a Russian ballet window'.

Within earshot of the Wilde disaster, many artists who were tolerant or themselves homosexual (or both) were cowed into accepting discretion as a moral virtue, and one which could be substituted for aesthetic virtue. Open secrets were considered preferable to openness. In the practice of literature, discretion sometimes meant a joyless abstention from expressing emotions. The open secret concealed a void. Homosexual writers borrowed the apologetic postures of Victorian freethinkers; regret for faith lost, permanent penitential discomfort and a promise not to proselytise. Alternatively, a novelist might disguise the sex of the people he wrote about. It was a small but far-effective treason for Proust to fake the sex of Marcel's lover and leave the Baron de Charlus alone in his grotesqueness as the major male representative of homosexuals.

In the climate of discretion, tolerant people were easily edged into an oblique anti-homosexuality parallel to the oblique anti-Jewishness of the same period. The 'Dreyfus case' was to anti-Jewishness what the 'Wilde case' (its almost exact contemporary) was to anti-homosexuality.

Practitioners of oblique anti-Jewishness didn't, of course, mind *Jews*– only flashy Jews. Oblique anti-homosexuals didn't mind homosexuals – only screaming homosexuals. (Quite a lot of oblique anti-homosexuals were, of course, homosexual themselves, just as quite a lot of the obliquely anti-Jewish were Jews.)

Applied as literary criticism, the lukewarm prejudice against screaming homosexuals prepared a further subversion of literary standards by inviting praise of screaming heterosexuals. If you mistake homosexuality for a vice, you become open to mistaking heterosexuality for a virtue. And when you substitute those false moral judgments for aesthetic judgments, you have created the literary climate that can mistake Ernest Hemingway for a good writer.

(The cult heroes of the literary anti-homosexual movement are seldom writers who just *are* heterosexual. The myth that heterosexuality is a moral virtue is better bolstered by figures like Hemingway and D. H. Lawrence whose work shews signs of a struggle [which can be mistaken for heroic] to reject homosexuality and opt for heterosexuality: screaming, indeed hysterical, heterosexuals, who have fabricated for themselves an hysterical personality [which can be mistaken for a work of literary invention].)

Publishing his books into the post-débâcle world, Firbank was discreet neither in life nor in writing, neither as a homosexual nor as an artist. His heroism, which was huge, was applied solely to art. His fictions made not the smallest or most ambiguous gesture towards letting themselves be mistaken for chronicles of real life, experiments in one of the recognised avant-garde schools or the work of a heterosexual. They were art or nothing; and so, because there was no recipient nervous network to take art, they were widely mistaken for nothing or next to it.

3. How Firbank Was Mistaken for Minor

NONE of this is to pretend that everything would have been fine for Firbank had he published before the Wilde catastrophe – any more than everything was fine for Wilde before the catastrophe. Philistinism was only licensed and massed in force by the prosecution of Wilde, not invented. Throughout his pre-disaster success Wilde was opposed, ridiculed, caricatured and condemned. It may be that his aesthetic mission made more noise than headway in a world where Rider Haggard and Marie Corelli were best-sellers.

Wilde was in fact in a necessity that has pressed many artists – and with particular stringency since the early part of the 19th century. Since the collapse of the intellectual structure of the Enlightenment in the French Revolution, and since the replacement of patronage by direct selling to a public who might want the time-eating quality of art without the art, imaginative artists have often been obliged to supply the missing intellectual structure themselves and practise as critics or theoreticians of aesthetics in order to prepare an aesthetic climate to receive their creations.

The *Maxims for Revolutionists* are correct enough: 'He who can, does. He who cannot, teaches.' But certain philistine periods of history place on him who can (of whom Shaw himself is the supreme example) the obligation to teach *as well as* do: because he is the only person who *can* teach the importance of what he supremely does.

Thus Bernard Shaw himself set about reforming the London theatre from a critic's stall before he enriched it with his dramatic inventions. Wilde (who was cut off before he could quite fulfil the inventive part of his programme), Beardsley, Baudelaire, Wagner and Shelley were all forced, by the same post-Revolutionary philistinism, to engage (though not all equally deeply) in comparable didactic-explanatory enterprises.

Firbank, however, made in that direction only the one brief excursion of his art-historical essay. He was unequipped for the personally public position an author takes when he utters non-fiction in his propria persona.

What disqualified Firbank was, of course, his shyness. Yet *why* was he *so* shy? It was not exactly *because* of the falterings of his educational career or the teeterings of his social standing. Rather, schooling and breeding (or, at least, income) were circumstances that might have made good his original shyness but failed and, in failing, made the shyness worse.

Neither was Firbank incapable of inventing a fictitious personality for himself to armour his shyness – in the manner of Bernard Shaw, who began only a little less shyly than Firbank and was in his youth no less exercised about his social position. But Shaw's invented persona was a public persona. Firbank had been warned by the Wilde trials that he was disqualified from public life. A *homosexual* Shavian persona would have been not armour but an extra vulnerability – the exact vulnerability of Wilde in the witness box, betrayed by his own wit. Firbank was shy because he was homosexual in a vindictively anti-homosexual world; and he remained shy because that world had been so successful in breaking Wilde that Firbank had taken warning not to adopt Wildean methods either to cover his shyness or to promote a literary climate receptive to his own books and thereby procure himself the literary success which he yearned after as the ultimate cure for shyness.

Though it had been warned off non-fiction polemic, Firbank's aestheticism did not go unexpressed. Part of it Firbank lived – through his habit of collection and cult, including his collection and cult of Wilde. And as a matter of fact Firbank directly extended that habit of living into his writing, which isolates and adores images as a collector does objects.

In that way, the texture of Firbank's work is itself a commentary on aesthetic appreciation as well as an instance and an occasion of it. But Firbank also invented a method of condensing the aesthetic of his books into the content of his books. His first-to-appear Firbankian work, *Vainglory*, is essentially *about* the creation of such a work. Its themes include the recovery and display in isolation of a poetic fragment. Its characters include the author of *Vaindreams*.

To create a book about creating such a book – and to invent a technique for describing the invention of such a technique – was a remarkable innovation as well as a remarkable creative act. Several artists have spontaneously taken much the same route: René Magritte with paintings of paintings; pop painters with paintings about paintings or about painting; and a great many novelists (not all of whom were necessarily uninfluenced by Firbank) who played variations on Firbank's theme of the novel within a novel-which-may-be-the-same-novel. (Nathalie Sarraute's *Les Fruits D'Or*, for instance, of 1963, may be coextensive with the novel of the same title which is the subject of her novel.)

Firbank's invention was, in fact, fertile of a great deal of 20th-century art. It was the obvious (once Firbank had brilliantly seen it) way for a novel to seal itself into its own autonomy now that novels were no longer required or able to cut themselves out a slice of time and place into which the excitements of plot sealed the reader, to his oblivion of real-life time and place.

Inhibited from projecting the aesthetics of his books into the world in advance of the books, Firbank made the aesthetics part of the books. He sealed the climate necessary to appreciating the book into the book's atmosphere.

Yet the message was not taken and the books were not appreciated. The reason, I think, was that strand after strand in Firbank's themes and techniques led back to Wilde. They did so because Firbank, as an analyst and theoretician of aesthetics, understood that the progress of aesthetics had been stopped short by the Wilde disaster. Firbank was taking up aesthetics from where Wilde had been cut off. However, anyone who was under the misapprehension that art is an evolutionary progress, and that the only art which matters is that which is leading the 'mainstream', could use

Firbank's return to where Wilde was cut off as a pretext for considering Firbank old-fashioned, which in the evolutionary view means minor.

Even so, that view would ordinarily have been hard to sustain, because it obliged the sustainer to ignore Firbank's enormous literary innovations of form and technique. It should be harder still to sustain now, when Firbank's innovations have been followed up, quite in the approved evolutionary manner, by numerous and various artistic progeny. What has enabled so many judges to stay blind to Firbank's conspicuous innovations (or to the fact that innovations which *are* recognised were originated by Firbank) is that Firbank went not just back but back specifically to Wilde. The Wilde storm is still rumbling round a few eminent places. Anyone still edgy about Wilde can still be edged into agreeing with the judgment[1] that 'there is nothing up to date in' Firbank. It is a strange judgment to be posthumously passed on Firbank, who published a play openly depicting and siding with homosexuals, by a novelist who refused, throughout his long life, to publish his own novel about homosexuality.

Firbank is judged a minor artist by those who still don't dare recognise Wilde as a major aesthete. Firbank's posthumous reputation has been damaged, as his life was, by the post-débâcle climate. As the débâcle becomes more distant, anti-homosexual spite and fear do not vanish. Often they are merely muted into condescension, much as the puritanical critical reaction 'disgusting' has been translated into 'boring'. The judgment that Firbank is a 'child-like' writer is perhaps simply borrowed from the tenet of vulgar psychology that homosexuals are 'immature' (a preposterous insult which reveals its preposterousness by becoming equally preposterous flattery if one substitutes, for 'immature', the synonym 'youthful').

The label 'minor', as affixed to Firbank, when it does not mean simply that he wrote short books, probably means equally simply that he was homosexual (and not discreet about it). Firbank is probably one of the distant victims of that small treason by Proust, who, if he would, might have obliged 20th-century minds to notice that homosexual writers are not necessarily minor. By putting everything, including aesthetic disquisitions, in, almost as ruthlessly as Firbank left almost everything out and obliged the reader to construe both content and aesthetic from the gaps, Proust became a major writer whose majorness can happily not be denied even by minds that judge on quantity.

Or perhaps not even a demonstration by Proust could have changed minds made up in advance. If condescension *wants* to find Firbank minor,

---

[1] Cf. Chapter VI, 4.

it is evidently capable of doing so, since it is capable of disregarding the biggest obstacle, namely his own œuvre. And it will of course select its texts to back itself up. Firbank, a novelist remarked during a television interview in 1970, 'said of his own work that it was mere thistledown. Well, I'd rather write thistle, to tell you the truth.' Firbank did indeed, in writing to his mother in 1914, call *Vainglory* 'only thistledown'. The letter is quoted in Miriam J. Benkovitz's Firbank *Biography* – which (or a review of it) was no doubt the interviewee's source. But it's symptomatic that it was the thistledown remark which, having blown in from the *Biography*, lodged in the interviewee's memory – and not another remark quoted in the *Biography*, Firbank's description of his own writing as 'aggressive, witty, & unrelenting'.

Since his death Firbank has continued to be assaulted by anti-homosexual prejudice, direct or oblique. Some time between 1930, when it was published, and 1970 when I borrowed it, a graffitist was direct enough to inscribe a margin in a London public library's copy of Kyrle Fletcher's *Memoir* of Firbank: 'Oh God! What a bloody, bloody PANSY! POOR DEAR!'

Oblique prejudice, rather than annotate the margin, distorts the text. Since oblique prejudice is against not queers but only screaming queers, its distortions consist of turning Firbank into a screaming queer: by twisting his delicate and idiosyncratic idiom of self-expression into the jargon of a caricature.

This seems the only way to explain the discrepancy between Kyrle Fletcher's account of two anecdotes, both of which I've already mentioned, and the anecdotes as they are re-told by Jocelyn Brooke in his 1951 volume on Firbank.[1]

One of the anecdotes concerns Firbank's goloshes remark (which I mentioned in Chapter VII, 4). Jocelyn Brooke expressly says he is taking the story from Kyrle Fletcher's *Memoir*. So the alterations in Jocelyn Brooke's version are confessedly Jocelyn Brooke's doing.

Kyrle Fletcher quotes verbatim the account of the man Firbank made the remark to. By his account, Firbank halted the cab, 'leaned out of the window and called to me. "I wish", he said, "you wouldn't call me Firbank; it gives me a sense of goloshes." '

This, re-told by Jocelyn Brooke, becomes: ' "I wish", he called back, in shrill and agonised tones, "I *wish* you wouldn't call me 'Firbank' – it gives me a sense of goloshes." '

Jocelyn Brooke has invented the 'shrill and agonised tones', in place of the neutral 'said' and 'called' of the person who heard the remark; and he has

[1] The distortion in the same book of a third Firbank anecdote is described in the note about Firbank and Aldous Huxley in Chapter VIII, 10.

invented the italicisation and repetition of the 'I wish'. Firbank has been re-made: into a screaming queer indeed. This re-made Firbank is forced to justify Jocelyn Brooke in introducing the story into his book, which he does expressly on the grounds that it 'shows just how irritatingly ninetyish he could be on occasion'.

For his version of the second anecdote Jocelyn Brooke conceivably had the justification of possessing a source other than Kyrle Fletcher's *Memoir*. However, he doesn't mention one – as he surely would if he had come by someone's unpublished reminiscences. And his volume as a whole is prefaced by a Note acknowledging its debt to Kyrle Fletcher's 'indispensable work'. Probably, therefore, he was again drawing on the *Memoir*. If he was, he was again distorting it – or, this time, replacing it by invention.

By the *Memoir*'s account (which I mentioned in Chapter VII, 3) of Firbank's behaviour, 'Once, when he was taken to meet an American staying in London, he paused in the doorway, looked once, muttered, "He is much too ugly", and walked away.'

Ifan Kyrle Fletcher called this 'curt treatment'. In Jocelyn Brooke's version, however, it becomes the opposite of curt. It is all a pansified dither. Related by Jocelyn Brooke, the story has become: 'when he was about to be introduced to some influential personage, he recoiled in horror, exclaiming in an all-too-audible stage-whisper: "My dear, I *couldn't* – he's *far* too ugly!"'

There is, of course, a particular reason why Firbank's curt remark, in the form recorded by Kyrle Fletcher, should provoke panic and, out of panic, distortion. As I pointed out when I first mentioned it, Firbank's remark is an echo of what Wilde said in the witness-box when he was asked whether he had kissed a certain boy: 'Oh, dear no. He was a peculiarly plain boy.'

Perhaps it was even from the 'Oh, dear' supplied by Wilde in 1895 that Jocelyn Brooke in 1951 fabricated the 'My dear' he unwarrantably attributed to Firbank.

The fabrication is delicate evidence that in 1951 the Wilde disaster was still lowering over English literary life and still to the detriment of Firbank.

4. Notes to Chapter XI

ODETTE eavesdrops on pp. 9–10 in the 1905 edition and on p. 18 in the *Complete Firbank*.

Oscar Wilde's account of his 'symbolic relations' to his age is in *De Profundis*

(*Epistola : In Carcere et Vinculis*), p. 466 in Rupert Hart-Davis's edition of *The Letters of Oscar Wilde*.

Wilde's *The Picture of Dorian Gray* was published in *Lippincott's Monthly Magazine* in June 1890. Of the 216 reviews which he said (in a letter of 13 August 1890) the magazine publication provoked, Wilde replied to three, by way of letters to the press. It is one of those (to the *St James's Gazette*, 26 June 1890) that Wilde speaks of 'pseudo-ethical criticism in dealing with artistic work'. In the *Fortnightly Review* of March 1891 Wilde published 23 aphorisms. Those, with revisions and two extra aphorisms, became *The Preface* to *The Picture of Dorian Gray* when it was published as a volume in April 1891. (*The Letters of Oscar Wilde*, edited by Rupert Hart-Davis, pp. 257, 270, 258, 298 and 263.)

André Gide's testimonial (translated by Bernard Frechtman) to Wilde's French is reprinted in *Oscar Wilde, A Collection of Critical Essays*, edited by Richard Ellmann.

Wilde wrote 'I shall have become a French author!' (by the time *Salomé* should have been published) in a letter to the Princess of Monaco published on p. 306 of *The Letters of Oscar Wilde* edited by Rupert Hart-Davis. The same volume describes the corrections to Wilde's French text of *Salomé* and quotes the *Echo de Paris* description on pp. 305–6 and pp. 303–4 respectively.

Sarah Bernhardt's response to the prosecution is described on pp. 300–1 of Hesketh Pearson's *The Life of Oscar Wilde*. The same book describes Gide's acquaintance with Wilde on p. 279. That is mentioned also on p. 241 of the English edition of Philippe Jullian's *Oscar Wilde*, which on the same page describes Proust's acquaintance with Wilde. Cocteau's remark, with the not very explanatory explanation 'as he had remained an incomplete narcissist', is reported in Robert McAlmon's *Being Geniuses Together 1920–1930*, p. 115.

Wilde's denial that 'morbid' can have meaning as aesthetic criticism is one of the extra aphorisms whose addition completed *The Preface to . . . Dorian Gray* (letter postmarked 16 March 1891, p. 289 in Rupert Hart-Davis's edition). His account of treating art as the supreme reality is in *De Profundis* (p. 466 in Rupert Hart-Davis's edition of the *Letters*).

Mrs Shamefoot is rumoured to be planning 'a Russian ballet window' on p. 87 of the Rainbow edition of *Vainglory* (p. 133 in the *Complete* Firbank).

Oscar Wilde was caricatured on the stage perhaps in Gilbert and Sullivan's *Patience* of 1881 and certainly in Charles Brookfield's *The Poet and the Puppets* of 1892 (p. 85 and pp. 316–17 of *The Letters of Oscar Wilde* edited by Rupert Hart-Davis).

The doing/teaching maxim is on p. 274 of the Penguin (1946) edition of Bernard Shaw's *Man and Superman*.

Bernard Shaw's accounts of his public persona, his youthful worry about his social position, and his early shyness are in his *Sixteen Self Sketches*, pp. 54, 20–9 and 56–64.

Firbank's 'thistledown' remark is quoted on p. 127 and his 'aggressive', etc.

description on p. 191 of the *Biography*. The television interview in which Edna O'Brien commented on the former is reprinted in *The Listener* of 7 May 1970.

Ifan Kyrle Fletcher's accounts of the two anecdotes are on p. 79 and p. 47 of the *Memoir*. Jocelyn Brooke's versions are on p. 20 and p. 35 of his 1971 *Ronald Firbank*.

XII

The Wilde Collection

1. Publications – and Publishers

BIBLIOGRAPHICALLY, Firbank was collecting relics of Wilde at least by the time he was 19. During his stay in Spain in 1905 (when Wilde was five years dead), Firbank wrote home to an English bookseller's asking them if they could get for him 'the copy of Wilde's "Happy Prince" sold at Mrs Brown Potter's Sale last week, & in which there is a dedication written by the author'.

(Chance was already endorsing Firbank with such pure Firbankianisms as the name Mrs Brown Potter.[1])

By the time (1915–19) of his stay in Oxford, Firbank had acquired a 'complete set of the large paper Wilde'.

The convention of special large-paper copies Firbank had, of course, acquired long before: on his own behalf. In Spain he was making a presentation of (and being photographed with) the large-paper volume containing one of the two stories in his own first book.[2] In this Firbank was emulating a habit generically of the Nineties[3] and specifically of Wilde – who had inscribed, for instance, a large-paper copy of ... *Dorian Gray*, in 1891, to his sweetheart Lord Alfred Douglas.

Beyond his first volume Firbank did not follow out Wilde's example of large-paper impressions. Probably it cost too much. Throughout his career, however, Firbank exercised command over the physical design of his own books. And in that, too, he was following the practice of Wilde – who, in the last year of his life, wrote to a fellow author: 'I am delighted you are interested in the cover of your book. I always *began* with the cover.'

Lecturer on house decoration and on dress, Wilde was a theoretician and

---

[1] Mrs Cora Brown-Potter was in reality a United-States actress who turned manager and was one of the people who, after the disaster, bought options on Wilde's idea for a play (*The Letters of Oscar Wilde*, edited by Rupert Hart-Davis, pp. 792 and 830). Violet Wyndham (*The Sphinx and her Circle*, pp. 72 and 39) records that in 1904 Mrs Brown-Potter appeared in a play whose cast included Mabel Beardsley and that she had, though 'only vaguely', the reputation of being homosexual.

[2] Cf. Chapter VI, 6.

[3] An Aubrey Beardsley example will crop up in a footnote to sub-section 2 of this chapter.

practitioner of *design* – a Wildean aesthetic concept which has had to be spontaneously revived this last decade or so. Wilde's concern naturally extended to the design of his own books, with the result, for example, that he wrote in 1893 to the publisher of the English translation (by Lord Alfred Douglas) of his *Salome*, which was illustrated by Aubrey Beardsley (who would have preferred, originally, to make the translation): 'Dear Mr Lane, The cover of *Salome* is quite dreadful. Don't spoil a lovely book. Have simply a folded vellum wrapper with the design in scarlet – much cheaper and much better.'

It was in that Wildean spirit that Firbank in 1915 sent the 'publisher' of *Vainglory* samples of paper as a guide to the choice of paper for *Vainglory*'s dust jacket, and a German book whose green stained edges he proposed as a model for his own book's.

In his systematic emulation of Wilde, Firbank did not stop short with adopting a couple of Wilde's publishing habits. He adopted Wilde's publisher – or, to be exact, half of Wilde's publishers.

The first book issued with the joint imprint (though the partnership had begun functioning earlier) of Elkin Mathews and John Lane was Wilde's *Poems* of 1892. In 1894 the partners split. ('Lane and Mathews are at last divorced,' reported Aubrey Beardsley.) Their authors were offered the choice of which partner to adhere to. Wilde offered to divide his works between them. But in the event Wilde was denied choice. Mathews didn't want him. Lane got him. (Wilde, not without reason, despised Lane to the point of giving his name to the – rather more sagacious, however – manservant in *The Importance of Being Earnest*.)

Ten years after the Wilde disaster, Firbank picked, for the publisher through whom to issue his first volume, the one of Wilde's formerly paired publishers who had behaved slightly the less abominably during the disaster. Elkin Mathews had the advantage of having turned against Wilde before the prosecution. (The work of Wilde's whose publication in volume form Mathews particularly didn't want to undertake was *The Portrait of Mr W.H.*) Consequently, when the prosecution was brought, Elkin Mathews was not in a position to do worse than write a letter to *The Times* (in order to disclaim all but a business relationship with Wilde) and give neutral, factual evidence for the prosecution at both Wilde's criminal trials.[1] John Lane, on the other

---

[1] One of the counts charged against Wilde was that he 'being a male person unlawfully did commit acts of gross indecency with another male person to wit one Edward Shelley'. Edward Shelley had been an employee of the yet unsplit Mathews and Lane. Elkin Mathews gave evidence to that effect at the first prosecution of Wilde and, after the jury disagreed in that case, repeated his evidence at the second trial. His letter to *The Times* was to deny that he introduced Edward Shelley to Wilde. (*The Trials of Oscar Wilde*,

hand, had the publishing of Wilde's books and was therefore able to withdraw them from sale at the moment of all moments when Wilde needed money and support.[1]

Ten years after publishing his first volume at his own expense Firbank attempted to find a publisher for his first Firbankian book. It seems to have been by a break with his pattern of Wildean precedents that he offered *Vainglory* to Martin Secker – who, however, refused it. Having thus failed to make a professional literary career as an alternative, Firbank then resumed his pursuit of Wilde. He offered *Vainglory* to a publisher Wilde had considered, Grant Richards – who also refused to publish it but agreed to 'publish' it at Firbank's expense.

Grant Richards remained Firbank's 'publisher' until Firbank, financially and ambitiously dissatisfied, made an excursion away from him with *Prancing Nigger*. Firbank did not, however, intend an excursion away from Wilde. He offered *Prancing Nigger* to Heinemann, to whom Wilde had in 1891 sold *Intentions* as a European paperback. When Heinemann refused *Prancing Nigger*, Firbank went back some steps in his Wilde quest by asking on what terms Elkin Mathews would 'publish' it for him. The negotiation was cut short by an offer for genuine publication by Brentano's. After his brief – by their doing – excursion with Brentano's, however, Firbank returned to Grant Richards.

Taking *Vainglory* to Grant Richards in 1915 was a step by Firbank in pursuit of Wilde because Grant Richards was the publisher whom Wilde, after his imprisonment, resolved to approach if Leonard Smithers would not take a novel Wilde had in mind. 'If he doesn't,' Wilde wrote in a letter in 1898, 'I am going to try Grant Richards. I hear he is daring, and likes to splash in great waters.'

That letter of Wilde's was to his friend Reginald Turner. In 1907 Firbank added the acquaintance of Reginald Turner to his Wilde collection. When he took *Vainglory* to Grant Richards in 1915 Firbank probably knew on Turner's excellent authority that he was following a route Wilde had sketched. He was indeed taking up English literature from where Wilde had been cut off.

edited by H. Montgomery Hyde, p. 187, p. 218, p. 299; *The Letters of Oscar Wilde*, edited by Rupert Hart-Davis, p. 312.)

[1] During the disaster Lane also (giving in to threats from his more self-righteous authors) sacked the ill and impoverished Aubrey Beardsley from his art editorship of *The Yellow Book*, which Lane had taken over, after the split, from the joint publishership. Wilde's only connexion with *The Yellow Book* was that a journalist thought – erroneously – he was carrying a copy of it when he was arrested.

2. A Collector's Piece

PRESUMABLY Firbank met Elkin Mathews when he fixed the terms on which Mathews 'published' his first volume in 1905. And in that case Elkin Mathews was probably the first person Firbank met who had known Wilde.

Elkin Mathews would thus become the first flesh-and-blood item in Firbank's Wilde collection. During the ten years between his first volume and *Vainglory*, however, Firbank acquired, in the course of his Wilde pursuit, many sources (Reginald Turner, for one) who could have told him that Elkin Mathews had been by no means an affectionate or even a barely loyal publisher to Wilde. Perhaps it was that information which made Firbank seek a different publisher for *Vainglory*, though it did not prevent him from approaching Elkin Mathews again with *Prancing Nigger*.

As soon as he had arranged to publish his first book through Elkin Mathews, Firbank boldly acquired the clou (or a possible clou) of his Wilde collection. Purporting to aim at a bibliographical item, Firbank acquired a flesh-and-blood one. He wrote out of the blue, asking how he could acquire a copy of one of his books (which was published, incidentally, by Grant Richards), to Lord Alfred Douglas – a collector's piece par excellence: indeed, the most notorious *piece* in England.

Firbank's letter mentioned that he was about both to go to Spain and to publish a book of his own. Douglas replied as author to author, and with an invitation for Firbank to visit him if his route to Spain was by way of London.

Perhaps Firbank's boldness as a Wilde-hunter had run too swiftly ahead of his shyness. He went to Spain leaving Douglas unvisited. But he continued the correspondence from Spain, had Elkin Mathews send Douglas a copy of his (Firbank's) book when it came out, and himself sent Douglas copies of two of the photographs[1] he had had taken in Madrid.

Douglas's letter in acknowledgement of the photographs perhaps set the tone of Firbank's lifelong concern about the viewpoint from which he was photographed or drawn.[2] Douglas preferred the full-face photograph to one of a side view.

There is perhaps an echo of the episode in Firbank's play *The Princess Zoubaroff* (whose close connexion with Douglas I will explore in Chapter XIV, 10): the Princess's fragment of conversation, 'I sent my new photo quarter-face to the Cardinal, and he said –'

When Firbank returned from Spain he at last met Douglas. He lunched with Douglas and his wife (Olive Custance, a poet) in October 1905. It was

---

[1] Cf. Plate 3 and Chapter VI, 6.   [2] Cf. Chapter VII, 5.

Lady Alfred Douglas who was embarrassed into the poetic-prosaic conceit[1] that 'Autumn herself' had supplied the flowers Firbank sent her the next day. The next week, it was Firbank who was host – at a performance of *Madama Butterfly* (an opera with whose heroine Firbank probably identified himself[2]). Douglas was already addressing him as Arthur.

In a literary mode, with Firbank seeking Douglas's advice about where to place the articles and poems-in-prose he was writing, Firbank pursued the acquaintance while he was at his series of crammers and then at Cambridge. Indeed, while Firbank was an undergraduate, Douglas played editor to a contribution by Firbank. Firbank's art-historical essay[3] of 1907 appeared in *The Academy*, of which Douglas had newly taken over the editorship.

In the following year it was Firbank who was – just – on the editorial side. At the request and on behalf of a fellow undergraduate, he solicited a contribution from Douglas to a university paper. Douglas complied, charging no fee except the insertion as editorial matter of a public-relations puff of himself written by himself. Douglas was attacked in undergraduate satire. He replied in his own paper, *The Academy*. His reply spread the dispute to another Cambridge paper – in which he was again ridiculed. Douglas threatened the libel action he so often threatened or brought during that long, sad, infuriated life so much of which was given to trying to win, after the event, the libel suit Wilde had ruined himself in bringing against Douglas's father.

This was the university literary scandal with which Firbank was distantly connected.[4] Firbank's part in the matter was merely to pass on the request to Douglas at the beginning and, at the end, to support Douglas's cause by writing a half cutting, half pompous letter to Douglas's opponent.

Douglas was paid 50 guineas to desist from legal action. The undergraduates involved were, no doubt unjustly, sent down. Firbank, who was not involved, drifted down with them. He had *nearly* figured in a cause célèbre with Oscar Wilde's lover.[5]

---

[1] (Cf. Chapter VII, 5). It might be unfair to Firbank to suggest that she needed much embarrassing into it. In 1897, before she married, Olive Custance was writing 11-page (plus two of verse) letters to Aubrey Beardsley. Having replied at length, Beardsley commented to Leonard Smithers: 'so I hope she will be good for a copy of *Pierrot*' (sc. *The Pierrot of the Minute*, Ernest Dowson's play which Smithers had just published with illustrations by Beardsley). A couple of days later, she had forced Beardsley to raise the value he set on his labours in sustaining the correspondence. He reported to Smithers: 'A huge letter this morning from Olive Custance. She must buy me in large-paper if she expects me to read her letters.' (*The Letters of Aubrey Beardsley*, 1971, pp. 250, 264, 267).

[2] Cf. Chapter VII, 3.   [3] Cf. Chapter IX, 7, 9 and 10.
[4] Cf. Chapter VII, 2.   [5] This thread will reappear in Chapter XIV, 10.

3. Collector's Luck?

FIRBANK let his acquaintance with Lord Alfred Douglas lapse by stages. The *Biography* records them, though confusedly: Douglas was dropped from the list of people to receive copies of Firbank's books;[1] by 1921 Firbank was privately describing Douglas as 'impossible' and denouncing his treachery towards Wilde. The treachery, Firbank said, would be apparent to posterity if *De Profundis* were to be published whole. In that instance he was evidently, as he perhaps was about Elkin Mathews, relying on fuller information received from his enlarged acquaintance among associates of Wilde.

And as a matter of fact Firbank could let Douglas go without detriment to his Wilde collection because at Cambridge he acquired an alternative flesh-and-blood clou: Vyvyan Holland.

Not that Firbank instantly decided Wilde's son to be a more valuable collector's item than Wilde's lover. In 1913 he snubbed (the *Biography*'s word) Vyvyan Holland for taking pleasure in Douglas's having lost some of his many lawsuits.

Firbank came across Vyvyan Holland so early in his Wilde quest either by astounding luck or by collector's cunning and assiduousness. If it was luck, it was luck with precision. Firbank went up in 1906 not just to the university but to the very college where Vyvyan Holland was already, and had been for a year past, an undergraduate.

Of Wilde's two sons, Cyril grew up to be killed by a sniper in the 1914–18 war and Vyvyan to become a professional writer. Vyvyan Holland's contribution to the Firbank *Memoir* is signed V. B. Holland – a name which in itself illustrates that society can't punish an individual, guilty or innocent, without also punishing undeniable innocents connected with him. It is not only the surname which has been obliged to disown Wilde. The very initials are an incognito by omission, since V. B. Holland had been christened V. O. B. – Vyvyan Oscar Beresford.

---

[1] The *Biography* states on p. 75: 'by 1916 Douglas was no longer among the friends designated to receive copies of Firbank's novels as they appeared.' However, it is not easy to reconcile that with the *Biography*'s statement on p. 148 that when *Inclinations* was published in 1916 Firbank arranged for a presentation copy to be sent to Alfred Douglas. And that statement in turn is irreconcilable with Firbank's handwritten list of recipients of *Inclinations*, a photograph of which appears opposite p. 22 in the *Bibliography*: Lord Alfred Douglas is not listed, but Lady Alfred Douglas is. (There is no need to suppose Firbank was snubbing Lord Alfred Douglas while keeping up social relations with his wife. All Firbank was keeping up was the ordinary upper-class convention whereby, for instance, invitations to husband and wife are sent in an envelope addressed to the wife. It was by following that convention that Firbank expressed his thanks to both Douglases after the first meeting by sending flowers to Lady Alfred Douglas.)

Hurried abroad at the time of the prosecution, the Wilde children, aged ten and nine respectively, were turned out of a Swiss hotel where they had been registered under their proper surname. Presently the children's clothes were re-marked with new name tapes and the children were set to practise writing their new signatures. (Holland was distantly a family name of their mother's.)

Vyvyan Holland afterwards recorded that he was told not only to leave the Oscar out of his name but to spell the Vyvyan Vivian 'as a further disguise' – in revulsion from which he in adult life insisted on Vyvyan. But in fact, although the son was indeed christened Vyvyan, Wilde himself, with a Firbankian and perhaps Irish negligence of detail (the verso of his sometimes Irishly pedantic scholarship), usually spelled his son's name Vivian. And the speakers in Wilde's Socratic dialogue *The Decay of Lying*, whom he must have named as a tribute to his children, are Cyril and Vivian.

(Some slapdashery by both Wildes characterised their relation to their second son. Perhaps it was through a vagueness of theirs that, after their deaths, no one survived who could tell Vyvyan Holland *why* he had been named Beresford. Certainly it was by what Lady Bracknell would have called carelessness that, by the time his mother registered his birth, neither parent could remember the exact date on which he was born. His birthday was registered as 3 November, that being the mean of the possible dates. As a result, Vyvyan Holland grew up with views different from his father's on a Firbankian topic: 'I am completely immune', he wrote in his autobiography, 'from the importunities of astrologers as, far from being able to tell them the exact hour of my birth, I cannot be certain of even the exact day.')

Vyvyan Holland went up to Trinity Hall through the simple association of events that when he was preparing to take Little-go he was put in the care of a recent graduate from Trinity Hall. A college of lawyers and hearties was not the obvious college for him, but he at once fitted himself to the college by agreeing to read law and taking up rowing.

For Firbank, on the other hand, Trinity Hall was an outrageous college. 'The choice of college was curious,' the *Memoir* remarks. The *Biography* adduces contemporary witnesses who wondered how Firbank's rooms escaped ragging by the hearties.[1] Vyvyan Holland, wrote, in his essay in the

---

[1] Forrest Reid (*Private Road*, p. 57) recorded that Firbank's rooms were ragged at least once. His evidence is not the best available. He wasn't in Firbank's college. Vyvyan Holland, who was, wrote, in his contribution to the *Memoir* (p. 107): 'strange as it may seem, his rooms were never "ragged" '. Forrest Reid also claimed to have seen Firbank, 'on a foggy November evening', being shaken by a drunken undergraduate in the street. Identifications in fog are suspect.

Memoir, 'I can imagine no college more inappropriate for Firbank than Trinity Hall at that period' and repeated the judgment in his autobiography: 'No college at the university, with the possible exception of Pembroke, could have been less suited to his character and temperament.'

In this wholly unlikely environment Firbank found the clou of his Wilde collection.

Perhaps it all happened by chance. Perhaps Firbank was directed towards his unsuitable college merely by the accident that his maternal great-grandfather, William Garrett, had (in the words of the *Biography*) 'matriculated at Trinity Hall'.

(The *Biography* gives some of the facts of William Garrett's career. But because it doesn't give the date of his matriculation it fails to remark the strangest of those facts: most of William Garrett's career took place *before* he went up to Cambridge. According to *Alumni Cantabrigienses*, he was born in 1783, and became 'Capt. 1st Carlow Yeomanry-Cavalry' in 1805, Sheriff of Carlow in 1806 and husband of Margaret Raymond in 1809. Not until 1818 was he 'adm. Fell.-Com.' at Trinity Hall. 'Fell.-Com.' I take to be for 'Fellow-Commoner', a term which the *Shorter Oxford English Dictionary* marks as practically obsolete and defines as a 'class of undergraduates in Oxford, Cambridge, and Dublin, who dine at the Fellows' table'. In William Garrett's case, to dine apart from his fellow-undergraduates might well have been a kindness to his age – which was, when he went up, 35-ish. A friend to whom I put the oddity of his case surmises that he decided in mid-career to become a clergyman. The guess seems all the more convincing because that was the profession of his son, Lady Firbank's father.)

Some time after mentioning William Garrett's matriculation, the *Biography* states that Lady Firbank 'had chosen Trinity Hall at Cambridge because her grandfather had matriculated there'. Evidence may exist in the family letters to support the 'because', but the *Biography* doesn't name it – or even any evidence that Lady Firbank *knew* that bit of her family history. What is said to be Lady Firbank's choice and its reason may be only the *Biography*'s knowledge of the family history and the *Biography*'s deduction from it.

Perhaps, therefore, it is Firbank's going to the same college as his great-grandfather which was coincidence, and his going to the same college as Vyvyan Holland which was deliberate.

4. ... Or Cunning?

FIRBANK could have gone to any college at Cambridge – or, indeed, at Oxford. In the event, he or his parents picked one of the least suitable that could be found in both universities put together – and that after the warning given by Firbank's failure at an unsuitable (though none would have been suitable) public school.

It isn't certain that Firbank knew there was a precedent in his mother's family for Trinity Hall. But, even if he did know, the family precedent might have needed backing up by a stronger attraction before Firbank let himself be inserted into a conspicuously unfavourable environment when more favourable ones were equally open.

Vyvyan Holland would certainly have been such a stronger attraction. In his fervour for Wilde, Firbank had already overcome both social danger and his own shyness in order to accost Lord Alfred Douglas. There is no doubt he would have willingly braved the heartiness of Trinity Hall in order to add Vyvyan Holland to his collection. The only doubt is whether he could have known that Vyvyan Holland was the prize to be had from doing so.

Nothing in Vyvyan Holland's contribution to the Firbank *Memoir* hints any method by which Firbank could have known. But then the *Memoir* essay, published in 1930 as by V. B. Holland, is written within the terms of Vyvyan Holland's incognito. All connexion with Wilde, and Wilde himself, go unmentioned. Vyvyan Holland describes introducing Firbank to Wilde's friend Robert Ross and trying, at Firbank's request, to introduce him to Wilde's friend Ada Leverson. But he neither mentions the conspicuously Wildean associations of those names nor offers any explanation of how he himself, Vyvyan Holland, as an apparently unconnected, virtually anonymous undergraduate, came to know such literary personages a generation older than himself.

When he recounts how, after they both came down (which they did in 1909), Firbank asked him to arrange a meeting with Ada Leverson, Vyvyan Holland's essay does make an allusion, obliquely, to Wilde. Ada Leverson was Wilde's 'Sphinx': quoting Wilde, Holland writes of her as 'the Gilded Sphinx of Golden Memory'. At the same time Holland makes it clear, as Firbank no doubt made it clear to *him*, that Firbank wanted to meet her for the sake of her literary associations.

However, the literary association Vyvyan Holland sketches in, with the implication that that was what Firbank was after, is a minor one. 'Anyone who had sat on the floor in the half-light of a studio party with Aubrey Beardsley', his essay says, 'would surely be able to give particulars of him which would not be within the knowledge of' Firbank's 'ordinary literary friends.' It is, of course, true that Firbank was an admirer and posthumously a disciple of Beardsley's; he no doubt did want to hear Ada Leverson's memories of Beardsley. But no ordinarily alert pursuer of literary history would seek out Ada Leverson primarily because she had known Beardsley. Firbank was certainly engaged primarily in his pursuit of Wilde and seeking out Ada Leverson because it was she who, with her husband, had given Wilde shelter while he was on bail between trials and because Wilde had nicknamed her after the sphinx image which obsessed his imagination and was adopted from Wilde's imagination by Firbank's.[1] Vyvyan Holland's essay displaced the centre of Firbank's interest in Ada Leverson: either because Firbank himself tactfully did so in asking Vyvyan Holland to arrange the meeting or as part of Vyvyan Holland's own habitual reticence about Wilde – or, most probably, for both causes.

The reticence has, of course, disappeared by the time (1954) of Vyvyan Holland's autobiography, which appeared not only with the author's first name spelt out in full and in, as he believed, its more Wildean form but under the explicit title *Son of Oscar Wilde*.

Vyvyan Holland was now giving an express account of the curious half-identity he had been obliged to bear. The autobiography fills in the previously silent part of his Cambridge experience: how at Cambridge he first came on some of his father's work, including *The Decay of Lying* with its use of his own and his brother's names ('I began to feel nervous lest someone should catch me reading the book and connect me with it in some way'); and how he ran into difficulties with his fellow undergraduates' curiosity about his parentage, since the answer that his father was an author led to questions about what his books were.

Those circumstances forced Vyvyan Holland to what he called 'a tissue of lies' in support of the incognito that was not of his own undertaking. He himself believed that he kept his identity secret from his fellow undergraduates until 1907, when he made a break, which was intended to be final but turned out to be temporary, in his Cambridge career. (Vyvyan Holland went up in 1905, Firbank in 1906.) 'It seems strange to me now', Vyvyan Holland wrote in *Son of Oscar Wilde*, 'that all the time I was at Stonyhurst and Cambridge my most intimate friends, such as Joshua Goodland, Gerald Seligman and Ronald Firbank, were quite unaware of my identity.'

By 'all the time I was at Cambridge', Vyvyan Holland in fact meant only

---

[1] The adoption will be discussed in Chapter XIII, 3-4 and 7-9.

the two years before the break of 1907, because he continues by saying that before he went down in 1907 he 'told one or two' of his friends who he was. Whether or not the one or two included Firbank he doesn't make clear. The only recipient of the information who is named is Joshua Goodland. But the inclusion of Firbank in the 'most intimate friends' (Vyvyan Holland was probably at that time, though for quite different reasons, as much a stranger to intimacy as Firbank was to remain all his life) suggests that Firbank may have been told. And there is another reason, which I'll mention in section 5 of this chapter, for being tolerably sure he was.

Before 1907 Vyvyan Holland had certainly not admitted his identity to Firbank. But that need not mean Firbank didn't know it. He would naturally conceal his knowledge, if he possessed it, from Vyvyan Holland until Vyvyan Holland had chosen to speak. Indeed, if the reason Holland implied for Firbank's wanting to meet Ada Leverson was the reason he was given by Firbank, Firbank went on being tactful even after Vyvyan Holland had spoken.

It is Vyvyan Holland's own autobiography which, without knowing it is doing so, suggests how Firbank might, unknown to Holland at the time and afterwards, have become aware who Holland was before Holland chose to tell him. It was during Vyvyan Holland's first year at Cambridge that he first encountered difficulties in keeping his identity from his fellow undergraduates. From the dons, however, he realised it was already too late to keep the secret. 'I suppose', his autobiography says when he describes his first year, 'all the dons were aware of my identity; the Master of my college must certainly have known. But although so many people were in the secret, I was not supposed to know that they knew, which put me into a cruelly awkward position.'

During the academic year through which Vyvyan Holland endured that cruel awkwardness at Cambridge, Firbank, newly returned from Spain, was being coached to get into Cambridge. By a typically Firbank educational passage, he first attended the London crammer's, Scoones', then moved to a tutor in Aberdeenshire, went on to another tutor, this time in Kent, and finally went back on his tracks by returning to the Aberdeenshire tutor.

All those tutors, it is safe to guess, maintained contact with the universities as a necessity to their job of getting pupils into the universities. Certainly, Firbank's Aberdeenshire tutor felt himself on good enough terms with one of the dons at Trinity Hall to write explaining that (as a result of a mistake by Firbank's Kent tutor, who had set him to work up the wrong gospel in Greek) Firbank would be unable to get through Little-go by the beginning of the academic year; and his recommendation that Firbank be allowed to go up and take the qualifying examination afterwards carried enough influence for the don to agree.

At the same time, Firbank was on terms close enough for gossip with his many crammers. In Aberdeenshire and in Kent he was a resident pupil. While he attended Scoones' in London, he lodged in the house of one of the tutors – and it was a house given to literary conversation. The *Memoir* quotes a letter to its owner which Firbank wrote long afterwards (putting one adverb into the English position and the other, by way of tribute to a French writer, in the French position[1]): 'Of course I have not forgotten, and very well I remember that it was at your house that I first heard of Dowson and read first Verlaine.'

Perhaps it was at the same house that Firbank first heard that Oscar Wilde's son was up at Trinity Hall and using the name Vyvyan Holland. The secret which Vyvyan Holland realised was common knowledge among the Trinity Hall dons would have an easy route to travel to one of Firbank's crammers, and thence to his pupils. If Firbank came to know of it, it would make a complete explanation at last of why he went up to a college whose unsuitability astounded his contemporaries, Vyvyan Holland ironically among them.

If Firbank's choosing Trinity Hall was indeed part of his pilgrimage of literary piety towards Oscar Wilde, it was another irony that met him when he arrived. For the cruellest of reasons, Oscar Wilde's son had not been brought up in a literary environment. It was Vyvyan Holland who sought out the just-arrived Firbank, and did so in a spirit of literary awe: because Firbank was said in college to be 'already a full-blown author with a published book to his credit'.

At their first meeting Firbank gave Vyvyan Holland a copy of his published book. In inscribing it he, with his usual negligence, mis-spelt[2] Vyvyan Holland's name.

5. A Birthday Dinner

A YEAR after Firbank's arrival, Vyvyan Holland began the interruption, as it turned out to be, in his Cambridge career. He came down from the university and went instead to Scoones', the London crammer where Firbank had been two years before him.

After a few days at Scoones', Vyvyan Holland became friends with one

---

[1] Cf. Chapter X, 11.
[2] Holland doesn't report whether or not the mis-spelling was on the point of the crucial Vyvyan–Vivian.

of his fellow pupils, Sir Coleridge Kennard. And, as Vyvyan Holland's autobiography relates, 'A week later he told me that he knew about me.' Vyvyan Holland was taken home to meet Kennard's mother, Helen Carew.

Sir Coleridge Kennard[1] had become a baronet in 1891 in unusual circumstances. His father[2] was already dead. The baronetcy was intended for his grandfather, Coleridge John Kennard, an M.P. for Salisbury – who, however, died (in 1890) after (in the words of *Debrett* for 1914) 'Her Majesty signified her intention of bestowing a Baronetcy' on him but 'before the patent was gazetted'. The solution was that, in 1891, his widow was (in the words of the same book) 'raised to the rank of a Baronet's widow' and (his son being dead) the baronetcy was 'conferred on his grandson'.

(It was by courtesy of the grandfather Kennard's yearning for a baronetcy that, in 1883, Frank Harris became editor of the *Evening News*. Kennard, a banker, financed the paper, but Harris got the job through Lord Folkestone, who was the effective boss because, Harris was informed, 'Kennard wants a baronetcy and Lord Folkestone can get it for him.' Harris found Kennard 'a fussy little person who seemed very anxious to keep the paper strictly Conservative'. He fussed indeed over the brashness of Harris's journalism. According to Harris, Kennard claimed to have spent £70,000 [presumably on publishing 'strictly Conservative' propaganda] towards his baronetcy, which he wanted not for himself but 'for my son'.[3] Kennard must have been a bad bargainer, since the promise was put off so long that it was eventually his grandson who took delivery.)

Sir Coleridge Kennard's widowed mother remarried[4] and became Helen Carew. She was an admirer of Oscar Wilde (my next sub-section will discuss

---

[1] Sir Coleridge Arthur FitzRoy Kennard, first baronet (of Fernhill). He was born in 1885 and went to Eton. *Debrett* for 1914 reports him a third Secretary, *Debrett* for 1945 a first Secretary, in the diplomatic service. He married in 1911 and was divorced in 1918. He re-married; his second wife died in 1931. Violet Wyndham (*The Sphinx and her Circle*, p. 94) adds the information that his friends called him Roy. I imagine that was for the FitzRoy in his name.

[2] Hugh Coleridge Downing Kennard, Lieutenant in the Grenadier Guards. He married in 1883 and died in 1886.

[3] Harris knew the son but (*My Life and Loves*, Volume 2, p. 209) says of him no more than *Debrett*: 'the son Hugh was in the Guards and soon afterwards got married'.

[4] in 1896. Her second husband was an Irish M.P., James Laurence Carew, Parnellite and Independent Nationalist. He died in 1903. It seems just possible that there was a connexion (which probably remained unknown to Firbank and Mrs Carew, since they did not meet until after his death) between his Irish family and Lady Firbank's. James Laurence Carew's maternal grandfather bore as first name Lady Firbank's maiden surname. (*Who Was Who* lists James Laurence Carew as son 'of [. . .] Laurence Carew [. . .] and Anne, o.d. of Garrett Robinson of Kilrainy, Co. Kildare'.) Perhaps his Irish nationalist politics were influential on his widow's tributes to Oscar Wilde.

the extent of her admiration) and had been a friend of his, though not, I surmise, a very close friend.[1]

However, she knew Wilde's close friends, including Robert Ross, who dedicated to her[2] the version of *De Profundis* he published in 1905.

Perhaps Helen Carew had learnt from the Wilde circle under what name Wilde's children were passing. Or perhaps her son recognised who Vyvyan Holland was because his identity was an open secret at Scoones', as it had been among the dons at Trinity Hall (in which case there is an extra probability that Firbank had earlier acquired the same information when *he* was at Scoones').

Mrs Carew passed on to Vyvyan Holland Robert Ross's wish to meet him and his brother; and Vyvyan Holland met Ross, together with Wilde's other close friend, Reginald Turner, at her house.

Three months later, while Vyvyan Holland was still at Scoones', Robert Ross gave a dinner for Vyvyan Holland's 21st birthday – which fell on that suppositional[3] day of November, in 1907.

The twelve people at that dinner were: Wilde's two sons; Sir Coleridge Kennard; Henry James (who had supported Wilde's joining the Savile Club); Sir William Richmond, R.A. (of whom Wilde had written in 1888 'I am dining with Willie Richmond at Hammersmith on Saturday'); Charles Ricketts and Charles Shannon[4] (who severally or jointly designed, wholly or in part, a total between them of ten of Wilde's books); William Rothenstein (from whom Wilde commissioned a drawing of Lord Alfred Douglas); Wilde's close friends Robert Ross, Reginald Turner[5] and (who fetched Wilde by cab from Pentonville Prison) More Adey; – and Firbank.

---

[1] She possessed and shewed Vyvyan Holland copies of Wilde's books inscribed to her. It was the first time Vyvyan Holland knowingly saw his father's hand-writing (*Son of Oscar Wilde*, Penguin, p. 163). However, neither as Helen Wyllie (*Debrett* lists her as the only daughter of James Wyllie [of, magnificently, Hove and Antibes]) nor as Mrs Kennard (in the strange circumstances of her son's baroneting, she was presumably never Lady Kennard, though her mother-in-law was) nor as Mrs Carew is she indexed in the Wilde *Letters* or in the *Life* by Hesketh Pearson.

[2] Ross dedicated his 1909 monograph on Beardsley to her son.

[3] Cf. sub-section 3 of this chapter.

[4] Charles Shannon made a pastel portrait of Firbank which is reproduced in Ifan Kyrle Fletcher's *Memoir*. Firbank's list (cf. Chapter IX, 5, footnote) of recipients for *Inclinations* includes 'Charles Shannon Esqre' (Firbank probably made a point of using the 18th-century form of the abbreviation rather than the shorter 20th-century 'Esq') as well as one of his other portraitists, Augustus John (cf. Chapters VI, 2 and VII, 1), Lady Alfred Douglas (cf. footnote to sub-section 3 of this chapter), 'Sir Coleridge Kennard Bart', Mrs Annesley Garrett (cf. Chapter VII, 4, footnote), E. J. Dent (cf. Chapter V, 6) and R. St C. Talboys (who will be mentioned again in Chapter XIII, 5).

[5] According to the *Biography* (p. 96) Reginald Turner took a dislike to Firbank even before Firbank finally alienated him with lilies in Florence (cf. Chapter VII, 5).

It is impossible that Firbank could have been invited to so intensely Wildean a gathering, in which Vyvyan Holland's identity was not merely no secret but the whole point, unless Firbank, too, knew – and was known by Vyvyan Holland to know – the secret.

That is why I think Firbank probably was among the Cambridge friends whom Vyvyan Holland spoke to openly before he went down in June 1907. But, even if Holland didn't speak that June, he had spoken before his birthday dinner in the November.

6. The Collection Expands

LUCK or calculation took Firbank to Vyvyan Holland. The next expansion in Firbank's Wilde collection – indeed, its ultimate completion – arrived certainly by luck; the luck whereby Vyvyan Holland, instead of staying isolated at Cambridge, went to Scoones'. As a result of that move, Vyvyan Holland himself came for the first time into contact with Wilde's friends. And Firbank, having already acquired Vyvyan Holland, was able through Holland to add the whole Wilde milieu to his collection.

Evidently Vyvyan Holland introduced Sir Coleridge Kennard to Firbank[1] even before the two met at the dinner for the 21st birthday. For Kennard recorded, as the occasion of his first meeting with Firbank, not that dinner in London but a visit by car to Cambridge, which Kennard made with Vyvyan Holland (and, 'for some reason', Kennard added, 'an old family butler' of Kennard's). Kennard was so enchanted by Firbank's conversation that he drove into a pond on the way back.

Firbank seems to have been enchanted in return. A story[2] he never published, *A Tragedy in Green*, bears the dedication 'To the Inspirer of the Tragedy, Sir Coleridge Kennard'.

In 1921 Firbank dedicated *Santal* to Kennard's mother, Helen Carew.[3]

[1] The *Biography* (p. 90) is vague about when Firbank and Kennard met and wrong about what Kennard was doing at the time. 'When Firbank first knew him', it says, 'Kennard was either at Scoones's in final preparation for taking his diplomatic examination or recently assigned to the Foreign Office.' In fact, Kennard was quite certainly not yet assigned to the Foreign Office. Vyvyan Holland's autobiography (Penguin edition, pp. 162–70) makes the sequence of events clear. Holland met Kennard in or soon after July 1907, when they were both at Scoones'. Firbank had certainly met Kennard by November 1907, when they were both at the dinner for Holland's 21st birthday. It was not until the summer of 1908 that Kennard took the examination for the diplomatic service.

[2] Cf. Chapter X, 2.

[3] The *Bibliography* mis-spells her Carewe, though the *Biography* gets her right. *Santal* is dedicated to her under her first name, which appears in Greek. (The first edition of *Santal* and the *Bibliography*, p. 34, in reporting it, get the Greek right, but the United-States edition of the *Biography*, p. 203, renders it as nonsense. The *Complete* Firbank

Firbank thereby added another figure to his Wildean pattern, by coming to share a dedicatee with Wilde. Wilde's dedication to Mrs Carew was, however, given posthumously, by Robert Ross acting, as it were, on Wilde's behalf – just as Helen Carew's service to Wilde was performed posthumously.

For it was Mrs Carew who anonymously gave[1] £2,000 to buy the site at Père Lachaise to which Wilde's body was moved in 1909 and to commission its surmounting sculpture from Jacob Epstein. She was scared of Firbank's scarab,[2] but on Wilde's tomb she placed that other Egyptian emblem, which brooded over both Wilde's imagery and Firbank's, the sphinx.

(I think it likely that Firbank honoured his scarab and Mrs Carew dreaded it or its significance for Firbank because they both knew from oral tradition a fact later recorded[3] by Ada Leverson: at the first night, 14 February 1895, of *The Importance of Being Earnest* Oscar Wilde, besides wearing in his buttonhole a green carnation,[4] wore on one of his fingers 'a large scarab ring.'[5])

Firbank added a minor, perfectionist touch to his Wilde collection when, round about 1920, he made the acquaintance of the sculptor of the hero's tomb. He even contemplated adding another skein to his bondage to Wilde by way of a plan, which remained frustrated, to have Epstein sculpt his portrait.

After he made his major haul of Wilde associates at Robert Ross's celebration in 1907 for Vyvyan Holland, Firbank was again backed by luck. Remaining at Cambridge while Vyvyan Holland was at Scoones', he might have lost touch with Vyvyan Holland and thus forfeited the means to add to his collection. However, Vyvyan Holland decided to abandon Scoones'.

---

lists Firbank's dedications at the back but leaves out the dedication of *Santal*, as well as part of the dedication of *Caprice*). Both the *Bibliography* and the *Biography* record that Mrs Carew wrote out the Greek form of 'Helen' for Firbank to use in his dedication. However, even though he prepared the wrong gospel for Little-go, Firbank was not in need of instruction in Greek script. (Witness, as Chapters XVIII, 3 and XX, 21 will insist, the texts of *Vainglory* and *Prancing Nigger*, as well as the dedication of *Caprice*.) But perhaps Mrs Carew mistrusted his spelling in any alphabet.

[1] Violet Wyndham records (*The Sphinx and her Circle*, p. 74) that Robert Ross announced the anonymous gift in December 1908. Later in the same book (p. 88) she names Mrs Carew as the donor and speaks of her as 'helped financially' in the enterprise by Sydney Schiff (Stephen Hudson), who was married to Ada Leverson's sister Violet.

[2] Cf. Chapter VIII, 5.

[3] in her essays on Wilde, reprinted in Violet Wyndham's *The Sphinx and her Circle* (p. 114).

[4] whose significance to Firbank will be discussed in Chapters XIV, 10–11 and XVI, 6.

[5] Perhaps (but this is mere guesswork) Wilde acquired it during the visit he and Lord Alfred Douglas made to North Africa in January 1895 while *The Importance . . .* was in rehearsal (Hesketh Pearson's *The Life of Oscar Wilde*, pp. 278–9).

He made a trip to North America and another (in the company of Sir Coleridge Kennard) to Venice, where he dropped his disguise and called himself Vyvyan Wilde until journalists drove him back into his pseudonym. On their way home Vyvyan Holland and Kennard stopped at Paris. Mrs Carew came out to meet them and shewed Vyvyan Holland the house where his father died and the Bagneux graveyard (whence she had not yet shifted Wilde's body to Père Lachaise). And then, after his return to England, Vyvyan Holland decided (in order to silence rumours that he had been sent down) to return to Cambridge.

Accordingly, Firbank and Vyvyan Holland passed their last year at Cambridge (1908 to 1909) in unison. It was in their last term that they gave in partnership the dinner to which Firbank contributed his father's sadly too old Moët.[1]

(In his contribution to the *Memoir* Vyvyan Holland named the Cambridge dinner of 1909 as the first time Robert Ross met Firbank. That, however, was a result of his writing in disguise, which obliged him to conceal the cause and closeness of his own acquaintance with Robert Ross; Vyvyan Holland was suppressing the occasion where Firbank did first meet Ross, namely Ross's 1907 dinner party for Vyvyan Holland, because Ross's celebration of his birthday placed Ross too detectably in loco parentis to Vyvyan Holland. But even in the account in the *Memoir* the suppression slips for a moment. In the paragraph before he says Ross and Firbank first met at Cambridge, Vyvyan Holland wrote 'Robert Ross came up to Cambridge to see me and Firbank' – which, though it could, just, be differently construed, would most easily imply that Ross already knew Firbank, as indeed Vyvyan Holland's autobiography later recorded he did.)

Because of the gap in Vyvyan Holland's Cambridge career, he and Firbank came down together (in 1909) although Vyvyan Holland had gone up the earlier by a year. It was after they both came down that Firbank made his attempt (which I mentioned in sub-section 4 of this chapter) to add Wilde's Sphinx to his collection. Vyvyan Holland had already met and made friends with Ada Leverson at the time when Robert Ross and Helen Carew were introducing him to his father's friends. Vyvyan Holland now (probably about 1912[2]) got Ada Leverson's permission to bring Firbank to call on her one Sunday afternoon at four. He lunched with Firbank at Curzon Street and then the two drove in a hansom cab to Mrs Leverson's house, 12 Radnor Street.

Firbank was dressed, according to Vyvyan Holland's essay in the *Memoir*, in 'a silk hat of Parisian proportions and the most remarkable pair of trousers

---

[1] Cf. Chapter IX, 3.   [2] See the note in section 7 of this chapter.

7 and 8 Ronald Firbank's rooms in Trinity Hall, Cambridge, 1907

9 Page from a Firbank notebook (from the notebook in the Henry W. and Albert A. Berg Collection, the New York Public Library)

10 Mrs Patrick Campbell and Sarah Bernhardt in *Pelléas et Mélisande* in 1904

11 Ronald Firbank, Chamonix, 1904
'... she murmured helplessly, as though clinging to an alpenstock, and not quite sure of her guide. Below her, so to speak, were the rooftops, pots and pans: Chamonix twinkling in the snow.' (*Vainglory*)

12 C. R. W. Nevinson's illustration to *The Flower Beneath the Foot* (1923) '... Etoile de Nazianzi'

13 The villa in Arcachon (Gironde) where Firbank spent the autumn of 1925 (photographed in 1971)

then in existence'. Vyvyan Holland remembered the trousers as 'mauve in *motif*, with black lines of varying thickness running down them'. The guests rang Mrs Leverson's doorbell; presently they were told by a servant that Mrs Leverson was not at home. Firbank, who at the time left Vyvyan Holland without speaking, later told him that he was convinced Mrs Leverson had looked out of the window and been frightened by his trousers – and that he had spent the rest of the afternoon cutting up the trousers and feeding them to his bedroom fire.

It was an episode that impressed Firbank's fiction.[1] Indirectly, his failure to make Mrs Leverson's acquaintance was remedied after the publication of *Vainglory* in 1915. Mrs Leverson gave her comment ('too Meredithian') to the book's 'publisher', Grant Richards, who passed it on to Firbank. In the next year there was another utterance by the Sphinx: on *Inclinations*. Eventually Firbank met Ada Leverson by accident. It was on one of his trips into Florence, when he was living in Fiesole in 1922. She was with the Sitwells, of whom she had become a close friend, and they introduced Firbank to her. Thereafter, as Ada Leverson's daughter, Violet Wyndham, records, Firbank ('generally bearing a large bouquet') used to call on her at her Florentine hotel and kept up the habit in London.

Perhaps it was for the sake of the indirect link with Wilde's friend William Rothenstein (whom Firbank had met at the dinner for Vyvyan Holland's 21st birthday) that Firbank agreed to Grant Richards's proposal that Albert Rothenstein be asked to illustrate *Inclinations* (1916). If it was indeed a Wildean tone he was after, it is not strange that Firbank was put out by the result. His collector's luck, faltering, had hit on an unpropitious moment: the middle of a war during which English anti-German fury prompted the change of many German-derived names, including (in 1917) the surname of the English royal family. Albert Rothenstein decided to change his surname to Rutherston, thereby hiding the publicly obvious connexion with his brother along with what was no doubt the secret charm for Firbank, the indirect connexion with Wilde. Author and illustrator wrangled through the 'publisher', Albert Rutherston holding out for the new, and Firbank for the old version of his name. In the end Grant Richards arranged a compromise not unlike the compromise which Firbank negotiated with himself over his own change of public name at the publication of *Vainglory*.[2] For *Inclinations*, 'Albert Rutherston' appeared as illustrator on the jacket and 'Albert Rutherston (Rothenstein)' on the title-page.[3]

---

[1] I will describe how in Chapter XIII, 8.
[2] Cf. Chapter VII, 4.
[3] The attraction of the Wildean link may have been reinforced, for Firbank, by a link

It was conceivably his Wilde quest that brought about a more largely effective contretemps in Firbank's life: his meeting, whenever that happened,[1] with Edward Marsh. Marsh was probably on Firbank's list of quarries – because (as Firbank very likely knew from acquaintance in common at Cambridge) he owned a letter from Wilde. The letter was not to Marsh, but it mentioned him, adumbrating a meeting that never in fact took place. Wilde wrote it in 1892 to a Cambridge undergraduate who was up with, and friends with, Marsh. Its recipient gave it to Marsh as a souvenir. Wilde had written: 'Come and see me when term is over, and bring your friend Edward Marsh, who has a charming name – for fiction.'[2]

Apart from Albert Rutherston, whose connexion with Wilde was at one remove, and Ada Leverson, whose acquaintance he didn't manage to make on his own initiative, Firbank added what was probably the final flesh-and-blood item to his Wilde collection in 1914. Firbank was in Italy when the war began but managed to get home by way of Paris. Before he settled on Oxford as his place of war-time retreat, Firbank stayed or lived in various parts of Great Britain, including[3] York (his souvenir of which will be mentioned in Chapter XV, 19) and Edinburgh. By Christmas 1914 he had rented a flat in Lincoln's Inn, whence he made journeys to Stratford-on-Avon and to Pangbourne in Berkshire (a neighbourhood in which he could contemplate the Wildean names Goring and, though Wilde altered the spelling, Chieveley); but he was living at Lincoln's Inn when it was bombed in the autumn of 1915 – the upset which drove him finally to Oxford.

It was during his 1914 stay at Edinburgh that Firbank visited John Gray. In 1893 Wilde had paid for the publication, by Mathews and Lane (half of whom Firbank acquired for his collection in 1905), of John Gray's volume of poems *Silverpoints*, which was illustrated by Charles Ricketts (whom Firbank acquired at the dinner for Vyvyan Holland in 1907). Gray had taken orders in the Catholic church and settled in Edinburgh, where a church was built specially for him by his patron and sometime literary

---

with one of his minor devotions: to (as I will discuss in Chapters XV, 6 and XIX, 18) the 1912 production by Granville Barker of *The Winter's Tale*. The costumes in that production were designed by Albert Rothenstein. (They are illustrated in *The Listener* of 13 January 1972, which prints a radio interview with the production's Perdita, Cathleen Nesbitt. (The designer is anachronistically referred to as Rutherston.)

[1] Cf. Chapter VI, 6.

[2] Wilde made quite a habit of charming his correspondents by versions of this remark. In 1889 he had written, to an Aubrey Richardson: 'What a pretty name you have! it is worthy of fiction. Would you mind if I wrote a book called *The Story of Aubrey Richardson*? I won't, but I should like to.' (*The Letters of Oscar Wilde*, edited by Rupert Hart-Davis, p. 252).

[3] Chapter XIX, 9 will be more specific about his itinerary.

collaborator, (Marc) André Raffalovich, the rich Anglo-Franco-Russian who, by material wealth and emotional blackmail, had in 1897 procured the conversion to Catholicism of a dying, terrified pauper, Aubrey Beardsley.

Firbank's biographer, in recording (from his letters) that while he was in Edinburgh Firbank visited Father Gray 'once at least', makes brief mention of Gray's associations with Wilde and Beardsley but remarks 'Apparently none of this meant a thing to Firbank; he commented on Gray only as the "nicest" of priests.' The comment is quoted from one of Firbank's letters to his mother. It is scarcely likely that Firbank would have reported to his mother that, in meeting Gray, he had completed his collection of living mementoes of the saint and martyr of homosexuality.

As a matter of fact, Firbank made further comments on Gray. But to find them it is necessary to read Firbank's books.

One of the inventions in *Vainglory* probably contains, besides an allusion to the Empress Eugénie's benefaction at Chislehurst,[1] an allusion (aptly transmuted into camp terms) to Raffalovich's grand gesture at Edinburgh: Mrs Henedge, newly converted to Catholicism, sets Ashringford by the ears when she builds a sumptuous Catholic church there specially for her tame Monsignor Parr (who, gossip, reports, 'has been hurrying to and fro all the morning, like St. Benedict at Monte Cassino').

Into his next novel, *Inclinations*, Firbank put Father Gray whole: in his proper location and disguised by no more than a change of colour in his surname. Mabel Collins, while she is in Athens, receives a letter from her mother, who is on a visit to Edinburgh (on the grounds that she is unlikely to emulate her daughter by seeing Athens itself, so she had better see 'the modern Athens'). From Edinburgh she writes: 'on Sunday we all went together to hear Father Brown. He spoke to us so simply, so eloquently, so touchingly [. . .] He reminds me just a little of St. Anthony of Padua. . . .'

7. Notes to Chapter XII

THE quotation from Firbank's 1905 letter to Robson & Co., booksellers, is published in the *Biography*, p. 68.

Firbank's possession of the large-paper Wilde is cited (in a quotation from F. J. A. Sanders) in the *Biography*, p. 144.

The inscribed large-paper . . . *Dorian Gray* is mentioned on p. 281 of Rupert Hart-Davis's edition of *The Letters of Oscar Wilde*. Wilde's letter (of 1900, to George Ives) about always beginning with the cover is on p. 816 of that edition. Wilde

---

[1] Cf. Chapter X, 9.

lectured on house decoration in the U.S.A. in 1882 and on dress in England in 1884 (*Letters*, p. 85 and p. 161). His letter about the *Salome* cover is on p. 348 of Rupert Hart-Davis's edition.

Firbank's *Vainglory* specifications are described in the *Bibliography*, pp. 18–19.

Wilde's literary relationship with Mathews and Lane, jointly and severally, is recounted in Rupert Hart-Davis's edition of the Wilde *Letters*, p. 312, p. 318 and pp. 365–8.

Beardsley's report of the publishers' split is on p. 75 in the 1971 edition of his *Letters*.

The terms of Firbank's agreement with Elkin Mathews are unknown but according to his bibliographer (p. 16) Firbank 'without doubt' financed the publication himself. The *Bibliography* records on p. 46 his proposal to return to Elkin Mathews.

Oscar Wilde's 1891 letter to William Heinemann about the publication of *Intentions* is on p. 294 of his *Letters*, edited by Rupert Hart-Davis.

Oscar Wilde's letter mentioning Grant Richards is on p. 746 of Rupert Hart-Davis's edition of the *Letters*.

The details of Firbank's acquaintance with Lord Alfred Douglas are in Chapters V–VII of the *Biography*. The *Biography*'s text throughout names Douglas's Cambridge opponent as Ragland Somerset, though in a footnote he appears as Raglan. As Somerset is the family name of the Lords Raglan, there seems a prima facie chance that the footnote is right and the text wrong. Firbank's letter to him is published on p. 101 of the *Biography*.

The information and the quotation about the childhood of Wilde's sons are from Vyvyan Holland's *Son of Oscar Wilde* (Penguin, p. 62, p. 65, pp. 30–1 and pp. 153–4).

That Vyvyan Holland's parents usually spelled his name Vivian is recorded in Rupert Hart-Davis's edition of *The Letters of Oscar Wilde*, p. 211.

Oscar Wilde's *The Decay of Lying* was published in *The Nineteenth Century* in 1889 and included in Wilde's volume *Intentions* of 1891.

Ifan Kyrle Fletcher's remark about the choice of Firbank's college is on p. 27 of the *Memoir*. The *Biography* discusses the matter on pp. 82–3. Vyvyan Holland's two remarks about it are in the *Memoir*, p. 107 and *Son of Oscar Wilde* (Penguin, p. 159).

The *Biography*'s references to William Garrett's matriculation are on p. 9 and p. 73.

William Garrett is recorded in Part II, Volume III, of *Alumni Cantabrigienses*.

Vyvyan Holland's 1930 account of Firbank's wish to meet Ada Leverson is in the *Memoir*, pp. 109–10. The quotations about Vyvyan Holland's incognito at Cambridge are from his *Son of Oscar Wilde* (Penguin, pp. 157–8 and p. 161).

The *Memoir* (p. 25) names the tutor Firbank stayed with while he attended Scoones' as Mr de V. Payen-Payne of 49 Nevern Square. It quotes Firbank's letter to him on the same page. The names and addresses of Firbank's other crammers are given, and the letter one of them wrote to Trinity Hall is quoted, in the *Biography*, pp. 76–8.

Vyvyan Holland's account of his first meeting with Firbank is in his contribution to the *Memoir* (p. 101). He described meeting Kennard, Helen Carew and Robert Ross, and the dinner for his 21st birthday, in *Son of Oscar Wilde* (Penguin, pp. 162–6).

Frank Harris's references to Coleridge Kennard are on pp. 108, 110 and 209 of *My Life and Loves*, Volume 2; he dates his editorship of *The Evening News* in Volume 3, p. 67.

The Wilde quotation about William Richmond is from p. 232 of Wilde's *Letters*, edited by Rupert Hart-Davis.

Sir Coleridge Kennard described his first meeting with Firbank in his Introduction to *The Artificial Princess*, 1934.

The reburial of Oscar Wilde is recorded in Hesketh Pearson's *Life*, p. 377, and Mrs Carew's expense in Vyvyan Holland's *Son of Oscar Wilde* (Penguin, p. 163).

Firbank's acquaintance with and desire to be sculpted by Jacob Epstein are mentioned in the *Biography*, p. 180.

Vyvyan Holland's journeys and his return to Cambridge are described in his *Son of Oscar Wilde* (Penguin, pp. 167–71). The quotation from his *Memoir* contribution about Robert Ross's Cambridge visit is from p. 108. He described his friendship with Ada Leverson in *Son of Oscar Wilde* (Penguin, p. 165).

Vyvyan Holland's account (*Memoir*, pp. 109–10) of his attempt to introduce Firbank to Ada Leverson implies that it took place a matter of months, though quite a large number of months, after he and Firbank came down (which was in the summer of 1909): 'Shortly after this' (sc. the Moët dinner for Robert Ross's visit to Cambridge) 'we both left Cambridge, and I lost sight of Firbank for some months, until one day he came to see me and asked if I could arrange for him to meet Ada Leverson.' However, Vyvyan Holland said that before the attempted meeting he 'lunched with Firbank at his house' and then drove with him by cab 'from Curzon Street to Radnor Street'. According to the *Biography* (p. 111), Firbank, after returning to London from Paris in summer 1912, lived with his mother 'briefly at 102 Queen's Gate and then at 33 Curzon Street'. If both the *Biography*'s account of Firbank's residences and Vyvyan Holland's memory of where he lunched are correct, the attempt on Ada Leverson cannot have been made before the autumn of 1912. But it is possible that Vyvyan Holland's memory had confused that luncheon chez Firbank with a later one truly at Curzon Street. (Ada Leverson's address is no help. The memoir by her daughter, Violet Wyndham, makes it clear that she lived in Radnor Street from early in the 1900s until after the 1914–18 war.)

Ada Leverson's comments on Firbank's books are quoted, from letters of Grant Richards to Firbank, in the *Biography*, p. 143 and p. 148. The *Biography* records the first Florence meeting on pp. 215–16. Subsequent meetings in Florence and in London (where, by that time, Mrs Leverson was living in an hotel in Curzon

Street) are mentioned on pp. 87 and 100 of Violet Wyndham's *The Sphinx and her Circle* (which does not, however, mention the introduction or the abortive meeting when Firbank wore mauve trousers). The same book records (pp. 84–8) the close friendship which developed after 1918 between Ada Leverson and the Sitwells.

The Rutherston/Rothenstein problem and solution are described in the *Bibliography*, pp. 22–3. The change of royal name to Windsor (from what is less certain) is chronicled in Harold Nicolson's *King George the Fifth*, p. 309.

Wilde's letter mentioning Edward Marsh was to Oswald Sickert, the painter's brother. It is on p. 314 of Rupert Hart-Davis's edition of the *Letters*. That Marsh never did meet Wilde but owned the letter is recorded in Christopher Hassall's *Edward Marsh*, p. 31.

Firbank's journeys in 1914–15 are recounted in the *Biography*, pp. 130–2 and 143–4. The *Memoir* (p. 51) adds Bath to his 1914 itinerary and supposes that he had just visited Bath with his mother and was living in Old Square, Lincoln's Inn, when the war began.

The *Biography*'s comment on Firbank's visit to John Gray is on pp. 131–2. Monsignor Parr's resemblance to Saint Benedict is on p. 137 in the *Complete Firbank*, and John Gray appears as Brown on p. 248.

XIII

The Crisis in the Wilde Collection

1. 'The Infamous St Oscar of Oxford, Poet and Martyr'

ACCIDENT gave it to Firbank to share Wilde's Irishness, and accident or perhaps Irishness gave it him to share Wilde's superstition.[1]

(If he didn't take warning from the small results of his own lucky publication days, Firbank might still have heeded the discrepancy between his hero's disaster and the soothsayings of Mrs Robinson, the Sibyl of Mortimer Street. 'Why did the Sibyl speak fair words?' Wilde wrote miserably from Holloway Prison while he awaited trial.)

Firbank also by nature shared with Wilde a devotional and cultist temperament. It was that temperament which directed both men to Catholicism – though Wilde, who had less of it, didn't arrive there until the latest possible moment – and which directed Firbank, who had more of it, to enlarge his natural sharings with Wilde by deliberate adoptions, as well as by some of which he was probably hardly aware, such as his adoption of Wilde's thick lips into his own Negroism.[2]

Indeed, besides sharing with Wilde the fact of conversion to Catholicism, Firbank contrived to make his own conversion one of his links, though a far-extended one, with Wilde. Hugh Benson, by whom Firbank chose to be received into the Catholic church, was, though remotely, an item in Firbank's Wilde collection, inasmuch as his brother, E. F. (Dodo) Benson was a friend of Lord Alfred Douglas's.[3]

Firbank *imitated* Wilde neither in life nor in literature. What he did was practise a literary equivalent of a practice belonging to the faith they were

[1] Cf. Chapter VIII, 5.   [2] Cf. Chapter IX, 11.
[3] It was in the Firbankianly significant setting of Egypt, at Luxor, that Robert Hichens (as he recorded in his Introduction to the 1949 reissue of his first novel) turned a previous acquaintanceship with Douglas into friendship and, through Douglas, met and became friends with E. F. Benson. Benson's success with *Dodo* inspired Hichens to ambition; Douglas's friendship introduced him (later, in England) to Oscar Wilde: the result, in 1894, was *The Green Carnation* (a book whose significance to Firbank will be mentioned in Chapters XIV, 11 and XVI, 6).

both converts to: the cult of the saints. That itself was one of his borrowings from Wilde. For Wilde, besides canonising Robert Ross (as Saint Robert of Phillimore[1]) in a pretty fable, satirically canonised himself: as 'the Infamous St Oscar of Oxford, Poet and Martyr'.

Prison, which debilitated his toughness of mind, reduced Oscar Wilde to the imitation of Christ. Before prison, he generally (though not wholly) kept his Christian idiom for his sentimental fables. Classical scholar and public didactic personality, he cast essays in the mould of Plato's Socratic dialogues and his own life in the heroic pattern laid down by Socrates. He stayed to stand trial and sentence, when he might have escaped, on the model of Socrates – and came to believe he had done it on the model of Christ.

Firbank, by contrast, was mentally convent-bred from the start. His cult of Wilde consisted always of invoking the saintly presence to his imagination. His methods included his collection of relics and witnesses, and his attempt to live his own career and his own imaginative life through forms sanctified by Wilde's observance of them – his adoption of, for instance, Wilde's publishing habits and concerns, one of Wilde's publishers and Wilde's cult of that comic, secular madonna, Queen Victoria.

Firbank's writings are studded with images from Wilde's: frequent wayside shrines, at which Firbank's genuflections in passing continually placed him again under the protection of his literary patron saint.

Firbank summed up his own art in the title and text of his most underestimated book, *Santal*. The summing-up is executed in the imagery not of Firbank's own religion but of Mohammedanism: Firbank's cultist art and temperament are more elemental than his cults Catholic and of Oscar Wilde. His sad Mohammedan hero sets out on his (possibly pointless) pilgrimage equipped with 'a few loose sticks of Santal to burn at passing shrines'.

2. A Hagiographical Imagination

BECAUSE his is a cultist temperament, Firbank's fantasy often and fluently takes a hagiographical turn. The very texture of his books is cultist in that it contemplates images isolated into holiness; and his great modern invention, the Firbankian novel, has abstracted part of its pattern from hagiography.

Indeed, given that all Firbank's writing is a contemplation of images, the

---

[1] – because he lived at 11 Upper Phillimore Gardens in Kensington. But by the time he gave the dinner for Vyvyan Holland's birthday he was sharing a house with More Adey at 15 Vicarage Gardens. (*The Letters of Oscar Wilde*, edited by Rupert Hart-Davis, p. 513; Vyvyan Holland: *Son of Oscar Wilde*, Penguin, p. 166).

image of contemplating an image is inevitably one of the most condensed and multi-significant of the images his books contemplate.

The dynamic images which set Firbank's fictional patterns moving are sometimes artistic (the Sappho fragment in *Vainglory*), sometimes saintly: and sometimes both. The London section of *Vainglory* spins round the Sappho fragment; and that, when the book shifts to a pastoral setting, has a saintly counterpart: a series of worn (fragmented) tapestries depicting the life story of Mrs Cresswell, an anchoress who is the local approximation, in Firbank's cathedral-city of Ashringford, to the 14th-century anchoress Julian (of the cathedral-city of Norwich).[1]

Mrs Cresswell, though locally much revered, cited and quoted, is not officially a saint. There are touches of heresy in her writings and of unorthodoxy in her life. This anomalous streak in her saintliness Firbank beautifully epitomised in her name. To outward view she is all modelled on the blameless and medieval Julian; but her name is appropriated from Madam Cresswell, a 'notorious bawd and procuress' (in the words of Brewer's *Dictionary of Phrase and Fable*) of 17th-century London.

Even the pre-Firbankian *Odette D'Antrevernes* sets off from Odette's attempt to make by prayer an appointment to have a vision of the Madonna. *The Artificial Princess* proceeds from the Princess's attempt to complete the Salome pattern by meeting the supposed saintly prophet. In *Santal* the prophet-saint is (though still once called a saint by the narrative) translated into the mental furniture of Mohammedanism.

In *Vainglory* the springs of the pattern are three, and two-thirds saintly: the Sappho fragment; Mrs Shamefoot's quasi-saintly aspirations to commemorative stained glass; and the memory, present and influential over Ashringford, of Mrs Cresswell, that nearly but not quite canonised saint of whom Miss Valley plans to write a biography which must be, like a Firbankian novel, nearly a hagiography.

The dramatis personae of Firbank's quasi-hagiographies naturally read hagiographies and contemplate (quasi-, Firbankian) saints. The Baroness

---

[1] Julian is perhaps slightly fused in Firbank's mind with her friend Margery Kempe. At what period Firbank conceived his Mrs Cresswell to have lived can be roughly inferred from the fact that Ashringford tries to look, to the eyes of Americans staying at the Cresswell Arms, as if it were still at 'the threshold of the thirteenth century'. Firbank, who (cf. Chapter X, 12) considered 1533 'lost amidst the shadows of the Middle Ages', may well have considered 1343–1413, which is the life-span of Julian, 'the threshold of the thirteenth century'. Margery Kempe is the author of an autobiography, Julian the author of *XVI Revelations of Divine Love* which was first printed, according to the D.N.B., in 1670. Firbank's Mrs Cresswell is the author of *The Red Rose of Martyrdom* and of an autobiography of which Mrs Shamefoot has a copy in the 1540 edition. (*Complete* Firbank, p. 123 [anchoress], p. 173 [the Cresswell Arms], p. 143 [Mrs Cresswell's books].)

Rudlieb (in *The Artificial Princess*) consults 'a pet Saint (a neglected long-shelved creature, one of her own discoveries: St. Aurora Vauvilliers)'.

As early as *The Artificial Princess*, the hagiographical content of Firbank's fiction is infecting the form. The story, itself about a saint, has to make room for the inclusion of a hagiography-within-the-story, 'the adventurous history' of the Baroness's private saint, who, after being captured by pirates and escaping 'on a loose board disguised as a man', returned to France and 'whilst on a round of visits to the Châteaux in Touraine,[1] had expired quite beautifully, one All Hallows Eve, at the Castle of Loches'.

This excellent picaresque excursion might be an episode-within-*Daphnis and Chloe*. Directly, however, it is probably inspired by the hagiography of Saint Rose of Lima which is narrated in a paragraph of Chapter VII, and illustrated by a masterpiece, in Aubrey Beardsley's novel *Under the Hill*. By 1923 the hagiographical form of Firbank's excursion had taken over the entire Firbankian novel. The full title of *The Flower Beneath the Foot* continues: *Being a Record of the Early Life of St. Laura de Nazianzi and the Times in which she Lived*.

Before it devised those Firbankian motifs and forms through which to express and define its own nature, Firbank's hagiographical impulse directed his writing into forms made sacred by his saint Oscar Wilde. *Odette D'Antrevernes*, in Firbank's first volume, is sub-titled[2] *A Fairy Tale for Weary People*: in evident tribute to Wilde's fairy tales. *Impression d'Automne*, which was published (as *Souvenir d'Automne*) in a magazine in the same year (1905), was sub-titled *A Poem in Prose* – after the Poems in Prose which Oscar Wilde had published in a magazine in 1894. And only a mind so conversant with the importance of Jack (Ernest) Worthing as to be able to forget him could have chosen to name a heroine (as Firbank named the heroine of his 1907 piece, *A Study in Opal*) Lady Henrietta Worthing.

Even the title of Firbank's second-to-appear Firbankian work, *Inclinations*, is shaped by Wilde's having collected four of his non-fictions under the title *Intentions*. But the nuance between the two titles signals a change of direction – the change precipitated by the Wilde disaster. Wilde's intention is to state his aesthetic expressly, in non-fiction essays and dialogues. Firbank has withdrawn his aesthetic to within the novel,[3] where it may read ambiguously. The intellectual background of Wilde's volume is classical scholarship; the setting of Firbank's fiction is tourism in contemporary Greece. Wilde deploys

[1] Cf. *Firbank and Tours* (Chapter X, 10).
[2] The *Bibliography* fails to record the sub-title of the 1905 edition. The *Biography* (p. 149) incorrectly implies that the sub-title was added for the 1916 edition (cf. footnote to Chapter VI, 6).
[3] Cf. Chapter XI, 3.

a Socratic dialectic, honouring that ancient Athenian milieu which took it for granted that wise men might fall in love with wise and handsome youths. Firbank crystallises brief, witty, lyrical images of women's inclinations towards women.

Some of Firbank's literary habits came from the same source as his early literary forms. To repeat lines from one work in another was a habit Firbank learned (though Firbank tried to eradicate it) from Wilde, who was much given to transposed epigrams.[1] And Firbank's perpetuation of characters from one work to another[2] is a borrowing, enlarged by Firbank, from the master who, before making her the eponymous heroine of a play, opened a short story at 'Lady Windermere's last reception before Easter'.

3. Firbank, Wilde and Sphinxes – 1

THE Sphinx is an apt emblem to crouch on Oscar Wilde's grave. It is truly the image that dominated Wilde's imagination, because it is the only image that ruled both his imaginative personalities: the personality that went clad in scarlet sins and costume jewellery – beneath which it is, all the same, sometimes possible to detect rustlings towards psychological disclosure; and the social, socialist wit, whose fantasies are constructed from the material of logic and whose aphorisms actually manage to capture psychological truths – and ('I summed up all systems in a phrase, and all existence in an epigram') to know that they do.

The Sphinx is an image from the ancient world, but not the classical ancient world. Wilde tried to exploit it for its exoticism (it is his non-biblical Salome, with no Richard Strauss to redeem it after him) and – which, in its psychological import, comes to much the same – for its monstrousness.

Like other mythic monsters that represent an unnatural mingling of species, the Sphinx stands psychological symbol of 'unnatural' sexual unions: a symbol primarily of incest (in which it again resembles the story of Salome) but one which can easily be read as a symbol of homosexuality – both because homosexual unions, too, are socially forbidden and because the Sphinx's mixed body can be interpreted as hermaphrodite: 'you exquisite grotesque!', Wilde addressed it in his poem *The Sphinx*, 'half woman and half animal!'

Firbank, whose œuvre is full of Wilde's Sphinx image, became in the end explicit about the Sphinx as the emblem of the naturalness of 'unnatural' sexuality. In his last (and unfinished) novel *The New Rythum*, it delivers its message in the code of heraldry. Mrs Rosemerchant alights from her car

[1] Cf. Chapters I, 2; VIII, 1; and X, 6.   [2] Cf. Chapter X, 2.

'between a couple of smiling Sphinxes, bearing a monogram and the device: *Take Nature as it comes*'.

Wilde's long poem *The Sphinx* (whose publication in 1894 afforded a nest of Firbankian precedents, since the publishers were Mathews and Lane, the designer was Charles Ricketts and there was a large-paper edition of 250 copies) is ingenious – and fairly atrocious. Wilde's verse is both less arresting and less nasty on the subject than Gustave Moreau's paint.[1] The versifier ends by dismissing the monster ('You wake in me each bestial sense') and asserting a faint preference for contemplating the crucifix.

The faintly Christian conclusion was logically unavoidable. It was only by the mores of Christendom that Wilde's predilections *were* bestial. Those, however, were the mores enforced. They thrust the mantle of sin on Wilde, who merely had the sense to dramatise the unavoidable as scarletly as he could. At the same time, he was aware that the mantle was a bad fit on his innocent and generous personality. By forcing him to wear it, society forced him to evolve his other self too: the wit who demonstrated by paradox that it was society which had got its morals upside down.

Wilde was brilliant enough to connect his brilliance with his supposed sins. 'What the paradox was to me in the sphere of thought, perversity became to me in the sphere of passion.'

It is this remark of Wilde's that caused Firbank to cause the naval officer in *Valmouth* to describe Achilles as 'the most paradoxical of all the Greeks', before going on to explain that his own 'middy-chum' is 'to me, what Patroclus was to Achilles, and even more'.

In psychological sequence, it was Wilde's 'perversity' that led him to paradox, not the other way about. But he was writing in prison, where society was punishing him for his 'perversity' and where he was in no state to vindicate 'perversity' as the quality that had led him to paradoxical truths about society.

The Sphinx, whose bodily form is a paradox incarnate, was the emblem of Wilde the paradoxicalist as well as of Wilde the faintly Christian sinner. In his personal mythology Wilde established a counterpart to the exotic monster Sphinx of the ancient world when he appointed his friend Ada Leverson, who was witty, literary, loyal, domesticated and yet, in so far as she was Jewish, exotic in her turn, to be 'the Sphinx of Modern Life'.

In pursuit of her habit of amicably satirising Wilde's among other con-

---

[1] Equally with Moreau's sphinx, Firbank (for reasons to be elaborated in Chapter XV, 13–14) would have liked what Aubrey Beardsley called 'one of his most beautiful works', which was owned by André Raffalovich, the friend of John Gray (whom Firbank collected; cf. Chapter XII, 6): a water-colour *Sappho* (Beardsley *Letters*, 1971 edition, pp. 218–19).

temporary works, his live Sphinx presently published a send-up of the Sphinx of his poem as 'The Minx'.

As a matter of fact, Wilde himself had sent up his Sphinx image even before he met Ada Leverson and before he published, though not before he wrote, his Sphinx poem. The volume of stories he published in 1891 included a short, proficient entertainment much in the narrative manner which Somerset Maugham later put into mass production. A worldly, uncharacterised narrator relates the tale as it was narrated to him by his friend Lord Murchison – who has suffered an infatuation with a beautiful and fashionable widow because she seems to possess a secret. She drops him hints of mystery, is out when he calls on her by appointment and is accidentally glimpsed by him going, veiled, into a shabby house. Only after the widow suddenly dies does Lord Murchison unveil her secret: by inquiring at the shabby house, where the landlady tells him that the widow used to rent a room solely in order to spend innocent afternoons alone. The worldly narrator assures his grieving friend that she was 'simply a woman with a mania for mystery'. The story's title is *The Sphinx Without a Secret*.

Though its manner is naturalistic, the story is one of Wilde's allegories. Consciously he is pointing out that mystery creates infatuation. Perhaps still consciously and certainly unconsciously, he is commenting on his own high-flown monstrous Sphinx: to the effect that, if society did not insist that 'the Love that dare not speak its name' was unspeakable, the monstrous Sphinx would turn out to have no secret that was not perfectly innocent. The beautiful widow fabricated a mystery about herself: society fabricated the mystery about Wilde's sexual tastes.

For Firbank, Wilde's Sphinx image probably incarnated the mystery Wilde had been to him in his childhood.[1] Indeed, if the riddles which the mythical Sphinx posed to passers-by represent the riddle that sexuality poses to children, Wilde's Sphinx waylaid the child Firbank with the riddle of Wilde's sexuality.

Wilde's high-flown and exotic Sphinx may have attracted Firbank along with Egyptology and superstition. Ifan Kyrle Fletcher was perhaps drawing on specific reports of Firbank's conversation when he described Firbank's mind as 'entangled by the mystery of the Sphinx'. However, as Ifan Kyrle Fletcher went on to remark, numinous awe didn't prevent Firbank from sending up Egypt. (The *Memoir* quotes: 'I dare say, dear, you can't judge of Egypt by *Aida*.'[2]) And a passage in *The Artificial Princess* demonstrates that

---

[1] Cf. Chapter XI, 1.
[2] The remark is made by the cathedral-laundress in . . . *Cardinal Pirelli* (p. 688 in the *Complete* Firbank).

it was not the high-flown but the satirical, commonsensical and deflationary Sphinx of Wilde's imagination that lodged in Firbank's.

The Artificial Princess was first published in 1934 (when Firbank was eight years dead) with an Introduction in which Sir Coleridge Kennard[1] gave the history of the manuscript. It had been 'put away amongst old papers in England before its author started on one of his numerous travels, forgotten and only remembered and retrieved during Firbank's last visit to London'.

More information about Firbank's retrieval of the book was sent by Firbank in a letter to Carl Van Vechten quoted in the *Bibliography*. Firbank told Van Vechten that, when he sorted his mother's papers after her death, he came on several early works of his own. In particular, he reported himself 'delighted' with 'a short novel (unfinished), The Artificial Princess'.

The *Bibliography* lists a typescript (of the first two sections of the book) in which the title has been changed from *Salome, Or 'Tis A Pity That She Would* (though between them the *Bibliography* and the *Biography* have made it impossible to detect the correct form of that early title[2]). The *Bibliography* also lists a typescript of almost the whole book, to which four completing pages have been added in Firbank's handwriting – though it has made it impossible to tell quite where the addition begins.[3]

Firbank's letter to Carl Van Vechten suggests that Firbank remembered the novel as being incomplete at the time when he abandoned it (though it is not totally impossible that he decided the ending to be insufficient only when he re-read the typescript). That he wrote of it to Van Vechten both as 'unfinished' and by the title *The Artificial Princess* makes it certain that, mentally at least, Firbank gave the book its new name before he gave it an ending.

According to the *Biography*,[4] it was in June 1925 that Firbank wrote to

[1] Cf. Chapter XII, 5.   [2] Cf. footnote to Chapter VI, 5.

[3] According to the *Bibliography* (p. 89), the handwritten pages contain the ending of the book as published. This handwritten ending, the *Bibliography* says, is added after the sentence in the typescript ' "A merciful end," the Baroness bewilderedly told herself.' The difficulty is that no such sentence occurs in the printed text. On p. 82 of the 1934 edition (p. 72 in the *Complete* Firbank), there is a sentence ' "A merciful end," the Baroness breathed, glancing up into the blue green of the night.' Perhaps the *Bibliography* means that Firbank replaced the last sentence of his typescript with the first sentence of his handwritten ending; but there's no way of knowing.

[4] (p. 288). My 'according to' is slightly sceptical or at least puzzled. The account in the *Biography* refers the reader to the same professor's *Bibliography*, and that has once again muddied the evidence. The *Bibliography* (p. 62) says that in June 1925 Firbank wrote to Van Vechten describing how he found the book while he sorted his mother's papers 'following her death in the spring'. However, Firbank's mother died in the spring (March) not of 1925 but of 1924. Perhaps the *Bibliography* and the *Biography* have dated Firbank's letter to Van Vechten 1925 in error for 1924. All that is certain about the recovery of the manuscript is that it happened after March 1924.

Carl Van Vechten describing his retrieval of the manuscript and in July to September 1925 that he revised and finished the book.

'At the time of his death' (Sir Coleridge Kennard's Introduction to the published novel goes on) Firbank 'was deliberating whether to publish it or not. He realised that he had drawn on it, from memory, in his later books and sent the story to Lord Berners, who was in Rome, for his opinion. Lord Berners was presumably too busy to offer the advice asked for and a few months later gave me the M.S.'

The habit of drawing on one work for lines to put into another was generated in Wilde and Firbank alike by the fact that they were non-naturalistic writers. Their narrative is not always tied closely to the context of a plot and their dialogue is often uncharacterised. Both wrote lines complete in themselves as statements of universal truth, as images or as snatches of unattributable conversation overheard. Such lines *can* be transposed, and they were particularly likely to be transposed by Firbank's method of working with a mosaic of strips of paper – a method Sir Coleridge Kennard described in the same Introduction, adding that, at the time he became acquainted with Firbank's method, Firbank was trying to use it to construct a play.

It was Wilde, however, who was the successful playwright – and who could therefore immediately count more on spoken words than on the same words submitting in print to cold comparison. And it was Wilde who was a teacher of society – who, wanting his sayings to be widely repeated, had no objection to repeating them himself. Firbank had to rely on the reading and (which its own nature tried to enforce) the re-reading of his œuvre. Consequently, although there was a Wildean precedent for doing so, Firbank probably[1] tried to avoid repeating himself in his published work.

He didn't always, however, succeed. True, his much-used poudre-de-riz sky[2] had appeared only in work he didn't publish (*Lady Appledore's Mésalliance* and *The Artificial Princess*) before he published it in *Vainglory*. But he published the voice like cheap scent[3] both in *Caprice* in 1917 and in *The Princess Zoubaroff* in 1920.

Verbally, *The Artificial Princess* had, during its long latency, been plundered by Firbank for work he wrote later and published. As well as the

---

[1] That is especially probable if his biographer (p. 155) is correct in supposing that, when Firbank crossed out phrases in his *Inclinations* notebooks, it was because he had transferred them to the finished work and wanted to avoid repetitions. Such crossings-out weren't, however, an invariable habit. Chapter XV, 9 will mention a line which Firbank published in 1920 but which stands un-crossed-out in one of his notebooks.

[2] Cf. Chapter VIII, 2 and Chapter X, 6.

[3] Cf. Chapter IX, 8.

poudre-de-riz sky, which had been published in *Vainglory*, *The Artificial Princess* contains a five-line song, beginning 'I am disgusted with Love', which had been published in *Vainglory* with only two words and some punctuation altered. In *The Artificial Princess* the song is said to be 'some words by a Court Poet'. It becomes 'a somewhat saturnine little song of Mrs. Cresswell' in *Vainglory* (where Miss Valley presently guys it by saying, in 'her chastest Cockney voice', 'I'm that disgusted with Love', and inspires her colleagues to treat it as, at the least, a spoken anthem).

The plunderings[1] *are*, however, only verbal. The theme and treatment of *The Artificial Princess* are unplundered in Firbank's other work – and are in their own right remarkably original as well as quintessentially Firbankian. If Firbank was truly anxious to avoid plagiarising himself, he could have allayed his anxiety by running down and altering the items he had used elsewhere – a no doubt tiresome but not difficult task, which would have taken less time than sending the manuscript out for Lord Berners's opinion. But in any case it was not very like Firbank's usual behaviour to be so gravely anxious about self-plagiarism – or he wouldn't have twice published, for instance, the cheap-scent voice.

It looks to me, therefore, as though the 'echoes' which Sir Coleridge Kennard's Introduction cites from Firbank's previously published works, by way of explaining Firbank's reluctance to publish *The Artificial Princess* when he rediscovered the typescript, are only the rationalisations for his hesitation which Firbank offered to acquaintances like Kennard – and to himself. I suspect that Firbank was suffering a deeper hesitation than he knew, and that his sudden and untypical terror of having, in works written in the meantime, plagiarised himself was a screen for a half-memory of having committed a half-conscious plagiarism at the time of writing *The Artificial Princess*.

That half-conscious (I surmise) plagiarism Firbank committed not on himself but on Oscar Wilde. Quite consciously and legitimately he had adopted Wilde's Salome theme. But he must have obscured from his own notice that he had borrowed also the joke of Wilde's *The Sphinx Without a Secret* and attributed it, without acknowledgment, to the Artificial Princess's emissary, the Baroness Rudlieb.

The Baroness is, by this point, a failed emissary. Instead of performing her mission, she has gone off on a frolic of her own. When she returns to court, she is disturbed by guilt – and 'To compose herself she thought of Carpaccio's St. Ursula in Venice, a woman without a trace of expression, with the veiled crêpe-de-chine look of a Sphinx. "Whoever said the Sphinx

---

[1] of which Chapter XVIII, 2 will mention another instance.

had a secret?" she wondered; and at this wonderful thought she was lifted into realms of abstract speculation, and was saved.'

4. Firbank, Wilde and Sphinxes – 2

THE moment when Firbank attributed that 'wonderful thought' to his Baroness and suppressed from himself the knowledge that Wilde had entertained it first was the crisis of his relation to Wilde.

Whenever an artist has by heredity (as Mozart had) a father who is also an artist and his artistic teacher or adopts (as Firbank did) an artist to stand to him as an artistic father, there is an artistic equivalent to the Oedipus situation to be lived through. And the resolution of that problem is as crucial to the forming of a creative personality as the resolution of the original problem in infancy and adolescence is to the forming of the private and personal personality.

For Firbank the Oedipus situation proper grew by a direct route into his artistically Oedipal relation to Wilde. The mystery of Wilde's sexual behaviour set its pattern on his original puzzle about sex;[1] and the pattern of the puzzle impressed itself on Firbank's literary work, to so much of which Wilde stood patron saint.

For his hesitation to publish *The Artificial Princess* when he recovered it after March 1924 Firbank could put forward the not totally convincing rationalisation that he had plundered the book for his other works. But not even a rationalisation is offered to solve the greater mystery of why he hesitated and indeed failed to finish the book and publish it at the beginning of his career – or, to be strict, at the beginning, as *The Artificial Princess* essentially is, of his Firbankian career.

It is in that essence that, I think, the answer lies. Certainly the answer is not that Firbank couldn't sustain his new, original and idiosyncratic idiom to the end of his first adventure in it. He all but finished the book at the time – if, indeed, he didn't then consider it finished. He certainly left his Baroness breathing of an ending.[2] The completion he supplied later is a matter of no more than 500 words, one and a half pages of print in a text that runs to 73. And those extra words are so totally and brilliantly in the tone of the rest that they had obviously been lying all along in Firbank's pre-conscious, needing re-invention but not invention. At the time of the original writing, Firbank brought his book to an emotional end and came so near to giving it its textual end that it is safe to judge that what stopped him short was not incapacity but inhibition.

[1] Cf. Chapter XI, 1.   [2] Cf. the footnote in sub-section 3 of this chapter.

The theft his text committed from Wilde was not the cause of that inhibition but a symptom.

Firbank's first Firbankian work was by definition the first work of his independence from Wilde. While he was writing it, Firbank's title for *The Artificial Princess* was presumably *Salome, Or 'Tis A Pity That She Would* (in one form or another): a title that pointed Firbank's adoption of Wilde's Salome theme. But, during the writing, that adoption, begun as pious tribute, must have revealed its other aspect.

Wilde's *Salomé* was a success – to the point at any rate of being a scandal. But Firbank can't have avoided noticing it was also scandalously bad. True, the one-act form of Wilde's play is a brilliant structure for building intensity to a climax; the structure brilliantly serves Richard Strauss's opera; and, in its English version, Wilde's *Salome* struck masterpieces from Aubrey Beardsley. But the poetic passages which the theme struck from Wilde himself are the most meretricious glints of the most fake jewels in his regalia.

Firbank of all people must have been aware of the fakeness of *Salomé* – because Firbank had imitated the Wilde of *Salomé* (in combination with Maeterlinck) in an early and unpublished 'dream play', *The Mauve Tower*, in which a Princess (of course), her hair 'plaited with rubies and strange mauve stones', breathes: 'The sea looks like a yellow fire, like a sheet of yellow flame . . . listen! how still it is . . . the birds have ceased to sing . . . All the palm trees are trembling, and yet there is no wind. Never before have I felt a night so hot. Oh! how dark it is, I cannot see the flowers, I can no longer see the moon.'

In the course of creating his own work on the theme of Salome, Firbank came to the crux of his Oedipal relation to Wilde: the point where the son was surpassing the father. Wilde had expressed his Salome image in the medium he was most masterly at, drama; and even so he had failed. Firbank, taking up Wilde's theme, was doing better with it – and in a medium Wilde had never mastered. As he wrote, Firbank was achieving two things Wilde never achieved: writing a good novel; and writing a good novel original in form.

By creating his first Firbankian work, Firbank ran into the guilt of outdoing Wilde. And he must have apprehended it as an irony or almost a punishment from fate that the Wildean theme on which he was outdoing Wilde concerned a prophet who was only the herald of a prophet greater yet. John the Baptist foretold his saviour as Wilde the great aesthetician prepared the climate for Firbank the great artist.

The guilt Firbank's Baroness runs into during the story resembles the guilt Firbank ran into during its writing: a dereliction of duty owed to a superior. The Baroness, sharing Firbank's turn for the cult of the saints, has recourse to a saint for consolation. By way of the image of a saint painted by Carpaccio she almost arrives at the image to which Firbank himself regularly applied for consolation: the thought of Wilde. But Firbank makes her stop short at a thought of Wilde's. The originator of the thought, whose image had once been potent of help, is suppressed. For the first time Firbank, having taken what he wanted from Wilde, had made it his Firbankian own.

In a later Firbankian work about another princess, Firbank restored his icon of Wilde – and made amends for his unacknowledged theft from Wilde by committing another and pointedly (as I shall explain in Chapter XIV, 10) acknowledging it.

5. A Minor Pupillage

THE guilt Firbank incurred by surpassing his master and making off with one of his jokes was endorsed by a lesser, parallel guilt. It is also in *The Artificial Princess* that Firbank claimed as his own something that originated with another of his literary masters – a lesser one, and, this time, one Firbank actually knew by personal acquaintance. And that apprenticeship, too, Firbank broke.

Miriam J. Benkovitz's *Biography* documents Firbank's relationship (which, luckily for documentation, was carried on as much through letters as through meetings) with Rollo St Clair Talboys,[1] a rather athletic aesthete whom Firbank met when Talboys was briefly a tutor and Firbank briefly a pupil at one of the first of Firbank's many crammers.[2] The acquaintance continued after both pupil and master had left the institution (Talboys became a master at Wellington), and Talboys behaved as overseer of Firbank's literary development.

In the course of commenting on Firbank's work Talboys gave more than advice. In 1904 he supplied both a title and a couple of phrases to a story by Firbank. The *Biography* quotes Talboys's phrases, 'the sins & sorrow of the whole world gathered in her wearied eyelids – & the red gold of her hair', and points out that Firbank incorporated them in his story: 'A woman, with a long pale face, leaning out of the clouds, the sins and sorrows of the whole world gathered in the wearied eyelids and the red-gold of her hair.'

The story in which Firbank incorporated Talboys's gift was *A Study in*

[1] – the influence of whose middle name on Firbank I mentioned in Chapter X, 12 and will mention further in Chapter XV, 17.

[2] According to the *Biography* (pp. 25-31), the institution was run by Alexander Macbean and was at Park Holm, Buxton, Derbyshire; Firbank was a pupil by May 1901 (when his age was 15) and met Talboys there in 1902.

Temperament (whose title was also a gift from Talboys), and in 1905 Firbank published it, along with *Odette D'Antrevernes*, as his first volume.

As a matter of fact, however, Firbank did not stop after making that use of Talboys's words. Having already published them in *A Study in Temperament*, he went on to write some of them into *The Artificial Princess*, appropriating them, as he did Wilde's joke, to the Baroness: 'She leaned back, her face almost grey, the sins and sorrows of all the world gathered for an instant in her tired green eyes.'

If Firbank *had* decided to publish *The Artificial Princess* towards the end of his life, he would have echoed not only work written after it but work written and published before it – and not written by himself. Perhaps it was a half-awareness of that double plagiarism, as well as of his plagiarism from Wilde, which prompted his uneasiness.

For although Talboys had originally made Firbank a gift of the words, Talboys was not approving when Firbank finally freed himself from all his apprenticeships and published as a Firbankian writer. (About *Vainglory* Talboys wrote to Firbank in 1915 'but I must not speak of that with the humiliating sense of misunderstanding'.[1]) And earlier still, before Firbank began Firbankian writing with the composition of *The Artificial Princess*, Talboys disapproved of Firbank's having exchanged Talboys's literary tutorship for the patron-saintliness of Wilde. In a metaphor either couched in Firbank's native imagery or influential on Firbank's imagery,[2] Talboys warned Firbank in 1904 against 'the cult of the purple orchid', which he called 'insidious & exotic poison [. . .] like the rank odour of dead men's sins'.

The warning was, as Firbank's biographer says, against 'decadence'. But it was also specifically against Wilde. Wilde was the dead man of whose 'sins' Firbank was indeed and very precisely making a cult.

Firbank incurred guilt when he ignored Talboys's advice and broke his apprenticeship to Talboys in order to enter himself apprentice to the dead man whose sins Talboys called rank; and that guilt must have been re-animated and redoubled when, by becoming the Firbankian author of *The Artificial Princess*, he broke, in turn, his apprenticeship to Wilde.

The crimes of Oedipus whereby Firbank, as a creative personality, became himself are marked by the two appropriations in *The Artificial Princess*: the unacknowledged theft from Wilde; and the misappropriation of the phrase Talboys had given to Firbank while Firbank was a Talboyish or even a

[1] This didn't stop Firbank's having Talboys sent a copy of his next book, *Inclinations* (cf. footnote to Chapter XII, 5).

[2] – as Chapters XIV, 10 and 11, and XV, 5 and 9 will explore.

proto-Wildean writer but whose use he might have discountenanced by a Firbankian writer.

It was probably because the parricides incidental to his self-creation were recorded in its texture that Firbank did not publish *The Artificial Princess* either later or at the time of writing. Having written it, however, and thereby created himself a Firbankian, he went on to write, in his Firbankian persona, *Vainglory*, which he did publish – and under his new writing name.

In *Vainglory*, Firbank's imagination wrought the apotheosis of the cult he had accorded to Wilde. Mrs Shamefoot becomes virtually a saint in her lifetime. ('I hear you are achieving sainthood by leaps and bounds!'). More miraculously still, she achieves, even before sainthood itself, the mark of sainthood, that commemorative monument in stained glass in Ashringford Cathedral, while her flesh-and-blood self is still living near by.

Mrs Shamefoot's apotheosis is an invention whose beauty and absurdity incarnate the beauty and alas, given the world, absurdity of Firbank's wish that Wilde (taken as the saintly type of all literary creators, Firbank himself included[1]) might have been accorded honour and a monument in his lifetime. Mrs Shamefoot's portrait in stained glass is Firbank's sighing wish that Helen Carew, rather than shift his corpse and honour it with an Epstein sphinx, had been able to remove Wilde's living body from Reading Gaol.

In being assumed into the baroque heaven of *Vainglory*, there to honour Wilde, Firbank's imagination was freed from his apprenticeship to, and his guilt towards, Wilde. By the same token he was freed of his apprenticeship to Talboys, which he had put off in order to bind himself to Wilde. Baroquely exalted, Firbank looked down with the distance of both his classicism and his satire on the heavily pre-Raphaelite phrase of Talboys's which he had put into both *A Study in Temperament* and *The Artificial Princess*. The eyes weary with the sins and sorrows of the whole world reappear, totally recast by satire, in *Vainglory*, attributed to the picture in stained glass of Mrs Shamefoot: 'The ennui of half the world is in her eyes – almost, as always.'

6. Creative Parricide

WRITING (though not to the very end) *The Artificial Princess* was the crisis of Firbank's literary Oedipus situation; and that crisis was forced on him by the crisis of his personal Oedipus situation.

In 1925,[2] when Firbank had taken out and up *The Artificial Princess*, one

---

[1] – as Chapter XV, 17 will say more emphatically.
[2] Cf. sub-section 3 of this chapter.

of his hesitating moves towards publication was to draft a foreword. Two versions of his draft are mentioned by the *Bibliography* as laid in to one of the typescripts. In one version Firbank said he wrote the book in 1906, and in the other he named 1910.

He wasn't necessarily, of course, contradicting himself. It is quite likely that he conceived or even began writing the book in 1906, the year in which he went up to Cambridge, and, after he came down, resumed it in 1910.

Certainly Firbank associated the book with Cambridge. One of his draft forewords says he composed the book 'while preparing for the Cambridge "Little go" '.[1] Perversely, however, that is the version which dates the book 1910. Even Firbank, who was 'preparing' (for the exam he ought to have taken before he went up) throughout his Cambridge career, can scarcely have gone on preparing after he had come down.

His other draft foreword gives different associations with the book's composition: 'It was about the time of the Maud Allen boom & the Straus cult (a little previous to the Russian Ballet) & the minds of young boys turned from their Greece towards the Palace Theatre, Vienna & Berlin.' This is the version Firbank labelled 1906.

Firbank's biographer seems to suppose that in 'the Straus cult' Firbank must have been referring to the arrival of Strauss's operas *Elektra* and *Salome* (to put them, that is, in order of arrival) in England. However, even in England, there was a cult of Strauss *before* the operas arrived. And in any case there is no need to assume that the travelled and proudly Parisian Firbank meant an English cult. Strauss's *Salome* reached Paris in 1907.

Likewise, 'the Maud Allen boom' does not necessarily date only from 1908, when Maud Allan danced *The Vision of Salome* (to music by Marcel Rémy and a story-line from Flaubert) at, as Firbank's associations include, the Palace Theatre, London (the theatre at which Sarah Bernhardt had rehearsed[2] Wilde's *Salomé* in 1892). Firbank's associations list Vienna and Berlin as well as the Palace Theatre; perhaps he had in mind that Maud Allan first gave her performance in Vienna in 1904 and took it round Europe before bringing it to London.

Neither is it much help towards dating the book that the text of *The Artificial Princess* actually makes reference to Richard Strauss's *Salome*. The reference gives, of course, the minimal information that that bit of the book was not written before Strauss's opera (which was first presented in December 1905). But the reference does not disclose whether, at the time

---

[1] This theme will be picked up in Chapter XIV, 1.
[2] – as Chapter XIV, 1 will mention again.

he made it, Firbank had himself heard Strauss's opera or only heard *of* it – and still less, if he had heard it, in which city.[1]

All the same, I think it is possible to pick out a passage in *The Artificial Princess* which does help the dating – and which suggests that, though Firbank may well have begun the book 'a little previous to the Russian Ballet', he was still writing it after he had made acquaintance (if only by hearsay) with the Russian Ballet.

By the Princess's account, the ceremonial at her mother's second marriage consisted of 'Just the Lord's Prayer in B and a chapter that sounded as though it were taken from Jean Cocteau or Maurice Rostand.'

Firbank might easily have known of Jean Cocteau as early as 1908. Firbank had some acquaintance[2] with, and a signed photograph of, Édouard de Max – the actor whom Cocteau described as one of the two great figures (the other being Sarah Bernhardt) of the French theatre during Cocteau's youth. Cocteau, too, had a signed photograph from de Max – and more: de Max arranged a public poetry-reading of Cocteau's work in 1908.

However, *The Artificial Princess* mentions Cocteau not alone but yoked (if disjunctively in syntax) to Maurice Rostand. I do not think it would have come to Firbank to link the two before 1910. For, according to Romola Nijinsky, it was in the Russian Ballet's Paris season of 1910 that 'an important group of young men' attached themselves to Diaghilev – and their 'leaders were Maurice Rostand and Jean Cocteau'.

I think it certain, therefore, that although he may have begun it earlier and continued it later, Firbank was engaged in writing *The Artificial Princess* during 1910. And, during the writing of it, he must have been forced to confront his relation to his adopted literary stepfathers: because in October 1910 his real father died.

It was that death which crucially formed Firbank's creative personality. I imagine that his literary adoptions, about which he was already guilty because he had abandoned Talboys for Wilde and then seemed likely to surpass Wilde, suddenly brought on him the more elemental guilt of the fact that they *were* adoptions. It was because he had been unable psychologically to adopt his real father that he had acquired the substitute literary fathers whom he betrayed.

The guilt the real son incurred when the real father died in 1910 was expressed by the literary son. To cast off his literary fathers was an atonement

---

[1] Firbank's references to Strauss (and their dating) will be discussed in Chapter XIV, 4.
[2] Forrest Reid's recollections of Firbank as an undergraduate (which he was between 1906 and 1909) include the item, presumably from Firbank's conversation, that 'Firbank had been staying in Paris with M. de Max, the actor' (Forrest Reid: *Private Road*, p. 57).

attempted too late for the suddenly recognised failure to adopt the real father enough to make substitutes unneeded. The text of *The Artificial Princess* embodies Firbank's two literary parricides. He steals from Talboys and is disloyal to his literary tutorship; he steals from Wilde and suppresses the very thought of Wilde from his consciousness. But in reality his two literary disloyalties did not bring him loyally back into reconciliation with his dead father. They carried him into his new creative personality. The book in which he assassinates his previous literary rulers is the one whereby he steps into his own kingdom of Firbankian idiom.

The Artificial Princess is in its psychological aspect Firbank's *Hamlet*.[1] But Firbank's Prince of Denmark is, of course, a Princess. And Hamlet's hesitation to kill became Firbank's own hesitations to publish.

Firbank met his guilt by abdicating the kingdom he had come into. He made his novel unpublishable by declining quite to finish it. Even when he eventually brought himself to recover and finish it, it was still an object so suggestive of guilt that he could not make up his mind to publish it – or even how to date it in the preface he (casting another hindrance in his own way) thought it would need if he did decide to publish. Perhaps his invention hit on, for once, a fortune-teller who was truly predictive (of himself) when he made the entertainments at the Artificial Princess's birthday celebrations include 'a Society Crystal gazer' who 'is not very definite, and muddles her dates'.

Firbank could not, of course, sacrifice his vocation permanently. He went on to compose, finish and publish *Vainglory*.

However, by offering up the sacrifice of his first work of Firbankianism, he made it possible for himself to preserve his piety towards Wilde. Thus he was able to take refuge under Wilde's saintly patronage at a time when his father's death made him deeply vulnerable, and he was able to invoke Wilde as patron of his future Firbankian adventures. Indeed, it was on a Wildean precedent that he perpetuated into his next Firbankian book, *Vainglory*, one of the personages, Monsignor Parr, from *The Artificial Princess*.

The text of *The Artificial Princess* plots to assassinate Wilde. But so long as Firbank refrained from publishing the text (and he managed, by hesitancy and seeking advice, to refrain all his life) he had not quite put the plot into execution, and had not publicly outdone Wilde on Wilde's own Salome theme. His Wilde collecting and genuflecting was licensed to continue long after – and because – he had abandoned the manuscript of *The Artificial Princess*.

Indeed, *The Artificial Princess* itself pays deliberate compliments (as well

[1] This motif will be taken up in Chapter XIV, 5.

as the involuntary compliment of an unacknowledged theft) to Wilde. It is by a bobbed curtsey to Wilde that 'There were Roses in the Rose Garden, which was remarkable where all was paradox.' And Firbank has taken the point of Wilde's anticipation,[1] through Lord Goring, of the psychoanalytic theory of narcissism. Firbank turns back to front, expresses in mirror-writing, Lord Goring's glance into a mirror after his pronouncement 'To love oneself is the beginning of a lifelong love affair.' In *The Artificial Princess*, 'The dancers crushed streaming by into the tent, where a frugal "Theatre Supper" was being served. The battle for precedence before the mirror was, in several cases, the commencement of a life-long feud.'

And in fact *The Artificial Princess* owes more, even, than its main (Salome) theme and several of its jokes to Wilde. The occasion of the princess's dance in the Bible is a feast 'when Herod's birthday was kept'. In Firbank's Salome novel, it is the Princess herself whose birthday is being kept. For that transposition, too, Wilde was responsible. The setting of *The Artificial Princess* is borrowed from Wilde's tale *The Birthday of the Infanta*.

(Firbank's Princess dances, instead of Salome's public dance of the seven veils, a private Tarantella. The choice of dance was very likely prompted by the Spanish background of Wilde's birthday princess, for it is very likely[2] that Firbank supposed that, in fact Italian, dance to be Spanish.)

Having taken over the setting, Firbank's creative consciousness continued to play on Wilde's tale even while it composed the narrative and descriptive texture of *The Artificial Princess*. In Wilde's tale, the court dwarf dies of a broken heart when he realises that the little princess is laughing at his ugliness, not his antics. Firbank's narrative goes out of its way to undo his fate in a half-sentence. At the birthday celebrations for Firbank's Princess, 'nobody smiled at the absurd antics of the King's Dwarf'.

All the same, the tragedy-in-a-Spanish setting of Wilde's dwarf was reflected – transmuted – in Firbank's œuvre. When Firbank had emancipated himself from his apprenticeship to Wilde, Wilde's imagery was free to return to him and he was free to put it to creative rather than cultist use. Firbank's first Firbankian work alludes to the imaginary Spain of Wilde's story. His last work is wholly set there (though Firbank's imagination has expanded Wilde's concept into a landscape wide enough to encompass Firbank's creations). The milieu of . . . *Cardinal Pirelli* owes less to the real-life Spain of Firbank's acquaintance than it does to Wilde's (via Velasquez's and Goya's) mood of ritual heartlessness even unto bizarre death.

[1] which I cited in Chapter I, 2.
[2] a likelihood established in Chapter X, 12.

7. Firbank, Wilde and Sphinxes – 3

WHILE he wrote *The Artificial Princess*, Firbank's mind was playing not only on Wilde's fictitious Sphinx, whose non-secret Firbank stole and gave to his Baroness, but on Wilde's live and lively Sphinx, who had parodied Wilde's other, high-flown Sphinx in *Punch*. Ada Leverson's parody was a dialogue between the poet and the Sphinx, which ended with the poet's suspicion that the creature was not a Sphinx at all but a Minx.

When he stole Wilde's Sphinx joke, Firbank united it to the art-historical information that was furnishing his mind at the time[1] and had his Baroness arrive at Wilde's idea via Carpaccio. Ada Leverson's Sphinx–Minx joke Firbank wove, much more amusingly as well as much more legitimately, into an art-historical joke of his own, one which (in keeping with his taste for archaic forms of painters' names[2]) plays on the English 18th-century habit of rendering the surname of Anton Raphael Mengs as Mynx. 'At Court the Princess was considered exquisite – a Largillière ... but her mother, the Queen, had never doubted her to be a Minx. "We have never heard of the painter", the Maids of Honour would say, curtseying.'

8. Firbank and the Sphinx in Person

IT was not only by way of her Wilde parody that Ada Leverson made an impression on Firbank's novel. She did so also in person – or, rather, by the unexpected absence of her person. The failure of the attempt[3] by Firbank, in mauve trousers and the company of Wilde's son, to meet Wilde's modern Sphinx certainly contributed to Firbank's abandonment of *The Artificial Princess*.

It may also have contributed to the text. But the relation of the failure in mauve trousers to the writing of the book can't be exactly fixed, because the date of the failure is uncertain and the book, though it was certainly being written in 1910, may have gone on being written later.

The attempted meeting took place either 1909–1910-ish (if Vyvyan Holland was right in remembering it as a matter of months after he and Firbank came down from Cambridge) or no earlier than the autumn of 1912 (if he was right in remembering Curzon Street as where he lunched chez Firbank beforehand).[4]

So when Firbank tried to meet Ada Leverson in person, he had perhaps already adapted her Minx joke, thieved Wilde's joke about another Sphinx

---

[1] Cf. Chapter IX, 6.   [2] Cf. Chapter IX, 7.
[3] Cf. Chapter XII, 6.   [4] Cf. the note in Chapter XII, 7.

and put away his manuscript incomplete (if, that is, the attempt was about 1912). Or perhaps he was in the middle of writing the text when he made the attempt (if it was about 1910, a matter of months after he came down) on the person who had occasioned or was associated with two passages in it.

And in curious fact it must have been the passage not about her own joke but about Wilde's which Firbank associated (whether before or after the event) with his failure to meet Ada Leverson. For Firbank stole the joke of *The Sphinx Without a Secret*, Wilde's story in which Lord Murchison keeps an appointment to call on the Sphinx-like widow and is told by a servant that she is not in. And that is precisely what Firbank and Vyvyan Holland were told when they kept their appointment with Wilde's Sphinx of Modern Life.

If the real event took place while Firbank was writing the book, that event was probably what impelled him to suppress Wilde while keeping the joke of Wilde's which the event must have called to his mind. For being rejected by Wilde's Sphinx must have seemed to Firbank, who was in any case becoming guilty of an attempted parricide on Wilde by surpassing him, a rejection, from beyond his Sphinx-ridden grave, by Wilde himself.

And indeed that must have been the interpretation Firbank set on the episode even if the episode happened *after* he had written Wilde's joke into his text. But, in that case, the rejection must have seemed to Firbank, superstitious anyway, and particularly about the Egyptian emblem of the Sphinx, doubly pointed: by virtue of being uncanny. Guilt must have seemed to come out of the tomb and in pursuit of him, since real life was fulfilling Wilde's (and Firbank's borrowed) fiction.

Either way, Ada Leverson affected *The Artificial Princess*. By being 'not at home' when Firbank called, either she made him suppress Wilde and thus incur a guilt to atone for which he abandoned his book or she seemed to add, to his guilt, a supernatural doom and an extra reason for offering up his book as a propitiatory sacrifice.

9. From the Sphinx's Point of View

NOBODY seems to have asked *why* the Sphinx broke the appointment she had given Vyvyan Holland and Firbank – nobody, that is to say, among Firbankians, and not Vyvyan Holland himself.

Perhaps Vyvyan Holland thought it would be impertinent in a man so much younger than herself to pick her up on her discourtesy. Evidently he *didn't* ask her for an explanation – or anyway didn't get one. His account reports both that Firbank afterwards attributed the rebuff to his trousers

('He was apparently under the impression that the Sphinx must have been looking out for us from an upper window and that the sight of his trousers had been too much for her and had decided her against the obvious risk of making his acquaintance') and that he, Vyvyan Holland, could offer no alternative: 'for aught I know this may have been the explanation'.

But it is, I think, possible to piece together an explanation more consonant with the character of the Sphinx – who had not avoided the risk of keeping Oscar Wilde's acquaintance even when he was on bail.

The Sphinx's action was in reality a message to Firbank, and a message couched in Wildean terms. Firbank failed to understand it because he was himself sending the Sphinx a message, also in Wildean terms. As he shewed by immediately assuming that the Sphinx had read them as too risky, Firbank intended his trousers to signal to the Sphinx that he was not a conventional moralist. He wanted to meet her because he wanted to hear about Wilde; and he was implying by his costume that she could speak to him frankly about Wilde.

He chose mauve for his trousers because mauve was the colour of 'decadence'. When Talboys cautioned[1] Firbank against 'the cult of the purple orchid', he picked on the deepest-dyed shade of decadence, the 'Tyrian purple' Wilde chose for the binding of his *Salome*; as Wilde himself explained, 'Bosie is very gilt-haired and I have bound *Salome* in purple to suit him.' Mauve[2] was the more insouciant, the less confessedly sin-laden aspect of purple. The 'connoisseurship' (in the subject of men) of one of the schoolgirls in *Concerning the Eccentricities of Cardinal Pirelli* is expressed: 'I can't explain; but I adore all that mauvishness about him.'

Firbank wore mauve when he called on Wilde's Sphinx because Wilde's Lord Goring left a party with the remark that he must look in at another, where 'I believe they have got a mauve Hungarian band that plays mauve Hungarian music.'

(As a matter of fact, Firbank, sheerly out of his supersaturation in Wilde, rewrote that Wildean concept in *The Artificial Princess*, attributing the mauveness, under another name, to the surroundings rather than to the music, but keeping the nationality of the band intact, give or take an Austro-Hungarian nuance. At the outdoors evening party for the Princess's birthday 'Under the trees, wrapped in nature's indigo, an orchestra, composed entirely of Zithers, commenced a serenade.')

However, so selfconscious was Firbank about his gesture that he instantly interpreted the Sphinx's absence as the failure of his own gesture – and did

---

[1] Cf. sub-section 5 of this chapter.
[2] Cf. Chapters VIII, 9 and XV, 5 and 9.

not notice that the Sphinx's absence was itself a gesture on her part, and one that made reference to another of Wilde's characters.

Vyvyan Holland, in asking the Sphinx to meet his fellow undergraduate, had of course explained why Firbank was seeking the interview. 'I called upon the Sphinx', Vyvyan Holland's account says, 'and told her of this young man and of his interest in her. The Sphinx, who was always, and indeed still is, perfectly charming, made an appointment to receive us on the following Sunday afternoon at 4 o'clock.'

For all her charm, however, the Sphinx might have been a touch justifiably piqued that the 'interest' of 'this young man' was transparently *not* 'in her', in her own literary right, but in her only for the sake of Wilde. I imagine it was then and there, during her conversation with Vyvyan Holland, that she decided to reply in terms of Wilde's story *The Sphinx Without a Secret*. Firbank was seeking her out as Wilde's Sphinx, so she could count on him to be conversant with the Sphinx part of Wilde's œuvre. And no doubt she herself was very familiar with the story in which Wilde had played with the name he later gave to her.

Even so, her memory of Wilde's story (which she couldn't look up, in Vyvyan Holland's presence, without giving her game away) was very slightly awry. She made an appointment with Vyvyan Holland for 'the following Sunday afternoon at 4 o'clock'. In Wilde's story, the widow-Sphinx gives Lord Murchison an appointment to call on her 'to-morrow at a quarter to five'; he calls, and she is mysteriously out; and *then*, to console him, she gives him a further appointment, which she in fact keeps, for 'Sunday at four'.

Ada Leverson had slightly (like the crystal gazer in *The Artificial Princess*) muddled her dates but her message is posthumously clear, though not clear to Firbank at the time. As Firbank and Vyvyan Holland waited outside her house on 'Sunday at four' eventually to receive only a dusty answer delivered by a servant, Firbank's vibrant trousers were radiating the message that he was a person to whom Wilde's Sphinx could safely divulge Wilde's secrets: and Ada Leverson, by sending her servant to report her not at home, was signifying that she was indeed Wilde's Sphinx but, to the young man who had sought her out as such, she was a Sphinx Without a Secret to tell him.

10. Notes to Chapter XIII

OSCAR WILDE's letter (of April 1895) about the Sibyl of Mortimer Street is on p. 389 of Rupert Hart-Davis's edition of the *Letters*. Wilde's canonisation of Robert

Ross is recorded on pp. 577, 583 and 720 of that edition, and his self-canonisation (which he reported, in 1898, to his fellow saint) on p. 720.

The pilgrimage equipment in *Santal* is on p. 494 in the *Complete* Firbank.

The Baroness's saintly consultation is on p. 49 in the *Complete* Firbank, and the hagiography-within-the-story on pp. 51-2.

The full title of *The Flower Beneath the Foot* appears in the first edition. It is not given in the *Complete* Firbank.

Extracts from *Impression d'Automne – A Poem in Prose* are published on p. 116 of *The New Rythum and Other Pieces*, which notes that the piece was published as *Souvenir d'Automne* in *Supplement* to *The King and His Navy and Army*, 2 December 1905.

Two of Wilde's Poems in Prose were published in *The Spirit Lamp* in 1893. Revised and with four others, they appeared in the *Fortnightly Review* in July 1894 (*Letters* . . ., edited by Rupert Hart-Davis, p. 356).

A brief account, which mentions the heroine's name, of *A Study in Opal* appears in the *Biography* (pp. 86-7), according to which Firbank's piece was published in *Granta* of 2 November 1907.

Wilde's remark that he summed up 'all existence in an epigram' (which I quoted in Chapter I) is from *De Profundis* (Epistola: In Carcere et Vinculis) and so is his paradox–perversity comparison. (Both are on p. 466 in Rupert Hart-Davis's edition of the Wilde *Letters*.)

The Oscar Wilde story that begins chez Lady Windermere is *Lord Arthur Savile's Crime* (magazine publication 1887; volume publication with other stories 1891). *Lady Windermere's Fan* was produced in 1892.

The smiling Sphinxes and their motto are on p. 78 of *The New Rythum*. The paradoxicalness of Achilles is on p. 398 in the *Complete* Firbank.

Probably Wilde worked on *The Sphinx* from when he was at Oxford till 1883. He published the poem in 1894. He met Ada Leverson in 1892. Her Sphinx–Minx parody appeared in *Punch* in 1894. (Rupert Hart-Davis's edition of the Wilde *Letters* documents these sequences on pp. 144, 342 and 357.)

'The Love that dare not speak its name' is the phrase from a sonnet by Lord Alfred Douglas which Wilde was questioned about when he was prosecuted (*The Trials of Oscar Wilde*, edited by H. Montgomery Hyde, pp. 235-6).

The *Memoir* speaks of Firbank and the Egyptian Sphinx on p. 41.

The two versions of 'I am disgusted with Love' come on p. 63 and p. 130 in the *Complete* Firbank. The song is guyed and anthemised on p. 166.

The plagiarised Sphinx passage in *The Artificial Princess* comes on p. 61 in the *Complete* Firbank.

According to the *Biography* (p. 34), Firbank himself later assigned the date 1900 to his *The Mauve Tower, A Dream Play*. The *Biography* (pp. 52-3) assigns the play to 1904. The passage I quote is from the extracts published (p. 117) in *The New Rythum and Other Pieces*.

The *Biography* quotes the contribution R. St C. Talboys made to Firbank's

A Study in Temperament on p. 44, but does not remark the repetition of the sins and sorrows of the world in *The Artificial Princess* (p. 52 in the *Complete* Firbank) or their satirical re-writing in *Vainglory* (p. 198 in the *Complete* Firbank).

Mrs Shamefoot's leaps and bounds are on p. 220 in the *Complete* Firbank.

Talboys's 1915 letter is quoted on p. 142, and his 1904 letter on p. 48, of the *Biography*, which quotes Firbank's two versions of his preface and dates his associations on p. 115.

The Strauss allusion in *The Artificial Princess* is on p. 36 in the *Complete* Firbank. Firbank's dating of the book is quoted in the *Biography*, p. 115. The details of Maud Allan's Salome performance are from William Mann's *Richard Strauss*, p. 44. The Cocteau–Rostand allusion comes on p. 35 in the *Complete* Firbank. Cocteau's account of Édouard de Max and of his own début is on pp. 34–9 of *Professional Secrets, An Autobiography of Jean Cocteau Drawn from his* [. . .] *Writings*, by Robert Phelps. The *Biography*'s account of Firbank's acquaintance with Édouard de Max is on pp. 47–8. The dating supplied by Romola Nijinsky is in her *Nijinsky*, 7.

The crystal gazer in *The Artificial Princess* comes on pp. 56–7 in the *Complete* Firbank.

Monsignor Parr in *The Artificial Princess* is on p. 67 of the *Complete* Firbank, and in *Vainglory* on p. 81.

The Rose Garden and the King's Dwarf are both on p. 56 of the *Complete* Firbank, the lifelong feud occasioned by a mirror on p. 71.

The end of Ada Leverson's Sphinx parody is quoted in Rupert Hart-Davis's edition of *The Letters of Oscar Wilde*, p. 357.

Minx turns painter on p. 27 in the *Complete* Firbank.

Wilde's accounts of the binding of *Salome* are in two of his letters, both on p. 333 in Rupert Hart-Davis's edition.

Lord Goring leaves the Chilterns' saying he is going on to the mauve Hungarian band in Act I of *An Ideal Husband*. Firbank's re-writing of the concept is on p. 65 of the original edition of *The Artificial Princess* (p. 61 in the *Complete* Firbank).

XIV

The Wilde Collection Concluded

1. A Princess of Scandal . . .

FIRBANK could have endorsed Oscar Wilde's 'French by sympathy, I am Irish by blood' – though, given that Firbank had a Unionist M.P. for a father whereas Wilde had an Irish-nationalist poet for a mother, it is unlikely Firbank would have gone on to endorse the nationalist half of the nationalist-aesthetic paradox with which Wilde continued: 'and the English have condemned me to speak the language of Shakespeare'. (It is, of course, *the* paradox of Ireland. Wilde had indeed 'summed up all' Irish 'existence in an epigram'.)

The imperial exile at Chislehurst set a pattern to Firbank's young imagination whereby he could figure himself as a princess, and first made French an attractive and nostalgic language to his ears. But for Firbank to learn enough French to write and publish in it required the further example of his saint Oscar Wilde. And if one asks exactly *what* example Wilde set him, what work Wilde wrote in French, the answer is *Salomé*: a work which re-instructed Firbank in considering himself a princess – and a princess, this time, explicitly and wilfully perverse. Firbank began to apply the lesson in the Princess of his play *The Mauve Tower*,[1] whose hair and speech alike he dressed in Wildean costume jewellery, and then he outdid the teacher with his Artificial Princess.

Wilde's *Salomé* occasioned a miniature Wilde scandal three years before the Wilde scandal proper. Sarah Bernhardt was already rehearsing for a production in London when the English censor banned the play, which he did in accordance with what Wilde called 'his silly vulgar rule about no Biblical *subject* being treated'. By treating the martyrdom of John the Baptist in a drama Wilde brought on himself a foretaste of his own martyrdom. He noticed the 'pleasure' the press took in his play's suppression; he noticed that Bernard Shaw and Ibsen's other champion, William Archer, were the only famous critics to support him; and the experience made him yet more strongly 'French by sympathy'. Indeed, Wilde would have avoided

[1] Cf. Chapter XIII, 4.

his ultimate martyrdom had he acted on the plan which immediately crossed his mind when his play was suppressed: to become a French citizen.

However, Wilde stayed in England – in pursuit of his lifelong courtship of danger. And in fact it must have been that courtship which drew him to Salome in the first place. The daughter of Herodias was a neat little package of scandal in her own biblical day (and her mother continued a scandalous figure into the middle ages, thanks to her muddled connexion with witchcraft). There was precedent enough by which Wilde could divine unerringly that he was picking on a princess who was a multiple time-bomb of scandal.

This in the event Salome proved: by detonating further scandals both when Aubrey Beardsley illustrated the English translation of Wilde's French play and when, five years after Wilde's death, Richard Strauss made the German translation into an opera. Robert Ross recorded: 'When "Salomé" was translated into English by Lord Alfred Douglas, the illustrator, Aubrey Beardsley, shared some of the obloquy heaped on Wilde.'[1] Strauss's opera was even more of a public success (running to productions in 50 different cities within two years of the first one in Dresden) and no less of a scandal. It worried the Kaiser (who was pacified into permitting the Berlin production only by the introduction of the star of Bethlehem into the final backcloth), Gustav Mahler was prevented by the church from producing it in Vienna (though the Breslau production was allowed to visit the city), and two attempted productions in New York were aborted by the influence of private patrons. The opera's journey to London (where it had to overcome the same objections which the Lord Chamberlain made to the play) took five years, mostly without hope. In 1908, two years before the opera did in fact arrive, Ernest Newman wrote: '*Salome*, presumably, we shall never hear on the stage in England.'

In Firbank's imagination Salome served as a concentrated symbol of scandal and, in particular, of the Wilde scandal – whose repetition in his own life (to which Salome was linked by being a princess) Firbank both dreaded and, Wilde-fashion, flirted with. Firbank's very fantasy was shaped by Wilde's catastrophic libel-suit; and a mere customs examination in his

---

[1] Ross continued: 'It is interesting that he should have found inspiration for his finest work in a play he never admired and by a writer he cordially disliked.' However, the notion that Beardsley didn't, at least when it first appeared, admire Wilde's play is contradicted by Beardsley's behaviour. Brian Reade (*Beardsley*, p. 336) points out that Beardsley not only volunteered an illustration to the play before he was commissioned but offered his own translation of the play to Wilde. Wilde preferred, however, to be translated by Lord Alfred Douglas, in whose honour he (cf. Chapter XIII, 9) had the translation bound in Tyrian purple, though (Hesketh Pearson, p. 230), dissatisfied with Douglas's translation, Wilde revised it himself.

own fiction brought to Firbank's mind Wilde's Salomesque self-stripping in cross-examination.[1] Perhaps it was the assonance between cross-examination and academic examinations that dictated Firbank's remarkable avoidance of the academic kind of examinations before and during his Cambridge career.[2] If so, it was inevitable that, when he later tried to set a date on his composition of the novel he presumably called, at the time of writing, by the Wildean title *Salome*, Firbank associated[3] it with when he was preparing for a Cambridge examination he never in fact took.

2. ... and of Domesticity

SAINT MATTHEW'S gospel does not accord Salome a name but speaks of her as the daughter of Herodias. Herod the Tetrarch has married his brother's wife, Herodias. John the Baptist preaches that the marriage is unlawful, and Herod therefore puts him in prison. At Herod's birthday, 'the daughter of Herodias danced before them, and pleased Herod. Whereupon he promised with an oath to give her whatsoever she would ask. And she, being before instructed of her mother, said, Give me here John Baptist's head in a charger.'

Oscar Wilde gave Salome the name she bears in Josephus, and restored John's name to the form Jokanaan. To the incestuous marriage between Herod and Herodias, Wilde added the further scandal that the manner in which Salome 'pleased' Herod was also incestuous. ('I have ever loved you,' Wilde's Herod says to Salome; '... It may be that I have loved you too much.') In Wilde, Salome exacts the oath from Herod *before* she consents to dance, and she demands the prophet's head not on her mother's instructions and in order to dispose of a political enemy of her mother's but because the prophet has refused her, Salome's, love.

When the head is delivered, Wilde adds the (indeed) final scandal of a touch of necrophilia. Salome addresses the chopped-off head: 'Ah! thou wouldst not suffer me to kiss thy mouth, Jokanaan. Well! I will kiss it now. I will bite it with my teeth as one bites a ripe fruit' – provoking Herod to tut-tut to his wife: 'She is monstrous, thy daughter, she is altogether monstrous.'

Firbank's contribution to this scandalous history was deliberately to import, into the royal household, what Wilde came scaringly near importing by accident: a domestic touch. In the Bible, Herod, though sorry, feels obliged to do as Salome asks 'for the oath's sake, and them which sat with

---

[1] Cf. Chapter VII, 3.   [2] Cf. Chapter VII, 2.
[3] Cf. Chapter VII, 2 and Chapter XIII, 6.

him at meat'. In *The Artificial Princess*, the great feast is sweetened and domesticated, the King's promise is swallowed into a subordinate clause, and Salome's public dance is repressed into privacy and a co-ordinate clause: 'the Princess, who had obtained the King's word, that she might ask, during dessert, for anything she pleased, had risen from her bath, and was dancing a Tarantella before the Mirror, in just a bracelet and a rope of pearls'.[1]

The same Firbankian touch domesticates Herodias: without, however, depriving her of either her regal or her baroque quality. 'The Queen had a passion for motoring. She would motor for hours and hours with her crown on' . . .

It was on the royal household of Judaea that Firbank developed this essential Firbankian technique of a domesticity deflationary and yet bizarre in its own right. Developing it was part of the parricide[2] which Firbank was committing on Wilde by re-writing Wilde's Salome story. Deflation was a weapon borrowed from Wilde the wit. Firbank was using it on Wilde the puffed-up and purply poetical.

Firbank learned the technique of deflation by domesticity from (as well as Wilde) a popular story: the folk tale about the Englishwoman who, on seeing Sarah Bernhardt play Cleopatra, commented (in the *Oxford Dictionary of Quotations*'s wording of the remark): 'How different, how very different from the home life of our own dear Queen!'

It is a story which Firbank, as a fellow-cultist (with Wilde) of Queen Victoria, would be *likely* to know. And *The Artificial Princess* bears witness that he *did* know it. A book the Princess receives as a birthday present is called *The Home Life of the Queen of Sheba*.[3]

(There is also a verbal echo of the folk tale in the thoughts which Firbank attributes to Eddy Monteith by way of comment on the English Ambassadress: 'What a contrast to his own Mamma – "so different," . . . and his thoughts returned to Intriguer – "dear Intriguer, . . ." ')

The domesticating joke that was applied to the Queens of England, Egypt and Sheba was applicable also to a more sinister woman from history. Firbank invented a book called *The Home Life of Lucretia Borgia*.[4] That fictitious book appeared in more than one of Firbank's early fictions, where it is read by more than one of his dramatis personae. He finally published it

---

[1] On the subject of the Tarantella, cf. Chapter XIII, 6. The rope of pearls will come into sub-section 7 of this chapter.

[2] Cf. Chapter XIII, 6.

[3] No doubt this is why the Princess presently (p. 42 in the *Complete* Firbank) commands 'a warm bath à la reine de Saba'.

[4] a work which has an almost nursery counterpart in *Valmouth* (p. 427 in the *Complete* Firbank): *Tales from Casanova*.

in *Vainglory*, where its author is Mrs Asp – whose name acknowledges its source to be the folk-tale comment on Cleopatra.

There are further strands to this Nilotic nexus. Oscar Wilde, in a letter to Leonard Smithers in 1900, wrote of Sarah Bernhardt as 'that "serpent of old Nile" ', the phrase which Shakespeare's Cleopatra says is one of Antony's names for her. In 1899 Wilde declared to Vincent O'Sullivan: 'The three women I have most admired are Queen Victoria, Sarah Bernhardt, and Lily Langtry. I would have married any one of them with pleasure.'

Either – or both – of those strands may be why Firbank's self-portrait in *Vainglory*, Claud Harvester, is, for at least part of the book,[1] married to a woman named Cleopatra.

No doubt those strands contributed also to the fact that Lady Something (in *The Flower Beneath the Foot*) 'once had a housemaid who had lived with Sarah Bernhardt, and oh! wasn't she a terror!'; and to the existence (in the same book) of the Café Cleopatra.[2]

In the private room above the Café Cleopatra, the 'mural imagery' is compounded from Firbank's[3] superstitious reverence for Egypt, his passion (by way of Wilde) for Sphinxes, his inability to spell correctly the Antony he meant, and, I surmise,[4] his taste for Tiepolo. 'She raised imploring eyes to the mural imagery – to the "Cleopatra couchant", to the "Arrival of Anthony", to the "Sphinx", to the "Temple of Ra", as though seeking inspiration. "Ah my God!" she groaned.'

3. Creature and Creation

THE *Artificial Princess* is consciously – indeed, by her own design – a Salome. In his first-composed Firbankian work, Firbank has already invented

---

[1] Chapter XV, 8 will elaborate this point.
[2] The immediate source of the Café will be identified in Chapter XX, 1.
[3] Cf. Chapter VIII, 5; Chapter XIII, 3, 4 and 7; and Chapter X, 12.
[4] I imagine that the *Arrival of Antony* which Firbank had in mind is the smallish Tiepolo (no. 91 of the National Gallery of Scotland, which records it as bought for the Royal Institution, Edinburgh, in 1845) where Antony, newly disembarked, kisses Cleopatra's hand. No doubt Firbank saw the painting on his 1914 visit to Edinburgh (when he added John Gray to his Wilde collection – cf. Chapter XII, 6). He published his interest in Tiepolo in 1915, in the fictitious Tiepolos in *Vainglory* (cf. Chapter IX, 6). In the mural decorations of the Café Cleopatra Firbank perhaps had in mind Tiepolo's decorative scheme at Palazzo Labia, Venice (for which the Edinburgh painting is a study). But the decorative scheme reads to me more as though Firbank had invented an Egyptian counterpart to the classical mythology of Tiepolo's less formal decorated walls at Villa Valmarana, outside Vicenza – a villa Firbank might have seen since it was near the Italian home of his Cambridge acquaintance (*Memoir*, p. 37), A. C. Landsberg.

the Firbankian novel which is partly about the invention of a Firbankian novel, just as his first-published Firbankian novel, *Vainglory*, makes mention of *Vainglory*, though its title is fictionalised (it is, after all, *in* a work of fiction) into *Vaindreams*.

'How I should care to be a new Salomé!' the Artificial Princess explicitly says; and her determination to become one creates the plot whose creation by Firbank has in reality created her.

She discovers 'something in Mamma's appearance that recalls Herodias, especially in the afternoon when she wears her furs'. The King, she discerns, 'would make a superb Herod'. As for herself: 'I have always suspected mine to be a Salomesque temperament.'

Thus Firbank's creature assembles the skeins of his creativity in her hand: 'And now, since Fate has placed us – how events repeat themselves – King, Queen, Princess – improbable people like ourselves, with a Prophet at our very gate, and the whole Court languishing for something new, it would be very ungrateful not to take advantage of the opportunity and make hay whilst . . .'

'Hay!' the Baroness comments.

In pursuit of her plot, the Princess entrusts the Baroness with a note (its envelope 'lilac, narcissi-scented') to the bruited Prophet, instructing her: 'do not return without his promise that he will come to my party tonight.' It is only by the intervention of 'the devil himself' (or Aleister Crowley[1]) that the Princess's plot comes unravelled and Firbank's is woven. The Baroness strays into a love affair of her own, the note goes undelivered and at the party the Princess welcomes a beautiful but unProphetic young man – to her embraces? to his death? or merely to discovery of the mistake?

The distortion of the Princess's plot achieves a distortion of the forerunner theme in the original. It is the Baroness who is sent out with a mission, as forerunner to the messianic Princess, and she falls down on the job. She becomes the disciple who betrays the messiah. ' "Cock-a-doodle, doooo . . ." ' (the oo-s prolonged to two lines of print), begins the last section of the book (part of the ending Firbank supplied long afterwards); and the dialogue concludes, in a masterstroke of Firbankianly unattributed lines and Firbankianly expressive punctuation:

'("Cluck-cluck?")

' "Cock-a-doodle . . ." '

---

[1] Cf. Chapter VIII, 6.

4. An Engaging Theme

FIRBANK'S Princess, who predicts that the King 'will certainly be made into an Opera after he is dead, and I daresay I shall be dragged into it, too', is evidently a Straussian.[1] Indeed at another moment in the book, 'seating herself, with the unreasonable look of an Iphigenia, upon a brittle, tattered and ornate throne, she began to hum a certain air by Strauss.'

The first (though posthumous) edition retains Firbank's italics and bad spelling: 'a certain air by *Straus*'.

(I can think of no occasion for Firbank, about 1910, to associate Strauss with Iphigenia. I doubt if Firbank can have been alluding to the performing edition of Gluck's *Iphigénie en Tauride* which Strauss prepared while [1889 to 1894] he was conductor at Weimar. So perhaps Iphigenia is another Firbankian negligence, like the spelling of the composer's name, and Firbank had in mind the heroine of Strauss's next great and scandalous opera after *Salome, Elektra* – which was first presented in Dresden on 25 January 1909 and first reached London on 19 February 1910. The 'unreasonable look' Firbank attributes to Iphigenia could reasonably be attributed to Elektra. And perhaps Firbank was half-mindful of the mythological fact that Elektra and Iphigenia are sisters.)

Firbank's imagination became almost as deep-engaged with the Strauss–Wilde figure of Salome as it was with the straight Wildean Salome. That Strauss had made a masterpiece where Wilde made a mistake could be read as a shewing-up of Wilde. But what Strauss music-dramatised[2] was Wilde's play, whose structure provides the structure of the opera.[3] So it is more likely that Firbank welcomed the greater artistic success of the opera as an opportunity to soften, in his own thoughts, his parricidal criticisms of Wilde.

---

[1] So are other Firbankian personages. The Duchess of Varna, for instance, in *The Flower Beneath the Foot*, breaks off a conversation (on p. 530 in the *Complete* Firbank) in order 'to listen to the orchestra in the café below, which was playing the waltz-air from *Der Rosenkavalier*'. 'It must make one', the Duchess comments, 'restless, dissatisfied, that yearning, yearning music continually at the door!'

[2] Cf. Ernest Newman in 1908: 'Strauss calls *Guntram* and *Salome* "Musikdramas" and *Feuersnot* a "Singgedicht". We may conveniently call them all three operas, declining to follow the Teutonic mind in its mania for giving different names to what is essentially the same thing.' (Newman's *Richard Strauss*, p. 104 in the 1921 reprint.)

[3] Cf. Robert Ross (undated Note): 'English musical journalists and correspondents always refer to the work as *founded* on Wilde's drama. [. . .] The music, however, has been set to the actual words of "Salomé" in Madame Hedwig Lachmann's admirable translation.' Ernest Newman: 'The libretto of *Salome* is based on Frau Hedwig Lachmann's German translation of Oscar Wilde's play; Strauss has done nothing more than abridge this for his own purposes.' (Newman's 1908 *Richard Strauss*; pp. 104–5 in the 1921 reprint.)

Firbank's concern with Salome was autobiographical (she is a manifestation of Princess Artie) and at the same time a strand in his Wilde pursuit (where her scandalousness represents the Wilde scandal). Salome motifs appear in Firbank's early pieces, written before he made Salome the centre of a whole novel; and (perhaps because he didn't at the time make it *quite* a whole novel, and never published it) Salome motifs continued to appear in work written after it.

It is,[1] for example, in Firbank's next-written and first-published Firbankian novel, *Vainglory*, that Mira Thumbler refuses to dance because 'I should feel far too like . . . *you know*.' 'The daughter of Herodias?' enquires Mrs Henedge (her vocabulary, for a rarity among Firbankian speakers, disdaining a reference to Wilde and being pedantically biblical: perhaps someone had lately *told* Firbank that Salome is not named in the Bible). Mira, like Salome, agrees in the end to dance. But by that swallowed pun of Firbank's narrative, the bribe is not a Prophet's head on a salver but her own on a canvas by George Calvally.

Vainglory, indeed, makes allusion, with archaeological thoroughness, to all the layers of the Salome complex. Besides its scrupulously worded reference to the biblical Salome, it makes mention of the *Salome* of, specifically, Strauss (although, according to the first edition, Firbank gives it a French accent as though it were the *Salomé* of Wilde). Winsome Brookes is allowed to disparage some of the opera. ' "For lack of humour", Winsome said, "I know of nothing in the world to compare with the Prophet's music in *Salomé*. It's the quintessence of villadom. It suggests the Salvation Army, and General Booth. It —" '

Vainglory's allusion to the *Salomé* of, specifically, Wilde is oblique. 'Next month', says an actress, 'I'm hoping to get Eysoldt over to play with me in Maeterlinck'.[2] Gertrud Eysoldt played Wilde's Salomé at Max Reinhardt's Kleines Theater in Berlin. (The production, which Strauss visited in 1903 because he was already intending to set the play, was in the German translation by Hedwig Lachmann which Strauss eventually used.)

Salome was still current in Firbank's mind when he was writing *The New Rythum*. Indeed, on one occasion in that unfinished novel, Firbank's thoughts associated Salome with the author whose work Eysoldt is to play in *Vainglory*, namely Maeterlinck. A voice heard singing[3] at a party in New York is said to be the voice of 'Farrar, or Garden'. Firbank has picked a pair of

---

[1] as I mentioned in Chapter IX, 9.
[2] This strand will recur in Chapter XV, 2; and Chapter XV, 15 will offer a further explanation of the actress's hope.
[3] This will be mentioned further in Chapter XV, 6.

singers who very plausibly might be in New York, the United-States soprano Geraldine Farrar and Mary Garden, a soprano who, born in Aberdeen, passed some of her childhood as well as much of her operatic career in the United States. For Mary Garden Firbank no doubt felt a particular reverence: because (after Strauss's opera was finally found admissible[1] there) she sang the rôle of Salome in New York; and again because she was the first person to sing (anywhere) the Maeterlinck–Debussy[2] rôle of Mélisande, which she did in English-accented[3] French.

Herod's title is, moreover, the only explanation I can surmise (though it doesn't explain all that needs explaining) of why, when Mrs Rosemerchant (still in *The New Rythum*) arrives at a charity committee meeting in Fifth Avenue, she should recognise, among the 'equipages [. . .] obstructing the roadway', 'Bertie Waldorf's handsome English horses of Tetrarch grey'.

(What Tetrarch grey *is* I don't know. Conceivably, since a tetrarchy is the fourth part of a kingdom, Firbank is implying that there were four horses, who made an impression of a greyness divided into four. More probably he is satirising fashion-writers', milliners' and paint-manufacturers' habit of giving names, often arbitrarily, to shades of colour. 'Dove grey' must have been forbidden by the fact that the next bit of the sentence is going to mention Mrs Mandarin Dove. For substitute Firbank perhaps just picked 'Tetrarch' out of his preoccupation with the household of Herod the Tetrarch.[4])

The preoccupation which continued thus late certainly began earlyish. Some of Firbank's allusions to (and one of his prettiest variations on) the theme of Salome belong to early work which he never published – though

---

[1] Cf. sub-section 1 of this chapter.

[2] Firbank's devotion to this coupling, and to that of Pelléas and Mélisande, will be explored in Chapter XV, 2 and 15.

[3] – a possible side-result of which will be mentioned in Chapter XV, 15, together with a possible further cause of Firbank's devotion.

[4] Or it is, of course, possible that 'Tetrarch' is a mis-transcription. Although the Introduction to *The New Rythum and Other Pieces* speaks of a typescript of *The New Rythum* which came to light after Heather Firbank's death, the catalogue of the Sotheby's sale published at the end of that volume lists no typescript of the book but only an autograph first draft and an autograph fair copy of the first six chapters. And perhaps it is unlikely that Firbank would have had the book typed while it remained (as in the event it always did remain) unfinished. (The unlikely wouldn't, however, have been unprecedented. According to p. 88 of the *Bibliography*, there is a typescript of the first two chapters of *The Artificial Princess* as well as two typescripts containing the all but finished final chapter.) If *The New Rythum* was set up in print from a transcript of Firbank's manuscript, it would be particularly prone to transcription errors. 'Tetrarch' might be one. And I think there is certainly one (or *some* sort of error, at least) at the top of the same (printed) page (78) where 'Tetrarch' occurs: 'impulsively changing her pen' should surely read 'impulsively charging her pen'.

in some happy cases the Salome items are among the extracts from early pieces which were published in 1962 in the same volume as *The New Rythum*.

That volume includes, for instance: ' "I am a work of art," she [Lady Georgia Blueharnis] sighed, "and this evening I feel nearly as wicked as Herodias." It was one of Lady Georgia's habits to find equivalents for all her worser feelings in the Bible.'

Lady Georgia's worser feelings are in Firbank's story *A Tragedy in Green*, which he cannot have written before the autumn of 1907 – the earliest moment, that is, at which he could have met Sir Coleridge Kennard, 'the Inspirer of the Tragedy'.[1]

Given that Kennard was introduced to Firbank by Wilde's son, and given that Kennard's mother was one of the quarries of Firbank's Wilde pursuit (because she was posthumously the dedicatee of a work by Wilde[2]), it was inevitable that the story Firbank dedicated to the son of Wilde's dedicatee should genuflect to *some* theme of Wilde's. Firbank perhaps picked on Salome's mother because Mrs Carew was Kennard's mother. And perhaps Wilde's Salome theme was already in Firbank's mind as the centre of an already-conceived or even already-begun *Salome, Or 'Tis A Pity That She Would*[3] (alias *The Artificial Princess*).

Another early story of Firbank's, one which, however, remains totally unpublished, is said by Firbank's biographer (who owns its typescript) to make an allusion to Richard Strauss's *Salome*. By the *Biography*'s dating, this story, *Her Dearest Friend*, is even earlier (by a couple of years) than the story Firbank dedicated to Kennard. But the *Biography*'s dating, which rests on the Strauss reference, seems to me deeply to be doubted.

The *Biography* lists *Her Dearest Friend* among Firbank pieces which can be dated by 'specific topical references': in this case, to 'Strauss's opera *Salome*, which was first presented on December 9, 1905'. The *Biography* then goes on to state that Firbank wrote *Her Dearest Friend* 'either in December 1905 or January 1906'.

Regrettably, the *Biography* gives no description of the Strauss allusion it says is in *Her Dearest Friend*. Perhaps the content of the allusion does something to justify the *Biography*'s dating. But, on the information the *Biography* gives, the *Biography*'s argument has left out the crucial consideration that Strauss's opera was first given on 9 December 1905 *in Dresden*. Firbank (according to the *Biography*) was at that time moving between his London crammer's (which he left on 8 December) and his crammer's in Aberdeenshire (where he had arrived 'by the second week in December').

---

[1] Cf. Chapter X, 2, footnote and Chapter XII, 5–6.   [2] Cf. Chapter XII, 5.
[3] Cf. Chapter VI, 5.

In stating that Firbank wrote *Her Dearest Friend* in the December or January, the *Biography* is making him allude to an opera he had certainly never heard.

There is, of course, no reason why Firbank should not have alluded to the *reputation* of Strauss's *Salome* well before he had an opportunity to hear the opera itself. Indeed, I believe he did make just such a hearsay allusion in another of his early pieces, which I will mention in a moment. No doubt Firbank, like most of the opera's audience outside Germany, heard *of* Strauss's *Salome* long before he heard *it*. But equally there is no reason why a reference to the opera's reputation should be written within two months of its first presentation in Dresden. Indeed, a reference to its reputation is more likely to have been written two years than two months after the work's Dresden début, because there was by then more reputation to refer to.

When *Salome* was mounted in Dresden, Strauss and his early orchestral works were tolerably well known in England. But neither of his earlier operas had been given in England.[1] His repute as an orchestral compseor may, however, have been enough to bring instantly to England some word of the stir made in Dresden by his newest opera. Firbank just possibly might have instantly picked up such a report, perhaps because he would be alert to any report connected with Wilde, perhaps because he was already interested in Strauss as a composer.

(He would have had opportunity to follow Strauss's orchestral works. On the whole, however, the allusions in his work suggest that Firbank was less fond of orchestral music[2] than of opera and ballet – and, perhaps, piano music, which he could play himself. On the grand piano belonging to the blatantly autobiographical hero of *Lady Appledore's Mésalliance* there stands 'an open piece of music by Debussy'.)

There is a thin chance that Firbank picked up a thin echo from Dresden and instantly alluded to it in a story. But he is much more likely to have written the allusion during the ensuing five years, while the opera moved, or was scandal-provokingly frustrated from moving, into the international repertory. The *Biography*'s implication that Strauss's *Salome* was 'topical' in England only within two months of its Dresden first night is absurd. In reality, the opera increased in topicality as it accumulated productions and scandals. It was actually *more* 'topical' in England in 1908, when Ernest Newman published his short book on Strauss, than it had been in 1905.

[1] – though an extract from *Feuersnot* was given a concert performance in 1902, and one from *Guntram* in 1903 (Ernest Newman: *Richard Strauss*, reprint p. 22 and p. 25).

[2] Chapter XVIII, 4 will name a piece of orchestral music which I think was of direct and particular influence on Firbank, but it is orchestral music which is entered by human voices.

Even in 1908 *Salome* was two years short of an English production,[1] and was as yet without hope of one, but its pre-publicity had by then grown to be enormous.

As a matter of fact, there is a reference to Strauss's *Salome* in another early Firbank piece, his one-act play *A Disciple from the Country*. Extracts from this play are, happily, published in the same volume as *The New Rythum*. They include the remark that the Salome story has 'quite recently' been made into an opera. If the *Biography* applied to the play the argument it seems to be applying to *Her Dearest Friend*, it would insist that the play, too, was written in December 1905 or January 1906. Instead, it proposes 1907 as the date of the play.

The simple fact, with no description attached, that it contains a reference to Strauss's opera can establish no more than that *Her Dearest Friend* was written after 9 December 1905. Firbank might have mentioned Strauss's *Salome* at any time from then on. In his own mind the opera was still topical ten years later, when he published the allusions to it in *Vainglory*. The external topicality of the opera was on the increase, in England, from 1905 till 1910, which was London's great Strauss year. *Elektra*, though the later composed, arrived the earlier by eleven months. *Salome* followed on 8 December 1910, having taken five years, almost to the day, on its passage from Dresden, its 'topicality' increasing with each year's delay.

If the dating of *Her Dearest Friend* rests on Strauss, the probability lies less towards 1905 than towards 1910. 1910 was, after all, almost certainly the year (or at least *a* year) in which Firbank was writing *The Artificial Princess*, with *its* Straussian references – a book whose date of composition Firbank himself, though in an imprecise way, associated with 'the Straus cult'.[2]

By the time (1915) he published Winsome Brookes's disparaging opinion of the Prophet's music in it, Firbank had obviously heard Strauss's opera. That is not to confuse Firbank with the personage in his fiction. Firbank may or may not have shared Winsome Brookes's opinion of it, but he certainly shared Winsome Brookes's acquaintance with the music.

The Straussian references in *The Artificial Princess*, being less particularised, leave it open whether Firbank had by then heard the music or was referring to it by reputation. (I do not think it would be impossible for

---

[1] though, as Ernest Newman records (reprint, p. 26), the dance was played in a concert in the Queen's Hall in November 1907; and an article by Terry Coleman in *The Guardian* (11 June 1971) records that, while the opera was still banned, extracts were sung, to a piano accompaniment played by Artur Rubinstein, at a performance in a private house in London (with Edward VII in the audience).

[2] Cf. Chapter XIII, 6.

Firbank to have attended an *Elektra* and still to mention its heroine under the name of Iphigenia.)

The Straussian allusion in Firbank's play *A Disciple from the Country* seems, on the other hand, to hint that when it was written Firbank had not heard Strauss's *Salome* but was going on hearsay.

In fact, the passage in the play makes *two* allusions to Salome: to the story; and to the opera. The first is a Firbankian ornamentation on the biblical story. That leads into a reference to the opera – a reference which is a version of the joke which Firbank incorporated into *The Artificial Princess* in the form of the Princess's prediction that the King 'will certainly be made into an Opera after he is dead, and I daresay I shall be dragged into it, too'.

The Princess speaks with certainty: about an opera which only fiction has placed in the future. But Mrs Creamway, who speaks the comparable joke in *A Disciple from the Country*, speaks (amusingly) on the strength of hearsay. 'They tell me the whole thing has been turned quite recently into a very tuneful opera. In these days nobody seems safe from being set to music...'

It is dangerous to amalgamate personage and author. Firbank may have been acquainted with what Mrs Creamway knew only by hearsay. And her 'They tell me' is amusing enough to be justified in its own right. Yet it may equally be that her 'They tell me' came to Firbank's mind because it echoed his own situation.

That is all the more likely if the *Biography* is correct in dating the play to 1907, which it does on the grounds that in 1907 Firbank joined two undergraduate dramatic societies at Cambridge, the implication being that Firbank was hoping for a production of a play of his own. If Mrs Creamway's hearsay allusion to Strauss does indeed reflect Firbank's not yet having heard the opera, then the dating of the play to 1907 can be slightly refined. The play is likely to have been written before May 1907. Up till May 1907 there seems to have been no production of Strauss's *Salome* in a city where Firbank might have attended it. But in May 1907 Strauss's *Salome* was given in Paris. It would have been very like Firbank to have gone over for it.

(In Paris *Salome*, following the French way with foreign operas, was sung in French. For Firbank that would have had the advantage that he could understand the opera. When *Elektra* and *Salome* finally reached England, they were sung in German – though even Firbank's probably considerable lack[1] of German can scarcely be the cause of his mistaking Electra for Iphigenia.)

The ornamentation which *A Disciple from the Country* adds (earlier in

---

[1] Cf. Chapter X, 12.

the same speech by Mrs Creamway) to the history of Salome is a felicitous Firbankian invention in Firbank's domestic[1] manner. To the scandal resonantly recounted in the Bible and grandiosely enlarged in Wilde's crown-jewelled prose, Firbank adds a twiddle in the idiom of Jane Austen. 'Only yesterday', Mrs Creamway says, 'I spent most of my morning hunting for a pamphlet which satisfactorily proves that Mary Magdalen was actually engaged to John the Baptist. It was only after the sad affair at the Palace that Mary really buckled to and became what she afterwards became.' It is after this inspired invention that Mrs Creamway continues, 'They tell me that the whole thing' – the sad affair at the Palace – 'has been turned quite recently into a very tuneful opera.'

Like the operatic joke, the invention about the Magdalen was transposed by Firbank into later work – and this time work which, unlike *The Artificial Princess*, he published. At the drop of the words 'St. Mary Magdalen', Mrs Shamefoot, in *Vainglory*, responds: 'I have her life upstairs! Did you know she was actually engaged to John the Baptist? Until Salome *broke it off*. It was only after the sad affair at the Palace' – etc. as in *A Disciple from the Country*.

In the earlier version there is a pamphlet proving the point. It persists into the later version in the form of a *Life* of the saint. Firbank's domestic invention ran true to his hagiographical imagination.[2]

And no doubt he was at his most deeply hagiographical when devising an ornament to a theme treated by his saint Oscar Wilde.

5. Emergence

FIRBANK'S invention translated the history of Salome into the common-sensible and social idiom of Jane Austen, the idiom in which people get engaged and (Firbank's italics of social scandal) *break it off*. Firbank's translation no more trivialised the story than Jane Austen's use of the idiom trivialised *her* subject-matter. On the contrary. Jane Austen's familial themes and Firbank's joke of domesticity are alike devices which analyse material into its psychological essentials. The Oedipus situation *is a domestic* situation. It was in an exact, as well as a perfectly serious, sense that I called[3] *The Artificial Princess* Firbank's *Hamlet*.

And as a matter of fact the Princess herself has equated Salome's family situation with Hamlet's. When she claims that her stepfather the King 'would make a superb Herod', she adduces in evidence a characteristic less of

---

[1] Cf. sub-section 2 of this chapter.   [2] Cf. Chapter XIII, 2.
[3] Cf. Chapter XIII, 6.

Herod than of Claudius: 'He has the same suspicious walk and the incurable habit of prodding curtains and expecting an ambush round every corner.'

Salome and Hamlet share a domestic crisis. In each case, the mother has remarried – and has married the father's brother. Firbank's Princess has borrowed this same crisis from Salome. 'Indeed the position in which Fate has placed me, to hers, exactly corresponds,' the Princess declares – and reviews the points of correspondence in conversation with the Baroness. ' "The resemblance *is* remarkable," ' the Baroness 'agreed tactfully, "your mother, like Herodias, *did* marry her brother-in-law, but somehow I never thought of them together before. I don't know why!" '

For Firbank this was an autobiographical situation. Not that his mother re-married and provided him with an uncle-plus-stepfather. (She did, however, in what was probably Firbank's imaginative model for Herodias's re-marriage, take a new name, as though she were re-marrying, at the occasion of a coronation: by becoming, when Firbank was 16, Lady Firbank, in Edward VII's coronation honours.[1]) It was Firbank who had emotionally put aside his real father in favour of literary stepfathers of his own choice.

His choice went first to Rollo St Clair Talboys, who warned him against the 'insidious and exotic poison' of 'dead men's sins'. Firbank then put aside that literary stepfather and took in his place precisely the dead man – the, to Firbank's mind, dead and canonised man – whom Talboys had warned him against.[2]

Firbank adopted the Salome theme from Wilde by way of paying pious tribute to his new stepfather, and then found himself in danger of assassinating Wilde too: by improving on him. And while[3] he was working on the book which constituted the improvement, Firbank's real father died.

Hamlet emerges from his crisis a murderer who is presently murdered: in both instances partly by accident, but the accident may be of the kind that is unconsciously willed. Hamlet is a half-voluntary suicide, capital-punishing himself, probably, for his unconscious concurrence in the fact of his father's death. Salome's guilt probably has the same occasion as Hamlet's, but it may be compounded by the guilt of her having also desired her father. Perhaps Wilde invented the stepfather's lust for Salome as a mirror-metaphor of Salome's lust for her true father. Wilde's princess is prepared to oust her mother from the affections of *any* of her mother's husbands. She lusts for the forbidden, whether a father or a holy man. Salome emerges a murderer (morally) and a monster – a monster whom, in Wilde's version, Herod orders to be put down, like a freak.

Firbank's Princess, on the other hand, emerges merely into mistakenness

[1] Cf. Chapter X, 8.   [2] Cf. Chapter XIII, 5.   [3] Cf. Chapter XIII, 6.

and a serene ambiguity: an ambiguity which is the witness to Firbank's having, himself, emerged a Firbankian. Princess Artie had 'come out'. True, he sacrificed his book to his guilt. The hesitations through which Firbank abstained from publishing it are Hamlet's half-voluntary moves towards self-destruction. But, by creating – and, although not publishing, not destroying either – his first Firbankian work, Firbank created himself a novelist independent both of Wilde's influence and of his own guilt towards Wilde.

6. Talismans

FIRBANK'S imagination adopted two talismans from Wilde's and played on them to the verge of obsession: Salome and the Sphinx. They are opposites: the Sphinx hugs her secret; Salome, compulsive strip-teaser, insists on brazenly disclosing the utmost of hers. Yet the talismans are complementary. The secret they respectively guard and flaunt is the same secret: the love that dare not speak its name. The unnatural and monstrous form of the Sphinx and the unnatural and monstrous conduct of the Princess both stand metaphor for the love unjustly called unnatural.

Wilde's long poem apostrophises the Sphinx as 'you exquisite grotesque! half woman and half animal!' and finally turns against her with 'Get hence, you loathsome mystery!' – a precursor of the cry with which Wilde's Herod rids the world of Salome, 'Kill that woman!'

Firbank put up none of Wilde's fight towards killing his 'half woman' self. He simply, mentally, *became* a woman. Indeed, he became '*that* woman'. Writing *The Artificial Princess*, he slipped into *being* Salome.

Had Princess Artie been persuaded to dance and divest, she would have disclosed herself a transvest.

Salome and the Sphinx, the talismans Firbank borrowed from Wilde, are emblems of the two complementary techniques Firbank developed for his narrative or discourse.

For paragraphs at a time, information is hugged between the Sphinx's paws. Pronouncements are cryptic. The reader–child–eavesdropper[1] is obliged to piece together answers to the riddles posed by multiple adult, knowing conversations. The riddles are all versions of the mythological riddle of the Sphinx: the great childhood puzzle about sex. And then an unaccountable social silence momentarily visits the talkative adults, and into it a solo voice flashes a phrase. It is clear and flaunting, going too far though never quite far enough. It is a tease *and* a challenge. It is the flash of Salome's

[1] Cf. Chapter XI, 1.

penultimate veil. It is always (there are fleas at the Ritz, mice at the British Embassy . . .) scandalous. And Firbank's personages break into scandalised chatter again, their comments sometimes totally couched in his conversing punctuation: '.............!.............?......!.....!!!'

7. What's in a Title – 1

FIRBANK'S original[1] name for *The Artificial Princess, Salome, Or 'Tis A Pity That She Would*, has presumably modelled its sub-title on the title of *'Tis Pity She's a Whore*, by John Ford (1586–?1640). It is not untypical of Firbank to have spoilt both the rhythm and the idiomaticness of the model by obtruding, in his derivative, an *a* between the *'tis* and the *pity*.

In external form, Firbank's novel is remarkably unlike a Jacobean drama.[2] But its text offers a large hint of how Firbank's literary aesthetic was tending: in the shape of an amusing allusion to, and a (correct apart from the line divisions) quotation from, a Jacobean drama by John Webster (?1580–?1625).

Firbank's Princess, in narrating how her newly widowed mother removed her family to the court of that royal brother-in-law whom she presently married, records her governess's premonitory allusion to another titled widow whose remarriage produced a crisis. ' "Did you never hear of the Duchess of Malfi," my Governess asked mysteriously, in tones that robbed us of our circulation, and without any more warning began to recite: "What would it pleasure me to have my throat cut with diamonds? or to be smothered with Cassia? or to be shot to death with pearls?" Personally' (the Princess goes unregardingly on) 'I was almost paralysed by the idea of a long drive on our arrival through crowded thoroughfares in an open landau, and being stared at, in an ugly crêpe hat trimmed with crêpe buttercups, my hair in a knot like a Chinaman's tail.'

Firbank's device of having the governess speak (or at least be misunderstood by her listeners to speak) of the Duchess of Malfi[3] as though she were gossiping about a contemporary was not so much mimicked as justly praised, in an act of complementing and complimenting symmetry, by Evelyn Waugh[4] when he put Webster's other great dramatic heroine on the tongues

---

[1] Cf. Chapter XIII, 3 (and Chapter VI, 5).
[2] 'I don't choose, my child, to think of some of the "works" we harbour,' says Father Mahoney in *Valmouth* (on p. 408 of the *Complete* Firbank). Mrs Hurstpierpoint replies: 'Those Jacobean dramatists, and the French erotic works of the eighteenth century, of course, would be free . . . but Père Ernest didn't reject them.'
[3] Cf. Chapter VIII, 4.
[4] Cf. Chapter VI, 3.

of his characters (while they are in Italy) as though she were a common acquaintance of theirs: 'Vittoria Corombona has asked us all to her ball on Saturday.'

I would guess that it was by way of criticism of Wilde that it first came to Firbank's mind to evoke Ford's play and quote Webster's. Webster's throat-cutting diamonds and penetrating pearls are summoned to serve as touchstone to the inventory of fakes which Wilde's Herod runs through in the hope of persuading Salome to accept his possessions in lieu of the Baptist's head as fulfilment of his oath: 'I have topazes, yellow as are the eyes of tigers, and topazes that are pink as the eyes of a wood-pigeon, and green topazes that are as the eyes of cats. I have opals that burn always, with an icelike flame, opals that make sad men's minds, and are fearful of the shadows. I have onyxes like the eyeballs of a dead woman. I have moonstones that change when the moon changes' . . . etc. etc.

Firbank's Salome novel was commenting that Wilde's Salome play had achieved only window-dresser's art nouveau when what it needed was Websterian baroque.

The novel itself began as a pious embroidery on Wilde and became the first work of Firbankianism. Just so, the Jacobean allusions, which began as a reproach to Wilde, turned into a definition of Firbankianism – a recognition by Firbank that his own art, which is an art of incongruities, is baroque.

Webster's baroquely shot pearls turn up again later in the narrative of *The Artificial Princess*, transformed into a weapon threatening, with baroque incongruity indeed, bats. The Princess, her hair half dressed (for the evening garden party that is to celebrate her birthday), sits 'at her bedroom window amusing herself by frightening the passing Bats with a rope of pearls'.

(Perhaps it is the very rope of pearls which, with a bracelet, is all the Princess wears during her Tarantella.)

This moon-glimpsed, baroque stroke through the night, that reads like a flash of high white impasto on the book's texture, must have pleased both Firbank's baroque eye and his flagellant disposition. For in *Vainglory* the motif has propagated itself by splitting into two. The lethalness of Webster's pearls (which remain baroque) has combined with a characteristic of Firbank's own[1] to produce a new and indeed bizarre mode of lethalness: 'And he's so miserably mean. Why, the collar of pearls he gave his first wife strangled her!' Meanwhile, what had been the Artificial Princess's regular 'pastime' is in *Vainglory* momentarily taken up by Mrs Shamefoot: 'With a string of pearls Mrs. Shamefoot flicked at a passing bat.'

[1] Cf. Chapters VII, 2 and IX, 5.

By 1920 the occupation has become almost a religious exercise, in pursuit of which a devotee can wear herself out almost to martyrdom. 'Those great fatigued eyes . . .', murmurs another Princess (Zoubaroff) to her protégée Enid – whose fellow-protégée, Nadine, expands: 'She does far too much! Last night she was chasing bats after midnight with a long white rosary.'

8. What's in a Title – 2

IT was by becoming Wilde's Princess Salome that Firbank became himself as a novelist; and in that first Firbankian novel he has already developed, by means of his impersonation, all the devices (which I shall write of more elaborately in Chapters XVI and XVII) of Firbankian baroque.

Out of his reproaches against Wilde's grandiose yet flat poeticisms Firbank has invented both his domesticities[1] and the baroque streaks that cross the texture of his discourse. In redesigning the (under the inflated flowing robes) classic structure of Wilde's play, with the result that what is in Wilde a dramatic climax is tucked into a corner of Firbank's story,[2] Firbank discovered a method of introducing the allusiveness and obliqueness of his statements into his very designs. Like his sentences,[3] his entire structures practise syncopation. When the emphasis falls, it fools expectancy. And, by investing himself in the Princess, Firbank was able to put the skeins of plot-making into her hands[4] and thereby invent the Firbankian novel about the invention of a Firbankian novel.

Firbank's crucial impersonation is noticeably a touch transvestite. His heroine is, if not quite a drag queen, a drag princess. 'Like a Virgin in a missal her figure lacked consequence – sex. "My tall-tall schoolboy," her mother would usually call her in her correspondence with neighbouring Queens.'

Firbank's impersonation has already carried him half way to his ultimate transvestism of the imagination, his obsession with homosexual love between *women* – that final twist of self-transformation through which he expressed[5] in his fiction much of his flirtation with scandal, much, probably, of his otherwise suppressed sense of social injustice, and almost all his tenderness.

He had already been carried all the way to the delicate transvestism of vocabulary which is the chief ingredient in Firbankian camp. The language in which the president of a republic can be a *Perfect Dear*[6] is already fluent in

---

[1] Cf. sub-section 2 of this chapter.   [2] Cf. sub-section 2 of this chapter.
[3] Cf. Chapter X, 11.   [4] Cf. sub-section 3 of this chapter.
[5] This motif will be discussed in Chapter XV, 9 and 13.
[6] Cf. Chapter VIII, 8.

The Artificial Princess. The Baroness, sitting (under her parasol) on the (open) upper deck of the blue tram as she obeys (thus far) the Princess's command to deliver the invitation to the Prophet, muses that the Prophet may be handsome 'or he may be only a frump'.

Probably it is in her capacity as a self of Firbank's that his Princess has no proper name. By becoming the Princess, Firbank became Firbankian; and it was with his first Firbankian publication, *Vainglory*, that he became Ronald instead of Arthur or A. A. R. Firbank.[1] It is one of the very oblique corners into which he squeezed his Wildean material that the heroine he borrowed from Wilde is called in the text simply the Princess, the name Salome being relegated to the title.

And even from there it was eventually expunged. Evidently, however, Firbank was inhibited from giving his novel its just title at the time he wrote it, in the same way, and perhaps for the same cause (namely guilt towards Wilde), that he was inhibited at the time (and long after) from publishing it.[2]

Indeed, Firbank's hesitation about finding a satisfactory and publishable title for the book is parallel to his hesitations about finding a satisfactory name for himself to publish under: not surprisingly, since the heroine (who in one manifestation or another is embodied in both the original and the final title) is a self of Firbank's.

Yet the mot juste had long been on the tip of Firbank's mental tongue. He had made much of the word *artificial* even before he wrote the novel that was eventually to bear the word in its title. Miss Tail, whose condemnation is recommendation, puritanically pontificates in *A Study in Temperament* that, in 'modern life', 'To be smart is to be artificial. To be artificial is to be smart.'

Perhaps it is slightly ambiguous praise of artificiality when, towards the end of the same story, her disappointed lover reflects that Lady Agnes 'doesn't seem able to *feel*, she has read so much that she has lost *herself*, she has become cold, artificial'. And indeed, at the end of the *Study* Lady Agnes, instead of deciding to elope, decides to dye her hair red.

However, Firbank re-instated *artificial* as a term of unambiguous praise when he sub-titled *Lady Appledore's Mésalliance* 'an artificial pastoral'. By the time of *Vainglory*, he had endorsed the temperament of which he had made the *Study* as his own. His self-portrait as Claud Harvester (author of *Vaindreams*) is numbered among 'artificial temperaments'.

Probably Firbank played with the word in obedience to Oscar Wilde's doctrine: 'The first duty in life is to be as artificial as possible. What the second duty is no one has as yet discovered.'

[1] Cf. Chapter VII, 4. [2] Cf. Chapter XIII, 3, 4 and 6.

(Wilde obeyed his own maxim when he invented that pinnacle of artificiality, a green carnation – in which invention Firbank's Artificial Princess tried, as I shall remark in sub-section 11 of this chapter, to emulate him.)

Certainly, during his play with the word, Firbank discovered, if not a second duty, a second significance. The artificial is the made-up. Firbank (in the originally theatrical usage) made up his face. (Lady Agnes in *A Study in Temperament* demonstrates *her* artificiality by applying a cosmetic to her hair.) At the same time, Firbank (in a childish idiom) made up fictions. (It is a childish idiom which Firbank as a child did use. He wrote to his mother: 'I hope you will like this piece of poetary I have written for you [. . .] I made it up all myself & as Joey[1] would say "did not look in a fairy book for it".')

One of Firbank's fictions was his own artificial temperament. He made up a personality (a minion's personality[2]) for himself when he made up his face.

An inventive player on names, including his own, Firbank did not neglect to exploit the happy chance[3] whereby he, who was everything the slang of the time meant by *arty*, was known to his family as Artie.

Yet that he was, precisely, *known* must have been one of the sources of Firbank's inhibition about giving his first Firbankian creation its just and obvious title. Obviously the Princess was Artificial: she was self-creating. She made up her own personality, by modelling herself on Salome, just as Firbank made up his personality in accordance with the pattern of saintliness laid down by the author of *Salomé*.

But to call the book *The Artificial Princess* while Firbank was still known as Artie would have made too nakedly Salomesque a revelation. It would have admitted who that tall-tall transvestite schoolboy truly was, and it would have confessed that it was he who, by impersonating a Wilde heroine, had made himself artist enough to challenge Wilde.

Firbank probably could not drive the Wildean allusion out of his book's title and replace it by an allusion to himself until Artie Firbank, along with Arthur and A. A. R., had wholly changed his name to Ronald.

Artie could not quite die until both his parents (the people who nicknamed him Artie and thus the people to whom par excellence he was *known* as Artie) were dead. One of them died while the book was being written.[4] It was after the death of the other[5] that Firbank was reminded – or let himself be reminded – of the book's existence. Only then, it seems, did he admit, through a half-pun half-metaphor, that the book's autobiographical heroine

---

[1] Firbank's elder brother, Joseph Sydney (*Biography*, p. 11).
[2] Cf. Chapter VIII, 2.   [3] Cf. Chapter X, 1.
[4] Cf. Chapter XIII, 6.   [5] Cf. Chapter XIII, 3.

was its author's infantile fantasy self. By renaming his heroine the Artificial Princess, Firbank proclaimed himself Princess Artie.

9. A Flick at a Passing Bat

I THINK there is a possibility that the Artificial Princess's pastime of frightening bats[1] was drawn into Firbank's thoughts by association with an anecdote about that imperial court at Chislehurst in whose legendary shadow Firbank first figured himself a princess.[2]

The anecdote might easily have reached Firbank (not directly, of course, but through common Cambridge acquaintance) from the anecdotal Edward Marsh, one of whose anecdotes so harmed Firbank.[3] The experience happened to Marsh's Cambridge friend and contemporary Maurice Baring. But it is Marsh's biographer who records it. And, after giving the preliminary explanation that 'Baring had recently spent a week-end at Chislehurst as a guest of the Empress Eugénie', Marsh's biographer quotes what is evidently Marsh's account: ' "One night a bat got into the passage and there was a fearful crisis, so the next night, when one actually came into the dining-room, and was only perceived by Maurice and the Empress, she said to him in a whisper '*Ne dites rien*' and nothing happened." '

Something is awry with the date of the story, which occurs in the section of Marsh's biography dealing with 1898–1902, years during which the Empress had not 'recently' been living at Chislehurst, which she left after the death of the Prince Imperial in 1879. Indeed, if Maurice Baring, who was born in 1874, was ever her guest at *Chislehurst*, he must have been a remarkably precocious one. And he can hardly have related the anecdote to Marsh as something that happened 'recently', as he didn't meet Marsh until he was an undergraduate.

Perhaps Marsh made a habit of ascribing his anecdotes to impossible dates and locales.[4] But the anachronistic persistence of Chislehurst in the story is interesting: the imperial exile there must have kept till the end of the century some legendary and evocative force in the minds even of people who hadn't themselves lived at Chislehurst.

If the story did drift to Firbank, it perhaps fixed in his imagination the idea that valour in confrontations with bats was a regal quality.

[1] Cf. sub-section 7 of this chapter.
[2] Cf. Chapter X, 9.
[3] Cf. Chapter VI, 6.
[4] Witness the impossible ascription of his encounter with Firbank to the locale of the Russian Ballet, which was out of action at the date (after Rupert Brooke's death) Marsh set on the encounter (cf. Chapter VI, 6).

Moreover, the Empress's whispered French would be an extra prompt to Firbank to think of the intruding bats in French. Not that Firbank needed prompting towards French. And neither did he need to hear the Chislehurst story before his imagination could frame the offensive defensive against bats conducted by his Princess – and by other, later, non-royal[1] Firbank heroines.

If he did hear it, the imperial anecdote gave Firbank no more than a touch of clothing for what was essentially a fantasy native to himself. The fantasy shews its nature distinctly through Firbank's French turn of mind. The French name for a bat, like more than one of its English names[2] and like its German name (which, thanks to his interest in opera, was probably a German word Firbank did know), labels the bat as a type of mouse. Firbank's Princess, his regal and bolder other self, frightens bats because Firbank was frightened[3] of mice.

10. Double Portrait: A Rakish Pair

WILDE'S (or perhaps Wilde's and Strauss's) *Salomé* reached out through Firbank's associative processes to touch and mark the vocabulary of Reggie Quintus, the companion (or the minion) of Lord Orkish in *The Princess Zoubaroff*, the play Firbank published in 1920.

As a rule, the influence which shapes Reggie Quintus's vocabulary is Firbank's own art-historical vocabulary – just as it is one of Firbank's own possible professions which Reggie practises when he supplements the rewards of minionship by a little picture-dealing on the side.[4] And the very name Reggie Quintus is a mutation of the imperial, regal and quaint Charles Quint of Firbank's own essay in art history.[5]

It is, however, by a violation of his usual Ruskin-turned ('Sebastian', 'Tintoret') art-historical vocabulary that Reggie describes the subject of one of the pictures (a Pinturicchio) which he peddles. You would expect him to call it a John the Baptist or (though Firbank would no doubt have mutilated the Italian words) a San Giovanni Battista. Instead, Reggie offers, Wildeanly, 'A "*Iokanaan*"'.

At least, that is what he offers in the *Complete* Firbank. The first edition, no doubt following Firbank (astray), has 'An "*Iaokannan*"' (and spells its painter Pinturricchio).

---

[1] Still: Enid is the protégée of a (though presumably not a royal) Princess. And Mrs Shamefoot aspires higher yet.

[2] And indeed bats are called 'flitter-mice' (or 'flittermice') in the texts of *Valmouth*, *Prancing Nigger* and . . . *Cardinal Pirelli* (*Complete* Firbank, p. 401, p. 604 and p. 669).

[3] Cf. Chapter VIII, 3. [4] Cf. Chapter IX, 8. [5] Cf. Chapter IX, 7.

This passage of dialogue, which is as perfect qua dialogue as its spelling is aberrant, occurs near the beginning of the last act. The Princess has constituted her villa a convent and herself its Abbess. Reggie is talking to Mrs Blanche Negress, who has turned nun.

REGGIE (*rising carelessly*). If the Princess should want a Pinturricchio for her chapel, by the way, I know where there's one to be found.
BLANCHE. Indeed.
REGGIE. An '*Iaokannan*'.
BLANCHE. Oh!
REGGIE. Or, I know of a topping Tintoret.
BLANCHE. Thanks . . . but I fancy she's on the scent of a *Sainte Famille* herself.

By speaking of John the Baptist under his Wildean name, Reggie introduces a touch of scandal (Salome's, and thence Wilde's) into the conventual world (though as a matter of fact the Princess Zoubaroff's convent is in no need of scandals from outside). The exclamation mark to Blanche's 'Oh', when she learns the picture's subject, is her response to scandal.

At the same time, Reggie's choice of word reveals Reggie's acquaintance with Wilde's play.

The acquaintance is hardly surprising. Reggie has (as I have already argued[1] and will presently expand) another significance as well: but in one of his selves he is, unmistakably, the person who transformed Wilde's *Salomé* into Wilde's *Salome* by translating it into English.

Reggie Quintus is more than a markedly Wildean young man. He is Wilde's young man. Firbank's double portrait of Reggie Quintus and Lord Orkish, minion and protector, is a portrait of Lord Alfred Douglas and Oscar Wilde.

That imperially derived name Reggie Quintus is also a rhythmic echo and an assonance[2] – Reggie Quintus: Bosie Douglas.

As a matter of fact (a matter no doubt influential on Firbank) the assonance between the names Bosie and Reggie had already been exploited by Robert Hichens. The Lord Alfred Douglas of *The Green Carnation*[3] is named Lord Reggie Hastings.

In portraying Wilde for the stage, Firbank was carrying to an utmost, baroque convolution his practice of patterning himself on Wilde as his

---

[1] in Chapter IX, 7.
[2] It was by a similar but wittier assonance that Firbank transformed the real-life Lord Tredegar into Lord Intriguer (cf. Chapter VIII, 5).
[3] a book whose influence on Firbank I shall mention again in sub-section 11 of this chapter.

private saint. What Wilde had done with the public scriptures Firbank was emulating in the terms of his private canon. In *Salomé* Wilde put a biblical saint on the stage – though not, thanks to the Lord Chamberlain's rule against biblical subjects, the English stage.[1] In *The Princess Zoubaroff* Firbank, had he found someone to finance a production,[2] would have put on the stage his private and personal Saint Oscar Wilde.

Firbank's name for his stage-portrait of Oscar Wilde was taken from the warning Firbank had received, from an earlier-adopted literary stepfather,[3] *against* Wilde.

Firbank was resurrecting on the stage the dead man whose 'sins' Rollo St Clair Talboys described to Firbank as poison. The stage-portrait of Wilde was the culminating creation of Firbank's cult of Wilde. Firbank christened the portrait after the phrase in which Talboys denounced the cult of Wilde, 'the cult of the purple orchid'.

Lord Orkish is an orchid botanically translated into an orchis, to which Firbank has by a final inspiration added that final *h* – which brilliantly tilts the whole towards the rakish and simultaneously, by the near-rhyme it summons, utters Firbank's literary-critical reproach against Wilde: Wilde in his purple-orchidaceous mood (the 'Tyrian purple' of *Salomé*[4]) is mawkish.

Wilde was not the only person Firbank portrayed as an orchid in literature;[5] and, about the time he was writing *The Princess Zoubaroff*, Firbank's own real-life passion for orchids prompted him to have himself portrayed (in paint) 'huddled up in a black suit by a jar of Orchids'.[6] Throughout his cult of orchids, I surmise, Firbank took an undisclosed, sly, rather Beardsleyan[7] delight in the fact (which he probably knew through his passion for horticulture, since it is not likely to have come into his in any case stunted study of New Testament Greek[8]) that *orchis* is the Greek for *testicle*.[9]

---

[1] Wilde's *Salomé*, banned in England when Sarah Bernhardt was rehearsing it, was eventually produced (but without Bernhardt) in Paris: in 1896, while Wilde was in prison.

[2] Cf. the attempt Lady Firbank made to finance a production by borrowing £1,000 from, appropriately, a picture-dealer (Chapter IX, 6).

[3] Cf. Chapter XIII, 5.   [4] Cf. Chapter XIII, 9.

[5] – as Chapter XV, 5 will expand.

[6] Firbank's description of himself in the painting of him by Alvaro Guevara (cf. Chapter VIII, 1).

[7] It was in the same slyness of spirit that Beardsley signed much of his work with a decorative motif which is a symbolic diagram of sexual intercourse.

[8] Cf. Chapter XII, 4.

[9] Another instance of the Firbankian language of flowers is the italicised warning given to her employee ('a slim Tunisian boy') by the Duchess of Varna (in *The Flower Beneath the Foot*), who, like other Firbankian personages, owns a flower-shop. ' "Be careful not to shake those *Alexandrian Balls*", the Duchess peremptorily enjoined, pointing to some Guelder-roses – "or they'll fall before they're sold!" ' (pp. 520–1 in the *Complete* Firbank).

In *The Princess Zoubaroff* the very baby (a boy, of course) is tenderly described as 'just like an opening orchid'.

As portraiture, Lord Orkish and Reggie make essentially a double portrait. It is the relationship between Wilde and Douglas which Firbank is depicting, and it is chiefly through their relationship that the portraits achieve a likeness.

However, Firbank has made sure that the portraits are severally recognisable, and his own intention to draw portraits unmistakable, by affixing to each portrait a label. Reggie is captioned, as I shall explain in a moment, in the stage directions of his first entrance into the play. Lord Orkish is marked as Wilde because Firbank has slipped into his lines one of Wilde's (feebler) jokes.

It was by this deliberate and highly conscious ascription of a Wilde joke to his portrait of Wilde in *The Princess Zoubaroff* that Firbank unconsciously made amends[1] for his unconscious theft[2] of a Wilde joke in his earlier fiction about another (and openly Wildean) princess.

I am convinced Firbank had no awareness he was making amends, because he had (I am convinced) no awareness that there was occasion for amends. But he unconsciously picked, for the point of restitution, a remarkably close counterpart to the point where he had committed the theft.

For *The Artificial Princess* Firbank stole the joke of Wilde's short story *The Sphinx Without a Secret*, a joke that is embodied in, and rather given away by, the story's title. Lord Orkish's joke is adapted from another of Wilde's short stories. In this even sketchier, less efficiently entertaining and perhaps rather snobbish story, a young gentleman who wants to marry but hasn't enough money meets a ragged old beggar, who is posing in the studio of the young gentleman's painter friend. The young gentleman gives the beggar a tip he can scarcely afford. But his investment of generosity produces a capital return when the seeming beggar turns out to be a millionaire whose mere foible it was to have himself portrayed in rags. The millionaire is generous in return. He endows the young gentleman's marriage.

The story is hardly more than a pun; and its dénouement line, in which the painter remarks 'Millionaire models [. . .] are rare enough; but, by Jove, model millionaires are rarer still!', is given away in advance (like the secret of *The Sphinx Without a Secret*) by the story's title: *The Model Millionaire*.

This pun Lord Orkish makes over to the purposes of the languid flirtation he conducts with Angelo, the footman[3] whom the stage directions describe as 'a boy of sixteen, fair, sleek, languishing, a "Benozzo Gozzoli" [. . .] He

---

[1] This is the amends by Firbank which I mentioned in Chapter XIII, 4.
[2] Cf. Chapter XIII, 3.   [3] Cf. Chapter IX, 7 and 8.

wears a trim black livery with' (of course) 'violet-coloured facings and shoulder-knots'.

> LORD ORKISH. I seem to have seen you.
> ANGELO (*displaying his teeth, smiling*). Via Tavolini!
> LORD ORKISH. I daresay.
> ANGELO. As a boy I vend flowers.
> LORD ORKISH. Via Tavolini?
> ANGELO. Now and then I would pose.
> LORD ORKISH. Pose?
> ANGELO (*gazing indolently over his shoulder-knots*). I'm a model.
> LORD ORKISH (*Ironic*). And so at last I behold a model footman!

It is by less recondite allusions that Firbank captions Reggie Quintus as a portrait of Bosie.

Indeed, an alert reader might guess who he is from the mere presages of his appearance in the play – presages allotted to the eleven-year-old Glyda, 'pale, plump, precocious', Firbank's inspired sketch of and invective against female pre-pubescence. 'I met some people in the lane', Glyda ('standing legs apart and swinging insolently her skirts') heralds: '[. . .] Apollo – and Lord Orkish.'

And when Reggie Quintus makes his Apollonian entrance, the stage directions say of him explicitly enough: 'Incredibly young. Incredibly good-looking. No one would suppose him to have figured as hero already in at least one *cause-célèbre*.'

As a matter of fact he figured in *the* cause célèbre.

Obviously Firbank was not portraying the married and not far from middle-aged[1] Douglas whom Firbank boldly added[2] to his incipient Wilde collection in 1905: and still less the fiftyish Douglas of the time when *The Princess Zoubaroff* was written.

Firbank's is an ideal (though not an idealised) double portrait of the lovers at the time of their romance: a portrait designed as an icon of homosexuality.

Since the portrait is of the lovers at the time when their love led to their cause célèbre, the Bosie-figure is, as Bosie was at that time, unmarried. It is the Wilde-figure who is married: again in keeping with the facts of that time. True, Lord Orkish doesn't live with his wife. To the two young men who have been left by their (nunned) wives, he says: 'I take it you'll live apart, as we do – Lady Orkish and I – by "mutual consent" .' But his being married provokes Reggie Quintus to resentment and a fine impasto'd streak

---

[1] Lord Alfred Douglas was born in 1870.   [2] Cf. Chapter XII, 2.

of a phrase: 'It made my flesh *creep* to see him in the white custody of a wife.'

Lord Orkish is in 'exile' – as, indeed, most of the dramatis personae have, to some extent, to be: for plausibility's sake, since the play is set in Florence. But the stage directions make the point only about Lord Orkish; and the word implies that, whereas the others might go back to England if they chose to, Lord Orkish couldn't. I don't think, however, that Firbank was reconstructing Wilde's exile after his imprisonment. (Wilde's wife died eleven months after his release.) I think Lord Orkish's is an ideal exile, background to the ideal portrait: the exile Wilde *ought* to have gone into *before* – or, rather, in order to prevent – the trials. The advice which Firbank gave his sister on financial grounds,[1] namely to live abroad, Firbank's play is posthumously giving to Oscar Wilde on more-than-financial grounds. Firbank himself learned to act on that advice from the results of Wilde's not doing so – though Wilde had put the advice to himself after the proto-Wilde-scandal occasioned by *Salomé*.[2]

Between Reggie Quintus and Lord Orkish Firbank preserves the relation in age as it was between Douglas and Wilde. For while Reggie is 'incredibly young' Lord Orkish is of 'a "certain age" '.

(To be, however, certain about his age is what was forced on Wilde in court, after his airy inaccuracy [which set Firbank both a precedent and a warning in the matter of lying about one's age[3]] during that libel suit whose disastrousness so echoed round Firbank's imagination.[4])

Lord Alfred Douglas's lord-ship Firbank has removed from him and awarded to his portrait of Wilde. No doubt Firbank, who prized it, felt it was better deserved there. More to the point, by swopping the lovers' rank Firbank emphasised the financial dependence, the sheer scrounging, of Bosie.

All the same, Firbank's fantasy made a note, though in code, of the factual relation in rank. If he promoted Wilde to lord, he promoted Lord Alfred Douglas by a yet larger grade, in so far as he named him after an emperor.[5]

The relation Firbank's double portrait preserves and points most carefully of all is the contrast between the two personalities. Reggie Quintus walks into the play *behind* Lord Orkish, and Firbank's stage direction exactly describes the slightly sullen ambivalence of the young Lord Alfred Douglas: 'his manner, which is somewhat "subdued", alternates between the demi-dazed and the demi-demure.' To Lord Orkish Firbank has given little of

---

[1] Cf. Chapter VI, 1.   [2] Cf. sub-section 1 of this chapter.
[3] Cf. Chapter V, 6 and 7.   [4] Cf. Chapter VII, 3.
[5] Cf. Chapter IX, 7.

Wilde's wit (which is distributed throughout the play and its conception, rather than gathered into aphorisms in anyone's mouth) but all Wilde's generosity of temperament: 'Enter LORD ORKISH. He is, despite "Exile" and a "certain age", all cheerfulness, gaiety and sweet good-humour. Behind him REGGIE QUINTUS. Incredibly young'. . . .

That the double portrait shews the pair as they were related at the time when Bosie in fact *was* incredibly young is the clue to how the Reggie-figure has become in itself a double image.

Reggie Quintus is both a portrait of Lord Alfred Douglas and, as I earlier[1] declared him to be, a self-portrait by Firbank.

All within the assonance of that *-ie* ending, Reggie is both Bosie and Artie.

Firbank begins to be superimposed on Douglas when Reggie Quintus speaks in Firbank's own art-historical vocabulary, and when Reggie Quintus sets about picking up an income through two of Firbank's own possible métiers, picture-dealing and some sort of ecclesiastical job.[2] And in one stage direction Firbank predominates over Douglas. Reggie Quintus is endowed with a distinctively Firbank habit[3] when he is described as 'regarding thoughtfully his white compact hands'.

The process of superimposition turns on two points where Firbank's image and Douglas's image are pinned together by real-life fact. From the two points of coincidence, the merging of the images proceeded into fiction.

The first pin concerns Reggie Quintus's use of Firbank's art-historical vocabulary. It was Lord Alfred Douglas who,[4] as editor of *The Academy*, published Firbank's 1907 essay in art history (on the significantly named subject of Charles Quint).

(It is by the blurring of the images round the pin of Douglas as editor that Reggie Quintus is said to have figured in the rather vague computation of 'at least one *cause-célèbre*!' Douglas and Wilde made one cause célèbre. But as a result of Douglas's being an editor [and Firbank's being an acquaintance of an undergraduate editor] Firbank himself had *nearly* figured with Douglas in what was *nearly* a cause célèbre.[5] The sum total was one and a bit causes célèbres.)

The second factual pin concerns Firbank's dropping Lord Alfred Douglas, emotionally at least, from his Wilde collection because he had become sure of keeping in the collection the no less valuable item of Wilde's son, Vyvyan Holland.[6]

---

[1] in Chapter IX, 7 and 8.
[2] Cf. Chapter IX, 8; Chapter VII, 2; and Chapter IX, 6.
[3] Cf. Chapter VIII, 1.   [4] Cf. Chapter IX, 7, 9 and 10 and Chapter XII, 2.
[5] Cf. Chapter XII, 2.   [6] Cf. Chapter XII, 3.

(It was in 1921, a year after he published *The Princess Zoubaroff*, that Firbank shewed himself wholly detached from Douglas by denouncing Douglas's treachery to Wilde.)

It is[1] by the instrumentality of Vyvyan Holland that, at one moment of the play, the image of Firbank blots out the image of Douglas in Reggie Quintus. The Princess speaks of Reggie Quintus as 'looking quite lawless' – an echo of the comment on Firbank which I conjecture Vyvyan Holland made to Firbank when they were at Cambridge and which he certainly published after Firbank's death, that there was something 'almost illegal' about Firbank.

That Firbank *wanted* to superimpose himself on Douglas in his double portrait of Wilde and Douglas is a glimpse into Firbank's fantasy life. His happy daydreams turn out to be as dominated by Wilde as his paranoid fantasies.[2]

As a matter of fact, Firbank learned another dread, besides that of prosecution, from the example of Wilde. Firbank compulsively abstained from food[3] because Wilde was fat and because Wilde had understood the psychology of over-eating.[4] (And then Wilde's son sought Firbank's advice on slimming.)

Firbank's relation to Wilde was a *devotion*, like a special devotion to a saint. It was a matter of drawing magical inspiration from Wilde. It was pointedly *not* a matter of Firbank's identifying himself with Wilde. So far from aiming to become Wilde, Firbank was afraid that such an identity might overtake him. He had encountered enough guilt in becoming a better writer-about-Salome than Wilde.

One of Firbank's defences against becoming Wilde was to take care not to become fat like Wilde. That defence he reinforced by making himself, in fantasy, an object to Wilde – a process he began by mentally becoming Wilde's creation, the Princess Salome. (Like Wilde's princess, Firbank spoke excellent French.)

So long as he was an object to Wilde, Firbank was not in danger of becoming Wilde. He tried to slim himself into remaining the slim young object that might have attracted Wilde's attentions.

Firbank's historically-backwards-looking imagination[5] fabricated a daydream which was a species of historical fiction. He reconstructed the relationship of Wilde and Bosie, made an icon of the idealised double-portrait, and then substituted himself, in the double-portrait, for Bosie.

Denouncing Bosie's treachery to Wilde, Firbank was asserting that he,

[1] as I mentioned in Chapter IX, 8.
[2] Cf. Chapter VII, 3.
[3] Cf. Chapter VIII, 4.
[4] Cf. Chapter I, 2.
[5] Cf. Chapter X, 9.

Firbank, would have loved Wilde loyally: an assertion all the more ardent because he had not managed quite to keep literary faith with Wilde.

The impetus that created Firbank's minion-impersonation[1] was the historical daydream in which Firbank himself took, but more loyally, Bosie's place in relation to Wilde. Sitting in the Café Royal, abstaining for slimness's sake from food, 'regarding thoughtfully' (and with the adverb so placed[2] as to *demonstrate* how excellent his French was) his white compact and beautiful hands, dreading what their flutter might in a witness box betray of him[3] and yet boldly insisting that they denote him, by their carmine nails, a minion, Firbank was signalling (it was the utmost of the many ghost stories he told himself[4]) that the ghost of Oscar Wilde should come and accost him.

Firbank was a Princess Salomé indeed. Having taken Wilde into his life to be a stepfather to him, Firbank made eyes (no doubt made-up eyes) at his stepfather.

11. A Wilde Flower

THE articles in which Firbank bound himself apprentice to Oscar Wilde[5] were committed to writing. They are to be found in *Lady Appledore's Mésalliance* (the 'artificial pastoral' which Firbank wrote probably in 1907 or 1908 and didn't publish,[6] though it is now to be read in the same volume as *The New Rythum*).

In the concentrated metaphor[7] of the story, Firbank was probably recording his expulsion (in 1907) from the paradise-garden of The Coopers, Chislehurst, and its emotional consequence, his reception (in December 1907) into the Catholic church at the hands of Hugh Benson. At the same time, Firbank was making, by the artificiality of his pastoral, a retort by satire to the back-to-nature message of Benson's novel *The Sentimentalists*.

Between those already packed layers Firbank wrote-in yet another significance: his apprenticeship to Wilde.

Here (as he did again in *The Princess Zoubaroff*[8]), Firbank accepted the association, which Rollo St Clair Talboys had proposed to him in a warning sense, between Wilde and an orchid. Having broken his apprenticeship to Talboys, Firbank wrote Talboys's warning against his new master into the

---

[1] Cf. Chapter VIII, 2.   [2] Cf. Chapter X, 11.   [3] Cf. Chapter VII, 3.
[4] Cf. Chapter VII, 3.   [5] Cf. Chapter V, 6.
[6] But it may later have occurred to Firbank to revise and publish it, since (according to the *Bibliography*, p. 90) he wrote on the titleleaf of the typescript: ' ?Revise considerably in places – If – '.
[7] some of which is explicated in Chapter X, 5 and 6.
[8] Cf. sub-section 10 of this chapter.

articles of his new apprenticeship. The orchid, however, which in Talboys's metaphor[1] was purple, has become decadent mauve.[2] And whereas, in the name Lord Orkish, Firbank was to represent Wilde as the flower itself, in *Lady Appledore's Mésalliance* Wilde appears as its cultivator.

It was not an astonishing metamorphosis for Wilde. He did, after all, claim to be the inventor of a flower.

Robert Hichens, the youngish journalist (presently Bernard Shaw's successor as music critic on the *World*) who had made friends at Luxor with Lord Alfred Douglas and Dodo Benson,[3] witnessed the arrival (late), at a fashionable first night, of Oscar Wilde wearing 'a large carnation dyed a violent green' and accompanied by a retinue of 'ultra-smart youths' with similar buttonholes. The sight provided Hichens with the title of his amusing novel in satire of Wilde and Douglas. *The Green Carnation* (which Hichens generously withdrew when Wilde was, as Hichens later[4] expressed it, 'attacked in the Law Courts)' was published in 1894 anonymously.[5] One of the many people suspected of writing it was Wilde himself – who disclaimed authorship of the book but asserted authorship of green carnations: 'I invented that magnificent flower [. . .] The flower is a work of art. The book is not.'

In inventing a green carnation Wilde invented a palpable paradox: a natural artifice, an emblem for Firbank's 'artificial pastoral'. As Wilde said in his *Phrases and Philosophies for the Use of the Young*: 'A really well-made buttonhole is the only link between Art and Nature.'

It is this artificial Wildean invention which Firbank's Artificial Princess hopes to emulate.[6] She sends the Baroness on her errand with the words: 'And now, don't forget, dearest, to bring me back in your basket an enormous water-melon, the kind they have in Palestine; and, if it were possible, I should so love a light green Rose. Up to now I have seen them only in hats, when they look like cabbages, or in paper sometimes at bazaars.'

In *Lady Appledore's Mésalliance* Firbank signified his apprenticeship to the super-inventor of flowers, Wilde, by sending his autobiographical hero to work, as under-gardener, under the supervision of the head gardener

---

[1] Cf. Chapter XIII, 5.
[2] (Cf. Chapter XIII, 9.) The orchid in *Lady Appledore's Mésalliance* is variously 'mauve' and 'mauve and black'.
[3] Cf. Chapter XIII, 1.
[4] in his Introduction to the 1949 reissue.
[5] though the second edition (as Hichens's 1949 Introduction calls what might nowadays be called, rather, an impression), which the book's success soon demanded, bore Hichens's name.
[6] as I mentioned in sub-section 8 of this chapter.

(whose name, Bartholomew, perhaps likens Wilde's martyrdom to that of Saint Bartholomew, which was by being flayed alive).

His qualifications for becoming Wilde's apprentice Firbank stated by naming his autobiographical hero Wildred. Was Firbank a well-read young man? At least, the pun answers, he was Wilde-read.

And Firbank had, in fact, read not only Wilde's writings but writings (even besides *The Green Carnation*[1]) *about* Wilde.

When Wildred arrives (which he does in the evening) to take up his new job, he attempts to see the head gardener. But the head gardener's daughter tells him: 'Father is not to be disturbed [. . .] he is sitting up all night with a sick Orchid.'

(On the next day Wildred manages to meet the head gardener, and the news is: 'The mauve Orchid is a little better this morning.')

Evidently Firbank had read (or had been told about) the fifth volume, which had been published in 1900, of Augustus Hare's *The Story of My Life*. There (in the entry for 21 June 1883) Augustus Hare retails some gossip about Oscar Wilde at a country house party 'going out shooting in a black velvet dress with salmon-coloured stockings, and falling down when the gun went off, yet captivating all the ladies by his pleasant talk'.

(It is by a very pure instance of either anti-aesthetic or anti-homosexual prejudice[2] that it could be reported and believed that Wilde fell down when his gun went off. The true shame to him, as the man who later devised a scathing definition against the wanton cruelty of fox-hunting, is that he spent quite a lot of his early manhood killing[3] 'time and pheasants'.)

'One day' (Augustus Hare's item of gossip, which he attributes to 'Mrs M. L.', who had supposedly met Wilde at the house party, continues) 'he came down looking very pale. "I am afraid you are ill, Mr. Wilde", said one of the party. "No, not ill, only tired", he answered. "The fact is, I picked a primose in the wood yesterday, and it was so ill, I have been sitting up with it all night." '

---

[1] It was the later and very different work of Robert Hichens which Firbank condemned at the end of *The Flower Beneath the Foot* (pp. 591-2 in the *Complete* Firbank), where the wedding procession in Pisuerga includes 'a brake containing various delegates and "representatives of English Culture" ', which 'rolled by at a stately trot – Lady Alexander, E. V. Lucas, Robert Hichens, Clutton Brock, etc. – the ensemble the very apotheosis of worn-out *cliché*'.

[2] Cf. Chapter XI, 3.

[3] as Wilde described it in a letter of 1878 published in Appendix A to Vyvyan Holland's *Son of Oscar Wilde*.

12. The Ultimate Knot in the Pattern

FIRBANK'S hagiographical and transvestite imagination invented (in *Valmouth*) 'the Blessed St. Elizabeth Bathilde, who, by dint of skipping, changed her sex at the age of forty and became a man'.

(Mrs Hurstpierpoint's response to the recital of this pious history is: 'A man –! Don't speak to me of *men*.')

Much of the wit of Firbank's technique is concentrated in the word (in the pious history) *dint*. The word is so well worn (but by literary rather than colloquial use) that its actual meaning has sunk beneath attention-level. It is across a dipping (a dinted) pavement-stone that the reader approaches, and looks up all the more sharply at, the bizarrely baroque monument to a saint which Firbank has erected at the close of the vista.

Firbank's fictitious saint borrows her surname from Saint Bathild (an Anglo-Frankish queen, of the seventh century). A touch, perhaps, of Firbank's own phobia[1] went to the choice and is to be heard in the first syllable of the surname. The rope of pearls used for frightening bats by the Artificial Princess (herself royal and in a sense Anglo-French, inasmuch as she was Salome and Salomé) has become the Bathilde's skipping-rope.

And indeed the saint herself is perhaps yet one more manifestation of the saint on whom Firbank patterned himself. At the age of (as he was obliged to admit[2] it was) 40, Oscar Wilde changed not his sex but the public image of his sex: at his trials.

The last of the acts by which Firbank patterned his life on Oscar Wilde's was perhaps one of the accidents that blessed Firbank or perhaps an achievement of unconscious will. If it was the latter, it, too, probably had a precedent in Wilde, who declared in the summer of 1900 'If another century began and I was still alive, it would really be more than the English could stand' and who did, indeed, die before the year and the century were out. Firbank finished his Wilde pilgrimage by dying, as Saint Elizabeth Bathilde had changed sex and as Saint Oscar Wilde had been put on trial, at the age of 40.

The final resemblance was certainly accidental, but suggestive of the pathetic fallacy that the influence of Wilde had entered Firbank's very bones. His corpse[3] resembled Wilde's in that both were dug up and re-buried.

[1] Cf. sub-sections 7 and 9 of this chapter; and Chapter VIII, 3.
[2] Cf. Chapter V, 6.
[3] Cf. Chapter VI, 1 and Chapter XII, 6.

13. Notes to Chapter XIV

WILDE'S 'Français de sympathie' etc. is from his letter of 17 December 1891 to Edmond de Goncourt. The Lord Chamberlain banned *Salomé* in 1892. Wilde's account of the censor's rule is from his letter of July 1892 to William Archer, to whom he wrote in 1893: 'I have not forgotten that you were, with the exception of George Bernard Shaw, the only critic of note who upheld me at all against the Censorship.' In a letter (to Arthur Fish) of July 1892, Wilde wrote: 'As regards the idea of my becoming a French citizen, I have not yet decided. I am very much hurt not merely at the action of the Licenser of Plays, but at the pleasure expressed by the entire Press of England at the suppression of my work.' (*The Letters of Oscar Wilde*, edited by Rupert Hart-Davis, pp. 304, 319, 332 and 318.)

Wilde's remark that he was still undecided about becoming French indicates that his plan was more serious than was known to Robert Ross, who wrote: 'Oscar Wilde immediately announced his intention of changing his nationality, a characteristic jest, which was only taken seriously, oddly enough, in Ireland.' (This and the quotation about Beardsley are from Ross's *A Note on 'Salomé'*, which is reproduced in an undated New York edition of the Wilde–Beardsley *Salome*. No date is given for the Ross Note either, but it is later than 1905, since it refers to the Strauss opera.)

In the 15th century the *Malleus Maleficarum* (I, I) mentioned women who (in Montague Summers's translation, which also glozes the passage) 'falsely imagine that during the night they ride with Diana or Herodias'.

The information about productions and aborted productions of the Strauss *Salome* is from pp. 41–62 of William Mann's *Richard Strauss*.

Ernest Newman's 1908 view of the impossibility of *Salome*'s being staged in England is in his *Richard Strauss* (1921 reprint, pp. 25–6).

The story of the daughter of Herodias is in *Matthew*, XIV, 1–12. The Artificial Princess's dance comes on p. 53 in the *Complete* Firbank, and the Queen motors on p. 30.

The Oxford Dictionary of Quotations (1941) puts the comparison between Cleopatra and Queen Victoria under Anonymous, citing, for its collection and recounting, Irvin S. Cobb: *A Laugh a Day*. (*The American College Dictionary* gives: Irvin Shrewsbury Cobb '1876–1944 U.S. humorist and writer'.) The anecdote is also recounted on p. 715 of the paperback edition of Lady Longford's *Victoria R.I.*

Eddy Monteith's similar thoughts are on p. 537 in the *Complete* Firbank, and the book about the Queen of Sheba on p. 39.

Mrs Asp is called 'the authoress of *The Home Life of Lucretia Borgia*' in *Vainglory* (p. 88 in the *Complete* Firbank). The information that Firbank used the title in earlier works is from Miriam J. Benkovitz's *Biography* (p. 121), which says that *The Home Life of Lucretia Borgia* is 'reading matter for the heroine of "A Tragedy in Green" and under a slightly different title for that of "The Wavering Disciple" '. The passage is not included in the extracts from *A Tragedy in Green* published in *The New Rythum and Other Pieces*.

The strands of the Nilotic nexus are in *The Letters of Oscar Wilde*, edited by Rupert Hart-Davis, p. 65, footnote and p. 834, and *Antony and Cleopatra*, I, v. Claud Harvester's wife is on p. 82 in the *Complete* Firbank, Lady Something's housemaid on p. 523 and the mural decoration of the room above the Café Cleopatra on p. 518.

The Artificial Princess wishes to be 'a new Salomé' on p. 32 in the *Complete* Firbank and discerns resemblances on pp. 35–6. She shews herself a Straussian on p. 36 of the *Complete* Firbank and (with Firbank's bad spelling) on p. 25 of the first (1934) edition of *The Artificial Princess*.

Mira Thumbler in *Vainglory* dances on p. 98 of the *Complete* Firbank, Winsome Brookes speaks ill of Strauss's Prophet's music on p. 150, and Eysoldt is expected in England on p. 87.

Strauss's visit to, and the details of, Eysoldt's *Salome* are recorded on p. 41 of William Mann's *Richard Strauss*, which mentions Mary Garden in 'the Manhattan production of *Salome*' on p. 61.

Geraldine Farrar lived 1882–1967; Mary Garden 1874–1967.

Tetrarch grey is on p. 78 in *The New Rythum and Other Pieces*, and Lady Georgia's Herodias equivalent for her worser feelings on p. 118.

The *Biography* dates *Her Dearest Friend* on p. 34 (note) and p. 71, and *A Disciple from the Country* on pp. 87–8. The Salome passage from the latter is on p. 123 of *The New Rythum and Other Pieces*. The *Vainglory* version of Firbank's Salome–Magdalen ornament is on p. 157 in the *Complete* Firbank, where the Artificial Princess likens the King to Herod on p. 36. The *Biography*'s account of Firbank's whereabouts in December 1905 is on p. 76.

Ernest Newman's 1908 (1921 reprint, p. 22) *Richard Strauss* records that Strauss's orchestral music began to be played in England in 1896 and Strauss himself began visiting England in 1897. Newman quotes *The Musical Times* as saying in 1902 that Strauss 'is gradually becoming known in England'.

The Debussy piano music in *Lady Appledore's Mésalliance* comes on p. 34 of *The New Rythum and Other Pieces*.

The dates of the Dresden and the London first performances of Strauss's *Salome* and *Elektra* are mentioned in Covent Garden programmes, that of the first Paris performance of *Salome* in *Richard Strauss Romain & Rolland : Correspondence*, edited by Rollo Myers, p. 142 and p. 82.

The Artificial Princess speaks of the position in which Fate has placed her on p. 32 of the *Complete* Firbank, and the Baroness tactfully agrees on p. 35.

The psychology of Hamlet was elucidated by Sigmund Freud, in *The Interpretation of Dreams*, V (D) (b), and by Ernest Jones. Freud commented on mythological riddles in, e.g., paper VI in Volume II of *Collected Papers*.

Mice are in the British Embassy in *The Artificial Princess*; fleas are in the Ritz and are commented on in *The Flower Beneath the Foot*: respectively, p. 71 and pp. 508-9 in the *Complete* Firbank (p. 80 and p. 32 in the first editions).

The Artificial Princess's governess's quotation (from *The Duchess of Malfi*, IV, ii) comes on p. 33 in the *Complete* Firbank. Evelyn Waugh's characters assume an acquaintance with the heroine of Webster's *The White Devil, Or Vittoria Corombona* in *Brideshead Revisited* (1947 edition, p. 89).

Bats are frightened, flicked at and chased on, respectively, p. 62, p. 154 and p. 707 of the *Complete* Firbank, where the lethal collar is on p. 158.

The Artificial Princess's figure's lack of consequence is described on p. 28 in the *Complete* Firbank. (In quoting, I have ignored the Firbankian paragraphing – by which a new paragraph starts with the Queen's name for her daughter.) The possible frumpishness of the Prophet is considered on p. 47 in the *Complete* Firbank.

Wilde's account of the first duty in life is from the *Phrases and Philosophies for the Use of the Young* which he contributed to *The Chameleon* in 1894 (and which are republished in *The Artist As Critic, Critical Writings of Oscar Wilde*, edited by Richard Ellmann).

Firbank's letter to his mother about making up poetary is of 30 October 1898 and is quoted in the *Bibliography*, p. 95.

The story of the Empress Eugénie and the bats is in Christopher Hassall's *Edward Marsh*, pp. 84-5.

The dialogue in *The Princess Zoubaroff* about the Pinturicchio Iokanaan and the topping Tintoret is on p. 95 of the first edition and pp. 754-5 in the *Complete* Firbank.

The details of the 1896 production of Wilde's *Salomé* in Paris are given in *The Letters of Oscar Wilde*, edited by Rupert Hart-Davis, p. 399.

The dating of the Guevara portrait, like Firbank's description of it, is in the *Biography*, p. 177.

The baby in *The Princess Zoubaroff* is compared to an orchid on p. 53 of the first edition and p. 729 in the *Complete* Firbank; Lord Orkish holds his Wildean conversation with the footman on, respectively, p. 70 and p. 740.

Oscar Wilde was released from prison in May 1897. Constance Wilde died in April 1898.

Wilde's first-night appearance wearing a green carnation and the inspiration Robert Hichens took from it are described in Robert Hichens's autobiography *Yesterday*, pp. 69-70.

Wilde's letter disclaiming authorship of *The Green Carnation* is on p. 373 in *The Letters of Oscar Wilde*, edited by Rupert Hart-Davis. The Princess hopes for a light green rose on p. 39 of the *Complete* Firbank.

The Blessed Saint Elizabeth Bathilde is on p. 426 in the *Complete* Firbank.

Wilde's declaration of the summer of 1900 is quoted in Hesketh Pearson's *The Life of Oscar Wilde*, p. 373.

XV

Princess Artie en Fleur

It is to be noted that sexual flower-symbolism, which, of course, is very widespread, symbolizes the human sexual organs by flowers, the sexual organs of plants; indeed, presents of flowers between lovers may perhaps have this unconscious significance.

Sigmund Freud,
The Interpretation of Dreams,
translated by A. A. Brill, VI (E)

1. How Does Your Garden Grow?

FIRBANK probably took an unspoken delight in the meaning of *orchis*, and he certainly punned on the gelding of guelder roses.[1] To attribute male sex organs to flowers gave him pleasure. (The headmistress of the girls' school in ... *Cardinal Pirelli* 'in private life was the Dowager-Marchioness of Pennisflores'.) The pleasure was, however, part of his pleasure in hermaphroditism. Predominantly, flowers (including orchids) figured to his imagination as female.

Indeed, he made that explicit in a pronoun. When the hero of *Lady Appledore's Mésalliance* asks after the health of the head gardener's patient,[2] the reply is that the mauve orchid is a little better but 'she is low, very low'.

Flowers were almost bound to seem female to the infant Firbank in the paradise-garden[3] at Chislehurst. There were four Firbank children. Only one of them was a girl. And her name was the name of a flower.

2. A Population of Flowers

FIRBANK'S rooms – and, indeed, his manner of life – were dressed with flowers.[4] His fictions are not only dressed but populated with flowers. Firbank fairly regularly gives capital initial letters to the names of flowers (and to the word 'flowers' itself[5]) because his flowers are people.

[1] Cf. Chapter XIV, 10.   [2] Cf. Chapter XIV, 11.
[3] Cf. Chapter X, 5.   [4] Cf. Chapter VII, 5.
[5] – in, for instance, the speech by the Princess Zoubaroff that will be quoted in subsection 10 of this chapter.

Both Firbank's floralism and his Christianity were probably influenced by Oscar Wilde's claim that Christ 'was the first person who ever said to people that they should live "flower-like" lives. He fixed the phrase.'

Possessing – to a more than botanical extent – sex, Firbankian flowers are capable of having or being denied a sex-life. Lady Appledore foreshadows her eventual 'mésalliance' with her under-gardener by demanding of him: 'But do you realize that Paeonies and Lobelia are not suitable together? that flowers can make the most undesirable marriages, just as –'. And in the royal Japanese garden in *The Artificial Princess* 'None of the flowers grew in the earth, but lived in celibacy in China pots.'

Firbank early began attributing thoughts and feelings to plants. His 1905 Poem in Prose, *Impression (Souvenir)*[1] *d'Automne*, describes (according to the *Biography*, whose account is borne out by the two very brief extracts published in *The New Rythum and Other Pieces*) the meditations of fallen leaves. His early, unpublished piece beginning 'The Roses were never called before seven' is (according to the *Biography*) about the roses' mourning the gardener's daughter.

(The name of the gardener's dead daughter is Winnie. By the time of *Vainglory*, from whose title-page he for the first time discarded his own first name, Firbank had turned satirical against his own early manner. In a conversation with Mrs Henedge, ' "The most wonderful name in all the world for any child", Winsome said, "is Diana. Don't you agree? Your gardener intended to call his daughter Winifred, but I was just in time!" ')

Firbank's literary sanction for vegetable personifications was Maurice Maeterlinck,[2] who (in *The Blue Bird*) lent power of speech to ten types of tree (as well as to the ivy). Firbank paid Maeterlinck direct tribute through the autobiographical hero of *Lady Appledore's Mésalliance*. The 'favourite books and music' which Wildred picks up before starting on his gardening life include Maeterlinck's *Ariane et Barbe-Bleue*.[3]

And perhaps the music by Debussy which is open on Wildred's grand

---

[1] Cf. the note on the subject in Chapter XIII, 10.

[2] – whose signature (according to the *Biography*, p. 28) Firbank collected in adolescence.

[3] Perhaps it is by copying Firbank's typescript (which she owns) of *Lady Appledore's Mésalliance* that Firbank's biographer has (*Biography*, p. 96) deprived Barbe-Bleue of his final *e*. However, the mistake is not necessarily Firbank's (or his Cambridge typist's): the text in the *New Rythum* volume (p. 34) gets *Barbe-Bleue* correct. In general this Maeterlinck play (which is of 1901) seems to suffer a fatality about names. Books about Maeterlinck, and also lists of translations of his work included in translations published by Methuen and by George Allen, often give the heroine's name as Ardiane. (This may be by some English fervour to get the *d* of *Ariadne* back into the name *some*where.) But the 1918 Charpentier (Paris) edition of Maeterlinck's plays names her firmly Ariane.

piano[1] is another tribute to Maeterlinck – whose *Pelléas et Mélisande*[2] Debussy had made into an opera in 1902. (As a fictional impresario Firbank put on a production in Cuna-Cuna. 'I understand him to be going to *Pelléas and Mélisande*,' runs a line of dialogue in *Prancing Nigger*, answered by 'He came to the Opera-house, but only for a minute.')

Firbank seems to have had a specialised fondness for operas made from plays[3] he held dear (and perhaps even a doubly specialised fondness for operas made from plays in which, as in both *Salome* and *Pelléas*, a woman falls in love with her husband's brother).

And by splendid converse he took specialised precautions against the thought that operas might be made from novels of a kind he held undear. The œuvre of Victoria Gellybore-Frinton[4] (in *The Flower Beneath the Foot*) consists, so far, of 'lurid studies of low life (of which she knew nothing at all)'. Her husband, the Hon. Harold Chilleywater, has been 'gently warned' by the Foreign Office that, if his career in diplomacy is to progress, 'the style of his wife must really grow less *virile*'. It is with the accuracy of both malice and genius that Firbank shapes the account Victoria Gellybore-Frinton delivers of her forthcoming novel and puts into her mouth the tellingly just words 'anticipating' and 'babelet'.[5] The climax of the plot is a 'tussle' between 'two brothers on the edge of the Kentish cliffs'. Victoria Gellybore-Frinton continues: 'Iris and Delitsiosa – Iris is anticipating a babelet soon – are watching them from a cornfield, where they're boiling a kettle for afternoon tea; and oh, I've such a darling description of a cornfield. I make you *feel* England!' To her account of her book Victoria Gellybore-Frinton adds, with modesty (and, in the strict use of 'pretends', an affectation of 18th centuryness that was probably Firbank's own[6]): 'Harold pretends it would be wonderful arranged as an Opera ... with duos and things and a *Liebestod* for Delitzi towards the close' – a suggestion which Firbank has Mr Limpness cut off with a 'No, no' and a gallantly (and, in

---

[1] Cf. Chapter XIV, 4.

[2] which sub-section 15 of this chapter will mention again.

[3] (Cf. Chapter XIV, 4.) Or perhaps Firbank's interest in opera drew his attention to certain pieces of literature, and vice versa. Maeterlinck's *Ariane et Barbe-Bleue*, reading matter which Firbank was attributing to the hero of *Lady Appledore's Mésalliance* circa 1907–8, was in 1907 made into an opera by Paul Dukas (according to p. 317 of Patrick J. Smith's *The Tenth Muse*).

[4] Cf. Chapter VI, 6.

[5] Firbank had previously tried out 'babelet' in the vocabulary of the eminent actress Mrs Mary in *Caprice* (*Complete* Firbank, p. 346).

[6] Firbank puts the same strict idiom into the mouth of the Princess Zoubaroff, who reports (*Complete* Firbank, p. 758) that the Pope 'pretends' that the liqueur she has invented 'will inspire him for Life'.

idiom, Irishly) rhetorical 'What would become of our modern fiction at all if Victoria Gellybore-Frinton gave herself up to the stage?'

(Firbank punishes Victoria Gellybore-Frinton a little further yet: by having her take the rhetorical question literally and confess in reply that hardly anyone 'is doing anything at present for English Letters' with the exception of herself and Lilian [Madam Adrian] Bloater – which latter I take to be Firbank's name, and a fine one, for Virginia [Mrs Leonard] Woolf.)

In *Vainglory* Firbank's tribute to Maeterlinck is a touch convoluted, being paid by way of Firbank's self-portrait as Claud Harvester. ' "Now that Maeterlinck is getting like Claud Harvester", the Professor, without tact, put in, "I don't read him any more." '

Yet Maeterlinck's presidency over vegetable symbolism abides in *Vainglory*. Mrs Shamefoot runs a flower-shop in Sloane Street. Its name (after Maeterlinck's play[1]) is Monna Vanna.

A yet classier flower-shop occurs in *The Flower Beneath the Foot*: owned (but clandestinely this time, for fear of 'sherrifs' officers') by the Duchess of Varna (who is in deep debt). The Princess Zoubaroff claims[2] that her flowers talk to her, but they don't do so audibly to the audience. It is on the Duchess of Varna's premises that Firbank's flowers achieve articulation. They complain, by night, in Maeterlinck-style repetitions and repetitions-with-slight-varations. 'My wires are hurting me: my wires are hurting me.' 'I have no water. I cannot reach the water.' And they squabble over social precedence, in the idiom of snobbish housemaids. 'You Weed you! You you you . . . *buttercup*! How dare you to *an Orchid*!' 'She's nothing but a piece of common grass and so I tell her!'

This at first sight over-prettified whimsy is in fact the mirror of the human plights in the book. The mirror distances the human pain and by the same token sets it in depth.

'It's uncomfy, isn't it, without one's roots?' says one of the plants – and thereby expresses the expatriate pain of Mrs Montgomery, whose search is for English *comfiness* (precisely) in the exoticism of Pisuerga. ('It's almost too warm for a fire' Mrs Montgomery murmurs to her fellow-expatriate Dr Babcock, 'but I like to hear the crackle!')

'I'm glad I'm in a Basket! No one will hurl *me* from a window to be bruised underfoot by the callous crowd.' So declares another flower – and mirrors

---

[1] which is mentioned by an actress in *The New Rythum* (p. 91); significantly, perhaps, of the directions Firbank's interests took, this play, too, was made into an opera: by Henri Février, in 1909 (Patrick J. Smith's *The Tenth Muse*, p. 317).

[2] a claim that will be reported in sub-section 10 of this chapter.

in advance the pain of Laura who, while 'the air' is indeed 'thick with falling flowers', watches from her convent window the royal wedding procession in whose interest she, the Flower of the title, *is* bruised beneath the foot.

The novel is a hagiography, its explicatory sub-title 'Being a record of the early life of St. Laura de Nazianzi and the times in which she lived'. Saint Laura is a Little Flower – but not of Jesus: or, at least, only of '*the Blue Jesus*' (the marvellous name by which 'all churchgoers' in Pisuerga know the Cathedral, which has a 'low white dome, crowned by turquoise-tinted tiles'). The enforced (or the at any rate without alternative) celibacy of Laura's final convent is the 'celibacy' of the flowers which live in China pots.

And, since flowers are girls, Mrs Shamefoot in her flower-shop, making up a lyre 'with some orchids and pink lilies, and numberless streaming ribands' (and wondering 'Remove a few of the orchids? No!') is the same figure as the Princess Zoubaroff numbering off little girls as future nuns for her convent:

> PRINCESS (*boxing*, con amore, *with her muff each little girl upon the ears as she goes by*). Nun! Nun! Nun!

3. Flower People

FLOWERS being girls, equally girls are flowers. It is not just that they are compared to flowers (not always as a compliment: 'Lady Wilson-Philipson has just arrived', says Lord Orkish, 'with an octet of daughters like cabbage-roses – so large, so pink, so fresh'). The equation is so confirmed that women in Firbank are subject to the same assaults as flowers are: by insect. Rapist insects, seeking perhaps to be suckled, attack Firbank's women: in gardens at night – when the décolletage of evening dress exposes them – or when they brazenly expose themselves. At the evening garden party for the Artificial Princess, the Mistress of the Robes is 'the cynosure of all eyes' – and of insects. Firbank's horror panics his prose into rhyme and near rhyme: 'The moths caught themselves in her crown, and beat their soft wings against the crystals on her gown; with a scream she felt their cold caress upon her throat and breast.'[1] And in *Valmouth* Mrs Yajñavalkya explains

---

[1] Perhaps it is rhetorical to say Firbank was *panicked* into this near-quatrain. Evidently he took care to avoid the distractions and false suggestions of words repeated non-significantly: witness (cf. Chapter VIII, 1) the alteration he made, in one version of his much-transposed poudre-de-riz sky, in order to prevent 'all over' from cancelling out 'overhead'. But his ear seems to have been less disturbed by the false emphases of unintended rhyme. The Mrs Van Cotton passage from *The New Rythum* (which, however,

(about her 'relative, Niri-Esther'): 'She cry for a sting ob a wasp dat settle on her exposed bosom. I tell her – at de window – she shouldn't expose it!'[1]

4. Language of Flower Names

'PEOPLE sometimes spoke (and especially ladies) of the language of flowers . . .' Thus Eddy Monteith's thoughts in *The Flower Beneath the Foot*.

Firbank and Milton are the great practitioners, in English literature, of the poetry of proper names.

Firbank, unlike Milton, often makes his proper names up.

Firbank's name poetry, which he exploits to the true Miltonic ends of sonorousness and evocation, is both personal and topographical – and it sometimes has tinges of both, as in Mrs Steeple (in *Vainglory*) or indeed (in the same book) Miss Chimney, Miss Valley, Mrs (later Lady) Barrow and the more geographically particularised Miss Wookie.

The habit of naming his personages from geography was yet another of the examples set Firbank by Oscar Wilde. Wilde, however, was a straightforward lifter, conjuring such dramatis personae as Lady Windermere, Jack Worthing, Lady Bracknell, Sir Robert Chiltern and Lord Goring directly from the map of England. Robert Hitchens stuck a pin through that custom of Wilde's when, to his portrait of Lord Alfred Douglas in *The Green Carnation*, he gave the surname Hastings.[2]

Firbank is seldom as direct as his exemplar. On one occasion when he *is* as direct (which is in the naming of a personage so minor that she appears [in *Vainglory*] only as the author of a postscript to a letter to Mrs Henedge), he is so by way of direct tribute to Wilde. As Firbank no doubt remarked during his trips to Pangbourne,[3] his Lady Twyford is a kinswoman, from a little further up the (railway) line, to Wilde's Lord Goring. (In *Inclinations* Lady Twyford, though remaining a mere reference, is disclosed to be a playwright.)

Perhaps Firbank's own ancestry caused him to mentally amalgamate railway lines with lines of descent.

As a rule Firbank enriches the Wildean example by invoking physical

---

Firbank might have revised had he lived to finish the book), which I quoted in Chapter X, 2, jogs along like doggerel and is almost divided into bars by the rhyme of *mind* with *behind*.

[1] – a passage which is the (Jamesian sense) donnée of my novel *The Finishing Touch*, as I would have signified by making it the epigraph had I had, when I wrote the book, the least consciousness that it was so.

[2] Cf. Chapter XIV, 10.

[3] (Cf. Chapter XII, 6.) Lady Twyford is on p. 216 (*Vainglory*) and p. 257 (*Inclinations*) in the *Complete* Firbank.

geography (Barrow, Valley) or by taking the *type* of English place names and filling it out with associative significance of his own inventing (though sometimes England provided him with names so deeply significant on their own that he needed only to transpose[1] them whole into contexts of his own inventing). A river in *Vainglory* is, splendidly, the Asz (a name which, convincingly English though it sounds in its eccentricity, I suspect Firbank of having borrowed from the label on a bottle of Tokay Aszu); a seat of nobility is Castle Barbarous; a country railway junction, at once expressively and plausibly, Totterdown. Mrs Shamefoot's search for a cathedral willing to enshrine her in stained glass provides a condensed sketch-map of English provincial life: 'I've Overcares in view [. . .] And then, there's Carnage. But somehow the East Coast never appealed to me. It's so stringy.'

(Perhaps the east coast didn't appeal to Firbank either. Frinton is on it. Perhaps he considered Victoria Gellybore-Frinton[2] 'stringy'.)

And Firbank populates the geography of his invention with such personages as 'Mr Sophax, a critic'; Mrs Whooper; Lady Anne Pantry (who so marvellously opens Chapter VII of *Vainglory*: 'Lady Anne Pantry was sitting in the china-cupboard'); Lady Anne's secretary, Miss Hospice; a curate named Mr (Peter) Pet; Lady Parvula (de Panzoust); Sir William West-Wind;[3] Lady Lucy Saunter; Mrs Thoroughfare (who fulfils one of Firbank's obsessions[4] by 'looking to-night like a good-natured sphinx'); Madame Poco;[5] the Hon. Edward Facile-Manners; Miss Miami Mouth (who opens *Prancing Nigger*). . .

Firbank's variation on a theme of Wilde's amounted to a revival and adaptation of a habit of Restoration comedy. And Firbank's re-invention (in 1915) of the mode was followed in places oblivious of Firbank: innumerable funny pages in journals (up to and including *Private Eye*), funny radio programmes, and middlebrow novels meant or not meant to be funny. Servants in the novels of Ivy Compton-Burnett are often named on Firbankian precedents. For Firbank's upper-class personages are waited on by maids called Sumph and ffoliott, and by butlers and manservants called Gripper,[6] Nit and ffines.

---

[1] Two such Firbankian transpositions (from Yorkshire and from Gloucestershire) will be mentioned in sub-section 19 of this chapter.

[2] Cf. Chapter VI, 6 and sub-section 2 of this chapter.

[3] Sir William West-Wind, who is announced by ffines in *Valmouth*, is presumably a kinsman of the Hon. Viola West-Wind who, in *Inclinations*, is announced by a butler named Queen (*Complete* Firbank, p. 472 and p. 303).

[4] Cf. Chapter XIII, 3, 4 and 7.

[5] the significance of whose name will be mentioned in Chapter XX, 24.

[6] Gripper is in service first at the Bishop's Palace in *Vainglory* and then at the Deanery in *Caprice*.

Twice in *Valmouth* Firbank breaks into a sheer and splendid catalogue of names. The Mayor reads out 'Congratulations [. . .] to Peggy Laughter, Ann and Zillah Bottom, Almeria Goatpath, Thisbe Brownjohn' . . . and so, plausibly and prodigally, on. ffines announces a classier catalogue: 'Sir Wroth and Lady Cleobulina Summer-Leyton, Sir Victor Vatt, Master Xavier Tanoski' . . . etc.

And perhaps the whole strain of proper-name poetry was inspired in Firbank (and his name games[1] and his jugglings with his own real first name[2] given an extra impetus) by similar lists of not quite wholly human names: in nurserymen's catalogues.

To Firbank, for whom flowers were people, it was evidently an inspiring and poetic circumstance that a rose could be Maréchal Niel or Dorothy Perkins.

(The English Ambassadress in Pisuerga first appears to Eddy Monteith 'with her hat awry, crammed with *Maréchal Niel* roses, hot, and decoiffed, flourishing a pair of garden-gauntlets'.[3] Dorothy Perkins makes the New York headlines in *The New Rythum*.[4])

Even when he merely adopts commonplace first names, Firbank frequently picks flowers. *Vainglory* contains a Rose, a Violet and a Lily (respectively, Mrs Asp, Mrs [Lady] Barrow, and Mrs Carteret Brown). *A Study in Temperament* runs, more exotically, to a Lobelia.

When he invents, Firbank's fantasy effloresces. Mrs Rosemerchant's name is extrapolated from Firbank's own[5] profuse purchasing. 'The younger Miss Flowerman', who is tossed (fainting) into *Vainglory*, is probably extrapolated from the heroine of the work mentioned, earlier in *Vainglory*, by the Bishop, when he is asked if he often goes to the theatre. ' "The last time I went", his lordship confessed, "was to see Mrs. Kendall in *The Elder Miss Blossom*." '[6] Miss Flowerman, however, by virtue of being a miss and a flower and yet a man, has enriched the example of her predecessor with a tinge of that ambiguity of sex which, still in *Vainglory*, tempts Winsome Brookes to the (again floral) pseudonym Rose de Tivoli.

The bucolic names congratulated by the Mayor of Valmouth include Rosa Sweet, Violet Ebbing, Tircis Tree and Lily Quickstep. It isn't surprising that the 'old air of France' sung by Mrs Thoroughfare is 'Le temps

---

[1] Cf. sub-section 12 of this chapter.
[2] Cf. Chapter VII, 4.
[3] Indeed, the Ambassadress's first name is (*Complete* Firbank, p. 510) Rosa.
[4] The headlines will be cited in sub-section 19 of this chapter.
[5] Cf. Chapter VII, 5.
[6] Firbank's early play *A Disciple from the Country* (*The New Rythum and Other Pieces*, pp. 120–6) contains a Mrs Blossome.

des lilas et le temps des roses'. The 'perfectly hysterical song' on whose wings 'Miss Wookie was being borne rapidly away' is *When Heliotropes Turn Black*.

Inevitably, *Vainglory*'s topography runs to Violet Villas. Inevitably, the Nijinsky ballet that Mrs Henedge adores in italics is *La Spectre de la Rose*. Inevitably, it is at 'the Château des Fleurs' that Prince Yousef of Pisuerga is accused by his mother of having gambled all night. And at the English library in Pisuerga even a book which is in fact *not* by Ronald Firbank bears a floral name:

' "*The Passing of Rose* I read the other day," Mrs Montgomery said, "and *so* enjoyed it." '

' "Isn't that one of Ronald Firbank's books?" '

' "No, dear, I don't think it is. But I never remember an author's name and I don't think it matters!" '

5. Portrait of the Artist as a Flower . . .

IT was by inventing an addition to the nurserymen's lists of varieties that Firbank wrought the most poignant of his self-portraits – in a novel (*Prancing Nigger*) from which he published an extract in advance under the title *A Broken Orchid*.

It was, of course, as an orchid that Firbank finally gave himself a flowery incarnation, an orchid being, to his imagination, a she with tinges of maleness. (Firbank's floral embodiment outdid Winsome Brookes's floral pseudonym for transvestism.) Perhaps it is the very orchid which Oscar Wilde, in *Lady Appledore's Mésalliance*, nursed back to health[1] – though the mauve[2] colour has been a touch rain-washed out by the neglect of critics and readers. Indeed, the hecticness of Firbank's first defiance of Rollo St Clair Talboys's warning[3] against 'the cult of the purple orchid' was, shade by shade, battered down – though simultaneously, shade by shade, Firbank was perfecting his defiance and his art. The 'purple orchid' has become mauve in *Lady Appledore's Mésalliance* – and, in *Prancing Nigger*, a final 'dingy lilac'.

At the 'Evening of Song and Gala' given for the Earthquake Relief Fund in the Villa Alba, Mr Mouth remarks 'the various plants that lined the way'. But 'in their malignant splendour the orchids were the thing. Mrs. Abanathy, Ronald Firbank (a dingy lilac blossom of rarity untold), Prince Palairet, a

---

[1] Cf. Chapter XIV, 11.
[2] Cf. Chapters VIII, 9 and XIII, 9; and sub-section 9 of this chapter.
[3] Cf. Chapter XIII, 5 and Chapter XIV, 10.

heavy blue-spotted flower, and rosy Olive Moonlight, were those that claimed the greatest respect from a few discerning connoisseurs.'

6. ... and as an Agriculturalist

FIRBANK, who juggled so extensively with his real-life first names,[1] left his real-life surname untouched. Perhaps one reason why it was sacrosanct was that it gratified Firbank's passion for plants, compounding as it does the name of a tree with a feature on which a landscape-gardener might plant the tree.

It was, I suspect, an arboreally punning self-portrait (with an allusion to his well-dressed-ness) that Firbank inserted in *Valmouth*, where, as Thetis Tooke makes her way towards attempted suicide, 'A labourer striding fugitively along in front of her, a young spruce-fir on his back (its bobbing boughs brushing the ground), perplexed her briefly.' Firbank's fantasy has placed him in the interesting, classical and art-historical situation of being (as he expressed it in *The Artificial Princess*) 'carried off all willingly-unwillingly like a creature in a Rape'.[2]

Perhaps it was as a florally ornamented hymn to his own name that Firbank had the company in *The New Rythum* entertained by 'someone singing – Farrar, or Garden, was it? – [. . .] *I know a bank whereon the wild thyme blows, Where oxlips and the nodding violet grows*'.

Mary Garden was a singer probably dear[3] to Firbank because she sang Salome and Mélisande. But her greatest hold on him must have been her surname.

When he made himself a gardener in fiction, Firbank provided his punning[4] self-portrait as Wildred with an arboricultural surname, suitable alike to the job of gardener and to the author's real surname: Forrester.

By a continuation of the same artificially pastoral line of thought, Firbank kept himself in, by name at least, countrified employment when he surnamed his self-portrait in *Vainglory* Harvester.

---

[1] Cf. Chapter VII, 4.

[2] That art-historical subject was much in Firbank's thoughts. The china-cupboard in which (cf. sub-section 4 of this chapter) Lady Anne Pantry so palpably sits turns out, further on in *Vainglory* (p. 169 in the *Complete* Firbank), to contain a collection of *Rapes* in porcelain (Firbank's italics and capital letter).

[3] (as I mentioned in Chapter XIV, 4.) Firbank perhaps had his pen-friend Carl Van Vechten in mind when he made Mary Garden sing at a fictitious party in New York. Robert Hichens (*Yesterday*, p. 177) recorded meeting Mary Garden in New York 'at an afternoon reception given by Carl Van Vechten and his attractive and youthful wife'.

[4] Cf. Chapter XIV, 11.

Gardening, forestry, harvesting: to Firbank they were Arcadian occupations.[1]

To his Harvester self Firbank attributes his own international nomadism[2] ('Certainly he had wandered . . .'); and Firbank adds that Claud Harvester 'had been into Arcadia, even,[3] a place where artificial temperaments so seldom get – their nearest approach being, perhaps, a matinée of *The Winter's Tale*'.

Claud Harvester's first name is taken from the Arcadian landscapes of the painter known in England as Claude.

('I sometimes wish, though', says the Marchioness of Macarnudo in . . . *Cardinal Pirelli*, 'I resembled my sister more, who cares only for amorous, "delicate" men – the Claudes, so to speak.')

Claud Harvester constitutes a landscape by Claude Lorraine playing setting to a Shakespearean pastoral: partly *The Winter's Tale* (the actress who is much taken with Claud Harvester has played Hermione); partly *The Tempest* (on the marvellously named Totterdown station, Mrs Shamefoot wonders – a thought that may have influenced Harvester's name – 'Where were *the sunburned sicklemen of August weary!*')

Long before *Vainglory* Firbank had permitted a personage of his inventing to take delight in the artificiality of pastorals on the stage. In *Mr White-Morgan the Diamond King*, an early or earlyish[4] Firbank story, the diamond king (whose sobriquet is perhaps a sophisticated extrapolation from a demon king in a pantomime of Firbank's childhood) is a 'self made nouveau riche' who buys a portion of Soho in order to pull it down and build himself not only a large house but a large garden. Perhaps that is what Firbank would have done with his grandfather Joseph's fortune, had it been he who was the self-made nouveau riche. To a party he gives in his garden, Mr

---

[1] Not all Firbank's gardening and pastoral names have Arcadian intentions. Two of a different tenor will be mentioned in sub-section 13 and sub-section 15 of this chapter.

[2] Cf. Chapter VII, 2.

[3] Perhaps this, as well as Poussin, directed Evelyn Waugh (cf. Chapters VI, 3; X, 2; and XIV, 7) to call Book One of *Brideshead Revisited* 'Et In Arcadia Ego'.

[4] *The New Rythum and Other Pieces*, which publishes an extract from it, marks this story as written when Firbank was 'aged about fourteen' – that is, about 1900. However, the *Biography* (pp. 67–70) dates it 1905: on, again (cf. Chapter XIV, 4), the 'topical references' theory. Firbank was the son of a politician. Yet the *Biography* assumes he was incapable of inventing, for fiction, a generalised general election. References in the story to London's forgetting (in the excitement of Mr White-Morgan's exploits) the general election, and to the 'Unemployed Question', are taken by the *Biography* to indicate that Firbank wrote the story in 1905, when the general election of January 1906 was, according to the *Biography*, 'prepared for and talked about'. Even on its own untenable premisses the argument in no way demolishes the *New Rythum* volume's dating of about 1900. There was a general election in 1900, too.

White-Morgan invites, among many others, the florally named Lady Violet Wilmington and her daughter. The daughter looks forward to the country air. 'If you call Old Cumpton[1] Street country air, my poor child!' murmurs the mother, and the daughter replies: 'It will be quite country enough for me, besides the real country bores me so, I am only fond of the country when I see it on the stage.'

When Firbank wrote of a matinée of *The Winter's Tale* in *Vainglory* he was perhaps fresh from seeing Harley Granville Barker's revolutionary (non-naturalistic) production at the Savoy Theatre of 1912.

It is even possible that the country which Lady Violet Wilmington's daughter had liked on the stage is also the country of *The Winter's Tale*, which Firbank was remembering through her mouth. There was a production he could have been taken to as an extreme child, the production at the Theatre Metropole in 1895, in which Henry Irving played Leontes – which was very probably enough like a pantomime to be thought suitable to be seen by a nine-year-old.

7. Arcady Beyond a Wall

SHEPHERDS in Arcady are not hard put to it to pick up a livelihood. 'For us' (sings the chorus of shepherds in Handel's artificial pastoral) 'the winters rain, For us the summers shine, Spring swells for us the grain, And autumn bleeds the vine.'

The pastoral names Firbank gave his self-portraits are small, concentrated, self-sufficient fantasies embodying Firbank's wish that autumn could be counted on to bleed the champagne grapes for him.

Wildred Forrester finds precisely what Firbank as a young man was looking for:[2] a job that will support him without any great or lasting forfeit on his part of leisure, amenity or gentility.

Wildred, who is a creature of Firbank's fantasy, finds his Arcadia among the plants in Lady Appledore's garden. Firbank, who had in inclement fact been expelled by the decline in his father's financial fortune from the garden of The Coopers, reconstructed the real garden by artifice (hence the artificiality of his pastoral) and with some exactitude in fiction. Wildred (a stranger – as Firbank had become) draws up 'before a long red brick wall'. He gets down from the cart that has brought him from the station. 'Over the garden wall, that seemed very old, Wildred could see the tops of fruit trees, through which the stars were shining. The wall ran along the high-

---

[1] Cf. Chapter X, 12.
[2] Cf. Chapter VII, 2 and Chapter IX, 6.

road for nearly a quarter of a mile, and seemed to end in a clock tower, that was probably the stables.'

Patently Wildred has alighted beside the long wall of old red brick that runs not along a highroad but along Hawkwood (or Botany Bay) Lane, Chislehurst.[1]

If you follow the wall along, past the house, you do indeed see the stables, a detached building in brick (the upper part tiled). Over the carriage arch there is indeed a clock tower – without (nowadays) a clock but with a weather vane.

Wildred's glimpse of the tops of fruit trees over the wall (nowadays conifers, roses and flowering shrubs can be glimpsed, but no fruit trees) became an icon of Firbank's nostalgia for The Coopers: a frozen last glimpse, as he departed, and the only glimpse to be had of the garden if, after his expulsion, he came back as a visiting stranger.

In his self-portrait as Claud Harvester, Firbank actually (and self-perceptively) incorporated the glimpse of the tops of the fruit trees as an item in his artistic personality.

The portrait is outlined, and Claud Harvester introduced into *Vainglory*, at the party Mrs Henedge gives to celebrate the recovery of a fragment of a yet remoter past, the lines by Sappho which Professor Inglepin has come upon in Egypt. (Into the same party Firbank introduces by allusion a fragment of a past fiction of his own, *Lady Appledore's Mésalliance*, in which he had reconstructed *his* past. Mrs Asp, in the course of '*talking servants* to Mrs. Thumbler', remarks: 'She was four years with Lady Appledore.') After making mention of Claud Harvester's visit to Arcadia, Firbank anatomises his writing. 'In style – he was often called obscure, although, in reality, he was as charming as the top of an apple-tree above a wall.'

8. Strawberry Harvest

THE jobs Firbank adumbrated, as sufficiently Arcadian, for himself in real life included something ecclesiastical and something to do with selling pictures – both of which, in Firbank's fiction, Reggie Quintus[2] comes rather nearer to managing to perform than Firbank himself did in real life.

Firbank's most successfully Arcadian creature is Wildred Forrester. He is, however, a creature of outright wish-fantasy. Wildred actually regains the lost paradise-garden of The Coopers: in his capacity first of husbandsman and eventually of husband. Firbank himself must have felt disqualified

---

[1] Cf. Chapter X, 4.
[2] Cf. Chapter IX, 8.

from both métiers, by a lack of robustness alike in his health and in his taste for women.

Indeed Firbank could not sustain the state of being a husband even in fiction. When Claud Harvester enters *Vainglory*, which he does towards the beginning, he has a wife (named, for sufficient Firbankian reasons,[1] Cleopatra). He arrives unaccompanied at the Sappho party given by Mrs Henedge (who 'could not endure his wife') and apologises for his wife's absence. By half way through, Claud Harvester's wife has gone unaccountably absent from the whole book, and others of the dramatis personae are discussing him thus: ' "I expect he'll fall in love some day with somebody," Lady Georgia exclaimed, injuring a silence, "and marry; or don't you think he will?" "Marry; who?" "Claud Harvester." "Why should he?" '

Although Wildred Forrester is the hero straightforwardly of a fantasy, it is a fantasy whose borders Firbank's imagination could extend into situations where they could be occupied by more truly Firbankian personages. The plant-peopled refuge from poverty which Wildred finds within the walls of a garden is the same refuge, with the same population, as Mrs Shamefoot and the Duchess of Varna severally find[2] within the walls of a flower-shop.

The text of *The Flower Beneath the Foot* admits at once that the Duchess is seeking refuge from notorious debts. *Vainglory*, however, maintains to begin with that Mrs Shamefoot keeps a flower-shop because 'It was her happiness to slap, delicately, at monotony by selling flowers' and 'She found in this by-life a mode of expression, too, which her nature craved.' But within a couple of pages Mrs Shamefoot's own account (of how she came to marry) discloses her family hard-up-ness: 'when I got engaged I was unconscious, or very nearly. I had fallen sound asleep, I remember, off an iron chair in the park. The next day he had put it in the paper; and we none of us could raise the guinea to contradict . . .'

Mrs Shamefoot's and Wildred Forrester's vocation for vegetables is shared by the Princess Zoubaroff. 'Your own garden, Princess, you know, is all our envy,' she is told by the owner of another garden (which she, in turn, has called 'a Paradise'[3]). The Princess, however, doesn't exercise her vocation professionally – or not in its vegetable aspect. In the language of Firbank's imagination, she is doing the same thing when she plucks and arranges women for her convent. And in exercising *that* vocation professionally the Princess Zoubaroff is carrying out Princess Artie's ambition of securing some sort of ecclesiastical job.[4]

Mrs Shamefoot perhaps actually combines her work on plants with

[1] Cf. Chapter XIV, 2, footnote.   [2] Cf. sub-section 2 of this chapter.
[3] Cf. Chapter X, 5.   [4] Cf. Chapter VII, 2.

Firbank's other potential job.[1] On the walls of her flower-shop 'hung charming flower studies by Fantin Latour, and by Nicholson, intermingled with some graceful efforts of her own – impressions, mostly, of roses; in which it might be observed that she always made a great point of the thorns'.

Some at least of her pictures you might think Mrs Shamefoot could scarcely afford to keep. Indeed, so thinks Mrs Mountjulian (previously the Duchess of Overcares and, before that, Miss Emma Harris), who admires Mrs Shamefoot's collection (which at this time of telling runs also to a Cézanne) and makes an indeed thorny point of repeating a conversation she had the previous night: in particular the remark (made to her by the florally *and herbally* named Sir Valerian Hanway) 'It's an anxiety for a poor man to own beautiful things.'

Mrs Shamefoot's comment discloses nothing (' "If she thought to embarrass me," Mrs Shamefoot said as soon as they were gone, "I'm afraid she failed!" '), but I suspect that her intention is not to own the 'beautiful things' for long but to sell them (including those by her own hand).

That he believed a house to need a garden Firbank affirmed early, through the folly built and planted by his diamond king, Mr White-Morgan.[2] He re-affirmed it in the last book he worked on. The 'bachelor-home' of Bertie Waldorf, in the New York Firbank's imagination created for *The New Rythum*, 'lay almost at the extremity of Upper Park Avenue. Planned from designs by Ronald Firbank, it possessed perhaps everything that a man might wish for except a garden.'

But as a matter of fact the design by Ronald Firbank has made good the want. By a culminating extension of his perception that a flower-shop is an indoor garden, Firbank has Bertie Waldorf throw, in his Firbankian house, a strawberry-picking party in indoor strawberry beds. It is the most artificial of Firbank's artificial pastorals.

9. Princess Artie, Trading as Ronald Firbank

TO keep a flower-shop was (perhaps still is) one of the few ways of making an income open to upper-class women who possessed no skill and didn't want to tumble out of 'Society'. Another way (which needed skill – but that could be hired) was to make and sell hats or dresses. Both types of business were usually conducted on a small scale but at the highest social level of chic. So far from dropping out of 'Society', the businesswoman exploited the fact that she was in 'Society' to provide her with her clientele. She lost no face. Her methods were so exactly like those of 'voluntary work' (that is,

---

[1] Cf. Chapter IX, 6.   [2] Cf. sub-section 6 of this chapter.

bullying contributions to 'charity' from social friends) that her business probably passed for a good cause.

Firbank's fiction, which invents or fictionalises from real life[1] upper-class owners of flower-shops, makes a trompe d'œil joke in the manner of Cervantes by not bothering to fictionalise upper-class dressmakers. *A Study in Temperament*, which Firbank included in the first volume he published, opens with Lady Agnes Charters glancing at her reflexion in a mirror. 'There is no one like Lucile for black,' she thinks at the beginning of the second paragraph.

And in *Vainglory* Mrs Henedge, calling on Mrs Calvally (whose husband has just left her), says: 'I was afraid [. . .] I should find you in one of Lucile's black dreams –'

Lucile was Heather Firbank's dressmaker. Trading as Lucile, much as Mrs Shamefoot's shop trades 'under the name of Monna Vanna', she was (according to the *Biography*[2]) a Lady Duff-Gordon.

Providing Lucile with a free puff in his first and second books didn't exempt Firbank from giving or lending[3] his sister money to pay one of Lucile's bills in 1924; and in 1925 he was writing to Heather that her annuity 'should go towards "Jones" the greengrocer as well as to "Lucile" the dressmaker'.

Heather Firbank, in whom her parents' passion for collecting had become a habit of keeping things (including magazines, between whose pages she further kept banknotes[4]), not only bought her clothes, extravagantly, from Lucile and other posh dressmakers but kept them. Her wardrobe now belongs to the Victoria and Albert Museum.

Her brother's transvestism of the imagination prompted him to an accuracy about women's clothes virtually fetishist. In *The New Rhythum* Firbank explicitly fictionalises himself as a designer of houses or house interiors ('Planned from designs by Ronald Firbank' . . .). But his whole œuvre is an implicit fictionalisation of himself as a designer of dresses. His female dramatis personae scarcely stir abroad unless swathed in a costume of Firbank's designing – with motifs often, of course, floral.

---

[1] According to the *Biography*, p. 120, the fictional flower-shop of Mrs Shamefoot is a 'hardly recognisable' version of the flower-shop run in real life by Lady Angela Forbes, with whom, the *Biography* says on the strength of a Firbank letter, Firbank in 1921 considered literary collaboration.

[2] which has not noticed the presence of Lucile in *A Study in Temperament* and *Vainglory*.

[3] I don't know which. The *Biography* (p. 269), which presumably has the fact from Firbank's letters, records it vaguely as 'he had assisted her in the payment of an overdue bill of £40 owed to her dressmaker.'

[4] Cf. Chapter VII, 2.

(Saint Laura de Nazianzi, asked what she will wear for the ball: 'A black gown and three blue flowers on my tummy.')

Firbank regularly sketched his clothes designs in words – and sometimes in pencil or watercolour, too. In 1904 he created an illuminated manuscript, *Ideas and Fancies*, which he wrote, in a sort of quasi-cursive majuscules, and decorated, in watercolour, with what (to judge from the page reproduced in *The New Rythum and Other Pieces*) might be sketches for fashion plates.

And in his notebooks he pencil-jotted drawings as well as phrases. A double-page spread [Plate 9] from a notebook Firbank used in the composition of *Valmouth* and *The Princess Zoubaroff* (works he published in, respectively, 1919 and 1920) intersperses words with drawings. On the left-hand page stands a presumably sainted nun. She seems to wear both wimple and halo – as well as being girt with such Firbankian emblems as an annunciatory branch (in flower) and a positive fetter of rosary (plus, perhaps, though it is too ghostly to read for sure, a church candle). Her habit is cut unorthodoxly low over a bosom fashionably and probably painfully[1] flattened to confront the 1920s. The facing page bears, besides blots from the left-hand page, two portraits of women in considerable hats.

Firbank's double page (which is in a notebook belonging to the Berg Collection, New York) was shewn in an exhibition (New York Public Library, 1969) of pictures by writers. (The exhibition's title was *Pen and Brush: The Author as Artist*, a twofold antithesis perversely designed to reduplicate misunderstanding. To the common refusal to acknowledge that authors as such *are* artists, it adds a confusion of its own. A great many of the pictures exhibited were done with a pen, not a brush.) The catalogue finds that Firbank's nun 'may well be Sister Ecclesia' from *Valmouth* – which indeed she may: but she may equally well, or perhaps, given the fashionable cut of her habit, more probably, be one of the nuns of Princess Zoubaroff's community, who, according to the stage-directions, 'look very pale, slim and Isis-like in their grain-coloured Nuns' toilettes'.[2]

The upper of the hatted women (the one who seems to sit on a bench or a sofa, accompanied by a bo-peep-ish parasol) the catalogue identifies as Mrs Hurstpierpoint, also from *Valmouth* (though by Firbankian fatality the catalogue mis-spells her as Hurstpierpont), on the grounds that Mrs Hurstpierpoint has been painted by Ingres and that Firbank has written, next to his drawing, 'How Ingres admired my hands. He quite worshiped'

---

[1] – a point which sub-section 10 will make more pointed.
[2] The nun in the drawing is well equipped to obey the *Princess Zoubaroff* stage direction 'smacking Eric smartly with her rosary' (*Complete* Firbank, p. 760).

(the mis-spelling is this time Firbank's) 'my little fingers –.' However, those words are spoken not by Mrs Hurstpierpoint or anyone else in *Valmouth*, but by the Princess Zoubaroff.

As a dress-designer in words (and a nuns'-habit-designer in occasional drawings), Firbank shewed a strong taste for Ingres, perhaps because Ingres was almost as vividly interested as Firbank in hands and in women's clothes. For her Sappho party Mrs Henedge hopes 'we shall all be as *Ingres* as possible, [. . .] since there's not much time to be Greek'. That Mrs Hurstpierpoint has been portrayed by Ingres[1] is explained by the fact that almost everyone in *Valmouth* is, thanks to the qualities of Valmouth air, virtually a centenarian. But it is by one of the deliberately bewildering anachronisms through which he expressed his taste that Firbank (who, as Claud Harvester, is 'an elaborate young man, who, in some bewildering way of his own, seemed to find charming the fashions of 1860') causes the Princess Zoubaroff to have been admired by Ingres, who died some nineteen years before Firbank was born.

Mentally, Firbank was in business in rivalry with Lucile[2] – and very likely also with his own inventions, Mrs Shamefoot and the Duchess of Varna. It no doubt provoked him to a little resentment that, in the pre-1914 world which he searched for a métier, the many occupations that were open to men and closed to women didn't appeal to him, whereas designing dresses or bouquets, which did, was less socially acceptable if done by a man than when done by upper-class women under pseudonyms. That resentment probably fused with another[3] more cardinal. But none of Firbank's social criticisms ever became explicit. They are to be read only in the direction and profusion of his fantasy.

Firbank early put two of his own sternest devotions, to fashion and to flowers, into the mouth of one of his inventions (a widow, as Firbank was to make himself for Carl Van Vechten[4]) – though perversely (or in obedience to Talboys's warning against purple flowers) he turns her against mauve.[5]

---

[1] Hers is a 'youthful', however, 'portrait from the hand of Ingres' (p. 401 in the *Complete* Firbank).

[2] Firbank probably shared the ambition, though he would deprecate the figure, of the dubious University student whom Charlie Mouth meets in Cuna-Cuna (*Complete* Firbank, p. 624): 'Pedro, Pedro, ardent and obese, who seemed to imagine that to be a dress-designer to foreign Princesses would yield his several talents a thrice-blessed harvest.' Indeed, the metaphor of harvest is perhaps a label affixed by the unconscious, marking the dream as Firbank's (or Claud Harvester's) own.

[3] to be mentioned in sub-section 14 of this chapter.

[4] (Cf. Chapter V, 6 and Chapter IX, 3.) The widow who voices Firbank's devotions is Mrs Fawley or Franley in *The Widow's Love* or *When Widows Love* (cf. Chapter X, 13)

[5] Cf. Chapters VIII, 9; XIII, 9; and XV, 5.

' "Nothing shall induce me to go into mauve", she said, "I shall be quite brave and live only for my dressmaker and for my garden." '

10. Il Faut Souffrir . . .

FASHION to Firbank was aboriginally Edwardian fashion: tight-laced to the point where the wasp-waist stung.

His clothes fetishism ministered to his erotic taste for pain. No doubt he knew, with pleasure, the maxim Il faut souffrir pour être belle.

At the same time, his clothes fetishism endorsed his flower fetishism: not only because flowers can be, and by Firbank's personages extensively are, worn but because flowers, besides being female, represented to Firbank female clothing. He felt his rooms naked when they were not dressed in flowers. Flowers were the frills and flounces, in interesting colours and delicate materials, which in the sobriety of his dandyism he denied his own body.

And flowers, too, ministered to masochism. Mrs Shamefoot punishes as well as puns when she makes a point of the thorns. In gardens flowers are staked out and bound up – to *canes*. In flower-shops they can be wired. Of Mrs Shamefoot 'it was declared that in all England nobody could wire Neapolitan violets more skilfully than she'.

Perhaps the flower who, in the Duchess of Varna's shop, complains 'My wires are hurting me: my wires are hurting me' is that dingy lilac blossom Ronald Firbank. He cried half, perhaps, in a masochist's ecstasy in submitting to 'discipline' – but half, also, in the pain of a disciplined artist. Firbank's method of composition[1] is remarkably like Mrs Shamefoot's: a wiring together of small bright efflorescences.

Perhaps he endorsed her 'I believe I'll be desired somehow more when I'm gone. What good am I here?' and hoped to receive in his own lifetime the answer she has from Lady Castleyard, 'My dear, you compose in flowers. You adorn life. You have not lived in vain.'

He did indeed compose in flowers.

To Firbank's mind flowers and literature too must suffer in order to be beautiful.

It was while he was trading as Claud Harvester that Firbank's mind brought together[2] the discipline of flowers and the discipline of fashion. While Claud Harvester converses at a party with an actress, ' "Surely", he reflected, "her hair must be wired?" '

---

[1] Cf. Chapter V, 2.
[2] Their culminating fusion will be mentioned in sub-section 19 of this chapter.

It is the discipline of fashion and horticulture alike that is dispensed by the Princess Zoubaroff. When she first discloses her new profession ('I often think I would rather like to run a Convent,' one which is, however, to be 'For little girls – not sour old women'), the Princess declares: 'I have passed through all the fads, I suppose, myself in furniture and pictures and books. And now all I ask for's a cell. Give me a room with nothing in it!'

(Adrian asks: 'It must need courage to be so eclectic?')

Indeed Zena Zoubaroff, Abbess, founder of a modern school of stoicism ('our austerities – our Rule –') for females only, is counterpart to Zeno, founder of the (masculine) school of stoicism of ancient Athens. However, the Princess's stoicism, as Firbank indicates by her surname, is ('I've had Austrian waltzes whirling through my head all day' and 'I'm inventing a delightfully potent liqueur to be made by the Nuns [. . .] We mean to call it yellow-ruin') more exuberant (which Firbank may well have thought was spelt exzoubarant).

It is not surprising that what the talking flora and fauna[1] of her garden disclose to the Princess Zoubaroff are the secrets of fashion.

> PRINCESS (*poetically*). I love the Flowers. They talk to me. I love the Birds. They sing to me!
> NADINE. What have they told you – if it's not indiscreet?
> PRINCESS (*elusively*). They say that Opera-cloaks this Spring are going to make one seven good feet across the shoulders.
> NADINE. Ah?
> PRINCESS. And that sandals shortly are coming in.

11. . . . et Maigrir

BY the perverse cruelties of fashion, the tight-laced waist must, even so, waste. Firbank, large consumer of fruits, surely thought of eating flowers – *the* delicate diet for slimmers,[2] and one tinged, to Firbank's personifying imagination, with the delicate deliciousness of cannibalism.

Firbank seems to hint at a naughtiness better left unpublished when the flowers sent by Mrs Henedge reach Winsome Brookes (whose figure is endangered by the food supplied by his landlady) and his companion Andrew. ' "Ah! here comes breakfast now", Andrew observed, as Mrs. Henedge's floral gift was ushered in upon a tray.'

Cannibalism is more explicit, if more circuitous, in a conversation further

---

[1] Cf. sub-section 2 of this chapter.
[2] Cf. Chapter VIII, 4 and Chapter XIV, 10.

on in *Vainglory*. This time it is not humans who eat the plants, but it comes to the same thing: all flesh is as the grass. Mrs Wookie laments the broken-down-ness of the fence round the churchyard where Brigadier Wookie is buried. 'It really isn't nice the way the cows get in and loll among the tombs. If it's only for the milk –'

And the notion of flower-eating launches a nonsense flight in *The Princess Zoubaroff*. It is nonsense that disguises a delicate psychological history of Firbank's own abstention from food: through the medium, as with so many of his autobiographies, of orchids.[1]

ADRIAN. I expect you're hungry after riding so far.
PRINCESS. I am!
ERIC. That's right.
PRINCESS. This morning my French cook got locked, by mistake, in the orchid-house, and I've had nothing to eat all day.

12. The Namer in the Garden

'[. . .] amid gardens made for suffering and delight [. . .] Lovely as Paradise, oppressive perhaps as Eden [. . .]'[2]

'And the Lord God planted a garden eastward in Eden [. . .] And Adam gave names to all cattle, and to the fowl of the air, and to every beast of the field; but for Adam there was not found an help meet for him.'[3]

IN that garden that runs eastward out of Chislehurst, Firbank perhaps had difficulty in *remembering* the names the nurserymen's lists ascribed to the flowers – a difficulty he later passed on to the Princess Zoubaroff and her protégée's husband:

PRINCESS. [. . .] Those purple, tragic roses. . . . Tell me, how are they named?
ADRIAN. I forget.

Perhaps Firbank made good his forgetfulness by invention – an activity he later passed on to the Duchess of Varna's flower-shop, where, in honour of the royal entente cordiale between Pisuerga and England, 'Many of the flowers had been newly christened, "Elsie" "Audrey", "London-Madonnas" (black Arums these), while the roses from the "Land of Punt" had been renamed "Mrs. Lloyd George" – and priced accordingly.'

---
[1] But for once even the first edition (p. 49) denies 'orchid' its capital.
[2] *Concerning the Eccentricities of Cardinal Pirelli*, VIII (p. 675 in the *Complete* Firbank).
[3] *Genesis*, II.

By such processes, perhaps, Firbank brought to perfection his art of nomenclature.

That art is a manifestation of his cultist, fetishist temperament – which attracted him, in the first place, to flowers, those emblems of female clothing, those marks of the presence of a shrine.

Firbank's thoughts worship. They dwell on a saint, an image of a saint, a literary image, a flower – or a name. They focus on names (which to his mind *are* flowers) with so vivid an intensity that the syllables fall separate – and can then be, by Firbank's mosaic method of composition, rearranged.

Having renamed Arthur Firbank Ronald Firbank, Ronald Firbank conjures up Winsome Brookes[1] out of Winston (Churchill), (Rupert) Brooke and Rupert Brooke's winsome handsomeness; causes Winsome Brookes to hesitate whether to rename himself Rose de Tivoli; and himself hesitates whether to rename Winsome as Sacheverell.

Firbank's naming, which probably began with nurserymen's lists, proceeded to something more on the model of the stud book. Reggie Quintus:[2] his dam is Bosie Douglas, he was sired by Lord Reggie Hastings, and you can read through his name to the regal stock of his ancestor Carolus Quintus or Charles-Quint.

At the same time you can read, in a rustic touch, Firbank's personal past: aptly since Reggie Quintus is also Firbank. The quaint 'Quint' is Henry James's Peter Quint, who goes back to a Shakespearean pastoral: not, this time, *The Winter's Tale*[3] but its seasonal counterpart, *A Midsummer Night's Dream*. In James's Peter Quint, Firbank read Shakespeare's Peter Quince – and thence back to the blossom[4] (was there a quince tree among the apples?) glimpsed over the wall of Arcadia.

Tredegar becomes Intriguer, Sevenoaks Sevenelms; Gossart represents the gosse Artie; a youth well read in Wilde is named Wildred; Crowley, correctly pronounced, takes diabolical wing as a crow.[5]

Even the pointedly reffined butler in *Valmouth* hiccups in name-games. The folk-lore figure of the drunken butler had factually occurred in Firbank's youth at Chislehurst, when his family dismissed a butler who was drunk while he served dinner. The episode (plus, perhaps, a family joke about it) was, I imagine, the germ of the onomatopoetic eruption of balkanised *b*-into-*v* conversions whereby the butler in *Valmouth* invents a further,[6] musical-

---

[1] Cf. Chapter VI, 6 and Chapter VII, 4.
[2] Cf. Chapter IX, 7 and Chapter XIV, 10.
[3] Cf. sub-section 6 of this chapter.
[4] Cf. sub-section 7 of this chapter.
[5] Cf. Chapters VIII, 5; VI, 6; IX, 9; XIV, 11; and VIII, 6.
[6] Cf. Chapter V, 6 and Chapter IX, 3.

comedic champagne widow, merges Beaujolais and Clos-Vougeot with Tokay and (a wine Firbank no doubt drank on the shores of the Loire in 1902 or 1904[1]) Vouvray, and comes finally, triumphantly and exclamatorily out with 'Château-Thierry!' as a circumvention of the unattemptable (the in the circumstances *too* liable to misconstruction) Château-Yquem: ' "Lulu Veuve? Veaujolais? Clos Voukay? Or Château-Thierry?" the butler broke the silence.'

('If ffines to-night was not enough to infuriate an archangel!' his employer, Mrs Hurstpierpoint, comments after dinner.)

Pursuing his creation of the Firbankian novel which is partly about the methods of creating Firbankian novels, Firbank (in his second-published Firbankian work, *Inclinations*) attributed his own technique of naming to one of the personages inside his book, Mabel Collins (and thereby incidentally justified me in disentangling, sometimes to the inclusion of French, his name chains):

' "There's a packet for Miss Hill. . . ." '
' "Take it away. It's not for us." '
' "I expect it's for me! Collins, Colline, Collina *Hill*. I thought it was advisable not to give my own name at any of the shops. . . ." '

(The Joycean Irish linguistic pungency protrudes through Firbank's mental Frenchness. Collina Hill is a colleen.)

13. A Sapphic Obsession – 1

COLLINA HILL or, rather, Mabel Collins is also the person who breaks Miss O'Brookomore's heart.

She does it by marrying Count Pastorelli, whose name incarnates the reverse of the innocence of Forrester and Harvester.[2] Count Pastorelli represents not artificial but sinisterly fake pastoral. 'Take my word for it,' Miss O'Brookomore forebodes when Miss Collins first picks him up on board ship, 'he's not so pastoral as he sounds.'

Count Pastorelli is, indeed, the satyr in Firbank's Arcadia: the intruding heterosexual. *The Princess Zoubaroff* is Firbank's prescriptive design for living in a mode which shall, by consent, exclude him. In both the novel and the play, the assertion of equal rights for homosexuality is made through the emotions of *women* homosexuals.[3]

From the childhood day when he and his brother named a dog Sapho in

---

[1] Cf. Chapter X, 10.   [2] Cf. sub-section 6 of this chapter.
[3] Cf. Chapter XIV, 8.

honour of Réjane and the French language,[1] Firbank was alert to exploit every association (witness the remarkable cinema programme advertised in such execrable Italian in *The Princess Zoubaroff*[2]) of the words *sapphic* and *lesbian* for their utmost value in bizarrerie or scandal.

Indeed, most of Firbank's personages must be in the situation declared by (a further[3] floral personage) Viola Neffal in *Inclinations*: 'The persons whom I should most have cared to meet were Walpole and Sappho.'

(I think Miss Neffal is more likely to have had in mind Horace than Sir Robert Walpole, but it is always possible she meant Hugh.)

It is not for its associations with Catullus, though it may be a touch for its associations with Swinburne and thus with flagellation,[4] that Firbank plays on the name Lesbia. Blanche Negress (in *The Princess Zoubaroff*) is the author of *Lesbia, or Would He Understand?* Mrs Rosemerchant (in *The New Rythum*) possesses 'Sargent's masterly study of *Lesbia Lukewarm*'.

A page later, Mrs Van Cotton[5] is 'ogling' the Sargent 'obliquely' – much as the Duquesa DunEden (in *Concerning the Eccentricities of Cardinal Pirelli*), in the course of viewing an exhibition of paintings by pupils of the College of Noble Damosels (the Guardia Nobile[6] transposed to Spain and the female sex?), raises 'a lorgnon, critically, before the portrait of a Lesbian, with dying, fabulous eyes'. The DunEden collection itself includes, among its classical statues, 'the "supposed original" of the *Lesbia of Lysippus*'.

A touch of scandal, at once sapphic and (artificially) floral, is, in *The New Rythum*, laid at the feet of another classical statue. A Hercules by Praxiteles ('the Prax Herc') is imported to the United States. The dockside party[7] that welcomes it is decorated by 'a wreath of cup-like, waxen flowers from the "Disciples of Sappho" ': fittingly, since the importing of the statue plays the same part in the imagist construction of *The New Rythum* as the recovery of the fragment of Sappho's poetry plays in that of *Vainglory*.

Perhaps Mrs Rosemerchant is one of the Disciples. She attends the dockside party with Heliodora,[8] the winner of a beauty prize – by whose

---

[1] Cf. Chapter V, 2.   [2] Cf. Chapter X, 12.
[3] Cf. sub-section 4 of this chapter.
[4] (Cf. sub-section 19 of this chapter.) One of the poems which Eddy Monteith (in *The Flower Beneath the Foot*, on p. 539 in the *Complete* Firbank) has, much in Firbank's own real-life fashion, had 'published for him by "Blackwood of Oxford" ', is an *Ode to Swinburne*. (There will be more about Eddy Monteith's poems in Chapter XX, 13.)
[5] Cf. Chapter X, 2.
[6] Cf. Chapter VII, 2.
[7] This is the social and art-historical gathering into which (cf. Chapter IX, 6, footnote) Firbank inserted Sir Joseph Duveen.
[8] – originally Dreadfuline (Hancock). Mrs Rosemerchant, sharing one of Firbank's own tendencies (cf. sub-section 12 of this chapter) renames her.

photograph Mrs Rosemerchant was 'arrested' while she read a magazine. 'It was a face of a wayward, Renaissance type, exciting enthusiasm and admiration – it was evident from the votes – almost equally from her own sex as from men.'

Perhaps *The New Rythum*, had Firbank finished it, would have enlarged that relationship into a serious love between women, like the love in *Inclinations* but reciprocated. Firbank's notes include: 'Great giant' (Mr Rosemerchant) 'goes to wife's room. Conjugal prerogatives – lovely pyjamas. Finds Heliodora. Scene. Mrs R. refuses to send her away. "She is sleeping dear tonight with me." hair-brushing continues. Great giant goes – returns, in the mood to do anything – even get into bed between them!' And, under the heading '*For finale tutto? suggestion*', Firbank wrote: 'The complete disappearance of Mrs Rosemerchant and of her young friend from the American scene made a profound sensation[...] Rumours from time to time reached New York that they had been seen together in Paris restaurants or in Egypt. While some believed they were living together in the mountains of Nirvana [...] Many, and particularly Mr Rosemerchant's friends, believed that he had quietly murdered them.'

In a new paragraph, Firbank added: '*N.B.* preceding chapter should be poetic lyric fantastic anything. Then cold snap as –'

In *Valmouth*, the 'little madcap negress' has 'torn to piecemeal' a copy of, inevitably,[1] *Les Chansons de Bilitis*. No less inevitably, Mrs Thoroughfare, when she first sits down to the piano to sing, begins 'Les – bia – ah-h. . . !'

Mrs Thoroughfare is continuing, with the words 'White Mit – y – lene [. . .] where the gir –', when Mrs Hurstpierpoint interrupts with a request for the 'old air of France',[2] 'Le temps des lilas et le temps des roses'. Firbank's floral obsession cuts short his lesbian obsession, which is thereby left, scandalous and emphasised, like dots of suspension hinting the unspeakable into the air.

With just so calculated a breath of scandal, at the party given (in *Vainglory*) for the recovered fragment of Sappho, 'The Lesbian wine (from Samos. Procured perhaps in Pall Mall) produced a hush.'

The same hush settles over the party chatter towards the end[3] of *The Artificial Princess*. Into it Firbank flashes his hint of Salome's veiling not quite removed: 'I hear that your wife and my wife . . . but I fancy there's

---

[1] – inevitably not only because of the female-homosexual content of the Chansons (published in 1894) but because the author, Pierre Louÿs, was a friend of Oscar Wilde.

[2] Cf. sub-section 4 of this chapter.

[3] – towards the end, that is, of the original stopping point. The conversation between the Baroness and Sir Oliver Scott, which I next quote, is from the final passage Firbank added after he recovered the book. (Cf. Chapter XIII, 3).

nothing in it . . .' A passage of party later, the theme is brought out again, with more brilliant orchestration:

> 'Tell me, Sir Oliver,' she demanded, 'have you ever been to Greece?'
> 'More than once,' Sir Oliver dryly replied, 'I even married, *en secondes noces*, a Lesbian . . .'
> 'A native of Lesbos? Just fancy that!' the Baroness marvelled, appraising a passing débutante, a young girl in a mousseline robe of palest Langue de chat.
> '*Née* a Demitraki.'
> 'A demi what?' the Baroness abstrusely twittered'. . . .

14. A Sapphic Obsession – 2

THE furnishings of his lesbian fantasies Firbank probably borrowed from real life.

No doubt the literary gossip of pre-1914 Paris directed his attention to two expatriates (of, respectively, United-States and Anglo-United States parentage) who, like Firbank himself at the beginning of his published career,[1] chose to write in French: Natalie Clifford Barney, poetic-dramatist on the subject of Sappho; and Renée Vivien, poet and translator of Sappho into French, who (as her friend Colette later chronicled in *Ces Plaisirs*[2]) died young in 1909 partly (and Firbankianly) of drink and self-starvation.

I imagine that Miss O'Brookomore and Miss Collins journey to Greece (in *Inclinations*), and that Mrs Thoroughfare sings (in *Valmouth*) of 'White Mit-y-lene', in tribute to the sojourns of Natalie Clifford Barney and Renée Vivien in the villa Renée Vivien owned at Mitylene.

Conceivably, however, intimations of Renée Vivien reached Firbank before she *was* Renée Vivien. She was born, in 1877, to the name Pauline Tarn, schooled on the Continent and then subjected to the husband-fishing social life of an English débutante. She rebelled, caused a homosexual scandal and eventually escaped to independence and her literary pseudonym in Paris.

In her exhaustive work *Sex Variant Women in Literature* (a work which mentions Firbank with appreciation and to which he would surely have been devoted), Jeannette H. Foster records in passing that the attempt to turn Renée Vivien into an orthodox English gentlewoman began when she was 16 (that is, about 1893) and that it took place in Chislehurst.

Perhaps, therefore, that remarkable provincial town provided Firbank's

---

[1] Cf. Chapter X, 11.   [2] 1932; republished in 1941 as *Le Pur et l'Impur*.

imagination not only with French, Catholic and imperial but also with lesbian trappings. Perhaps the national scandal about Oscar Wilde in 1895, which so deeply and formatively impressed Firbank, fused in his mind with the (roughly contemporary) local scandal about a homosexual *woman*. Ultimately, therefore, it may have been Chislehurst that created Firbank's creative obsession with *female* homosexuality.

It was an obsession not just with a subject of social scandal but with a scandalous social injustice.

Firbank's transvestism of the imagination made him not merely a woman but a queer woman; and instantly he noticed that imagination had placed him in a less dangerous position than fact permitted to his real-life self.

The fluency with which he invents florists discloses Firbank's slight social criticism of the ease for a woman, and difficulty for a man, of taking up that profession:[1] the fertility of fantasy whereby he dots his work with lesbian occasions discloses his strong resentment of the difficulty society imposed on men, in comparison with women, in making profession of homosexuality.

It is as though he never stopped making the comparison which Chislehurst perhaps forced on him in childhood, between the outcomes for Oscar Wilde and for Renée Vivien.

The deepest tribute Firbank's imagination paid to Wilde was to invent dozens of situations whose content pointed out that, had Wilde been a homosexual *woman*, there might have been (as there was for Renée Vivien) an almighty family scandal but there could not have been imprisonment.

Perhaps Firbank's accusation that his sister wasted money (on, for instance, her dressmaker[2]) is a disguise for the accusation that, by being heterosexual, she was wasting an opportunity.

Firbank's social criticism is to be read only in the tendency of his invention. Yet the dramatic form of *The Princess Zoubaroff* obliged his invention to reveal its tendency more explicitly than in his novels. In *The Princess Zoubaroff* alone, Firbank is openly socially prescriptive, though his prescription for society has to be read only in the play's design, not in its speeches. The design is for happy homosexuality. Two married couples part and take up homosexuality. The play even answers, quite in non-fiction terms, the social question of what homosexual people should do about parenthood.

The play's dramatic design is symmetrical: but its prescriptive design is worked out exclusively through its women. The two young husbands merely go off, equally away from their wives and out of the action of the play, on a

---

[1] Cf. sub-section 9 of this chapter.
[2] Cf. sub-section 9 of this chapter.

trip together. It is the wives who remain to be visibly woven into the design of the Princess's convent.

Lord Orkish and Reggie Quintus make a decorative frame, a Greek commentating chorus, to the grand lesbian enterprise of the Princess's Zenoesque[1] and Teresan[2] religious order. Evidently, therefore, it wasn't simply fear of being censored if he put a pair of homosexual men on the stage that made Firbank expel the husbands from most of the play. He had positive reasons for writing his social prescription through women: it gave expression to his own mental transvestism, and at the same time it stated one of the items in his social criticism.

The content of Firbank's invention is continually pointing out that that threat of imprisonment, with its consequences of blackmail and mercenariness, corrupts the possibilities of love between men. His tenderness can be incarnated only in images of love between women.

(Perhaps *The New Rythum* was intended[3] to contain such an incarnation: a 'poetic lyric fantastic anything' incarnation.)

It is the bizarre mating, in a boat becalmed on a lake, between Olga and Vi (Mademoiselle Blumenghast[4] and the Countess of Tolga, in *The Flower Beneath the Foot*), whose strangeness Firbank evokes with passionate exactitude, as though it were the mating of exotic crested water birds (their crests liable to disarrangement – 'Tell me, Olga: Is my hat all sideways?'); and indeed on shore there is (Count Cabinet) an unseen observer-through-a-telescope. And it is the broken homosexual heart of Gerald(ine) O'Brookomore, on the occasion of Mabel Collins's desertion to Count Pastorelli,[5] that Firbank expresses in Chapter XX of Part I of *Inclinations*, a chapter whose text consists of 'Mabel!' uttered eight times between the inverted commas of Miss O'Brookomore's agonised thought.

---

[1] Cf. sub-section 10 of this chapter.

[2] Like Cardinal Pirelli (cf. Chapter II, 3), the Princess evidently has a devotion to Saint Teresa of Ávila. The Princess is able to pattern herself on Saint Teresa to the point of likewise founding an order. When she has turned Abbess, the stage directions (p. 757 in the *Complete* Firbank) have the Princess salute Lady Rocktower by 'kissing her à la Sainte Thérèse'.

[3] Cf. sub-section 13 of this chapter.

[4] Blumenghast is another (cf. sub-section 4 of this chapter) of Firbank's floral names: the little German Firbank knew (cf. Chapter X, 12) inevitably included the German for *flowers*. Firbank's Blumenghast in turn perhaps contributed to Mervyn Peake's *Gormenghast* – in which another imagination has converted Firbank's floral element into gore and gourmandise.

[5] Cf. sub-section 13 of this chapter.

15. Flowers at Shrines

FIRBANK lays garlands through his fiction. His flowers, flower names and chains of flowery association serve multiple purposes: as decorative elements, as clothing, as dramatis personae – and as celebratory sacrifices laid before a shrine.

Flowers mark a shrine, which marks a saint. Inevitably, the odour of sanctity is, for Firbank, floral. Because the martyr and quasi-saint Mrs Cresswell is buried there, Ashringford Cathedral is permeated by a sweet smell; and, as the Bishop of Ashringford explains, 'On some days it's as delicate as a single cowslip. On others it's quite strong, more like syringa.'

Firbank's own literary pursuit is of Oscar Wilde. Patterning himself on that saintly model, he dedicates the flowers of his invention to the martyr who invented a green flower.

Parallel to the pursuit of Wilde which Firbank is conducting by writing his books, there run, in counterpoint, the pursuits conducted by or inside the books: the hagiographical line of narrative ('. . . a Record of the Early Life of Saint Laura de Nazianzi'[1]); the plot devised by its own heroine as she patterns herself on an Oscar Wilde heroine;[2] and the hagiographical pursuits and devotions of the dramatis personae themselves.

In a quick-frozen instant of reported (party) speech, Mrs Henedge is caught 'comparing the prose of a professional saint to a blind alley'. Mrs Shamefoot, besides aspiring to be (by a canonical impossibility) a live acknowledged saint, has a (highly apocryphal) *Life* of a saint upstairs.[3] The Baroness Rudlieb prays to a saint yet more apocryphal, 'one of her own discoveries: St. Aurora Vauvilliers'.[4] The Princess Zoubaroff emulates the career[5] and Cardinal Pirelli sees a vision[6] of Saint Teresa: and the Cardinal asks her to disclose to him the saintly pattern, her way of perfection.

The Baroness Rudlieb, too, 'sprayed her face with spirits of Roses'[7] and read a chapter from *The Way of Perfection* in circumstances where Saint Aurora Vauvilliers would have been 'too exciting'; and indeed the Baroness's own name is Teresa.

Hagiography combines, in *The New Rythum*, with two other Firbank passions, art history and gardening, to produce a new Raphael ('an exquisite variation', the text art-historically remarks, 'of *La Belle Jardinière* in the Paris Louvre'): the *Madonna with a hoe* (collection: Mrs Otto Van Cotton).

Hagiographically, Firbank even names the actress in *Vainglory* Miss

---

[1] Cf. Chapter XIII, 2. [2] Cf. Chapter XIV, 3. [3] Cf. Chapter XIV, 4.
[4] Cf. Chapter XIII, 2. [5] Cf. sub-section 14 of this chapter.
[6] Cf. Chapter II, 3. [7] Cf. sub-section 2 of this chapter.

Compostella: after the shrine at Compostela of Saint James the Elder, patron saint of Spain.

That's not, however, all there is to Miss Compostella, who makes a supreme (and in its content fascinating) example of the complexity of Firbankian naming. Hers is, as well as a shrine, one of the less airily Arcadian of Firbank's gardening names. It begins as *compost*. No wonder Miss Compostella feels attracted to Mr Harvester.

Moreover, Firbank has, for once, method in his aberrant spelling. By slipping the extra *l* into the name of the Spanish shrine, Firbank makes his actress into a Stella: a name semantically apt for a star in general (as Firbank had probably noted from its being the name of the operatic star in Offenbach's *Tales of Hoffmann*) and a particular tribute to the grand Edwardian prototype of starry actresses, (Beatrice) Stella, Mrs Patrick Campbell.[1]

That in turn is why Miss Compostella is 'hoping to get Eysoldt over to play with me in Maeterlinck'.[2] Gertrud Eysoldt in fact played Wilde's Salome. So, but for the Lord Chamberlain, would have done an actress who shares her final -dt, Sarah Bernhardt. Firbank fictionally casts Eysoldt and Compostella in Maeterlinck in memory of a production of Maeterlinck that cast Bernhardt together with Stella (Patrick Campbell). It took place at the Vaudeville Theatre in London in 1904 (and went on tour in 1905), and for Firbank it must have been an occasion unforgettable in its union of his devotion to Maeterlinck, his devotion to persons associated, as Bernhardt was, with Wilde and Wilde's *Salomé*, and the campest, campbellest of his obsessions.[3] Mrs Patrick Campbell played Mélisande to the transvest[4] Pelléas of Sarah Bernhardt [Plate 10].

The *Pelléas et Mélisande* of Bernhardt and Mrs Patrick Campbell was played in French – despite Mrs Patrick Campbell's confession:[5] 'and oh

---

[1] The signatures of actresses which, the *Biography* records (pp. 28–9), Firbank collected when he was about 15, include those of Sarah Bernhardt and 'Mrs Campbell' (by which I assume the *Biography* means Mrs Patrick Campbell). Osbert Sitwell (*Memoir*, p. 128) names Mrs Patrick Campbell (with Pavlova and Isadora Duncan) as the people Firbank 'most adored in the theatre'. Conceivably, Firbank's interest in Mrs Patrick Campbell was associated with his interest (cf. Chapters VI, 6, IX, 5 and X, 6) in the Churchill family, since Mrs Patrick Campbell married George Cornwallis-West, who had been married to Lady Randolph Churchill.

[2] Cf. Chapter XIV, 4.

[3] Cf. sub-sections 13 and 14 of this chapter.

[4] It is probably by pious tribute to another Bernhardt drag rôle that when (on p. 87 in the *Complete* Firbank) Mrs Steeple 'imprudently perhaps, disclosed to Winsome Brookes her opinion of Miss Compostella', she 'laughed and laughed [...] "Her H-H-Hamlet was irresistible!" she repeated.'

[5] The confession was made when she remembered the production, much later (1928) in writing to Bernard Shaw (p. 269 in Alan Dent's edition of their *Correspondence*).

lor! my French'. The precedent that perhaps justified Mrs Patrick Campbell had been set two years earlier, at the first production of the Maeterlinck-Debussy opera, by Mary Garden. In a letter to *The Times* recently, Edward Garden records that Debussy was 'enraptured' by Mary Garden's performance, that she sang the French words with an English accent, and that Maggie Teyte succeeded her in the rôle 'mainly because highbrows considered it essential that Mélisande should have an English accent'.

No doubt when Firbank introduced Mary Garden's voice into *The New Rythum* he was impelled by the assonance between her English-accented Maeterlinck and Mrs Patrick Campbell's, as well as by her Salome and her surname.[1]

And perhaps by the time he was writing *The New Rythum* yet another item had joined the list of the signposts directing Firbank's devotion towards Mary Garden. In her *Sex Variant Women in Literature*, Jeannette H. Foster gives a résumé of James Gibbons Huneker's novel *Painted Veils*, published in New York in 1920, in which a fictitious female opera singer fights a duel, over a third woman, with Mary Garden. Dr Foster notes that gossip at the time of publication held the fictitious singer to be in fact a portrait of Mary Garden.

16. Cultus

FOR Firbank the pursuit of literary saints and their relics was emotionally the same act as the pursuit of saints Catholic or apocryphal and *theirs*. Firbank tracking down the books and disciples of Oscar Wilde demonstrates the same state of mind as Lady Parvula self-declaredly (in *Valmouth*) 'agog to see the tooth, too, of St. Automona Meris[2] (Do you imagine she ever really ate with it horrid Castilian garlic *olla cocida*? Or purple *pistos insalada*? She and Teresa together, in some white *posada*, perhaps, journeying South)'.

Or perhaps, given the motive of terror in Firbank's superstitiousness, it was terror rather than curiosity that he transformed into comic masterpieces. His cultist state of mind may most particularly resemble that of Mrs Hurstpierpoint, the owner of Saint Automona's tooth, who, as the most inspired (together with *King Lear*'s) thunderstorm in literature reaches directly above the house, bids her maid 'Lift the lid of the long casket – and pick me a

---

[1] Cf. Chapter XIV, 4 and sub-section 6 of this chapter.

[2] It is Saint Automona who (as related in the *Complete* Firbank on p. 426, where she has acquired a particle and become Saint Automona di Meris), by spitting into the mouth of a novice who was yawning, begat (bespat) Saint Elizabeth Bathilde who, in one of Firbank's sex-metamorphotic flights, changed sex at 40 by dint of skipping (cf. Chapter XIV, 12 and sub-section 18 of this chapter).

relic' (and, to the query 'Any one in particular, 'm?', replies 'No; but not a leg-bone, mind! A leg-bone relic somehow –').

Literary and liturgical pursuit fused, for Firbank, about the word *cult*.

Cult (or, in Latin, *cultus*): 'veneration or worship' – one sub-division of which is particularly 'that secondary veneration which Catholics give to saints and angels'.[1]

It was in its full Catholic sense that Firbank transferred both the mental deed and the technical term for it to the arts. A cult was what he believed had been accorded (by himself as well as the world at large) to Richard Strauss.[2] A cult was what he believed should be made of great writers – not, however, in lieu of popularity. *Cult* can be wielded as a stick on Firbank only by people who forget his Catholicism. He hoped for, but didn't get, catholicity of readership, too. Osbert Sitwell was right:[3] Firbank *was* 'simple enough' to expect to be a best seller. Through his other self, Claud Harvester, Firbank expressly denied that cult belonged only to 'minority' writers. 'Of course' (it is said of Claud Harvester in *Vainglory*) 'Claud's considered a cult, but everybody reads him!'

As Claud Harvester's horticultural name indicates, Firbank (who usually *was* alert to words down to their last syllable) had remarked the cult in horti*cult*ure. Plants might be the objects of, as well as objects dedicated in, a cult. 'If *I* worship anything' (confesses the saintlily and horticulturally named Miss Compostella) '[. . .] it's trees. . . .'

Firbank's declaration that he, in the persona of Claud Harvester, was considered a cult yet read by everybody was made in advance not only of the fact but of the possibility. Harvester's book *Vaindreams* did not exist to become the centre of a cult or to be read by anybody until Firbank's book *Vainglory*, in which it had its whole existence, was published; and *Vainglory* was Firbank's first-published Firbankian and cultable book. What Firbank was declaring was his expectation.

It was an expectation so visible to people who knew him that more than one of them vouched to him for his being, in the eyes of a third party, the object of a cult. (It would have been futilely heroic to offer to vouch for the other item of his expectation.) Helen Carew (who had enshrined Oscar Wilde as a cult object by entombing him[4]) promoted, in 1918, the meeting of Firbank and the Sitwell brothers by writing to Firbank that the Sitwells had 'a cult' of him.[5]

---

[1] *A Catholic Dictionary* (William E. Addiss and Thomas Arnold).
[2] – 'about the time of the [. . .] Straus cult' (cf. Chapter XIII, 6).
[3] Cf. Chapter I, 3.   [4] Cf. Chapter XII, 6.
[5] Lord Berners was an acquaintance Firbank acquired in the same year from the same

In 1922, Firbank himself tried to live up to what he had expected for Claud Harvester. With the defiance of having the Atlantic between them he explained to Carl Van Vechten that the reason why even his fellow-Briton J. C. Squire had never heard of him[1] was that he was a cult.

The word was brought back across the Atlantic to Firbank in 1924. Philip Moeller, bearing an introduction from Carl Van Vechten, sought Firbank out in Rome and assured Firbank that Van Vechten (whom Firbank had never met except by letter) was 'a sort of high priest of the cult'. Firbank (Moeller reported back to Van Vechten), 'squirmed like a very sly lizard, in a sort of oncoming and, at the same time, reticent delight'.

The cult was probably never much of a reality in Firbank's lifetime, though afterwards memories might mistakenly date it back. Evan Morgan, writing 20 years after the event, could speak of 'the Firbank cult which had already started' at the time (1920) of *The Princess Zoubaroff*.[2] Martin Secker is probably more to be relied on, with his implication that the cult began after Firbank's death, and chiefly with Ifan Kyrle Fletcher's *Memoir* of 1930. Solicited, evidently, for information for the *Memoir*, Martin Secker replied: 'My only distinction [. . .] is that I declined to publish both his first and second novels [. . .] not being gifted with second sight, I had no idea that one day he would become a cult and that monographs would be devoted to him and his work.'

In so far as there was a cult in his lifetime, it had to be chiefly supplied by Firbank. The ultimate occasion of his profuse flower-buying is that he had to buy his own flowers to place at his own shrine. No doubt it was because Philip Moeller, standing at Firbank's door in Rome, had spoken of 'the cult' that Firbank so particularly[3] lamented, when he invited Moeller in: 'But there aren't any flowers! None! None!'

17. Premature Canonisation

IT did not escape Firbank's Catholicised mind that canonisation, and the consequent cultus of a saint, are expressly forbidden by the Catholic church until the saint is dead.

He must have feared that there was a correspondingly inexorable natural law of literature (and there *almost* is) whereby 'envy and calumny and hate'

source. Mrs Carew sent Firbank (in Oxford) first assurances that Lord Berners admired him and then Lord Berners (*Biography*, p. 166).

[1] Cf. Chapter I, 3.
[2] Cf. Chapter VIII, 5.
[3] Cf. Chapter VII, 5.

(in the words Shelley wrote of one of the bitterest examples of the near-law's functioning) do not permit the recognition of a great writer until the great writer is dead.

Firbank heaped flowers at his own living shrine for fear of the truth of the opening words of the song he has Miss Tooke hum in *Valmouth*:

> 'When I am dead
> Ah bring me flow-ers,
> Spread roses and forget-me-nots.'

Forgetting-a-writer-not usually *is* posthumous.

It was that fear which Firbank expressed through Mrs Shamefoot, his fellow composer in flowery images:[1] 'I believe I'll be desired more somehow when I'm gone.'

It was likewise through Mrs Shamefoot that Firbank's imagination devised a way round the law of the church and of literary nature.

His imagination was beautifully prolific of unorthodoxies in general. The reason why Mrs Cresswell is only a quasi-saint is explained by the Bishop of Ashringford: 'she would have been canonised, but for an unfortunate remark.' (It comes in her florally named work, *The Red Rose of Martyrdom*.) ' "If we are all a part of God," she says, "then God must *indeed* be horrible." '

Even art-historically, Firbank's fantasy is heretical. In Lord Brassknocker's collection (in *Vainglory*) Firbank socialises the end of the gospel story just as in *The Artificial Princess* he domesticated[2] its forerunner. ' "A Last Supper at *two tables*", Mrs. Pontypool said confidentially, "struck one as – scarcely –" '

In the answering comment, 'Not if it was Veronese,' Firbank art-historically alludes to the difficulties Veronese had in 1573 with the Inquisition, who bade him paint out a dog (in a painting of his of either the Last Supper or the Feast at the house of Simon) and replace it by a Mary Magdalen. Conceivably it was this line of thought which Firbank's imagination presently enlarged into its cardinal indeed heresy: Cardinal Pirelli's sublimely canon-law-defying 'eccentricity', whose unorthodoxy stands patent metaphor for sexual unorthodoxy, of baptising a dog.

But the unorthodoxy which Firbank obsessively plays on is premature (that is, within one's lifetime) canonisation.

When the Artificial Princess addresses the envelope that is to bear her invitation to the hermit whom she has selected for the rôle of John the Baptist, she discloses his name to be St John Pellegrin (a Firbankian play on the name spelt St John and pronounced Sinjun that was probably spun from

---

[1] Cf. sub-section 10 of this chapter.   [2] Cf. Chapter XIV, 2.

Firbank's contemplation of R. St Clair (pronounced Sinclair] Talboys).[1] The Princess Zoubaroff has scarcely started her nunnery before Reggie Quintus remarks to one of her nuns: 'Your Abbess, I'm told, is quite scoring as a Saint.'

(Perhaps Firbank knew that Hugh Benson[2] had been called 'a Saint' by, in Benson's biographer's words, 'the more indiscreet of his penitents'. Benson, unlike Firbank's imagination, took care to remain, if only just, within the bounds of orthodoxy. To a penitent whose indiscretion went so far as to put in writing the belief that Benson was a saint, he replied: '*Never* never again must you even hint to me such things.')

In *A Disciple from the Country*,[3] Firbank invented Stella Creamway, of whom it is said 'people talk of her as Saint Angelica, it will be her own fault if she doesn't marry *at least* a Bishop [. . .] Stella is artistic, in a Cathedral she would find scope for her tastes. Erecting a window to herself [. . .]'

So established is Stella as a living saint that Mrs Blossome (whom I mentioned in sub-section 4 for the sake of her floral name) walks from Warwickshire to London in hope of a miraculous cure by saintly virtue. ('No really nice woman', comments Mrs Creamway, 'would walk all the way from Warwickshire.')

Both the notion of putting up a window to oneself (with its touch, perhaps, of church windows at Chislehurst[4]) and the bishop-marrying Firbank put into *A Study in Opal* (which, as an undergraduate, he published in *Granta* in 1907). His Wildeanly surnamed heroine,[5] Lady Henrietta Worthing, marries a bishop and sets about getting herself into stained glass; but her husband dies, and she has to improve the design into one for a double window.

It is in *Vainglory* that this much-transposed fantasy achieves perfection. The bishop-marrying component is allotted to Mrs Henedge: it is in Mrs Shamefoot, who expresses Firbank's fear openly, that Firbank expresses the apotheosis of the stained-glass item. Mrs Shamefoot is so obsessed by 'her desire to set up a commemorative window to herself' that she joins in no party conversation. 'Mentally, perhaps, she was already three parts glass.'

Putting her case for a window in Ashringford Cathedral to the Bishop of Ashringford, Dr Pantry, Mrs Shamefoot almost lays open claim to sainthood in her lifetime: 'Dear Doctor Pantry, were I to proclaim myself a saint you'd

---

[1] (Cf. Chapter X, 12); Firbank evidently remarked, in the course of his contemplations, that St John's Wood is *not* pronounced Sinjun's Wood – whence, in a conversation in *Caprice* (p. 370 in the *Complete* Firbank) that is partly in French ('If I tell you, I'll have to tell you in French'), it is rendered as 'Bois St. Jean'.
[2] Cf. Chapter VIII, 6.   [3] Cf. Chapter XIV, 4.
[4] Cf. Chapter X, 9.   [5] Cf. Chapter XIII, 2.

probably not believe it –' 'Indeed I assure you I've no misgivings,' the Bishop replies. And even before she sends out the invitation cards for 'her vitrification' Mrs Shamefoot has 'such a curious-funny dream. People were digging me up for reliques . . .'

Eddy Monteith in his bath passes through a series of saintly metamorphoses. 'Beneath the rhythmic sponge, perfumed with *Kiki*, he was St. Sebastian, and as the water became cloudier, and the crystals evaporated amid the steam, he was Teresa . . . and he would have been, most likely, the Blessed Virgin herself but that the bath grew gradually cold.'[1]

Mrs Shamefoot suffers a similar interruption in the development of an idea of emulating, if not quite becoming, the Virgin. Her aspirations to stained glass would have been supererogatory had not her evening thoughts been cut off by the close of Chapter VIII of *Vainglory*. 'Star beyond star, the sky was covered. The clouds, she observed, too, appeared to be preparing for an Assumption.'

Sir Coleridge Kennard knew that Firbank's heretical fantasy of premature canonisation was autobiographical; but he didn't know he knew. It was merely as a figure of speech that he wrote, in the Introduction he supplied after Firbank's death to *The Artificial Princess*, that Firbank's being, when he arrived at Cambridge, already a published author 'surrounded Firbank with a halo. Indeed I think that his nervous habit of clawing at his head, on which all his biographers have laid such stress, was really a definite effort on his part to keep that object in its place.'

18. Portrait of the Artist as the Messiah ('She Will Provide')

WHY, however, once imagination has burst through the heresy barrier, stop at 'that secondary veneration'?

In *The Artificial Princess*, which is already taking diabolical[2] wing, that inevitable question is in the presence of, though not yet fully combined with, Firbank's mental transvestism.

Not only is the Princess herself a 'tall-tall schoolboy'.[3] Not only do the Baroness's camp thoughts[4] conceive that the Prophet may be a frump. Not only does the Baroness end by making party conversation[5] about natives of

---

[1] The stations of the metamorphosis are saintly favourites, all of them, of Firbank's own. The Virgin is the quasi-dea-ex-machina of *Odette*; Saint Sebastian attracts (cf. sub-section 19 of this chapter) Firbank's masochism; Firbank's devotion to Saint Teresa is chronicled in Chapter II, 3 and in sub-sections 14–16 of this chapter.
[2] Cf. Chapter VIII, 6.   [3] Cf. Chapter XIV, 8.
[4] Cf. Chapter XIV, 8.   [5] Cf. sub-section 13 of this chapter.

Lesbos while she appraises a girl the colour of whose dress is 'palest Langue de chat'. The Baroness also experiences a strangely metamorphotic sensation, whose nature perhaps partly explains why, when Firbank imaginatively made himself female, he inhabited women who love women, not women who love men. Having let herself be 'carried off all willingly-unwillingly like a creature in a Rape',[1] by her lover, Max, and thereby diverted from her errand on the Princess's behalf, the Baroness suffers, on her return to the palace, a moment when 'her guilt tripped forth, a ripple'. And the shape her guilt assumes to her sensations is: 'She felt suddenly a little masculine, that she was wearing his lips, his eyes, his way. . . .'

That motif of sex-metamorphosis has already, in *The Artificial Princess*, combined with theology and art history to produce a transvestite heresy: a female crucifixion. 'The Baroness fixed enormous eyes on a Crucifixion by a pupil of Félicien Rops[2] – a pale woman seen stretched upon a Cross in a silver tea gown, with a pink Rose in her powdered hair.'

From that point Firbank's imagination explored deeper into the Baroness's sensation of metamorphosis, in such conversations as this (in *Valmouth*):

> Mrs. Hurstpierpoint repressed a grimace.
> 'Nowadays', she murmured, 'a man . . . to me . . . somehow . . . oh! he is something so wildly *strange*.'
> 'Strange?'
> 'Unglimpsable.'[3]
> 'Still, some men are ultra-womanly, and they're the kind I love!' Mrs. Thoroughfare chirruped.
> 'I suppose that none but those whose courage is unquestionable can venture to be effeminate?' Lady Parvula said, plunging a two-pronged fork into a 'made' dish of sugared-violets served in aspic.

At the same time Firbank's autobiographical fantasy was pushing beyond premature canonisation into the concept of deification itself.

Indeed, Firbank's self-portrait as Wildred Forrester, who becomes gardener to Lady Appledore, is deified in a dream of Mrs Hurstpierpoint's in *Valmouth*. ' "I thought last night, in my sleep", she murmured, "that Christ was my new gardener." '

And all Firbank's autobiographically inspired transvestite explorations

---

[1] Cf. sub-section 6 of this chapter.
[2] Cf. Chapter IX, 5 and 6.
[3] The sense is perhaps explicated by a later passage in the same dinner-table conversation. Lady Parvula claims: 'I once peeped under a bishop's apron!' To Mrs Thoroughfare's 'And what ever did you see?', ' "Well . . . I saw", Lady Parvula replied (helping herself to a few *pointes d'asperges à la Laura Leslie*), "I saw . . . the dear Bishop!" '

are deified in his masterpiece of literary camp, counterpart to the private masterpiece of his Haiti postcard[1] and, like that, coloured Negro: the thought which (in *Prancing Nigger*) visits the Archbishop of Cuna as he delivers, 'in full and impassioned swing', an 'extemporary address' – 'Imagine the world, my friends, had Christ been born a girl!'

Perhaps what *in particular* prompted Firbank to reply to J. C. Squire's ignorance of him by promoting himself as an object of cult was pique at J. C. Squire's initials.

19. Fladge

IN Firbank's invented picture 'by a pupil of Félicien Rops', pearls about the crucified woman's throat 'bound her faster to the cross'.

Firbank was fairly interested in what the pornography market[2] nowadays calls bondage. It is a token of his interest that he lent his most intimately significant flowers to a bondage metaphor for the Gala evening[3] in *Prancing Nigger*, where the dancers' feet are 'fettered with chains of orchids'.

Neither did he forbid his personages to consult, as pornography or as methods of mental revenge, accounts of more elaborate sado-masochistic machines. 'Lady Barrow' (so begins Chapter XX of *Vainglory*) 'lolled languidly in her mouse-eaten[4] library, a volume of medieval Tortures (with plates) propped up against her knee. In fancy, her husband was well pinned down and imploring for mercy at Figure 3.'

Perhaps it was as a self-imposed instrument of torture that Firbank interpreted 'spiked garters'[5] – of which a servant in *Valmouth* is overheard to say 'I always know instinctive when the Mrs. has on her spiked garters.'

Firbank's speciality, however, was (in modern and perhaps[6] also in Firbankian idiom) fladge, one of the obsessive interests (the other being 'pretty

---

[1] Cf. Chapter VIII, 8.
[2] – to which my indispensable guide has been Gillian Freeman's *The Undergrowth of Literature*.
[3] Cf. sub-section 5 of this chapter.
[4] Between Firbank's phobia of mice (cf. Chapter VIII, 3) and the pearls with which the Artificial Princess and Mrs Shamefoot severally lash at bats (cf. Chapter XIV, 7) the connecting rope is perhaps the pearls of bondage in the Rops-esque crucifixion. Even, perhaps, *ropes* of pearls led to *Rops*.
[5] Katherine Mansfield seems to have set a more aggressive interpretation on something similar. Witness her *Journal* (1911): 'He gathered me up in his arms and carried me to the Black Bed. Very brown and strange was he ... It grew dark. I crouched against him like a wild cat. Quite impersonally I admired my silver stockings bound beneath the knee with spiked ribbons [...] How vicious I looked! We made love to each other like two wild beasts.'
[6] as Chapter XIX, 14 will suggest more specifically.

boys') which[1] prompted Evelyn Waugh to accuse him of a 'coy naughtiness'.

The last sermon of Cardinal Pirelli's life is 'on the theme of Flagellation' (not, as a hurried or unFirbankian reader might suppose, *the* Flagellation).

Firbank's taste for being beaten was already formed when, at the age (in his biographer's estimate) of 'less than twelve', he wrote in a notebook a piece of doggerel named *The Lay of the Last Nurserymaid* (the manuscript of which is owned, and the text of which is published, by his biographer).

The verse begins with 'the child' bent over a chair and the nursemaid's hand raised. But an intruding step mounts the stair and an interrupting voice calls 'the nurse a terrible name'. The raised hand pauses and lets the stick tumble to the floor.

It is perhaps the culminating imperceptiveness of the *Biography* that it simply doesn't notice the disappointment of 'the child' in the verse. Indeed, it manages to discuss the verse in terms of aggression by Firbank against others. It is probably right in taking Firbank's mother to be the interrupter of the flagellation scene, but it seems to suppose Firbank was grateful for his deliverance. Ifan Kyrle Fletcher lacked the verse to call in evidence, but observed Firbank's books and personality. Those made it clear to him that masochism was an important element in Firbank's psychology, and he remarked that Firbank 'came to derive a perverse pleasure from being hurt'.

Indeed, it would be hard for anyone who had actually read Firbank's books to miss the point.

> 'The mistress, I presume, is with the scourge', the butler announced, peering impassably around.
> Lady Parvula placed her fan to her train.
> 'Let her lash it!' she said. 'In this glorious room one is quite content to wait.'

Through a service hatch in the same book (*Valmouth*) Mrs Thoroughfare hears 'the eternal *she she she* of servants' voices', including, 'You could hear her a-tanning herself before cock-crow this morning in her room. Frtt! but she can swipe.'

And Mrs Shamefoot (in *Vainglory*), searching for a house, has 'already made an offer for the Old Flagellites Club'. ' "It should suit her. That long flaying room would make an exquisite drawing-room." '

For the location of the Flagellites Club Firbank borrowed from the real-life map of England – a Wildean practice;[2] but unlike Wilde Firbank was not in quest of merely neutral names, that should sound convincing without

---

[1] Cf. Chapter VI, 3.   [2] Cf. sub-section 4 of this chapter.

being libellous. The minster-city of York, which Firbank visited[1] twice during the composition of *Vainglory*, contains a street name too exquisitely to Firbank's purposes to be passed over: Whip-ma-whop-ma-gate. By 1915 he had imported it to the cathedral-city of Ashringford in *Vainglory*. The Flagellites Club is 'at the corner of Whip-me-Whop-me Street'.[2]

Meanwhile, in the wholly imaginary country of *The Artificial Princess*, the very 'National game' is 'Whipping Tops'.

The Flower Beneath the Foot almost re-enacts the scene of Firbank's doggerel *Lay* about the nurserymaid. The Honourables Eddy Monteith and Lionel Limpness are no sooner reunited in Pisuerga than they fall to the entertainments again of their childhood at an English school. 'Turn over, Old Dear, while I chastise you!' 'Put it down, Lionel, and don't be absurd.' 'Over we go. Come on.' The interrupter is, this time, the English Ambassadress. 'Clad in the flowing circumstance of an oyster satin ball-dress, and all a-glitter like a Christmas tree (with jewels), her' asyntactical[3] 'arrival perhaps saved her guest a "whipping".'

Eddy Monteith's protests are, of course, no more designed to prevent the assault than the child in the verse is grateful to be 'saved' *his* whipping. Indeed, it is from Eddy's own 'portable altar' that Lionel has snatched up the weapon – 'what looked to be a tortoiseshell lorgnon to which had been attached three threads of "cerulean" floss silk', and which is in fact a discipline, an object which in Firbank's œuvre holds the value of a fetish. (Perhaps it is the name *discipline* for a whip to be used in self-scourging as a religious exercise which the pornography market has enlarged to mean exercises more generally sado-masochistic.) Planning to (when he gets the chance) turn his family home, Intriguer[4] Park, into a Jesuit college, 'if only to vex his father's ghost', Eddy Monteith delights in the thought that 'the crack of the discipline in Lent would echo throughout the house!'

Taken though he was with Jesuit colleges, Firbank was even more taken with nunneries. Having plundered the street-map of York for Whip-me-Whop-me Street in *Vainglory*, he exploited the map of rural England (and

[1] According to the *Biography* (p. 123 and p. 131), he was in York in the autumns of 1913 and 1914 (Cf. Chapter XII, 6).

[2] In Firbank's next book, *Inclinations*, Miss Gerald(ine) O'Brookomore enquires of Miss Collins 'Hasn't the eccentricity of living near York ever occurred to your mother?' The joke is about provincialism; but the 'eccentricity' which Firbank's thoughts truly associated with York is perhaps betrayed by a passage a few lines earlier in the same conversation. Miss Collins remarks that she loves her fiancé (of that period) best when he says 'What'. Miss O'Brookomore explains that he says it 'like the crack of a cart-whip'. 'A whip? Oh, Gerald –', says Miss Collins. (*Complete* Firbank, pp. 247-8).

[3] Cf. Chapter X, 12.

[4] Cf. Chapter VIII, 5 and sub-section 12 of this chapter.

Gloucestershire in particular) to lend him religious communities of both sexes for *Valmouth*: 'the Nuns of Sodbury and the Oblates of Up-More'. His concentration, however, is on nuns, and it is owed to their uniting two of his obsessions. They wield the discipline, and they are an all-female community.

What Firbank understood of all-female communities is clear from the Princess Zoubaroff's imperious want: 'Poor little woman – I want her *so* much.' Nadine, stage-directed to drop her eyes, asks: 'You want her? What for?' 'For my community.'

What he understood of the use, in such a community, of the discipline, appears in the conventual exchange[1] in *The Flower Beneath the Foot*: 'Now you're here, I shall ask you, I think, to whip me.' 'Oh, no . . .'

Before she is initiated into such dialogue in the convent, Laura (the Flower of *The Flower Beneath the Foot*) has had a run-in: by entering the 'Ecclesiastical set at Court', where she experiences 'the charm, the flavour of the religious world'. The flavour is of cocoa ('hasty informal lightly-pencilled notes [. . .] such as: "I shall be pouring out cocoa after dinner in bed"'). The 'charm' lies in messages, verbally delivered by 'a round-eyed page', such as: 'The Marchioness will be birched to-morrow, and *not* to-day.'

A discussion in *The New Rhythum* about what to award as 'cotillion favours' associates flagellation with another Firbankian motif, this time transvestism. 'For the fifth figure let us provide vanity bags for the gentlemen and moustache-brushes for the ladies' is succeeded by another suggestion: 'Say, everybody, why not whips?'

That the pornography market was not much different in Firbank's lifetime from now, and that Firbank's gifts could easily have adapted themselves into the knack of writing for it, are attested by a minor quirk among the theatrical personages in *Caprice*: 'Miss Whipsina Peters, a daughter of the famous flagellist'. (In 1962 the Olympia Press published a novel called *Whipsdom*.)

Indeed it is possible that Firbank *did* write for the pornography market. Though concluding that there is no firm evidence either way, the *Bibliography* reports that some booksellers believed that *Count Fanny's Nuptials*, which was published in 1907 as by 'Simon Arrow', was in fact by Firbank.

It would be a pretty irony if, by writing pornography (which is, however, usually accounted even less lucrative to its authors than other fiction), Firbank for once made some money by a book.

However, if Firbank *did* write *Count Fanny's Nuptials* it was probably not for money but for the sake of patterning himself on Oscar Wilde, who was

---

[1] which I quoted (in misapplication) in Chapter X, 12.

widely, though probably wrongly, reputed to be the author of *Teleny*, a homosexual 'physiological romance' published in 1893.

From his title, Simon Arrow's Count Fanny looks to me as though he had an interesting and distinguished lineage in English literature. It is a lineage Firbank might well have taken sly delight in furthering, since it falls beautifully in with Firbank's literary tastes. C. W. Beaumont, in whose Charing Cross Road bookshop Firbank exercised them, described his tastes as 'rather "ninetyish", although he was interested in eighteenth-century French literature of the more frivolous type [. . .] He was very fond of the word "restful"; all the books he liked he termed "restful". Even a study in the baroque such as Beardsley's *Venus and Tannhäuser* he would term "restful".'

If one deletes the *French* and the *frivolous*, leaving 18th-century literature in general, the description of Firbank's literary tastes is a description of what I surmise to be the lineage of *Count Fanny's Nuptials*. In 1734 Alexander Pope attacked Lord Hervey under the names[1] of 'Sporus' and 'Lord Fanny'. Lord Fanny I take to be a direct ancestor of Count Fanny, and Sporus an indirect one – by a line that leads through, precisely, Beardsley's *Venus and Tannhäuser* (alias *Under the Hill*).

In Beardsley's novel, Venus's servants present a ballet, whose characters include Sporion. I surmise that Beardsley extrapolated Sporion from Pope's Sporus – whose other pseudonym is Lord Fanny; a surmise confirmed by the fact that Sporion's hands are (mysteriously[2]) said to have 'such unquenchable palms lined and mounted like Lord Fanny's in *Love at all Hazards*'.

Anyone who shared Firbank's taste for Beardsley[3] and the 18th century might have concocted Count Fanny on Beardsley–Pope precedents. There is, however, a tiny, far from conclusive sign that Firbank had, at least, paid strong attention to Pope's Lord Fanny. 'Has she been in Shakespeare before?' runs a question in the theatrical chatter of *Caprice*. 'From the time she could toddle; in *A Midsummer Night's Dream*, when not quite two, she was the Bug with gilded wings,' goes the answer – and goes, indeed, so fast and plausibly that the reading mind almost accepts that Bug as com-

---

[1] – in, respectively, the *Epistle to Dr Arbuthnot* and *The Second Satire of the Second Book of Horace*.

[2] – at least to me; I cannot guess if the work Beardsley names is a book or a ballet or whether he made it up or whether it is another item in the Lord Fanny literary lineage.

[3] Portions of Beardsley's novel were published in *The Savoy* in his lifetime, and portions in a John Lane volume in 1904. It was in 1907 that Leonard Smithers brought out the whole work, unexpurgated; and in 1907 (according to the *Bibliography*) that *Count Fanny's Nuptials* was published.

panion to Moth and Mustardseed. But as a matter of fact 'this bug with gilded wings' is Pope's epithet for Sporus–Lord Fanny.

Firbank's familiarity (as reader if not writer) with the pornography market is attested by the list of the books to be found in Bertie Waldorf's Firbank-designed house:[1] '*A Plea for the Separation of the Sexes*. A treatise on *The Value of Smiles*.[2] *Queens of the Rod and Birch*. The *Life and Times of Gaby Deslys*. *The Holy Bible* (Authorized Version). *Valmouth* – a presentation copy, it seemed, from the author.'

Only a deep-versed sado-masochist could wring the authority of 'discipline' from the Authorised Version – as well as hinting, by merging the 'Authorized' into the following 'author', that he wrote it. And, as a matter of fact, Firbank is responsible for more books in the list than *Valmouth*. *A Plea for the Separation of the Sexes* may well be a disguise of *The Princess Zoubaroff*, whose plea is in non-fiction terms exactly that. Even the life and times of Gaby Deslys are in a sense the life and times of Firbank: Firbank is Claud Harvester, and Claud Harvester is 'the Gaby Deslys of literature'.[3]

Firbank's technique of compiling efflorescent *lists*, a technique seeded perhaps in the first place from nurserymen's catalogues, is exercised on personal names,[4] on book titles and on things. I have already quoted[5] his list-in-a-footnote of ecclesiastical objects stolen perhaps on a precedent set at Chislehurst. Later in the same novel (*The Flower Beneath the Foot*) Firbank lists objects likewise ecclesiastical, the contents of a nun's cell. The prize blooms in the first list are hagiographical: 'the Tongue of St. Thelma'; and '4¾ yards of black lace, said to have "belonged to" the Madonna'. The most numinous two objects in the second list are, respectively, homosexually-floral and flagellant. 'A crucifix, a text, *I would lay Pansies at Jesus' Feet*, two fresh eggs in a blue paper bag, some ends of string, a breviary and a birch were the chamber's individual if meagre contents.'

Firbank adumbrated a union between flagellation and his cult of flowers in *The Princess Zoubaroff*, where Lady Rocktower remembers school days that have gone a step further into fantasy than those shared by the Honourables. 'School, in my time, was not the soft place it is to-day [. . .] As a

---

[1] Cf. sub-section 8 of this chapter.

[2] This item of reading matter Bertie Waldorf shares with (*Complete* Firbank, p. 676) Cardinal Pirelli.

[3] The signature of Gaby Deslys, too (cf. sub-sections 2 and 15 of this chapter) was in the collection of Firbank's adolescence. In 1923 Carl Van Vechten, either sharing or knowing of Firbank's cults, told Firbank (according to the *Biography*, p. 240, which quotes a letter of Van Vechten's) that he had hung two photographs of Firbank, sent him by Firbank, in his bathroom 'somewhere between Gaby Deslys and Mary Garden (cf. Chapters XIV, 4 and XV, 6).

[4] Cf. sub-section 4 of this chapter.   [5] in Chapter X, 9.

young girl I used to be whipped with furze.' (Firbank's punning mind was making play, I think, with the title in translation of the prototypical masochistic novel, by the eponymous Leopold von Sacher-Masoch, *Venus in Furs*.)

It is in his last work[1] that Firbank truly enshrined flagellation in flowers. Mrs Rosemerchant justifies her floral name (and Firbank returns to his original, as I conjecture, inspiration[2] in the fact that 'named varieties' of flowers are simultaneously flowers and people) in the 'singularly hectic number' of the magazine whose headlines Mrs Rosemerchant is scanning just before she is 'arrested'[3] by the prize-winning beauty. (Girls and flowers alike win prizes in beauty contests.)

The ('glowing', of course) headlines run: 'Fifth Av. Scandal [. . .] New York's New Vice: Society Women Birched With Roses. Multi-Millionairess Whipped With Thorns. Widow of Defunct Senator Mandarin-Dove Declares For *Gloire de Dijon* While Mrs Culling Browne[4] Says Dorothy Perkins Are Best.'

20. Miracle-Working Icons

LADY Barrow consults a volume of tortures 'with plates'. Pictures, for Firbank's personages, are hypnotic objects or fetishes, icons that focus concentration for purposes of fantasy or of devotion. Lady Parvula is agog to see, besides Saint Automona's tooth, 'your Ghirlandajo and the miracle-working effigy'.

Two of Firbank's novels themselves focus their composition about icons. In *Vainglory*, the icon, the object not only of the personages' but of the novel's devotion, is the fragmented literary image of Sappho. In *The New Rythum* the icon (the 'Prax Herc') has become three-dimensional, but it is still fragmented. ' "Fingers five by three, phallus ten by eight; restored . . ." An insurance-officer was conscientiously verifying that all was as it should be' after the statue's arrival at the docks in New York.

In both books parties are given in the icon's honour. The icon is the focus-point of cult.

Both as a cult-object and in its fragmentation, the icon at the heart of *Vainglory* and *The New Rythum* stands metaphor for Firbank's own literary technique[5] of fragmented imagism. The miracle-working properties of

---

[1] *The New Rythum*, where (p. 106) 'With a birching match earlier in the afternoon, it had been for the matron a busy day.'
[2] Cf. sub-section 4 of this chapter.   [3] Cf. sub-section 13 of this chapter.
[4] – culling, no doubt, rosebuds while she may.   [5] Cf. Chapter V, 2–3.

icons (of, for instance, the 'miracle-working effigy' which Lady Parvula is agog to see) have become the miracle of fiction: the conjuring of imaginative realities out of 'airy nothing', the 'willing suspension of disbelief for the moment'.

The metaphor is sustained, fragmented into tinier pieces but disseminated, by the theme of devotion to icons sacred or profane which permeates Firbank's work and life. Firbank the hagiographer is the Catholic face of Firbank the connoisseur. Brought-up, though not always in his adult life paid-up, as a collector, an art-historical essayist on the subject of an emperor's portrait, much given to having his own face rendered an icon by portraitists and photographers, as well as to building cults round photographs of other people, Firbank lent his iconographical temperament to his novels, whose discourse is thickly art-historical, and to his dramatis personae, who regularly collect, inspect, sell, think about, make or sit for statues and paintings.[1]

Firbank's icons at once serve his imagist technique and express his cultist temperament, which turned his life into a pilgrimage in pursuit of Oscar Wilde. His concern, in life and in writing, is to isolate an image and render it holy – 'miracle-working': by sharpening the focus and the exclusiveness of his concentration on it. Firbank's literary technique is an extension of the mental technique of another miracle-worker and conjurer, masturbation fantasy. Icons are invoked by Firbank by methods derived from Lady Barrow's invocation of the plates in the volume of tortures.

It is as an emblem or fetish of their own literary technique that Firbank's fictions wield the 'discipline'. Firbank's personages may be invited ('Turn over, Old Dear') to share its pleasures or may take them ('New York's New Vice') by orgy, but the discipline is an instrument essentially of self-scourging in solitude.

Even the person-to-person whipping scene in Firbank's childish flagellatory doggerel is given the detachment and impersonality that belong to scenes in masturbation fantasy, where alone a single person is both the active and the passive lover, both the do-er and the spectator. In Firbank's verse there is no 'I and she' or 'he and she'. There is not even 'her hand'. It is impersonally 'the' hand and 'the' child. The rhyme begins:

> The hand was raised
> The child was there!

---

[1] Cf. Chapter IX, 2, 5 and 7; Chapter VIII, 1 and 5; Chapter X, 7; Chapter IX, 6; and sub-section 13 of this chapter (collecting and inspecting); Chapter IX, 8 and sub-section 8 of this chapter (selling and making); Chapter XIII, 3 (thinking about); Chapter IX, 9, Chapter XIV, 4 and sub-section 9 of this chapter (sitting for).

The detachment of the actors from their actions and responses brings to my mind Freud's account of 'the phantasy "A Child is Being Beaten" [. . .] which occurs so commonly in girls'. (Firbank is hardly an anomalous instance.) 'The peculiar rigidity which struck me so much', Freud commented, 'in the monotonous formula "a child is being beaten" can probably be interpreted in a special way. The child which is being beaten (or caressed) may at bottom be nothing more nor less than the clitoris itself, so that at its very lowest level the statement will contain a confession of masturbation.'

Perhaps there is a similar statement, to the effect that sexual experiences are valuable only as providers of images for masturbation fantasies, in the Baroness Rudlieb's thoughts as she begins her straying love affair with Max. 'After all one did not expect to enjoy these adventures much at *the time*; it was only afterwards, from a sofa, in recollection, to the sound of a piano that they began to seem delightful.'

Perhaps the mare[1] whose withers give off powder when she is whipped is an adaptation of a flagellant-maquillant masturbation fantasy of Firbank's own.

Certainly Firbank, in the course of his public praises of the beauty of his own hands,[2] made an all but explicit statement of masturbation. 'When I'm alone I'm never lonely' (Robert McAlmon reports him as saying), 'because my hands are beautiful.'

The unjustly ill repute of the in reality neutral (morally, socially, aesthetically) activity of masturbation has damaged the repute of fiction.[3] It would be a constructive irony were society at last to do justice to the neutrality of masturbation and the positive goodness of fiction through noticing that Firbank created great fiction by techniques brought to perfection 'from a sofa' in a solitude that was 'never lonely'.

21. Notes to Chapter XV

THE headmistress's name in private life is on p. 670 in the *Complete* Firbank.

Oscar Wilde on a flower-like life is on p. 484 in Rupert Hart-Davis's edition of his *Letters*.

The celibate flowers are on p. 65 in the *Complete* Firbank. The earlier work of Victoria Gellybore-Frinton is described on p. 541 in the *Complete* Firbank, and she describes her new book on p. 559.

The plant personifications in the early pieces are described in the *Biography*, pp. 70–1. Winsome Brookes disparages the naming in an earlier Firbank piece on p. 189 in the *Complete* Firbank, and the Debussy opera in *Prancing Nigger* is on

---

[1] Cf. Chapter VIII, 1.   [2] Cf. Chapter VIII, 1.   [3] Cf. Chapter I, 4.

p. 613. The name and location of Mrs Shamefoot's shop are on p. 98 in the *Complete* Firbank, the Princess Zoubaroff's claim on p. 706, and the secrecy of the Duchess of Varna's 'little business venture' on p. 520.

The flowers' conversation in *The Flower Beneath the Foot* is on pp. 578–9 in the *Complete* Firbank, Mrs Montgomery's reflexions on a fire on p. 572 and the wedding procession on p. 592. The novel's full title is given in the first edition of 1923. The Blue Jesus is described on p. 500 in the *Complete* Firbank.

Mrs Shamefoot's floral lyre is on p. 99 and p. 104 in the *Complete* Firbank, the Princess Zoubaroff's nun-making on p. 750.

The octet of cabbage-rose daughters is on p. 738 in the *Complete* Firbank, the moths' cold caress on p. 55, the sting ob a wasp on p. 417, and Eddy Monteith's thoughts on the language of flowers on p. 537.

Mrs Shamefoot's views on the East Coast are on p. 157 in the *Complete* Firbank.

In my catalogue of Firbankian names, the first five are from *Vainglory* and the next four from *Valmouth*. Madame Poco is from *Concerning the Eccentricities of Cardinal Pirelli*, and the Hon. Edward Facile-Manners from *The New Rythum*. Sumph and Gripper are in *Vainglory* (and Gripper also in *Caprice*), ffines and Nit in *Valmouth*, and ffoliott in *The Flower Beneath the Foot*. ffoliott is thus spelt in the *Complete* Firbank, but the Brentano's 1924 edition of *The Flower Beneath the Foot* gives the name a capital initial letter. Perhaps the United-States printer simply could not believe the small one.

Firbank's own catalogues of Firbankian names are on p. 441 and p. 472 in the *Complete* Firbank.

The English Ambassadress is crammed with Maréchal Niel roses on p. 537 of the *Complete* Firbank, and Dorothy Perkins roses make a headline on p. 72 of *The New Rythum*. Mrs Rosemerchant is in *The New Rythum*. Miss Flowerman faints on p. 204 of the *Complete* Firbank; Winsome Brookes considers re-baptism on p. 107; the Bishop speaks of the theatre on p. 146; Mrs Thoroughfare's song is on p. 430 and Miss Wookie's on pp. 168–70; Mrs Henedge adores Nijinsky on p. 79; Prince Yousef is suspected of gambling on p. 502 and Firbank of writing *The Passing of Rose* on p. 532.

The publication of 'A Broken Orchid (From Sorrow in Sunlight)' (*Sorrow in Sunlight* being Firbank's own title for *Prancing Nigger*) in the October 1923 issue of *The Reviewer is* recorded in the *Biography*, pp. 233–4.

The varieties of orchid in the Villa Alba are listed on p. 631 of the *Complete* Firbank; the spruce-fir is on p. 460 and the willing-unwilling creature on p. 49; Claud Harvester's visit to Arcadia is mentioned on p. 82, the rôle of Hermione on p. 110, the sunburned sicklemen on p. 114, and the Marchioness's sister's taste on p. 662.

Handel's chorus of shepherds (and nymphs) is in *Acis and Galatea*.

Lady Violet's exchange with her daughter is from the extract from *Mr White-Morgan the Diamond King* published on pp. 115–16 of *The New Rythum and Other*

Pieces. The story's description of its hero as a 'self made nouveau riche' is quoted in the *Biography*, p. 69. Both volumes give digests of the story.

Wildred arrives outside Lady Appledore's garden wall on p. 38 of *The New Rythum and Other Pieces*. Mrs Asp and Mrs Thumbler talk servants on p. 88 in the *Complete* Firbank.

Claud Harvester's married and unmarried states are on p. 82 and pp. 155–6 in the *Complete* Firbank, Mrs Shamefoot's shop, engagement, pictures and tiff with Mrs Mountjulian on pp. 98–103, and the Princess Zoubaroff's garden on p. 706. The designs of Bertie Waldorf's house are on p. 96 of *The New Rythum*.

The *Biography* records Lucile's real name on p. 129. It quotes Firbank's letter about how Heather Firbank should use her annuity on p. 270 and gives its date on p. 267.

The Victoria and Albert Museum exhibited Heather Firbank's clothes in 1960 (Alan Harris's Introduction to *The New Rythum and Other Pieces*).

Laura describes her dress for the ball on p. 504 in the *Complete* Firbank.

Firbank's saintly sketch is reproduced and discussed on p. 51 of the exhibition catalogue, *Pen and Brush*, by Lola L. Szladits and Harvey Simmonds. The same notebook page is more extensively reproduced, as Plate VIII, in the *Biography*.

The nuns' habits are described on p. 755 in the *Complete* Firbank, the Princess Zoubaroff speaks of Ingres's admiration on p. 706, Mrs Henedge's Ingres hope is on p. 79 and Claud Harvester's 1860 tastes are on p. 82.

Jean Auguste Dominique Ingres died in 1867.

The widow's devotions are on p. 116 of *The New Rythum and Other Pieces*.

Mrs Shamefoot's skill at wiring is on p. 99 in the *Complete* Firbank and the consolation she receives on p. 179; Claud Harvester's application of wiring to hair is on p. 86; the Princess Zoubaroff's eclecticism is on pp. 707–8, the Rule of her convent on p. 757, her Austrian waltzes on p. 750 and her yellow liqueur on pp. 757–8. The message of the birds and the flowers to her is on p. 706 in the *Complete* Firbank and p. 15 in the first edition of the play.

Winsome's floral breakfast is on p. 107 in the *Complete* Firbank, Mrs Wookie's fears for the milk on p. 160, and the Princess Zoubaroff's hunger on p. 727 (p. 49 in the first edition).

Adrian and the Princess Zoubaroff are forgetful on p. 15 of the first edition (p. 706 in the *Complete* Firbank).

The Duchess of Varna's flowers are renamed on p. 579 in the *Complete* Firbank.

The dismissal of the Chislehurst butler is recorded (from family letters) on p. 13 of the *Biography*. The wines of ffines are on p. 407 in the *Complete* Firbank, and his employer's comment on p. 409.

Miss Collins explains the evolution of her shopping pseudonym on p. 241 of the *Complete* Firbank, and Miss O'Brookomore doubts the pastoralness of Count Pastorelli on p. 237.

Miss Neffal speaks of Sappho and Walpole on p. 224 in the *Complete* Firbank, and Mrs Negress's heroine Lesbia is mentioned on p. 723. The Sargent is on p. 85

of *The New Rythum*. The Lesbian portrait is on p. 674 in the *Complete* Firbank and the supposed Lysippus on p. 663.

The Disciples' wreath is on p. 93 in *The New Rythum*, Heliodora is re-named on p. 82 and Mrs Rosemerchant's eye is arrested on p. 72. The quotations from Firbank's notebooks are from the extracts published on pp. 108-9 in *The New Rythum and Other Pieces*.

Les Chansons de Bilitis is on p. 467 in the *Complete* Firbank, Mrs Thoroughfare's cut-short song on p. 429, the 'Lesbian' wine from Samos on p. 85, the scandal which has nothing in it on p. 72 and the conversation between the Baroness Rudlieb and Sir Oliver Scott on p. 73.

The becalmed act of love is on p. 565 in the *Complete* Firbank, the sideways hat on p. 568 and the chapter of *Mabel*s on p. 284, and the odour of sanctity on p. 143.

Mrs Henedge's blind alley is on p. 87 in the *Complete* Firbank. The Baroness reads Saint Teresa on p. 65 in the first edition of *The Artificial Princess* (p. 61 in the *Complete* Firbank). The variant Raphael is on p. 81 of *The New Rythum*.

Mrs Patrick Campbell's part in *Pelléas et Mélisande* is described on p. 17 and pp. 268-9 of Alan Dent's edition of *Bernard Shaw and Mrs. Patrick Campbell : Their Correspondence*, and in Alan Dent's biography *Mrs. Patrick Campbell*, from which I borrow Plate 10.

Edward Garden's letter about Mary Garden's Mélisande is in *The Times* of 7 October 1970.

Lady Parvula de Panzoust is agog to see the tooth on p. 410 of the *Complete* Firbank, the thunderstorm is overhead on p. 425, Claud Harvester is a cult on p. 156 and Miss Compostella worships trees on p. 158.

Helen Carew's letter to Firbank about the Sitwells is described on p. 168 of the *Biography*, and Firbank's to Van Vechten on p. 218.

Philip Moeller's account of his meeting with Firbank is on pp. 82-4 of the *Memoir*. The quotation from Martin Secker is from p. 56 of the *Memoir*.

Miss Tooke hums on p. 436 of the *Complete* Firbank, the Bishop explains Mrs Cresswell's heresy on p. 143, Veronese is discussed on p. 117, the Artificial Princess addresses her letter on p. 31, and Reggie Quintus saints the Princess Zoubaroff on p. 753.

The unofficial sainting of Hugh Benson is described in Volume II, pp. 236-7 of C. C. Martindale's *Life* of Benson.

Stella Creamway's sainting and tendency to stained glass is on p. 121 of *The New Rythum and Other Pieces*. Lady Henrietta Worthing's similar tendency is described in the *Biography*, p. 87.

Mrs Shamefoot's mental three parts are on p. 87 in the *Complete* Firbank, she discusses her sainthood with the Bishop on pp. 144-5, her vitrification cards are expected on p. 196 and she recounts her dream of being dug up on p. 178; Eddy Monteith's bath (in *The Flower Beneath the Foot*) is on p. 536 and the clouds prepare on p. 130.

The Baroness is carried off as if 'in a Rape' on p. 49 in the *Complete* Firbank and feels suddenly 'a little masculine' on p. 61; the crucifixion by a pupil of Rops is on p. 32, the effeminacy conversation on p. 406, Mrs Hurstpierpoint's dream on p. 450, and the improvised address by the archbishop on pp. 614–15.

The fettering orchids are on p. 629 in the *Complete* Firbank, the tortures in the mouse-eaten library on p. 193, the spiked garters on p. 464, and the Cardinal's last sermon on p. 693.

Katherine Mansfield's spiked ribbons are on pp. 45–6 in the 'Definitive Edition' (1954) of her *Journal*.

Firbank's early flagellation poem is published and discussed but not recognised for what it is on pp. 20–1 of the *Biography*. The *Memoir* is perceptive on the subject of Firbank's masochism on pp. 45–6.

Lady Parvula de Panzoust has to wait through a scourging on p. 401 in the *Complete* Firbank and the overhear before cock-crow is on p. 464. The long flaying-room is on p. 193 in the *Complete* Firbank, the location of the club on p. 138, the national game on p. 43, the Honourables' flagellation scene on p. 538 and Eddy Monteith's intention for Intriguer on p. 537.

The 'Nuns of Sodbury' and their companion pieces are on p. 440 in the *Complete* Firbank, the Princess Zoubaroff's want on p. 732, the request for a whipping on p. 590 and the charm of the religious world on p. 553. The cotillion favours are on p. 79 of *The New Rythum* and Miss Whipsina Peters on p. 336 in the *Complete* Firbank.

The *Bibliography* reports on *Count Fanny's Nuptials* on pp. 95–6. Publication details of *Teleny* are given in the Icon edition of 1966, introduced by H. Montgomery Hyde. C. W. Beaumont's account of Firbank's literary taste is quoted in the *Memoir*, p. 49. Publication details of *Under the Hill* are given in John Glassco's edition. The Bug is transposed into *A Midsummer Night's Dream* on p. 355 in the *Complete* Firbank.

Bertie Waldorf's books are listed on p. 101 of *The New Rythum*. Claud Harvester is likened to Gaby Deslys on p. 156 in the *Complete* Firbank, where the lists of ecclesiastical objects are on p. 565 and p. 590.

Lady Rocktower remembers her schooldays on p. 748 in the *Complete* Firbank, and the vicious headlines are in *The New Rythum*, p. 72.

An English translation of Sacher-Masoch's *Venus in Pelz* (1870) appeared in 1902 (Foreword, p. 12, Faber 1971 translation).

The insurance officer inspects the Herc on p. 94 of *The New Rythum*. Freud discusses the beating fantasy in *Collected Papers*, Volume V, XVII. The Baroness expects to enjoy herself afterwards on p. 53 of the *Complete* Firbank. Robert McAlmon reports Firbank's claim not to be lonely on p. 80 of *Being Geniuses Together 1920–1930*.

PART FOUR

IN PRAISE OF FIRBANK'S FICTION

' "*I suppose I'm getting squeamish! But this Ronald Firbank I can't take to at all. Valmouth! Was there ever a novel more coarse? I assure you I hadn't gone very far when I had to put it down.*"

' "*It's out*", Mrs. Bedley suavely said, "*as well*", she added, "*as the rest of them.*"

' "*I once met him*", Miss Hopkins said, dilating slightly the retinae of her eyes. "*He told me writing books was by no means easy!*" '

The Flower Beneath the Foot

Contents

OF PART FOUR

In Praise of Firbank's Fiction

Chapter XVI	DEVICES OF FIRBANKIAN BAROQUE	396
1	Aerial Tactics – 1	396
2	Aerial Tactics – 2	397
3	Air	398
4	Aerial Strategy	399
5	A Change of Air	399
6	A Particularised Generalisation	400
7	The Perpetual Convert	402
8	The Immortal	403
9	The Economist	404
10	The (Misleadingly) Wit	405
11	Paradise Reframed	407
12	'I am all Design'	408
13	Notes	409
Chapter XVII	MAUVE INTO FAUVE (MORE DEVICES OF FIRBANKIAN BAROQUE)	411
1	Mauve into Fauve	411
2	The Two Voices	413
3	'Exquisite Feeling & Beauty'	416
4	A Weep on the Grass	417
5	Trailers	419
6	The Aeration of Irony	420
7	Concerto Form	422

8	Overhear . . .	426
9	. . . into Fragment	427
10	A Monument	427
11	Leaning	429
12	Notes	431

Chapter XVIII FANFARE (*Vainglory* – 1) 432

1	Image and Shadow	432
2	Prelude (as Fugue)	433
3	Prelude (as Grand Prelude)	439
4	Prelude and Ode	445
5	Notes	450

Chapter XIX THE PASTORALS AND THE FIRST
TRAGEDY (*Vainglory* – 2; *Inclinations*; *Caprice*;
Valmouth; *The Princess Zoubaroff*; *Santal*) 451

1	Monumental Pun . . .	451
2	. . . into Literary Pun	452
3	Distribution	452
4	Fugue	454
5	Harvest Cycle	456
6	Counter-Fugue	457
7	Redistribution	457
8	Tutti and a Syncopated Stress	458
(9	Itinerary)	461
10	Patterns of Irony	462
11	Diptych	463
12	The Extraordinary Caprice	471
13	The Thread . . .	476
14	Mrs Yaj's Profession	478
15	. . . and the Material	481
16	A Classical Bridge Passage	485
17	Play	486
18	Casa Heartbreak	491
19	Heartbreak	499
20	A Short but Important Prayer Mat	501

IN PRAISE OF FIRBANK'S FICTION 395

Chapter XX THE THREE LATE TRAGEDIES (*The Flower Beneath the Foot; Prancing Nigger; Concerning the Eccentricities of Cardinal Pirelli*) 509

1. Death Arab 509
2. Conversions and Versions 510
3. Streamers and Riddles 511
4. Court Life . . . 512
5. The Flower and 'the gardener, (poor dear)' 514
6. . . . and Non-Life . . . 518
7. . . . and Une Vie Courte 519
8. 'The error is so slight . . .' 521
9. The Archduchess Artie 524
10. Where? 526
11. Boiseries and Recesses 531
12. Six, major caesura, Six, minor caesura, Three 532
13. Six 533
14. 'Ssssh' 539
15. Six; Three 540
16. 'Cynical & "Horrid" ' 545
17. The Old Rythum 546
18. Requisite Chastity 549
19. Purposely Unshaded 551
20. Focus 552
21. Binding 554
22. Où? 556
23. Earthquake 557
24. 'Ahi; this death' 558
25. The Mountains of Nirvana 566

XVI

Devices of Firbankian Baroque

1. Aerial Tactics – 1

FIRBANK'S writing consists of his giving his images space to be contemplated in.[1]

His technique is to *aerate* his books.

Indeed, his pages are quite visibly aerated by the deployment on them of white space.

It is neither chance nor an arbitrariness in Firbank that puts so much white space on the paper and distributes it so irregularly. The gaps directly correspond to acts of fiction. Firbank's left-hand margins are frequently indented, and his right-hand margins are repeatedly invaded by uneven blanks, *because* of his wiry reliance on dialogue, usually in short lengths (playwright's lengths, by the measure of *The Princess Zoubaroff*), and *because* of his brief paragraphing,[2] which is not wantonly imposed (as it is by popular newspapers that distrust their readers' ability to read more than two sentences in a block) but which follows the rapid and jagged changes of direction in his discourse.

Firbank's discourse and dialogue are often (most often, I think, in *Inclinations*) interspersed with songs or verses, and those occasion yet broader encroachments by white space, between which the poems trail like garlands.

Because the setting-out of the page follows the nature of the material which has to be thus set out, the frequent white spaces on the page correspond to mental white spaces, to tiny pauses, in the reader's mind. The indentation for a new speaker or a new paragraph marks the pause in which the reader changes his mental tone of voice. The white space that moves in on the text when the text changes from prose to verse marks the pause of adjustment between reading different kinds of rhythm.

Firbank's pages are more frequently and variously invaded by white space than pages by most writers because his texts impose more pauses and

[1] Cf. Chapters V, 2 and 7 and XV, 20.
[2] Cf. Chapter X, 6.

adjustments on the reader. The aerated *look* of his pages is a visible analogue of the aeration of his literary texture.

Firbank puts the analogue to use as a method of expression. Layout, on a Firbank page, is almost notation. It maps the pauses and emphases in his matter.

The same is true of Firbank's expressive punctuation.[1] It is expressive not only by its significance but through its look.

Firbank's idiosyncratic (in fact, simply 18th-century) capital letters raise momentary hurdles in the reader's track (and perhaps, by slowing him down, return him a moment's 18th-century selfconsciousness above the surface of his 19th-century immersion in the book[2]).

Firbank's frequent dots of suspension (not simply French, but a borrowing and adaptation from French usage) impose a rallentando that gives the reader time to contemplate the images' ambiguity. . . . At the same stroke, the dots ventilate the page, by their actually airy look. Dots are almost perforation.

'I wanted', Firbank wrote to Grant Richards in 1916 about the proofs of *Inclinations*, '[. . .] more capital-letters & dots instead of dashes. . . .'

Firbank's italics, too, create a pause in perusal. Italics for emphasis slide the reader down into an instant's groove; the italics of foreign words (including words in languages made up by Firbank) halt him before he raises his efforts (and the pitch of his mental voice) to surmount them. Those pauses, too, are *visible*: in the gaps left by the comparative thinness of italic type (or, in some of Firbank's foreign words, Greek type).

In 1918 Firbank said to Siegfried Sassoon: 'I adore italics, don't you?' (a remark Sassoon ought surely to have reported as 'I *adore* italics, don't you?' or, with a subtler point and avoiding confusion with the italics merely of screaming queerdom,[3] as 'I adore *italics*, don't you?')

2. Aerial Tactics – 2

FIRBANK aerates his books also by devices which have no visible analogue and which are peculiarly Firbankian.

Within his sentences he holds back the reader's pace and then tumbles it onwards by the idiosyncratic (in fact, simply French) positioning of his adverbs.[4] Within the texture of his discourse as a whole, he makes an equivalent effect by his acute changes (sometimes almost reversals) of direction between one block of discourse and the next.[5]

[1] Cf. Chapter X, 12.   [2] Cf. Part One.   [3] Cf. Chapter XI, 3.
[4] Cf. Chapter X, 11.   [5] Cf. Chapter V, 2 and 3.

Those devices are part of the fiction, inasmuch as they create the tone - which in Firbank *is* the fiction: Firbank of all authors would vanish if his works were re-told by someone else. In themselves, however, they are devices without imagist content. They create invisible irregular spaces in the reader's progress: jagged areas of pure transparency through which the reader contemplates Firbank's images.

Firbank deploys also spaces which *have* imagist content. When he puts an image inside a line of dialogue, his reader views the inside image in a perspective, down an avenue, which is itself an image. When Firbank's personages contemplate images, their contemplation is itself an image – though it is also a device that instructs the reader how to contemplate the images in the book and how to make a cult of the book's author.

Indeed, many of Firbank's images are set up as ironic reflectors. They flash dazzlement out of the book at the reader, forcing the reader into self-consciousness and into consciousness of that fact which naturalistic fiction often conceals,[1] the fact that the book *has* an author. The space Firbank ironically creates by that method is the distancing of reader from book, of writer from book, and of reader from writer. 'Isn't that one of Ronald Firbank's books?' asks a client in Mrs Bedley's English circulating library in Pisuerga; isn't, the question demands of the reader who comes on it in *The Flower Beneath the Foot*, *this* one of Ronald Firbank's books?

3. Air

BY devices with and without fictional content, Firbank creates analogues, symbols, metaphors and illusions of space. He surrounds his images with inviolable borders of distance. He riddles the texture of his books with gaps, airiness and, sometimes, draughts. And at the same time he infuses and circumfuses all his fictions with fictitious air.

Climate and weather are an indispensable item, almost a hero, in Firbank's fiction. They create spaces, through which other images are viewed; but because they are themselves images these spaces are not pure transparencies but tinted varnishes.

Tropical climate is to *Prancing Nigger* what sky is to a rococo ceiling. Firbank can decorate it with the passing of a butterfly or cloud it with swarms of menace.[2] And against its brilliance he can darken his personages into silhouettes of tragedy.

---

[1] Cf. Chapter I, 1.   [2] Cf. Chapter XV, 3.

Cherif's pilgrimage in *Santal* is dried up by the desert, a Firbankian space that is also a metaphor of waste.

Valmouth scintillates with 'Valmouth air'.

4. Aerial Strategy

YET 'Valmouth air', besides pervading the book, is the nucleus from which the book has grown.

And Firbank, besides being a tactician of textural spaces, is a strategist: a baroque designer who encloses grand spaces and relates them to each other.

The climate of *Prancing Nigger* is both pervasive tropicality and the earthquake.

Events in Firbank's weather turn out to be the central explosive or convulsive points from which the reader can apprehend his baroque designs whole. Indeed it is from these points that the designs declare themselves baroque. The earthquake in *Prancing Nigger* and thunderstorms in *Vainglory* and *Valmouth* are the compositional centres (not necessarily the centres of the plot): the centres from which all the themes and motifs of the fiction (not the events in the story) are flung or convulsed into movement.

A baroque iconographer as well as designer, Firbank apprehended the upper air to be the sphere in which daimonic beings move (invisibly, though some are perhaps briefly precipitated into visibility by the thunderstorm in *Vainglory*) and create eddies palpable in spheres below: 'a girls'-school passed with its escort of [. . .] fantastic Demons flying above them (invisible) criss-cross through the air'. . . .

5. A Change of Air

IT is part both of the beauty and of the economic structural strength of Firbank's designs that his tactics echo, and thereby reinforce, his strategy.

His acute changes of tactical direction have a counterpart in his strategy: his regular device of a shift in the whole fiction's locale.

He subjects his books to tactical aeration: and to a strategic change of air.

The shift is made within the terms of the fiction. Some of the fictional material is lent to the constructing of a bridge passage between the two locales – a bridge passage that may take flight as suddenly and engagingly as the 'Ponte di Sospiri' in the Bishop's Palace at Ashringford which 'broke, quite unexpectedly, from the stairs with all the freedom of a polonaise'.

Vainglory fashions its own fictitious and internal ponte di sospiri, indeed *gets* itself to Ashringford, by borrowing from the English convention that members of 'Society' leave London at the end of 'the Season'. *The Flower Beneath the Foot* uses the same bridge passage but socially promotes and exoticises it into the Court's removal to the Summer Palace. . . . *Cardinal Pirelli* combines summer retreat with retreat from scandal.

Vainglory and *Prancing Nigger* detach a thread of the fictional material and set it to cross the bridge passage in the form of a journey undertaken by the personages. In *Inclinations* and *Santal*, the journey is a pilgrimage and is itself a segment of the fictional material: travelling, shifting locale, is itself one of the two locales.

With the exception (for which there is poignant cause) of *Valmouth*, all Firbank's Firbankian novels undergo a change of air. So does the proto-Firbankian *Lady Appledore's Mésalliance*. Even that under-age pre-Firbankian heroine whom Firbank's narrative regularly calls 'little Odette d'Antrevernes' undertakes a journey, though a suitably little one: into the château garden.

The Princess Zoubaroff maintains a dramatic unity of place, but its pattern spins round the absence, on a journey, of two husbands during most of the action.

6. A Particularised Generalisation

FIRBANK'S fictions shift setting not by reflexion of his own nomadism but as a twin symptom, with his nomadism, of themes in himself.

It is not even that his travels – or, at least, any in particular of his travels – supplied furniture for what his imagination had anyway sketched. The colouring in his books is intense and intensely particularised, but it is not 'local colour'. It is localised to Firbank's world, not to any part of the geographical world; and it performs purely Firbankian functions as an image in its own right and as an aeration-device.

Siegfried Sassoon, who like many of Firbank's acquaintance was surprised to discover that he was 'business-like' and 'had travelled widely', asked which was his favourite country and received the magnificent and Firbankian reply 'Lotus land, of course!'

What Firbank took from his experience of the world's geography was an intensification of his Firbankianness.

The furniture of his books is an intense particularisation of a generalised alienness, Negroism or exoticism.

Against his exotic backdrop (Bakst-drop?) Firbank can set an essence of Englishness in exile: 'And for a solemn moment their thoughts went out in unison to the sea-girt land of their birth – Barkers', Selfridges', Brighton-pier, the Zoological gardens on a Sunday afternoon' (a sentence of *The Flower Beneath the Foot* which encapsulates in advance much of the œuvre of Graham Greene). Or he drags across his exoticism an essence of Englishness on the traipse: ' "I feel his books are all written in hotels with the bed unmade at the back of the chair." '[1]

Mrs Yajñavalkya is an exotic in exile in an English seaside health-resort: an exotic particularised in her exoticism but generalised as to the exotic locality she comes from. She is 'Oriental' and 'negress' in the same breath – indeed in a single sentence.[2] The Mouth family are exotics in their native land: but *what* land? (*Did* Firbank visit Haiti?[3]) And both Mrs Yaj and Mrs Mouth speak, besides French and Firbank's invented exotic language, Firbank's French-based dialect[4] of exotic English. So far as its reflexions in his fiction are concerned, Firbank's experience of Touraine was the same thing as his experience of the West Indies (themselves closer in his imagination to the East Indies than geography sanctions[5]) and the same thing as his experience or non-experience of Haiti.

To understand the generalised quality of Firbank's exoticism is crucial to understanding what sort of writer Firbank is.

Exoticism itself is indispensable to him. It is both a contributor to and a metaphor of the bizarreness of his images in their own reverberant right; and at the same economical stroke it creates an aesthetic climate for the appreciation of the baroque strangenesses of his designs.

And the fact that Firbank's is a *generalised* exoticism denotes him an imaginative creator, not a reporter of flat facts observed in exciting places.

Recognising that the generalness of his exoticism was an essential part of the definition of his talent, Firbank emphasised its importance by means of a Wildean flow of paradox on the subject.

He told Aldous Huxley he was going to the West Indies 'so as to collect material for a novel about Mayfair'.[6] And he framed his preface to the

---

[1] The comment (p. 533 in the *Complete* Firbank) is spoken in Mrs Bedley's library, on the subject of the books of 'Robert Hitchinson'. (They include *The East is Whispering*.) As Firbank demonstrated at the end of *The Flower Beneath the Foot*, where Robert Hichens, under his own name unblended with that of a publisher, is included in the 'ensemble' which Firbank's text calls 'the very apotheosis of worn-out cliché', neither Hichens's generosity to Wilde nor even the garden in Hichens's best-selling title could make Firbank forgive Hichens (who had known Wilde in person) for abandoning the Wildean milieu of his first book, satirical though that was, in favour of writing novels like *The Garden of Allah*, which was published in 1905 and turned into a theatrical success, too, in London and the United States (Cf. Chapters XIII, 1 and XIV, 10 and 11).
[2] Cf. p. 413 in the *Complete* Firbank. [3] Cf. Chapter VIII, 9.
[4] Cf. Chapter X, 11. [5] Cf. Chapter X, 12.
[6] Cf. Chapter VIII, 9 and the *Memoir*, p. 73.

United-States edition of *The Flower Beneath the Foot* between two further versions of the same topographical paradox.

His preface begins: 'I suppose the Flower beneth the Foot is really Oriental in origin, although the scene is some imaginary Vienna.' And its last sentence runs: 'Ah, the East. . . . I propose to return there, some day, when I write about New York.'

7. The Perpetual Convert

IN Firbank's life and fiction alike, the shifts of locale are a response to his sense of having been excluded from his Chislehurst home (that exclusion to which all his social exclusions were assimilated) and to his expectation of being soon excluded from life itself.

He travelled in search of health – and presently, I suspect, from a restlessness that was itself a symptom of his illness.

His constant travels were the bodily equivalent of his multifarious superstition. He travelled in hope of hitting on not merely a health-giving but a propitious climate.

Valmouth alone of his novels sticks to a single setting: because 'Valmouth air' virtually guarantees a life expectancy of a century.

All the same, lightning might descend through even Valmouth air; and after even a century of life on earth there might be the possibility of immortal life to make arrangements for. Accordingly, Mrs Hurstpierpoint collects saintly relics, and wards off danger from thunderstorms by invoking their miraculousness; and she collects, indeed enforces, conversions to Catholicism in order to purchase heavenly insurance. Mrs Hurstpierpoint's culminating investment (like one of Firbank's own major literary and by-identification investments) is in Negroism. Her conversion of Niri-Esther counts as a 'double conversion': both because Niri-Esther's baby is included in the deal and because it is a conversion from heathenism (instead of mere protestantism). Niri-Esther's 'salvation', Mrs Thoroughfare assures Mrs Hurstpierpoint, 'in my estimate, Eulalia, should be equivalent quite to a Plenary-perpetual Indulgence'.

Mrs Hurstpierpoint has borrowed her pattern from Firbank: from his collection and invocation of relics of the 'Infamous St Oscar of Oxford, Poet and Martyr'; and from his own (in the pattern of Wilde) conversion to Catholicism.

Catholicism was, as well as being Wildean (and, in ultimate literary tradition, gothick[1]), the faith of Chislehurst. When Firbank entered Catholicism

[1] Cf. Chapter VIII, 8.

he entered Chislehurst regained. The lost, mortal, imperial-and-Catholic town put on the pretensions of eternity.

Catholicism presented itself as Firbank's Valmouth air, a setting he had no need to shift because it was both home and the promise not of a mere century's but of eternal life.

Finally, however, Firbank believed not the promises of Catholicism but the promises of his own imagination speaking through and transfiguring Catholicism. His emotions were invested less in his Catholicism than in his conversion. None of his Firbankian works could be mistaken for the work of a believing Catholic. But they are all unmistakably the work of a convert.

What, however, Firbank was a convert *to* is almost as unlocalised as his exoticism.

The act of being converted, in his life and in his fiction (where persons are converted into Catholics, saints, stained glass and persons of the other sex) is a thematic equivalent to his shifts (in life and fiction) of locale – and almost a continuation of his (in life) superstition. Firbank was all but a modern-life convert to the religion of ancient Egypt.

Firbank's thoughts are working towards himself when a conversation, in *Vainglory*, about Mrs Henedge's impending conversion to Catholicism works up to the Bishop of Ashringford's remark, 'Many people [. . .] are very easily influenced. They have only to look at a peacock's tail to think of Brahma.'

If Firbank's device of a shift of locale within a single book is formally and psychologically equivalent to a conversion, the shift of setting between his previous books and *Santal* actually has the imagist content of a conversion. For the purposes of *Santal* Firbank translated not just Odette's quest of the madonna but the whole apparatus of Firbankian imagery (camp, talismanic values and saintly patterns of perfection included) out of Catholicism and into Islam.

8. The Immortal

CHANGES neither of his wintering-place nor of his fortune-teller could give Firbank assurance that his health would hold out for even a half, let alone a whole, century.

And for his immortal life he again trusted his imagination, not his religion. He meant to be immortal in his books. Like Mrs Shamefoot herself, he located immortal life not in *being* a saint but in being depicted and incarnated as a saint (a worker of artistic miracles) in a work of art.

In his miracle-working saint Oscar Wilde Firbank ultimately patterned himself not on the occasional Christian and not, even, on the convert but on the aesthete.

On Mrs Shamefoot's aspirations to immortality in glass Firbank's text comments 'It was the Egyptian sighing for his pyramid, of course' – naming a religion older than Christianity and one whose monuments had lasted (if fragmentarily[1]) longer than the eternal city (whose claims to eternity are paradigmed in the properties of 'Valmouth air' and in which Firbank finally shewed himself an unwilling disbeliever by dying: in the eternal city).

Firbank still needed his Egyptian talismans and gypsy consultations. He needed luck if he was to live long enough to finish building his pyramid; luck again to get it sufficiently noticed by mankind to be sure it wouldn't be demolished and sanded over the moment he was dead; and luck to insure the continuance of his income, which he needed not only to live on but to be immortal on, since it must pay for the posthumous publication of his collected edition.

(The *posthumous* collected edition was itself a concession, by Firbank, to his realistic assessment of his life expectancy. Originally, his ambition was to act out in literary form his fantasy of being canonised while he was yet alive[2] and, perhaps, to outdo the elegant cheek with which, in 1895, Max Beerbohm had published *The Works of Max Beerbohm* when he was 23. 'It would be wonderful', Firbank told Vyvyan Holland, 'to have one's complete works published whilst one is still alive.')

Accordingly, Firbank sought propitious publication days, underwent shifts of his own locale in hope of finding a place propitious for writing in, and fought off in fantasy the threats which he conceived to be eroding his income along with his mortal life – activities all of which he, by a supreme act of miraculous conversion, transformed into the imagist material and the structural devices of the monument he was creating.

9. The Economist

THE attempt to dodge premature death by the shifts of superstition, geographical restlessness and the invocation of saints gave Firbank much of his material. The rational expectation that he would, nevertheless, die young dictated the extreme economy[3] of his methods.

His inventiveness was huge. But there was no likelihood that he would

---

[1] After reading his re-discovered fragment of Sappho in *Vainglory*, ' "Christianity, no doubt", the Professor observed, with some ferocity, to Monsignor Parr, "has invented many admirable things, but it has destroyed more than it has created!" ' (*Complete Firbank*, p. 94).

[2] Cf. Chapter XV, 16 and 17.   [3] Cf. Chapter VI, 7.

have time and energy to impress on the world his imaginative richness by sheerly and repeatedly splurging it across the world.

Circumstance pushed him where aesthetics pulled him: to the tactics of marking the richness of his imagery by setting each image in a pause in which its importance reverberates.

Those tactics he was in turn obliged to build into the very system of his strategy, creating perspectives which economically perform two functions: as funnels down which the reader, during his reading, contemplates an image; and as structural components of the whole design, with the result that they are themselves motifs in the image of the book that can be contemplated, entire, from outside the book.

The shift of locale in a Firbankian novel can be used expressively, as the vehicle of an image. An adaptation of Firbank's own restlessness, it can incarnate the quest of a personage within the fiction or the questing mood of the whole fiction, in which case it may be echoed by the fugal structure of the whole.

At the same time the shift functions as an aeration-device. The shift repeats on a big scale the shape of Firbank's smaller and more frequent aeration-devices, his white space and his pauses for change of direction.

That repetition is itself a motif in the total pattern. It marks the relation of the immediate texture of Firbank's writing, with its many small pauses and small shifts of direction, to the *sort* of union of motifs through which he puts together his structures as wholes.

A Firbankian novel juxtaposes the major blocks of the fiction to one another at the same sharp angles as the Firbankian page juxtaposes paragraphs. The shift of locale often marks the transition from one major block to the next. It is equivalent to the pause between movements in music or to the angle (in Firbank's case, usually an unexpected one) at which the central section meets the east (or, indeed, oriental) wing.

The shift of locale is a monumental structural pause in the progression of the work. It imposes a major pause, a grand hiatus, on the reading mind. It is a pause during which the image contemplated by the reader is the image of the whole book as a design, because it is during the shift-of-locale pause that the reader apprehends the relation, in tone and structure, of one block to the next.

10. The (Misleadingly) Wit

FIRBANK'S fiction-reading contemporaries had probably, on the instructions of both fashion and experience, ceased to *expect*, when they saw a fireworks display, that the fireworks were mounted on a structure that was anything more than makeshift, ephemeral and not meant to be seen.

It may be by one of the ultimate results of the Wilde disaster that, within Firbank's lifetime, the witticism degenerated into the wisecrack: into, that is, an opportunist purchase of present laughter detached from, or actually destructive of, the long-term effectiveness of (whether work of art or coherency of nonfiction thought) its vehicle. The wit of Voltaire, Gibbon, Shaw and Wilde belonged to the (emotionally considered) left. Perhaps it was the social and socialist charges packed subversively into Wilde's aphorisms which frightened society into degrading wit along with Wilde, and the right into taking over the witticism in its degraded form. By the Twenties the wisecrack, in a philistine vacuum detached alike from social philosophy and from art, was a cosh chiefly for knocking out liberalising and tolerant aspirations. It was no longer Lady Bracknell's retardative gestures that were punctured; it was everyone who thought the world could be advanced or improved who was bludgeoned. The automatically derisible people were believers in social equality, heeders of Freud, vegetarians and other practitioners of non-violence, 'avant-garde' or merely 'modern' artists, 'progressive' educationalists, and women who wanted a métier beyond husband-minding.

Firbank's fictions emancipate both women and proletarians: by the same method whereby Wilde's plays emancipate women. (Wilde's wishes towards the emancipation of the proletariat were expressed chiefly in nonfiction form, by his socialism.) Firbankian servants are as likely as their employers to bear surnames with the upper-class beginning *ff*. And, though their speech includes the phraseology and sometimes the grammar of the servants' hall[1] ('I always know instinctive when the Mrs. has on her spiked garters'), it takes a turn as delicately French and Firbankian as their employers' speech (it's 'when the Mrs. has on her spiked garters', not *when she has her spiked garters on*) and is cast in the same cultivated idiom of ambiguity. 'Naturally' says a Firbank lady's maid on setting eyes on the Acropolis, 'one sees it has its old associations. . . .'

In their fictional emancipation of women, Firbank and Wilde alike were at the creative advantage of not bothering to simulate or prop-up heterosexuality in themselves. Consequently they had no emotional inducement to swallow those myths of inherent psychological differences between men and women behind which society hides its imposition of social inferiority on women. Since they did not believe in the myths and had no emotional

---

[1] As Chapter XVIII, 2 will remark, the servants' hall could also lend phraseology to Firbank's text.

need to believe in them, the myths could not operate as either an intellectual or a taboo barrier blocking the investment of some of the author's own personality in women he created.

The prostitutes of London are said to have danced for joy at Wilde's conviction, on the grounds that he had taken trade from them. Women's Liberation should make him amends by blessing the fact that he created Mabel Chiltern and Cecily Cardew women *and* created them witty.

Firbank's fictions, emancipated, modern and witty, were issued into a society which regularly directed wit *against* emancipation and modernism, and which used wit to the neglect or defiance of structure. Expectation did not equip Firbank's contemporaries to notice that his witty fictions were modern, and still less to notice that much of their modernity lay in their structure, since so many contemporaries assumed, from the existence of the fireworks (which no one could miss), that there *was* no structure.

One contemporary who made that assumption had the grace to admit later that he had been wrong. Siegfried Sassoon wrote in 1945: 'His earlier books had amused me, but I regarded them as the elegant triflings of a gifted amateur. Misled by their apparent lack of construction, I failed to see that he had a deliberate technique of his own.'

In 1924 Firbank welcomed the invitation to write a preface to the United-States edition of *The Flower Beneath the Foot* in the explicit hope that his doing so would help towards 'removing the prejudice' concerning his 'supposed [. . .] lack of design'.

Least of all could those of Firbank's contemporaries who went on expectation (or by the reviews) notice that the modernity of Firbank's structures lay in his revival and adaptation of the baroque method of constructing and that, thanks to his tense and terse economy of means, each firework of his wit is simultaneously: an image impressed, in its own existential right, on the mind's eye; a decorative element; and that detonation which is the motive point from which baroque compositions hurl their components through space.

11. Paradise Reframed

FIRBANKIAN fiction came into being through Firbank's impulse to regain Chislehurst. The Firbankian shift of locale is an edging round towards getting back to that one true propitious and permanent home.

Impulse and direction are obvious in *Lady Appledore's Mésalliance*.[1] Wildred is dispossessed of home and income; he shifts to the setting of

---
[1] Cf. Chapter X, 5 and 6.

Lady Appledore's garden – which becomes, by virtue of his marriage, his home and the seat of his income.

Lady Appledore's Mésalliance is Firbank's rewriting of the Christian myth. Man is expelled from the garden of Eden (where money grows on trees and an income drops into his Arcadian lap) but becomes, by conversion, qualified to regain it in the form of paradise.

In his fully Firbankian fictions Firbank has converted the blatantly wish-fulfilling fantasy at the end of that story into an impulse of imaginative art.

Paradise no longer appears as a place or state in the fiction. Firbank became increasingly sceptical of its existence as he increasingly furnished his books with, and spoke through the images of, high ecclesiastical camp. He ceased to believe in Catholicism because he was himself inventing it.

The idea of paradise, taken out of the fiction, has been transformed into the fiction itself. Inventing the beauty and permanence of the book, Firbank has created paradise.

Concerning the Eccentricities of Cardinal Pirelli, Firbank's last completed book, published after his death, is his Firbankian rewriting of the proto-Firbankian *Lady Appledore's Mésalliance*.

The shift of locale (which is now structurally used, to create the baroque spaciousness into which Firbank explodes the book's themes) is again to a garden. The garden of Cardinal Pirelli's retreat, however, belongs to 'the disestablished and, *sic transit*, slowly decaying monastery of the Desierto'.

Firbank's Catholic faith was long disestablished, and he sets the Cardinal to reflect explicitly on the transitoriness and slow decay of Christianity. ('It looked as though Mother Church, like Venus or Diana, was making way in due turn for the beliefs that should follow: "and we shall begin again with intolerance, martyrdom and converts", the Cardinal ruminated, pausing before an ancient fresco depicting the eleven thousand virgins, or as many as there was room for.')

It is the garden of the Desierto which is[1] 'Lovely as Paradise, oppressive perhaps as Eden'. Firbank's text confesses that the original Eden at Chislehurst was stifling. (Firbank had become sceptical of its perfection because he was himself re-creating it.) It is the paradise of Firbank's book which is – by all his devices for introducing space – aerated.

12. 'I am all design'

BY necessity, because he did not expect to live long, Firbank was not only strategist but grand strategist. The structure of his œuvre as a whole is,

---

[1] as I quoted at the beginning of Chapter XV, 12.

however, organic, not artistic. Almost each of his books contains a thematic trailer for the next. Because he was so short of time, Firbank made a rigorously systematic exploitation of the material he found deposited in his mind.

The same terrible pressure of time which made him systematic in his private literary life obliged him, in each work, to economic design and, as part of his economy, to a reliance on design as an incarnation in itself of his meaning and his imagery.

It was a factual description of himself as an artist which he gave when he wrote, in a letter of 1924, 'I am all design.'

Urgently mortal, he was driven to design immortal structures. Startled and startlingly, Cardinal Pirelli reflects in and of his cathedral: 'the great fane (after all) was nothing but a cage; God's cage; the cage of God! . . .'

God can be caged. Firbank, like his Cardinal, can and will die. The baroque-cathedral structures of Firbank's books are the cages of Firbank's immortality.

13. Notes to Chapter XVI

FIRBANK'S 1916 letter about capitals and dots is quoted in the *Biography*, p. 146.

His adoration of italics is reported by Siegfried Sassoon in *Siegfried's Journey 1916–1920*, p. 136.

'Isn't that one of Ronald Firbank's books?' is asked on p. 532 in the *Complete* Firbank.

The passing of schoolgirls and demons through *The Artificial Princess*, which I quoted in Chapter X, 1, comes on pp. 45–6 in the *Complete* Firbank, the Ponte di Sospiri on p. 165.

Barkers', Selfridge's, etc. are on p. 572 in the *Complete* Firbank, where the value of Niri-Esther's conversion is computed on p. 467 and p. 471, and the Bishop's Brahma remark is on p. 147.

Siegfried Sassoon's report about Lotus land is in *Siegfried's Journey 1916–1920*, p. 136.

Vyvyan Holland recorded Firbank's ambition of publishing his complete works in his contribution to the *Memoir*, p. 111.

Mrs Shamefoot sighs for her pyramid on p. 87, the spiked garters (which I quoted in Chapter XV, 19) are spoken of on p. 464, and the Acropolis has old associations (in *Inclinations*) on p. 251, in the *Complete* Firbank.

Siegfried Sassoon reported being misled on p. 137 of *Siegfried's Journey 1916–1920*.

Firbank's counterattack on the belief that he lacked design is quoted in the *Biography*, p. 258, from a letter.

The gardens of the monastery are described on p. 675, and Cardinal Pirelli reflects on the transitoriness of Christianity on p. 679, in the *Complete* Firbank.

Firbank's 'I am all design' letter (which I quoted in Chapter V, 5) is quoted in the *Biography*, p. 155.

God is caged on p. 697 in the *Complete* Firbank.

XVII

Mauve into Fauve (More Devices of Firbankian Baroque)

1. Mauve into Fauve

NAKEDLY baroque as a putto's bottom, and yet already jouncing in the rhythms of jazz, *Vainglory* emerged in 1915 – and with it 20th-century fiction.

What it emerged *from* were the pale mauve delicacies of the fin-de-siècle: the lavender-bag moral conventionalisms of Oscar Wilde in his sentimentalist, melodramatist or sheer tripehound mood, according to which 'vice' was something treasured by a spinster in a drawer marked Nameless; the flora-and-fauna flutings of Maeterlinck; the chiffon simplicities (the simplicities of a window-dresser with an earnest message) of Puvis de Chavannes, the Maeterlinck of painting.

Firbankianism emerged by the same impulse towards 20th-century-ness which transformed impressionist painting (an attempt on the extremes of naturalism, a snatch, made through delicate nuances of scotch mist, at fidelity to things' appearance at a given instant) into the tropical tapestries of Gauguin and the near-eastern miniatures[1] on a bold scale of Matisse.

It was a revolution made not by rejecting previous (and often in themselves revolutionary) themes but by adopting them and turning them round to face in the opposite direction.

Beardsley was bouncily proud to receive, in 1893, 'great encouragement from Puvis de Chavannes'. Yet Beardsley had already twisted the tails of Puvis de Chavannes's nightshirts into baroque swags and had devised, as he said, 'quite a new world of my own creation', in which 'The subjects were quite mad and a little indecent', consisting of 'Strange hermaphroditic creatures wandering about in Pierrot costumes or modern dress'.

Picasso borrowed from Puvis de Chavannes the sweet-pea colours and the sweetness of mood in which his blue and pink personages wander about (or

[1] 'On a dark canvas screen were grouped some inconceivably delicate Persian miniatures' (*Vainglory*; *Complete* Firbank, p. 75).

droop) in *their* modern-Pierrot costumes. And then he turned (or twisted) his sweet personages round and displayed their 'primitive' (frequently African) face.

In *Vainglory* itself, Mrs Shamefoot, picknicking ('Mrs. Shamefoot re-helped herself to Clicquot') on Totterdown station (or, structurally considered, camping out on the bridge passage between *Vainglory*'s two locales[1]), is 'looking to-day incomparably well, draped in a sort of large sheet *à la* Puvis de Chavannes,[2] with a large, lonely hat suggestive of *Der Wanderer*'.

By 1916 Firbank had adopted Gauguin:[3] by 1917 and *Caprice*, his personages are 'pirouetting to a nigger band', which plays 'wild rag-time with passages of almost Wesleyan hymnishness – reminiscent of Georgia gospel-missions; the eighteenth century in the Dutch East Indies'. ...

(This reminiscence is also a prediction: of *The New Rythum* and *Prancing Nigger* and perhaps even of Firbank's East/West Indian confusion.)

Jazz became to Firbank what Negro masks were to Picasso.

Indeed, in celebration of *Prancing Nigger* (a book which Firbank described as 'purposely a little "primitive", rather like a Gauguin in painting' and which contains 'The latest jazz, bewildering, glittering, exuberant as the soil, a jazz, throbbing, pulsating, with a zim, zim, zim, a jazz all abandon and verve'), Lord Berners, thinking he heard the arrival of Firbank, whom he was expecting for luncheon in Rome, experienced 'a sudden impulse [. . .] to put on a Negro Mask and surprise him by appearing at one of the windows'.

(Lord Berners in fact merely frightened a passing small boy off his bicycle – to no harm, but to the collecting of a crowd, into which Firbank presently arrived. Told the history, Firbank said, 'That will teach him to concentrate in future.')

Jazz, however, only underlined and coloured Firbank's rhythms. His tactics were syncopated from the start, thanks to the French placing of his adverbs: he was already holding back the beat in order to create a pause of aeration: he was himself writing a French-based patois in English before he coloured it Negro and invented Negro mouths and Mouths to put it in.

How to syncopate his strategy (through the unexpected, exotic, incongruous expressive and revelatory emphases in his treatment of his themes) Firbank learned by re-sorting his originally fin-de-siècle subject-matter. By holding faster than Wilde had done to Wilde's aesthetic, Firbank turned

---

[1] Cf. Chapter XVI, 5.
[2] The first edition (pp. 77–8), very likely by Firbank's doing, leaves the *s* off *Chavannes* and the central *c* out of *Clicquot*.
[3] Cf. Chapter IX, 11 and the black woman whom Miss O'Brookomore in *Inclinations* 'called a *Gauguin*'.

Wilde's wit against Wilde's melodrama, transformed both, and created a 20th-century baroque.

2. The Two Voices

THE two stories in the pamphlet-thin volume which Firbank, aged 19, published in 1905 speak through the two personae of Oscar Wilde.

A Study in Temperament studiously mimicks Wilde the wit. The very temperament it studies is the artificial one (later given to Claud Harvester) which creates itself (or in a significant pun makes itself up) by obeying Wilde's 'The first duty in life is to be as artificial as possible.'[1]

Lady Agnes Charters[2] is noted ('It is so nice', the text Wildeanly notes, 'to be noted for something!') for her golden hair – which (in a tribute yet more Wildean to make-up) 'her women friends charitably attributed to Art'. Lady Agnes reads (or at least hopes to be surprised reading) Maeterlinck and receives four persons for afternoon tea: Mrs Corba (a proto-Firbankian rearrangement of cobra[3]), who introduces the first published of Firbank's flower people (' "I have brought Lobelia", remarked Mrs. Corba, standing aside to show her daughter'); an American 'poetess' named, by an Anglo-French pun on queue, Miss Hester Q. Tail, who betrays herself for an intellectual nouveau-riche by scintillating like a Wilde adventuress in a blaze of near-Wildean near-aphorisms ('modern life is only remarkable for its want of profile,[4] and lack of manners'); and Lord Sevenoaks,[5] who invites his hostess to run away with him.

(Lady Agnes admits to not being happy with her husband but Wildeanly adds: 'but then, so few women are – at least, in our set'.)

By the end of the evening and the tale (on which Miss Tail may further be a pun), Lady Agnes has shelved answering her suitor but has decided to make up her temperament and her person yet more fiercely (' "Yes, I shall certainly dye my hair red", she said'[6]), and the influence of Wilde the sentimentalist has obtruded only once.

---

[1] Cf. Chapter XIV, 8.   [2] whose name I discussed in Chapter X, 12.

[3] Of the Baroness Rudlieb the narrative of *The Artificial Princess* reports (p. 29 in the *Complete* Firbank): ' "She is so splendidly feminine," the Courtiers would say. "What fastidious joie de vivre!" "She is a Cobra", thought her maid, who understood her to perfection.'

[4] Lobelia, who (as Chapter VIII, 1 mentioned) is a self-portrait or self-profile of Firbank's, 'didn't like the remark about profiles. Lobelia had no profile' . . .

[5] Cf. Chapter VI, 6.

[6] That Firbank closed the story (and indeed his first book as a whole) on 'red'–'said' is another (cf. Chapter XV, 3) instance of his ear's being not much troubled by rhymes in his prose.

He enters, indeed, as a shadow of the twist to the pathetic fallacy (in which Wilde simply, and typically, replaced nature by art) which is the donnée of *The Picture of Dorian Gray*. Firbank leaves Lord Sevenoaks unanswered beside, precisely, a picture: the 'mystical Madonna' whose eyelids, wearied with the sins and sorrows of the whole world, were a gift to Firbank from Wilde's predecessor and enemy in Firbank's literary life, Rollo St Clair Talboys.[1] (The gift included the colour of the madonna's hair, which is pitched between the two states of Lady Agnes's. It is 'red-gold'.) After Lady Agnes has unsatisfyingly drifted away from Lord Sevenoaks, 'The Madonna looked down on him from the wall, and her eyes seemed to dim with tears!'

By contrast, Firbank's other 1905 story, which stands first in the volume,[2] despatches its heroine to *her* appointment with the madonna quite thoroughly and blatantly under the patronage of Wilde's sentimental mood – and it keeps the rendezvous under the scarlet cloak of Wilde the melodramatist.

The 'innocence' of Odette d'Antrevernes, who eavesdrops adult conversation (from, which is probably significant,[3] bed) but doesn't truly understand it, probably[4] commemorates Firbank's own nine-year-old's incomprehension of adult references to the Wilde scandal.

Odette herself might be older or younger than nine. One of the most displeasing, Walt-Disneyish tricks the story practises is to try to win the reader to what it describes as Odette's 'pretty baby voice' while preventing any precision in the reader's guesswork about how babyish a baby she is – a half-repressed metaphor, perhaps, of an ambiguity in Firbank himself (an ambiguity about sex expressed, via the theme of sexual 'innocence', as an ambiguity about age[5]) and a symptom of his pre-Firbankian unease in projecting himself as a little girl, albeit a pious, French and aristocratic little girl.

Odette more easily understands stories designed for children: 'the Curé [. . .] would tell little Odette beautiful stories about the Saints and the Virgin Mary.' From the curé's stories Odette picks herself a saintly exemplar and makes the resolve: 'She too, like little Bernadette, would speak with the Holy Mary.'

---

[1] Cf. Chapter XIII, 5.
[2] Indeed, it stood alone in the large-paper printing, and was to do so again in the 1916 republication.
[3] Cf. Chapter XV, 20.
[4] Cf. Chapter XI, 1.
[5] Indeed, Firbank's story tacitly practises about its heroine's age some of the coyness which Firbank later practised about his own on Carl Van Vechten and which Firbank learned not from the writings but from the life of Oscar Wilde (cf. Chapter V, 6).

Firbank had already picked *his* saintly exemplar. For his story about a child (who probably represents his childhood self in relation to Wilde), he took as pattern those of Wilde's writings that were designed for (or partly for) children. It is the (more effective because more artificial) simplicity of Wilde's fairy-tale idiom that Firbank is trying to catch in the coarse trap of arranging for both his heroine and her pattern-saint to bear names ending in the diminutive -ette, a diminutive Firbank further shrinks with his label 'little'.

On uncomfortable tiptoe Firbank's narrative conducts its ambiguously 'baby' heroine, who believes she is on her way to meet the madonna, to a further test of her innocence. It ushers her by night into the château garden, pauses (in a counterpart to Lady Agnes's reading Maeterlinck) to animate some flowers with human and pious feelings,[1] and then leads Odette to a woman who is lying weeping on the grass.

Odette at first assumes that the visitor must be the madonna, but she turns out to be a prostitute – or, as Firbank puts it, in Wilde's most creakingly absinthe-soaked tones, a 'sad wreck of a human soul', with 'painted cheeks and flaming hair' and a 'terrible expression' in her 'dreadful eyes'.

The prostitute suffers 'a frenzy of mad laughter' that presently turns into 'terrible sobs'. It is now the prostitute's turn to mistake Odette's identity. She takes her first, because of her nightdress and bare feet, for a fellow prostitute ('You've begun early, my dear!') (but quite *how* early?) and presently for an angel.

Odette has made the second mistake virtually inevitable, because (to the prostitute's 'Who are you?') 'Odette in her baby voice whispered back, "I have been sent by the Holy Virgin to make you well." '

And indeed Odette, by her coincidental arrival, performs the office of an angel. It turns out that the prostitute was on the point of throwing herself into the Loire. Odette goes on to perform a near-miracle. After their conversation, the prostitute promises: 'I am going to try and find work – honest work'.

(The difference between the two stories is that Miss Hester Q. Tail speaks in the accents of a Wilde adventuress, the prostitute in *Odette D'Antrevernes* in those of a Wilde adventuress repentant.)

Odette's quasi-miracle is achieved, presumably, by grace of her 'innocence'. She returns to the château still ignorant of what her interlocutrix's previous

[1] (Cf. Chapter XV, 2); 'she picked a great bouquet of flowers to offer to the Virgin. Some of the flowers were sleeping as she picked them, and Odette thought, with a little thrill of delight, at' (sic) 'their joy on awakening and finding themselves on the Holy Mother's breast.' (Odette still thinks *at* the flowers' joy in the revised text of 1916 given [cf. Chapter VI, 6] in the *Complete* Firbank.)

work *was* but feeling 'somehow changed' by the realisation that 'Life was cruel, Life was sad.'

3. 'Exquisite Feeling & Beauty'

FIRBANK'S later attitude to the twaddle of *Odette D'Antrevernes* was ambivalent.

He chose to revise the story (though he didn't and couldn't revise the twaddle out of it) and to republish it in 1916, by which time the story was eleven years old and from its manner suspect, like its heroine, of being older, whereas Firbank had demonstrated himself, by publishing *Vainglory* and *Inclinations*,[1] to have meanwhile become a Firbankian and modern artist.

Yet though he republished it Firbank didn't thrust the story, either published or republished, on his acquaintance's attention. His Cambridge acquaintance, of course, remembered[2] the halo of kudos which the original publication had set on the undergraduate Firbank. But Osbert Sitwell, whom Firbank met[3] within a couple of years of putting his baby heroine back into print, adds, to his mention[4] of Firbank's 1905 volume, the firm footnote: 'Firbank often in later years talked to me about his work, but never for one moment did he mention this book. He had always given me to understand that *Vainglory* was his first published volume.'

One of Firbank's reasons for republishing *Odette* was undoubtedly the reason (or excuse) he gave Carl Van Vechten, namely his wish to please his mother – to whom he dedicated the republication and who found in the story 'exquisite feeling & beauty'.

Perhaps when she did so Lady Firbank was reading through the manifest (and twaddling) content to the unconscious content and there perceiving a compliment to herself. For even without its later dedication the story is an act of devotion by Firbank to his mother. Indeed, when you add, to the theme of *Odette D'Antrevernes*, the slightly gratuitous, guest-star appearance of the madonna in *A Study in Temperament*, Firbank's first-published volume as a whole looks a singular tribute to (mythologically) the madonna and (psychologically) the mother.

In particular, *Odette D'Antrevernes* commemorates and would like to undo the first of the exclusions Firbank suffered, the universal experience of being excluded from the mother's breast at weaning. Firbank is not only

[1] According to the *Bibliography*, *Inclinations* was published in the June of 1916 and the revised *Odette* in the December.
[2] Cf. Chapters XII, 4 and XV, 17.
[3] Cf. Chapter XV, 16.
[4] in his contribution to the *Memoir* (p. 121).

Odette. He is also (in the first of his flower impersonations) the sleeping flower which Odette picks and which would experience such joy if it awoke to find itself 'on the Holy Mother's breast'.

The ultimate source of Firbank's narrative's slipperiness on the subject of Odette's age is Firbank's guilty suspicion that he was a touch old to be a suckling.

Amalgamating the French imperial past of Chislehurst with his experience of Touraine,[1] Firbank has refashioned The Coopers, Chislehurst, into a château on the Loire. That is a social promotion for his family, but he has not simply converted his mother (already half-crowned, in her court dress and new title, at the real-life coronation of 1902[2]) into a French aristocrat. Pointedly, Odette is an orphan. (The story has translated the withdrawal of the mother's breast as the withdrawal of the mother toute entière.) Odette-Firbank does not adventure by night outside the security of Château Coopers except in hope of recovering a yet greater security which she once had but lost. The story offers Lady Firbank the very highest promotion: from the dignity of mother to that of 'the Holy Mother'.

(The same stroke tacitly, of course, promotes her child. Odette's getting herself, fairly intentionally, mistaken for an angel was the first manifestation of that canonising and transvesting line of self-portraiture which led Firbank to urge, through the Archbishop of Cuna-Cuna:[3] 'Imagine the world, my friends, had Christ been born a girl.')

4. A Weep on the Grass

FIRBANK republished *Odette* as a gesture, consciously, of his unbroken loyalty to his mother. But I think the republication was also a gesture towards re-establishing his loyalty to his literary adoptive father, a loyalty which had, between the publication of the story in 1905 and its republication in 1916, been broken.

Firbank was finally weaned two years after the original publication: when, in 1907, he was expelled from The Coopers.

His first weaning made him, as *Odette D'Antrevernes* demonstrates, susceptible to the madonna-myth of Catholicism. His final weaning, which cut him off from the French-Catholic myth of Chislehurst (Eugénie for madonna-empress), made him a Catholic.

Firbank became in 1907 an Odette who could no longer return to the château, though he accomplished a return in wish by writing *Lady Appledore's Mésalliance*.

[1] Cf. Chapter X, 9 and 10.   [2] Cf. Chapter X, 8.   [3] Cf. Chapter XV, 18.

That story, because it contradicts the argument of a novel by the priest who received him,[1] was an early sign of Firbank's refusal to accept the Catholic church as a final and satisfactory substitute for The inaccessible Coopers. At the same time, the story indicated where Firbank had transferred his loyalty: Firbank wrote into it the articles[2] of his apprenticeship to Oscar Wilde.

In 1910, however, Firbank became an Odette half-orphaned in real life. His father's death obliged Firbank to re-make his relation to his literary master and adoptive father, Wilde.[3] He responded by attacking Wilde the melodramatist: by, that is, writing *The Artificial Princess* (alias *Salome, Or 'Tis A Pity That She Would*), in which he outdid Wilde by treating Firbankianly Wilde's theme of Salome.

Salome's situation was, because Firbank had taken Wilde to himself as a stepfather, Firbank's own psychological situation.[4]

In the course of outdoing Wilde in treating that situation, Firbank stole one of Wilde's jokes.[5] Firbank, who dreaded being stolen from because he apprehended it as a filching-away of his own life,[6] no doubt interpreted the theft on his own part as an act of assassination against Wilde.

He appeased Wilde's ghost by not publishing *The Artificial Princess*. He did, however, publish later Firbankian works whose Firbankianness he had created in *The Artificial Princess* by acts of literary assassination on Wilde. Perhaps in 1916 Firbank was taken (as he was again towards the end of his life) by a wish to publish *The Artificial Princess* – and beat it down by, instead, republishing *Odette*.

He didn't republish *A Study in Temperament* (though it is, albeit a more blatantly imitative, a more accomplished work). He had no need to. He had never quarrelled with Wilde the wit. He offered Wilde amends by republishing on its own the story in which he had paid to Wilde the sentimental melodramatist the tribute of tumbling into every soggy or bathetic pit left by Wilde's careless progress.

Perhaps he was offering Wilde more than amends. The prostitute in *Odette D'Antrevernes* is one of the moods of the temperament of Lady Agnes in *A Study in Temperament*. The prostitute has 'flaming hair' and 'painted cheeks'. Lady Agnes has gold hair which she decides further to inflame, and 'Lord Sevenoaks looked from the painted face of the Madonna to the painted face of Lady Agnes.'

Lady Agnes's temperament Firbank presently admitted to be his own, by giving it to his open self-portrait as Claud Harvester. Perhaps the republica-

---

[1] Cf. Chapter X, 6. [2] Cf. Chapter XIV, 11. [3] Cf. Chapter XIII, 6.
[4] Cf. Chapter XIV, 5. [5] Cf. Chapter XIII, 3. [6] Cf. Chapter VII, 3.

tion of *Odette* admitted that the temperament of the prostitute was likewise Firbank's. (Firbank takes most of the major rôles in the story – heroine, flower [which in Firbank is always a major rôle], prostitute – leaving Lady Firbank the rôle only of the dea ex machina who never actually appears and who may or may not be supposed to have brought the whole happening about.)

The prostitute in *Odette D'Antrevernes* is Firbank's minion self[1] – who perhaps forever remained, from a worldly point of view, incomprehensible to his child self: Odette never understood what the adults were saying about the Wilde trials, but only that 'Life was cruel' and society was given to putting homosexuals in prison. The minion's cheeks are painted (or powdered) as a signal to Oscar Wilde, and in 1916 he *again* flung himself on the grass weeping because Oscar Wilde, whom he had assassinated, had still not come out of the château to accost him.

5. Trailers

FIRBANK'S first volume, like most of Firbank's volumes,[2] contains trailers for his œuvre to come.

The first volume's trailers are discernible, however, only by hindsight. Stylistically, both stories scream 'Wilde'. But no one could have predicted that five years later Firbank would be beating up Wildeanism so thoroughly as to refashion it into Firbankianism.

The refashioning was of style and structure, tactics and strategy. It was a revolution in the 20th-century artistic manner,[3] in which the subject-matter stayed constant. For there the subject-matter already is in the first volume, but latent and barely recognisable because it is not yet disclosed down the structural avenues of a Firbankian baroque design.

Lady Agnes Charters makes herself up as she goes along. Odette resolves to pattern herself on Saint Bernadette. Between them they point directly towards *The Artificial Princess*, in which the Princess renders herself truly artificial by making up her own life-pattern, on the model of the Wildean and New Testament personage of Salome, as the book goes along.

The 1905 trailers point also beyond *The Artificial Princess*: to *Vainglory*, the book which makes itself up, by enshrining and making a cult of its own fragmentary method in a rediscovered fragment of Sappho, and by being *about* itself (under its pseudonym, *Vaindreams*); to Firbank's cult of Wilde

---

[1] Cf. Chapters VIII, 2 and XIV, 10. [2] Cf. Chapter XVI, 12.
[3] Cf. sub-section 1 of this chapter.

and his personages' cult of other heretical saints; to the hagiographical form of *The Flower Beneath the Foot*.

That Firbank would work out his treatment of those adumbrated themes in a book taking the form and using the material of, precisely, *The Artificial Princess* is signalled in both the tales in his 1905 volume.

Indeed, *The Artificial Princess*, in frustrating the Princess's wish to re-create herself as Salome, follows exactly the same narrative-outline as *Odette D'Antrevernes*. The skeleton of both stories is that the heroine makes an appointment with one person and keeps it with another.

Odette plans to meet the madonna in the footsteps of Saint Bernadette. That the Princess would plan to meet *her* quarry, the Baptist-surrogate, in the biblical footsteps of Salome is signalled in the other 1905 story, *A Study in Temperament*. (The signal is put into the mouth of Lobelia, who thereby shews herself to be a self-sketch by Firbank in the matter not only of floralness and profile[1] but of propensity to cult.) ' "I should have loved to have lived in the Bible period", said Lobelia religiously. "How beautiful to have followed the Saints",[2] Lobelia was engaged to a clergyman.'

6. The Aeration of Irony

Odette D'Antrevernes and *The Artificial Princess* have the same plot but place on it different emphases.

Their difference is the difference between fin-de-sièclism and Firbankianness.

Odette means to meet the madonna and meets her (by the scale of conventional morals) exact opposite. The irony is symmetrical, tidily packaged and entirely, indeed, *dependent* on conventional morals: if the reader questions the moral conventions, the irony vanishes.

Firbank learned the entire package from Wilde's commercially packaged anecdotes: from the story of Wilde's, for instance, whose hardly more than verbal irony symmetrically contrasts 'millionaire model' with 'model millionaire' (the joke Firbank borrowed and gave to Lord Orkish, thereby labelling him a portrait of Wilde),[3] a story whose irony depends on its accepting the conventional distribution of money and snob-status in defiance of Wilde's own moral socialism.

In theme *Odette D'Antrevernes* is even closer to an anecdote which Wilde

---

[1] Cf. sub-section 2 of this chapter.
[2] The reprint in *The New Rythum and Other Pieces* substitutes for this comma an exclamation mark at the end of Lobelia's speech, presumably in the belief (which may, however, flatter Firbank) that the comma in the first edition is a misprint.
[3] Cf. Chapter XIV, 10.

eventually began to make into a play but which he also told by word of mouth to several of his acquaintance. His auditors included Robert Hichens, who not long afterwards discovered Wilde's story to be the theme of 'the famous romance, *Thaïs*, by Anatole France', though Wilde had given Hichens 'no hint that it had ever been treated by another, or that it had perhaps been founded on or suggested by a legend'.

Firbank later marked in his fiction[1] that he, too, had made the discovery that Wilde's theme had 'been treated by another'.

The story that was passing as Wilde's concerned an Alexandrian prostitute who tries to win over an early Christian desert anchorite to sensuality, while he, arguing back, tries to convert her to asceticism : both attempted conversions succeed, and the two characters symmetrically swop rôles.

Wilde gave his anecdote (and the play he began to write on its theme) a title: *La Sainte Courtisane*. If Firbank's quest for Wilde brought the title to his knowledge before 1905, the title itself, detached from the story's content (which may have been less accessible), perhaps formed the donnée of *Odette D'Antrevernes*. Firbank's courtesan is 'sainte' inasmuch as she appears in the place which Odette expects to be occupied by the madonna. The tale, which embodies Firbank's childish puzzling over the sexual problem presented by Wilde, was perhaps the answer Firbank's fantasy supplied when he tried to decipher the paradox of Wilde's title and puzzle out how a courtisane could be sainte.

(By November 1907 Firbank's quest for Wilde had taken him to Vyvyan Holland's 21st-birthday dinner,[2] where he met Charles Ricketts and became in a position to know that, when Ricketts asked Wilde in 1895 how his play on the Sainte Courtisane theme was going, Wilde replied that the courtesan 'continues to say wonderful things, but the Anchorite always remains mute. I admit her words are quite unanswerable. I think I shall have to indicate his replies by stars or asterisks.' Perhaps Firbank received the reported words as Wilde's blessing on Firbank's system of speaking punctuation.)

The symmetrical Wildean irony whereby *Odette D'Antrevernes* inexorably conducts its reader to the single pre-determined point of the story is, in *The Artificial Princess*, opened out to create a design that encloses space – space which Firbank infuses with the atmosphere of uncertainty. The Princess sends an invitation that bids St John Pellegrin[3] to her party: at her party she welcomes not the opposite of a saint but a young man related to the expected saint at a tangent, a merely rather Rupert Brookeish young man ('She was surprised, and not displeased, to notice that he wore a Gardenia in his

---

[1] as Chapter XVIII, 4 will mention.   [2] Cf. Chapter XII, 5.
[3] whose name I remarked on in Chapter XV, 17.

buttonhole, and that his hair – a dusky gold – seemed decidedly waved') who, in his well-mannered turn ('he kissed her hand'), seems, though surprised, not displeased by her Baptist-alluding conversation: ' "When I knew you were coming I wired for Lampreys; I thought they might tempt you. What is a Lamprey? Well, really I scarcely know; surely a sort of *Locust*", she enquired with a searching look.'

The Princess's mistake turns not, like Odette's, on 'innocence' but on ignorance, an ignorance deliberately induced in the Princess by her messenger the Baroness Rudlieb, who fails to confess that she has failed to deliver the Princess's invitation. The Baroness, however, has been led astray from her mission by the devil himself. One of Firbank's methods of opening up the irony is to extend his pattern into a black and baroquely thunderclouded dimension of the supernatural: he replaces by images and personages the merely conceptual and grossly sentimental ambiguity whereby *Odette D'Antrevernes* leaves it uncertain whether it is chance or the supernatural agency of the madonna that has brought Odette so opportunely to the prostitute's redemption.

Whichever the agency, *Odette D'Antrevernes* has patly manipulated everything for the (conventionally judged) best. *The Artificial Princess* thrusts its ambiguity beyond the borders of the book, dazzling the reader after he has finished by the problem of *how* the Princess intends to wreak the fate of John the Baptist on her unknowing captive-guest. Firbank has introduced into the substance of the work the effect of suspended menace which, on a lesser scale, he maps by his punctuation with dots. His supreme aeration device is to aerate his own irony.

7. Concerto Form

WHEN he broke up the constricting symmetry of his subject-matter and the narrowness of its point, Firbank became free to invest his talent for symmetry in his design.

The business of *The Artificial Princess* is transacted in a day, the Princess's birthday. The book is a book of hours,[1] aching through its richly and arthistorically[2] furnished spaces towards the culminating birthday party. It is a concerto (the Princess the solo instrument, laying down the themes and the tone of even the passages from which she is absent) in the three beautifully paced and counterbalanced movements of early afternoon; high afternoon to dusk; and night.

[1] And indeed, soon after the beginning of the second section, 'In a corner of the tram sat a Priest, reading a Book of Hours'. . . .   [2] Cf. Chapter IX, 6.

The first movement[1] is set in the Palace. The Princess enunciates (to the Baroness) the dominating theme of the book: the resemblance between her family situation and Salome's, and her own imperative will to fashion the resemblance into an identification. The Princess's will persuades the Baroness to undertake the necessary errand, and the Baroness is sent off bearing the birthday-party invitation which is meant to draw the chosen John the Baptist into his slot in the nexus. Alone, the Princess steps on to a balcony and is startled by the passing, through the texture of this first section, of a motif premonitory of the next: 'a bird skimmed past her with a satin quilt'. (The Princess's grandmother, like a gargoyle on the floor above, calls down: 'My dear, [. . .] did you notice that irregular looking bird? I'm afraid it means *we are about to have a War*.')

In a four-line coda, separated by asterisks from the body of the first movement, the Princess takes her first step towards establishing herself as a Salome to the Herod played by the King, and again Firbank lends to the statement of a structurally vital theme the italics of emphasis: 'Ten minutes later the whole palace was in an uproar. The Princess had commanded a Warm[2] bath à la reine de Saba,[3] and before she had it, she wished to *speak with the King*.'

The second movement accomplishes the Firbankian shift of locale[4] – and, a further aeration, the Firbankian opening-up of the supernatural dimension.

The second movement follows (andante – it is all 'wrapt in summer haze') the Baroness's excursion: from 'the Platz under the Linden trees' by white omnibus to the Flower Market ('with its lazy fountain designed from an early drawing of Verrocchio'), and thence by the blue tram to the Barrier, the outer-limit, evidently, of the city, since, when the Baroness descends, 'How lovely it was to be in the Country again!!'

But it also turns out that 'the Princess had looked at an old time-table'; if her messenger is to deliver the invitation to the prophet, she must board yet a third conveyance, the pink tram.

(Firbank has extrapolated the colours of his trams from the colours of tram tickets: evocative synecdoche.)

Because she has been persuaded into a clandestine mission, the Baroness is from the outset subject to guilt.

Indeed her guilt and her reluctance are the suck-back of the onward and impetuous wave represented by the Princess's will. The Baroness's theme is the Princess's theme played backwards.

---

[1] The first edition names the three sections chapters; the *Complete* Firbank merely numbers them.   [2] The capital letter is the first edition's.
[3] Cf. Chapter XIV, 2.   [4] Cf. Chapter XVI, 5.

At each interchange on her strangely jointed journey the Baroness goes in fear of being spotted: by, she thinks most probable, the Queen, who might at any moment drive past in pursuit of her eccentric passion for motoring.

As the Baroness proceeds and changes vehicle, Firbank plays hide-and-seek with her fears, letting events fall on her in syncopated stresses, a fraction of a beat before or beyond her expectations.

At her first stop, the Flower Market, 'the Queen was nowhere in sight'. There passes, however, though again not in sight, a motif that takes up the demonic premonition that skimmed across the first movement: the invisible 'escort of Nuns, and fantastic Demons' that accompanies the girls' school.

That passing is succeeded by a visible and flesh-and-blood passing. In her horsedrawn painted coach, the Mistress of the Robes rumbles by: seen by the Baroness but unable to see her, by virtue of a hat whose size precludes the turning of the wearer's head.

Besides, the Mistress of the Robes is in a hurry, already late for 'a last rehearsal of her play': her quick, intent, noisy passage drags across the second movement a snatch of the material of the third.

The Baroness continues her mission. At her next stop, in open country, she is yet more vulnerable to being seen – and she *is* seen, but not according to expectation, and not by any of the dramatis personae of the court (or not, anyway, of her familiar court). The warning scribbled across the first movement by the 'irregular looking bird' and invisibly reiterated by the demons is fulfilled by the devil in his disguise of a crow (or Crowley).[1] In the upper dimension, he wheels above the Baroness: 'he plucked a feather from his breast and willed . . .'

She, in the earthly dimension, becomes 'impatient for the pink tram' and increasingly afraid that a passing car will contain the Queen.

In her panic of guilt the Baroness is almost run over by one of the passing cars, which stops just in time and proves to be bearing Max, 'a young man whom her husband had often sworn to kill'.

Not until the Baroness, still reluctantly (indeed, 'all willingly-unwillingly like a creature in a Rape'[2]), has been persuaded to entrust herself to Max, and delivery of the Princess's invitation to Max's chauffeur, is there 'a flash of diamonds, and the Queen whirled by in a cloud of dust'.

The Baroness continues her excursion in Max's car. As the afternoon haze declines and the time that should have been used to the fulfilment of the Princess's pattern is lost, Firbank again invokes a book of hours: in the course of the guilty Baroness's invoking[3] of her 'pet saint', Aurora Vauvilliers,

[1] Cf. Chapter VIII, 6.   [2] Cf. Chapter XV, 6.
[3] Cf. Chapter XIII, 2.

whose 'adventurous history' includes setting sail 'one languid summer evening with just a faithful maid and a Book of Hours . . .'

Driven through what has become indeed a languid evening, followed by the crow, calling (at a glimpse of a goat and in satire, perhaps, on the pagan whimsies of early E. M. Forster[1]) 'Stop, stop [. . .] I think I see Pan', the Baroness is taken by Max to 'an old haunted Inn'. Dusk becomes night; Max and the Baroness sit down to dinner; the second movement drifts towards the Baroness's resignation[2] to not expecting 'to enjoy these adventures much at *the time*' . . .

Then, with a sharp cut to the previous locale ('Far off, in the Palace' . . .) Firbank gives the second movement *its* coda. The Princess is dancing her version of Salome's dance as a private tarantella, having already made her next move as Salome in relation to the King – though this time her move is folded into a subordinate clause[3] ('the Princess, who had obtained the King's word, that she might ask, during dessert, for anything she pleased'), since the Baroness and the devil have already rendered the fulfilment of the Salome pattern less likely.

The last movement returns to the setting of the first – or, rather, to its Firbankian annexe, the Palace gardens, transformed into 'a City of Flowers, and Lights'. The movement is a scherzo – indeed a party: the garden-party by night which celebrates the Princess's birthday and incidentally commemorates[4] the birthday of Wilde's Infanta. The scherzo proceeds rapidly, decoratively and with full orchestration: the pomp of the court, the scandals and intrigues of courtiers, the fragmented chatter of the concourse, and the performance of the presaged play whose author holds the position at court of Mistress of the Robes.

(Was it an unrecognised memory of Firbank's novel that made Virginia Woolf [Lilian Bloater[5]] reassemble Firbank's syllables and name the author of *her* open-air play, in *Between the Acts*,[6] Miss La Trobe?)

Through the party noise the reader has almost to seek the bassoon notes of the Baroness's guilt, as she insinuates herself inconspicuously into the

---

[1] Firbank was probably (cf. Chapter XIII, 6) composing *The Artificial Princess* when E. M. Forster published his stories about a faun in Wiltshire and about the enchanting of an English boy in Italy by Pan (whose footsteps the narrator mistakes for a goat's). *The Celestial Omnibus* appeared as a volume in March 1911, the six stories in it having been previously published in magazines.
[2] Cf. Chapter XV, 20.
[3] Cf. Chapters XIII, 6 and XIV, 2.
[4] Cf. Chapter XIII, 6.
[5] Cf. Chapter XV, 2.
[6] which was published posthumously: like (and seven years later than) *The Artificial Princess*.

gathering and evades the Princess's questions about the prophet (whom the Baroness is supposed to have met in the course of delivering him the Princess's letter). Then, as the culmination of her guilt, the Baroness receives secret word that Max's plan for having the letter delivered has gone as astray as the Baroness's own mission. Having been taken on a round-about journey that recapitulates her own (and the form of the second movement), the letter is returned to the Baroness unopened. But the Princess, confident that her will has prevailed on the Baroness to procure the result she wants, is already conducting her encounter with a mistaken identity.

Through the party noise the Princess's words to the anonymous young man still sound firm, wilful, leading, solo. But they echo now in the silence of irony. The devil having counter-willed, the Princess is exerting her will on a delusion.

Perhaps acts of artistic creation have an issue as ambiguous as the Princess's will towards self-creation.

Firbank conjures up the party to a finale. Through the party noise, what would have been the coda to the last movement, the Princess's final move as Salome, her declaration of love or (as the bird perhaps presaged) war in relation to the young man, can't – ever – be heard.

8. Overhear...

ODETTE (Firbank) eavesdrops adult conversation (about the Wilde scandal) and doesn't understand.[1]

When he had become an adult himself, Firbank became in real life a collector and connoisseur of overheard remarks either non-understandable (because the context was unknown) or open to misunderstanding: 'he would be', the *Memoir* reports, '[. . .] excited about [. . .] an *incongruité* he had overheard in the train.'

By the time[2] of *The Artificial Princess* Firbank was a virtuoso of the overheard. The book's finale is constructed from fragments of party conversation overheard by the reader. Firbank's fragments may defy interpretation ('Such a cat! I would, dear, if I could only move my poor hips') or expose themselves to several interpretations ('Would you mind not hurting me with your fan?') or single-mindedly invite misinterpretation (in this case, on the very theme, though transvested, of the enigma which probably puzzled

[1] Cf. Chapter XI, 1 and sub-section 2 of this chapter.
[2] I mean the time when Firbank wrote the bulk of the book, a time I think was circa 1910 (cf. Chapter XIII, 6). The ending Firbank added at a date after March 1924 (cf. Chapter XIII, 3) is an extension that uses the method he had already established. All my quotations here are from the section written circa 1910.

the infant Firbank): 'I hear that your wife and my wife . . . but I fancy there's nothing in it . . .'

The motif of overhearing, mentioned in *Odette D'Antrevernes* but not put into practice by the story's literary method, is acted out in *The Artificial Princess*.

In *The Flower Beneath the Foot* it becomes *both* a motif in its own right *and* acted out. Overheard fragments constitute part of the vehicle for the history of that misconstrued overheard fragment which, perhaps actionably, puts fleas in the Ritz.

9. . . . into Fragment

THE incongruities Firbank collected in real life were conspicuous in their incongruity because the noise of the train had drowned out their context.

Perhaps it was his real-life expertise that conducted Firbank to his literary appreciation of Sappho, the context round whose images has often been suppressed by the historical chance that the poems were not preserved whole but only in fragments quoted by other writers.

On his appreciation of Sappho's accidentally isolated images Firbank built his technique of deliberately isolating his own: a technique that consists of suppressing much of the expected (by the conventions of naturalistic fiction) context and substituting those aerated spaces in which his images have room to be conspicuously incongruous or ambivalent.

Firbank's contemplation of images originated, in unlonely solitude, 'from a sofa'.[1] His technique for displaying them in a monstrance of conspicuity originated in a train.

10. A Monument

FOR the expected, tidy point of anecdotes in Wilde's manner Firbank substituted the ironic sense of dots of suspension.

That, too, had its counterpart in Firbank's real life, where Firbank would end his stories with conversational dots or would drown out a coda by the private party-noise of his tragic laugh. 'Frequently his stories were left unfinished. Either his mind would fly off at a tangent, leaving his listeners to bridge the gap, or he would lose his climax in torrents of hoarse, helpless laughter.'[2]

[1] Cf. Chapter XV, 20.
[2] This account in the *Memoir* (p. 31) is supplemented by Vyvyan Holland's contribution (p. 104): 'He always stopped his recitals with a wave of his hand and his far-away, rather

The Artificial Princess is Firbank's ironic commentary on Wilde's *Salomé*.

Firbank, who as a raconteur 'would lose his climax in torrents of hoarse, helpless laughter', wrote his comment on the necrophilic climax of Wilde's play (Salome's 'Yes, I will kiss thy mouth' to the Baptist's detached head) by sardonically refraining from writing it. He simply lost *his* Salome's climactic move in the funny and sad conversations of a garden-party by night.

Firbank was attacking his literary stepfather for failing to make a work of art of Salome and her stepfather.

He was judging Wilde inadequate to both the tragedy and the comedy of the Salome scandal – and, by implication, to the tragedy and comedy of the enigma that was Wilde's legacy to the child Firbank, the Wilde scandal.[1]

That Wilde's drama was undramatic, his poetical prose anti-poetic, his lists of exotic gems more banal than bizarre Firbank pointed out[2] by invoking Webster (' "Did you never hear of the Duchess of Malfi?" ') and by shooting lethal Websterian flights ('frightening the passing Bats with a rope of pearls') across the fabric of his book.

That Wilde, stretching for tragedy, fell into unwilled comedy Firbank remarked by his own deliberate and psychologically observant domestication ('that she might ask, during dessert, for anything she pleased'), his positive Queen-Victoria-isation ('*The Home Life of the Queen of Sheba*'),[3] of the court and of its scandalous princess – whose lover-victim may, quite domestically, be 'a frump'.[4]

Firbank's own baroque flights are juxtaposed to his most deliberate low notes. He is composing in baroque incongruities, re-writing Wilde's high thin monotone of a vocal line in the form of a versed and versatile coloratura whose extremes both low and high are beyond Wilde's compass.

It is the bizarre custom of Firbank's Queen to insist 'while motoring on mending her punctures herself, and it was no uncommon sight to see her sitting with her crown on in the dust. Her reasons for doing so were complex; probably she found genuine amusement in making herself hot and piggy; but it is not unlikely that the more Philistine motive of wishing to edify her subjects was the real cause. She had been called a great many things, but nobody had ever said she was proud; this was her pride. . . .'

Firbank's paragraph, which the reader comes on in his text as expectedly-

hoarse laugh, just when they were beginning to reach what we imagined were about to be the most interesting parts, and left us to guess at the mystery and romance. It was very tantalising, but very effective.'

[1] Cf. Chapter XIV, 1.   [2] Cf. Chapter XIV, 7.   [3] Cf. Chapter XIV, 2.
[4] Cf. Chapter XIV, 8.

unexpectedly as citizens of that Firbankian country come on their queen sitting on the highroad, is a baroque monument. Into its design, which is as complex as the Queen's motives, Firbank introduces the perfect incongruous word 'piggy' – in the way baroque statuaries introduce the bare buttocks of a mourning boy angel among the graven allegorical persons and draperies of a tomb.

Like a baroque tomb, Firbank's design proceeds by contrasts. White marble and black marble, juxtaposed, afford each other a setting of irony. In the midst of high-life we are in the low comedy of flesh and its liability to death.

Firbank incarnates his contrasts in his syntax (in his negative that expresses a positive 'no uncommon sight') and in paradox (the Queen's pride in not being proud, a paradox Firbank had adapted, for his exposure of a queen, from the defensive sophistries of hagiography).

The paradoxical form is a borrowing from Wilde. So is (from Wilde's aesthetic) Firbank's antithesis between art and edification.[1]

It was an indeed monumental irony that Firbank should build a commemoration of Wilde's aesthetic theory, a free-standing monument to the free-standingness, the autonomy, of works of art, in the book that consists of his assassination of Wilde's artistic practice.

Wilde's straight-pathed axioms, which are witty *because* they take the shortest distance between two points, Firbank twists into barley-sugar columns.

Firbank makes the baroque contrast between pomp and mortality. The Queen sits 'with her crown on in the dust': the sculpted crown surmounts a tombful of dusty emptiness. It is the pride of monarchs to commission monuments to the humility of their endings, and the pride of artists to suppose their monuments immortal, outlasting artist and patron alike: but when Wilde built *Salomé* to stand as an immortal commemoration of his own temperamental propensity to stir up scandal about him, he built badly.

The puncture *The Artificial Princess* inflicts on Wilde no queen could mend.

11. Leaning

FIRBANK had, in fact, leaned very hard on the whole edifice of Wilde's œuvre, splintering its smugly gabled points and bursting it open to the

[1] The same point, that edification is philistine, is made by Winsome Brookes when (cf. Chapter XIV, 4), in a still Wildean but now also Straussian connexion, he describes the prophet's music in Strauss's *Salome* as suggestive of the Salvation Army.

creation of a whole extra storey, a demonic dimension which actually presents what Wilde had alluded to grandiosely as evil but kept offstage like the rumour of a ghost making bumps in the attic.

Leaning, Firbank re-directed the thrusts of the Wildean edifice (turning their irony outward, so that it is often the reader whom they threaten to run through), and created his own syncopation by re-distributing Wilde's stresses. The Salomesque climax is so underemphasised that it has become inaudible. Salome's dance is locked in to the domestic seclusion of a bathroom. (In *Vainglory* it was suppressed further still, into a merely alluded-to narrative pun.[1]) The boon Salome begs of the King is enclosed in the oblique angle of a subordinate clause.

Wilde's paradoxes turned logic upside down but left it logic. His aphorisms and axioms are direct point-to-point links, and direct person-to-person communications, their manner declarative. Those too, Wilde's declarations, Firbank leaned on, squashed down and folded away in oblique angles. From Firbank's subordinated statements you can sometimes pick out the substance of a Wildean aphorism and, by straightening it out, re-erect it in its original upright stance of assertion or inquiry or, catechetically, both. 'Naturally, it would be treason to speak with candour of the King, but he would make a superb Herod,' Firbank's Princess remarks. 'What is treason?' a Wildean stooge enquires between her lines, and the indefatigably aphoristic ghost of Oscar Wilde faintly replies 'Treason is speaking with candour of kings.'

Besides folding away Wilde's logic (and thereby transforming it into a quite different article of furniture with a quite different literary purpose), Firbank was able to perforate the logical lines of causation which conduct Wilde's anecdotes to their determined ends. The logic of Firbank's structures is so exact that he can dissolve the logic of his material into non-logic. Firbank's 'later novels', Evelyn Waugh remarked,[2] 'are almost wholly devoid of any attributions of cause to effect'.

Even into the earlier novels Firbank has already, by letting in air, admitted a glimpse of the prettily scudding clouds of surrealism. His rococo ceilings are (logically) composed from the material both of logic and of illogic: clouds advance through them marshalled and compact or in disconnected wisps resembling the personal untidiness of the Baroness Rudlieb ('But probably her secret lay simply in her untidiness; she had made it a study [. . .] A loose strand of hair . . . the helpless angle of a hat'[3]) or the abstruse and bird-brained ('The Baroness abstrusely twittered' . . .) processes of her thought.

---

[1] as Chapter IX, 9 mentioned and Chapter XVIII, 4 will expand.
[2] Cf. Chapter VI, 3.   [3] Chapter XVIII, 2 will mention a twin to this passage.

Having put in the solid colours of his tramway system by borrowing from tram tickets, Firbank sets a system of surrealist logic to scud through the catechism which is transacted (in masterly and very Jane-Austenish *semi-indirect* speech) between the conductor ('he clipped her ticket *with a bell*') and the Baroness: 'And why was the tram painted blue??? Surely heliotrope or palest amber would attract more passengers? What! colour made no difference? No? How strange!'

12. Notes to Chapter XVII

BEARDSLEY'S accounts of Puvis de Chavannes's encouragement and his own new world are in a letter (dated by the editors circa 15 February 1893) on p. 43 of the 1971 edition of his *Letters*.

The sheet à la Puvis de Chavannes is on p. 115 in the *Complete* Firbank, the Wesleyan rag-time on p. 371.

Firbank's 'primitive' letter is quoted in the *Biography*, p. 240.

The zim zim zim jazz is on pp. 603-4 in the *Complete* Firbank.

The account of Lord Berners and the Negro Mask is in Lord Berners's words, quoted by Ifan Kyrle Fletcher in the *Memoir*, pp. 84-5.

Lady Firbank on 'feeling & beauty' is quoted in the *Bibliography*, p. 26.

The content and the history (including Wilde's reply to Charles Ricketts) of Oscar Wilde's *La Sainte Courtisane* are given on pp. 238-9 of Hesketh Pearson's *Life*. Robert Hichens's account of Wilde's recounting the story to him and his charge of plagiarism against Wilde are on pp. 66-8 of Hichens's autobiography *Yesterday*. In his *De Profundis* letter Wilde recorded that he 'conceived' and 'almost completed' *La Sainte Courtisane* and another play in 1893-4, during Lord Alfred Douglas's absence abroad, but was interrupted by Douglas's return: 'The two works left then imperfect I was unable to take up again' (p. 427 in Rupert Hart-Davis's edition of Wilde's *Letters*). Violet Wyndham (*The Sphinx and her Circle*, p. 60) records that the manuscript of Wilde's play *La Sainte Courtisane* was safe-kept by Ada Leverson during Wilde's trials and imprisonment and returned to him by her in Paris in 1898, when he lost it by leaving it in a cab.

Firbank's excitement about incongruities overheard in the train is recorded on p. 38 of the *Memoir*.

XVIII

Fanfare *(Vainglory - 1)*

' *"What am I to play to you?"* Winsome asked of Mrs. Henedge. *"A fanfare? A requiem?"* '

Vainglory (Chapter II)

1. Image and Shadow

FIRBANK'S conversational theorising[1] about the mot juste was put into perfect practice in 1915, when he gave his first-published Firbankian novel the title *Vainglory*.

He achieved not just the mot juste but the exactly right *word*: an exploitation of, essentially and in particular, the *English* language.

Isolated[2] by the simple fact of being the title, the word is an effulgent image in itself: a bravura aria by Handel, with trumpets.

The plumed word announces and incarnates the baroque substance[3] of the book and is presently echoed by one of the baroque metaphors which compose that substance: 'In smoke-like, dreamy spirals streamed the elms, breaking towards their zeniths into incredible *ich diens*' – the signatures, with flourish, of Artie Firbank, Princess of Wales (or at least of Monmouthshire[4]).

And already the flourish casts a sad shadow. Firbank was boldly issuing a fiction of a new type, and one which implicitly explained its new method. He set on it a title that remarks that the enterprise is a glory and yet in vain.

The shadowed half, too, of the title-word has its echo in the book's substance. The book *Vainglory* is pursued, inside its content, by its fictitious and hopeless self, Claud Harvester's book *Vaindreams*.

Firbank is already implying the explicit theme of *Santal*: pilgrimages (his own, by means of *Vainglory*, into the canon of perpetual remembrance of English literature [or 'half-way up', as Miss Compostella's thoughts place

---

[1] which the *Memoir* records (cf. Chapter V, 6).

[2] Cf. Chapter V, 2 and Chapter XVI.

[3] which the *Memoir* (p. 93) recognises: 'the heavy outline and bold colouring of baroque *Vainglory*'.

[4] Cf. Chapters VI, 2 and IX, 4.

Claud Harvester, Mount Parnassos] or Mrs Shamefoot's, inside *Vainglory*, into the canon of saints) lead to the emptiness of the desert.

The spaces with which Firbank aerates his fiction[1] include emptiness, the literal meaning of vanity.

2. Prelude (as Fugue)

Vainglory is designed as a prelude-and-fugue: one in which the prelude, too, is fugal.

Not all Firbank's models of artistic form were adapted from music. He borrowed from painting and architecture as well. But it is on the strength of a touch more than personally perceived analogy that I call *The Artificial Princess* a concerto and *Vainglory* a prelude-and-fugue.

Firbank's conscious and intellectual apprehension of form was probably developed through music: because he played the piano.[2] His architectural eye, I surmise, was trained unconsciously: by connoisseurship and being brought up at The Coopers,[3] rather than by execution.

Originally, perhaps, Firbank intended a direct collaboration between music and his literary talent. An early poem of his is catalogued[4] under the title and direction 'The Wind and the Roses (To be set to Music)'.

No doubt it is that early wish which grew, passively, into Firbank's appreciation of opera and, actively, into Winsome Brookes – who is not only, like Firbank, a pianist but also a composer of opera.

Firbank's own fictions, however, including even his play, are less like operas without music than like pieces that give literary expression to forms of the type incarnated in instrumental music.

There is a pointer to the formativeness of musical form in the title that Firbank either set or allowed to be set[5] on the chapter (Chapter VIII) of *Valmouth* which Osbert Sitwell published in advance in the spring number of *Art and Letters* in 1919:[6] 'Fantasia for Orchestra in F Sharp Minor'.

That the chapter was called a fantasia *for orchestra* is appropriate. The texture of *Valmouth*, like that of *Vainglory* (where Mrs Henedge presides as

---

[1] Cf. Chapter XVI.   [2] Cf. Chapter XIV, 4 and Plates 7 and 8.
[3] Cf. Chapter X, 4.

[4] in the catalogue of the 1961 Sotheby's sale, reprinted in *The New Rythum and Other Pieces* (p. 127). The poem (whose title the *Biography* cites with an ampersand for the 'and') will be mentioned again in Chapter XIX, 3.

[5] Osbert Sitwell's account (*Memoir*, p. 127) doesn't record which. A letter (quoted in the *Biography*, p. 172) from Sitwell to Firbank on the subject of the publication speaks of the piece simply as 'Chapter VIII'.

[6] (Cf. Chapter VII, 3); *Art and Letters*, Volume II, New Series (Spring 1919), pp. 64–79.

hostess 'orchestrating fearlessly her guests'[1]) and unlike that of, say, *Inclinations*, is indeed orchestrated. On the contents page of the magazine, however, Firbank's piece was listed under the shortened title of 'Fantasia in F Sharp Minor'. Perhaps Osbert Sitwell, through personal acquaintance with Firbank's (piano) forte, was editorially thinking of the chapter as piano music – which might help explain Osbert Sitwell's lapse of memory when, giving his account of the matter a decade afterwards, he misnamed the piece 'Fantasia in A Sharp Minor'.[2] No doubt A sharp minor, as a minor key containing seven sharps, seemed to Osbert Sitwell the nearest equivalent to Firbank's oblique and 'difficult' tone in general. But, if Sitwell was thinking of A sharp minor particularly in terms of a keyboard, then his was a positively creative lapse of memory: the seven sharps of A sharp minor include, on a piano, five black notes – a black reflexion of Firbank's, and *Valmouth*'s, Negroism.

The 'F Sharp Minor' of the title which the piece in reality bore is, I imagine, a simpler pun: in which the F is for Firbank, the 'sharp' for his literary tone and the 'minor' an ironic reflexion in Firbank's self-depreciating manner. Authors are never taken at face value except when they are ironic at their own expense. Perhaps by putting or allowing to be put that gently anti-Firbankian title on Chapter VIII of *Valmouth* Firbank inadvertently put his own thumb-print first on that soiled and sticky critical label 'minor'[3] that still clings to his work.

The prelude to *Vainglory* is set in London, and it occupies the first five of the novel's 24 chapters.

Each of the five prelude chapters is transacted at a different London address. In musical terms, the prelude is a round, the onset of each new chapter constituting a new entry. And the fictional framework of its subject-matter is, precisely, the London round.

The prelude proceeds in the manner of Firbank himself as he made by cab his haunted round of farewell visits to his London acquaintance.[4]

Suitably, Chapter I opens in medias res of a social call.

Its first words have to place the tone not just of the prelude but of the whole ensuing book. Consequently, they consist not of an immediately locating statement but of one of Firbank's flying conversational streamers – which is rendered startling by the suppression, for the time being, of context and location: ' "And, then, oh yes! Atalanta is getting too pronounced." '

(Mrs Henedge's consoling reply is that it is better 'to be pronounced than to be a bag of bones. And thank goodness Atalanta's not eccentric! Think

---

[1] *Complete* Firbank, p. 85. The orchestration of Mrs Henedge's party is further discussed in sub-section 4 of this chapter.
[2] *Memoir*, p. 127.   [3] Cf. Chapters VI, 4 and XI, 3.   [4] Cf. Chapter VIII, 7.

of poor little Mr. Rienzi-Smith who lives in continual terror lest one day his wife may do something really strange – perhaps run down Piccadilly without a hat. . . .'[1])

The suppression of context round Atalanta *is*, however, no more than temporary. This is not (yet) one of the surrealist occasions when Firbank dispenses with logic. Logic and locality are essential to his fugal construction. He has merely reversed the logical order of disclosure. Quickly he restores context to the opening remark ('It was the end of a somewhat lively review') and builds locality round it: 'Lady Georgia Blueharnis owned that house off Hill Street from whose curved iron balconies it would have seemed right for dames in staid silks to lean melodiously at certain moments of the day.'

(I suspect that Firbank intended the staid silken rhythm of the passage to be yet further weighted by the pedantry of giving the balconies their 18th-century stress: balCONies.)

To 'that house off Hill Street' Mrs Henedge has come with the intention (within the fiction) of inviting Lady Georgia to a small party of her own in honour of Professor Inglepin's discovery, in Egypt, of 'an original fragment of Sappho' – and with the structural function of thereby inviting the next entry in the round.

Before she can deliver her news Mrs Henedge has to sit out an incursion of Blueharnis children, who arrive in the company of their 'fräulein'[2] and a windmill whirr of Firbankian streamers ('It ran away in Berkeley Square' . . . 'On her head were two very tall green feathers'), the book's first, and still very tightly concentrated, nucleus of surrealism.

Mrs Henedge has also sat out Lady Georgia's account ('apt to be a strain') of a 'mother's rôle', an account of which the book's opening words are the climax.

Although Firbank fills in the context of that opening remark about Atalanta, about Atalanta herself there is no context to fill in. She opens the book *because* she is at a tangent to its fictional substance. Atalanta's, it turns out, is the peripheral rôle of bridesmaid – and that at a wedding peripheral to the main personages. Follow up Atalanta and you arrive (in

---

[1] The Wagnerian name Rienzi-Smith seems to have arrested Virginia Woolf in the same way as the Mistress of the Robes in *The Artificial Princess* who, I surmise (cf. Chapter XVII, 7), later emerged as Virginia Woolf's Miss La Trobe. Maureen Duffy has pointed out to me that Firbank's Rienzi-Smith of 1915 has, in Virginia Woolf's *Mrs Dalloway* of 1925, become Rezia Smith (in which the Rezia=Lucrezia, under the influence perhaps, of *Vainglory*'s *The Home Life of Lucretia Borgia*) and the situation is turned the other way about, since it is Virginia Woolf's Rezia Smith who 'lives in continual terror' of what her husband may do.   [2] Cf. Chapter X, 12.

Chapter III) at the wedding of Nils and Isolde: a wedding whose fictional raison d'être is merely to strike glancingly on Mrs Shamefoot's consciousness and thereby provoke her to remember the extensively casual circumstances of her own engagement;[1] a wedding whose own emptiness of imagist content and structural function is reflected, by beautiful contrast, in the idiosyncratic circumstantialness of the *objects* amassed round it. This is the wedding that provokes from Mrs Henedge the Irish and probably Wildean wedding-present[2] of a pack of cards bought in Chelsea and 'supposed once to have belonged to Deirdre'. And the wedding cake (as Mrs Henedge discloses to Lady Georgia in Chapter I) consists, in that Firbankian (and again perhaps, in its devotion to the Queen, Wildean) image which[3] is as grotesquely, bulbously baroque as a floral chamberpot, of 'an exact replica of the Victoria Memorial'.

Opening with a pronouncement about Atalanta is itself a pronouncement about Firbank's narrative manner: the manner *is* tangential. A reader who interprets Atalanta's prominent position according to the rules of orthodox narrative will pursue a clue that conducts him to a series of decorative and entertaining images which, however, as a series, leads nowhere. The opening of *Vainglory* gives notice that Firbank has destroyed the seeming narrative-logic of anecdotes that make towards a fixed and limited point, and has substituted the self-justifying logic of his oblique juxtaposition of statement to statement and image to image.

Yet the fictional tangent has private relevance. It makes a concealed statement about *what* Firbank has destroyed. *Vainglory*, as the *Memoir* remarked, 'commemorates the death of Arthur Firbank, a charming dilettante, and it proclaims the birth of Ronald Firbank'. It is in fact Firbank himself who has become 'too pronounced' in style (and, perhaps, in femininity of literary figure) to pass any longer for Arthur Firbank, author of such sub-Wildean anecdotes as *Odette D'Antrevernes*. In the course of restoring context to Lady Georgia's remark about Atalanta, Firbank's narrative lets slip the private information that Atalanta is another signature (or perhaps the visiting-card) of Artie (Firbank). 'Too pronounced' though she is in public, Atalanta is in her home circumstances under-pronounced. Her mother abbreviates her to 'At'y'.

Like Mrs Henedge's invitation, Lady Georgia's house off Hill Street has to wait out other matters (seven brief paragraphs of Chapter I) before it is sited. Chapters II, III and IV, on the other hand, site themselves, in their structural slots on the London round, with the directness of, indeed, a street directory.

[1] Cf. Chapter XV, 8.   [2] Cf. Chapter VIII, 7.   [3] Cf. Chapter V, 2.

Chapter II (the entry of Mrs Henedge's party) begins: 'Mrs. Henedge lived in a small house with killing stairs just off Chesham Place.'

(Firbank creates a baroque incongruity by importing the killing stairs from the idiom of below stairs.[1] The smart – or perhaps 'just off' smart – London address suffers the deflationary superimposition of an image as domestic,[2] as *of domestics*, as housemaid's knee.)

Chapter III begins as if it were instructing you how to find the way: 'Just at the beginning of Sloane Street, under the name of Monna Vanna, Mrs. Shamefoot kept a shop.'[3]

Chapter IV begins with, positively, an address: '13 Silvery Place was the address of Mrs. Henedge's latest genius' (who is Winsome Brookes).

Chapter V, the last of the prelude, keeps symmetry with the first by opening with a line of dialogue (a rather Wildean one, both in its pathetically fallacious content and in its Irish and 18th-century declarative cadence), though this time it is free to be a line that instantly locates the chapter at a fifth London address, Miss Compostella's:[4] ' "I wonder you aren't ashamed, Sumph", Miss Compostella said to her maid, "to draw the blinds up every morning on such a grey sky." '

Across that grey sky Firbank sets drifting the disconnected (or connected by a beautiful illogic) images of surrealism: by means of Miss Compostella's drifting ('She held out long arms, driftingly') morning meditations, from bed, on the view through her window.

It is a view of and through a window that might have been painted (a decade or two later) by René Magritte. Like Magritte's window pictures, it plays on a frame within a frame. It is through 'the vigilant bars' of a suspended cage (containing a stuffed canary, which Miss Compostella sometimes, 'by mistake', addresses with 'Angel! Sweet! Pet! Pretty!') that Miss Compostella contemplates the more distant view of 'a cold stone church by Vanbrugh'.

Firbank is using the symmetry of classicising architecture (contemplation of which probably developed his own effortlessly symmetrical and classicising sense of design[5]) as a paperweight, to hold down and lend a compositional centre to his surreal drift.

The 'austere and heavy tower' of the Vanbrugh church 'did not depress' Miss Compostella. Its solidity becomes the centre of her cloud fantasia. 'Flushed at sunset, it suggested quite forcibly a middle-aged bachelor

---

[1] Cf. Chapter XVI, 10.   [2] Cf. Chapter XIV, 2.   [3] Cf. Chapter XV, 2.
[4] It is in 'Sacred Gardens', where 'The address alone, she hoped, would be a sufficient protection, and so spare her the irksomeness of a chaperon.'
[5] Cf. Chapter X, 4.

with possessions at Coutts. At times she could almost think of it as *James*....'[1]

Firbank's classicising eye has arranged to answer the tight nexus of surrealism introduced by the Blueharnis children into the first chapter of the prelude by the full-blown, the indeed tumbling surrealist petals in the last.

That the mind through which the petals fall would be Miss Compostella's he presaged in the second chapter, by attributing to Miss Compostella a wispiness of personal appearance transferred almost verbatim from the untidiness attributed to the Baroness Rudlieb in *The Artificial Princess*.[2] (The Baroness's untidiness, too, is the outward reflexion of a surrealist turn of thought.)

By Chapter V of *Vainglory* the London season is (within the fiction) running down. Miss Compostella contemplates, as well as the view, a hiatus of five weeks in the exercise of her profession of acting. Structurally, the prelude has accomplished its first four revolutions and now, in the fifth, like a catherine wheel towards the end of its spin, it begins to turn out of true and to throw off irregularly timed, high-powered dazzles and blotches of imagery.

Impatience is entering the structural succession of one London address to another. The catherine wheel is working itself loose from its pin: and preparing to leap into the dark. The opened-out texture of Chapter V, the surrealist gaps in which its images are presented to the reader's contemplation, and Miss Compostella's own contemplation of distance and of exotic geography ('It was noon! Sultry noon – somewhere in the world. In Cintra now . . .') presage that the man-about-town round is to be overtaken by the Firbankian major shift of locale. And that, indeed, is what Chapter VI announces, with the directness of a railway time-table, in its opening words: 'To Ashringford from Euston is really quite a journey.'

---

[1] Saint James, perhaps, of Compostela (cf. Chapter XV, 15).

[2] (Cf. Chapters XIII, 3 and XVII, 11); 'But probably her secret lay simply in her untidiness; she had made it a study. Untidiness, with her, had become a fine art. A loose strand of hair . . . the helpless angle of a hat; and, to add emphasis, there were always quantities of tiny paste buttons in absurd places on her frocks that cried aloud to be fastened, giving her an air of irresponsibility which the very young Courtiers seemed to find quite fascinating' (*The Artificial Princess*; *Complete* Firbank, p. 29). 'Probably, as his wife' (sc. Claud Harvester's wife) 'had hinted once, her secret lay simply in her untidiness. She had made it a study. Disorder, with her, had become a fine art. A loose strand of hair . . . the helpless angle of a hat . . . And then, to add emphasis, there were always quantities of tiny buttons in absurd places on her frocks that cried aloud, or screamed, or gently prayed, to be fastened, and which, somehow, gave her an air of irresponsibility, which, for simple folk, was possibly quite fascinating' (*Vainglory*; *Complete* Firbank, p. 86).

3. Prelude (as Grand Prelude)

THE first five chapters of *Vainglory* perform two simultaneous functions; and in performing the second they can be read as the prelude not only to the rest of *Vainglory* but to the rest of Firbank's œuvre.

Firbank is fugally placing his figures for the grand fugue to which he makes the transition at Chapter VI. From Chapter I, into which he introduces Mrs Henedge as 'the widow of that injudicious man the Bishop of Ashringford', the London round is headed towards Euston and Ashringford (via Totterdown[1]). That he will, when the season gives him fictional pretext, transpose his fiction into the pastoral mode Firbank promises by bringing to Mrs Henedge's Sappho party in Chapter II the pastorally named[2] and characterised ('He had been into Arcadia, even') Claud Harvester – and also Mrs Calvally, 'who brought with her, somehow, into the room, the tranquillity of gardens'.

Suitably, Mrs Calvally enters Mrs Henedge's house pursued by a butterfly.[3] Mrs Calvally is already in fugue.

Simultaneously with its immediate functions in the fiction, the prelude is discharging that large duty which falls on pioneer works of art in philistine and hostile periods.[4] It is explicating, even while it practises, its own artistic method, and enclosing within its own fictional walls the aesthetic by which it can be appreciated in the world outside.

That its decoration is conceived according to the aesthetic of the rococo *Vainglory* establishes by beginning in 'that house off Hill Street' which has, besides the external decoration of curved iron balCONies, a drawing-room which an act of backwards-pioneering taste has hung with the 'blotches of rose and celestial blue' of a Tiepolo[5] Stations of the Cross.

(I think it was in order to create an internal echo of the book's fugal form that Firbank invented a *series* of paintings by Tiepolo instead of a perhaps more characteristic altarpiece or ceiling.)

With the next twist of his London round Firbank pioneers yet further back – or archaeologises yet further down. It is the archaeologist and palaeographer Professor Inglepin who discloses the pin that skewers Firbank's images together, the pin from which the fabric of *Vainglory* hangs (at, no doubt, an oblique ingle): the technique of fragmentation practised by Sappho and the accidents of history.

[1] (Cf. Chapter XV, 4); 'Only an inconvenient morning train, or a dissipated evening one – described in time-tables as the Cathedral Express – ever attempt at concentration. Normal middle-day persons disliking these extremes must get out at Totterdown and wait.'   [2] Cf. Chapter XV, 6.   [3] Cf. Chapter VII, 3.
[4] Cf. Chapter XI, 3.   [5] Cf. Chapter IX, 6.

Between his 18th-century aesthetic and the classicism of the Greek classics Firbank's text has already stated a fusion: in Chapter I, where it ascribes Lady Georgia's house off Hill Street to 'Grecian-Walpole times'.

The fragment the Professor has discovered in Egypt is presumably written on one of those scrappily preserved pieces of papyrus (or, sometimes, parchment) whose discovery (chiefly in Egypt) and decipherment or conjectural restoration (chiefly in Berlin and London) added, in the 19th and early 20th centuries, a sudden augment to the corpus of fragments of Sappho's work that had been preserved by being quoted, a line, phrase or word at a time, by other writers of antiquity by way of illustration to their points about style, metre, grammar or dialect.

The occasion when the Professor unveils his discovery to an audience of Mrs Henedge's London acquaintance is marshalled by Firbank, with virtuosity, in the traditional lines of such set-pieces in fictional comedies of English manners, where the set-piece assembles the dramatis personae and relates them to (and differentiates them from) one another.

Already, however, Firbank is practising on the traditional assembly that method of pioneering (by going back to a yet earlier tradition) by which he is destroying the tradition under which the assembly was marshalled.

Suppressing the context round his personages and their lines of dialogue, he breaks off or disrupts the relationships between them, tumbling them into bizarre proximities or separating them by surrealist gaps, leaving personalities and speeches exposed as autonomous images: images that are all the more there for leading nowhere.

As the guests seize (sometimes from each other) their chairs and transform themselves into an audience waiting to hear the Sappho fragment, their own conversation has already suffered a disintegration into a non-logical series of context-less Sapphic fragments. 'But if they had meant to murder me', one of them is 'mysteriously murmuring' to Mrs Henedge's pet monsignor, 'they would not have put chocolate in the luncheon-basket.' Immediately afterwards Miss Compostella is 'heard to exclaim vaguely above everyone else' the fragment: 'My dear, *when an angel* like Sabine Watson . . .'

Firbank first *applies* his context-drowning, train-noisy[1] technique and only afterwards gives it sacramental body in his fiction, in the form of the fragment his already fragmented audience is waiting to hear.

The Professor's discovery turns out to read (in translation; Firbank does not vouchsafe a Greek text for it): 'Could not, for the fury of her feet'.

The total absence of strings in the fragment leading to anything beyond itself dizzies the audience. ' "Could not . . ." ' Mrs Thumbler 'murmured

[1] Cf. Chapter XVII, 8–9.

helplessly, as though clinging to an alpenstock, and not quite sure of her guide. Below her, so to speak, were the rooftops, pots and pans: Chamonix twinkling in the snow.'[1]

Puritanically-pruriently hopeful of *some* traditionally logical significance, Monsignor Parr asks: 'But no doubt there is a *sous-entendu*?' But the Professor's opinion is that Sappho probably 'did not even mean to be caustic'.

Loosed on its audience, the fragment just lies in the middle of the assembly, suggesting nothing, not even something suggestive: a precise, a perfect fictional image of the lapidary existential *thereness* of Firbank's fictional images, a tiny stony exact mirror of Firbank's unwinking irony.

The Professor has uncovered the deepest, most archaic layer in Firbank's reconstruction of aesthetics.

(Firbank was perhaps helped towards his appreciation of Sappho's time-nibbled scraps by the imagist theory and practice of Ezra Pound,[2] who was perhaps inspired in turn by *Vainglory*. Two years before the appearance of *Vainglory* Pound published the advice that the essence of imagism was to be found in 'Sappho, Catullus, Villon [. . .]' In the year after *Vainglory* Pound published, under the title *Papyrus*, his translation of three [or, dependent on restoration, four] recovered but incomplete and non-consecutive words by Sappho.[3])

Disconcerted by his audience's being disconcerted, Professor Inglepin utters on Sappho's behalf what amounts to (though it is presented in the distorting-mirror of a satirical view of professors) Firbank's own apologia, an anatomy of the Firbankian imagist and context-suppressing technique: 'Here is an adventurous line, separated (alas!) from its full context. Decorative, useless, as you will; a water-colour on silk!'

Firbank was evidently aware[4] that his Sapphic adventurousness was also Chinese.[5]

---

[1] Cf. Plate 11.

[2] Firbank was likely to know of Pound's work simply through being interested in literature, but his attention might have been directed particularly to Pound through (cf. Chapters VII, 1 and VIII, 1 and 3) Wyndham Lewis, who (according to *Ezra Pound, A Critical Anthology*, edited by J. P. Sullivan) met Pound in 1910, or through (cf. Chapter XII, 1) Elkin Mathews, Firbank's 'publisher' of 1905, who (according to the same Critical Anthology) published work by Pound in 1909 and 1911.

[3] Hugh Kenner (in an essay republished in *Ezra Pound, A Critical Anthology*, edited by J. P. Sullivan) gives an account of the Sappho fragment (which he remarks is on parchment, not papyrus) and of the publication of Pound's translation in *Lustra*, 1916.

[4] The water-colour on silk metaphor suggests that Firbank came by his awareness by analogy with visual arts. Ezra Pound was probably not an influence this time; his chinoiseries in (American) literature appeared only in the same year as *Vainglory*. And, unless musicologists have exaggerated the depth and duration of English deafness to his music, Firbank is unlikely to have known Gustav Mahler's chinoiseries in (German)

By a stroke of vivid and satirical anti-naturalism, Firbank brings the fashionable audience forward, to overcome its own discomposure and (mainly) to support the Professor, with a bombardment of Sapphic erudition. Before the Professor's recital, there rose from the audience a chorus of Sappho-like fragmentary lines; and that chorus is matched, after the recital, by a counter-chorus of the real thing.

Mrs Asp compares the Professor's Sappho fragment to three others (one of which she cites in Greek). The Professor takes her up ('As Mrs. Asp explains' . . .) and cites five more. Even Mrs Calvally murmurs 'And isn't there just one little tiny wee word of hers which says: *A tortoise-shell*?'

There is. (It reads χέλυννα and was preserved by the fifth-century A.D. lexicographer Orion in commenting on its dialect variation from the standard Attic form of the word[1] [which means primarily *tortoise* and thence *lyre*].) With the exception of one which the Professor calls 'I fear me, spurious', all Firbank's fragments of Sappho are authentic and for Firbank surprisingly,[2] if not quite totally, accurate.[3]

One of the inaccuracies, however, is probably a sly[4] Firbankian joke in Greek – or at the least a learned[5] slip[6] of his pen.

literature set to music, *Das Lied von der Erde*, composed (according to the E.M.I. recording) in 1907–9 and first (posthumously) performed (according to the Philharmonia score) in Vienna in 1911. It is perhaps a shade more likely that, led by his passion for the Russian Ballet to Igor Stravinsky, Firbank knew or heard of Stravinsky's 1913 setting of *Three Japanese Lyrics*.

[5] Perhaps it was the Chinese-ness of Firbank's technique which attracted the translator-from-the-Chinese Arthur Waley, who (as the *Bibliography*, p. 51, records) wrote the Introduction to the 1929 collected (and limited) edition of Firbank's work. And in 1929 Evelyn Waugh (cf. Chapter VI, 3) compared Firbankian comedy to 'the abiding and inscrutable wit of the Chinese'.

[1] Pp. 306 and 307 in Volume I of the Loeb *Lyra Graeca*, edited by J. M. Edmonds.
[2] Cf. Chapter X, 12.
[3] Mrs Asp's three fragments (the second of which I will discuss more thoroughly in my next-but-one footnote) can be found on, respectively, pp. 224, 252 and 220 in the Loeb *Lyra Graeca*, Volume I. The first of the Professor's citations, 'the poet's *With Golden Ankles*, for instance', is perhaps a slip of Firbank's pen for the fragment (Loeb, p. 196) which, if literally translated, reads 'Recently [to] me the golden-sandalled dawn'. The Professor's next three authentic fragments are free but in spirit accurate translations of fragments whose texts are given on respectively, pp. 300, 274 and 306 in the Loeb edition.
[4] Cf. Chapter XIV, 10.
[5] Firbank has Mrs Asp quote 'Γέλλως παιδοφιλώτερος' (though he gives the proper name Gello its alternative spelling with a single *l*). The fragment, which is preserved in Zenobius, in fact reads (in, for instance, the Loeb edition, p. 252, and in Liddell and Scott's Lexicon, which quotes it from Zenobius) Γέλλως παιδοφιλωτέρα. The meaning is 'fonder of children than Gello', Gello being, as Zenobius explains, a Lesbian (geographical sense) bogeywoman who causes children to die young. In Sappho's version the person who is fonder is female. Firbank has given the comparative a masculine ending.

All Firbank's Sappho quotations are from material preserved in literary sources. It looks as though the edition of Sappho he used as springboard for his satire on papyrus finds was one which didn't include papyrus finds.

Supported by Mrs Asp and Mrs Calvally, the Professor is snubbed by Mrs Steeple, who remarks 'disparagingly' (and very much in the manner of Firbank's 1969 biographer finding[1] a 'decline in power' to be 'sadly apparent' in Firbank's own final fragment of work, *The New Rythum*): 'I should say that Sappho's powers were decidedly in declension when she wrote the Professor's "water-colour".'

Mrs Steeple is stupid enough to judge a fragment a falling-off by comparing it with a poem in extenso. Yet even she is erudite enough to quote in extenso. She insists, 'rapidly, occult, archaic, before anybody could stop her', on declaiming to the company the Ode to Aphrodite[2] (which is that intensely rare object, a longish poem by Sappho that has been preserved entire[3]).

The translation Mrs Steeple recites ('Zeus-begotten, weaver of arts deceitful, From thy throne of various hues behold me' . . .) is on Gilbert Murrayish lines and conspicuously less successful than *Vainglory*'s renderings of the fragments at capturing Sappho's sophisticated and decorative simplicity of idiom. Indeed, Sappho's Ode has been done over into purest fake Swinburne (a thing which Swinburne himself, to his credit, hesitated to do[4]). It is perhaps the second of Firbank's tributes, in *Vainglory*, to Swinburne[5] – the first being delivered in the novel's opening line and consisting of that

Consciously or unconsciously he has taken pedophilia to be pederasty and transposed the sex of Sappho's homosexuality.

[6] By an unlearned slip, the *Complete* Firbank (p. 92) misprints the phi as a psi. The mistake is not made in the 1930 Duckworth *Vainglory* in the (cf. Chapter VI, 2) Rainbow Edition or in the first edition.

---

[1] (Cf. Chapter VI, 7); the opinion is expressed on p. 276 of the *Biography*.

[2] the one (since fragments exist of other odes by Sappho to Aphrodite) that begins Ποικιλόθρον' (Loeb, p. 182).

[3] The Ode to Aphrodite is no exception to the rule that Firbank's Sappho comes from literary sources; it was preserved in the work of Dionysius of Halicarnassus.

[4] 'I have wished, and I have even ventured to hope, that I might in time be competent to translate [. . .] the divine words [. . .] That hope, if indeed I dared ever entertain such a hope, I soon found fallacious. To translate the two odes and the remaining fragments of Sappho is the one impossible task [. . .] Where Catullus failed I could not hope to succeed; I tried instead to reproduce in a diluted and dilated form the spirit of a poem which could not be reproduced in the body.' (Swinburne in *Notes on Poems and Reviews*, 1866, extracts [including, on p. 51, the portion I have quoted extracts from] from which are reprinted in *Swinburne, The Critical Heritage*, edited by Clyde K. Hyder).

[5] to whom Eddy Monteith, in *The Flower Beneath the Foot*, has paid (cf. Chapter XV, 13) the tribute of an *Ode to Swinburne*.

multiply meaningful name Atalanta. At'y — Artie — Claud Harvester; and Claud Harvester in Arcadia is *Atalanta in Calydon*.

The creaking diction of the translation declaimed by Mrs Steeple is in the manner of 19th-century English classical scholarship (witness the aptly named Butcher and Lang rendering of Homer). And Mrs Steeple's hideous version of Sappho *is* a scholarly performance, which observes Sappho's metre, line by line and indeed syllable by syllable, through the seven four-line verses.

For want of a better surmise I take this scholarly performance to be Firbank's own,[1] an exercise preserved, perhaps, from one of the many fragments of his academic education.[2] (Even so, there is evidence, which I will adduce in my next sub-section, that Firbank relied on a crib – and a bowdlerised one.)

Within the terms of *Vainglory*, however, the translation might be by Professor Inglepin: both on the point of scholarliness and because the diction accords with the mock-Tudor 'I fear me' which Firbank satirically puts in the Professor's mouth.

As a matter of fact, the discrepancy in manner between the translation of the Ode and the translations of the fragments matches a small unevenness in the narrative manner of *Vainglory* itself. Traditional locutions fit the Professor's speech with satiric felicity. But though Firbank's intention may be equally satirical they look less happy when he inserts them into his own text, where he, not one of his personages, has to sponsor them.

In his surrealist chapter on Miss Compostella's morning meditations, Firbank is entirely justified, by a doubleness in his purpose, when he writes: 'Round the bed in which we surprise her hung a severe blue veil.' Miss Compostella is being *placed* (still in bed so late in the morning) as an actress, and her maid, Sumph, as a connoisseur of acting. It is by a beautiful and witty aptness that Sumph's drawing the blind up on that shamingly grey sky becomes the raising of the curtain which, as if in an old stage direction, *surprises* the personages of the drama.

Traditionalisms seem, however, less securely distanced in Chapter IV,

---

[1] At least it is clear what the translation in *Vainglory* is *not*. It is not the translation by J. A. Symonds or the one by Sir Edwin Arnold or the one by F. L. Lucas in *The Oxford Book of Greek Verse in Translation*. And indeed I surmise that to quote any fairly recent translation by someone other than himself might have brought Firbank into a difficulty (which might not have troubled him but would surely have been raised by his 'publisher') over copyright (which under the 1911 Act existed for 25 years after an author's death).

[2] Cf. Swinburne in 1866: 'We in England are taught, are compelled under penalties to learn, to construe, and to repeat, as schoolboys, the imperishable and incomparable verses of that supreme poet; and I at least am grateful for the training.' (*Swinburne, The Critical Heritage*, edited by Clyde K. Hyder, p. 51).

which Firbank opens with the address of Mrs Henedge's 'latest genius' and the information that Mrs Henedge is in the habit of describing him as 'a young boy'. Firbank's text proceeds: 'The young boy, gentle reader, was Winsome Brookes.' The text then puts in the figures of Winsome and Andrew at home, and goes on to advise: 'Let us follow these bright ornaments.'

Perhaps the echo of the fugal structure is not quite strong enough to justify the 'follow' – nor the satirical purpose (which seems to reflect more on narrative than on Winsome) to justify the sarcastic 'bright ornaments'.

A 'dear reader' in *The Artificial Princess*, at the moment when the Mistress of the Robes clatters across the nervous Baroness's errand,[1] is more truly justified by Firbankian purpose. At the intersection of two skeins in his material Firbank bumps the reader momentarily out of the book altogether and into selfconsciousness.

Vainglory's 'gentle reader', on the other hand, is subjected to satire with a wobble in it. Firbank turns his disdain like a ray-gun on the traditional narrative props he is rejecting, yet he leans some of his own narrative's weight on the props, trusting them to make the transition between Winsome's postal address and the image of Winsome at home there.

It is as though Firbank's nerve for his vainglorious enterprise has for a moment failed. He doesn't quite dare to quite suppress the connective tissue of context. He doesn't entirely trust himself simply and starkly to juxtapose Winsome's address and Winsome. Temporarily he retreats from the idiom of Sapphic fragments: back into the over-carved diction whereby scholarship tried to represent (and in effect misrepresented) Sappho whole.

4. Prelude and Ode

TRANSLATED, however, into some, no matter which, idiom, Sappho's Ode to Aphrodite was indispensable to *Vainglory*.

Its least (though still considerable) usefulness to Firbank is that a portion of its content makes a further suggestion of fugue. Invoked, the goddess promises Sappho: 'Whoso flies thee, soon shall he turn to woo thee.'

Mrs Steeple's version is, as a matter of fact, a mis-translation. The gender of the participles in the Greek makes it clear that Aphrodite is offering to secure for Sappho the affections of whichever *female* person Sappho has set her heart on. The promise should read: 'soon shall she turn to woo thee'. Either Firbank was quoting a bowdlerised translation or, if the translation is his own, he was following a bowdlerised crib. Had he been working direct

[1] Cf. Chapter XVII, 7.

from the Greek, he would never have muffed so excellently Firbankian a point.

Irrespectively, however, of the sexes concerned, the essential idea of a flight reversed into a pursuit was to another Firbankian purpose. The Greek poem conveniently brings to mind the Greek visual arts' counterpart to a fugue, namely a frieze: the very image to which,[1] later in *Vainglory*, Firbank makes his personages compare Claud Harvester's *Vaindreams*. 'His work calls to mind a frieze with figures of varying heights trotting all the same way.'

Sappho's 'soon shall she turn' remarks, as it were, that a fugue can be inverted and run, like a film strip, back to front. That suggestion too Firbank took up: in later work (*Inclinations*); in the internal structure of that very chapter of *Vainglory* where Sappho's words are quoted, since the chapter puts its fugue into reverse after the recital of the Ode; and in the description of Claud Harvester's work, which continues: 'If one' (of the trotting figures) 'should by chance turn about it's usually merely to stare or to sneer or to make a grimace.'

All the same, useful though it is piecemeal, it is as a complete image (a concept imaged in its survival complete) that the Ode to Aphrodite is most valuable to Firbank's purpose.

It is valuable through being an invocation, and through being an invocation to, in particular, *that* goddess.

For the purpose of his grand strategy, in so far as he was writing a prelude to his entire Firbankian œuvre, Firbank was enabled to begin his revolutionary enterprise under the auspices of the classical tradition of beginnings. His œuvre, no less than Lucretius's *De Rerum Natura* (a work as revolutionary as *Vainglory*), is prefaced by an invocation to (to latinise her) Venus.

At the same time, the Ode is the structural hinge on which Firbank turns the prelude considered as prelude to, specifically, *Vainglory*. Moreover, within the five chapters of that prelude, the cardinal chapter is the second, the chapter of Mrs Henedge's party; and the structure of that chapter in itself turns on the Ode to Aphrodite.

Mrs Steeple having, with her declamation of the Ode, set the fashion for party pieces, Mrs Henedge decides to act on a plan she sketched to herself at the beginning. The company she has assembled has been first disconcerted, and then set almost squabbling,[2] by the principal event; Mrs Henedge sets

---

[1] Cf. Chapter X, 7; and Plates 7 and 8.

[2] Mrs Henedge's invitation to music averts the squabble that is arising round the Professor's Sappho-prompted remark to Monsignor Parr (cf. Chapter XVI, 8) that Christianity 'has destroyed more than it has created'.

out to calm her guests by means of a fugal sequence of party performances.

All the contributions from the guests have musical associations: aptly, since from early on in the party Mrs Henedge has been 'orchestrating fearlessly her guests', and Firbank's text has been orchestrated throughout. George Calvally arrives accompanying his wife and 'unhappy, perhaps, at playing, if even for only a few hours, an oboe to her violin'; and the Professor announces his reading of the fragment by interrupting the fragmented party talk, 'breaking in like a piccolo to Miss Compostella's harp'.

First Mrs Henedge invites Winsome Brookes to the piano. 'A fanfare? A requiem?' he offers – and eventually plays some of his own compositions (those bits of his opera *Justinian* which Firbank so closely[1] modelled on Rupert Brooke's real-life literary compositions).

Mrs Henedge's next invitation is to Mrs Shamefoot: to sing.

Mrs Shamefoot (after demur) begins: 'Ah! je suis fatiguée à mourir!', words which lead into 'O mon miroir fidèle', a passage which in turn leads to: 'Vénus, réponds-moi.'

Firbank's round within a round (round of party turns within the London round) has described an exact cycle. As a result, one invocation is superimposed on another: Vénus on Aphrodite.

The fusion of images liberates in Firbank enough psychological energy for him to pursue the archaeologising motif he introduced through the Professor.

The significance of the words Mrs Shamefoot sings is personal to her: 'dis-moi que je suis belle et que je serai belle éternellement! éternellement! éternellement!'

She is singing (to a glass – 'O mon miroir') her quest for eternity in the beauty of stained glass. Firbank has set to music the sigh his text attributed to Mrs Shamefoot earlier in the chapter: the sigh of the Egyptian 'for his pyramid'.[2]

And as a matter of fact (a fact no doubt present to Firbank's at least preconscious thoughts), this French and musical sigh *is* the sigh of an Egyptian.

What the words are is personal to Firbank.

Mrs Shamefoot is singing the address to the mirror, followed by the address to Venus, from the second act of Massenet's opera (which is set in Egypt) *Thaïs*.

('Ah! tais-toi, voix impitoyable!', Mrs Shamefoot sings, 'voix qui me dis: "Thaïs ne sera plus Thaïs! . . ."')

---

[1] Cf. Chapter VI, 6.
[2] Cf. Chapter XVI, 8.

Thus Firbank marks that he (like Robert Hichens) had discovered that the anecdote which Oscar Wilde told under the title *La Sainte Courtisane* had indeed (its story is the story of Massenet's opera) been 'treated by another'.[1]

(Perhaps Firbank's fusion of Sappho's Aphrodite with Massenet's Vénus was helped by the knowledge that Massenet also composed a *Sappho*.[2])

Between Sappho's Aphrodite and Massenet's Vénus Firbank has reversed the direction of his archaeological drive.

At first he went in pursuit (using the Professor as explorer) of the rock-bottom stratum of his own new aesthetic. Now, reversing the fugue, he burrows upwards again, cataloguing on his way the aesthetic strata which he rejected (or which he fled from) en route to Sappho.

The sequence of party pieces (there are three in all) at Mrs Henedge's Sunday[3] evening is a history of Firbank's aesthetic past.

In Winsome Brookes's/Rupert Brooke's party turn, Firbank rejects his own Cambridge fin-de-sièclism.

In Mrs Shamefoot's excerpt from *Thaïs* he rejects Wilde the sentimental Christian plagiarist, together with his own Wilde-influenced fiction published ten years before *Vainglory*, *Odette D'Antrevernes*, that tale of a figure who, expected to be sainte, turns out to be a courtisane.[4]

In the last of the amateur entertainments (certainly *Vainglory* 'commemorates the death of Arthur Firbank, a charming dilettante'[5] – an amateur entertainer) which Mrs Henedge invites from her guests, Firbank rejects Wilde the melodramatic author of *Salomé*, together with his own novel *The Artificial Princess* (*Salome, Or 'Tis A Pity That She Would*), in which he re-worked Wilde's Salome theme.

For the third and last of Mrs Henedge's invitations is to Mrs Thumbler's daughter, Mira Thumbler: 'My dear, won't you dance for us?'

(Again, Mrs Henedge's request is timed to avert a social disaster – and, in image, an aesthetic one, the puncturing of Firbank's chinoiserie method. 'Her hostess gathered by' Mira's 'silhouette that the temptation to poke a finger through a Chinese vellum screen, painted with water-lilies and fantastic swooping birds, was almost *more* than she could endure.')

---

[1] Cf. Chapter XVII, 6.

[2] The date of Jules Émile Frédéric Massenet's *Thaïs* is 1894, of his *Sappho* (thus spelt in *The Oxford Companion to Music*, whence I take these dates) 1897. Patrick J. Smith's *The Tenth Muse* records (pp. 317–18) that the libretto of *Thaïs* is by Louis Gallet but not whether Gallet based it on (cf. Chapter XVII, 6) Anatole France.

[3] Mrs Henedge to Lady Georgia in Chapter I: 'And I'm having a small party at my house, on Sunday, with his assistance, to make the line known.'

[4] Cf. Chapter XVII, 6.   [5] Cf. sub-section 2 of this chapter.

Mira, like Mrs Shamefoot before her, demurs. Mira's demur takes the form: ' "Oh, forgive me, please", she exclaimed, "but I should feel far too like . . . *you know*!" '

Mrs Henedge supplies (confidently restoring what has been lost from the fragment) 'The daughter of Herodias?'; and George Calvally ('that perfect painter', as the text has earlier explained him) supplies what the completion of the story requires, a murmur to the effect 'Anything you might ask for . . .'

What Mira asks for is to sit to him for her portrait.

The Artificial Princess leaned hard enough on Wilde's treatment of the Salome story to push its main emphases aside into oblique angles and subordinate clauses.[1] But in *Vainglory* Firbank rejects even *The Artificial Princess*. He redistributes Wilde totally. Salome's request is digested into a narrative pun[2] and becomes a request for her own head on a canvas.

(Even so, a trace of the process remains, unstressed, in the form of the ruined fragments of a verbal pun. Salome's biblical request reads: 'Give me here John Baptist's head in a charger.' That charger-dish has become, I suspect, a charger-warhorse[3] and re-emerges, re-arranged, in the name of Mira's John the Baptist: charger – cavalry – Calvally.)

For the sequence of three rejected performances which constitutes the second half of Chapter II of *Vainglory*, Firbank again[4] had a musical model.

The model this time is not a generic musical form but a specific piece of music (one which involves a specific piece of literature). It is not in musical form a fugue, but it is in a sense an opened-out fugue. It is what might result if you gave a fugue literary form (where the separate strands have to have different contents, and where they have to follow one another as wholes, not merely as entrances, because literature cannot arrange for several lines to sound simultaneously) but continued to express it in music.

The last movement of Beethoven's Ninth Symphony is prefaced by the orchestra's beginning to perform, and then rejecting (by cutting itself off), themes from (in sequence) the previous three movements.

The musical entertainments chez Mrs Henedge reject Firbank's past œuvre and preface his future œuvre on the model of Beethoven's preface to the last movement of his last sympathy.

Beethoven presently reinforces the already literary scheme of his three rejections by words themselves. The human voice enters the orchestral work: the musical rejections are voiced by the baritone in (Beethoven's) words 'O

---

[1] Cf. Chapter XVII, 11.   [2] Cf. Chapters IX, 9 and XVII, 11.

[3] I wonder if some unformulated recognition of the pun in *Vainglory* influenced Osbert Sitwell's story of Firbank's accusing Harold Nicolson 'of having stolen his charger' (cf. Chapter VI, 8 and *Memoir*, p. 129).

[4] Cf. sub-section 2 of this chapter.

Freunde, nicht diese Töne!' – and the rejected orchestral Töne are replaced by the setting, for orchestra and voices, of Schiller's Ode to Joy.

Firbank attained his Beethoven model for his own three musical rejections by bringing his round of amateur entertainments in yet another full cycle, and thereby achieving yet another superimposition. Chapter II of *Vainglory* builds up to the dizzying anticlimax of the Sappho fragment and thence staggers to the plateau of Sappho's Ode to Aphrodite. From there the second half declines, a fugue run backwards, on the literary model of Beethoven. Its downward slope is contoured in three stages, three coincidences and fusions of image: Ode to Aphrodite – address to Venus – Ode to Joy.

5. Notes to Chapter XVIII

THE incredible ich diens are on p. 211 in the *Complete* Firbank.

Ifan Kyrle Fletcher's remark about the death of Arthur Firbank, dilettante, is on p. 58 of the *Memoir*.

Swinburne's *Atalanta in Calydon* appeared in 1865.

The 'dear reader' in *The Artificial Princess* is on p. 46 in the *Complete* Firbank.

Salome's biblical request is in *Matthew* XIV, 8.

XIX

The Pastorals and the First Tragedy (*Vainglory* [1915]-2; *Inclinations* [1916]; *Caprice* [1917]; *Valmouth* [1919]; *The Princess Zoubaroff* [1920]; *Santal* [1921])

1. Monumental Pun . . .

THE language of unspoken puns, whereby Mira Thumbler[1] becomes Salome,[2] emerges again on Totterdown station.

Mrs Shamefoot and 'her old crony, Mrs. Barrow of Dawn' drink Veuve Clicquot from a picnic basket and anatomise the episcopal politics of Ashringford, while they wait for the Ashringford connexion (and Firbank establishes the connexion[3] between his London round and his grander Ashringford fugue[4]).

Near them there is compiled on the platform a baroque (and exotic) monument: one of Firbank's finest Salome-veiled hints of the unspeakable.[5]

Surrounded by smaller cases ('My dear, what a dreadful amount of etceteras you appear to bring,' Mrs Barrow observes to her crony), 'like a small town clustering about the walls of some lawless temple',[6] Mrs

---

[1] Mira's surname is itself a multiple half-spoken pun. As the name of her father, 'the restorer of Ashringford Cathedral' (*Complete* Firbank, p. 88), it is a comment on his practice of architecture: Thumbler = Fumbler. As the name of Mira, who dances, Thumbler = Tumbler (to which a touch of the pigeon may adhere). However, Mrs Calvally remarks to her husband, as they go home (*Complete* Firbank, p. 98) after Mira's Salomesque dance chez Mrs Henedge: 'It's extraordinary that a little skimped thing like Miss Thumbler should fascinate you!' – a remark which suggests that Mira is also Hans Andersen's tiny heroine Thumbelina.

[2] Cf. Chapter XVIII, 4. [3] Cf. Chapters XVI, 5 and XVII, 1.
[4] Cf. Chapter XVIII, 2. [5] Cf. Chapter XIV, 6.
[6] I think the temple is partly The Temple, frequented by lawyers. The pun is an exotic version of that whereby Vyvyan Holland called Firbank, at a college mainly of

Shamefoot's 'principal portmantcau' is a rose-coloured[1] chest 'which, with its many foreign labels, exhaled an atmosphere of positive scandal. No nice maid would stand beside it.'

The foreign labels are autobiographical[2] to Firbank – and likewise, he would hope, the atmosphere of positive scandal. Indeed, the monumental pile is a monument to his minion impersonation.[3] The entire conceit is (as well as a presage of what will happen to Ashringford when the train finally delivers Mrs Shamefoot there) a concealed pun on the word *baggage*.

2. . . . into Literary Pun

THAT pun in the bridge passage undergoes a telling transformation when *Vainglory* establishes itself at Ashringford.

The concealed *baggage* becomes a concealed *trollop*. Firbank's Ashringford is Anthony Trollope's Barchester re-satirised.

Trollope and *trollop* were, of course, indistinguishable to Firbank's inveterate bad spelling.

Indeed, in 1903 or so, in his correspondence with his lesser literary mentor Rollo St Clair Talboys,[4] Firbank fantasised himself for fun a girl-friend named Edna – and described her as a 'little trollope'.

(*Vainglory* might be described as more than a little Trollope.)

3. Distribution

THE fugue which constitutes the body of *Vainglory* is topographically distributed over three main fixed points in Ashringford and its neighbourhood.

It is a plan whose type is borrowed (especially, of course, at its episcopal fixed point) from Trollope, though the firmer constructional genius of Jane Austen shews through from the background.

Indeed, a few efflorescences from Jane Austen have grown through the trellis and into the foreground.

The genteel, gossipy and financially reduced existence at Ashringford

---

incipient lawyers, 'almost illegal', which Firbank later transformed into the 'lawless' look of Reggie Quintus (cf. Chapters IX, 8 and XIV, 10).

[1] of (cf. Chapter XV, 1–6) course. But the portmanteau, besides being floral in its own right, has been influenced by the temple with clustering town to which it is compared. A tinge of its tint is borrowed from John William Burgon's famous line about Petra: 'A rose-red city – half as old as Time!'

[2] as sub-section 9 of this chapter will detail about the composition of *Vainglory*.

[3] Cf. Chapters VIII, 2 and XIV, 10.

[4] (Cf. Chapter XIII, 5); the 'little trollope' is quoted, with an implied date of circa 1903, in the *Biography*, p. 35.

of Mrs Wookie and her daughter, Miss (Kate) Wookie, is a re-creation of the situation in Highbury of Mrs Bates and Miss Bates in *Emma*.

In token of her literary descent, Miss Wookie (in speaking of an idiosyncrasy of her own [one rather like that of the Queen in *The Artificial Princess*], 'You know I collect motor numbers, which obliges me frequently to run out into the road. . . .'[1]) assumes the very idiom of Jane Austen's personages (or of Wilde's personages when *they* echo Jane Austen[2]): 'I hope I'm not so vulgar as to bang a door, still, when I saw him coming, I confess I shut it!'

And it is from *Pride and Prejudice*, from the unexpected marriage of Charlotte Lucas to the unspeakable clergyman Mr Collins,[3] that *Vainglory* has borrowed the unexpected marriage of Miss Wardle to that (according to Mrs Wookie) 'disgrace to his cloth' Mr Pet.[4]

The function of the 'great house' in a Jane Austen novel is discharged in *Vainglory* by Stockingham, the Blueharnis country place,[5] which gathers together the itinerant dramatis personae because Lady Georgia invites her London acquaintance to stay during the summer.

A less great house, Dawn, is a subsidiary gathering-place for permanent residents – except when Mrs Barrow (who becomes Lady Barrow when her husband becomes Sir Sartorious as a reward for 'doctoring the Asz'[6]) can contrive to hear the ominous family raven and escape to London.

And the third fixed point, inhabited by permanent residents but also attracting tourists, is the episcopal nexus. The Cathedral itself (Saint Dorothy's), where Mrs Cresswell, Ashringford's heretical saint, is buried in the floral odour of sanctity[7] and in whose tower Mrs Shamefoot aspires to be windowed, is surrounded, like Mrs Shamefoot's portmanteau on the platform, by a clustering small town: the Cresswell Arms; the 'municipal museum in Ghost Street' (visited in an aesthetic frame of mind[8] by Miss

---

[1] The text in the *Complete* Firbank (p. 137) omits the 'out' in 'run out into the road'. The 'out is given in the first edition (p. 116). [2] Cf. Chapter V, 6.
[3] This motif will reappear in sub-section 11 of this chapter.
[4] Perhaps here again a verbal echo confirms how much of *Pride and Prejudice* had stuck unnoticed in Firbank's memory. A 'sudden noise below seemed to speak the whole house' (of the recently married Collinses) 'in confusion', a confusion that turns out to be caused by the arrival at the gate of Lady Catherine de Bourgh; and Elizabeth Bennet comments 'And is this all? [. . .] I had expected at least that the pigs were got into the garden.' Perhaps that comment reappears in Mrs Henedge's complaint at Ashringford: 'Well, I never know what goes on, except when the sow gets into the Dean's garden. And then I hear the screams.' (*Pride and Prejudice*, Pan edition, p. 119; *Complete* Firbank, p. 191).
[5] A perceptive friend has pointed out to me *why* Lady Georgia Blueharnis's house is called Stockingham: BLUE (harnis) STOCKING (ham).   [6] Cf. Chapter XV, 4.
[7] Cf. Chapters XIII, 2 and XV, 15.
[8] (Cf. Chapter XVI, 10); Sumph remarks 'Whenever I'm able I like to encourage anything that's Art' (*Complete* Firbank, p. 176).

Compostella's and Mrs Henedge's maids); and the Bishop's Palace – whose Trollopean personnel comprises Doctor and Lady Anne Pantry; whichever of the Bishop's eleven sisters whose turn (by rotation) it is to be in attendance; and Miss Hospice ('Lady Anne was fond of her secretary because of her wild, beautiful handwriting, that seemed to fly, and because she really did enjoy to snub the Bishop's sisters'[1]), to whom Firbank attributes some (by his biographer's attribution) early verses of his own.[2]

Doctor Pantry Firbank named, I surmise, by extrapolation from a bishop's apron – which suggested to Firbank butlers, and thence pantries.

Trollope's own episcopal naming Firbank borrowed not for the residents of the Bishop's Palace but for the aspirant to permanent residence in the Cathedral in glass. From Trollope's Bishop's wife, Mrs Proudie, Firbank's thoughts went to Proudfoot. Thence, by a beautiful (and beautifully justified) inversion, Mrs Shamefoot.

4. Fugue

'A fugue and a breath of air', Lady Anne said, 'should be quite enough.'
Vainglory (Chapter XIV)

THE 'figures of varying heights trotting all the same way'[3] through Firbank's fugue are in pursuit of their hearts' desires – desires which also are of varying heights.

The breaths of air that Firbank sets between his figures are the gaps between pursuit and attainment. It is the hearts' desires which are in fugue, in perpetual escape from their pursuers.

('Bold Lover, never, never canst thou kiss.' Firbank's Grecian frieze is inscribed on a Grecian urn.)

Through one of the carefully positioned gaps in his composition Firbank has carelessly allowed Mrs Claud Harvester to tumble[4] – no doubt because Mrs Harvester (named Cleopatra after the trollop of all time) was, like the 'little trollope' Edna, a fantasy, not a heart's desire.

The tallest figure in pursuit of the tallest ambition (a tall story, a tall storey, the tower of Saint Dorothy's) is Mrs Shamefoot in pursuit of eternity and demi-canonisation in a towered window.

Mrs Shamefoot's pursuit is an attempt to bring her own career into

---

[1] Cf. Chapter X, 11.
[2] The *Biography* (p. 35) identifies the four lines that begin 'Poor pale pierrot through the dark boughs peering' (*Complete* Firbank, p. 133; *Vainglory*, 1915, p. 108), in which Miss Hospice 'attempts to out-Chatterton Chatterton', as part of Firbank's own poem *The Wind & the Roses* (cf. Chapter XVIII, 2).
[3] Cf. Chapter XVIII, 4.   [4] Cf. Chapter XV, 8.

parallel with that of Ashringford's earlier half-saint, Mrs Cresswell. To begin with (until she invokes higher help), Mrs Shamefoot is frustrated: by, for instance, such fobbing-off suggestions of alternatives as Doctor Pantry's recommendation of a brass in the Cathedral floor. (But to that Mrs Shamefoot makes inspired anwer. ' "But brass", she said, "would lead to rubbings. I know so well! Persons on all fours, perpetually bending over me." "I can see no objection to that." "I don't think my husband would like it." ')

About the portmanteau figure of Mrs Shamefoot with its aspiration to a 'lawless temple' trot the lesser pursuits and evasions.

Miss Valley, the biographer, is evaded by the life history of Mrs Cresswell, which she hagiographically aspires to chronicle. Just as Firbank, in the course of his own hagiographical pursuit of Wilde, found Wilde's son, so Miss Valley comes on a descendant of Mrs Cresswell working in the Ashringford laundry. To this small boy Firbank gives the regal name Reggie which, via lawlessness/illegality,[1] he associated with Vyvyan Holland. Indeed he may have associated Reggie Cresswell's duties with the legal profession; for, as Miss Valley puts it, 'this carrier of dirty linen ... is Reggie ... Cresswell – a descendant of the saint....'

Mrs Henedge is evaded by Rome (to which she aspires to build a monument, a Catholic church,[2] at Ashringford – scandalously, since she is the widow of the previous Bishop) and by the genius to which she aspires to play patron in her protégé Winsome Brookes.

Winsome is evaded by his own genius – and by a decision about whether he should or shouldn't, for his début as a concert pianist, change his name (to the floral transvestism of Rose de Tivoli[3]) as Firbank changed his[4] for the Firbankian début he was making with *Vainglory*.

Even Winsome's minion, Andrew, 'goes' (by Winsome's account) 'stumbling along towards some ideal; it's difficult to say quite what'.

Miss Compostella is frustrated in her pursuit of Claud Harvester and of avant-garde status.

(Mrs Steeple, the declaimer in Chapter II of the Ode to Aphrodite, is introduced into that chapter by Firbank's text with: 'One burning afternoon in July, with the thermometer at 90, the ridiculous woman had played *Rosmersholm* in Camberwell. Nobody had seen her do it, but it was conceivable that she had been very fine.' That a rival should champion Ibsen south of the river demands a comeback from Miss Compostella. She makes it, again through Firbank's text, two pages later: at dinner, where she

---
[1] Cf. sub-section 1 of this chapter (and Chapters IX, 8 and XIV, 10).
[2] Cf. Chapter XII, 6.   [3] Cf. Chapter VI, 6.
[4] Cf. Chapter VII, 4.

confides a remark to her neighbour while 'she cut a little wild-duck with her luminous hands'.[1])

The gaps which in *Vainglory* stand between the personages and fulfilment of their ambitions are not straight distances, of the kind which could be reduced by simple acceleration. They are those jagged, mosaic gaps in terms of which Firbank composes.

The pursuits in *Vainglory* are conducted sub specie aeternitatis *and* in the light of a thought of Mrs Cresswell's. 'Has not Mrs. Cresswell (in a trance) described heaven as *another* grim reality?'

The tragi-comic atmosphere Firbank infuses into the spaces between pursuer and ambition, thereby aerating[2] his book, consists not just of the vanity but also of the idiosyncraticness of human wishes.

5. Harvest Cycle

THE *Vainglory* fugue is transacted inside the confines of Claud Harvester's frieze, *Vaindreams*.

(But Claud Harvester himself – or his œuvre – is unconfined. At his début in Firbankianism Firbank closed no literary possibilities to his self-portrait. Claud Harvester is a novelist ['As a novelist he was almost successful. His books were watched for . . . but without impatience.'], a playwright [' "Never mind, Mr. Harvester", Lady Georgia was saying to him, "I'm sure your play was exquisite; or it would have had a longer run." '] and a poet [waiting for the Sappho fragment, Lady Listless is 'perched uncomfortably on Claud Harvester's *New Poems*'].)

And the transaction-time of the fugue is enclosed within the pastoral significance[3] of the name Harvester. The seeds of the book are sown at the Sappho party, which takes place in the spring.[4] High summer, with its cardinal propensity to thunderstorms, is passed at Ashringford. By the final chapter Mrs Shamefoot has reaped the harvest of vitrification within her

---

[1] Miss Compostella's Ibsenism is consonant with the career of her half-namesake (cf. Chapter XV, 15) Stella Patrick Campbell, who (according to Alan Dent's *Mrs. Patrick Campbell*) in 1896 played the Rat Wife in the first English performance of *Little Eyolf* before going on to Hedda and other Ibsen rôles. By the last chapter of *Vainglory* Miss Compostella's avant-gardisme has advanced to 1907: she is to play Pegeen Mike (in J. M. Synge's *The Playboy of the Western World*) in the Greek theatre at Stockingham. However, the next conversational breath, 'I see she's reviving *Magda*', re-establishes her Mrs Patrick Campbellism, *Magda* being a play (by Hermann Sudermann) in which Mrs Patrick Campbell first played in 1896 and did indeed more than once revive.

[2] Cf. Chapter XVI.   [3] Cf. Chapter XV, 6.

[4] 'Dear Julia' (sc. Compostella), 'I've seen nothing of her since the Sappho supper-party Mrs. Henedge gave in the spring' (*Complete* Firbank, p. 187).

lifetime. 'Achieving sainthood by leaps and bounds', she remains at Ashringford in proximity to herself-in-glass. She is waiting, ultimately, for death ('I am afraid I frighten Lady Anne. . . . Old Mrs. Wookie made me some advances with a *face-cloth* she had worked me for my demise. . . . And I've become quite friendly with the Pets. He has such character. Force. I am leaving him a lock of my hair.') and, immediately, to witness the autumn at Ashringford. (Lady Castleyard says: 'I think the autumn here should be simply sublime.')

6. Counter-Fugue

WITH only one pair of personages does Firbank invert his fugal purpose.

He sows a love affair at that indeed seminal Sappho party, where George Calvally becomes a John the Baptist fascinated by the dancing of the 'little skimped thing',[1] Mira Thumbler. In the ensuing fugue Firbank turns Calvally and Mira, alone among his personages, to face one another and permits them to trot through his frieze to a meeting.

Their happy adultery runs (beneath a poudre-de-riz sky[2]) in counter-fugue to the pastoral pursuits and frustrations at Ashringford. Theirs is an adultery conducted 'through the slow, deep streets of the capital' – in London out-of-season.

Their achieved happiness, when they finally run away together to Italy ('And he went away with such an overweight of luggage. . . .' Mrs Calvally reports to Mrs Henedge, who comments 'I expect he took his easels!'), constitutes a further obstacle in the pursuits of others: an obstacle less to Mrs Calvally, who quickly recovers 'all her old tranquillity of gardens' and pointedly *doesn't* go into 'one of Lucile's black dreams'[3] in order to mourn the loss of her husband's affections, than to Mrs Henedge's building mania. (George Calvally had been going to paint the frescoes in Mrs Henedge's church.) ' "It is certainly unfortunate", Mrs. Henedge complained, "that the daughter of my architect should run away with my painter." '

7. Redistribution

ECHOING and counterpointing the book's fugal and counter-fugal structure, Firbank practises beautiful, virtuoso reversals (like that in *Vainglory*'s opening line) of the traditionally logical order of disclosure.

[1] Cf. sub-section 1 of this chapter.
[2] (*Complete* Firbank, p. 151); cf. Chapters VIII, 2; X, 6; and XIII, 3.
[3] Cf. Chapter XV, 9.

Mrs Cresswell and the Cresswell Arms are introduced by allusion, and even that 'somewhat saturnine little song of Mrs. Cresswell', *I am disgusted with Love*,[1] is recited (by Lady Georgia, at Stockingham, in the Greek theatre ['Darling Georgia! Why will she always withdraw to the gladiators'[2] seats?']), long in advance of the explanation of whom Mrs Cresswell *was*.

("But Mrs. Cresswell", she enquired, "who was she – exactly?" "Primarily", the Bishop replied, "she was a governess. And with some excellent people too.")

By the same technique practised on a smaller scale, Firbank submerges the context round a line of dialogue and leaves it startlingly stranded, like Miss Hospice's remark (to Lady Anne), 'I've told Gripper again to sponge the stretchers', and then triumphantly restores context with an explanation but no loss of poetic excitement: 'The bi-weekly Ambulance Classes at the Palace, so popular socially, were, it must be owned, on a parallel with the butter-making at Trianon.'

8. Tutti and a Syncopated Stress

IT is by a similar rearrangement of the expectations of conventional logic that Firbank distributes the stresses of his narrative in relation to the grand orchestral passages in his texture.

There are in *Vainglory* three major orchestral tutti,[3] three social set-pieces which assemble and concert the separate lines of the fugue: the Sappho party in Chapter II;[4] the dinner party which Lady Anne Pantry gives at the Bishop's Palace and which occupies Chapter XIV; and the assembly at Ashringford, in Chapter XXII, of residents and visitors in celebration of Mrs Shamefoot's window.

The first and last of these social tutti coincide with the first and last of the main narrative stresses in the pursuit conducted by Firbank's tallest frieze-figure, Mrs Shamefoot. The Sappho party states her ambition to be windowed; the assembly in Chapter XXII celebrates her achievement of it. But the middle stress of Mrs Shamefoot's pursuit falls, in two parts (cause and, possibly, effect), just before and just after (in Chapters XIII and XVI) the middle social set-piece, Lady Anne's dinner of Chapter XIV.

Lady Anne's dinner-party counterpoises Mrs Henedge's supper-party. It

---

[1] Cf. Chapter XIII, 3.

[2] Firbank no more distinguished Greeks from Romans than (cf. Chapter X, 12) Italian from French.

[3] or tuttis; I don't know how to form the English plural of an Italian plural which is an English singular.

[4] Cf. Chapter XVIII, 3.

does so by taking up and amplifying the other-than-literary associations set in train by Sappho's presiding over the supper.

Lady Anne's dinner (she was scorned the lower status of a tea-party) is a conference: 'for women alone'. It begins as an assembly of emancipated women ('Lady Anne accepted a conferential cigarette from Mrs. Barrow of Dawn') and beautifully takes on a hint of the outline of a witches' sabbat.

(Its burden is that of *A Plea for the Separation of the Sexes*.[1])

Mrs Cresswell's poem is given an impromptu performance as a fugue for (fake cockney[2]) speaking voices. The guests recite a solo line apiece (slogans, perhaps, of women's emancipation – or witches' runes) and come together in chorus for the last line (which is the same as the first). ' "I'm that disgusted with love", the ladies chanted charmingly all together.'

Like Mrs Henedge's, Lady Anne's social evening dissolves into music (though Lady Anne, less exorbitant, is satisfied with 'a fugue and a breath of air') and dancing – but dancing more Sapphic than Salomesque: 'Notwithstanding, upon the veranda, Miss Valley and Aurelia' (the Bishop's sister) 'were sketching out a valse.'

Miss Valley is perhaps celebrating a forward step in her biographical ambition. At an earlier point in the dinner party she has been conducted by Lady Anne to the Ponte di Sospiri (which 'connects us to the cloisters') to inspect the series of Mortlake tapestries that depicts Mrs Cresswell's life.

The Mortlake tapesty series, like the Tiepolo series, echoes the fugal form of *Vainglory* (and the frieze form of *Vaindreams*).[3] Along the tapestry series Firbank runs his fugue in reverse. 'Lady Anne commenced the inspection, starting instinctively at the end. And the end, as she pointed out, was simply frantic Bacchanals. After (*à rebours*) came the Martyrdom.'

Thus Firbank turns his reversed fugue into a tribute to J.-K. Huysmans's *À Rebours* and, through that, to Firbank's own local martyr, Oscar Wilde.[4]

The reversal in the order of Mrs Cresswell's tapestried life (and death) is echoed in the valse sketched by her biographer and the Bishop's sister. 'Aurelia reversed. "Mrs. Shamefoot won't die", she said, "unless we kill her." '

---

[1] (one of the books which [cf. Chapter XV, 19] Firbank placed in Bertie Waldorf's house in *The New Rythum*); the point is explicitly made in *Vainglory* in a conversation (*Complete* Firbank, p. 179) between Mrs Shamefoot and Lady Castleyard: ' "Do you suppose, if there were no men in the world, that women would frightfully mind?" '

[2] Cf. Chapter XIII, 3.

[3] Cf. Chapter XVIII, 3 and 4.

[4] 'The book in *Dorian Gray* is one of the many books I have never written, but it is partly suggested by Huysmans's *À Rebours*' (Oscar Wilde in 1892; *Letters*, edited by Rupert Hart-Davis, p. 313).

Aurelia is discussing the question about which Lady Anne has called the conference: whether Mrs Shamefoot should get her window.

But it is not anything said at the conferential dinner which determines the fact that she does get it, the fact celebrated in the third and last social tutti.

It is in the last social set-piece that the streamers of conversation flap most surrealistically (just as it is in the last of the five chapters of the prelude that Firbank opens out his images to admit surreal space[1]).

The Sapphic fragmentation of technique, whose nucleus was delivered in the first tutti, explodes in the third.

The dialogue looks on the page like a transcription of a Sappho papyrus from which time has eroded the left-hand side:

' "... A day together."
' "... Rabbits."
' "... As tall as Iss'y."
' "... Precedence!"
' "... A regular peruke."
' "... An interesting trio!" '

It is from this heated bubbling that Mrs Shamefoot steps into the chill solitude of the Cathedral, there to spend a frightening night alone with her window.

She has attained her window neither through nor despite the dinner-party conference of Chapter XIV, but (perhaps) because she opened Chapter XIII with 'Wierus, Furiel, Charpon, Charmias!'

Watching her (from an 'Anne settle', where she lies 'in a rather beautiful heap'), Lady Castleyard comments: 'If the devil won't come, [. . .] we can't force him.' Mrs Shamefoot is piqued: 'Not come? Why, he's taken all the wave out of my hair.' Lady Castleyard concedes: 'It certainly *is* less successful, from the side.'

Whether or not as a further result of the devil's intervention, there follows (two chapters *after* the dinner-party) 'the accident', as it first appears, by allusion, in Lady Georgia's conversation – which turns out, on Firbank's held-back, syncopated stress, to consist of the felling of part of the Cathedral structure by lightning.

In the rebuilding Mrs Shamefoot is vitrified.

Thus Firbank justifies Miss Missingham's inclusion of Ashringford Cathedral in her work with the Hugh-Benson-suggestive title, *Sacerdotalism and Satanism,*[2] together with his own inversion of the name Proudfoot into Shamefoot.[3]

[1] Cf. Chapter XVIII, 2.   [2] Cf. Chapter VIII, 6.
[3] Cf. sub-section 3 of this chapter.

After 'Hannah was telling us the night it fell she noticed devils sort-of-hobble-stepping beneath the trees', there is no doubt what *kind* of foot it is that occasions Mrs Shamefoot shame.

(No wonder that Lady Castleyard, visiting Mrs Shamefoot at the end of the book in her autumnal trance of sainthood achieved, remarks [on the subject of antique shops]: 'And the last time I was here I unearthed such a sweet old chair with hoofs.')

Ashringford's medieval saint was heretical, the modern counterpart who follows in her pattern diabolic.

And indeed Mrs Shamefoot (whose propensity for hagiographically following out saintly patterns is patterned on Firbank's own) follows the pattern of Mrs Cresswell's life (as tapestried) to the point, even, of the 'frantic Bacchanals'.

On her vitrification day, 'According to *The Ashringford Chronicle* there'll be almost a procession.' 'Oh, nothing half so formal. . . .'

But then a rout is indeed not half so formal.

It looks at first as though the celebrations are to be limited to 'Children singing; scattering flowers', because of the Bishop's objections: 'The *panther skins* upset him. . . .'

But presently Lady Anne sits sewing a panther skin on the Palace lawn.

('To make it less schismatical, I believe I'm going to take off the tail.' 'Oh no. Give it a careless twist.')

Thus Firbank opposes the unofficial (indeed, careless) vestments of paganism, panther skins and tails, to the Bishop's lawn.

It is another of his concealed puns: a dangerous concealed entrance decoratively and architecturally designed into the baroque monument (of incongruity) constituted by *Vainglory*.

Vainglory is a collage, a counterpoint of superimposed images: an etching of an English cathedral city across which Firbank drags the warm spotted colour of Titian s bacchanal rout.

(9. Itinerary

HINTS of the relation, itself fragmentary,[1] of Firbank's topographically fragmented way of life to his literary technique are to be had from the time-table of the composition of *Vainglory* that can be extracted from the *Biography*'s[2] account.

Late 1912: After an autumn visit to Venice, Firbank was living in Laura

---

[1] Cf. Chapter XVI, 6. [2] pp. 117–33.

Place, Bath and began to write *Vainglory* [which was at that stage set, scarcely imaginably, in Venice].

I conjecture that it was Bath which provoked some of *Vainglory*'s Jane-Austenism.[1] Surely, too, Mrs and Miss Wookie have borrowed their surname from the nearby topographical feature of Somerset, Wookey Hole. And perhaps it was because Firbank had recently seen the rock formation called the Witch of Wookey that his fragments from Sappho include the one about Gello, the bogeywoman of Lesbos.[2]

May 1913: Firbank went from Bath to Salisbury.

July 1913: Firbank began a French tour.

Autumn 1913: Firbank returned to England and visited York, whence [with the substitution of a street for a gate] he transposed[3] Whip-ma-Whop-ma Gate to Ashringford.

End of 1913 and first half of 1914: Firbank was in London, at an address now unknown.

June 1914: He visited Paris.

July 1914: He went to Rome, Assisi [whence perhaps Saint Clare[4] made contributions to Mrs Cresswell], Perugia and Florence.

2 August 1914: Firbank spent his last night in Florence barefooted and nightshirted watching lightning over the Palazzo Vecchio – whose tower perhaps contributed as much as Salisbury and York to Saint Dorothy's, Ashringford.

3 August 1914: Firbank was in Venice, whence he returned to England [via Como] because war had begun.

September 1914: Firbank visited York, Harrogate, Edinburgh [and John Gray[5]], Glasgow, Durham, Carlisle.

Early December 1914: Firbank submitted *Vainglory* to Martin Secker, who refused it.[6]

End of 1914: Firbank was living in a flat at 19 Old Square, Lincoln's Inn.)

10. Patterns of Irony

Vainglory is a complex grand fugue for full orchestra, symphonic in its breadth.

Firbank's next two books (which he published in 1916 and 1917) are certainly not slighter in the slighting sense. They do, however, select fewer

---

[1] Cf. sub-section 3 of this chapter.
[2] Cf. Chapter XVIII, 3.   [3] Cf. Chapter XV, 19.
[4] circa 1194–1253; cf. the discussion of Mrs Cresswell's date in Chapter XIII, 2.
[5] Cf. Chapter XII, 6.   [6] Cf. Chapter XV, 16.

and narrower, though possibly even tougher, threads of material (threads drawn out, as a matter of fact, from themes already present in *Vainglory*) and fashion them into patterns which imprison a violent intensity of emotion.

The sadness in *Vainglory* is in *Inclinations* pitched as a cry. *Caprice* is the first of Firbank's tragedies.

If *Vainglory* is a frieze in low relief, Firbank for his next two books melted down its material and spun it into two relentless designs in wrought iron.

11. Diptych

'In Arcadia', Miss O'Brookomore declared, 'I intend to coil my hair like rams' horns.'

Inclinations (Part I)

MR COLLINS, the anti-hero of *Pride and Prejudice*, present as a ghost in *Vainglory*,[1] has positively given his name to the anti-heroine or the, at least, anti-ingénue of *Inclinations*, Mabel Collins.

Perhaps it is because the name is a borrowed fit that Firbank shrugs it a little to and fro, causing Mabel Collins to devise her shopping pseudonym[2] by means of an associative chain ('Collins, Colline, Collina *Hill*') that exposes Firbank's tactics with names as analytically as the Sappho supper-party in *Vainglory* exposes his strategy with images.

And indeed it is the double theme of that supper-party, Sapphic Greek and Sapphic sexuality, which is pursued in the first (and major) part of *Inclinations*.

The impetus which moves that first half comes from Gerald(ine) O'Brookomore, and it begins as an impetus of Firbankian hagiography:[3] towards following out an exemplary pattern.

Biographer, author of *Those Gonzagas*, Miss O'Brookomore has evidently patterned herself on the biographer, author of *The Home Life of Lucretia Borgia*,[4] in *Vainglory*, Mrs Asp – whom indeed, by a Firbankian perpetuation,[5] Miss O'Brookomore meets in the second chapter of *Inclinations*.

Miss O' Brookomore's biographical researches bear a fictitious fruit in the epigraph to *Inclinations* (in, that is, the first edition; the epigraph is suppressed from the *Complete* Firbank, and the *Bibliography* records only its existence, not its text). In a snatch of 17th- or 18th-century conversation (which comes out rather Irish in tone), Firbank invokes the scandalousness of flirting with

[1] Cf. sub-section 3 of this chapter.   [2] Cf. Chapter XV, 12.
[3] Cf. Chapter XIII, 2.   [4] Cf. Chapter XIV, 2.
[5] Cf. Chapter X, 2.

the Holy Father (a secondary assault on the incest taboo) as guardian angel to the scandalous homosexual theme of his book: ' "*Besides, I never ventured once to carry you with me to any conference I had with the Pope for fear you should be trying some of your coquettish airs upon him.*" – Lady Kitty Crockodile to Miss Lydell.'

(*Crockodile* may be mimicking the spelling of the period; or it may just be Firbank's spelling.)

In the direct exercise of her profession, Miss O'Brookomore again acts out Firbank's hagiographical impulse, as well as practising a professional orderliness of mind (coupled with a disorderliness, probably reflective of Firbank's own state of mind, about the alphabet) that licenses Firbank to compile one of his most numinous talismanic lists.[1] The labels (painted on 'tinted pearl') in Miss O'Brookomore's card index run 'Reminiscences. Anecdotes. Apologias. Crimes. Follies. Fabrications. Nostalgia. Mysticism. Trivia. Human Documents. Love Letters. His to Me: Mine to Him.'

A Mortlake tapestry incidentally mentioned on the opening page of *Inclinations* might be filed under the first of Miss O'Brookomore's labels, in reminiscence of Mrs Shamefoot's pilgrimage through *Vainglory* in the tapestried steps of Mrs Cresswell.[2]

Miss O'Brookomore herself, who is patterned on all her biographical subjects to the extent of seeing a bodily likeness between herself and each of them, plans to follow the example of her present subject, Mrs (Kate/Kitty) Kettler, geographically as well: 'I intend taking a fairly extensive trip in *her* footsteps.'

The footsteps lead to Greece. 'What would I not give', Mabel Collins declares (on her knees), 'to go with you!' And Gerald O'Brookomore's own inclinations lead her to propose it.

'Was it solely Vampirism that made me ask her?' Miss O'Brookomore wonders.

Mrs Shamefoot's diabolism assumes, in Miss O'Brookomore, the cast of a vampire, giving her very headgear ('a bewildering affair with a vampire-bat's-wing slanting behind') the sinister wings against which other Firbankian heroines phobically flick.[3] But it is not in the end Miss O'Brookomore who is sinister.

From their first verbal riffle through their itinerary (a riffle in which Firbank's virtuosity with dialogue indicates climax by a change of preposition), Miss O'Brookomore and Miss Collins are bound for Claud Harvester's pastoral destination (though that is now conceived less as the

---

[1] Cf. Chapter XV, 19.   [2] Cf. sub-section 8 of this chapter.
[3] Cf. Chapter XIV, 9.

background to *The Winter's Tale*[1] than as that wood near Athens in *A Midsummer Night's Dream*[2]):

' "At Corinth! . . ."
' "At Aulis!"
' "At Athens!"
' "At Epidauros!"
' "At Mycenae!"
' "In Arcadia!"
' "It would be like a fairy dream." '

After three brief chapters of prelude in England, *Inclinations* is in train in the train.

'Reading in the train would upset anyone' is the sympathetic comment of Miss Collins, who is not much given to reading anywhere ('The only books I care for are those about Farms').

'I was renewing my acquaintance with the classics,' Miss O'Brookomore intellectually answers.

She is not alone in the exercise.

As the pilgrims progress, together with Miss O'Brookomore's lady's maid, Palmer (whose name incarnates the fact of pilgrimage[3]), they accumulate round them a cast of other ladies and their maids (and, sometimes, husbands).

The cast includes Miss Arne, who is spun from the same Stellar[4] material as Miss Compostella in *Vainglory*: 'I'm Miss Arne. Mary Arne – the actress. [. . .] I often say I'm the only Lady Teazle!'[5]

Miss Arne, too, is renewing her acquaintance with the classics. 'I'm on my way to Greece to study Lysistrata. [. . .] As I told the silly critics, I mean to treat her as a character-part.'

At the skirts of the cast there trails, unwelcome to Miss O'Brookomore,

---

[1] Cf. Chapter XV, 6.

[2] And indeed when they (and several other travellers) reached Athens, ' "I spent most of" ' the day ' "in a wood on the Marathon Road", Mrs. Arbanel said, "with *A Midsummer Night's Dream*. . . ."

' "Hermia! Lysander! Oberon! Titania! Oh dear!"

'Miss Collins showed her culture.

' "Bottom", she added.'

[3] 'Palmer [. . .] A pilgrim who had returned from the Holy Land, in token of which he carried a palm-branch or palm-leaf [. . .]; often simply = *pilgrim*' (*Shorter Oxford English Dictionary*).

[4] Cf. Chapter XV, 15.

[5] And Bernard Shaw did indeed say 'Mrs Patrick Campbell struck me as being exactly right, for modern purposes, in her performance' as Lady Teazle in 1896 (*Our Theatres in the Nineties*, Volume II, p. 171).

Mabel's shipboard pick-up ('He will keep bumping into me'), Count Pastorelli.

Athens, however, fills up with the safely English – or English-speaking, since they include the drunken Australian Miss Dawkins, a Siegfried figure in perpetual quest of her mislaid parents, who becomes a 'huge recruit' drilled by Miss Arne into preparing to play Lampito to Miss Arne's Lysistrata.

The influx of English 'Society' into Athens allows Firbank to place, in one of the antique shops his upper-class tourists frequent, the pack of cards that once belonged to Deirdre[1] re-written into the classical shape of a tea-set that 'belonged to Iphigenia – in Tauris'.

With yet more inspired precision he places an 'Even so' in his upper-class tourists' dialogue and hinges on it one of his most delicate reversals of logic into surrealism.

' "I'm told the measles in Athens just now is very bad." '

' "Even so, I must say, I find the city dull." '

It is Mrs Cowsend who finds Athens dull, and she does so because Mr or Professor (Firbank's titling varies) Cowsend is given to passing 'the entire day poking about the Pnyx. . . .'

Firbank probably hesitated over giving Cowsend a professorship for fear of pointing too blatantly out that he is a mere echo of Professor Inglepin in *Vainglory*.

But other *Vainglory* themes are amplified.

The visit in that book of two aesthetic maids to a museum[2] is in *Inclinations* expanded into the expedition[3] of a whole posse to the Acropolis.

Climbing the slope, they discuss past employers (' "Once", Mrs. Arbanel's maid declared, "I took a situation with a literary lady – the Scottish-Sappho" ') and present employers equally literary and equally Sapphic. It is remarked in italics of Miss O'Brookomore that *'When she's with Miss Mabel she looks quite different.'*

Among the employers, the dinner-party of *Vainglory* 'for women alone' is opened-out, in *Inclinations*, into the yet more emancipated gesture of (at Salamis) an all-women shooting-party.

There, too,[4] an accident occurs whose nature Firbank discloses only on a held-back beat. It turns out that one of the shooters has been accidentally shot (dead).

The victim turns out to be Miss Arne.

(It is the first time Firbank kills off an actress.)

[1] Cf. Chapter VIII, 7. [2] Cf. sub-section 3 of this chapter.
[3] Cf. Chapter XIV, 10. [4] Cf. sub-section 8 of this chapter.

And still Count Pastorelli pursues Mabel Collins through Greece.

From him Miss O'Brookomore snatches Mabel away on ever hastier, ever more relentless travels. Her pursuit of a Sapphic pastoral idyll has turned into a fugue from Count Pastorelli, in which she and Mabel are always packing and moving on.

And Miss O'Brookomore (as Mabel explains to Count Pastorelli, whose arrival at their hotel prompts the packing) 'always sings as she packs! Just making it up as she goes –'

Firbank is aerating his text with lines of verse.

And so identified is he with Miss O'Brookomore's plea-by-flight for the separation of the sexes that the folkish ballad he has her make up as she goes is Firbank's autobiography, his confession to being a princess (child of that old Tory knight, Sir Thomas), to being the sole survivor of the three Firbank sons, and to being (like the form of Miss O'Brookomore's name) Irish.

> For I am the old King's daughter,
> The *youngest*, sir, said she!'[1]

the ballad begins. It continues

> One night I sat upon the stairs
> And heard him call my name![2]
> I crept into the darkness
> And covered my head for shame.

And its last complete verse runs

> My sister Yoland she is dead
> And Ygrind is no more. . . .
> They went away to Ireland,
> And nobody knows where they are!

'Oh, what', inquires Miss O'Brookomore's song, 'will tomorrow bring?' The answer, for Miss O'Brookomore, is the disruption of the ancient Greek pastoral by the conquering Roman, Count Pastorelli.

'Take my word for it,' Miss O'Brookomore warned when Mabel first met him, 'he's not so pastoral as he sounds.'

And neither, for the matter of that, is Mabel – for all her pseudonym of Hill and her taste exclusively for books about farms. When Mrs Cowsend

---

[1] Firbank echoed the cadence in 1925 in his letter to Carl Van Vechten (cf. Chapter V 6): 'I am a *spinster* sir, & by God's grace, intend to stay so.'
[2] – an echo, I suspect, of Firbank's childhood flagellatory poem (cf. Chapter XV, 19): 'A step on the staircase, a voice there came.'

offers to entertain her in Athens with a trip to 'the royal gardens' (Chislehurst again, no doubt), Mabel replies: 'Unfortunately I'm not overfond of flowers. Gardening in the rain was one of our punishments at home.'

No more is Mabel, for all her schoolgirlishness ('Once I ate nineteen méringues. . . .'), so ingenuous as she seems. Professing to Miss O'Brookomore to find the Count's persecution tiresome, pressing indeed her hand against Miss O'Brookomore's in a spasm of union, Mabel in fact responds more than a little 'willingly-unwillingly like a creature in a Rape'[1] to the irruption of the heterosexual satyr[2] into Arcady.

Besides the Firbankian criterion whereby Mabel is condemned by her dislike of flowers, Firbank wields against her her dislike of books ('I never open a book unless I'm obliged'). He uses literacy as a moral criterion exactly as Jane Austen uses it, in the book from one of whose personages Mabel is named, to distinguish the goodies from the baddies among the Bennet girls. When Mabel elopes with her Count, breaking Miss O'Brookomore's heart into a chapter of eight fragments each crying 'Mabel!',[3] she sends Miss O'Brookomore the news in a letter whose illiteracy is modelled on that of Lydia Bennet's elopement letter.'[4]

Having borrowed Mabel's elopement from Jane Austen, Firbank uses (for the only time) Jane Austen's technique for separating the major sections of her fictions. He breaks *Inclinations* in the middle, and starts the chapter-numbering from the beginning again for Part II.

Inclinations is thus a diptych, with the major Firbankian change of locale in the middle.

To Greek pastoral he opposes Yorkshire pastoral. At her parents' splendidly bovinely named home, Bovon, Mabel (now 'the Countess'[5]) waits, with her baby, for her husband.

Explaining that the Count is detained in Italy by 'the Vintage' Mabel waits through the country neighbours' curiosity, the envy-stirred sexual aspirations of her ineducable[6] younger sister, her father's sarcasm (lifted entire from Mr Bennet's in *Pride and Prejudice*), a straying visit from Miss

---

[1] Cf. Chapter XV, 6.
[2] Cf. Chapter XV, 13.
[3] Cf. Chapter XV, 14.
[4] I have described Jane Austen's use of literacy as a criterion in my introduction (pp. xiv-xv) and notes (p. 307) to the Pan *Pride and Prejudice*.
[5] Firbank's diptych form is partly modelled, I suspect, on that of Henry James's *The Golden Bowl*, whose two halves are called 'The Prince' and 'The Princess' and where, as in *Inclinations*, it is an Italian title that is thus shared by marriage and a half-Italian baby that's in danger of tumbling through the gap between the parents. (Chapter XV, 12 mentioned another instance where I think Firbank borrowed from Henry James.)
[6] Cf. Chapter X, 12.

Dawkins, and the dinner-party Mrs Collins gives in her married daughter's honour and defiance of neighbourly suspicion that the daughter is not in fact legally married at all.

In 1925, nine years after he published the book, Firbank re-wrote and expanded the dinner-party.[1] His expansion included an expansion of his Negro imagery,[2] the introduction of a guest with the splendid name-and-title of The Farquhar (a Firbankian tribute to several things, among them, by way of George Farquhar, Restoration drama), and a reference to Mussolini ('her tongue tripped heedlessly from Mussolini to Miss Arne'[3]).

That reference of 1925 was to Mussolini as an already world-famous fascist.[4] But another reference, in the dialogue of a later chapter ('In olive oil; garnished "Mussolini-wise" '), belongs to the text Firbank published in 1916 and must have been, when it was written, a reference to Mussolini as a not very widely known-of revolutionary socialist[5] (whom Firbank had perhaps read about in Italian newspapers during his journeying in 1914[6]).

Though he re-wrote Chapter IV of Part II, Firbank didn't take the opportunity to explicate a crux two chapters further on that has since troubled commentators. It occurs, like the Mussolini garnish, when a letter from the Count has at last named a date (but will he, even so, postpone it?) for his arrival in Yorkshire, and Mabel's parents are discussing how to feast him. Mabel specifies that he likes 'a soufflé too, so long as it isn't *led*'. Perhaps it's a double pun too recondite to be deciphered; or perhaps 'led' is just Firbank's bad spelling for (in the sense of Pb) *lead*.

Perhaps Firbank was disturbed in the execution of his joke by remembering a significant occasion when he had used (and mis-spelt) the word *soufflé*. During his Edinburgh stay in 1914 he revised *Vainglory*, read it through and wrote to his mother that it was a 'souflé'.[7] Perhaps when the writing of *Inclinations* summoned that memory, his doubt of his powers caused his powers to falter.

---

[1] The *Memoir* (p. 88) quotes a letter of his: 'I have also written an entirely new, and as yet unpublished, dinner-party chapter scene for *Inclinations*.' The *Complete* Firbank prints both versions.
[2] I mentioned these additions in Chapter IX, 11.
[3] misprinted in the *Complete* Firbank (p. 305) as 'Miss Anne'.
[4] The *Biography* (p. 233) quotes a letter of Firbank's of 1923 (when he was living in Bordighera) which describes the local ironmonger as 'an attractive looking Fasciste'.
[5] *Valmouth* (1919) contains (*Complete* Firbank, p. 475) 'the Bolshevik member for Valmouth, Sir William West-Wind' (a kinsman no doubt of one of the 1925 dinner-party guests in *Inclinations*, 'Miss Viola West-Wind, a young girl of the County with a little Tatler-painted face').
[6] Cf. sub-section 9 of this chapter.
[7] The *Biography* cites the letter on p. 132.

There is a companion problem in Part I, at Miss Arne's funeral, where I think Firbank's accidentally bad spelling has combined with an intended pun on the drummers who provide the (presumably muffled) funeral music:
'Miss Collins slipped an arm about her companion's waist.
' "Oh . . . It's the Dance of the Hours, Gerald!" '
' "Dance of the Drumerdairies, my dear." '

Firbank enlarged and elaborated the dinner-party in Part II in order, I imagine, to make it a more perfect counter-weight to the shooting-party in Part I. By making the dinner-party a more equal match to the shooting-party, he was the better able to suggest, through form alone, that, just as the shooting-party was attended by disaster, so will the dinner-party be. *Inclinations* does not pursue its narrative to the point where the Count must either keep or break his promise to join his wife, but whichever he does, after the close of the book, the result will not be happiness.

Because its tempo is slowed by waiting for the Count, Part II emotionally balances Part I, though it is in fact only six chapters set against 21.

Indeed, Part II could not have progressed beyond six chapters, because it lacks the book's motivating force, Miss O'Brookomore's inclinations. All Part II can do is play sounding-board, echoing back and distorting the themes she has set in motion in Part I.

The second wing of Firbank's diptych is a stagnant counter-fugue, which comments by opposites on the fugue (the Count's pursuit, Miss O'Brookomore's defensive flight) of Part I.

That the Count pursues Mabel until they elope and delays afterwards is Firbank's comment on marriage: on marriage considered as the consequence of ignoring the plea for the separation of the sexes.

The bored, bovine, pastoral but unidyllic emptiness of Part II ostensibly reflects the Count's absence from Yorkshire. In reality Part II aches with the withdrawal from the book of Miss O'Brookomore, mentioned only in the visiting conversation of Miss Dawkins (where it provokes ' "Oh, that woman." Mrs. Collins shuddered') and the reminiscences of Mabel, where it encounters parental censorship.

Mrs Collins would even like to censor, to cancel retrospectively, the whole Grecian journey: 'Had I known what sort of woman she was!'

(*What* sort Mrs Collins specifies: 'I'm told she's a noted Vampire.' And to Mabel's ingenuous-disingenuous 'What do Vampires do?', the answer is 'What don't they!')

Part II consists of the hollowness of Mabel's married and maternal life: a hollowness which Firbank makes a reverberation of Miss O'Brookomore's eightfold cry, in Part I, of 'Mabel!'

12. The Extraordinary[1] Caprice

'Do you know Mr. Harvester?' Mira asked. [. . .] 'I should so much like to meet him.'

'My dear, what an extraordinary caprice!'

Vainglory (Chapter II)

Caprice (though not as it stands in the *Complete* Firbank[2]) is prefaced by a ghost from the Sappho supper-party in *Vainglory*. The book's dedication, 'To Stephen Hammerton',[3] is followed by a fragment,[4] in Greek, of Sappho.

'What countrified girl', it inquires, 'who doesn't know to pull her skirt down over her ankles, is exciting your heart?'

The fictional world of *Caprice* is spun, however, from another nucleus: one which, extended into *Inclinations* by way of Miss Arne, is represented in *Vainglory* by Miss Compostella, Mrs Steeple and, most autobiographically, Claud Harvester. 'He had groped so. . . . In the end he began to suspect that what he had been seeking for all along was the theatre.'

Caprice is Firbank's *Romeo and Juliet*: an early, poetic and perfect tragedy.

Its heroine (who puts on a production of *Romeo and Juliet* with herself as Juliet) dies, like Juliet, of an accident consequent on the pure intensity of her romantic love – which is, however, not for a man but for the theatre.

The countrified girl of the epigraph is in the fiction Miss Sarah Sinquier: Sarah because in ambition she is Siddons and Bernhardt together; and Sinquier, whose first syllable at least Firbank intended to be pronounced in English, not French ('this *Miss Sin—*, the new star with the naughty name'), primarily because, I take it, she swallows the blandishments of her exploiters hook, line and sinker.

Sarah Sinquier is the innocent whom Mabel Collins only seemed to be.

Caprice begins (in Westmorland) as pastoral: with a great clangour of church bells[5] (hagiographically particularised according to the saints their

---

[1] The *Bibliography* (p. 28) records that Firbank and his mother took offence when Grant Richards advertised *Caprice* as 'like nothing else on earth'.

[2] which gives the dedicatee's name in its list of dedications at the end of the volume but omits the Greek quotation.

[3] I can find out nothing about him. And the *Biography* doesn't mention him. (The *Bibliography* records the dedication without comment.)

[4] The epigraph as printed in the first edition differs in one word from the Loeb text. By leaving out four words Firbank made the fragment even more fragmentary than it is, though his omission doesn't disturb its sense or continuity. Like the passages cited in *Vainglory* (cf. Chapter XVIII, 3), the *Caprice* fragment (Loeb, p. 254) is one of those preserved in literary sources. No doubt Firbank was still consulting the same edition of Sappho.

[5] I don't think it totally impossible that some half memory of the opening of *Caprice*

churches are dedicated to) in, as Miss Sinquier spells it out to the reporters to whom she is already, in fantasy, granting an interview, 'the sleepy peaceful town of Applethorp (three p's)'.

Another Ashringford (Miss Sinquier's father is Canon Sinquier, and the family lives at the Deanery), Applethorp preserves in its name that Chislehurst apple blossom which[1] contributed to the heroine's name and to the description of her home in Firbank's early pastoral, *Lady Appledore's Mésalliance*, and which in *Vainglory* makes Claud Harvester's literary style 'as charming as the top of an apple-tree above a wall'.

Canon Sinquier takes the same delight in his daughter's amateur theatrical recitations as Lady Firbank took in her son's dilettante writing. Miss Sinquier, however, quits her Arcadia voluntarily – and indeed surreptitiously, having first clandestinely secured an appointment in London with a teacher of dramatic art.

Making (in Chapter IV) the Firbankian change of locale (in the reverse direction to the London-to-pastoral change in *Vainglory*), Miss Sinquier leaves behind her, as regrettably not portable, several family treasures (including Deirdre's cards and Iphigenia's tea-set,[2] now re-written [by transvesting the sacrificed Iphigenia into a sacrificed biblical son] into suitability for a clerical household as 'an antique bush-knife of barbaric shape, supposed to have been *Abraham*'s'). She slips away from the Deanery to 'London – City of Love', taking with her only the thousand-pounds'-worth of pearls she has inherited from her godmother.

The first vulture in her path is a dead one. Before Miss Sinquier can keep the appointment, the drama teacher has died.

At a loss in London, Miss Sinquier looks round Regent Street for 'some nice tea-shop, some cool creamery . . .', and spots the Café Royal.

It is in the Café Royal that she falls into theatrical company and the clutches of the shady Mrs Sixsmith, who is prepared to help Miss Sinquier to the fulfilment of her ambitions while 'wondering (as middlewoman) what commission she should ask'.

Mrs Sixsmith's name Firbank put together, I surmise, from *fix*, *sick* and a famous rôle of Mrs Patrick Campbell's, the title part in *The Notorious Mrs Ebbsmith*.[3] It is likewise from Mrs Patrick Campbell that Mrs Sixsmith gets 'her constant Juno', a 'minute' dog whom Firbank describes as 'griffin-

---

was wrought into the virtuoso campanological opening of Thomas Mann's *The Holy Sinner*.

[1] Cf. Chapter XV, 7.
[2] Cf. sub-section 11 of this chapter.
[3] by A. W. Pinero; Mrs Patrick Campbell first played the part in 1895.

eared' – a misunderstanding, perhaps, on Firbank's part, since Mrs Patrick Campbell's dog, Georgina, was[1] a Belgian griffon.

Theatricalism provides the book's bizarre decorative background, into which Firbank sets such exotic artificial nosegays as the inclusion of Pope's 'Bug with gilded wings' among Titania's courtiers[2] and (a line of dialogue that outdoes even Miss Arne's determination to treat Lysistrata 'as a character-part'[3]) 'I well recall her as the "wife" in *Macbeth*.'

(Firbank didn't, however, wholly neglect in *Caprice* his most usual[4] source of ornamental allusion, the visual arts. Mrs Sixsmith, for instance, places 'a hand to her hip in the style of an early John',[5] a gypsy pose pendant to Firbank's later description[6] of John's drawing of Firbank as 'rather "gypsy" '.)

Against this indeed theatrical backdrop Firbank brings about the exploitation of Miss Sinquier.

Through the offices of Mrs Sixsmith she sells her pearls (which become, at one remove, more of Firbank's baroque lethal pearls[7]) and is induced to spend the proceeds on mounting her own London season, thereby providing an easy living for a rabble of scroungers.

Air-borne on the realising of her fantasy, Miss Sinquier disobeys her parents' newspaper-advertisement advice ('Come back. All shall be forgiven', an early instance of a now very pop joke, to which Miss Sinquier replies, by letter, 'Really I don't know what there can be to "forgive" ') and rents an unsoundly built theatre called The Source – a name whose source in Firbank's thoughts was evidently Sadler's Wells since, as Miss Sinquier (presagingly) explains in her letter home, 'They say the theatre contains a well *beneath the stage*, which is why it's known as the Source.'

However, the theatre in Firbank's mind was less the real-life Sadler's Wells than the faintly fictionalised[8] eponymous theatre in *Trelawny of the*

---

[1] according to p. 20 of Alan Dent's edition of the *Correspondence* of Mrs Patrick Campbell and Bernard Shaw.   [2] Cf. Chapter XV, 19.
[3] Cf. sub-section 11 of this chapter.   [4] Cf. Chapter IX, 6.
[5] Presumably the text of *Caprice* originally contained other allusions to Augustus John. Without remarking on this one, the *Bibliography* (pp. 27–8) records 'allusions in the text, later removed, which Firbank feared might offend' John – who provided *Caprice* with its frontispiece.   [6] 1922 (cf. Chapter VIII, 5).   [7] Cf. Chapter XIV, 7.
[8] Originally, Pinero explained the Wells of his title as standing for Bagnigge-Wells, 'formerly a popular mineral spring in Islington, London, situated not far from the better-remembered Sadler's-Wells [. . .] but, as a matter of fact, Bagnigge-Wells, unlike Sadler's-Wells, has never possessed a playhouse'. Later, Pinero added to his text a note stating: 'On the occasion of the revival at the Old Vic' (1925) 'I struck out all mention of Bagnigge-Wells from the programme and frankly described the Company of the "Wells" as "of Sadler's-Wells Theatre" '.

"*Wells*", the 'comedietta' (of 1898) by Pinero (whose presence in Firbank's thoughts is attested by the contribution to Miss Sixsmith's name made by another of Pinero's heroines, Mrs Ebbsmith). The theatrical milieu of *Caprice* is Pinero's sentimental view of 'the Profession' turned inside out to display its seaminess.

While she prepares for her expensive début as Juliet, Miss Sinquier lives in her theatre, kept company by May Mant, a rival parasite to Mrs Sixsmith.

May Mant is Miss Sinquier's Mabel Collins: similarly equipped with an ineducable hoyden sister but better versed than Mabel in feigning love ('Kiss me.' 'I love you.' 'Pet', runs one of her exchanges with Miss Sinquier) and capable of assuming a butch rôle. Indeed, in Miss Sinquier's theatre company Miss Mant plays 'Page' (her and Firbank's capital) to Paris – in 'a pair of striped "culottes" ' (which are conceivably a vengeful literary resurrection by Firbank of the mauve striped trousers he destroyed after his failure, in them, to meet Ada Leverson[1]).

Living in the theatre, Miss Sinquier and Miss Mant fall into the habit of eating in the stage boxes. The consequent crumbs attract mice, to catch the mice Miss Mant sets traps, and it is in one of the traps that Miss Sinquier (whom Sir Oliver, Mrs Sixsmith's shady associate, has prophetically called 'his "little mouse" '), dancing in triumphant solitude on the stage after her first night as Juliet, is caught.

There is a touch of '*triste* obscurity'[2] about the exact manner of her end but it seems likely that, trapped, she sinks through the stage into the well beneath: in which case, her solitary dance, like most solitary dances in Firbank, is probably Salome's, the well beneath the stage is probably the well where John the Baptist is imprisoned in Wilde's *Salomé*, and Sinquier is certainly to be pronounced sinker.

Firbank gives *Caprice* a circular, in-my-end-is-my-beginning ending, in contrast to his usual open (opening on a sense of dots of suspension) endings. The change of locale is repeated in reverse. The book shifts back to Applethorp for Miss Sinquier's funeral, which is attended by Mrs Sixsmith, who, insinuating herself into Canon Sinquier's affection by describing how 'We laid her, star-like, in the dress-circle – out on Juliet's bier . . .', remembers covetously the family treasures Miss Sinquier has mentioned and begins to plan a career of, the daughter being dead, exploiting the father.

For his last-but-three paragraph, Firbank brings in the Applethorp bells with which the book began, his wording structurally the same but varied by

---

[1] Cf. Chapters XII, 6 and XIII, 7–9.
[2] Cf. Chapter VIII, 5 and *Complete* Firbank, p. 581, footnote.

a paraphrase here and an alternative conceit there like ornaments on the returned vocal line in a da capo aria.

Firbank fashioned his first tragedy from his own dreads: his phobia of mice;[1] and his fear that his money was being filched.[2]

Miss Sinquier adventuring into the theatre with her small fortune and being defrauded of it when she finances her own production is Firbank entering English literature with his private income and being obliged to subsidise literature by financing his own books.

Firbank lent Miss Sinquier his own entrance-hall to the world of scroungers, the Café Royal, where Firbank himself was 'always paying for drinks'.[3]

Perhaps when he valued Miss Sinquier's pearls at a thousand pounds he was already planning that a thousand pounds must be the sum he left[4] to pay for his posthumous collected edition.

Certainly he already knew that in being offered no alternative to financing his own books, a process which limited both the number of copies printed and the publicity and critical attention they received, he was being exploited.

However, like many writers, Firbank was debilitated by the act of creating a book into doubting, immediately afterwards, the value of what he had done.[5]

It is this fairly regular post-creative reaction on his part, a reaction not uncommon among good artists, that has left self-disparaging remarks by Firbank (like his description of *Vainglory* as a soufflé or thistledown[6]), lying about to be picked out of unsympathetic biographies by unsympathetic readers in preference to his juster accounts of his own talent ('aggressive, witty & unrelenting') – and in preference, too, to reading *Caprice* and reading through it to the bitterness of Firbank's statement that he was being defrauded.

What Firbank, like Miss Sinquier, was defrauded of was not simply a financial return and not simply a return in terms of fame. Miss Sinquier's is a tragic as well as an ironic history because her quest is not only for applause but for love. What she prays immediately before her début is: '... Soften all hostile hearts and let them love me ...'

Taken by his usual doubts when[7] he sent the finished but unrevised typescript of *Caprice* to Grant Richards, Firbank wrote: 'I fear you will find Caprice "nothing".'

---

[1] Cf. Chapter VIII, 3. [2] Cf. Chapter VII, 3.
[3] Cf. Chapter VII, 2. [4] Cf. Chapters V, 4 and VI, 2.
[5] Cf. Chapter IV, 1. [6] Cf. Chapter XI, 3 and sub-section 11 of this chapter.
[7] 19 June 1917, according to the *Bibliography* (p. 27), from which I have taken the quotation from Firbank's letter, together with the publication details.

Evidently Grant Richards didn't think it quite nothing, though he either failed to notice or brazened out its content. In *Caprice*'s end was the continuation of Ronald Firbank's exploitation. Shamelessly Grant Richards made arrangements to 'publish' *Caprice* in an edition of 500 copies (this of the book which, in Ifan Kyrle Fletcher's assessment in 1930,[1] of all Firbank's work 'perhaps [. . .] has made the most direct appeal to his admirers'), for which Grant Richards charged Firbank £70, plus £25 for the illustration, plus £21 for printing the illustration and the dust-jacket.

13. The Thread . . .

THE Firbankian thread of Negro decoration[2] entered *Inclinations* in 1916: with 'the Negress you' (sc. Miss O'Brookomore) 'called a *Gauguin*. . . .'

It was pursued in *Caprice*: at Applethorp, by way of the recitation with which Miss Sinquier soothes[3] the Canon ('I care no longer for all other negresses'); and in a London that 'flared with lights', where a 'nigger band' plays an 'agile negro melody, wild rag-time with passages of almost Wesleyan hymnishness'.

In *Valmouth* the thread was gathered into a major motif: Mrs Yajñavalkya.

In being amplified, Firbank's Negro strain lost whatever specificness it had (which was not much: it is only to a generalising eye that Gauguin's islanders *are* Negro, and the 'nigger band' in *Caprice* plays in proximity to a 'Buddha shrine').

Mrs Yajñavalkya is the first and one of the most telling of the creations of Firbank's genius for particularised generalisation.[4]

Her name, with its Slav-looking ending and its Spanish-suggestive tilde over the *n*, is nevertheless Indian.

(The *Biography*[5] states that Firbank named Mrs Yajñavalkya 'after the Hindu goddess of the same name'. I cannot find the goddess in reference books, but the *Encyclopaedia Britannica*'s article on Sanskrit records a male and human [if a touch mythical] Yajñavalkya, who is regarded as the reviser of a set of Vedic sacrificial texts and hymns.)

Mrs Yajñavalkya herself inclines slightly (but only slightly) less towards Hinduism than towards Islam. 'O Allah la Ilaha', she exclaims in Chapter III as she ministers to Mrs Tooke, letting slip in the same paragraph that

---

[1] *Memoir*, p. 58.   [2] Cf. Chapters VIII, 9 and IX, 11.
[3] 'Recite, dear, something; soothe me,' says the Canon, who evidently means by *soothing* much what Firbank meant (cf. Chapter XV, 19) by 'restful'.
[4] Cf. Chapter XVI, 6.   [5] p. 159.

her late husband was named Mustapha. But by Chapter V she is, though still invoking Allah, paying Lady Parvula a compliment that takes the Hinduish form 'In a like rig-up you would stir de soul ob Krishna, as de milk-maid Rádhá did' and (besides herself quoting William Blake – 'My mother bore me in the southern wild, And I am black but O! my soul is white') commending the readings-aloud of her putative niece from the work of Rabindranath Tagore. By Chapter VII she is advising Mrs Tooke to try the Talmud as a change from the Bible, though herself claiming 'I miss a mosque, Mrs. Tooke, and de consolation ob de church,' but in Chapter IX she is put in mind of 'Dai-Cok [. . .] De Japanese God ob Wealth'.

An attempt to pin Mrs Yajñavalkya herself down to geography would meet the same end as Lady Parvula's to pin her down to specifying the provenance of her supposed niece:

' "Then your niece", Lady Parvula pressed, "is from Taihaiti?"

'But Mrs. Yajñavalkya was abstruse.'

It is with the same abstruseness that Mrs Yajñavalkya speaks of her original home as, variously and vaguely, 'de East' and 'de jungle' – and that Firbank's text calls her an 'oriental', a 'negress' and a 'mulattress'.

Mrs Yajñavalkya is the whole extra-European spectrum of exotic colour.

She is the first speaker in print (for I imagine that Firbank spoke it to himself as a child) of Firbank's invented foreign language, and the first speaker also of (at least in a primitive version) his invented foreign patois in English.

In Mrs Yajñavalkya's English, *v* sounds become *b* ('lub' and 'ob'), *th* becomes *d* (which makes it necessary for Firbank to render *though* as 'dô' in order to distinguish it from *do*) and *w* sometimes becomes *v* ('alvays' and 'von' [= *one*]).

This last transposition contains a beautifully Firbankian muddle. Internally, it contradicts Mrs Yajñavalkya's own English: if she can pronounce a *v* sound in 'alvays' and 'von', there is no reason why she couldn't pronounce it in 'love' and 'of'. Moreover, her need to substitute *v* for *w* in English is contradicted by her native language, which contains *w* sounds: '*Ah mawardi, mawardi*', for instance, and '*Owesta wan?*'

(Mrs Yajñavalkya's native language also contains sounds that ring remarkably like echoes in Firbank's mind of schoolroom recitations of Greek verbs ['*Ah didadidacti, didadidacti*'], as well as a formation [*Ukka – kukka!*] that looks almost Yiddish-ish – whence, perhaps, her recommendation of the Talmud.)

Like Lady Appledore's well-born gardener,[1] Mrs Yajñavalkya causes

[1] Cf. Chapters X, 6 and 11.

surprise by speaking French. (To Lady Parvula's astonished 'You know French?', she replies 'Like ebberything else!') And certainly there are[1] places where her English is based on French: when, for example, she remarks that her maid reads her medical dictionary 'dô I defend her ebber to open it'. But at other places Mrs Yajñavalkya's English crumbles into pure Italian: 'My niece, Niri-Esther, she fill de flower vases so full dat de water' (an untransposed *w*) 'do all drip down and *ro-vine* de carpet'.

14. Mrs Yaj's Profession

IT is with the brilliant, multi-coloured and tough thread of Mrs Yajñavalkya that Firbank stitches together his many layers of material in *Valmouth*.

For *Valmouth*, like *Vainglory* (and unlike the two novels between), is one of Firbank's complex, symphonic-scale designs. It includes large set-pieces, sometimes counterparts to set-pieces in *Vainglory*: another climactic thunderstorm (during which Mrs Hurstpierpoint takes comfort from her collection of saintly relics[2]); a dinner-party that resembles Lady Anne's inasmuch as men are, verbally at least, excluded – by being judged 'unglimpsable';[3] an amplification of the witches'-sabbatarian murmurs present at Lady Anne's dinner, in the form of a party to which the guests came 'as to a sabbat'[4] and a doublet of the Mrs Cresswell tapestries (plus a touch of Mrs Shamefoot), in the shape of a depiction in stained glass of the life of Saint Automona (whose tooth is one of Mrs Hurstpierpoint's pious relics).

Vainglory, however, could count on Firbankian shifts of locale to disclose and confirm its structure, marking where the prelude ends and the grand fugue begins, and distinguishing the themes that trot parallel through Ashringford from the Mira–Calvally counter-theme transacted in London.

To *Valmouth* that device is unavailable, because it is all transacted in the environs of Valmouth. The book is a monument that can't display its design by setting it out in groundplan: its masses have to be piled on top of each other on a single spot.

And indeed *Valmouth* is composed in fewer (eleven) but on the whole longer chapters than *Vainglory*.

To bring its blocs into relation with one another, *Valmouth*, more than *Vainglory*, needs a single instrument composed of material from within the fiction. That is what Mrs Yajñavalkya is, and she is, precisely, *within the fiction* by the same token that the fiction is and must stay within Valmouth.

[1] Cf. Chapter X, 11.   [2] Cf. Chapter XV, 16.   [3] Cf. Chapter XV, 18.
[4] This party set-piece occupies Chapter VIII of *Valmouth*, the chapter which Osbert Sitwell published on its own (cf. Chapter XVIII, 2).

The essence of the sea-side town of Valmouth is that it is a health resort.

The influence of 'Valmouth air' towards longevity is instanced by the statue in the market square to 'Valmouth's illustrious son': '*b.* 1698, *ob.* 1803'. Indeed, one of the titles Firbank originally proposed for the book was *The Centenarians of Glennyfurry*.[1] The title became (by way of *Glenmouth: A Romantic Novel*, under which name the book is announced in advance in the first edition of *Caprice*) *Valmouth, A Romantic Novel*, but the centenarians remained: the sabbat-like party is a party for centenarians.

And indeed the principal personages of *Valmouth* are of incalculable age. Mrs Hurstpierpoint has been painted by Ingres.[2] Mrs Thoroughfare is capable of remarking (during that thunderstorm): 'Dear mother was the same. [. . .] Whenever it thundered she'd creep away under her bed, and make the servants come and lie down on top . . . (it was in the eighteenth century of course . . .)'

Yet to the servants (the present ones) Mrs Thoroughfare is (to distinguish her from Mrs Hurstpierpoint) 'the young mistress'.

Partly, I suspect, Firbank called the book a romantic novel in the sense of *historical romance*. Had its personages lived in any climate but Valmouth's they would, by now (by, that is, the book's present tense), have been historical characters.

And indeed for the frontispiece Firbank chose an already existing drawing by Augustus John 'of a lady in eighteenth century dress'.[3]

The impulse by which Firbank created his sea-side health resort was the same sad autobiographical impulse whereby Jane Austen began to create hers, Sanditon.

Valmouth was Firbank's wish, which he satirised by reminding himself of the displeasures of senility, that there truly might exist an English sea-side town (in 1916 he had tried Torquay, where the wind blew the proofs of his revised *Odette* towards the sea[4]) that could guarantee him against his fears of living a life as exceptionally short as those passed in Valmouth are long.

Firbank's fears rested on the fact of his two brothers' early deaths. The donnée of *Valmouth* probably resides in a fact which the *Biography* tosses, unremarked on, into its statement that Firbank arrived at the name he at first intended to give his sea-side town, Glennyfurry, by corrupting the

---

[1] according to the *Bibliography*. The *Biography* (p. 160) gives the place name as 'Glenfurry'.

[2] Cf. Chapter XV, 9.

[3] quoted in the *Biography*, p. 175. A Negro shades her with an umbrella.

[4] (Cf. Chapter II, 3); Firbank interpreted the incident as 'a *favourable omen* for America!' (*Biography*, p. 216, quoting a letter from Firbank to Grant Richards).

name of a Welsh town, Glyndyfrdwy:[1] Glyndyfrdwy 'was the Welsh town where his brother had died'.

(The Welsh influence was not wholly lost when Firbank changed Glennyfurry into Valmouth. Since Welsh *v*'s are pronounced *f*, Valmouth is simply Falmouth [in Cornwall; Firbank's thoughts remained, after Torquay, in the West of England] given a Welsh spelling.)

The action of *Valmouth* is confined to Valmouth because its personages would crumble like mummies were they exposed to any but its healthgiving air.

Within that fixed environment the person who can move agilely, visiting and ministering to every social layer, is the health-giver: the masseuse, Mrs Yajñavalkya.

Whether or not Firbank was malapropising when he described her as speaking 'ubiquitously',[2] he had in mind that she *is* ubiquitous. Herself exotically outside the European class system, she is the insinuating principle that squirms between all its strata, making and unmaking relationships and matches between them, democratically passing under the insinuating abbreviation 'Mrs Yaj'.

If 'Valmouth air' keeps people alive, Mrs Yaj's skill keeps their interest in life alive. She is an insinuating principle by virtue of being an erotic principle. ' "Only", Mrs. Yajñavalkya comfortably sighed' (in reaffirming her rule never to 'take' gentlemen), ' "I like to relieve my own sex" ' – a service she carries to the point of trying to procure Dairyman Tooke as a lover for Lady Parvula.

Mrs Yaj's profession is Firbank's play on the chain of resemblances, verbal and active: massage – masturbation – flagellation.

'I alvays try', Mrs Yaj inspiredly declares, 'to end off wid a charming sensation.'

As an image, Mrs Yaj is Firbank's tribute to the restorative properties of his two favourite[3] sexual sports.

(The texts[4] revised by the real- or realish-life Yajñavalkya are *sacrificial*; and the *Yajña* part of the name means *sacrifice*.)

As the principle of erotic vitality, Mrs Yaj is the impetus that inspires, unites and sometimes tangles all the knots of the pattern.

Mrs Yaj is to *Valmouth* what Puck (another failed matchmaker) is to *A Midsummer Night's Dream*.

And, as Puck through rhyme equals *fuck*, Mrs Yaj equals Mrs Fladge.

---

[1] Thus the *Biography* (p. 159). The *Concise Oxford Atlas* gives the name in the form Glyn Dyfrwy.
[2] Cf. Chapter X, 12.
[3] Cf. Chapter XV, 19 and 20.
[4] Cf. sub-section 13 of this chapter.

15. . . . and the Material

THE two principal levels between which Mrs Yaj mediates are levels of dottiness: one (socially) high, the other tumbledown, both leaving, in the logic of their thought processes, gaping lacunae which Firbank could express by dots (did he indeed associate his flexible punctuation of dots with *dottiness*?) and shape to the images of his surrealism.

His high level consists of the highly wrought, high baroque, high Catholic (to the point of heresy) cults practised,[1] and the Catholic conversions enforced[2] à la Raffalovich,[3] by Mrs (Eulalia) Hurstpierpoint and Mrs (Eliza/Betty/Elizabeth) Thoroughfare.

They inhabit (the Jane Austen 'great house'[4] of *Valmouth*) Hare Hatch House, whose name, according to the *Biography*, Firbank took from 'the village he saw repeatedly as he traveled between Oxford and London, Hare Hatch, complete with Hare Hatch House'. Take it from real life Firbank most probably did (as, I imagine, he took the ornamental name of the mistress of the house from Hurtpierpoint in Sussex). But in the case of Hare Hatch House the borrowing from life has a particular point. It is a tribute to Colney Hatch, a district whose eponymous lunatic asylum made it an English-idiomatic synonym for craziness: Colney, pronounced *coney* = rabbit = (almost) *hare*.

Hare Hatch possesses nothing so lowly (so, almost, low-church) as a private chapel. It has its own 'House-basilica': dedicated, with dedicated Firbankian masochism, to 'Nuestra Señora de la Pena'.

Nuestra ('Father's in Nuestra now' Mrs Thoroughfare familiarly remarks) is the site of those 'mystic windows' which, besides adding to Mrs Hurstpierpoint's terror in the thunderstorm ('My dear, in my opinion, the lightning's so much more ghastly through the stained-glass windows!'), depict tableaux from 'the astonishing Life' of Saint Automona, a series which, while its totality expresses Firbank's hagiographical impulse, includes monuments to Firbank the horticulturalist[5] and Firbank the mental dressmaker:[6] '[. . .] Automona with a purple heartsease, pursuing a nail-pink youth [. . .] Automona meeting Queen Maud of Cassiopia:– "You look like some rare plant, dear!" Her growing mysticism. [. . .] Her austerities. Her increasing dowdiness. Her indifference to dress. She repulses her couturier: "Send her away!" Her founding of Sodbury.[7] Her end.'

[1] Cf. Chapters XIV, 12 and XV, 16. [2] Cf. Chapter XVI, 7.
[3] Cf. Chapter XII, 6. [4] sub-section 3 of this chapter.
[5] Cf. Chapter XV, 6. [6] Cf. Chapter XV, 9.
[7] (Cf. Chapter XV, 19); the (*Complete* Firbank, p. 428) 'Convent of Arimathaea, at Sodbury hard by Hare'.

So pious a household as that at Hare Hatch, ecclesiastical to the very appointments of its dinner table (as its worldly guest, Lady Parvula de Panzoust, unwittingly discloses: ' "And so you've lost Père Ernest", Lady Parvula murmured, humbling a mitred napkin with a dreamy hand'), naturally includes its own ecclesiastics: the replacement[1] for Père Ernest,[2] the seemingly Irish Father Colley-Mahoney;[3] and a nun (on loan from the convent at Sodbury) whose ecclesiasticism is inherent in her professional name, Sister Ecclesia.

Firbank introduces Sister Ecclesia into the book during the thunder-storm. It is one of his most apocalyptic baroque contrasts: for Sister Ecclesia herself is (in one of his most conspicuous malapropisms) 'Proscribed to silence'.

Sister Ecclesia's penitential silence (which she is permitted to break thrice yearly, but only in solitude on the sea-shore) is the cause of her becoming another Firbankian personage who appears to be already sainted. As she is by nature garrulous, her lips move though they do not utter, with the result that 'Strangers sometimes took her to be a saint, in touch with heaven.'

The household at Hare Hatch, of which Mrs Hurstpierpoint is mistress though the heir (but will those ladies ever die?) is Mrs Thoroughfare's world-wandering naval-officer[4] son, Dick, stands in no need of Mrs Yaj's services. At Hare Hatch flagellation is administered in its proper form. ' "May a woman know, dear", Mrs. Hurstpierpoint softly said, "when she may receive her drubbing?" ' (Mrs Thoroughfare turns out to be too tired, and answers 'Ask Ecclesia' – of whom 'Mrs. Hurstpierpoint was wont to say, her arm seemed born for a birch.') Indeed, at Hare Hatch even Firbank's anti-Parliament joke is transformed to flagellatory purpose;[5] and

---

[1] By the last chapter Mrs Thoroughfare has an inkling that the replacement himself 'very soon may be resigning his post [. . .] Such a pity! None of the chaplains ever stay long. . . . They seem to dislike Eulalia hauling them out of bed o' nights to say Midnight Masses for her.'

[2] A footnote to Chapter XIV, 7 cites Père Ernest's unrestrictive attitude to books.

[3] I call him *seemingly* Irish because I think that Firbank developed Colley-Mahoney from the Italian for hand baggage, colli a mano. (Mahoney is another of those deceivingly spelt names which, I suspect [cf. Chapters X, 12 and XV, 17], Firbank was alerted to by the St Clair in Rollo St Clair Talboys. With his defective Italian [cf. Chapter X, 12], Firbank may well have wrongly supposed that in the phrase *colli a mano* the *mano*, too, went into the plural; so it was probably from *colli* and *mani* that he synthesised Colley-Mahoney [pronounced Mahny].) Indeed I suspect that, through a probably unconscious Firbankian chain of Wildean association, Firbank considered Father Colley-Mahoney a natural successor to Père Ernest on account of Lady Bracknell's disapproving cry, when she learns the origins of Ernest (Worthing), 'A hand-bag?'

[4] Cf. Chapter IX, 5.

[5] (Cf. Chapter IX, 3); the visitors to Valmouth in search of health include 'horrid

Mrs Hurstpierpoint is arranging, through the Abbess of Sodbury, to have one of her birches blessed by the Pope ('Has His Holiness complied with the almond-twigs?')

All the same, Mrs Yaj contrives to insinuate her influence into Hare Hatch House: by way of its heir. Dick Thoroughfare, while voyaging in the unspecific zone of Firbankian exoticism, has contracted a marriage whose authenticity is even more in doubt than Mabel Collins's ('Their own rites, so it seems, are far simpler. All they do is *simply* to place a hand each to the torso of the Beloved') and whose social unorthodoxy is a yet clearer mirror of Firbank's own sexuality; for Dick's bride, sent home to Valmouth in advance of himself, proves to be the black niece or unspecified relative who has been staying with Mrs Yaj. 'I'll refuse to believe' (Mrs Thoroughfare affirms) 'this little madcap negress was ever born a Tahaitian princess [. . .] or that Mrs. Yajñavalkya of Valmouth is only her nurse.'

The last social set-piece of *Valmouth* is built round the first of Firbank's unorthodox christenings by a cardinal (Doppio-Mignoni on this occasion): the double christening, in the basilica of Hare Hatch, of Dick Throughfare's half-black baby daughter, Marigold, and of his black bride Niri-Esther (who is already pregnant again).

From the ceremony Dick Thoroughfare himself, though returned to Valmouth, is absent – consistently with his career as a breaker of hearts. His breakages include the heart of Lieutenant Whorwood,[1] who has accompanied Dick to Valmouth and who 'as he lagged along in the faint boreal light behind his friend [. . .] resembled singularly some girl masquerading as a boy for reasons of romance'; and the heart of Thetis Tooke, who is prevented from committing suicide (in, suitably to her name, the sea) 'for reasons of romance' only by the coincidence with her attempt of one of Sister Ecclesia's thrice-yearly trips to the shore.

Thetis Tooke belongs to the more tumbledown of the strata of Valmouth society between which Mrs Yaj negotiates. The Tookes are bucolic squires, enriched by Henry VIII, since whose time their minds have mouldered with their farm buildings. They are still christened with classy classical names like Thetis but have forgotten how to interpret them. It is Dick Thoroughfare

parliament-men', and (when Lady Parvula dines at Hare Hatch in Chapter IV) Mrs Thoroughfare relates: 'Last Epiphany in a fit of contrition we sent a tiny *enfant du chœur* [. . .] into town for a couple of whips. They duly appeared. But two such old vote-hunters. . . . "My God," Eulalia said, "we asked for whips and Thou sendest *scourges*." '

[1] whose name is no doubt (like the cardinal's) a projection of Firbank as (cf. Chapter VIII, 2) minion; Cardinal Doppio-Mignoni and Lieutenant Whorwood represent sacred and profane minionship. (A Jack Whorwood plays Tybalt in Miss Sinquier's company in *Caprice*; *Complete* Firbank, p. 378.)

who explains to Thetis Tooke that the sea-goddess Thetis was the mother of Achilles (and he takes the opportunity to explain Achilles's love of Patroclus in the Wildean terms of paradox[1]).

The dottiness of the Tookes' thought processes is daisy-pied. Of David 'Dairyman' Tooke even Mrs Yaj fails to make a lover for Lady Parvula; but of Thetis Tooke Firbank, turning her rusticity to favour and to prettiness, makes a would-be Ophelia, who seeks her watery death with the meditation ' "It exasperates me though to think of the trouble I gave myself over maquillage. Blanching my face and fingers (and often my neck and arms . . .) surreptitiously in the cream-cans, before their consignment to Market, when all the while," she mumbled, fumbling convulsively amid the intricacies of her veil, "he'd sooner have had me black!" '

For Granny Tooke, one of Mrs Yaj's loyallest customers, Firbank invents a dialect which enters into a dialectic with Mrs Yaj's unspecified exotic patois. Mrs Tooke's language compounds the rustic with the stately idiom of the Book of Common Prayer (' "Belike," she said, "by God's grace to-morrow night we'll both have a bit of a fling. Oh-ay, I do mind the nestful of field-mice we had in the spring-cart last year" '). And on occasion Mrs Tooke is infected by Mrs Yaj's Frenchness to the point of latinity: '[. . .] furnishing the tag-rag and bobtail there was standing about with all manner of *immund*[2] remarks. . . .'

Through Mrs Tooke's grass-overgrown thoughts Firbank lets gleam that peasant blood-lechery towards livestock ('following with a poulterer's discerning eye the careless movements of the farm pigeons as they preened themselves on the gross gargoyles of the church') which, in the transmuted context, two years later, of *Santal*, drove Cherif from home and expressed what I take to be the crypto-vegetarian in Firbank himself.[3]

The daisy-pied surrealism of the Tookes was popularised in 1932 by Stella Gibbons's *Cold Comfort Farm*. In Jocelyn Brooke's view, *Valmouth* satirised 'those "rural" novelists later to be satirized more directly by Stella Gibbons'. But the direct line seems to me to run, rather, from *Valmouth* to *Cold Comfort Farm*, which seems to have borrowed Firbank's very nomenclature. Besides its Firbank-*type* names (Mrs Smiling; Mouse Place), *Cold Comfort Farm* gives its rustic household a family name, Starkadder, that reads as though it was unconsciously compounded from the topographical names of the Valmouth district, Spadder Bay and Spadder Tor (which

---

[1] Cf. Chapter XIII, 3.
[2] Or perhaps it is just that Mrs Tooke is speaking in italics the English of (*Shorter Oxford English Dictionary*) 1621.
[3] Cf. Chapter VIII, 4.

Firbank himself probably compounded from buckets-and-spades observed in 1916 at Torquay[1] and Torbay); and one of the Starkadder sons seems to take his christian name, Seth, from Mrs Hurstpierpoint's gardener (who is mentioned in Mrs Hurstpierpoint's unforgettable dream[2]).

(It was also in 1932 that Mrs Hurstpierpoint's gardener re-emerged in Evelyn Waugh's *Black Mischief* as 'Seth, Emperor of Azania'.)

There is no sourness about the success (Femina Vie Heureuse Prize for 1933, Penguin edition in 1938, with many subsequent reprints) of that funny novel *Cold Comfort Farm* except in comparison with the non-success of its even funnier (as well as sad) predecessor. *Valmouth*, first published 13 years before *Cold Comfort Farm*, did not go into Penguin until 23 years after *Cold Comfort Farm* did. And Firbank might have lived a vie heureuse indeed had he been awarded (though especially, of course, one labelled Femina) *any* literary prize.

16. A Classical Bridge Passage

HAVING written *Vainglory* on the traipse, Firbank began *Inclinations* in London.[3] Bombing drove him, in the autumn of 1915, to Oxford,[4] and it was at Oxford that he finished *Inclinations*, wrote *Caprice* and (outstaying the war) wrote *Valmouth*.

In September 1919[5] he went from Oxford briefly to Bath, where he corrected the proofs of *Valmouth*. Later in the month he moved to London and took a flat at 48 Jermyn Street. *Valmouth* was issued in November 1919.

Firbankianism, by that point, consisted of a solid and symmetrical monument: the two sharp cries, *Inclinations* of pain and *Caprice* of agony, framed between the two symphony-sized social and complex compositions *Vainglory* and *Valmouth*, whose assonance of form Firbank marked when he decided to make the title of the second alliterative with the initial work of Firbankianism.

[1] (Cf. sub-section 14 of this chapter); Tor 'probably cognate with Gaelic *tòrr* [. . .] a high rock, a pile of rocks [. . .] a rocky peak' (*Shorter Oxford English Dictionary*).
[2] (Cf. Chapter XV, 18); it is at the sabbat for centenarians (and on p. 450 in the *Complete Firbank*) that Mrs Hurstpierpoint (bringing Firbank's identification with Christ to a climax in the item that there is a precedent for them both to be mistaken for gardeners) recounts: 'I thought last night, in my sleep, [. . .] that Christ was my new gardener. I thought I saw Him in the Long Walk there [. . .] "Oh, Seth," I said to him . . . "remember the fresh lilies for the altar-vases. . . . Cut all the myosotis there is", I said [. . .] And then, as He turned, I saw of course it was not Seth at all.' (With wonderful unimpressionability, Mrs Hurstpierpoint's interlocutor replies merely 'Is Seth leaving you?').
[3] Cf. sub-section 9 of this chapter.
[4] Cf. Chapter IX, 5.
[5] The datings in this paragraph are according to the *Biography*.

It was a cadence that closed the first section of his œuvre.

There followed the equivalent, within his œuvre as a whole, of a Firbankian shift of locale.

It accompanied a shift from the solitude of Firbank's war-time retreat back into society, including the society of Evan Morgan,[1] whose refusal of the dedication of *The Princess Zoubaroff*, the major work of section two of Firbankianism, provoked Firbank to revenge via Eddy Monteith in the opening work of section three.

Returned to society, Firbank took advantage of the freedoms restored by the restoration of peace: freedom first to live in London, where he wrote *The Princess Zoubaroff*, and then to travel abroad – to North Africa, where he wrote *Santal*.

The two books constitute a bridge passage in his œuvre. They are organic developments of themes inherent in section one and at the same time organic and evolutionary movements towards the three great tragic novels that followed them.

Some apprehension, perhaps, that they are transitional works has caused them to be mistaken for transitory. But Firbank's bridge, if scrutinised without preconceptions, proves to be among his most firmly classical designs.

17. Play

[. . .] he began to suspect that what he had been seeking for all along was the theatre. He had discovered the truth in writing plays.

Vainglory (Chapter II)

IT is an instructive paradox that Firbank's first-issued Firbankian novel contains a self-portrait of the author as, not solely[2] but quintessentially, a dramatist.

Like most particulars about him (except his briefly married state), Claud Harvester's discovery through writing plays of his talent for writing plays is autobiographical to Firbank.

Firbank (as well as joining dramatic societies when he was an undergraduate[3]) had been writing plays all along (the *New Rythum* volume includes extracts from two surviving earlyish examples[4]) and freely transposing

---

[1] Cf. Chapter VIII, 5.
[2] Cf. sub-section 5 of this chapter.
[3] Cf. Chapter XIV, 4.
[4] *The Mauve Tower* (*a dream play in seven scenes*) and *A Disciple from the Country* (*a one-act play*): cf., respectively, Chapters VIII, 9, XIII, 4 and XIV, 1; and Chapters XIV, 4 and XV, 17.

his données to and fro between dramatic and narrative works.¹ And the earliest title he had in mind for *Prancing Nigger* was not *Sorrow* but *Drama (or, possibly,² A Drama) in Sunlight*.

Claud Harvester's discovery is, however, only a portion of the truth about Firbank, who discovered his talent and taste for writing plays not only through writing plays but through writing Firbankian novels.

Although Firbank did not publish a play until 1920, by which time his œuvre contained four Firbankian novels, it was from dramatic technique that he developed the technique of the Firbankian novel rather than the other way about.

Indeed, dramatic effectiveness (an effectiveness, that is, carried chiefly in the medium of dialogue and rendered intense by a confinement of context resembling the restrictions imposed by the dramatic unities) was Firbank's first and most familiar literary idiom – inevitably, since his literary apprenticeship³ was to Oscar Wilde and since theatre, rather than narrative, is what Wilde had to teach.

It was an act of justice that when Firbank did publish a play it included a deliberate and (by allusion) labelled portrait of Wilde.⁴

Not that the Firbankian novel is merely a play done over into narrative, in the manner of the-book-of-the-film. Its technique is truly, and by truly fictional methods, developed *from* dramatic technique. By no means does it limit itself to dramatic means. Unlike the Shavian novel,⁵ the Firbankian novel has not renounced entering the private minds of its personages or following them into solitude.

However, the Firbankian novel does stretch dialogue to the performance of everything that dialogue *can* perform (which is a good deal more than most novels *ask* it to perform). It was from the theatre that Firbank learned his reliance on cross-fires of dialogue in brief bursts (which sometimes leave behind them diagrammatic bullet-paths of dots). And he often accompanies his personages' brief speeches by an isolated significant action ('[. . .] Lady Parvula murmured, humbling a mitred napkin with a dreamy hand') of the kind that might be singled out and given the significance of a necessary move by being stated as a stage direction.

Indeed, Firbank's imagism, which composes, isolates (or frames) and fixes

---

¹ Cf. Chapter XV, 17.
² (Cf. Chapter VII, 4); it is typical of the relation between Professor Benkovitz's *Bibliography* of Firbank and her *Biography* of him that the *Bibliography* (p. 45) quotes Firbank as saying that his novel was called *Drama in Sunlight* and the *Biography* (p. 234) has him name it *A Drama in Sunlight*. Both books cite the same Firbank letter (to Carl Van Vechten, 19 June 1923).   ³ Cf. Chapter XIV, 11.
⁴ Cf. Chapter XIV, 10.   ⁵ Cf. Chapter II, 5.

a series of vividly visual impressions, is itself a dramatic craft carried out by fictional methods. He stage-manages his crowd scenes and presents them, momentarily frozen into tableaux, as though within a proscenium arch – catching and freezing his tableaux at the high baroque moment just before or (as on the delayed beat that discloses Miss Arne's death through her shooting-companions' reaction to it[1]) just after their social relationships burst apart. His dialogue rings with curtain lines, ambivalent and open-ended or on the minor-key final note of an epigram whose stresses have been redistributed. Equally, he opens chapters ('Lady Anne Pantry was sitting in the china-cupboard') or initiates passages (as when his narrative *surprises* Miss Compostella in bed[2]) as though he were raising the curtain on them. Or he can raise the curtain on the bare announcement of a new chapter (Chapter X of *Vainglory*, for instance) and *then* bring on his personages ambulant and already conversing: 'And your own tomb, dear Doctor Pantry, what is it going to be?'

In constantly intensifying his dialogue by gathering and confining it in scenic nodules, Firbank was influenced, I think, as in other matters,[3] by Henry James: perhaps by the practice in James's novels but more probably by the preaching, in James's prefaces to them, of James's 'dramatic' or 'scenic' method in the composing of narrative.[4] But James builds up to the impressiveness of an impression of solidity. Firbank pares down[5] to the impressiveness of the isolated image. James adapted his method from the serious drama or perhaps from what he mistook for it. Firbank, consonantly with his taste for jazzy entertainments,[6] borrowed rather from the theatre of revue. A Firbankian novel is a sequence of indirectly related vivid glimpses, each of which is revealed, pointed and then, by the Firbankian spaces and silences, blacked-out.

How organically section one of the Firbankian œuvre, which is entirely

---

[1] Cf. sub-section 11 of this chapter. [2] Cf. Chapter XVIII, 3.
[3] Cf. Chapters IX, 7 and XV, 12 and sub-section 11 of this chapter.
[4] 'The material of *The Ambassadors*, conforming in this respect exactly to that of *The Wings of the Dove*, [. . .] is taken absolutely for the stuff of drama; so that, availing myself of the opportunity given me by this edition for some prefatory remarks on the latter work, I had mainly to make on its behalf the point of its scenic consistency. [. . .] it sharply divides itself [. . .] into the parts that prepare, that tend in fact to over-prepare, for scenes, and the parts, or otherwise into the scenes, that justify and crown the preparation. [. . .] These alterations propose themselves [. . .] as the very form and figure of *The Ambassadors*; [. . .] we have treated scenically, and scenically alone, the whole lumpish question of Strether's "past"; [. . .] the scene in question [. . .] is normal and entire, is really an excellent *standard* scene [. . .]' (from James's Preface to *The Ambassadors*).
[5] 'I think nothing of fileing fifty pages down to make a brief, crisp paragraph, or even a row of dots!' (cf. Chapter V, 2).
[6] Cf. Chapter VIII, 9.

novels, developed into section two, which includes a play, is demonstrated by a letter Firbank wrote within a month of publicly beginning, with the appearance of *Vainglory*, section one. In May 1915 he (besides incidentally predicting what became, in 1919, Mrs Yaj's profession) predicted in outline the constituents of Firbankianism section two (1920–1), namely a North-African novel and a play. 'I would adore' (he wrote to Grant Richards[1]) 'to write a really charming soothing[2] novel. A sort of Moorish massage . . . Or a play – that would begin before the theatre opened & evapourate while the "Star" was still en toilette de ville.'

And indeed the 'Star' element in Miss Compostella *did* persist after *Vainglory*: into the actress-motif in *Inclinations* and into dominance in *Caprice*.

Immediately after *Vainglory*, however, Firbank evidently had it in mind to enlarge the surrealist play of ideas in that book into an actual play.

In *Vainglory* Miss Compostella's surrealist reflexions are framed, in the surrealist manner afterwards adopted by Magritte, by her window; and that scene is further framed within the 'severe blue veil suspended from oblong wooden rings' which surrounds her bed, and which Firbank's narrative treats as a theatre curtain[3] when it discovers her in the manner of a stage direction.

('Above it, a china angel upon a wire was suspended to complete the picture,' the narrative adds, itself thereby completing the picture of a picture-frame stage by an allusion at once to the external frame [the presiding figure-heads or masks at the keystone of the proscenium arch] and to the content of drama, by way of a touch of deus ex machina.)

That idea, which in *Vainglory* is already, on the pretext of Miss Compostella's profession, theatrical in content and allusion, Firbank considered transposing into the palpable theatre through his notion of a play in which the theatre should represent a theatre and the proscenium arch perform the framing function of a proscenium arch.

Perhaps Firbank's notion originated in his reflecting that he could make better use than Pinero did of the setting of the fourth act of *Trelawny of the "Wells"*, where 'The SCENE represents the stage of a theatre, the footlights and proscenium arch of the actual stage being the proscenium arch and the footlights of the mimic stage.'

Pinero uses his staged stage to transact the rehearsal of a play-within-his-play, at the same time as unravelling the threads of his play as such. Firbank's

---

[1] in a letter of 11 May 1915, quoted on p. 143 of the *Biography*.
[2] Cf. the soothing and restful footnote to sub-section 13 of this chapter.
[3] Cf. Chapter XVIII, 2 and 3.

play was never to reach the point of the play-within-the-play but was to 'evapourate' (into Firbankian dots of suspension) before the fictitious curtain went up.

It was not, however, in the theatre that Firbank's essentially theatrical conceit eventually expressed itself but in his novel about the theatre – a novel in which he found a more telling way of inverting an idea of Pinero's[1] as well as a more condensed fusion of fiction and the fiction-within-the-fiction.

Whether by the further influence of Henry James or, which seems more likely in this case, through a simple psychological resemblance to James, Firbank took the Jamesian course of writing a novel about the theatre by way of compensating himself for the theatre's failure to come and demand his dramatic works (a demand which a professionally competent theatre would have made the instant *Vainglory* disclosed his genius for dialogue). The notion of a before-the-play 'reality' which should turn out to *be* the play became the novel in which Miss Sinquier plays out the rôle of Juliet in the course of playing the rôle of Juliet.

Caprice so thoroughly exploited the theatre as subject-matter that when Firbank did publish a play it could not be, as he had in 1915 thought of making it, a play about the theatre.

Indeed for the time being *Caprice* summed up Firbank's impulse to theatre. His previously habitual theatrical thread is absent from *Valmouth*, having gone underground before issuing in the only form *Caprice* had left possible, a veritable play.

When that happened, Firbank took the warning he had uttered through the content of *Caprice*. It looks as though from quite early in the genesis of his play Firbank intended[2] to put it into print and circulation at his own expense but not to fall, like Miss Sinquier, into the mouse-trap of financing a production himself.

It was the printed book that Firbank was counting on to attract a backer (and, indeed, a cast).

That no doubt is why the intensity of his fury against Grant Richards as his 'publisher' began with Grant Richards's 'neglecting to push'[3] the volume.

---

[1] Cf. sub-section 12 of this chapter.

[2] That Firbank early decided to publish the play I argue from his having (according to the *Biography*, p. 182) shewn the proposed dedication to Evan Morgan 'long before' the text went to the printer's. The dedication of an unpublished (even if it had been also a produced) play wouldn't have been much of a love offering.

[3] an accusation Firbank made in a letter (quoted in the *Biography*, p. 197) to his mother, 9 April 1921.

In the first half of November 1920, at a time when the play was already in print (though not yet issued[1]) and Firbank already in North Africa at work on *Santal*, Firbank was entertaining hopes that, if a financial backer could be found, Lillah McCarthy[2] would play the Princess.

By July 1921 he had hopes that Edith Evans, to whom he had sent a copy of the play, would join the company;[3] he had sought an estimate of how much backing would be needed; and he was trying, through his mother, to raise £1,000-worth of it from a source appropriate to the play's art-historical decoration, Duveen.[4]

18. Casa Heartbreak

ALL those projects petered out. Firbank never saw the play performed.

On a Jamesian precedent he had *not* meant to follow, he suffered (less agonisingly than James, because it did not happen at such close quarters, but perhaps for that very reason even more woundingly) the heartbreak of being rejected by the theatre.

One of Firbank's unfulfilled projects for the play discloses something of the play's nature and also, I think, contains a modification of the idea[5] Firbank had in 1915 for a play set in a theatre represented by the theatre. He considered that *The Princess Zoubaroff* might be performed not in a theatre but in a drawing-room.

He must, I think, have had in mind (no doubt in the image of The Coopers, Chislehurst) a drawing-room opening on a garden.

The action of *The Princess Zoubaroff* takes place entirely in a garden: 'The garden of the Casa Meyer' at Florence.

The concept of a real theatre representing a fictitious theatre had become the concept of a real garden encroaching on and merging with the fictitious garden which the play would create on the other side of, probably and appropriately, french windows.

It is a concept symbolic of that 'artificial pastoral' genre which Firbank established with *Lady Appledore's Mésalliance, An Artificial Pastoral* (into

---

[1] According to the *Biography*, Evan Morgan accepted the dedication when Firbank shewed it him and rejected it only after he had seen, in print, the volume it was to accompany. His insistence that the dedication be deleted caused 'publication' of the volume to be postponed until 26 November 1920.

[2] I will discuss the significance of this choice in sub-section 18.

[3] By 1971 Dame Edith Evans had (as she kindly told me by letter) no recollection of the incident.

[4] Cf. Chapter IX, 6; Firbank's schemes for a production are described in the *Biography*, pp. 190 and 204–5.

[5] Cf. sub-section 17 of this chapter.

which he transcribed the image of The Coopers, Chislehurst in detail)[1] and whose artificiality he wrote into the final title[2] of *The Artificial Princess*, a book where the garden in the narrative is used as a theatre.

Like the garden in *Lady Appledore's Mésalliance*, the garden in *The Princess Zoubaroff* is the garden of The Coopers, Chislehurst. And in fact[3] Firbank has labelled it as such, simultaneously claiming The Coopers as (still) his home. Although the owners of the house at Florence are called in full Sheil-Meyer,[4] Firbank introduces the garden into the first stage direction, setting the scene for the entire play, as 'the garden of the Casa Meyer'. By a typically Firbankian confusion[5] of Italian with Latin, Firbank is affirming it to be the garden of 'casa mea', 'casa mia', 'my home'.

The Princess Zoubaroff is the culmination of Firbank's pastoral mode. (Oscar Wilde necessarily appears in the play, as he did in Firbank's earlier 'artificial pastoral', in pastoral association with a flower.[6]) The play observes the same seasonal half-cycle as *Vainglory*,[7] its changes recorded in the state of the Sheil-Meyers' garden. (Act I is directed to take place in '*Early summer*'. The setting of Act II is '*Same as Act I., only the trees have changed their tints. Some are orange, some are scarlet. Red creepers. Autumn flowers.*' Act III occupies the '*Same scene. A few of the trees have shed their leaves. It is Winter.*') And this time the pathetic fallacy of the vegetable fertility cycle includes the birth (to the Sheil-Meyers) of a baby.

The pastoral mode again suggested to Firbank's thoughts Arcadia, to which Claud Harvester in *Vainglory* and Miss O'Brookomore in *Inclinations* had been pilgrims. 'Nestling', as she is stage-directed to do against the Princess Zoubaroff (who is newly returned from 'oh such a heavenly ride. Half way to Vallombrosa!'), Enid Tresilian observes 'Your habit smells of Arcady. . . .'

(Dress-designer and art historian, Firbank has directed the Princess to wear 'a riding-habit, rather Vanloo, fringed with sables. In lieu of a riding-crop she holds a fan.')

And Arcady Firbank again takes in its fully Greek sense. Indeed it is a

---

[1] Cf. Chapter XV, 7.
[2] Cf. Chapter XIV, 8.
[3] a fact I am grateful to Maureen Duffy for pointing out to me.
[4] But with a small alteration of spelling (which certainly would have been no obstacle to Firbank), the Sheil part of the name merely repeats the *Casa* in 'Casa Meyer'. *Shiel* (according to *The Shorter Oxford English Dictionary*) is a Scottish and north-country word for 'a small house, cottage'.
[5] Cf. Chapter X, 12.
[6] In the play he appears as Lord Orkish (cf. Chapter XIV, 10) and in *Lady Appledore's Mésalliance* (cf. Chapter XIV, 11) as the cultivator and sick-nurse of an orchid.
[7] Cf. sub-section 5 of this chapter.

falling-off in his Hellenism that marks the beginning of Enid's indifference towards her husband: 'His Hellenism once captivated me. But [. . .] the *Attic* to him means nothing now *but Servants' bedrooms*.'

('What leaf-fringed legend haunts about thy shape Of deities or mortals, or of both. In Tempe or the dales of Arcady? [. . .] O Attic shape!' Firbank's Greece is again[1] read off a Grecian Urn.)

And Hellenism, as in his novels, again urges on Firbank that thought of Sappho. But in *The Princess Zoubaroff* Sapphism is of universal application and Firbank is prescribing it to society.

It is symptomatic of the state of literary understanding that one of the few Firbankians not to form a condescending or outright dismissive opinion[2] of *The Princess Zoubaroff* was Ifan Kyrle Fletcher: one of the few, that is, with practical experience in the theatre.[3]

The knack of reading a dramatic script and palpably imagining the work in performance is every bit as technical as reading and imagining the performance of a musical score; but, since literary technology is seldom recognised as technical,[4] it is quite common for amateurs and even for professionals like impresarios to lack this essential expertise and have no knowledge that they lack it, since they have no knowledge that such a thing exists.

It was Ifan Kyrle Fletcher who recognised[5] that in drama Firbank's 'master was Congreve. To read *The Way of the World* and *The Princess Zoubaroff* is to become aware of relationships stronger than those of blood and more enduring than those of contemporaneity.'

And indeed *The Princess Zoubaroff* is another of Firbank's concealed literary puns.[6] The entire play is a play on the contrast between the Way of the World and the Way of the Cross; and Firbank has set on both Ways an idiosyncratic interpretation.

The Way of the World is for him the heterosexual conventions, including marriage. The Way of the Cross is the scarcely unworldly Way followed by the Princess and her protégées. 'It must take an exceptionally "good" woman', Lord Orkish comments, 'to forsake husband, son, friends, society to follow the Way of the Cross.' But, as the deserted husband points out, 'she hasn't deserted her *friends* at all'.

---

[1] Cf. sub-section 4 of this chapter.
[2] Jocelyn Brooke (in his 1962 pamphlet, p. 18) held that *Santal* 'exemplifies (like *The Princess Zoubaroff*) the limitations of its author'. Miriam J. Benkovitz (*Biography*, p. 193) holds that *The Princess Zoubaroff*'s 'characterization is thin, its dialogue forced, its material without focus; and as drama, which it purported to be, it is entirely too static'.
[3] Cf. Chapter VI, 2.   [4] Cf. Chapter I, 5.
[5] *Memoir*, p. 64.   [6] Cf. sub-sections 1 and 2 of this chapter.

The texture of Firbank's play alludes to Congreve's both in detail and at large. Firbank has set up his Lady Rocktower as a puritanical (at least in heterosexual matters) counter-fortification to Congreve's Lady Wishfort (a keep to which the entrance has been sold). And it is from Congreve's skilled marching and counter-marching of his dramatis personae through the paths of Saint James's Park in the pastoral second act of *The Way of the World* that Firbank has learnt how to deploy and permute the residents and visitors in the garden of the Sheil-Meyers' house.

The artificiality of Firbank's pastoral is that of artificial high comedy. His dialogue is couched in a non-naturalistic idiom of extreme flexibility. Lady Rocktower has borrowed it direct from Congreve (with a tinge, perhaps, of Congreve via Lady Bracknell):

LADY ROCKTOWER (*fairly floored*). Why on earth did you marry?
ERIC [. . .]. I was only half-serious when I proposed.
LADY ROCKTOWER. And she accepted you?
ERIC. I never expected to be taken quite *au pied de la lettre*.
LADY ROCKTOWER. Fool.
ERIC. I beg your pardon?
LADY ROCKTOWER. I said insensate!

Lady Rocktower's idiom, it becomes clear when she switches her interrogation about their marriage to Eric's wife (with 'Tell me dear. Were you solicited besides?', a question Enid queries with 'Was I – ', obliging Lady Rocktower to translate her question into 'Did anyone else ask you?'), is not always comprehensible to the younger generation, who themselves speak the language of 1919–20 ('Sorry to be late, old girl'; 'And you shall play us each at pills after, what?') in a stylised version resembling the one invented by P. G. Wodehouse.

(The younger idiom is less contradictory than it seems of Lady Rocktower's classical diction; in structure, P. G. Wodehouse's own prose is very much that of the early 18th century.)

To accompany his personages' fluent and easy delivery (it is only mirror-faithful naturalistic dialogue that is either unspeakable by actors or unlistenable-to by audiences), Firbank has developed a non-naturalistic stagecraft for handling the personages themselves. With invisible efficiency he gets them on and off stage in the course of their pastoral quests; and by means of their entrances and exits he sets up and delimits his scenes.

In the French[1] (or indeed in Congreve's) manner, Firbank numbers a new scene whenever there is a change of personnel on stage, though the

[1] Cf. Chapter X, 11.

action is continuous from one scene to the next. By this notation he marks that he has transferred his imagist method from his novels (and especially from the grand social set-pieces in his novels, where his images are particularly embodied in dialogue) back to its place of origin, the theatre.

Each of the scenes in his play is a self-contained self-definition of relationships, its crossfires and ricochets confined, defined and visibly diagrammed, in the manner of a tableau, within the invisible space–time box of the scene; and each scene is related to the one before and the one after not only by the continuity of the action but by imagist and picturesque juxtaposition.

Firbank has, in fact, divided his text into sections much as though it *were* an orchestral score. Unlike his immediate tactics, which consist of decorative and amusing (*and*, on occasion, musically allusive[1]) stage directions that make his text from line to line as readable as a novel, his strategy of layout defies unversed reading but awaits a producer prepared to, precisely, *conduct* the text. Firbank has already marked the strategic dispositions a producer would have to make for himself but might make less felicitously. A producer need only obey the text to bring the non-naturalistic idiom to life – an orchestral idiom that summons in each particular voice not when representationalism demands but when the texture does.

Throughout scene 16 of Act II, for instance, the nurse, seated in full view beside the marble statue of the Virgin in the garden, is reading aloud (to 'a squadron of small children'). But her voice enters the audible texture of the scene only twice, on the separate occasions of two discontinuous paragraphs of the fairy tale (probably a tribute to Wilde) she is reading from. The fairy-tale extracts become Firbankian-Sapphic fragments, and Firbank interposes them, into the other matter transacted in the scene, with an effect of conspicuous baroque incongruity and also, since they unwittingly reflect and comment on the other matter, with secret baroque symmetry.

Firbank's text is indeed *orchestrating* the dramatis personae: as Mrs Henedge orchestrated the guests at her Sappho party (and as Firbank's narrative orchestrated the Sappho-party chapter).[2]

The linked series of small scenes that constitutes the skin of *The Princess*

---

[1] on the occasion, for instance, of the end of Act II: 'PRINCESS (*boxing*, con amore, *with her muff each little girl upon the ears* [. . .])'.

[2] Cf. Chapter XVIII, 2 and 4; Firbank was attracted to the metaphor of orchestration – because, I imagine, it reflects and explains his technique. Not only is Mrs Henedge in *Vainglory* 'orchestrating fearlessly her guests'; Miss O'Brookomore, in *Inclinations*, mixes a salad (and expresses her anger and fear) while 'Orchestrating olives and tomatoes'; and in *Valmouth* the climactic thunderstorm is announced by the 'lament of the peacocks' of Hare Hatch, 'orchestrating, with barbarity, [. . .] their strident screech with the clangour of the chapel bell' (*Complete* Firbank, pp. 85, 246 and 421–2). (The garden in *The Princess Zoubaroff* incidentally contains 'a peacock or two'.)

Zoubaroff is as flexible and as unobtrusive in movement as the segments of a roll-top desk, curving over the year's half-circle which the play encompasses and at the same time defining and disclosing the form of the play as an autonomous object.

If Firbankians have failed to read through the play's flexible surface and the practical notation of its text to the form beneath, it is not, I surmise, because the mood of the play is too delicate but because its assertions are too bold and so is the design that incarnates them.

In Firbank's Arcady almost everyone is homosexual: not just and inevitably the idealised double-portrait of Oscar Wilde and Bosie[1] but even such middle-distant (from the central action) figures as Mrs Blanche Negress[2] (an author who shares more than her profession with Sappho, since she 'can safely say I prefer the society of other women to that of men' and enters Act II, scene 17 'wearing a tailor-made "Redfern"[3] and a man's cravat) and Lady Rocktower herself who, having elicited by interrogation that Eric's feelings towards his wife are not 'carnal', comments ('Half to herself') 'He must have the blood of an Esquimau!'

In *Inclinations* Firbank lamented the irruption into Arcady of the anti-pastoral[4] heterosexual. *The Princess Zoubaroff*, by contrast, is a demonstration of how homosexuality can, rationally and happily, *work*. The pastoral background to the pan-homosexual figures is invoked prescriptively, as a metaphor of the *naturalness* of homosexuality; and the play's design is a prescriptive design, a 'plea for the separation of the sexes'[5] by means of a re-sorting of the socially conventional groupings.

Starting from his two newly married couples, Eric and Enid[6] Tresilian[7] and Adrian and Nadine Sheil-Meyer, Firbank does not simply re-align them

---

[1] Cf. Chapter XIV, 10.
[2] Cf. Chapter IX, 11.
[3] Eric Partridge's *A Dictionary of Slang* . . . dates this term 1879–1915, derives it from the name of a celebrated tailor and describes the garment in question as 'a perfectly fitting lady's coat or jacket'. Perhaps Firbank's allusion to the tailor is further fruit of his knowledge, via Chislehurst gossip, of the habits of the Empress Eugénie (cf. Chapter X, 9). In 1886, the year of Firbank's birth, during the Empress's summer holiday as Queen Victoria's guest at Osborne Cottage on the Isle of Wight, the governess Agnes Carey (*The Empress Eugénie in Exile*, p. 213) wrote home: 'the girls' (the Empress's nieces) 'are trying on a number of very pretty yachting dresses their aunt is having made for them at Redfern's (the original Redfern, who started in a modest little shop here in East Cowes).'
[4] Cf. sub-section 11 of this chapter.
[5] Cf. Chapter XV, 19.
[6] The pairing of Eric and Enid is a late fruit of Firbank's study of French literature. *Erec et Enide* is a 12th-century Arthurian romance by Chrétien de Troyes.
[7] a surname Firbank perhaps picked up while he was in the West of England (cf. sub-section 14 of this chapter).

in homosexual symmetry. True, he sends the two young men off together; but he has both young women succumb to the Princess Zoubaroff – through whose six discarded husbands[1] Firbank has read a dissatisfaction with heterosexual coupling that can be set at rest only by the Princess's compiling round herself the multiple and all-female household of a convent. Thus Firbank makes himself able to deploy an elaborate baroque symmetry which matches a pair of men, Adrian and Eric (who are echoed on the ideal plane by Lord Orkish and Reggie), not to a homosexual pair of women but to a whole institution of female homosexuality.

Firbank's design for society does not totally cancel heterosexuality. Nadine is pregnant before her husband goes off with his boyfriend and by Act II (by which time early summer has been replaced by autumn) she has given birth to a son. Firbank's design includes the scheme that the women should communally enjoy the pleasure of seeing the baby through infancy and that the men, also more or less communally, should take over the pleasures of parenthood from then on.

Firbank's plea for the separation of the sexes comprises a plea for their temporary union in order to engender children and then a plea for the fair division of the consequent work and pleasure between them.

Behind the languor of his play's mood Firbank was proposing, to a 'problem' which 1920, if it would mention its existence at all, insisted on treating in sackcloth and ashes, a solution brisk, reasonable, utilitarian, social, unsentimental and, generally, in tone and import, Shavian.

Indeed, the homosexual social contract implied in *The Princess Zoubaroff* is precisely what Shaw might have put forward had temperament inclined him and puritanism permitted him to expand his permissive personal tolerance towards homosexuality into a positive and programmatic play about homosexuality.

And as a matter of fact it was Shaw, I conjecture, whose example inspired Firbank to the enterprise.

The quasi-musical notation of Firbank's eloquent punctuation in his novels is perhaps a borrowing[2] from Shaw's published plays at large; and

[1] 'PRINCESS. [. . .] (*Grimly.*) When I want to impress a stranger, I carry their miniatures on my wrist – three on each arm.'

[2] (Cf. Chapter X, 12). In the autumn of 1923 Carl Van Vechten secured Firbank his first genuine publisher, Brentano's. Writing to inform Firbank, Van Vechten explained Brentano's as Bernard Shaw's United-States publisher (*Biography*, p. 247). I do not know whether it was the influence of that explanation on Firbank or the influence of Shaw directly on Firbank or, indeed, the influence of Shaw on Brentano's which brought it about that Brentano's edition (1924) of *The Flower Beneath the Foot* adopts throughout the Shavian–Jane Austenish spelling *shew* for what in Firbank's earlier publications had been *show*.

almost certainly it is from that source that Firbank adopted, for *The Princess Zoubaroff*, the device of making his play readable as well as performable by using the stage directions as a decorative member.

However, Shaw's œuvre contains a specific, as well as general, inspiration to Firbank: *Heartbreak House*, the play which (besides incidentally offering Firbank the model of its pastoral third act, set in a garden) incarnates the merger Firbank was seeking for *The Princess Zoubaroff* between lyrical mood and programmatic social design.

The mood of *Heartbreak House*, whose sub-title is *A Fantasia in the Russian Manner on English Themes*, has been transferred to *The Princess Zoubaroff* in the shape of the tacit Russianness of the name of the Princess who presides over the play and its title.

(The Russianness of *Heartbreak House* is Anton Tchekov's. 'Heartbreak House', the Preface begins, 'is not merely the name of the play that follows this preface. It is cultured, leisured Europe before the war. [. . .] A Russian playwright, Tchekov, had produced four fascinating dramatic studies of Heartbreak House, of which three [. . .] had been performed in England.' On the strength, perhaps, of those pre-war English performances, Firbank had early seen a likeness between Tchekov's mood and Firbankianism – or so I conclude from the *Biography*'s incidental record[1] that in 1915 Firbank tried to get Grant Richards to send [presumably in hope of an appreciative review] a copy of *Vainglory* to George Calderon, who, according to the *Biography*, 'had written a preface to an edition of Chekov's plays'.[2])

It was, I think, the fact that even so successful a dramatist as Shaw had by then become published *Heartbreak House* in a volume in 1919, before the play had been performed, which licensed and heartened Firbank to publish *his* unperformed play in 1920 and hope that the volume would attract a production.

And the production Firbank was hoping for was conspicuously Shavian. Lillah McCarthy, who[3] in Firbank's plans was to play the Princess, was an actress-manager at the middle of the Shaw–Granville Barker dramatic renaissance. Besides being the first wife of Granville Barker[4] (and the Hermione[5] in his 1912 production of *The Winter's Tale* which, I suspect,

---

[1] *Biography*, p. 140, which cites letters from Firbank to Grant Richards.

[2] By 1917 Firbank evidently felt the need to defend Tchekov against the pretentiousness of some of his admirers. Witness Mrs Smee's speech in *Caprice* (*Complete* Firbank, p. 376): 'O Russia! Russia! land of Tchekhov', etc. etc.

[3] Cf. sub-section 17 of this chapter.

[4] She divorced him at his request in 1917 (p. 196 of C. B. Purdom's edition of Bernard Shaw's Letters to Granville Barker).

[5] a rôle also taken by Miss Compostella in *Vainglory*.

inspired the Arcadia of Firbank's pastoral mode[1]), she had been, for Shaw, his first Ann Whitefield (in *Man and Superman* in 1905), his first Jennifer Dubedat (in *The Doctor's Dilemma*, 1906) and his first Lavinia (in *Androcles and the Lion*, 1913).

For Firbank in 1917 she became, I suspect, Mrs Mary, the actress-manager from whom Miss Sinquier tries to get a part.[2] But by 1920–1 Firbank was hoping, I think, to become a second Shaw to her.

Although the Preface to *Heartbreak House* was already noticing, in June 1919, that 'the widespread notion that the shock of the war would automatically make a new heaven and a new earth [. . .] is already seen to be a delusion', Firbank's post-war move out of retreat and back into London society did, I think, coincide with a belief on his part that Heartbreak House, that 'cultured, leisured Europe before the war' which was Firbank's Europe, might be preparing to make, at least, a new disposition of the social rules. Leaping into the most social as well as the most Shavian of the arts, Firbank designed a Shavian-Tchekovian prescription of what society should be.

He saw himself on the verge, I think, of assuming that homosexual Shavian social persona[3] which in the real-life event the exemplary martyrdom of Oscar Wilde forbade.

But in *The Princess Zoubaroff* Firbank had re-designed Oscar Wilde – as an ideal, as circumspect enough, unlike the reckless real-life Wilde, to go into voluntary 'exile',[4] and, most boldly of all, as *happy*.

The Princess Zoubaroff is Firbank's *Heartbreak House*: but a happy *Heartbreak House*.

19. Heartbreak

THE vision of happy homosexuality must have soured in the instant when Evan Morgan rejected Firbank's love by rejecting the dedication of his play.

Firbank's vision of himself designing, from the stage, a programme whereby post-war society might build a society fit for homosexuals to live in must have curdled more slowly, as slowly no news came in and it became obvious that society, through its most social artistic institution, the theatre, was going to do nothing whatever about *The Princess Zoubaroff*.

Before the play was due to be 'published' Firbank took advantage of that other peace-time freedom, to travel, and resumed his habit of solitary

---

[1] and perhaps Firbank's agreement to the choice of illustrator for *Inclinations* (cf. Chapters XII, 6 and XV, 6).
[2] and into whose mouth (cf. Chapter XV, 2, footnote) Firbank put the word 'babelet'.
[3] Cf. Chapter XI, 3.   [4] Cf. Chapter XIV, 1 and 10.

nomadism. He went by way of France to North Africa. In September 1920 he corrected the proofs of *The Princess Zoubaroff* in Algiers. By October he had conceived *Santal*. Travelling during October and November (Constantine, Timgad, Batna, Biskra, Tunis), he made notes for *Santal*, wrote to ask his mother to send him an Everyman translation of the Koran and wrote to Grant Richards suggesting that *Santal* be given an advance announcement in *The Princess Zoubaroff*.[1] (It wasn't.[2])

Firbank believed that *The Princess Zoubaroff* had been issued, according to schedule, on the propitious[3] date of 9 November, when he received (at Tunis, on 11 November) word from Grant Richards of Evan Morgan's refusal.

'Publication' was put off until 26 November, in order that the dedication might be deleted.

The deletion has left its scar in the printed book, where the page that bears on one side the half title and on the other the Dramatis Personae list is glued on to the stump left by cutting off the page on which the dedication was printed.

The excised dedication, 'To the Hon. Evan Morgan in Souvenir Amicale of a "Previous Incarnation" ', was, of course, an allusion to that moment[4] of Egyptological and reincarnational fervour in which Firbank had swept the newly met Morgan off to the British Museum to see his 'original', the mummy of Rameses: and perhaps it was also a more secret allusion not so much to a previous as to an ideal incarnation in which Evan Morgan and Firbank represented that happy pair, Lord Orkish and Reggie or Oscar Wilde and Bosie, in the play which was Firbank's offering to Evan Morgan.

Firbank spent Christmas 1920 in Tunis. He made expeditions in the new year (Sfax,[5] Gabès, Kairouan; Carthage, Sidi bou Saïd). In the first week of March 1921, at Tunis, he finished *Santal* (whose printed text ends with the locational line '*Algiers, Tunis*'), a brief story about a pious pilgrimage that leads into solitude and the delusionariness of visions.

The influence of Bernard Shaw is still detectable in *Santal*: in the shape of the book's crypto-vegetarianism.[6]

[1] The *Biography*'s account of Firbank's travels, based on his letters, is on pp. 184-8.
[2] At least, it wasn't *in* the book. The announcement may have been made on the dust-jacket which is missing from my copy. (The front of the dust-jacket [which made use of the frontispiece, by Michel Sevier] is reproduced in the *Biography*.)
[3] Cf. Chapter VIII, 5.
[4] Cf. Chapter VIII, 5 and *Memoir*, p. 47.
[5] 'Mr. Sophax, a critic' (*Vainglory*, Chapter II).
[6] Cf. Chapter VIII, 4.

20. A Short but Important Prayer Mat

IF Evan Morgan's reason for declining the dedication of *The Princess Zoubaroff* truly was, as his solicitors' letter[1] to Grant Richards implied, his shock, when he read the play, at 'its general tone towards the Catholic Church', he cannot have read *Valmouth* or, indeed, *any* of Firbank's previous Firbankian books.

Firbank, that emotional perpetual convert,[2] had been detached from actual belief in Catholicism ever since he had been actually converted to it.

His sole expression of an immersed, undistanced and uncynical piety dated from *before* his conversion: *Odette D'Antrevernes*.

When he resumed his nomadic habit of frequent changes of air,[3] Firbank resumed also its emotional analogue, his religious convertibility.

His ambiguity[4] towards *Odette D'Antrevernes* had evidently not been allayed by his revising it, in 1916, into *Odette*. Three months or so before the conception of *Santal* in the autumn of 1920, Firbank had been reminded of the existence of *Odette* by a request from its solitary fan, Lady Firbank, for twelve specially bound copies of the 1916 edition.[5] It must have been forced on his notice that *Odette* was the sole totally non-Firbankian work in his œuvre. Perhaps, in that uncertainty about his health which is expressed in the *non*-nomadism of *Valmouth*,[6] he felt that the donnée of *Odette* was not yet in a fit state for him to die on.

He conceived *Santal*, therefore, as an *Odette* subjected bodily to the Firbankian change of locale.

The French Catholic orphan girl brought up by her aunt becomes the North-African Mohammedan orphan boy given a home by his uncle and aunt. Odette's tiny pilgrimage into the château garden to meet the madonna, her token of the internal Firbankian shift of locale, is enlarged into Cherif's deliberate decision, prompted by his aunt's blood lust,[7] to leave his foster home and enter on what turns out to be a limitless quest. With the ultimate object of asking his company on a pilgrimage to Mecca Cherif sets off in

---

[1] Cf. Chapter VIII, 5.
[2] Cf. Chapter XVI, 7.
[3] Cf. Chapter XVI, 5–6.
[4] Cf. Chapter XVII, 3.
[5] The *Biography*, p. 183, records (from letters) Lady Firbank's request in 'the summer of 1920' and Firbank's overseeing of the early part of the preparations.
[6] Cf. sub-section 14 of this chapter.
[7] 'Coming back one day, he found her in the kitchen with Mabrouka holding the very knife, while on the Moorish-chest in a stream of gushing blood, lay the lamb.
  ' "I think *cutlets*", Amoucha was saying.
  ' "But be guided by me, dear, now won't you," Mabrouka replied, " about the leg?" '

search of a hermit known to him only by pious hearsay and 'thought by some even to be the Prophet himself'.

Even the prostitution motif in *Odette*, that gleam obliquely reflected from Firbank's fantasised minion self,[1] is transposed into *Santal* in the form of Ibn Ibrahim, whose sinister 'babouched' steps through the Souk Cherif dreads because 'He had amassed vast wealth, rumour had it, in the traffic of handsome youths', and whom Cherif presently overhears, sighing (as he sits 'beneath a little rustic temple') the words 'My lazy, drowsy darling' to 'a slim Tunisian boy'.

Aptly Firbank marked *Santal* North-African though its colour is, as another flight of his 'Hellenism',[2] a pan-Sapphic declaration only less declarative than *The Princess Zoubaroff*, by dedicating the story to Helen Carew[3] by her first name written in Greek form (Helenē) and Greek script: Hellenism as Helenism.

Firbank was quite aware of (and perhaps took a transvestite pleasure he would not mention in writing to his mother in) the fact that he was transmuting his earlier heroine into a North-African boy: 'I want to rewrite Odette in an Arab setting – a child seeking Allah'.[4]

As if to work on his imagination by working, in imagination, on his senses, he decided: 'I shall call the story "Santal", which is the name of a perfume of the East.'

It is a perfume perhaps cognate in name with sandalwood.[5] (There is also[6] a Santal tribe in West Bengal.) And it is evidently a perfume that can be contained in and released from incense. The marabout who tells Cherif of the hermit is burning 'sticks of Santal'; and Cherif himself, when he sets off alone on his quest, takes with him (in Firbank's own hagiographical frame of mind) 'a few loose sticks of Santal to burn at passing shrines'.

The name of his hero it seems conceivable that Firbank borrowed (and Arabised) from Colette's Chéri.

(Curiously, Colette, too, was in Algeria in 1920. *Chéri* seems[7] to have been published in volume form about December 1920, but it was serialised first in

[1] Cf. Chapter XVII, 4.
[2] Cf. sub-section 18 of this chapter.
[3] Cf. Chapter XII, 5.
[4] This, the quotation in my next paragraph and the 'scenery' quotation a few paragraphs on are from a letter of Firbank's to his mother (from Constantine, 7 October 1920), quoted in the *Biography*, p. 187.
[5] According to *The Shorter Oxford English Dictionary*, the *sandal* in *sandalwood* is ultimately derived, via Latin, from Sanskrit.
[6] as I learned in 1971 from the advance programme for the appearance at Sadler's Wells of the Kalashetra Indian Dance Theatre.
[7] from pp. 94–6 of Margaret Crosland's *Madame Colette* . . .

La Vie Parisienne, a copy of which Firbank might have bought in French-speaking North Africa.)

What Firbank achieved with *Santal* was to translate his pastoral lyricism into a desert song ('I shall try & make the descriptions of scenery beautiful & keep the whole thing as simple as possible') and to convert not only piety but camp out of the idiom of Catholicism and into the idiom of Islam.

No one can suppose Islam (unlike protestantism[1]) inherently less susceptible to camp than Catholicism who has seen exhibited in the Topkapi Museum at Istanbul the object which the English translation of the guidebook catalogues as 'a short but important prayer written in brilliants'.

Firbank wrought the conversion of his imaginative world in brilliants – and with his dress-designer's (and gardener's) touch:[2] ' "Salaam!" he made reply, raising a hand to a turban of frayed *crêpe* jauntily wreathed with Jasmine'.[3]

With the same unperturbed accomplishment and the same slyly baroque delight in the resulting incongruity with which he had set down the creatures and furnishings of his imagination in an English cathedral town, Firbank now set them down in 'the street Bab-Azoun' (and allowed them to deliver his, no doubt, comments on the Everyman edition[4]):

> 'I find, myself, the Koran,' Mabrouka confessed, 'just a wee bit bewildering.'
>
> 'There is nothing to absorb a woman much in the Koran,' Amoucha agreed. ' "Given in at Mecca"; "Handed in at Mecca"; it reminds one, doesn't it, of the Post Office?'
>
> 'I've noticed,' Embarka[5] remarked, 'that Mecca born men are nearly always naughty.'
>
> 'You veiled women notice more than others,' Mabrouka murmured [...]
>
> 'Better a bad Mussulman than a good Christian! as the adage goes.'
>
> 'Oh, my dear – a Christian!' Mabrouka shuddered.
>
> 'To me, they all look just like white tired parakeets,' Amoucha said.

---

[1] Cf. Chapter VIII, 8.

[2] Cf. Chapter XV, 6 and 9.

[3] Firbank's capital (cf. Chapter XV, 1–3) of respect for the personalness of flowers (*Santal*, 1921, p. 20) has been dropped from the *Complete* Firbank (p. 487).

[4] Cf. sub-section 19 of this chapter.

[5] The 'widow Embarka (who was of negro-extraction)' is a reflexion of Firbank's pro-Negroism (which he could scarcely have left out of his North Africa), who in the extravagance of her passion for western gadgets anticipates in miniature the Mouth family in *Prancing Nigger*; for 'Having squandered her husband's meagre fortune upon the purchase of a Gramophone, she was dependent now [...] upon her friends' (*Santal*, 1921, pp. 12–13).

Firbank trailed across his text several deliberate and delighted traces of the fact that a mental translation had taken place, such as[1] his narrative's calling the hermit a saint ('Yes, he would seek the Saint among the remotest places of the hills') and Amoucha's declaration entirely in the tones of English dowagerhood: ' "I shall never forget," she said, "I was *née* an Abdelhafid." '

One trace is perhaps less deliberate. Amoucha's ravishment of a claim, ' "Believe me," she was saying, "my last couscous, before Ramadan-Eve, was a ravishment to the sense" ', presently evokes from the widow Embarka the economic dictum, which I believe to be culinarily incorrect,[2] 'In order to make a couscous [. . .] there must first be rice!'

No Firbankian work has been more snubbed than *Santal*. The fashion for dismissing it was perhaps begun by Lord Berners[3] and has continued long after fashion treated Lord Berners in the same way. Some Firbankians are probably simply unable to recognise Firbank's world in its North-African trappings – thereby shewing themselves to have made the mistake in the first place of thinking Firbank's an observed instead of an imagined world.

At some point after writing it, Firbank himself joined the snubbers of *Santal*. Three years after finishing it Firbank declared that it had bored him even while he was writing it. But the good opinion he expressed of the book immediately after finishing it argues that to be a false memory, engendered by his dislike of the book – a dislike which began later than he retrospectively believed but which certainly grew rapidly and bitterly. By 1923 Firbank was wielding *Santal* almost as a term of abuse, remarking of Hunter Stagg's[4] friend Montgomery Evans that *Santal* was the only book of Firbank's he was likely to enjoy.

Against *Santal* Firbank obviously experienced a much stronger – and also a much more delayed – reaction than the usual writerly doubts he entertained after producing, for instance,[5] *Caprice*.

Santal was no doubt attacked retrospectively in his mind by his memory

---

[1] *Santal*, 1921, pp. 29 and 15 respectively; the couscous discussion quoted in my next paragraph is on pp. 12–13.

[2] Couscous: 'Semoule des Arabes. Ragôut préparé avec cette semoule' (*Larousse de Poche*, in an edition of the same decade as *Santal*.) *Semoule* is usually made from wheat, but the word can be used of substances made from the grains of any cereal, including rice. It is therefore not impossible for a dish made from rice to be a couscous; but I think the widow Embarka is wrong in saying that rice is *necessary* to the making of a couscous.

[3] The *Biography* (p. 207) quotes a late expression by Lord Berners (in a letter of 1948 to Jocelyn Brooke) of the headmasterly view, which is probably more or less the view Lord Berners held all along, that *Santal* is 'not up to the standard of the kind of thing one expected'.

[4] (Cf. Chapter VII, 2); *Biography*, p. 244.   [5] Cf. sub-section 14 of this chapter.

of the circumstances in which he composed it: the smart left by Evan Morgan's instant rejection, and the slow hurt imposed by the theatre's slow rejection, of *The Princess Zoubaroff*.

Moreover, in the autumn of 1920, during his sojourn in North Africa, Firbank conceived another donnée besides that of *Santal*. The second donnée became *The Flower Beneath the Foot*, which Firbank wrote next after *Santal*.

It is in the preface to *The Flower Beneath the Foot*, which he wrote for its United-States publication, that Firbank recounted the co-existence of the two donnéees and made his declaration 'my tale of Islam began to bore me unutterably, & I longed to begin the Flower.'

The boredom with *Santal* probably belongs to the period when Firbank wrote that preface, not to the period when he was writing *Santal*. But it is probably true, as well as justifiable as a literary judgment, that while he wrote *Santal* he was *even more* excited about the future book than about the present one.

Psychologically Firbank probably used his anticipatory excitement as a vehicle to carry him into the future and beyond the hurt given him by his experience with the theatre. It is a symptom, I think, of his giving up his vision of himself as a Shavian dramatist (who might have written Shavian prefaces to his dramas), and reverting to the Jamesian rôle of a novelist rejected by the theatre, that, when he equipped *The Flower Beneath the Foot* with its preface, he gave it a preface in the manner of Henry James's prefaces to his novels: a preface, that is, tracing the book's genesis to small and by-chance observations of real life.

The personages of *The Flower Beneath the Foot* Firbank traced to persons seen, and speculated or fantasised about, during that North-African autumn of 1920. An unknown woman ('almost assuredly an American', Firbank added, perhaps hoping to appeal to the United-States readership for whom the preface was designed), seen in 'a supper-restaurant in Algiers', became the Queen of Pisuerga. The Prince was created from, first, an Arab boy seen asleep beside the sea and, presently, dozens of similar Arab boys: '*wonderful boys*', Firbank's preface calls them, in the italics perhaps of indiscretion or perhaps of his attempt to attract attention to his book by raising a ghost of the Wilde scandal in the safely distant United States.

The clinging together of 'two shed rose-leaves in a Moorish fountain' (rose leaves or, as Firbank probably meant, rose petals being *persons*[1] to Firbank) inspired the love affair on the lake[2] of that florally named pair Vi and Mademoiselle Blumenghast.

[1] Cf. Chapter XV, 1–3. [2] Cf. Chapter XV, 14.

(Firbank's preface calls their love affair a 'soul-trip'. Perhaps the attempted Americanism was again designed for the audience of the United-States edition; or perhaps Firbank was practising for his New York novel, which he had conceived nearly a year before and in whose cause he sought a dictionary of American colloquialisms as a source of 'racy [. . .] expressions of the soil'.[1] In a letter he wrote Carl Van Vechten not long after writing the preface,[2] Firbank made an attempt similar to his 'soul-trip' at an expression of the American soil. Commenting on his receipt, from Brentano's, of the first money he had ever earned by a book, he remarked: 'As you know, with the St Martin Street[3] edition there was not much "swanny cloak" for the author!')

There was reason enough, in his wounds and in his excitement, which carried him over the wounds, about another book, for Firbank's memory to turn against *Santal*. But the profuse and reasonable reasons were perhaps only veils for the true cause, which Firbank could not admit to be reasonable. In turning against *Santal* he was, I think, attacking its earlier form, *Odette*.

That attack, which had far more literary justice, Firbank could not admit in its own right to his consciousness because *Odette* was a pious tribute to his mother.[4]

After finishing *Santal* in the spring of 1921, Firbank left North Africa and returned slowly to England (in order to arrange for *Santal*'s 'publication', which Grant Richards undertook only after Firbank changed some of the dialogue, which had shocked Grant Richards) by way of Sicily, Italy and Paris.

He made a long pause in Rome, where he had *Santal* typed (by a Russian princess[5]) and where he committed an act unconsciously designed, perhaps, to reassure himself that in re-casting *Odette* as *Santal* he had not unwritten the piety *Odette* incarnated towards his mother. He went three evenings running[6] to a Viennese operetta named *Die Schöne Mama*.

Firbank's anger against *Santal* is most conspicuous, and most destructive of Firbank's own interest, in his preface to *The Flower Beneath the Foot*. The preface is blatantly trying to capture a United-States audience for *The*

---

[1] Cf. Chapter X, 11.

[2] The preface was written between May and July 1924. The letter to Carl Van Vechten (quoted on p. 258 of the *Biography*) is of 25 September 1924.

[3] The books Firbank published through Grant Richards bear on the title-page 'London Grant Richards Ltd. St Martin's Street'.

[4] Cf. Chapter XVII, 3.

[5] Cf. Chapter X, 12.

[6] April 11, 12 and 13 (1921), according to the *Biography*, p. 199, which cites Firbank letters.

Flower Beneath the Foot. But to do that by denigrating another of his books ('my tale of Islam began to bore me unutterably') was to the opposite of Firbank's advantage: Brentano's had already adumbrated their plan, which Firbank was strongly counting on, of publishing his whole œuvre in the United States. To announce that *Santal* bored even its author was a positive anti-advertisement for himself.

Firbank was goaded into that act against his own interest by, I think, the fact that he wrote the preface to *The Flower Beneath the Foot*, with its strong anti-advertisement for *Santal*, at the moment of all moments when he could not permit himself to recognise that the anger he directed against *Santal* belonged properly to its earlier incarnation, that tribute to Lady Firbank, *Odette*. Firbank agreed to write the preface on 17 May 1924.[1] Lady Firbank had died on 25 March 1924.

But perhaps this same preface which re-affirms Firbank's loyalty to his dead mother by attacking *Santal* because it had dared to oust *Odette* contains an expression of relief. It is like the admission[2] in . . . *Cardinal Pirelli* that the garden of Eden (or the garden of The Coopers, Chislehurst, under the presidency of Lady Firbank) had been 'oppressive'. Surely it was because Lady Firbank was dead that Firbank *could*, whether in the carelessness of his new freedom or in the hope of attracting scandalised attention, state, publicly and in his own signed person, that Arab '*boys*' were '*wonderful*'.

Although he retrospectively turned against it, Firbank formed a juster opinion of *Santal* when it was newly finished. He thought, correctly, that it was 'slight' (too slight to be taken to a new 'publisher', though his dissatisfactions with Grant Richards were prompting him to seek one). But, when[3] he told his mother from Tunis that he had finished the book, he told her that in it the 'fascination of the East' was 'caught and fixed'; and when, in Rome, he read the book in its Russian typescript, he passed the judgment that it would last as long as an Eastern rug.

To some such not only durable but highly decorative object *Santal* deserves comparison: a prayer mat, perhaps, devoted to no religion but potent, as a cult object, in conjuring and focusing Firbank's unlocated exoticism and his free-range susceptibility to religious conversion: or, since all its brilliant decoration is gathered at the beginning and the end trails

---

[1] and he sent the preface to Brentano's on 10 July 1924 (*Bibliography*, p. 43, citing letters).

[2] Cf. Chapter XVI, 11.

[3] Firbank's immediate judgments on *Santal* are recorded in the *Biography*, pp. 195 and 200, which cites Firbank letters of March 1921 (from Tunis) and of April and May 1921 (from Rome).

away, with Cherif's endless quest, into dots of suspension and into Firbankian space (now rendered as desert, drought and impending death), a runner . . . (one which is, in the Firbankian manner, also a trailer, pointing towards the exoticism and tragedy of the next, the final, section of his œuvre . . .).

XX

The Three Late Tragedies (*The Flower Beneath the Foot* [1923]; *Prancing Nigger* [1924]; *Concerning the Eccentricities of Cardinal Pirelli* [1926])

'(Oh you gardens of Palaces... ! How often have you witnessed agitation and disappointment? You smooth, adorned paths... ! How often have you known the extremes of care... ?)'
The Flower Beneath the Foot (VII)

1. Death Arab

DURING his North-African autumn of 1920, while he was in Constantine, Firbank went to a flea-infested cinema and saw a silent film in which Theda Bara played Cleopatra.[1]

The synthetic anagrammatised name Theda Bara (Death Arab) states major themes present in both the novels Firbank conceived in North Africa, *Santal* and *The Flower Beneath the Foot*. That, combined with the eternal promise of Cleopatra, is probably what drew him to the cinema. And his experience there exerted in turn a particular influence on *The Flower Beneath the Foot*.

Firbank's concern with the Egypto-Wildean image of Cleopatra[2] had, of course, begun much earlier. It was in *Vainglory* that he had temporarily married himself (as Claud Harvester) to a Cleopatra.

But his cinema-visit at Constantine was, I think, the immediate source of three motifs in *The Flower Beneath the Foot*: the Café Cleopatra (centre of the demi-reputable social life of Kairoulla[3]); the fleas which the English

---

[1] The *Biography* (p. 186) reports this fact from Firbank's letters to his mother.
[2] Cf. Chapter XIV, 2.
[3] 'The Capital of Pisuerga', as Firbank's footnote explains, punning in punctuation (cf. Chapter X, 6).

Ambassadress mistakenly believes to infest the Kairoullan Ritz;[1] and the incident in the opening chapter where Laura de Nazianzi, in her capacity as maid of honour, reads aloud to the Queen, and the Queen presently complains: 'She reads at such a pace, [. . .] and when I asked her *where* she had learnt to read so quickly, she replied "On the screens at Cinemas."'

2. Conversions and Versions

IT was from Constantine that Firbank reported to his mother the conception of *Santal*:[2] 'I want to rewrite Odette in an Arab setting.'

North Africa, by playing on Firbank's religious convertibility, evidently set his thoughts towards literary conversions. *The Flower Beneath the Foot* is also, though much less closely and explicitly, a rewriting: of an unpublished and probably unfinished Firbankian novel, namely (though it probably did not yet bear that name)[3] *The Artificial Princess*.

Odette, which Firbank chose to re-work into *Santal*, was itself a revision of *Odette D'Antrevernes*. Perhaps *The Artificial Princess* proposed itself as a second candidate for conversion because it was already a re-working of Wilde's re-working of a story from the New Testament.

And perhaps his early novel about the daughter of Herodias was summoned back into Firbank's thoughts when (during that autumn 1920 to spring 1921 in which he was writing *Santal* in North Africa) he went to the opera in Tunis and heard Massenet's *Hérodiade*.[4]

However, in Firbank's second act of literary conversion, the element of re-working is much less important: because *The Artificial Princess* is so much less in *need* of re-working than *Odette*.

As Firbank acknowledged by taking out the manuscript, finishing it and contemplating publication, *The Artificial Princess* remained a creation valid in its own right even after *The Flower Beneath the Foot* had come into existence.

Odette is (twice over) a botched and falsified sketch which happily turned out to be convertible into *Santal* (though that result made Firbank angry with *Santal*[5]).

The relation between *The Artificial Princess* and *The Flower Beneath the Foot* is just as intimate, but it allows both books their autonomy. They are alternative versions of the metaphor in which Firbank incarnated his own

---

[1] Cf. Chapter VII, 3.   [2] Cf. Chapter XIX, 20.
[3] Cf. Chapters XIII, 3 and XIV, 8.
[4] This fact is recorded (from Firbank's letters) in the *Biography*, p. 194.
[5] Cf. Chapter XIX, 20.

childhood situation at The Coopers and, in doing so, incarnated the universal[1] and essentially domestic[2] situation of the child who continues his unageing life in the unconscious of every adult.

3. Streamers and Riddles

THE metaphor (which borrows[3] the imperial trappings of Chislehurst, the talismanic dress in which Mrs Firbank was quasi-crowned Lady Firbank, and even the disappearance of ecclesiastical objects from the imperially patronised church opposite The Coopers) consists of a royal court.

It is the setting of the Home Life[4] of His Infant Majesty the Ego, that heir apparent who is always finally disappointed of his kingdom.[5]

It is in this setting that the child listens-in to adult conversations which, because he only partly understands them, disintegrate in his ears into fragmented, contextless streamers of Firbankian dialogue[6] or pose him riddles in the manner of that Wilde-beast the Sphinx.[7]

The Flower Beneath the Foot is the book which gives Firbank's technique of dialogue an embodiment *in* the fiction.

Naturally the fragment that is so grievously misconstrued by Lady Something, the English Ambassadress, is overheard *at court*. Lady Something has her misinformation from the authoritative lips of the quintessential parent, the King himself – to whose conversation she has been 'blandly' listening.

> 'I could not be more astonished', the king declared, 'if[8] you told me there were fleas at the Ritz,' a part of which assertion Lady Something, who was blandly listening, imperfectly chanced to hear.
>
> 'Who would credit it!' she breathed, turning to an attaché, a young man all white and pensieroso,[9] at her elbow [. . .]
>
> 'Won't you tell me though,' the young man murmured gently, with his nose in his plate.
>
> Lady Something raised a glass of frozen lemonade to her lips.

---

[1] Cf. Chapter X, 8. [2] Cf. Chapter XIV, 2 and 5.
[3] Cf. Chapter X, 7, 8 and 9. [4] Cf. Chapter XIV, 2.
[5] Cf. Chapters IV, 1 and X, 8. [6] Cf. Chapters XI, 1 and XVII, 8 and 9.
[7] Cf. Chapters XIII, 3 and XIV, 6.
[8] The Brentano's 1924 edition misprints the 'if' with a capital *I*, but the first edition (Grant Richards, 1923) has the small *i*.
[9] Under the influence, I suppose, of Milton, the *Complete* Firbank (p. 508) has changed this word to 'penseroso'. But for once Firbank (or Richards) was right. The (modern) Italian *is* 'pensieroso'.

'Fleas,' she murmured, 'have been found at the Ritz.'
'............!............?.......!.....!!!'¹

Thus, in the second chapter, a streamer of dialogue is misconstrued and the misconstruction provokes a responding streamer shot, by Firbank's perforating dots, to eloquent ribbons.

In the sixth chapter, it is the Sphinx's riddles of Firbank's technique that achieve embodiment in a riddle *in* the fiction:

'Guess who is at the Ritz, ma'am, this week!' the Countess demurely murmured.
'Who is at the Ritz this week, I can't,' the Queen replied.
'*Nobody!*'
'Why how so?'
'The Ambassadress of England, it seems has alarmed the world away. I gather they mean to prosecute!'

For naturally the child who repeats what he thinks he has heard is liable to punishment – which takes the Wildean–Firbankian form of an impending legal action.²

Yet 'even now' (by, that is, the tenth chapter), 'notwithstanding her writ', the Ambassadress 'would say to every other visitor that came to the villa: "Have you heard about the Ritz?? The other night we were dining at the Palace, and I heard the King," *etc.*'

Through the metaphor of the Ambassadress at court (child at parental table), Firbank has exactly captured children's perseverance in the fantasy-theories by which they explain to themselves the riddle of sex. It is exactly the psychological truth he failed to capture when he prettified the sexual ignorance of Odette.

4. Court Life . . .

BOTH *The Artificial Princess* and *The Flower Beneath the Foot* open in royal palaces.

The similarity or identity of the two courts in Firbank's creative mind is established by an office common to them, that of Mistress of the Robes.

It is the Mistress of the Robes at the neo-Herodian court who, by her activity as dramatist, sets the galloping pace of the last movement of *The Artificial Princess*.³

Her office is the connecting thread between the end of one book and the

---

[1] a remark grievously curtailed in the *Complete* Firbank (p. 509); cf. Chapters X, 12; XIV, 6; and XIX, 18. [2] Cf. Chapter VII, 3. [3] Cf. Chapter XVII, 7.

beginning of the other. The Mistress of the Robes at the court of Pisuerga appears in the opening sentence of *The Flower Beneath the Foot*, taking precedence, even, over her sovereign.

Her title, together with her sovereign's, sounds in the opening words the decorative tone of the whole book, which plays on the metamorphosis of the titles *her Majesty* and *his Highness* into 'her Dreaminess' and 'his Weariness': a play which comments, perhaps, on the metamorphosis of Mrs into Lady Firbank and the non-transmission of a title to her son, who lacked even the aristocratic badge of a distinctive first name.[1]

Simultaneously, and this time presumably not by conscious design, the opening sentence sounds the tone of Firbankian negligence proper to the book that contains Firbank's reference to 'the singular tense'.[2] Pedantically considered, the first sentence of the book is a grammatical blunder: 'Neither her Gaudiness the Mistress of the Robes, or her Dreaminess the Queen were feeling quite themselves.'

After her conspicuous début, however, the Mistress of the Robes vanishes into the background of the rest of the novel.

Within the fiction, her duty is merely to introduce into it (as indeed, the narrative implies, she has recently introduced at court) the maid of honour who is amusing the Queen, during her bout of feeling not quite herself, by reading aloud to her (too fast). The maid of honour is, the narrative of the first chapter presently discloses, the niece of the Mistress of the Robes.

(The degree of kinship was probably suggested by contagion from *The Artificial Princess*, where the Princess is, in the Salome pattern, niece as well as stepdaughter to the King.)

Having marked the continuity between *The Artificial Princess* and *The Flower Beneath the Foot*, the Mistress of the Robes marks, by introducing her niece, their divergence.

At the neo-Herodian court the heir is a Princess. It is in her that Firbank invests his own identity – and also his creativity: for it is the Princess who creates the book by trying to impose on circumstances and events the pattern of the Salome story.

The royal family of Pisuerga, on the other hand, has two sons: his Weariness Prince Yousef; and 'his Naughtyness,[3] Prince Olaf', a small boy

---

[1] Cf. Chapter VII, 4.   [2] Cf. Chapter X, 12.

[3] Firbank was prone to spellings on this model. The *Biography* (p. 253) quotes a letter to his sister in which he wrote '*happyness*'. The Brentano's 1924 edition of *The Flower Beneath the Foot* preserves (on p. 81) the spelling 'Naughtyness', but the *Complete* Firbank (p. 531) corrects it to 'Naughtiness'. (In his handwritten preface, which sub-section 8 will mention further, Firbank wrote 'Wearyness' but corrected it to 'Weariness'.)

At the end of the same chapter, the *Complete* Firbank (p. 535) prints: 'And taking his led by the hand through the book by his governess, Mrs Montgomery, who is British and preparing him for Eton.

5. The Flower and 'the gardener, (poor dear)'

FIRBANK'S selfhood is invested in neither prince. His chief though not sole representative in the book is the reading maid of honour: Laura Lita Carmen Etoile de Nazianzi, 'sometimes called among her friends', as a footnote explains, by the name Rara.

As the flower who is finally crushed beneath the foot, Laura is another floral self-portrait of Arthur Annesley Ronald Firbank, sometimes called among his friends by the name Artie, a name which increasingly was, however, rare indeed.

Laura's first name (besides horticulturally suggesting *laurel*) is a reference to her enforced vocation for the convent. A laura (according to *The Shorter Oxford English Dictionary*) was, in the terminology of Christian antiquity, an 'aggregation of detached cells, tenanted by recluse monks under a superior, in Egypt and elsewhere'.

And, as a matter of fact, the same conventual reference is made by her surname. Nazianzi has acquired, since Firbank coined it, the nasty association of *Nazi*. But to Firbank it suggested Nazareth. Laura's destiny is to be a Nazarene; and the *anzi* ending, tacked on to the root in her surname, records (by way of the Italian *anzi* in its oppositional sense of *however*) that her destiny is accomplished in opposition to her heart's wishes.

The last of Laura's christian names, Etoile, is a literal translation of the Stella component in Miss Compostella.

Naughtiness by the hand, the royal governess withdrew.' Both the first edition (p. 91) and the Brentano's edition (p. 89) render the sentence as: 'And taking the little prince by the hand, the Royal Governess withdrew.'

Since the first British and United-States editions agree, the different version in the *Complete* Firbank cannot be explained by a fact recorded in the *Bibliography* (p. 43): for the United-States edition, Firbank sent Brentano's a set of proofs which had been corrected for the British edition but not used for it.

The *Bibliography* further records that Firbank sent Brentano's, with the proofs, a letter requesting three alterations.

One is the correction of a misprinted 'Three' to 'Thee' in 'But to Thee I cling'. The misprint occurs on p. 128 of the first edition. It is corrected on p. 128 of the Brentano's edition.

Firbank's other two requests were for the alteration of 'his Lankiness, Prince Olaf', which occurs on p. 22 and p. 84 of the first edition, to (according to the *Bibliography*, p. 43) 'his naughtiness, Prince Olaf'. The Brentano's edition makes these changes, on p. 16 and p. 81, but with the spelling 'Naughtyness'. So perhaps the *Bibliography*, in transcribing the request Firbank made to Brentano's, has accidentally corrected his spelling.

If, moreover, the Etoile is read in conjunction with the Nazarene surname that immediately follows it, the result discloses what *variety* of flower is trodden beneath the foot. Etoile de Nazianzi is the white-flowered lily (*Ornithogallum umbellatum*) called Star of Bethlehem.

This interpretation might seem too tortuous to be true. But it is confirmed by the illustration [Plate 12][1] which Firbank commissioned for *The Flower Beneath the Foot* from C. R. W. Nevinson.[2] The heroine is shewn wearing a chaplet (or a halo) of flowers, and the whole picture has a floral border; and the flowers in both are[3] Star of Bethlehem.

Firbank's francophile mind was playing not only on the French (Etoile) for part of the flower's English name but simultaneously on its French name. *Brewer's Dictionary of Phrase and Fable* records that Star of Bethlehem is known to French peasants as 'la dame d'onze heures' ('because it opens at eleven o'clock'). Firbank's heroine is a dame d'onze heures because she is carried off to her convent at the eleventh hour.

The naming of his Flower heroine is the culmination of Firbank's language of flowers[4] – and of that procedure in forming names which I suspect[5] he developed in the first place from catalogues of flowers.

Obviously, all the components of Laura's name are susceptible of interpretation, though I may not have more than partly solved them.

The first two christian names, Laura Lita, run together to make their owner a Lorelei. That is Laura's rôle in the Queen's eyes: she is a temptation the Prince must be forced to resist.

On its own, Lita (which I take to be a diminutive of some such name as Carmelita, on the analogy of Rita from Margarita) suggests *litany* or *liturgy*. So Lita plus the Carmen which follows it add up to something like a sung mass, a further reference to Laura's life in the convent.

However, Laura's pet-name Rara indicates that she is a rara avis, finally caged in the convent.[6] So the Carmen in her name is also the rare bird's sad, caged song

And indeed, when a sister comes to collect Laura from court and take her

---

[1] The Nevinson illustration is called a 'decoration' in the first (Grant Richards) edition, where it is reproduced in bright blue and white. Reproduced in tan on white, it is also the frontispiece to the first United-States (Brentano's) edition.

[2] Cf. Chapters VI, 6 and VII, 3.

[3] The identification can be checked against, for instance, the photograph of Star of Bethlehem in R. Genders: *Bulbs all the Year Round* (facing p. 160).

[4] 'People sometimes spoke (and especially ladies) of the language of flowers . . .' (*The Flower Beneath the Foot*, V).

[5] Cf. Chapter XV, 4.

[6] This motif will be expanded in sub-section 15.

to the convent, Firbank's text is aerated by a snatch of song which drifts into the Palace from the preparations going on in the garden for the Prince's wedding supper. It is sung by a boy's voice, 'sweet as a robin's'; and its words are

> Flap your wings, little bird
> O flap your wings –.

At the same time, the Carmen in the heroine's name makes (as Michael Levey has pointed out to me) allusion to Théophile Gautier's poem *Carmen*,[1] whose second verse reads

> Les femmes disent qu'elle est laide
> Mais tous les hommes en sont fous,
> Et l'archevêque de Tolède
> Chante la messe à ses genoux.

(The *Memoir*[2] records that Firbank read Gautier during his stay in Touraine; the archbishop of Toledo is a purely Firbankian personage; and the archbishop's devotions in the poem bring back the Carmen in Laura's name to suggestions of a sung mass.)

Among the people who address Laura de Nazianzi as Rara is Prince Yousef. She is in love with him, and he, at the beginning of the book, with her. His mother the Queen deplores the possible marriage: 'She's so housemaid. . . .' But the Prince, who means to marry Laura,[3] defends her: 'She saves us from *cliché*.'

Firbank's self-portrait as Laura de Nazianzi shares the sex of his self-portrait as the Artificial Princess (alias Princess Artie). Indeed, Laura shares the Princess's touches of trans-sexualism. The Princess is her mother's 'tall-tall schoolboy';[4] and when Prince Yousef looks for Laura de Nazianzi at the royal ball the narrative remarks that 'he caught a glimpse of the agile, boyish figure of his betrothed'.

But the method whereby Firbank-as-Laura plans to come into his kingdom is that of his masculine (and arboriculturally surnamed) self-portrait as Wildred Forrester (in *Lady Appledore's Mésalliance*): by marriage.

And indeed when *The Flower Beneath the Foot* was published Firbank restored himself to the métier which he had, as Wildred Forrester, exercised chez Lady Appledore: that of gardener. Playing on the title whereby his

---

[1] *Émaux et Camées.*   [2] p. 22.
[3] '[. . .] and he could not help rejoicing inwardly, that, *once* his wife, it would no longer be possible for her to enjoy herself exactly with whom she pleased.' (This, like the account of Laura's figure, is from Chapter II of *The Flower Beneath the Foot*.)
[4] Cf. Chapter XIV, 8.

book was a flower, Firbank wrote[1] to Carl Van Vechten: 'its parfum is what concerns me most, & if it is exotic & elusive & bafflingly embaumé, the gardener, (poor dear), will be glad.'

The Artificial Princess is (unknown to herself) frustrated in the imposition of her royal will on events: by her emissary's carelessness and the machinations of the devil. Laura is frustrated by the weakness of the Prince's royal will. Prince Yousef cannot hold out against his parents' machinations for a marriage that will ally their royal family with that of England.

He marries, instead of Laura, an English princess – and is not saved from cliché. His wedding procession includes a carriage that contains 'the very apotheosis of worn-out *cliché*'.[2]

The Artificial Princess is squeezed by the Princess's will into the pattern (or an unintended variation on the pattern) of the biblical anti-saint, the witch's child,[3] Salome. But *The Flower Beneath the Foot* tumbles, against Laura's will and through the weakness of Yousef's, into the pattern of a hagiography.

The end of the book leaves Laura no alternative to the convent. There, after the close of the narrative, she becomes a saint. As its sub-title[4] points out, the novel is written in purported retrospect: as a record of the youth of the heroine whom one of its footnotes calls 'the future saint'.

On the page following its dedication,[5] the book bears, by way of epigraphs,[6] two of its heroine's agonised sayings:

Some girls are born organically[7] good: I wasn't.

[1] in a letter (quoted in the *Biography*, p. 209) of 17 January 1923 – that is (according to the *Bibliography*, p. 37) publication day of the first (the English) edition.
[2] in the person of, among others, Robert Hichens (cf. Chapter XIV, 11).
[3] Cf. Chapter XIV, 1 and 13.
[4] According to the *Biography* (p. 216), a month or so before finishing the novel Firbank asked Grant Richards to announce it in advance under the title *A Record of the Early Life of St. Laura De Nazianzi and The Times in Which She Lived*. Grant Richards preferred the alternative title Firbank had supplied, *The Flower Beneath the Foot*. At Grant Richards's suggestion, Firbank's first choice became (with the addition of a connecting *Being* at the beginning) the sub-title (which is not, however, given in the *Complete* Firbank).
[5] 'To/MADAME MATHIEU/AND/MADEMOISELLE DORA GARNIER-PAGÈS'. I don't know who they were or are. Neither, apparently, does the *Bibliography*, which simply records the dedication, or the *Biography*, which doesn't mention it. From the line divisions I guess that the first name is short for 'Madame Mathieu Garnier-Pagès', and that the two were mother and daughter. I wonder if they are descendants of the Garnier-Pagès who was a member of the provisional government established in Paris at the revolution of 1848.
[6] They are not given in the *Complete* Firbank. The *Bibliography* merely records the existence of two epigraphs, without quoting them.
[7] Since it doesn't quote the epigraphs, the *Bibliography* leaves the context of his query a mystery, but it does record (p. 38) that Grant Richards questioned Firbank's spelling,

> It was about my eighteenth year that I conquered my *Ego*.
> IBID.

6. ... and Non-Life ...

LAURA de Nazianzi becomes a saint only because she is prevented from becoming a lover.

Her agony at being forced into sainthood is Mrs Shamefoot's pursuit of sainthood reversed.

In Mrs Shamefoot Firbank stated his ambition of building, while he was yet alive, an immortal monument to himself in works of art.

In *The Flower Beneath the Foot* he attained his ambition. He must have known, while he was writing it, that it was a great book. What he wrote into it was the cost to him of its greatness.

The Flower Beneath the Foot is an accounts-book: an account of the huge debit-column in Firbank's life, the absence of love, balanced against his credit as a great writer.

The bitterness of his emotional accounting within the book burst into his dealings about the book: in the form of financial accounting. It was over *The Flower Beneath the Foot* that Firbank's dissatisfaction with Grant Richards erupted into a quarrel about money.

Three months after the book was issued Firbank was, in his correspondence with Carl Van Vechten, adding up the accounts of his investment in his own literary career and finding he had 'never seen back *one* farthing piece' of the money he had paid to have his books published. He briefly hoped that *The Flower Beneath the Foot* would sell enough copies to create him a credit balance in his running account (the proceeds from one book going to the costs of the next) with Grant Richards. But instead of seeing even one farthing back Firbank received Grant Richards's statement to the effect that Firbank owed Grant Richards 3*s*. 6*d*. Firbank engaged a firm of accountants or solicitors[1] to go through Grant Richards's accounts.

It was an ironic acting-out, in financial terms and on the subject of the book as a commercial commodity, of the book's content as fiction.

which read 'organicly'. Evidently Grant Richards won. The word is spelt 'organically' in the first edition.

[1] The *Bibliography* (which records Firbank's financial quarrel with Grant Richards over *The Flower Beneath the Foot* on pp. 39–42) doesn't say what it was a firm of, but names it as W. B. Peat & Company. Firbank's case was taken up by the Society of Authors, which in May 1924 obtained a settlement from Grant Richards in respect of all the books Firbank had published with him. He paid Firbank £54. 0*s*. 2*d*. It would be incorrect to call that sum profit (because Firbank had been keeping himself since he began to write *Vainglory*, the first of his books to be 'published' by Richards). It was Firbank's return on the cost of publishing eight books over nine years.

Laura's saintly goodness is Firbank's literary goodness. It was Firbank who was saving English literature 'from *cliché*'.

However, as *Odette D'Antrevernes* bears witness, Firbank hadn't always written well. Translated into autobiography, the epigraph to *The Flower Beneath the Foot* would read: 'Some writers are born organically good: I wasn't.'

The book (which, like all Firbank's books, is about itself as a book) is Firbank's statement that he became a good writer by the process whereby Laura became a saint: confinement to a laura.

Firbank created himself as a writer by living as a 'recluse monk' in a series of isolated cells: his hotel rooms abroad and rooms in clubs in England.

Unlike the nunned Laura, Firbank was not condemned to bodily chastity. He could have sexual intercourse, at least while he was abroad, though he probably often had to buy it. But he lived solitary. What was denied him was the possibility of living with someone of his choice. If you never live with someone, you in a sense never live.

Firbank achieved artistic sainthood through an enforced chastity not of the body but of the heart.

What forced chastity on him *The Flower Beneath the Foot* makes explicit. The Artificial Princess's ambition is frustrated by a mere waywardness in the Baroness, reinforced by a supernatural intervention personified in a form that can be laughed at, the punning Crow who represents Crowley.[1] But the force which excludes Laura from love is expressed without laughter or the disguise of a superstitious mythology. It consists of the machinations of parents.

Moreover, the ambition to which the royal parents sacrifice Laura is an alliance with the royal family of, specifically, England.

It was the ruling social conventions of England, enforced through his mother, which confined Firbank to a cell and excluded love from his life.

7. . . . and Une Vie Courte

JUST after his mother's death Firbank (without knowing he was doing any such disloyal thing) expressed[2] his release from the convent-walls she had set about him by expressing, in his preface to *The Flower Beneath the Foot*, his appreciation of the '*wonderful boys*' of North Africa, one of whom had begotten his Weariness Prince Yousef on Firbank's imagination: 'I beheld an Arab boy asleep beside the summer-sea, & to myself I murmured: "His Weariness, the Prince!" [. . .] a short while afterwards, in another town, his

---

[1] Cf. Chapter VIII, 6.   [2] Cf. Chapter XIX, 20.

Weariness I saw again. Everywhere, in fact his Weariness, or his simulacrum, appeared; all Princes, all weary – *wonderful boys* – wearier, even, than me!'

All, however, that Firbank was truly released from was circumspection: in picking up Arab (or any other) boys, and in publishing his admiration of them. It was too late to go back and marry the Prince. The Arab boys were not in fact wearier than Firbank. Perhaps they were suffering (as his excitement suggests he supposed) from sexual lassitude. But he was weary, and ill, to death. Lady Firbank died too late to release him into the possibility of living with someone he loved – or even, in its barest sense, of living much. He survived her by a mere couple of years.

Firbank's sense of 'too late' was expressed, on a different subject, in writing to his sister three months after their mother's death, when he had just been visited (and caught flowerless[1]) in Rome by Carl Van Vechten's friend Philip Moeller. 'I feel alarmed by his sudden advent into my life & of these new friends my books are bringing me. I feel often far too tired & their sympathy comes too late to make a *personal* success of my literary one – !'[2]

During his long pause in Rome[3] on his way back to England from North Africa, Firbank was told by a fortune-teller that, provided he lived through a couple of sticky dates in the immediate future, he would survive to the age of 72. Obviously, he wanted to believe. But his disbelief, his knowledge of the short span he could rationally expect[4] and his ultimate dismissal of the supernatural gypsydom he tried to take to his comfort[5] are all written into *The Flower Beneath the Foot*: by way of its divergence from *The Artificial Princess*.

In *The Artificial Princess* the baroque dimension coincides with the force of frustration: both are personified in the laughable Crow. In *The Flower Beneath the Foot*, the force that frustrates Laura's impulse to life and love appears nakedly as what it is, parental selfishness. All the same, there is a baroque dimension in *The Flower Beneath the Foot* (whose structure echoes that of *The Artificial Princess* fairly exactly). But it adopts its proper, monumental, highest-baroque personification, and is given nakedly the name of Firbank's true enemy: 'the Angel of Death'.

The Angel of Death (at the end of the book's first movement) carries off the old and eccentric Archduchess Elizabeth (Lizzie) of Pisuerga; and the

---

[1] Cf. Chapter VII, 5 and *Memoir*, pp. 82–3.

[2] quoted, from a letter to Heather Firbank of 6 June 1924, in the *Biography*, p. 260.

[3] (Cf. Chapter XIX, 20). The prediction is recorded, from Firbank's letters to his mother of April 1921, in the *Biography*, p. 199.

[4] Cf. Chapter VI, 7.

[5] Cf. Chapter VIII, 5, 6 and 7.

Queen's unnoticing, egoistical cruelty while the old woman dies prefigures the unnoticing, egoistical cruelty with which, at the end of the whole book, she (whose machinations are responsible) sees Laura carried off to the deathly life of the convent.

The idea of objects being stolen from him was interpreted by Firbank as theft of his life.[1] *The Flower Beneath the Foot* is a monument to his sense of how small a store of life he still possessed. That, I think, is why it was over *that* book that he expressed his cumulative belief that Grant Richards was in effect stealing from him. And no doubt it was because *that* book had been illustrated by C. R. W. Nevinson that Firbank's delusions, when time was indeed short for him, appointed the Nevinsons conspirators in the supposed theft of his scarf.

Inevitably it was in *The Flower Beneath the Foot* that Firbank gave metaphorical explicitness to the interpretation he set on robbery.

His selfhood is invested in the old Archduchess of Pisuerga, the first object of the Queen's cruelty, as well as in Laura, who is the second. The book is a double tragedy. It counterpoints the brief stretch of life left to the old woman against the long saintly life-in-death placed before the young one.

The Archduchess is introduced into Chapter II with the words: 'she was looking as the Grammar-books say, "meet" to be robbed, beneath a formidable tiara, and a dozen long strands of pearls.' By Chapter VI, the destiny implied in 'meet' is fulfilled. The Archduchess has been robbed indeed – of her life.

Between writing his first and writing his second version of the metaphor of a court, Firbank had become pressingly aware of the pun inherent in *court*. *The Flower Beneath the Foot* is a baroque contrast, playing on the divergence of *court*, the royal Anglo-French noun, from *court*, the curt French adjective.

And in the middle of the two senses there glimmers, coinciding with the half-formed substance of Firbank's paranoid delusions, yet a third *court*: the court of law that threatens Lady Something because she (in Firbank's own manner) courts the danger of libel.

8. 'The error is so slight . . .' (Cf. Chapter X, 12: Firbank and the Rules)

WHEN he came to write his preface[2] to the United-States edition, Firbank had by no means lost touch with the spirit of *The Flower Beneath the Foot*.

---

[1] Cf. Chapter VII, 3.   [2] whose text is printed as an appendix to this book.

Having given the novel itself an ungrammatical opening sentence,[1] he gave the preface an opening sentence that contains a spelling mistake (in his rendering of his book's very title): 'I suppose the Flower beneth the Foot is really Oriental in origin [. . .]'

Unlike the same mistake when he made it in writing to Grant Richards about the book's finances,[2] the spelling mistake in the preface was accessible to Firbank's readers, at least in the United States, from the start. Brentano's reproduced his handwritten preface in facsimile.[3] As if to underline Firbank's disregard of orthodoxy, the preface goes on to commit a malapropism. It is in the exact opposite of its orthodox sense that Firbank uses the word *nadir* when he remarks, of the Queen: 'an alliance with England, poor woman, was the nadir of her dreams!'

In the text of the novel itself, on the subject of another state alliance, this time with Dateland, Firbank put into the Queen's mouth the malapropism from which Grant Richards failed to dissuade him,[4] 'depreciated' in the sense of 'deprecated'.

It was in writing *The Flower Beneath the Foot* (and in afterwards writing about writing it) that Firbank was most conspicuously, even by Firbankian standards, defiant of the orthodoxies of expression in English.

At the same time, it was in *The Flower Beneath the Foot* that he shewed himself most mindful of the existence of the rules of orthodox expression and the discipline of grammar.

His mindfulness speaks through the lethal image[5] in which the Archduchess Elizabeth of Pisuerga looks 'as the Grammar-books say, "meet" to be robbed'.

The same awareness of grammar-books illuminates that brilliant imagist

---

[1] Cf. sub-section 4 of this chapter.

[2] The *Bibliography* (p. 41) quotes Firbank's letter of 18 June 1923 with the spelling 'Beneth'.

[3] The *Biography* (p. 258) records that, a few days after he sent Brentano's the preface, Firbank sent them a letter asking that the word *fabric* in the preface be changed to *evolve*. (The context is Firbank's rather Jamesian use of *fabric* as a verb, in the in any case rather Jamesian [cf. Chapter XIX, 20] remark: 'It did not occur to me, at the time, I believe, to fabric a story from so singularly little.') The alteration is not made in the Brentano's edition; and indeed, since the preface is reproduced in facsimile, it could not have been, unless Brentano's had sent the original back across the Atlantic or had employed a forger. The *Biography* unfortunately makes no comment, but the request it reports Firbank as making suggests that, at that time, he didn't *know* that Brentano's intended fascimile reproduction.

[4] Cf. Chapter X, 12; 'For the aggrandisement of the country's trade, an alliance with Dateland is by no means to be depreciated' (p. 501 in the *Complete* Firbank and p. 13 in the 1923 *The Flower Beneath the Foot*, in both of which Firbank's 'depreciated' stands uncorrected). [5] Cf. sub-section 7 of this chapter.

glimpse[1] which Firbank places in the perspective of an exchange between the King of Pisuerga and the court physician:

> 'Whenever I go out,' the King complained, 'I get an impression of raised hats.'
> It was seldom King William of Pisuerga spoke in the singular tense, and Doctor Babcock looked perturbed.
> 'Raised hats, sir?' he murmured in impressive tones.
> 'Nude heads, doctor.'

But in the same breath which shews him aware of the rules Firbank contrived, with his indeed singular 'singular tense', to break the rules of the very terminology of the rules.

And, as a matter of fact, both Firbank's awareness of the rules of English expression and his defiance of them were bound to be at their highest pitch in *The Flower Beneath the Foot*: because that book is his highest protest against the rules of English behaviour.

No wonder he malapropised twice on the subject of state alliances. State alliances, affirmed by royal marriages, are the novel's metaphor for the heterosexual conventions.

And the idiom of court life, whereby a king is 'We' and not 'I', is the book's metaphor for the rigid grammar of conventional life, whereby *he* must remain strictly *he* and not merge into *she*.

The Flower Beneath the Foot is the substantiation of my hypothesis[2] that in defying the rules of the English language Firbank was defying the English social rules about sex.

That his rebellion was cardinally against the social rule which forbade the merging of a *he* into a *she* is substantiated by one of the most brilliant decorative inventions in *The Flower Beneath the Foot*.

In this episode there is a grammatical mistake, and it is on the cardinal question of gender.

This time, however, it is not Firbank himself who makes the mistake.

He has given his own grammatical mistake an embodiment *in* the fiction, just as he gives fictional embodiment, in the same novel, to his technique of overheard fragments and his technique of riddles.[3]

The mistake is made by the personage whose title enshrines one of Firbank's unorthodoxies of spelling,[4] 'his Naughtyness, Prince Olaf' – a pupil who is 'as the Grammar-books say, "meet" to be' drilled in English grammar by his governess, Mrs Montgomery (whose own English *h*'s are insecure).

[1] Cf. Chapter V, 2.
[2] In Chapter X, 12.
[3] Cf. sub-section 3 of this chapter.
[4] Cf. sub-section 4 of this chapter.

'[. . .] and now, let me hear your lessons: I should like,' Mrs Montgomery murmured, her eyes set in detachment on the floor;[1] 'the present-indicative tense[2] of the Verb *To be*! Adding the words, Political h-Hostess; – more for the sake of the pronunciation than for anything else!'

And after considerable persuasion, prompting, and 'bribing', with various sorts of sweets:

'I am a Political Hostess,
Thou art a Political Hostess,
He is a Political Hostess,
We are Political Hostesses,
Ye are Political Hostesses,
They are Political Hostesses.'

'Very good, dear, and only one mistake. *He* is a Political h-Hostess: Can you correct yourself? The error is so slight. . . . . .'

9. The Archduchess Artie

TO the Archduchess Lizzie of Pisuerga, 'Very old and very bent, and (even) very beautiful', Firbank attributes two bizarreries of behaviour (both connected with still or running water).

Arriving late for the state dinner which the King and Queen of Pisuerga give in Chapter II for their royal visitors from Dateland, the Archduchess excuses herself to the King with: 'Forgive me, Willie [. . .] but it was so fine that after tea, I and a Lady went paddling in the Basin of the Nymphs.'

It is, Firbank's narrative explains, because she was 'Forbidden in youth by parents and tutors alike the joys of paddling under pain of chastisement' that the Archduchess now 'liked to slip off to one of the numerous basins or natural grottos in the castle gardens, where she would pass whole hours in wading blissfully about'. While she wades she sings snatches 'from the vaudevilles and operas [. . .] in favour in her day, interspersed at intervals by such cries as: "Pull up your skirt, Marquise, it's dragging a little my friend below the knees . . ."'

Even in explicating the Archduchess's eccentricity Firbank's narrative dooms her by means of it (as surely as he dooms her through introducing her as looking ' "meet" to be robbed').

King William replies to her apology by enquiring 'How was the water?'

---

[1] I am following the (in this instance very strange) punctuation of the first edition, where the grammar lesson is on pp. 172–3.

[2] Evidently Firbank did in fact know what a tense was.

By way of answer, 'The Archduchess repressed a sneeze: "Fresh", she replied, "but not too . . ."'

And after the narrative has given its account of her eccentricity, ' "I fear our Archduchess has contracted a slight catarrh", the Mistress of the Robes,[1] a woman like a sleepy cow, observed, addressing herself to the Duke of Varna upon her left'; to which the Duke replies: 'Unless she is more careful, she'll go paddling once too often.'

The Archduchess is not more careful. By Chapter V she is 'Swathed in furs, on account of a troublesome cough contracted paddling'. By Chapter VI she is on her deathbed.

And there she is still pursuing her other eccentricity, her true vocation. 'Propped high, by many bolsters, in a vast blue canopied bed, the Archduchess lay staring laconically at a diminutive model of a flight of steps, leading to what appeared to be intended, perhaps, as a hall of Attent, off which opened quite a lot of little doors, most of which bore the word "Engaged." '

Three chapters earlier, Firbank's narrative has given an account of this eccentricity of the Archduchess's – incidentally anticipating in two sentences the entire and intricate plot of Gabriel Chevallier's comic novel *Clochemerle*. 'The most philanthropic perhaps of all the Royal Family, her hobby was designing, for the use of the public, sanitary, but artistic, places of Necessity on a novel system of ventilation. The King had consented to open (it was expected appropriately) one of these in course of construction in the Opera Square.'

The Archduchess Lizzie is a Princess Artie who has missed the throne and been relegated to the position of a princess royal.

Firbank, whose protest against the social conventions this novel is, is identified with the Archduchess in both strands of her unconventionality. It is the perpetuated 'slight catarrh' of Firbank's childhood which, by the time he wrote *The Flower Beneath the Foot*, had increased into 'a troublesome cough'. And he, too, was a designer of bizarre artistic monuments on an indeed novel (and for use in novels) system (of ventilation or aeration).

In the Archduchess's œuvre ('Your Royal Highness never repeats herself!'), one of the earlier works is positively identifiable as one of Firbank's earlier works.

> 'Have you been to my new *Pipi*?' she asked.
> 'Not yet –'
> 'Oh but you must!'

---

[1] Cf. sub-section 4 of this chapter.

'I'm told it's even finer than the one at the Railway Station. Ah, from musing too long on that Hellenic frieze, how often I've missed my train!' the Duchess of Cavaljos[1] murmured, with a little fat deep laugh.

It is a description of the frieze-structure, and the Sapphic (or Hellenic[2]) motifs, of *Vainglory*. ('His work calls to mind a frieze with figures of varying heights trotting all the same way.'[3]) The Archduchess's *Vainglory* is sited at the Railway Station because[4] 'To Ashringford from Euston is really quite a journey.'

Structures of the sort designed by the Archduchess were no doubt likely places to seek '*wonderful boys*', the source of pleasures Firbank no doubt felt he pursued in adult life because in youth he had been forbidden them 'by parents and tutors[5] alike'. And indeed the structures designed by the Archduchess lent their French name (or probably, with more immediacy, their French North-African name) to the fictional kingdom in *The Flower Beneath the Foot*. The word is wrenched into a Spanish- or Portuguese-sounding disguise (where it nevertheless preserves its characteristic *w* sound, plus the unEnglish fact that that sound is indicated by a group of vowels), but Pisuerga is still, recognisably,[6] *pissoir*.

10. Where?

PISUERGA is indeed a good place to meet '*wonderful boys*'; and a great many of the boys to be met there are, like the boys in Firbank's preface, North-African.

The flower-shop clandestinely owned[7] by the Duchess of Varna trades under the name '*Haboubet of Egypt*'. The shop trades falsely, since the flowers said to come from the Land of Punt in fact come from the Duchess's country estate. But the manager is 'a slim' (and genuine) 'Tunisian boy', Bachir, who speaks ('Itchiata wa?') a revival of the language of Mrs Yaj.[8]

---

[1] who, incidentally, is the Mistress of the Robes.   [2] Cf. Chapter XIX, 18.
[3] Cf. Chapter XVIII, 4.   [4] Cf. Chapter XVIII, 2.
[5] particularly, no doubt, the tutor who warned Firbank against 'the cult of the purple orchid' (cf. Chapter XIII, 5).
[6] That is not all that is recognisable in Pisuerga, a name that is almost as crammed and cryptic as Laura's. Indeed, Pisuerga refers to Laura's fate as well as to the Archduchess's. To go into a convent is for Laura a pis-aller. The nature of the pis-aller is made clear by the -uerga component in Pisuerga, through the simple and linguistically plausible transformation of *u* into *v*, so that -uerga becomes *verga*. Via French (*vierge*), Laura's fate is virginity. Via Italian, convent-life includes the wielding of the 'discipline': verga – rod; vergare – to flog.
[7] Cf. Chapter XV, 2.   [8] Cf. Chapter XIX, 13.

And when there is extra business Bachir is helped by his friend Ouardi, 'an Armenian boy'.

The royal wedding in Pisuerga naturally brings even more extra custom to the flower-shop,[1] and the extra labour then taken on consists of 'betarbouched boys in burnooses'. It is true that 'by no means all of those assembled in the little shop, bore the seal of Islam', but remarkably many of them do (or the seal, at least, of Firbank's North-African sojourn): Sidi, 'an olive-skinned Armenian youth', Lazari Demitraki, 'a blonde boy with a skin of amber', and such passing and time-passing visitors as 'a Levantine Greek known as "Effendi darling" ' and the 'dark-cheeked Tunisian' who is employed at the Count of Tolga's 'private Hammam Baths'.

Clearly Firbank was correct in spirit when he began his preface: 'I suppose the Flower beneth the Foot is really Oriental in origin.'

Yet despite the near-eastern origin of so much of its population and also, by the sound of it, of the very name of its capital city (Kairoulla: Cairo plus Kairouan?[2]), Pisuerga itself is in Europe.

Indeed, Firbank creates Black Mischief (of the kind subsequently exploited by Evelyn Waugh) out of the meeting between the occident and the near-orient which opens the book in the form of the state visit to Pisuerga of 'King Jotifa and Queen Thleeanouhee[3] of the Land of Dates'.

'They're in European dress, dear?', the Queen inquires of Prince Yousef, who has been sent to meet the visitors at the station.

' "The King had on a frock coat and a cap. . . ."

' "And she?"

' "A tartan-skirt, and checked wool-stockings."

' "She has great individuality, so I hear, marm," the Countess[4] ventured.'

But by the time of the royal banquet, to which the royal party makes its entrance 'to the exhilarating' (and wittily, *Handelianly* barbaric) 'strains of King Goahead's War-March', the royal visitors have changed down (or up) into 'the loose-flowing vestments of their native land', together with its loose-flowing customs.

Indeed, it is on learning that in Dateland one eats from shells rather than from plates that the King of Pisuerga remarks 'I could not be more astonished [. . .] if you told me there were fleas at the Ritz.'[5]

---

[1] as well as occasioning a change (to associations with England) in the false descriptions of the flowers (cf. Chapter XV, 2).

[2] (Cf. Chapter XIX, 19). Perhaps Kairoulla is also a cerulean city (full of heavenly boys).

[3] promoted (as Chapter X, 2 remarked) from the 'Ex-Princess' of that name mentioned in *Inclinations*.

[4] of Tolga.   [5] Cf. sub-section 3 of this chapter.

The 'babouched feet' which in *Santal* sum up 'the fascination of the East'[1] in the sexual menace extended towards Cherif by Ibn Ibrahim, reputed trader in boys, belong in *The Flower Beneath the Foot* to Queen Thleeanouhee.

The sexual menace *she* extends is in the direction of Lady Something, wife of the British Ambassador at the court of Pisuerga.

And that Pisuerga itself is of the west is emphasised in the reply ('Unhappily Pisuerga is not the East, ma'am!') which Lady Something returns when, at a reception at the British Embassy, Queen Thleeanouhee makes her an indeed loose-flowing proposition: ' "Let us go away by and by, my dear gazelle", she exclaimed with a primitive smile, "and remove our corsets and talk." '

Pisuerga is firmly placed in Europe, but its Europeanness is generalised Europeanness. Pisuerga is an equivalent in occidental terms to the unspecific Afro-Asia which Firbank created to be the unseen homeland of Mrs Yaj.

Kairoulla apart (and even that is lent a latinate ending), place names and personal names in Pisuerga offer a mixture of the latin with the Slav which might be expected of Roumania. Cavaljos, like Pisuerga itself, has Iberian associations; Nazianzi is Italianate; Varna and Tolga (Olga, Volga) seem Slav (though Varna is in fact perhaps a Firbankian phonetic rendering of the end bit of *Nirvana*[2]).

Yet despite this conspicuous and presumably deliberate mongrelism, Firbank's preface, after acknowledging the 'Oriental' origin of the book, states: 'the scene is some imaginary Vienna'.

And, during the gestation of the book, Firbank insists further on in the preface, 'A kind of nostalgia (which *may* only have been waywardness) turned all my thoughts towards Vienna. And it was a veritable craving for Vienna, too.'

The connexion of the composition of the book with the thought of Vienna was not a false memory. Firbank considered going to Vienna in order to write *The Flower Beneath the Foot* there, and three months before it was finished wrote to his mother:[3] 'How different my book would have been had I gone to Vienna, for of course one's surroundings tell. Probably it would have been more brilliant & flippant, but not so good as the steady work I hope to do here.'

'Here' was, temporarily, Florence. Firbank in fact wrote *The Flower*

---

[1] Cf. Chapter XIX, 20.

[2] a concept which, by the time he was making notes for *The New Rythum*, he had localised to the point of attributing mountains to it (cf. Chapter XV, 13).

[3] In a letter of 25 February 1922, quoted in the *Biography*, p. 214.

Beneath the Foot in surroundings whose mongrelism perhaps 'tells' in the result. He began it (in July 1921)[1] in Versailles, pursued it (in autumn 1921 to spring 1922) at Montreux, where there were mice in the châlet,[2] and (having gone there by way of Florence) finished it in May 1922 in Fiesole.[3]

Firbank was telling the truth when he recorded that he had Vienna in mind. Yet, with the exception of his borrowing the Austrian imperial title *Archduchess* for the daughter of a monarch, there is paradoxically little in the book itself that hints, with any exclusiveness, at even an 'imaginary' Vienna.

The 'Promenade' at Kairoulla, where the *'screen artiste'* whips her powdered mare (who may be a Firbank self-portrait),[4] might be the Prater but might equally be the Row. Likewise, the clientele of the Café Cleopatra, 'officers, or artistes from the Halls', might be borrowed from the dramatis personae of a Viennese operetta (*Die Schöne Mama*,[5] perhaps) or they might inhabit any European capital. Even the music at the Café, the Rosenkavalier waltz,[6] might be played at any café in Europe. The proprietress's surname, Wetme, is Germanic in form but determined by strictly English (and nursery) associations (prompted, probably, by the Archduchess's philanthropic hobby); and the Germanic sound of the name is anyway cancelled by its always appearing preceded by *Madame*. Even the nearly impeccably Germanic surname Blumenghast is in the book for its floral associations, and it too is negatived: by both a *Mademoiselle* and the Slav first name Olga.

In fact, the specific items which made Firbank call the scene of *The Flower Beneath the Foot* 'some imaginary Vienna' are not to be found in *The Flower Beneath the Foot* at all. They are in its predecessor in Firbank's imagination, *The Artificial Princess*.

In 1924 Firbank wrote his preface to *The Flower Beneath the Foot* and insisted that, during the gestation of that book, nostalgia 'turned' his thoughts 'towards Vienna'. In 1925[7] he was drafting (but not finishing) his preface[8] to *The Artificial Princess*, which he was considering publishing. In that preface, using almost the same phrase, he applied the turning of his thoughts towards Vienna to its proper object. He dated the original composition of *The Artificial Princess* to the period of 'the Straus cult', a period

---

[1] The dates and itinerary are according to the account the *Biography* gives from Firbank's correspondence. That account is confirmed by the date- and place-lines at the end of the novel, which read: '*July, 1921, May, 1922. Versailles, Montreux, Florence.*'

[2] Cf. Chapter VIII, 3.

[3] It was on a trip he made to Florence while he was living at Fiesole that Firbank at last met Ada Leverson (cf. Chapter XII, 6).

[4] Cf. Chapter VIII, 1.   [5] Cf. Chapter XIX, 20.   [6] Cf. Chapter XIV, 4.

[7] according to the *Biography*.   [8] Cf. Chapter XIII, 6.

when, he said, 'the minds of young boys turned from their Greece towards the Palace Theatre, Vienna & Berlin.'

It is the imaginary kingdom in *The Artificial Princess* whose personal names and places names are linguistically Viennese. It is at that court that the courtiers bear such Germanic names as Fräulein Anna Schweidler[1] and Baroness Rudlieb. It is in that book that the Baroness's lover bears the name Max, and that 'You take the white omnibus in', Germanically, 'the Platz'.

Firbank put his punctuation-pun[2] of spelling *capital* with a capital into both novels – and came to believe that they indeed shared a capital.

Geographically considered, they don't: but Firbank was psychologically right, since both royal courts represent The Coopers.

So convinced was he of the continuity of setting between the two books that when, some three years after writing *The Flower Beneath the Foot*, he added a final passage of 500 words or so to *The Artificial Princess*[3] he added it in the spirit of the earlier part of *The Artificial Princess* but in the idiom of *The Flower Beneath the Foot*: not its geographical idiom (which would have been inappropriate, since Kairoulla is in fact so unViennese), but the idiom of expression and nomenclature.

The extra 500 words include, in the context of Firbank's lesbian obsession, the exchange:[4]

' "*Née* a Demitraki."

' "A demi what?" the Baroness abstrusely twittered [. . .]'

The two lines contain two echoes of *The Flower Beneath the Foot*: a blended echo of that book's expressions 'she inconsequently chirruped' and 'she abstrusely murmured';[5] and a direct echo of the blonde and amber Lazari Demitraki who frequents the Duchess of Varna's flower-shop.

The obstinate perceptiveness with which Firbank insisted that *The Flower Beneath the Foot* was set in an imaginary Vienna has the same source as his obstinate blindness to the book's quite unViennese character: his identification with the Archduchess Lizzie.

It is the Archduchess who provokes the only specifically Viennese references in the book. On her deathbed she starts, as the Queen's cruel thoughts put it, 'suddenly cackling about Vienna'. ' "I recollect the first time I heard the *Blue-Danube* played!" she broke out: "it was at Schonnbrunn – schönes Schonnbrunn – My cousin Ludwig of Bavaria came – [. . .]" '

---

[1] Cf. Chapter VIII, 6.   [2] Cf. Chapter X, 6 and sub-section 1 of this chapter.
[3] Cf. Chapter XIII, 3 and 4.   [4] Cf. Chapter XV, 13.
[5] The *she* who chirrups (in Chapter XII) is Mrs Montgomery, the *she* who is abstruse (in Chapter XIV) the Queen.

(It is a cousinship which puts the Archduchess's baroque building-mania on an hereditary basis – and perhaps derives the monumental nature of Firbank's literary works by heredity from his grandfather's métier.)

Firbank was afraid that the progress from slight catarrh to troublesome cough would lead to his, as to the Archduchess's, death. He could not blot out but he tried to obfuscate the connexion between *The Flower Beneath the Foot* and Vienna for fear that the Archduchess, dying, contemplating her last work of art and remembering Vienna, should prove to be a self-portrait of Firbank, writing what might be his last work of art and remembering that earlier work of art in which he had set his own childhood in, indeed, 'some imaginary Vienna'.

11. Boiseries and Recesses

HAVING borrowed its capital pun, *The Flower Beneath the Foot* borrowed also the concerto form[1] of *The Artificial Princess* – but stretched it further, and let light and air into it in patterns yet more rococo.

The Flower Beneath the Foot was written at the point of perfect equipoise between Firbank's weariness ('wearier, even, than me!') and the economy of means[2] which that forced on him.

The book is full of Firbank's weariness, which has seeped not only into the title of 'his Weariness, the Prince' but into the very images. The Countess of Tolga is remarked to have 'the air to-night of a tired business-woman'; and King William of Pisuerga has 'the air of a tired pastry-cook'.

Yet the novel is the opposite of fatigued or fatiguing. Firbank is too weary to weary his readers. He has no energy to waste on images of second-best potency. He cannot be tempted into dwelling on anything to dulling-point.

The result is the most intense concentration of intense images he ever assembled, and also, because he had no time to swoop more than once on each image and must therefore swoop with infallible accuracy, the most breathtaking of all his demonstrations of his reliance on his perfected technique.

In *The Flower Beneath the Foot* the brevity and exactitude of the strokes whereby Firbank minimally puts in each motif before he swoops on the next have become, as in the paintings of Watteau, a metaphor *in* the technique of the poignancy of the subject-matter, which is the brevity of life and love.

It is the most direct reciprocal mirroring Firbank achieved between technique and subject.

[1] Cf. Chapter XVII, 7.   [2] Cf. Chapter XVI, 9.

That no doubt is why it is in *The Flower Beneath the Foot* that Firbank gave fictional incarnations to so many items of his technique.

The items include (besides[1] his overhear method, his riddling method and his very grammatical mistakes) his habit of ambiguously half-bodying forth images by means of deliberate gaps in his fabric.

His preface relates that, after the conception of 'her Dreaminess' and 'his Weariness', 'then, quite naturally, &[2] cosily, figures & objects composed themselves about them. The Queen's Ladies – her hectic Maids, the Palace, the Furniture [. . .]'

The Furniture deserves his specific mention of it. It is an important member of the fiction.

Not only do story-telling[3] tapestries half-conceal 'the silver *boiseries*[4] of the walls', just as the incidents and decorations of Firbank's fabric half-conceal (and counterpoint) his filigree construction. There are also deliberate, and palpably Firbankian, gaps. 'Between the windows were canopied recesses, denuded of their statues by the Queen's desire, "in order that they might appear suggestive".'

12. Six, major caesura, Six, minor caesura, Three

THE Firbankian shifts of locale are accomplished in *The Flower Beneath the Foot*, as in *The Artificial Princess*, at the pauses between movements.

The second movement of *The Artificial Princess* takes the Baroness merely on a high afternoon's excursion away from the Palace and back. *The Flower Beneath the Foot* employs *Vainglory*'s occasion to make a longer and larger shift: the occasion of the break between 'the Season' (whose duration is decreed by the royal court) and the 'canopied' (or at least sun-shaded) recess in the country for high summer.

The off-stage shifts in *The Flower Beneath the Foot* stretch further still. The fabric of the book is penetrated by rumours of, and indeed the results of, journeys yet more distant.

Vainglory, having shifted to the country for the summer, leaves Mrs Shamefoot permanently there in stained glass. But *The Flower Beneath the Foot*, like *The Artificial Princess*, fully returns in its third movement to the setting of its first.

Indeed, it returns not just to the same setting but to a similar occasion.

---

[1] Cf. sub-sections 3 and 8 of this chapter. [2] Another *quite* is here crossed out.

[3] 'depicting the Loves of *Mejnoun and Leileh*'; perhaps the tapestries were an orientalised re-working of (cf. Chapter X, 12) the ten-year-old Firbank's novel *Lila*.

[4] mis-rendered '*boisèries*' in the first edition (p. 12).

The first movement begins with the arrival in Kairoulla of the King and Queen of Dateland. The last movement ends in the presence at Kairoulla, for their daughter's marriage to the Prince, of the King and Queen of England (King Geo and Queen Glory, Firbank's double portrait of George V and Queen Mary – a portrait like a tinted, slightly shabbied and sun-faded loyal photograph pinned up by one of the book's English exiles in a tropical place).

The last movement of *The Flower Beneath the Foot* is, like that of *The Artificial Princess* but more ironically, a rapid scherzo which climbs to its climax in a celebration: not, this time, for the birthday of a Princess but for the wedding of a Prince.

True to concerto form, the first is the major movement. It consists of six chapters, transacted in Kairoulla. At the end of the sixth chapter, the Archduchess's death gives the movement a monumental close and imposes on the book its major caesura.

The second movement is spent in the country. In bulk it is slightly shorter than the first (60 pages, in the first edition, to 99). But bulk can take no account of pace. The second movement is longer in time than in bulk, because it is bound to a slow dreaminess by the pastoral spell of high summer.

It is the chapter divisions, which are themselves structural divisions, that denote the proportions of the structure. The second movement matches the first. Each consists of six chapters.

The caesura after the second movement is minor. The book is making a lesser shift: moving back to a place where it has been before. It is the less deeply cleft pause between the slow and the last movement in a concerto, a pause small enough to be webbed-over, in some concertos, by transitional music.

The final movement of *The Flower Beneath the Foot* balances each of its predecessors: by halving the number of chapters but doubling the pace.

6 : 6 ; 3.

13. Six

THE shift of locale that is to dig a moat at the end of the first movement is adumbrated from the beginning.

It is on the opening page that the Countess of Tolga, making her way to the Royal apartments (where the Queen, not feeling quite herself, is being read to by Laura), is waylaid by the Countess Medusa Rappa[1] with a wager

[1] She is named, I imagine, as a rapper of knuckles and a petrifier with gorgon looks, a notion which tallies with her appearance on the 'Promenade' in Chapter III 'bolt upright,

that (as a result of the Queen's not feeling quite herself) 'another week would find the Court shivering beneath the vaulted domes of the Summer-Palace'.

Since he first used it in *Vainglory* as the fictional vehicle for his structural shift of locale, the change from the Season to the summer recess must have become personally poignant to Firbank.

The shift of locale in his designs is itself psychologically related to his personal nomadism. From the time he came out of his war-time retreat and resumed his international peace-time wanderings, his nomadism was no longer entirely free-range. A pattern was forced on it, to the negative extent that his health could no longer bear a winter in England.

(After his sojourn in North Africa, Firbank returned to England in May 1921. He spent the first part of the summer in London, but left England in July and didn't return until June 1922, when he stayed for another London summer. In 1922 he risked a further return in the autumn, arriving in October and leaving [for Italy] in November. He was in England again for the summer of 1923, and in 1923 again risked an autumn visit, but earlier in the year: he arrived in September and was away by October. In 1924 he came to England in March, because Lady Firbank died; but he was back in Rome by April. His next and last visit to England began at the end of April 1925 and lasted till August. In February 1926, he offered, from Egypt, to return to England before the spring if his sister wanted him to.[1] Evidently she didn't – or didn't insist; and it was another summer visit to England he was planning when he died in Rome in May 1926.)

The result was that for Firbank the London Season was always curtailed. He could only snatch a few weeks of its beginning in the autumn or catch its summer ending (though he sometimes then stayed on in 'the slow, deep streets of the capital' where George Calvally and Mira Thumbler had conducted the out-of-Season counter-fugue of their love affair[2]).

It is his own sense of being cut short in his enjoyment of a capital city in its Season that Firbank transfers to *The Flower Beneath the Foot*.

And perhaps his thoughts, which punned in the book on capital (city) and capital (letter), touched also on the third sense of the word; with the result that the curtailment, by illness, of his seasons in the capital seemed to

---

her head carried stiffly staring with a pathetic expression of dead *joie-de-vie* between her coachman's and footman's waists'. But in practice her most schoolmistressly act is to felicitate the English Ambassadress on the existence of (according to the 1923 first edition, p. 20) 'Shakespere', and to remark that her favourite Shakespearean work is 'Julia *Sees* Her' (a play with which the English Ambassadress, in the cultural tradition of the English upper class, proves imperfectly acquainted).

[1] His letter to her is quoted on p. 291 of the *Biography*.
[2] Cf. Chapter XIX, 6.

include also that cutting-off of his financial capital which Firbank always interpreted as the cutting-off of his life.

The first movement of *The Flower Beneath the Foot* consists of a 'brilliant season' in the capital of Pisuerga; and its brilliance is heightened by the threat from the beginning that it may be cut short.

It is the gossip-columnist's paragraph 'I hear on the best authority that before the Court goes to the Summer-Palace later on, there will be at least *one* more Drawing-room' that gives urgency to the pilgrimage of the nouveau-riche Madame Wetme. 'Madame Wetme's religion, her cruel God, was the *Chic*'. The cruel god urges her to achieve presentation at court at the one 'drawing-room' certainly remaining to the Season; and she sets about getting an invitation by playing on the high birth and low income of the Duchess of Varna.

For Laura the threat, though she does not know it, is more stringent: a threat to cut off her happiness with Yousef. It is with the Queen's whim that the power lies to cut short the Season; and it is the Queen's whim that eventually cuts short Laura's happiness.

Already on the opening page the Queen is being assimilated in image to an arbitrary Fate; she is being seen as a queen of death.

What does in fact cut the Season short is a royal death. 'And suddenly the Angel of Death passed by and the brilliant season waned.' The Queen and the Angel of Death are twinned presences at the Archduchess's deathbed, the Queen's unmoved cruelty endorsing, and assimilated to, Death's.

The threat of brevity that impends over the brilliant Season becomes a metaphor of the brilliant brevities with which Firbank touches in his material and touches it, thereby, with evanescence.

His first chapter and a half put in the royal families of Pisuerga and of Dateland.

The Queen of Pisuerga is just dismissing the idea of amending her 'condition' by an immediate removal to the Summer-Palace when the royal visitors arrive off-stage. ' "Dr. Cunliffe Babcock[1] flatly forbids it," the Royal woman declared, starting slightly at the sound of a gun: "That must be *the Dates*!" she said.'

In Chapter II Firbank brings 'the Dates' on-stage, to the accompaniment of King Goahead's War-March,[2] and places Queen Thleeanouhee in the perspective of a construction whose 'although' reverses the expected as surreally as the 'Even so' (that is, despite the measles) by which Athens is judged dull in *Inclinations*.[3] Of Queen Thleeanouhee 'It was told that, in

---

[1] Cf. sub-section 8 of this chapter. [2] Cf. sub-section 10 of this chapter.
[3] Cf. Chapter XIX, 11.

the past, her life had been a gallant one, although her adventures, it was believed, had been mostly with men.'

The visit of 'the Dates' lends substance to the 'wildest' of the Queen of Pisuerga's lethal 'whims'. This is the whim which proves ultimately lethal to Eddy Monteith. For the Queen's hope is that, in return for the financial benefits of the trade alliance with Dateland, the Pisuergan parliament will vote support to an expedition patronised by the Queen: 'a party to excavate (for objects of art) among the ruins of Chedorlahomor, a *faubourg* of Sodom.'

(The faubourg must be named *after* Chedorlahomor, who is a person, not a place. Firbank amalgamated the Authorised Version's protestant version of the name, Chedorlaomer, with the Douai translation's[1] Catholic rendering, Chodorlahomor, and arrived at a synthesis which *both* suggests Cheddar Gorge *and* includes the component 'homo'. He made his selection from the same source that yielded him Elsassar:[2] the beginning, in the 14th chapter of *Genesis*, of the story of Sodom and Gomorrah.)

Within the same compass Firbank begins to fill in the court. He outlines the Queen's 'hectic' maids of honour, who include, besides Laura, 'Olga Blumenghast, whose exotic attraction had aroused not a few heartburnings (and even feuds) among several of the grandes dames about the court'; and he sketches some of the grandes dames themselves, who include the Countess Yvorra (mentioned first in predictive association with a 'curé or two' and developed presently into the prurient leader of the pious faction at court) and the Countess of Tolga, who by Chapter III will be confiding to the Duchess of Varna that Olga Blumenghast is her only consolation, and of whom, by Chapter V, the Archduchess will remark: 'She looks at other women as though she would inhale them.'

Half way through the second chapter Firbank's mobile narrative looks out from the Palace over the rest of Kairoulla – through the paired eyes of Laura and Yousef, sweethearts in the dark Palace garden during the party for the Dateland visitors.

From the garden Laura points, with her fan, down to ' "the column of Justice and," she laughed a little, "of *Liberty*" '.

(Firbank's italics are of predictive irony.)

' "And there," he pointed inconsequently, "is *the Automobile Club*!" ' (the Prince's inconsequence of mind an image of his eventual inconstancy of heart).

---

[1] Perhaps it was having read the two Versions side by side that led Firbank to specify (cf. Chapter XV, 19) that the books in Bertie Waldorf's house in *The New Rythum* include '*The Holy Bible* (Authorized Version)'.

[2] Cf. Chapter X, 9.

He identifies for her the lights of the Café Cleopatra; and she points out to him the Convent of the Flaming-Hood, believing that she is shewing him only her past.

It is a past (as her reverie recapitulates when she gets ready for bed, in 'The Bachelors' Wing' in the Palace, at the end of the chapter) that consists of her attending boarding-school at the convent – a period during which she felt a brief impulse towards turning nun, 'more, perhaps, to be near one of the nuns whom she had *idolised* than from any more immediate vocation'.

Unaware that Yousef's infirmity of purpose will make the convent her future, Laura ends the chapter by falling asleep as she plans her wedding with Yousef and prays for 'all the sisters at the Flaming-Hood – above all Sister Ursula. . . .'

Chapter III plunges where Chapter II has pointed: directly into the Café Cleopatra and the ambitious (or Chic-religious) thoughts of Madame Wetme; and then on a tour of Kairoulla in the company of the Duchess of Varna, who visits her clandestine flower-shop and proceeds to the Palace (where Queen Thleeanouhee is making overtures to the English Ambassadress, and where the first gift by way of overture to a royal alliance with England has arrived, in the essentially English shape of a pet dog) before she makes her way, via the 'Promenade', to the rendezvous where Madame Wetme tries to buy her patronage.

The narrative's freedom to tour Kairoulla is enlarged by Chapter IV, which at first circulates without fixed location, reporting the envies and snobberies of the English in Kairoulla on the question of who has been invited to the forthcoming party at the British Embassy. When the circulating chapter finally sites itself, it is in the aptest (to fiction and technique alike) of locations: Mrs Bedley's English circulating library. There the clients (who include Mrs Montgomery with Prince Olaf[1] at hand) complain that the smallness of the stock causes the same book to circulate to each reader repeatedly. They demonstrate that the English lower middle class is no better versed in literature than the ambassadorial class; for although Mrs Bedley's clients want, in their boredom, to get hold of the books of Ronald Firbank, they discuss them with neither appreciation[2] nor knowledge.[3] They add to the anthology, which is one of the things *The Flower Beneath the Foot* incidentally constitutes, of exact observations and reports of the language the English actually speak. It is not until Chapter XII that Mrs Montgomery reproves her royal pupil (for damning democracy) with 'Cs, Cs'; but it is in the library that Mrs Montgomery asks Mrs Bedley if the book she has ordered

---

[1] Cf. sub-section 4 of this chapter.   [2] Cf. the epigraph to Part Four.
[3] Cf. Chapters XV, 4 and XVI, 2.

is in yet, and Mrs Bedley puts on her spectacles, searches the drawer where she reserves books for favourites, and replies: '*Mmnops.*' And another aspect of the clientele's Englishness abroad is emphasised (and Laura's fate again threatened) by the masterstroke of social comedy that brings into the library (with a request for *Valmouth* or *Inclinations*) a nun from the convent of the Flaming-Hood, after whose 'twinkling' (and unsatisfied) departure one of the clients comments: 'Once a Girton girl always a Girton girl.'

Chapter V enters the cause of Chapter IV's disputes, the British Embassy. The narrative's arrival at the Embassy coincides with that of Eddy Monteith. He has come to join the expedition to Chedorlahomor (which is setting off from Kairoulla because it is under Pisuergan royal patronage) – and to assuage the wound Firbank received from Evan Morgan.[1]

However, since Firbank has vengefully arranged for the Ambassadress to mistake him for one of the extra cloakroom staff[2] taken on for the Embassy party which has caused Chapter IV's dissension among the English, Eddy himself has wounds, which he assuages in that scented, saint-haunted bath[3] from which he demonstrates, in speaking to his valet, his Berlitz-School Italian.[4]

He is still in towels from his bath when he is accosted by Embassy staff and wives: his 'former school chum, Lionel Limpness – Lord Tiredstock's third (and perhaps most gifted) son', who tries to impose on Eddy that episode of flagellation which is a re-working of Firbank's early piece of flagellatory verse, *The Lay of the Last Nurserymaid*;[5] Victoria Gellybore-Frinton[6] ('V.G.F.' to Lionel Limpness), literary wife of the diplomatist 'the Hon. Harold Chilleywater';[7] and the Ambassadress, Lady Something, herself.

The nursery setting of Firbank's *Lay* has tinged the whole scene. The Ambassadress insists on administering medicine to Eddy Monteith, and does it in nursery manner: 'Toss it off like a brave man, Mr Monteith (nip his nostrils, Mr Limpness).' Eddy takes refuge in a volume of his own poems whose contents prove coloured by the same source. Besides his no doubt flagellatory *Ode to Swinburne*,[8] there is 'a sweet thing suggested by an old Nursery Rhyme' and a poem that strikingly begins:

> I heard the clock strike seven,
> Seven strokes I heard it strike.

[1] Cf. Chapters VIII, 5 and XIX, 19.
[2] Cf. Chapter VIII, 5.
[3] Cf. Chapter XV, 17.
[4] Cf. Chapter X, 12.
[5] Cf. Chapter XV, 19.
[6] Cf. Chapters VI, 6 and XV, 2.
[7] Cf. Chapter VI, 6.
[8] Cf. Chapters XV, 13 and XVIII, 3.

Perhaps it was an unconscious apprehension of the nursery setting of the episode that caused the *Complete* Firbank to render[1] Eddy Monteith's volume of verse as 'a volume of *Juvenilia* published for him by "Blackwood of Oxford" '. The first edition prints '*Juvenalia*' and is surely right, though Firbank was no doubt punning on *juvenile* and Juvenal.

Eddy is too exhausted or too sulky to attend the party at the Embassy, to which the chapter descends without him, there to report the occasion largely through the pen (until its nib catches fire) of the gossip-columnist who put the fear of the god Chic into Madame Wetme. To the Embassy portraits of the King and Queen of England, there has been added a new portrait, of their daughter Princess Elsie; and Laura de Nazianzi, though she attaches 'not the faintest importance to the rumours afloat', feels 'a little heartshaken. . . .'.

It is the next chapter that introduces the Angel of Death.

Chapter VI is framed between his two appearances,[2] in the first sentence and in the penultimate, when 'the Angel of Death (who had sat unmoved throughout the day) arose'.

The chapter is designed as a monumental tomb. Between the baroque angelic presences at the ends there stretches the marble chill of the Queen's cruelty. She too has sat unmoved throughout the day, writing in advance the telegrams to be sent out when the Archduchess shall have died, and exclaiming, when the Archduchess begins 'cackling about Vienna',[3] '*Ssssh*, Lizzie – I can never write when people talk!'

14. 'Ssssh'

THE Queen's '*Ssssh*' is the most extreme version of an incident Firbank had used before as an image of heartlessness.

Mrs Sixsmith, parasite on Miss Sinquier in *Caprice*, is composing a note (to make arrangements that will ultimately lead to the spending of Miss Sinquier's money) when Miss Sinquier chances on her parents' 'Come back' advertisement in the newspaper.[4] ' "I can't epistolise while you make those *unearthly* noises", Mrs Sixsmith complained.'

And Enid, in *The Princess Zoubaroff*, unperturbedly writing letters while

---

[1] p. 539.
[2] which may have been distantly suggested by the source that provided Chedorlahomor, namely the story of Sodom and Gomorrah: 'And there came two angels to Sodom at even' (*Genesis*, XIX, 1).
[3] Cf. sub-section 10 of this chapter.
[4] Cf. Chapter XIX, 12.

her husband, Eric, prepares to leave for a trip of indefinite length, remarks:[1] 'I can't write letters while Eric is fidgeting about.'

I think it is an image that reflects Firbank's sense of his own cruelty to himself, an epitome of the profit-and-loss account[2] which is the theme of *The Flower Beneath the Foot*: the conventions have condemned him to live solitary, but solitude is what he needs if he is to write.

15. Six; Three

FOR the second movement (which he opens at Chapter VII) of *The Flower Beneath the Foot*, Firbank shifts both his centres of Kairoullan life to the country and sets them down at a lake-side he perhaps borrowed from his stay in Switzerland while he was writing the book.[3]

The court, in crêpe for the Archduchess, is in the Summer-Palace (with the dog that was the royal gift from England), where King and courtiers face the insulting residence, on an island in the middle of the lake and in exile from the capital, of the fallen statesman, Count Cabinet,[4] with the 'mignon youth'[5] who is a fallen choirboy from the Blue Jesus.[6]

Meanwhile the British Embassy has rented for the summer the Villa Clement – a name which (like Clemenza in . . . *Cardinal Pirelli*) is a Firbankian prayer for mercy in the midst of cruelty and perhaps also for the clement weather without which he could not visit England.[7] And indeed the twofold removal does permit Firbank to insert a clement chapter of English social comedy (the Ambassadress's involvement in her slander suit, the literary opinions of Victoria Gellybore-Frinton) between the severities and the intensities of life at court.

The first three chapters of the slow movement are transacted at court at the Summer-Palace. Slowed to a pastoral sadness, they sing a subdued threnody for the Archduchess and interleave the dying melody of Laura's diminishing chances of love and freedom with the asperities of the religious dedication that is to imprison her.

Such attempts as Laura and Yousef make towards a lovers' meeting are easily headed-off, in those pastoral longueurs where everyone takes walks,

[1] on p. 707 in the *Complete* Firbank, where Mrs Sixsmith epistolises on p. 352.
[2] Cf. sub-section 6 of this chapter.
[3] Cf. sub-section 10 of this chapter.
[4] Cf. Chapter X, 9.
[5] Cf. Chapter VIII, 2.
[6] Cf. Chapter XV, 2.
[7] (Cf. sub-section 13.) Perhaps the name was also another gesture of respect (cf. Chapter IX, 6 and p. 330 in the *Complete* Firbank) towards *La Clemenza di Tito*.

by the unrelenting royal parents. Yousef still seems to resist their pressure towards the English marriage. He is still (betraying his kinship to Cherif[1] in more than the similarity of their names) repelled by the bloodlust which, when they met in childhood, he saw the English princess display in the hunting-field. But ' "We had always thought you too lacking in initiative," King William said (tucking a few long hairs back into his nose) "to marry against our wishes." '

Countess Yvorra asserts her leadership of the pious faction at court by proposing an expedition to the island to reclaim Count Cabinet. In the manner of Mrs Hurstpierpoint[2] (but with an emotional edge sharpened by the profit-and-loss theme of the book, with an expertise borrowed from Firbank's foreign travelling, and with Firbank's own religious convertibility, liberated by North Africa, nearly assimilated to the convertibility of currency), Countess Yvorra cynically calculates that the salvation of a soul so deeply lost 'should be worth hereafter (at the present rate of exchange, but the values vary) . . . a Plenary perpetual-indulgence'. But the Count runs away from her evangelical attempt and leaves her to be repulsed by his 'mignon youth': 'an adolescent, with Bougainvillea at his ear', the evangelist reports afterwards, 'came and looked out with an insolent grin, and I recognised Peter Passer from the Blue Jesus grown quite fat.'

From court gossip Laura learns not only that Yousef is likely to betray her finally by marrying Princess Elsie but that he has betrayed her in the past by numerous small and surreptitious sexual initiatives. One of his mistresses, the florally and punningly named dancer April Flowers, is black; and Laura laments in the manner of Thetis Tooke[3] the preferring of a black to herself.

Thinking yearningly of her schooldays in the convent and driven by hurt to prefer the pure kisses of Sister Ursula to the now lost kisses of Yousef, which were flavoured with 'tobacco and *charcuterie*' (perhaps Laura is a crypto-vegetarian[4] too), Laura takes refuge in the 'Ecclesiastical set at Court', whose 'flavour' is of cocoa and mild flagellation[5] – a training run, it is to prove, for the major disciplines of the convent (where, on Laura's eventual arrival, Sister Ursula confides to her: 'I was scourged, by Sister Agnes, but yesterday, with a heavy bunch of keys, head downwards, hanging from a bar').

And from the president of the 'Ecclesiastical set', Countess Yvorra, Laura hears presages of her eventual caging, as the Countess discusses with her

---

[1] Cf. Chapter XIX, 20.   [2] Cf. Chapter XVI, 7.
[3] Cf. Chapter XIX, 15.   [4] Cf. Chapters VIII, 4 and XIX, 19 and 20.
[5] Cf. Chapter XV, 19.

confessor (Father Nostradamus) the problem of choosing a 'cage-companion' for her canary. 'Why not let it go?' Laura asks, and is told severely 'A hawk might peck it.'

Laura is pet-named 'Rara' as a rara avis indeed.[1] She is the rare bird whom the Queen cannot leave free but must see safely nunned in order to put temptation out of Yousef's reach. Freedom is for common birds like Count Cabinet's minion Peter Passer; Peter in Latin Sparrow.

At the culmination of the first three chapters of the second movement, Prince Yousef leaves for England.

Firbank then interposes Chapter X, his respite in the form of social comedy at the British Embassy's summer villa.

When he returns the book to the Summer-Palace he has heightened its mood from resignation to intensity.

The last two chapters of the second movement (Chapters XI and XII) are two brilliant, coloratura, perfectly (and baroquely) built arias (or each a whole scena and aria) which, flung off in passionate succession to one another, give the movement its solid and dramatic close.

There is no verbal comment on Laura's pain. The comment, which is the ironic one that other people's loves *are* fulfilled, is made structurally: by the fact that these other loves are the structural climax of Laura's slow progress to disillusion.

In Chapter XI[2] the Countess of Tolga undertakes a kindlier expedition than Countess Yvorra's to the island. Knowing that Count Cabinet likes to be reminded in his exile of the capital, she puts on a quite unsuitably sophisticated and winter dress and proposes to take him, by sailing boat, a basket of pears ('those big burley-worleys'). Dispensing with boatmen (on the grounds that today they 'seem all so ugly'), she takes with her, 'on an impulse she was never able afterwards to explain', Olga Blumenghast.[3]

The Countess might have understood her own impulse had she been versed in Firbank's cryptic language of the Sapphic-Hellenic. Her over-sophisticated dress is 'stencilled' with 'a crisp Greek-key design'.

For it is on this boating-trip that the pastoral spell turns into the slow-motion enchantment of a dream.

(Firbank is perhaps invoking dream-sensation when, at the end of the chapter, he brings night down on the lake with tropical swiftness and cites

---

[1] Cf. sub-section 5 of this chapter.
[2] 'chapter, (I *think*,) *eleven*', Firbank says in his preface when he mentions the contents of this chapter – betraying that during the writing of the book he had been highly conscious of his structural chapter divisions (cf. sub-section 12) and that he did in fact recall them correctly afterwards.
[3] whose 'exotic attraction' and its consequence were quoted in sub-section 13.

'the scientists' theories on Time and Relativity' as possible answers to 'such riddles' as why Northern climates have twilight but in Pisuerga 'Night pursued Day, as though she meant it'.)

The slowness of the slow movement slows into an actual becalming. The expedition never reaches the island. Instead, Count Cabinet witnesses through his telescope that bizarre water-borne, stillness-gripped mating that seems[1] to set against the caging of the rara avis the exotic sexual rites of water birds.

' "Tell me, Olga: Is my hat all side-ways?"
' "............" '

With that exoticism Firbank contrasts the cosiness of domesticity.

By Chapter XII the court is already packing-up to leave the Summer-Palace and return to the capital.

The scena of Chapter XII begins with Prince Olaf's bringing his governess news from her own country: 'My brother's betrothed! So need I go on with my preparation?'

He need. Mrs Montgomery proceeds to administer her classic lesson in English grammar, 'I am a Political Hostess.'[2]

After the lesson Mrs Montgomery collects her post, which consists of a direct reminder of life in the capital: 'a picture postcard of a field mouse in a bonnet, from her old friend Mrs Bedley'. (The message reads: 'We have *Valmouth* at last [. . .] and was it you, my dear, who asked for *The Beard Throughout the Ages*?')

The scena breaks into aria (or, strictly, duet) when the court physician, Dr Cunliffe Babcock, taps ('Do I intrude?') at Mrs Montgomery's door. Not satisfied by Firbank's having united a cunt and a cock in his very name (and underlined the meaning by making Mrs Montgomery pet-name him 'Cunnie'),[3] the doctor has arrived, bearing champagne ('Bollinger, you naughty man'), in quest of union with Mrs Montgomery. Theirs is a tour-de-force duet of Englishness in exile, as their thoughts in union go out 'to the sea-girt land of their birth – Barkers', Selfridges', Brighton-pier, the Zoological gardens on a Sunday afternoon'[4] and Mrs Montgomery murmurs 'It's almost too warm for a fire [. . .] but I like to hear the crackle!'[5]

---

[1] Cf. Chapter XV, 14.
[2] Cf. sub-section 8 of this chapter.
[3] Perhaps it was formations like this and the pun, in the Duchess of Varna's flower-shop, on Alexandrian balls and guelder roses (cf. Chapters XIV, 10 and XV, 1) that caused Firbank, while he was writing the book, to tell (or warn?) his mother that *The Flower Beneath the Foot* was (in, probably, Lady Firbank's idiom rather than his own) 'vulgar'. (His letter, of 20 March 1922, is quoted on p. 209 in the *Biography*.)
[4] Cf. Chapter XVI, 6.   [5] Cf. Chapter XV, 2.

The champagne makes him unsteady and her chirruping.[1] Yet even when he grabs her she remembers her *h*'s: 'H-Help!'

The chapter, and with it the second movement, ends on the brilliant discord of a violent irony: 'Thus did they celebrate the "Royal Engagement."'

It is in the clashing overhang of that climax that the last movement begins, almost surreptitiously, to pursue its scurrying pace.

Returned to Kairoulla, the book immediately enters the Duchess of Varna's flower-shop, which the approach of the royal wedding has rendered over-busy and over-populated (chiefly with North Africans,[2] but Peter Passer is present, come to town for the celebrations and 'to advance his fortunes, in ways best known to himself').

It is in the shadow, it is almost as an echo, of the exiled yearnings of Mrs Montgomery and her lover that, when the flower-shop is shut up for the night, the flowers *speak*[3] their pain: the yearnings of those that are exiled from their roots; the constriction of those that are wired too severely, as Laura is by the conventions and aspirations of the court.

And since they quarrel over social precedence ('you . . . *buttercup*! How dare you to *an Orchid*!'[4]), this opening chapter of the last movement is a counterpart to the dissensions, on the same subject, of the exiled English in the first movement.

The flowers' colloquy is interrupted by the clandestine return of the Duchess of Varna to rob her own till, so that, equipped with 'quite a welcome sheaf of the elegant little banknotes of Pisuerga', she may make her final escape from the persecutions of her creditors and of Madame Wetme (whom the Duchess has failed to get invited to court). The Duchess scribbles a press handout ('*The Duchess of Varna has left for Dateland*') for Kairoulla's gossipy newspaper, and the colloquy of the flowers closes over her departure.

It is more summarily yet that the next swift chapter, which returns to court, marks the yet more permanent departure of Eddy Monteith. The Queen permits one of her Ladies to read her the news of the expedition she has patronised to Chedorlahomor but insists on the lectrice's 'Omitting (skipping, I say) the death of the son of Lord Intriguer'; with the result that it is a footnote which records his death from 'the shock received by meeting a jackal while composing a sonnet'.

The reading is interrupted by the arrival of a nun to fetch Laura. The Queen, who has forgotten the appointment, scrabbles about for an im-

---

[1] 'she inconsequently chirruped' (cf. sub-section 10).
[2] Cf. sub-section 10 of this chapter.   [3] Cf. Chapter XV, 2.
[4] This, no doubt, is why Firbank's preface speaks of the book as 'my Flower, which really is as much a country-buttercup as a cattleya orchid'.

In the event, Firbank never fulfilled the rhythm of having *Prancing Nigger* 'published' by the 'publisher' of his earliest volume. *Prancing Nigger* was published, in the ordinary meaning of the word, by Brentano's. But Firbank's 'rhythmic' remark is perhaps a token that producing *Prancing Nigger* had made him notice a certain internal rhythm in his creativeness.

Firbank's first great baroque construction, *Vainglory*, was followed by two books conceived not merely on a smaller scale but in fewer dimensions of complexity. It is not that *Inclinations* and *Caprice* are inferior designs to *Vainglory*. They are designs in a mode where the design *cannot* constitute so much of the fiction.

Vainglory, a work equally of synthesis and of analysis (hence the beauty of its design), must have cost Firbank a vast effort of sheer *thought*. Perhaps what he experienced after it was a recuperative need to create works more palpably and concentratedly of synthesis. *Inclinations* and *Caprice* are very purely and visibly *inventions*, products of the magical faculty which conjures something into thereness in the book, where nothing (where, indeed, no book) existed before.

Perhaps it was only after thus reassuring himself of his powers of pure, magical synthesis that Firbank could bend his imagination to constructing *Valmouth*, which is another of the complex books that are created by the same designing stroke which simultaneously analyses them.

Vainglory was a work of Firbank the monumental mason. It was followed by two works by Firbank the painter, works that proceed linearly rather than by enclosing spaces, works whose designs are patterns, to be read flat. *Inclinations* is perceptibly a diptych, the meeting of two panels of complementary pattern. *Caprice* leads the solo line of Miss Sinquier's adventures through a predatory background.

Recuperated, Firbank constructed the complex edifice of *Valmouth* and followed it with two books which, being themselves transitions to the next section of his œuvre, do not repeat with exactitude the relation of *Inclinations* and *Caprice* to *Vainglory* but perhaps served the same recruiting purpose.

The Princess Zoubaroff, it is true, is scarcely a recession from complexity. Rather, it is outside the terms of the rhythm that governs the novels. It is a complexity in another mode. But the deliberate[1] simplicity of *Santal*, which again follows a solo line, Cherif's experience, and takes it through a background much flatter and emptier than that of *Caprice*, is simple enough to count double.

And it was, evidently, simple enough to recruit Firbank's forces for the most complex of all his works, *The Flower Beneath the Foot*, whose donnée

[1] 'I shall try [. . .] & keep the whole thing as simple as possible' (cf. Chapter XIX, 20).

he conceived as a twin simultaneously with *Santal* but which he did not permit himself to write until he had gathered himself by finishing *Santal*.[1]

After the monument of *The Flower Beneath the Foot* Firbank again, as after the monument of *Vainglory*, produced two paintings.

In a comparison with *Inclinations* and *Caprice*, Firbank's increasingly strangled sense of being short of time has made the second pair of masterpieces more intense in their tragedy and more tour-de-force in their technique. The colouring is fiercer in *Prancing Nigger*; the impasto and the impressionism are more passionate in . . . *Cardinal Pirelli*. For it is possible to be quite precise about what sort of paintings they resemble. *Prancing Nigger* is, by Firbank's own description,[2] 'rather like a Gauguin'; . . . *Cardinal Pirelli* is a portrait by Velasquez.[3]

By what looks like an incipient habit of twin conceptions (and, if it was, it was probably because of the recuperative relation between his painting-type books and his monuments), Firbank conceived the donnée of *The New Rythum* while he was still gestating the donnée of . . . *Cardinal Pirelli*. Just as, according to his preface, he 'longed to begin the Flower' while he was still writing its twin, *Santal*, so, two years later, he declared[4] that he 'pined' to begin his 'American novel', *The New Rythum*, but was going to set himself to the long task of writing his Cardinal book first.

Perhaps, therefore, *The New Rythum*, had he finished it, would have been a baroque architectural complex, to gather himself for which Firbank needed to complete his Cardinal picture. Or perhaps one of his private and possibly unconscious reasons for calling it *The New Rythum* was a hope of breaking the 'rhythmic' cycle he had perhaps glimpsed after writing *Prancing Nigger* in accordance with it.

In one respect, what exists of *The New Rythum* resembles the flat patterning of *Prancing Nigger*. Firbank is using North-American idiom, including 'racy [. . .] expressions of the soil',[5] to give the book a linguistic climate exactly as he uses his Anglo-French Negro patois in *Prancing Nigger*.

That need not, however, argue that *The New Rythum* was to be more flat than monumental. After all, the patois which supplies the backdrop to *Prancing Nigger* was first introduced to lend an exotic irradiation to the enclosures of three-dimensional space in *Valmouth*.

---

[1] Cf. Chapter XIX, 20.

[2] which is quoted in the *Memoir*, p. 81.

[3] (Cf. Chapter VI, 6.) Cardinal Pirelli's desperate last bribes offered to his favourite choirboy include 'How would you like my Velasquez, boy? . . .'

[4] a declaration quoted by the *Biography* (p. 246) from a letter from Firbank to Carl Van Vechten, from Lisbon, 8 September 1923.

[5] Cf. Chapter XIX, 20.

And *The New Rythum* already possesses the ingredients of a monumental Firbankian design, in that it counterpoints several groups of personages and pursues more than one line of experience. In the section which is already written, Firbank would probably have made a few small-sized but effective alterations that would have sprung the pages into higher relief. In the notes for the rest, there is a sign that the structure was conceived in three dimensions. Firbank's[1] 'N.B. preceding chapter should be poetic lyric fantastic anything. Then cold snap as –' reads to me as though Firbank was imagining in the terms of a type of composition scarcely practised in *Prancing Nigger* and . . . *Cardinal Pirelli*, whereby the 'preceding chapter' was to be an architectural perspective funnelling the reader's view of the next, in the way that Chapters XI and XII of *The Flower Beneath the Foot* are,[2] without mentioning Laura, ironic perspectives on Laura's pain.

18. Requisite Chastity

THE summer of 1922, after he had finished *The Flower Beneath the Foot* in Fiesole in May, was one of Firbank's summers in London.[3] There he had himself drawn by Wyndham Lewis;[4] was drawn by Augustus John on John's spontaneous initiative; arranged for *The Flower Beneath the Foot* to be 'published' by Grant Richards in an edition containing drawings of Firbank by both draughtsmen (as well as the illustration in the language of flowers by C. R. W. Nevinson[5]); and conceived the book that became *Prancing Nigger*.

In pursuit of his book, Firbank decided to go to Jamaica. To Carl Van Vechten he proposed by post that he should go on from Jamaica to New York. To his mother he proposed that she should try to book him a passage to Jamaica at the special (and smaller) 'college fare'[6] – a comic attempt to cut financial corners which Firbank probably thought necessitated, and which perhaps truly was necessitated, by his having just contracted[7] to pay the cost plus $33\frac{1}{3}$ per cent of producing a thousand copies of *The Flower Beneath the Foot*.

Carl Van Vechten replied that March or November would be a more suitable time than August for a Firbank visit to New York.

---

[1] Cf. Chapter XV, 13.
[2] Cf. sub-section 15 of this chapter.
[3] Cf. sub-section 13 of this chapter.
[4] Cf. Chapter VIII, 1 and 3.
[5] Cf. sub-section 5 of this chapter.
[6] a reduced fare (according to p. 224 of the *Biography*, which is presumably following Firbank's correspondence with his mother) available at off-peak travelling seasons to undergraduates.
[7] according to the *Bibliography*, p. 38.

Firbank's biographer seems to hint that Van Vechten dreaded some homosexual conspicuousness or scandal from Firbank, but he can scarcely have expected Firbank to be less homosexual in March or November.

If the evidence for Van Vechten's fear is the interview the *Biography* cites[1] with Van Vechten in 1953, perhaps the supposed fear was merely Van Vechten's after-gloze on Firbank's reply to the put-off from Van Vechten, the reply being that Firbank doubted if he had the 'chastity requisite for America . . . especially in March'.

It is a reply which can look like an answer to a query raised by Van Vechten (or thought by Firbank to have been raised by Van Vechten) about whether Firbank was chaste enough for Van Vechten to parade in New York. It might, however, be camouflage for a quite different consideration.

Perhaps Van Vechten preferred November or March to August on the simple grounds that New York emptied for the summer and that in the spring or autumn Firbank would be able to meet more people. (If Van Vechten truly was afraid of scandal, it was nonsensical for him to propose November or March, because those were the periods when Firbank would also be able to scandalise more people.) Van Vechten was, in fact, simply proposing that Firbank should visit New York at one of the high points of the season.

Van Vechten surely had no awareness that he was touching Firbank's sense of being excluded, by his illness, from exactly those heights of the London Season – a personal exclusion which Firbank's imagination had just transformed into the urgency and evanescence that attend the image of the Season in *The Flower Beneath the Foot*.[2] Firbank, who could barely risk spending March and November in London, could certainly not have endured them in the climate of New York. That he doubted whether he had the requisite chastity 'especially in March' was a brave version of the statement that he knew he lacked the requisite health, especially for March in New York.

Firbank had no more success in his other proposal. He sailed at the full fare: for Cuba, where he landed on[3] 26 August 1922 and where he stayed in Havana and in Santiago, and whence he went on to Jamaica but not to New York (or, his biographer considers, to Haiti[4]).

From Jamaica he told his mother[5] that Cuba 'gave me all I needed for another novel'. In October he was back in London, making the changes in

---

[1] p. 225.   [2] Cf. sub-section 13 of this chapter.
[3] the dates of Firbank's visits to Cuba and Jamaica are recorded, from his correspondence, in the *Biography*, pp. 224-5.   [4] Cf. Chapter VIII, 9.
[5] in a letter of 19 September 1922 from Kingston, Jamaica, quoted in the *Biography*, p. 225.

The Flower Beneath the Foot which Grant Richards insisted on for the avoidance of libel.[1] By November he had fled the English winter and was writing his 'another novel' at Bordighera.

19. Purposely Unshaded

FROM the moment of its conception it was a novel designed to be seen flat, inasmuch as the background was to be a decorative element in the same plane, and with the same importance, as the figures.

Before he left for Cuba, Firbank described[2] his donnée in terms that bring the brilliance of the 'background' into the foreground: 'a negro novel with a brilliant background of sunlight, sea and as tropical' as he could contrive.

Carl Van Vechten's cleverness in making *Prancing Nigger* the book's United-States title (a title so irrefutably apt that, after the first English edition under Firbank's own title,[3] it was adopted in England as well) was to have picked on a phrase from Mrs Mouth's conversation that epitomises the book by tacitly suggesting that the prancing figure is seen in silhouette, its blackness a matter of the presentation as well as of pigment, its area a flat dark decorative motif fitted into the brilliant tropical patterns.

After he finished the book (in June 1923, when he was still in Bordighera[4]), Firbank's description[5] of it still mentioned the background first and counted that to the book's chief credit: 'as a bit of colour & atmosphere it is the best of all my others'. He still rated the figures only *as* important as the background, not more: 'some of the figures negroes & Spanish South Americans are as wonderful as their setting!' And his last emphasis, like his first, was placed on the fierce and bizarre colour ('its vivid unusualness') with an addition that makes explicit the book's existence in a single plane without recessions into perspective: '& the crude touches left purposely unshaded'.

The book is indeed, as Firbank described it when he offered it in vain to Heinemann, 'purposely a little "primitive", rather like a Gauguin in painting – extremely gay'.[6]

[1] Cf. Chapter VII, 3.
[2] in a letter to his mother from London in July 1922, quoted on p. 224 of the *Biography*.
[3] Cf. Chapter VII, 4.
[4] though not still at the same address; according to the *Biography* (pp. 226–7 and 233–4), Firbank first stayed at the Hotel Bristol, moved at the end of November 1922 into the Villa Sans Souci and moved thence, in January 1923, to the Villa Olivetti.
[5] in a letter from Bordighera to his mother, written on the day he finished the book, 17 June 1923 (and quoted in the *Biography*, p. 234).
[6] This, which is quoted on p. 46 of the *Bibliography*, is presumably a fuller version of the quotation on p. 81 of the *Memoir* which I mentioned in sub-section 17.

It is a flat strip of significant patterning, from which the inscrutable faces of islanders peer, in mid-close-up, from the same decorative plane as the faces of exotic flowers.

20. Focus

NONE of the faces in *Prancing Nigger* is in the full and scrutinising close-up that Firbank obtained by perspective methods in *The Flower Beneath the Foot* and by portrait-painting methods in . . . *Cardinal Pirelli*.

Prancing Nigger holds its principal figures at middle distance, where the pattern requires them to be.

This it achieves in the first place because, uniquely among Firbank's novels, it focuses its attention on the large unit of a whole family.

The strip shape of the total book is served from the beginning by the distributed focus, which strings out the Mouth[1] family to the reader's eye. Parents, son and two daughters are presented in a row, like a family in a painting by ('purposely a little "primitive" ') a child.

When Firbank told[2] Aldous Huxley that he was going to the West Indies in order to collect material for a novel about Mayfair, he played down the paradox of what he was about. In reality, it was the influence of Jane Austen, discernible in *Vainglory*,[3] which was expanded in *Prancing Nigger*. Firbank's high, fauve paradox is to have placed Jane Austen's social unit, the family, against a tropical setting, and to attribute to the 'primitive' Mrs Mouth the great problem of mothers in Jane Austen's formal society, namely to balance the marriageability of daughters against their perilous seductibility.

Mrs Mouth's problem is the reason why Firbank's Gauguinesque tapestry includes not only exotic flowers but the insects they attract. Mr Mouth remarks 'how many skeeter-bugs dair are 'bout dis ebenin' in the vicinity of the Mouth home. ('De begonias in de window-boxes most lik'ly draw dem,' Mrs Mouth explains.) Miami Mouth has to take off her apron of ivy leaves (her sole garment) ''cos it seemed to draw de bees'. They are all, these menacing swarms, Firbankian rapist or rapine-ist insects;[4] they are attracted to the flower-like Mouth girls and play on the girls' seductibility or, more fatalistically, on their propensity to have their hearts broken by circumstances.

It is partly because she undertakes her Jane-Austenish social responsibility as a mother that Mrs Mouth wants to move her family from provincial Mediavilla (where her daughters are growing up capable of commenting

---

[1] Cf. Chapter IX, 11. [2] Cf. Chapter VIII, 9.
[3] Cf. Chapter XIX, 3. [4] Cf. Chapters XV, 3 and XVI, 3.

'No! really. De ideah!' when the idea in question is that of wearing clothes) to the capital, Cuna-Cuna. Mrs Mouth has set her own heart on 'a Villa with a watercloset' but she is also concerned about 'de finishing ob *mes filles*'.

Thanks to her ambition, the Firbankian shift of locale is adumbrated, as it is in *The Flower Beneath the Foot*,[1] from the outset.

Mr Mouth, however, holds out for almost four chapters, in a piety that counts villas with waterclosets among 'vanities an' innovations'.

In both his piety and his obduracy, Mr Mouth affords Firbank beautifully Firbankian occasions.

It is thanks chiefly to his piety that the currents of verse which aerate the warm pages include chill northern winds of revivalist hymnology,[2] which bite into the context with a surrealism complementary to the inherent surrealism of such an 'esoteric song of remote tribal times' as

> I am King Elephant-bag,
> Ob de rose-pink Mountains!

And it is against his obduracy that Mrs Mouth has occasion to fling the arabesques of her vocabulary. Mr Mouth is, again perhaps on a Jane Austen model, a paterfamilias more addressed than addressing. Mrs Mouth cajoles and batters him with her virtuoso variations on *nigger* ('say, higger, lub'; 'Prancing Nigger, lemme say sumptin' more!'), and she wields that not inherently contemptuous[3] word (though she can *make* it contemptuous) almost as if it were the German *Mann*: 'it seem no more dan yestidday dat I put on me maiden wreath ob arange blastams to walk wid me nigger to church.'

Mr Mouth is won to the shift of locale: for 'de sake ob de chillen's schoolin' '.

In Chapter V the move is made, parents and daughters travelling by caravan, Charlie Mouth making his own slower, young-bachelor way, pursuing butterflies as he goes. He arrives in Cuna-Cuna later than his family (indeed, in Chapter VIII), and on his route he passes through those

---

[1] Cf. sub-section 13 of this chapter.

[2] Perhaps Firbank was influenced by a dinner in 1921 at the Eiffel Tower in London, where (according to the *Biography*, p. 202) Iris Tree recited hymns, including Salvation Army hymns. The Salvation Army appears, with tambourines, in Chapter VIII of *Prancing Nigger* as 'the Army of the Soul'. However, Firbank had already, in *Vainglory*, permitted Winsome Brookes to cite the Salvation Army in disparagement of Strauss (cf. Chapter XIV, 4); and in Chapter VIII of *Inclinations* Mabel Collins receives a letter from her mother that strikes a thrillingly nordic chill into Greece through a paragraph that marvellously begins 'Listening lately to the Y.M.C.A. singing "There is a Green Hill" '.

[3] Cf. Chapter VIII, 9.

presumably internal and inland Customs where he makes his Wildean-Firbankian[1] declaration of '... Butterflies!'

21. Binding

FIRBANK'S decorative panel is divided into three sections, but its divisions are not the deep clefts of his monumental works. Rather, the book resembles a chronicle picture which represents side by side events that take place at different times, which can be apprehended at a coup d'œil and in which because of the simultaneous presentation, people and events never, in a narrative sense, quite get anywhere.

The Mouths go to Cuna-Cuna and are, variously, amazed by and corrupted by its sophistications. (Firbank must have discovered with delight in the West Indies a ready-made Firbankian self-portrait. He takes Charlie Mouth agape into a bar in Cuna-Cuna, and makes him a 'little dazed after a Ron Bacardi'.) To the reader, however, the sophistications of Cuna-Cuna are infinitely less conspicuous than its exoticisms, and its exoticisms are the same as those of Mediavilla. For the reader, though the Mouths move, they never arrive in a different place.

This flat, chronicle-picture effect Firbank achieved by bringing the exoticisms of the background so conspicuously into the foreground that the three segments of his picture are bound into one by the continuous decorative pattern.

The various motifs of his pattern Firbank achieved by transplanting them and naturalising them in the exotic setting.

It is by an ultimate, metamorphic wriggle of his own religious convertibility that he creates the exotically 'tribal' background of belief. The black magic of *The Artificial Princess* and *Vainglory*[2] has become 'de Obi man', who sells 'luck-balls'. Mrs Hurstpierpoint's application to saintly relics during the thunderstorm[3] is translated into Charlie Mouth's 'clasping a fetish' during the earthquake. Firbank's own ghost-story phobias and fantasies[4] furnish the Mouths' conversation in the caravan to Cuna-Cuna:

'"... if a Wood-Spirit wid two heads an' six arms were to take hold ob you, Mimi, from behind?"

'"I do nothin' at all," Miami answered briefly.

'"Talk not so much of the jumbies, Chile, as de chickens go to roost!" Mrs Mouth admonished.'

Even Firbank's own obsession with Sappho can take exotic root in the

---

[1] Cf. Chapter VII, 3. [2] Cf. Chapters XVII, 7 and XIX, 8.
[3] Cf. Chapter XV, 16. [4] Cf. Chapter VII, 3.

sophisticated society of Cuna-Cuna, among those 'Spanish South Americans' whom he called[1] 'as wonderful as their setting'. Vittorio Ruiz improvises at his piano: ' "Ah Atthis, it was Sappho who told me –" tentatively he sought an air.'

But the aeration of his own text by the spindly letters of the Greek alphabet[2] Firbank reserves for the fate of Edna Mouth's cat. Perhaps the act of once more composing dialogue in Mrs Yaj's idiom reminded Firbank of Mrs Yaj's quotation[3] from Blake, 'And I am black but O! my soul is white.' *Prancing Nigger* is an extended ironic play on the antithesis of black to white. Edna's cat (named Snowball) is white. Arrived at Cuna-Cuna, she bears black kittens. It is a prediction of what will happen to her black owner among the white Spanish South Americans at their ironically named Villa Alba. Pursuing her mother's social ambitions to the villa of Madame Ruiz, 'arbitress absolute of Cunan society', Edna falls victim to her son, the playboy[4] and dilettante composer of an opera on Sapphic themes, Vittorio Ruiz. Ruiz = ruin. Firbank insists on the tragicness of what happens to Edna by using the word περιπέτεια of what has happened to Snowball: he has picked the Aristotelian word for (in Liddell and Scott's explanation) 'the sudden reverse of circumstances on which the plot of a Tragedy hinges'.

The decorative element that most firmly binds the book into unity is not, however, the Greek language but the idiom of Mrs Yaj,[5] which so pervades *Prancing Nigger* as to give the book a linguistic (and no less tropical) climate as well as its meteorological one.

Prancing Nigger persists in Mrs Yaj's *v* into *b* transformations, and Mrs Mouth keeps up Mrs Yaj's French. The Mouths' villa in Cuna-Cuna, she boasts to Charlie when he eventually reaches the capital and is reunited with his family, 'is dat mignon'.

(Or perhaps, given the ease with which Firbank slipped from *mignon* into *minion*,[6] the description truly applies to the subject of the Mouths' other great boast: 'An' since we go into S'ciety, we keep a boy in buttons!'[7])

The idiom of *Prancing Nigger* is enriched by the addition, to the two chief ingredients of Mrs Yaj's idiom, of a strain of pidgin or piccaninny English. *Bimeby* for *by-and-by* and *kimpoged* for *composed* set off a series of

---

[1] Cf. sub-section 19 of this chapter. [2] Cf. Chapter XII, 6 footnote.
[3] Cf. Chapter XIX, 3.
[4] He is also a half-sharer of a Firbankian characteristic (cf. Chapter VIII, 1): ' "Let me come, Mother dear," he murmured without interrupting, "over the other side of you; I always like to be on the right side of my profile!" '
[5] Cf. Chapter XIX, 13.
[6] Cf. Chapter VIII, 2.
[7] who may be connected with (cf. Chapter VII, 3) Firbank's 'boot-buttons' delusion.

gently explosive distortions in the surface of the book's fabric. Sometimes they gather the force almost of a malapropism. (Perhaps Firbank was incarnating his own propensity to malapropism[1] in *Prancing Nigger* as he did his own propensity to bad grammar in *The Flower Beneath the Foot*.[2]) There are presages of surrealist rents in the reality and identity of objects in a world where a water melon is a *watteh-million*. And in fact these tiny linguistic disturbances are metaphors of the book's grand cataclysm. The tremors that Firbank passes through the linguistic fabric run parallel to the earthquake.

22. Où?

AT Chapter V, with the shift of locale, Miami Mouth is already divided against herself, because she is leaving her sweetheart, Bamboo, behind in Mediavilla. By the same token Miami is already a little set apart from her sister who, being heartwhole, is in hope of adventure in Cuna-Cuna.

There is a small rift, as well as the actual change of locale, dividing off the first stage of Firbank's pattern from the next. It is answered at Chapter XI by the major rift, the earthquake itself, which separates the middle section from the last.

Firbank's imagination was projecting his own death in the images of childish terror, to which the extinction of one's own consciousness represents the bottom falling out of the external world.

Yet he covered the rift with the sad cynicism of the adult's knowledge that the world will in fact continue. The earthquake turns out to have done small damage in Cuna-Cuna. Charlie is scared but unhurt. The final segment of the pattern remains in continuity with the first.

Having assured that continuity, Firbank is able to hold back the effect of the earthquake, render it a delayed shock indeed, by erupting its consequence, on one of his syncopated stresses,[3] into the middle of his final section.

The Mouths attend a charity gala (for the earthquake relief fund) at the Villa Alba, where the decorative orchids include[4] 'Ronald Firbank (a dingy lilac blossom of rarity untold)'. Edna vanishes, to her seduction by the son of the house; the rest of the family goes sadly home without her; and at

---

[1] Firbank, who could write (cf. sub-section 8 of this chapter) *nadir* for *zenith*, was in no better a position to send-up Mrs Malaprop (the *Biography*, p. 271, quotes him as writing to Heather Firbank in 1925 ' "Your letters are all omissions"! As Mrs Malaprop says') than to (cf. Chapter X, 12) hold the Berlitz School against Eddy Monteith.

[2] Cf. sub-section 8 of this chapter.

[3] Cf. Chapter XIX, 8.   [4] Cf. Chapter XV, 5.

home they receive news¹ that Miami's sweetheart in Mediavilla has died in the earthquake.

Only then is the rift between the sisters manifest. Edna, taken up (as briefly, no doubt, as his previous mistresses) by Vittorio, cuts loose from her family and is cut off by her father's piety. The end is a reversal of the end of *The Flower Beneath the Foot*. It is Edna and Vittorio who watch, from the balcony of the flat he has set her up in; and it is the pious, single and heart-broken sister who marches, to the accompaniment of protestant hymns ('Time like an ever-rolling stream Bears all its sons away' ...), in the religious procession below.

But the procession is not going anywhere, not even, like the wedding procession in *The Flower Beneath the Foot*, into an unloving marriage. It is bound by a garland of hymnology into the timeless unity of the pattern, a pattern which is meaningful of questions but which directs the eye to no answers.

Firbank scrutinises fate: earthquakes that swallow up sweethearts, consumption that consumes authors.

The pattern of flowers, insects and suffering but undisclosing faces that constitutes *Prancing Nigger* asks the precise questions posed by, and written on, Gauguin's painting of 1897: 'D'où venons-nous? Que sommes-nous? Où allons-nous?'

23. Earthquake

FIRBANK's earth did open under his feet: in the month (March 1924) that *Prancing Nigger* was published. Lady Firbank died.

After finishing *Prancing Nigger* in Bordighera in June 1923, Firbank passed one of his summers in London. He spent it in having the earthquake chapter in *Prancing Nigger* separately typed, in order to send it to Carl Van Vechten, at Van Vechten's request, to be separately published in *The Reviewer*;² in setting the Society of Authors on Grant Richards;³ and in seeking a publisher to replace Richards – which in practice meant waiting summerlong for Heinemann's finally unfavourable decision on *Prancing Nigger*.

In August 1923 Firbank went to Spain, and conceived ... *Cardinal*

---

¹ Perhaps the delayed news echoes the delayed news of the consequences of the counter-part to the earthquake in (cf. sub-section 16) *Vanity Fair*, namely the Battle of Waterloo.
² which the *Biography* describes (p. 219) as a magazine published in Richmond, Virginia. According to pp. 233–4 of the *Biography*, Firbank's chapter appeared in October 1923: as (cf. Chapter XV, 5) *A Broken Orchid (From Sorrow in Sunlight)*.
³ Cf. sub-section 6 of this chapter.

Pirelli in Seville. He went on to Portugal, and in September twin-conceived[1] *The New Rythum* in Lisbon.

He made a brief early-autumn visit to London and heard of the possibility that Brentano's might publish *Prancing Nigger*. By later autumn he was in the more clement climate of Rome, where Lord Berner's ugly Psyche[2] bruised Firbank's psyche but where, in November 1923, word reached him that Brentano's intended to make him a professional writer.

Firbank received the news, he wrote to Carl Van Vechten, as though it were 'the "Annonce[3] faite à Marie" '. It was a simile, on the subject of the publishing of the book, which by likening Firbank to the madonna played a pretty variation on that apotheosis,[4] *in* the book, of all his transvesting and apotheosising fantasies, 'Imagine the world, my friends, had Christ been born a girl!'

Adding a postscript to his letter to Van Vechten, Firbank named the most suitable place of worship in the world (and happily it was at hand) for him to give thanks in for the publication of the book that is the utmost demonstration of his infinitely convertible pantheism: 'I am going round to pray now in the Pantheon.'

In December 1923, in his flat in Palazzo Orsini in Rome, he began writing . . . *Cardinal Pirelli*, which he was working on when he had to face the English March of 1924.

24. 'Ahi; this death'

IF *Prancing Nigger* is unique in Firbank's œuvre because it focuses on a family, . . . *Cardinal Pirelli* is unique in that it is a solo portrait.

Caprice and *Santal* follow solo lines of experience. But the soloist chiefly *sees*, and is only in glimpses seen. . . . *Cardinal Pirelli* is a depiction.

Far from intending to keep it, as he wanted to keep *Santal*, 'as simple as possible', Firbank declared in advance[5] that . . . *Cardinal Pirelli* 'will be very short & very elabourate & condensed'.

Following his custom,[6] Firbank trailed threads of continuity from previous books to the new one and laid down threads to be resumed later. Sisters of the Flaming-Hood, in a convent of which order Laura was enrolled in *The*

---

[1] Cf. sub-section 17 of this chapter.
[2] Cf. Chapter VII, 4.
[3] The *Biography* (p. 251), quoting Firbank's letter of 17 November 1923, from Rome, prints this word as 'Announce'. The mistake might or might not be Firbank's.
[4] Cf. Chapter XV, 18 and *Complete* Firbank, p. 615.
[5] in a letter of 17 May 1924 to Stuart Rose of Brentano's, quoted in the *Biography*, pp. 261-2.
[6] Cf. Chapter X, 2.

Flower Beneath the Foot, are to be seen in Clemenza. Cardinal Pirelli, reading, as he sups, a work of devotion placed on a 'menu-stand formed of a satyr sentimentalising over a wood-nymph's breasts', recalls that just such a devotional book once won him a convert: 'A Mrs. Mandarin Dove. American. Ninety million sterling.' Restored to her own country, Mrs Mandarin Dove is in *The New Rythum*.

The transition from *Prancing Nigger* to . . . *Cardinal Pirelli* is a transition from South American Spaniards to Spanish Spaniards. Naturally the same families recur, gaining an extra *s* on the ocean crossing to make their piety the more pointed. Princess Altamisal has left her card at Madame Ruiz's villa in the last-but-two chapter of *Prancing Nigger*; 'the Altamissals' attend the christening on the opening page of . . . *Cardinal Pirelli*.

And indeed the germ of that baroquely eccentric christening is perhaps to be glimpsed in *Prancing Nigger*, where Madame Ruiz owns 'a pomeranian of parts, "Snob"; a dog beautiful as a child'.

Put that together with Miss O'Brookomore's remark[1] 'After all, [. . .] isn't heaven a sort of snobbism? A looking-up, a preference for the best hotel?', and with the fact that Firbank himself in boyhood named a dog,[2] and you move towards that ultimate degree of religious snobbery where the Duquesa DunEden insists that Don Alvaro Narciso Hernando Pirelli, Cardinal-Archbishop of Clemenza, should pronounce over her week-old police-dog the words: 'And thus being cleansed and purified, I do call thee "Crack"!'

True to his Jane Austenish groundplans, Firbank distributes life in Clemenza over several fixed points and more than one social layer.

The point of highest fashion is the DunEden palace, which is so high, indeed, in fashion that the women of its milieu enjoy an exclusive disease: ' "Boheara", the new and fashionable epidemic, diagnosed by the medical faculty as "hyperaesthesia with complications" '. I imagine Firbank conceived it to be the result of drinking too much tea.[3]

Inevitably it was an 18th-century word that Firbank incorporated in the name. Boheara is an addition to the great 18th-century catalogue of imaginary diseases like 'the vapours' (1711) and 'the hyps'[4] (1705).

(Firbank told an acquaintance that he had invented Boheara and then caught it himself.[5])

---

[1] in *Inclinations* (and on p. 261 in the *Complete* Firbank).
[2] The name was, of course, Sapho (in its French spelling after Daudet); cf. Chapter V, 2.
[3] 'Bohea [. . .] 1701 [. . .] The name orig. of the finest kinds of black tea' (*Shorter Oxford English Dictionary*). [4] sc. hypochondria.
[5] But Firbank can't have told him, as the *Biography* (p. 292) claims, that he invented it for Pirelli.

The College of Noble Damosels, an institution prepared to admit the Duquesa DunEden's baptised dog ('A bitch, of course. . . .') as a pupil, contains and condenses more than one of Firbank's obsessive images. Writing of its President (the Dowager-Marchioness of Pennisflores[1]), Firbank slips into the Frenchness of Mrs Yaj; wanting, no doubt, to avoid writing 'the present President', yet wanting also to distinguish her from the medieval founder of the college, Firbank calls her 'the actual President'. The President is attended by two quintessentially Firbankian presences: Fräulein Pappenheim who has 'no experience of the pains of Aphrodite caused by men'; and Muley, the President's Negro maid, who (by, this time, Firbank's intention) speaks the idiom of Mrs Yaj (and speaks, indeed, the beginning of a middle-eastern limerick in it, 'Dair was once a young lady ob Fez –') and who finds it 'impossible to forget that the great basilica of Clemenza was a Mosque profaned'.

In the basilica and its surrounding buildings (a torrid Ashringford cathedral close), Firbank assembles, besides choirboys, an underworld of back-stage workers. The cathedral laundress, speaking Firbank's transvestism, is amazed at 'the time a man takes to slip on a frilly'. The cathedral secretary, besides remarking on the grossness of candles,[2] speaks Firbank's diabolism when, to a woman who wants to arrange for a brief mass, he observes: 'We say all but the Black.' And in the Cardinal-Archbishop's Palace, the superintendent, Madame Poco, spies on her employer. She has 'crossed the borderland that divides mere curiosity from professional vigilance' and has been bribed by 'certain monsignori' to report on the Cardinal.

The full import of Madame Poco's striking name Firbank strikes home in Chapter VI, the most sustainedly sinister passage he ever wrote. It contains the concentrated culmination of two of the images that haunted his imagination, and is itself the culmination of his own sense of being haunted – or hunted.

In accordance with 'the social status of a Spy', Madame Poco trails the Cardinal, a poco a poco indeed, through the Palace and basilica precincts at dusk, to the tolling accompaniment of the basilica bells – which include a bell said by tradition to contain 'fused into its metal one of the thirty pieces of silver received by the Iscariot for the betrayal of Christ': last, sinister incarnation of Deirdre's cards, Iphigenia's tea-set and Abraham's knife.[3]

And the image of Salome, so innocently-ambiguously embodied in the Artificial Princess, is likewise gathered to a sinister culmination in Madame Poco, who has already rehearsed before her mirror the steps she will take

[1] Cf. Chapter XV, 1.   [2] Cf. Chapter VIII, 3.   [3] Cf. Chapter XIX, 12.

when she finally catches the Cardinal out: *steps*, in the literal sense, for she has 'evolved an eerie "Dance of Indictment" ', in which 'Finger rigid, she would advance ominously with slow, Salomé-like liftings of the knees' on the Cardinal and proclaim 'I denounce thee, Don Alvaro.'

At the end of Chapter VI, her ominous and secret advance catches the Cardinal merely in prayer. But his is a temporary reprieve, borrowed, perhaps, thanks to the fusing[1] of Salome's situation in Firbank's mind with Hamlet's, from the reprieve accorded Claudius in prayer. Firbank has been inexorably stalked through the precincts of his creation by the imminence of his own death.

Yet though there are many milieux in . . . *Cardinal Pirelli* there is only one personage. The milieux are put in with Firbankian brilliance in their own right. ('They say', murmurs a woman poet, 'I utter the cry of sex throughout the Ages'; to which the response of the Duchess-Dowager of Vizeu is to 'spread prudishly her fan' and declare 'Since me maid set me muskito net afire, I'm just a bunch, me dear, of hysterics.') With equal brilliance of design, all the surrounding milieux, even when they turn their back on him, point attention to the central figure. The very ladies who attend the convalescence (from Boheara) party at the DunEden Palace, in 'focusing languishly the Cardinal', focus the book on him, too.

' "He is delicious in handsomeness to-night!" '

' "A shade battered. But a lover's none the worse in my opinion for acquiring technique", the Duchess of Sarmento declared.'

A frisson of mass hysteria runs through his flock at sight of the Cardinal's handsomeness; 'broken sobs of either sex' are provoked by the dicta he delivers at the inspiration of 'what prurient persons might term, perhaps, a "frolic" '.

It is a response borrowed and amplified from the response of *his* parishioners to the hero of *The Monk*. In . . . *Cardinal Pirelli* Firbankian camp is most conspicuously re-united with its literary original, 18th-century gothick.[2] A whole Monk Lewis sub-plot is condensed and carried to the heights of high comedy it had been silently begging to reach all along in half a sentence of Firbank's account of the Foundation Day performance at the College of Noble Damosels, where one of the pupils sings an aria[3] to an accompaniment played by 'a young nun with a face like some strange white rock, who was inclined to give herself married airs, since she had been debauched, one otiose noon, by a demon'.

Vividly, however, as the surroundings exist, they exist *as* surroundings.

---

[1] Cf. Chapter XIV, 5.   [2] Cf. Chapter VIII, 8.
[3] The aria is *Gaze not on Swans*, 'from the new opera, *Leda*'.

The book bends on them that even, distributed focus which holds the Mouth family at mid-distance. The details are of milieux, not of individuals, and so they serve or set off the sole individuality in the book. The social milieux of Clemenza are the heroic drapery behind the sitter, set trembling or swishing by *his* swishing past in 'the militant bravoura of a skirt'.[1]

Even the sextet of specially favoured choirboys that foams about the Cardinal is merely the high white impasto that squiggles-in the lace of his vestments.

Firbank perhaps whipped up his froth of choirboys from a memory of Hugh Benson's wish[2] 'to form a small choir – a quartette, perhaps'. And Benson's 'ideal', which was 'to have a boy who could sing, as my servant,' is fulfilled by Cardinal Pirelli, who in his summer retreat is waited on at table by the most favoured of the favoured boys, the Chiclet.

As with the fixed points in the surrounding social life, so with the book's shifts of locale: they serve the centralness of the central figure.

Word runs round the Foundation Day assembly at the College: '*Cardinal Pirelli has fled the capital!*'[3] He has in fact prudently withdrawn to his summer retreat in the country, the 'decaying monastery of the Desierto', where Firbank lends him his own devotion to Saint Teresa of Ávila.[4]

It is a shift that permits the book to become one of those portraits that shew three views of the single sitter's face. The first section (Chapters I to VII, with an exception at Chapter IV) displays the Cardinal's customary profile as he is seen at his see in Clemenza.

The central section (Chapter IX) presents a Pirelli in retreat, relaxed (it is still only 'idly' that he is 'considering his Defence'), and with 'his physiognomy in repose': a front-face depiction, perhaps, and as if for that reason[5] most pointedly and personally Firbankian. The garden of the monastery is the garden of The Coopers, admitted now to be, as well as 'Lovely as Paradise', 'oppressive perhaps as Eden'.[6]

---

[1] that touch of drag which (cf. Chapter VIII, 3) the Cardinal is unwilling 'to forgo altogether' in the disguises in which he seeks nocturnal adventure in the city, with the result that he passes sometimes as 'a caballero from the provinces' and sometimes as 'a matron'.

[2] Cf. Chapter VIII, 6.

[3] It is hard to understand how the 'city of Clemenza' can be a capital – even of a province; for Clemenza 'is in white Andalucia', and Andalusia, as an old kingdom, had its own capital, Granada. (As a modern region it has two: Granada for East Andalusia and Seville for West.) I think Firbank must have borrowed the capital from *The Flower Beneath the Foot* or *Prancing Nigger*, a seeming inadvertence pressed on him by his own sense (cf. sub-sections 13 and 18) of being held in near-permanent retreat from the capitals of England and the United States.   [4] Cf. Chapter II, 3.

[5] Cf. Chapter VIII, 1.   [6] Cf. Chapters XV, 12 and XVI, 11.

The 'tranquil court' of the monastery is visited by the Firbankian butterfly,[1] which is pursuing a Firbankian (that is, homosexual) mésalliance: 'a rose-red butterfly pursued a blue', and at the sight the Cardinal thinks 'I believe the world is all love, only no one understands.'

And the Cardinal is visited in his garden by the local parish priest,[2] Father Felicitas, who tells him which of the parishioners have died since the Cardinal's last summer visit to the country. 'Ahi; this death . . .' the Cardinal comments.

In the last two chapters, the Cardinal has returned to Clemenza. But he has turned round to confront his enemies. He means to cross the frontier and face judgment at Rome. He is displaying his other profile to the portraitist. But before he can fulfil his intentions his face slips and, rather than displaying, he reveals himself.

Even Chapter IV, a peep-hole let in to the first section of the book, a chapter shifted in locale from Clemenza to Rome, to the Vatican (and, in it, another garden), to the Papal thoughts themselves, affords merely another view of the sitter. Chapter IV is a baroque vision from on high enshrined at the top left of the composition, an eye of God inset in the canvas. The Cardinal's ultimate superior, the Pope, looks distantly down on 'the scandals of Clemenza' and decides reluctantly that he must act on reports reaching him of the Cardinal's 'eccentricities'.

They include, perhaps, the report of Monsignor Silex who, attending the eccentric christening in the first chapter, urges himself to 'gather force to look about him. Frame a close[3] report. The Pontiff, in far-off Italy, would expect precision.'

Monsignor Silex's unrelenting name[4] betokens the force gathering indeed against Cardinal Pirelli.

And perhaps the substance of the whole book consists of some such report sent back to Rome or drawn up, after the Cardinal's death, by a Vatican judge. In *Concerning the Eccentricities of Cardinal Pirelli*, the *Concerning* is perhaps a Latin *De*. The title is a counterpart to *A Record of the Early Life of St. Laura de Nazianzi*. . . . The book is, this time, an anti-hagiography.

Or, rather, it is a portrait of Firbank's secular saint.

In Cardinal Pirelli Firbank at last created a cardinal he had often fantasised.

---

[1] Cf. Chapter VII, 3.

[2] a scene perhaps created by an inversion of Firbank's own experience during the August of 1921, when he was writing *The Flower Beneath the Foot* at Versailles and (as the *Biography* records on p. 210) accepted the invitation of the English chaplain to sit in his garden in the evenings.   [3] which I read in the sense of 'secret'.

[4] 'silex [. . .] A hard stone, flint, [. . .] granite' (Lewis).

He had tried projecting the fantasy on to more than one of his acquaintance but it was an ill fit or was shrugged off by the wearer.

'It had long been a standing joke', Evan Morgan wrote in his after-account[1] of the affair of the *Princess Zoubaroff* dedication,[2] 'that I should be called "Cardinal Morgan".'

When Evan Morgan had shrugged off the fantasy, Firbank played at it in reverse with Carl Van Vechten. This time it was Firbank who was the church dignitary, adopting the other half of Cardinal Pirelli's title, Archbishop. Van Vechten addressed a parcel to Firbank under his false title; it was delivered to the Archbishop's Palace and thence returned to its sender.[3]

In the play whose dedication Evan Morgan declined, Firbank sketches Cardinal Pirelli off-stage. He is the Cardinal of whom Reggie Quintus says 'I'm hoping to be a Cardinal's secretary soon.'

In the play, Reggie finds better financial support in his occupation of minion to Lord Orkish, that ideal Oscar Wilde who has prudently crossed the frontier and gone into 'exile' before he can be brought to judgment.[4]

Evan Morgan shrugged off Firbank's prescription for happy homosexuality. Firbank admitted, at the approach of death, that he was no longer a young object to Oscar Wilde.[5] He fused his own identity with Wilde's on the points of grotesqueness and 'eccentricities' – all of which are metaphors of the sexual eccentricity Firbank shared with Wilde: to administer to a dog a sacrament which convention reserves to another species is to spend on a boy the love which convention directs to the other sex.

The great scarlet splurge of his Cardinal is the most tragic and the fullest of Firbank's self-portraits, and it is a portrait of Firbank in Wilde's tragic robes. Pirelli is Wilde unidealised by prudence, the Wilde who went to judgment (on his eccentricity) and to death.

Firbank had brought Oscar Wilde back to the Spain which Wilde imagined in the manner of Velasquez for his tale *The Birthday of the Infanta*,[6] the tale to which Firbank made allusion,[7] by way of the Velasquez-style court dwarf, at the birthday celebrations of his own Artificial Princess.

Packing his passport, rehearsing what he will declare at the Customs (a

---

[1] quoted on p. 33 of the *Bibliography*.
[2] Cf. Chapters VIII, 5 and XIX, 19.
[3] The story is reported in the *Biography*, p. 246, footnote.
[4] Cf. Chapter XIV, 10.
[5] Cf. Chapter XIV, 10.
[6] which is perhaps why Cardinal Pirelli's most fashionable christening is attended by the Infanta Eulalia-Irene (who assumes an 'affected slight confusion' at sight of the dog father 'Tail away, sex apparent'.
[7] Cf. Chapter XIII, 6.

flask of brandy and a novel soon to be put on the Index) as Charlie Mouth declared butterflies and Oscar Wilde declared he had nothing to declare except his genius, the Cardinal is drawn aside from his purpose by love. He enters the dark cathedral, meaning to mitigate the punishment of being shut in with the mice which he has visited on the Chiclet for his crime of chasing them.[1] The boy leads him a baroque dance among the baroque monuments;[2] to the flicker of forked lightning through the chancel window.

Cardinal Pirelli begins to make, after all, his Customs declaration: 'I declare I feel quite rompish!' But his heart is already hurting him.

Rendering himself rompishly baroque by 'setting a mitre like a wondrous mustard-pot upon his head', the Cardinal begins to chase the boy, as the boy chased the mice, round the cathedral.

In their bizarre obstacle-race plus dance plus dialogue of flirtation, which is watched secretly by Madame Poco (who thinks 'Old ogre: why can't he be brisk about it and let a woman back to bed?'), the Cardinal is at once at his most Firbankian and his most Wildean.

When the boy teases the Cardinal, it is a Firbankian trait he teases: 'You'd do the handsome by me, sir; you'd not be mean? [. . .] you'd be surprised, your Greatness, at the stinginess of some!'

The Cardinal, like Firbank himself,[3] is scarcely to be budged from his stinginess even by the promise of sex; and, as the chase and the chapter continue, it truly is the life[4] of the Cardinal's heart that is being filched away.

When the Cardinal cajoles the boy, it is in the very cadences of Oscar Wilde.

' "And always be obedient, dear child", the Cardinal was saying; "it is one of the five things in Life that matter most."

' "Which are the others, sir?" [. . .]

' "Never mind now. Come here."

' "Oh, tral-a-la, sir." '

(' The first duty in life is to be as artificial as possible. What the second duty is no one has as yet discovered.'[5])

The Cardinal pursues on, cajoling the boy, slapping at him, offering him bribes[6] and passing on to the boy his literary reflexions: 'If only Oriental literature *sprawled* less.'

---

[1] Cf. Chapter VIII, 3.
[2] The boy is himself a baroque monument made mobile: a cupid. ('Witching as Eros', the narrative comments.) Indeed he is a child version of Madame Wetme's (cf. sub-section 13) 'cruel god', 'the Chic'. The boy is the cruel small god, the Chiclet.
[3] Cf. Chapter VII, 2.   [4] Cf. Chapter VII, 3.
[5] Cf. Chapter XIV, 8.   [6] Cf. sub-section 17 of this chapter.

It is a pursuit that, in a literary classical allusion, crosses another frontier than the one the Cardinal had meant to cross: 'Olé, the Styx.'

Stripped, by the ardency of his pursuit and the jutting bits of the monuments he dodges among and clambers over, of all his clothes except his mitre, the Cardinal makes good his final Customs declaration (Oscar Wilde's final declaration and self-disclosure at the bar of judgment), 'As you can perfectly see, I have nothing but myself to declare,' and dies, of a heart attack, naked in homosexual pursuit but crowned.

25. The Mountains of Nirvana

BEFORE he finished . . . *Cardinal Pirelli*, Firbank knew, imaginatively as well as by rational calculation, that he was dying.

He had expected, I think, that his mother would outlive him, as she had outlived her other two sons. When she didn't, he probably lost such last belief as he maintained in the promise of eternity held out by the church, whose embrace he had entered when he was expelled from that territorial and extended mother, The Coopers.

After Lady Firbank's funeral he went back to Rome, locked himself in his room and only by night snatched at the food which a restaurant left at his door. But he received pious comfort from, which may have seemed ironic to him, Evan Morgan, who accompanied him to pray in the crypt of Saint Peter's.[1]

He stayed in Rome, moving to a different flat in[2] June 1924 and to yet another in November 1924. His restlessness was probably a manifestation of his illness. He finished . . . *Cardinal Pirelli* in February 1925.

But he didn't at once write the twin-conceived novel, *The New Rythum*, which he had earlier 'pined' to begin.[3] His mother's death, presaging his own, reactivated the impulse (one of whose early warnings had in 1920 prompted him to transpose *Odette* into *Santal*[4]) to put his œuvre into a fit state to be left as his monument.

At first a vehicle for his purpose seemed presented by Brentano's intention to publish all his books, old and new, in the United States.

At Brentano's request, he wrote a preface to *Caprice* and sent it to them for their edition of the book.

He revised *Vainglory*[5] for their edition.

On his own initiative (but, I surmise, in the hope that Brentano's would

---

[1] a fact reported on p. 254 of the *Biography*.
[2] These dates are from the *Biography*.
[3] Cf. sub-section 17 of this chapter.
[4] Cf. Chapter XIX, 20.
[5] Cf. Chapter VII, 4.

publish an edition of that book, too) he re-wrote the dinner-party chapter of *Inclinations*.[1]

At the end of April 1925, he left Rome for London and had . . . *Cardinal Pirelli* typed. One copy of the typescript he sent to Brentano's for the United-States edition. But for the English edition he made arrangements that must have cost some swallowing of pride to both contracting parties: the book was to be issued in England, at Firbank's expense, by Grant Richards.

I imagine Firbank expected that Brentano's payment for the United-States edition would cover his expenditure on the English one.

But while he was spending his summer in London he heard that Brentano's would not, after all, publish *Caprice*[2] and then that Brentano's had decided, 'on religious and moral grounds' against publishing . . . *Cardinal Pirelli*.

Firbank had ceased to be a professional writer.

The convenient vehicle for the tidying of his œuvre had been snatched away, but the impulse could not vanish because it was generated by the approach of death. Firbank left London in August 1925 and spent the autumn in Arcachon [Plate 13],[3] the brash little resort town on the Atlantic coast, not far from Bordeaux, where he finished his revision of *The Artificial Princess* and gave it its ending.

In October he moved on: to winter in Egypt. Thence he sent out a piece of local tourist-trade craft as his Christmas card. On the stiff cover (some $3\frac{1}{2}$ inches wide and $2\frac{1}{2}$ deep, pierced at the left by a green ribbon bow), a monkey in light blue trousers faces the bird-headed ancient Egyptian moon god. The outline and the caption, 'ĀḤ – TEḤUTI and the Ape', are printed, the colours put in by hand. On the middle pages, two small grey photographic views merge unevenly into their white surround. The first inside page is printed with the legend 'With best wishes for a Merry X'mas' and, beneath, a dotted line. Along this row of his favourite punctuation mark, Firbank has signed 'Ronald Firbank', and added '25', in violet ink.

In Egypt Firbank began to write *The New Rythum*, and, in the spring of 1926 made arrangements with the Society of Authors (suggested to his

[1] Cf. Chapters IX, 11 and XIX, 11.

[2] I am indebted for this information, as for most of the factual information in this sub-section, to the *Biography*. But neither from the *Biography* nor from the *Bibliography* can I search out what became of the preface written for the edition of *Caprice* that never appeared.

[3] The *Biography* (p. 287) gives Firbank's address as 'the Villa Primrose, boulevard de la Plage'. This may be how Firbank, orthodox for once, spelt the name of the villa in his letters; indeed, it may be how the name was spelt in 1925: but by 1971 Firbankian spelling had prevailed and, as Plate 13 bears witness, number 265 Boulevard de la Plage is named 'Primerose'.

thoughts, perhaps, by their good offices in his quarrel with Grant Richards – who, however, was now restored to the position of Firbank's sole 'publisher') for the issuing at his expense of a collected edition of his œuvre 'in the event of the death of the author within five years' of the date of the deed. The date was 23 April 1926. (Did Firbank *choose* the date on which Shakespeare's birthday is celebrated?) The author was dead within a month.

Concerning the Eccentricities of Cardinal Pirelli was issued, at the author's expense, about five weeks after his death.

In the autumn of 1926 scatty newspaper stories appeared to the effect that Firbank, so unnewsworthy during his life, was not dead but had mysteriously vanished.

'The complete disappearance' (run the notes for the unwritten part of *The New Rythum*) 'of Mrs Rosemerchant and of her young friend made a profound sensation [...] some believed they were living together in the mountains of Nirvana.'[1]

Firbank, however, was a corpse, to be shifted from one graveyard to another, fulfilling his Wildean pattern[2] without volition.

He lives only a life in death in his œuvre, as Laura lived a death in life caged in the convent, and as the God Firbank no longer believed in was caged[3] in the imaginative edifice of the cathedral at Clemenza.

---

[1] Cf. Chapter XV, 13 and sub-section 10 of this chapter.
[2] Cf. Chapter XIV, 12.   [3] Cf. Chapter XVI, 12.

Appendix

TEXT of Firbank's Preface to *The Flower Beneath the Foot*, published in facsimile of his handwriting in Brentano's edition of 1924.

I suppose the Flower beneth the Foot is really Oriental in origin, although the scene is some imaginary Vienna. The idea came in Algeria while writing Santal. One evening (or it may have been early morning) just as the lights were being extinguished of a supper-restaurant in Algiers, a woman, almost assuredly an American, sailed unconcernedly in, & sank down with charming composure at a table not far from mine, & to myself I murmured: "her Dreaminess, the Queen!" Later, in the radiant dawn, just outside, I beheld an Arab boy asleep beside the summer-sea, & to myself I murmured: "His Weariness, the Prince!" And from these two names the Flower just came about. It did not occur to me, at the time, I believe, to fabric a story from so singularly little; but a short while afterwards, in another town, his Weariness I saw again. Everywhere in fact his Weariness, or his simulacrum, appeared; all Princes, all weary – *wonderful boys* – wearier, even, than me! And his Weariness recalled her Dreaminess, & then, quite naturally, & cosily,[1] figures & objects composed themselves about them. The Queen's Ladies – her hectic Maids, the Palace, the Furniture, the Gardens &, above all, the ambitions of her Dreaminess the Queen for his Weariness[2] the Prince – an alliance with England, poor woman, was the nadir of her dreams! Thus, gradually, characters & dialogue came together[3] in my mind, & my tale of Islam began to bore me unutterably, & I longed to begin the Flower. A kind of nostalgia (which may only have been waywardness,) turned all my thoughts towards Vienna. And it was a veritable craving for Vienna, too. I remember it was at Touggourt in mid-Sahara while assisting at a sunset from the minarette of a Mosque, that I found the Duchess of Varna's court-dress – the green of Nile water. "Vi" & Olga's little soul-trip on the Lake, chapter, (I think,) *eleven*, suggested itself while watching two shed rose-leaves in a Moorish fountain. Such clinging, tender, courageous little rose-leaves they were – curious ones as well. Other elements, of course, went towards the shading and formation of my Flower, which really is as much a country-buttercup as a cattleya-orchid!

Ah, the East ... I propose to return there, some day, when I write about New York.

Ronald Firbank

[1] originally '& quite cosily'; Firbank crossed out the 'quite'.
[2] originally spelt 'Wearyness', and corrected.
[3] Firbank crossed out 'arranged themselves' and substituted 'came together'.

Books, Magazines and Articles Cited

(*Memoir*: see I. K. Fletcher. *Bibliography* and *Biography*: see M. J. Benkovitz.)

Adam International Review, Number 300, 1965; Curwen Press.
W. E. Addis and T. Arnold: *A Catholic Dictionary*; revised edition, Virtue, 1952.
Queen Alexandra's Christmas Gift Book; Daily Telegraph, 1908.
Antony Alpers: *Katherine Mansfield, A Biography*; Cape, 1954.
Alumni Cantabrigienses; Cambridge U.P., 1947.
Anonymous: *Teleny* (1893); Icon Books, 1966.
Art and Letters, Volume II, New Series, Spring 1919.
Jane Austen: *Emma* (1815–16); Oxford, 1960.
—— *Northanger Abbey* and *Persuasion* (1818); Oxford, 1965.
—— *Pride and Prejudice* (1813); Pan, 1967 (original volume and chapter divisions cited on p. 291).
Jane Austen's *Letters* to her Sister Cassandra and others; edited R. W. Chapman; Oxford, 1959.
(See also B. C. Southam.)
J. E. Austen-Leigh: *A Memoir of Jane Austen* (second edition, 1870); reprint (with *Persuasion*), Penguin, 1965.
The Aylesford Review, Summer 1966; St Albert's Press.
Aubrey Beardsley: *Under The Hill* (*Venus and Tannhäuser*); edition, with completion, by John Glassco; Grove Press (Evergreen Black Cat), U.S.A., 1968.
The *Letters* of Aubrey Beardsley; edited Henry Maas, J. L. Duncan and W. G. Good; Cassell, 1971.
(See also Brian Reade.)
Miriam J. Benkovitz: *A Bibliography of Ronald Firbank*; Hart-Davis, 1963.
—— *Ronald Firbank, A Biography*; Knopf, New York, 1969.
(British edition Weidenfeld & Nicolson, 1970).
Robert Hugh Benson: See C. C. Martindale.
Robert Blake: *Disraeli* (1966); University Paperbacks (Methuen in association with Eyre & Spottiswoode), 1969.
Brewer's Dictionary of Phrase and Fable; revised by Ivor H. Evans; Cassell, 1970.
Jocelyn Brooke: *Ronald Firbank*; Arthur Barker, 1951.

Jocelyn Brooke: *Ronald Firbank and John Betjeman*; published for the British Council and the National Book League, Longmans, 1962.
Brigid Brophy: *Black and White, A Portrait of Aubrey Beardsley*; Cape, 1968 (U.S. edition Stein & Day).
—— *Black Ship to Hell*; Secker & Warburg, 1962 (U.S. edition Harcourt, Brace & World).
—— *Don't Never Forget*; Cape, 1966 (U.S. edition Holt, Rinehart & Winston). (See also B. C. Southam, editor.)
Sir Bernard Burke: *A Genealogical and Heraldic History of the Landed Gentry of Great Britain and Ireland*; Harrison, 1898.
Agnes Carey: *The Empress Eugénie in Exile*; Eveleigh Nash and Grayson, 1922.
Miguel de Cervantes Saavedra: *The Adventures of Don Quixote*; translated by J. M. Cohen; Penguin, 1950.
Gabriel Chevallier: *Clochemerle*; translated by Jocelyn Godefroi, 1936; Secker & Warburg, 1966.
Chrétien de Troyes: Arthurian Romances, translated by W. W. Comfort; Dent, 1913.
Jean Cocteau, edited by Robert Phelps: *Professional Secrets (An Autobiography of Jean Cocteau Drawn from his Lifetime Writings)*; translated by R. Howard; Farrar, Straus & Giroux, New York, 1970.
J. M. and M. J. Cohen: See Penguin.
Colette: *The Pure and the Impure*; translated by H. Briffault (*Ces Plaisirs*, 1932; *Le Pur et l'Impur*, 1941); Secker & Warburg, 1968.
Cyril Connolly: *The Condemned Playground* (1945); Routledge, 1946.
Concise Oxford Atlas; Oxford, 1952.
Concise Dictionary of National Biography; Oxford, 1930.
Margaret Crosland: *Madame Colette, A Provincial in Paris*; Peter Owen, 1954.
Alan Dent: *Mrs. Patrick Campbell*; Museum Press, 1961.
(See also Bernard Shaw.)
Douai translation (The Holy Bible translated from the Latin Vulgate [. . .] Douai A.D. 1609; Rheims, A.D. 1582); Burns Oates & Washbourne (1914).
George Eliot: *Middlemarch* (1871–2); Blackwood, 1892.
Henry Fielding: *Amelia* (1751); Dent, 1930.
(A. A.) Ronald Firbank: *An Early Flemish Painter*; Enitharmon Press, 1969.
—— *Caprice*; Grant Richards, 1917.
—— *Concerning the Eccentricities of Cardinal Pirelli*; Grant Richards, 1926.
—— *Inclinations*; Grant Richards, 1916.
—— *Odette D'Antrevernes, A Fairy Tale for Weary People* and *A Study in Temperament*; Elkin Mathews, 1905.
—— *Santal*; Grant Richards, 1921.
—— *The Artificial Princess*; with an Introduction by Sir Coleridge Kennard; Duckworth, 1934.

—— *The Flower Beneath the Foot, Being a Record of the Early Life of St. Laura de Nazianzi and the Times in which She Lived*; Grant Richards, 1923; (with a Preface by the author; Brentano's, New York, 1924).
—— *The New Rythum and Other Pieces*; with an Introduction by Alan Harris; Duckworth, 1962.
—— *The Princess Zoubaroff*; Grant Richards, 1920.
—— *Vainglory*; Grant Richards, 1915.
—— *Valmouth*; Grant Richards, 1919.
The Complete Ronald Firbank; with an Introduction by Anthony Powell; Duckworth, 1961.
(Joseph Firbank: See F. McDermott.)
Ifan Kyrle Fletcher: *Ronald Firbank, A Memoir*; with Personal Reminiscences by Lord Berners, V. B. Holland, Augustus John, R.A., and Osbert Sitwell; 'The Reminiscences by Osbert Sitwell are reprinted with some alterations from the limited edition of THE WORKS OF RONALD FIRBANK (1928)'; Duckworth, 1930.
(See also Society for Theatre Research.)
E. M. Forster: *Abinger Harvest* (1936); Penguin, 1967.
—— *The Celestial Omnibus and Other Stories* (1911); Sidgwick & Jackson, 1936.
Jeannette H. Foster: *Sex Variant Women in Literature*; Frederick Muller, 1958.
G. S. Fraser: *The Modern Writer and His World*; revised edition, Deutsch, 1964.
Gillian Freeman: *The Undergrowth of Literature*; Nelson, 1967.
Sigmund Freud: *Collected Papers*; Volume III, translated by A. and J. Strachey; Hogarth Press (1925), 1953. Volume IV, translated under the supervision of J. Riviere; Hogarth Press, 1953. Volume V, edited by J. Strachey; Hogarth Press, 1950.
—— *Group Psychology and the Analysis of the Ego* (1921); translated by J. Strachey (1922); Hogarth Press, 1949.
—— *Totem and Taboo* (1919); translated by A. A. Brill; Penguin, 1942.
P. N. Furbank: *Reflections on the Word 'Image'*; Secker & Warburg, 1970.
Théophile Gautier: *Émaux et Camées*; Gründ, Paris.
Maxwell Geismar: *Henry James and his Cult*; Chatto & Windus, 1964.
Roy Genders: *Bulbs all the Year Round*; Faber, 1955.
Augustus J. C. Hare: *The Story of My Life*: Volume V; George Allen, 1900.
Frank Harris: *My Life and Loves*; Volumes 2 and 3; Obelisk Press, Paris, 1948.
(Rupert Hart-Davis: See Oscar Wilde.)
Christopher Hassall: *Edward Marsh, Patron of the Arts, A Biography*; Longmans, 1959.
Robert Hichens: *The Green Carnation* (anonymously, 1894); reissue with Introduction; Unicorn Press, 1949.
—— *Yesterday*; Cassell, 1947.
Heinrich Hoffman: (*Struwwelpeter*, 1847); *The English Struwwelpeter* [...] Routledge, undated.

Vyvyan Holland: *Son of Oscar Wilde* (1954); Penguin, 1957.
(See also I. K. Fletcher.)
H. Montgomery Hyde (editor): *The Trials of Oscar Wilde*; William Hodge (1948), 1960.
Clyde K. Hyder (editor): *Swinburne, The Critical Heritage*; Routledge & Kegan Paul, 1970.
Henry James: *The Ambassadors* (1903); with Preface, 2 volumes, Macmillan, 1923.
Ernest Jones: *The Life and Work of Sigmund Freud*; edited and abridged by Lionel Trilling and Steven Marcus; Penguin (Pelican), 1964 (U.S. edition Basic Books, 1961).
Ernest Jones: 'The World of Ronald Firbank', review (of *Five Novels of Firbank*, New Directions) in *The Nation*, New York, 26 November 1949; Volume CLXIX, pp. 520–1.
(E. Jourdain: See E. Morison.)
Kelly's Handbook to the Titled, Landed and Official Classes; volumes of 1900, 1921 and 1924.
(Hugh Kenner: See J. P. Sullivan, editor.)
John Anthony Kiechler: *The Butterfly's Freckled Wings, A Study of Style in the Novels of Ronald Firbank*; Schweizer Anglistische Arbeiten; Francke (Bern), 1969.
Rudyard Kipling: *Stalky & Co.* (1899); Macmillan, 1922.
Madame de La Fayette: *La Princesse de Clèves* (1678); Gründ, Paris.
(F. Lamont: See E. Morison.)
Larousse de Poche (C. and P. Augé); Paris, 1926.
Serge Lifar: *A History of the Russian Ballet* [. . .]; translated by Arnold Haskell; Hutchinson, 1954.
Elizabeth Longford: *Victoria R.I.* (1964); Pan, 1966.
Longus: *Daphnis and Chloe*; (together with Parthenius, etc.); text edited and with a translation by G. Thornley and J. M. Edmonds; Loeb Library; Heinemann, 1962.
Lyra Graeca, Volume I; edited and translated by J. M. Edmonds; Loeb Library; Heinemann 1963.
LM ('Lesley Moore', Ida Baker): *Katherine Mansfield, The Memories of LM*; Michael Joseph, 1971.
Maurice Maeterlinck: *Théâtre*: Volume III (including *Ariane et Barbe-Bleue ou La Délivrance Inutile*, 1901); Charpentier, Paris, 1918.
Gustav Mahler: *Das Lied von der Erde*; score with editorial note from Universal Edition; Philharmonia, Vienna, 1962.
Malleus Maleficarum; translated by Montague Summers (1928); Pushkin Press, 1951.
Thomas Mann: *The Holy Sinner* (*Der Erwählte*, 1951), translated by H. T. Lowe-Porter; Penguin, 1961.
William Mann: *Richard Strauss, A Critical Study of the Operas*; Cassell, 1964.

Katherine Mansfield: *In a German Pension* (1911); Penguin, 1964.
—— *Journal* of Katherine Mansfield; edited by J. Middleton Murry; definitive edition, Constable, 1954.
—— Katherine Mansfield's *Letters* to John Middleton Murry 1913–22; edited by J. Middleton Murry; Constable, 1951.
(See also Adam; LM; A. Alpers.)
Edward Marsh: *Memoir* (of Rupert Brooke); prefaced to *Collected Poems* of Rupert Brooke, 1918; Sidgwick & Jackson, 1954.
(See also C. Hassall.)
C. C. Martindale, S.J.: *The Life of Monsignor Robert Hugh Benson*; 2 volumes; Longmans, 1916.
Robert McAlmon: *Being Geniuses Together 1920–1930*; revised and with supplementary chapters by Kay Boyle; Michael Joseph, 1970.
Frederick McDermott: *The Life and Work of Joseph Firbank, J.P., D.L., Railway Contractor*; Longmans, 1887.
Elizabeth Morison and Frances Lamont (A. Moberly and E. Jourdain): *An Adventure* (1911); third edition with additional matter; Guy Chapman, 1924.
National Gallery of Scotland; Catalogue of Paintings and Sculpture; Edinburgh, 1957.
Ernest Newman: *Richard Strauss*; with a personal note by A. Kalisch; (1908); John Lane, 1921.
John Henry Newman: *Apologia Pro Vita Sua* (1865); Longmans, 1890.
Harold Nicolson: *King George the Fifth*; Constable, 1952.
—— *Some People* (1927); Constable, 1934.
Romola Nijinsky: *Nijinsky* (1933); Penguin, 1960.
Rev. T. P. O'Beirne: *The Wood on the Stony Hill, A Short History of St Mary's Catholic Church, Chislehurst, Kent*.
The Oxford Companion to Music (P. A. Scholes); Oxford (1938), 1950.
The Oxford Dictionary of English Christian Names (E. G. Withycombe); Oxford (1945), 1963.
The Oxford Dictionary of Quotations; Oxford, 1941.
Eric Partridge: *A Dictionary of Slang and Unconventional English* (1937); Routledge & Kegan Paul, 1967.
(Mrs Patrick Campbell: See Bernard Shaw; Alan Dent.)
Hesketh Pearson: *The Life of Oscar Wilde* (1946); Methuen, 1949.
(*Pen and Brush*: See L. Szladits.)
The Penguin Dictionary of Quotations (J. M. and M. J. Cohen); Penguin (1960), 1964.
Robert Phelps and Peter Deane: *The Literary Life*; Farrar, Straus & Giroux, New York, 1968.
Arthur W. Pinero: *Trelawny of the "Wells", An Original Comedietta in Four Acts* (1898); Samuel French, 1936.
(C. B. Purdom: See Bernard Shaw.)

Brian Reade: *Beardsley*; Studio Vista, 1967.
Forrest Reid: *Private Road*; Faber, 1940.
Leopold von Sacher-Masoch: *Venus in Furs* (*Venus in Pelz*, 1870); English translation by Jean McNeil 'from a French rendering' by Aude Willm; together with an essay by Gilles Deleuze; Faber, 1971.
(Sappho: See *Lyra Graeca*.)
Nathalie Sarraute: *Les Fruits d'Or*; Gallimard, Paris, 1963. (*The Golden Fruits*, translation by Maria Jolas; Calder, 1965.)
Siegfried Sassoon: *Siegfried's Journey 1916–1920*; Faber, 1945.
Bernard Shaw: *Androcles and the Lion* (performed 1912–13; published 1916); Penguin, 1946.
—— *Heartbreak House* (1919); Penguin, 1964.
—— *Man and Superman* (published 1903; performed 1905); Penguin, 1946.
—— *Our Theatres in the Nineties* (1932); Constable, 1948.
—— *Sixteen Self Sketches*; Constable, 1949.
—— *The Doctor's Dilemma* (performed 1906; published 1908); Penguin, 1946.
—— *The Irrational Knot* (1880); Constable, 1924.
—— Bernard Shaw's *Letters* to Granville Barker; edited by C. B. Purdom; Theatre Arts, New York, 1957.
—— Bernard Shaw and Mrs Patrick Campbell: *Their Correspondence*; edited by Alan Dent; Gollancz, 1952.
The Shorter Oxford English Dictionary on Historical Principles (1933); revised edition Oxford, 1959.
Osbert Sitwell: *Laughter in the Next Room* (Volume IV of *Left Hand, Right Hand, An Autobiography*); Macmillan, 1949.
(See also I. K. Fletcher.)
Patrick J. Smith: *The Tenth Muse, A Historical Study of the Opera Libretto*; Gollancz, 1971.
Society for Theatre Research (editors and publisher): *Ifan Kyrle Fletcher, A Memorial Tribute*; 1970.
Susan Sontag: *Against Interpretation*; Farrar, Straus & Giroux, New York, 1966.
B. C. Southam (editor): *Critical Essays on Jane Austen*; Routledge & Kegan Paul, 1968.
Francis Steegmuller: *Flaubert and Madame Bovary* (1939); Collins, 1947.
Gertrude Stein: *Look at Me Now and Here I Am, Writings and Lectures 1909–45*; edited by P. Meyerowitz; Penguin, 1971.
Richard Strauss and Romain Rolland: *Correspondence*, etc.; edited by Rollo Myers; Calder & Boyars, 1968.
(See also E. Newman.)
J. P. Sullivan, editor: *Ezra Pound, A Critical Anthology*; Penguin, 1970.
(Charles Algernon Swinburne: See Clyde K. Hyder, editor.)
L. L. Szladits and H. Simmonds: *Pen and Brush, The Author as Artist*; catalogue of an exhibition [. . .]; The New York Public Library, 1969.

The *Life* of Saint Teresa of Ávila By Herself; translated by J. M. Cohen; Penguin, 1957.
Jean Terrasson: *The Life of Sethos* [...]; anonymously, Paris, 1731; translated by (Thomas) Lediard; London, 1732.
W. M. Thackeray: *Vanity Fair* (1847–8); Chatto & Windus, 1948.
Flora Thompson: *Lark Rise to Candleford* (1939; 1941; 1943); Oxford, 1954.
The Topkapi Palace Museum; text by Z. Erkins; Istanbul.
Carl Van Vechten: *Nigger Heaven* (1926); Knopf, New York, 1927.
Evelyn Waugh: *Black Mischief* (1932); Penguin, 1951.
—— *Brideshead Revisited* (1945); Chapman & Hall, 1947.
—— 'Ronald Firbank'; article in *Life & Letters*, II, March 1929, pp. 191–6.
Oscar Wilde:
—— *The Artist as Critic, Critical Writings of Oscar Wilde*; edited by Richard Ellmann; W. H. Allen, 1970.
—— *The Importance of Being Earnest, A Trivial Comedy for Serious People By the Author of Lady Windermere's Fan* (no mention of Wilde's name in the volume); Leonard Smithers, 1899.
—— The *Letters* of Oscar Wilde; edited by Rupert Hart-Davis; Hart-Davis, 1962.
—— The *Works* of Oscar Wilde; Spring Books, 1963.
(See also: R. Ellmann, editor; H. M. Hyde; H. Pearson; H. Wyndham.)
A. E. Wilson: *Christmas Pantomime*; Allen & Unwin, 1934.
Colin Wilson: *Bernard Shaw, A Reassessment*; Hutchinson, 1969.
(E. G. Withycombe: See Oxford.)
Leonard Woolf: *Beginning Again, An Autobiography of the Years 1911–1918*; Hogarth Press, 1964.
Virginia Woolf: *Between The Acts* (1941); Penguin, 1953.
—— *Mrs Dalloway* (1925); Penguin, 1964.
Horace Wyndham: *Speranza, A Biography of Lady Wilde*; Boardman, 1951.
Violet Wyndham: *The Sphinx and her Circle, A Memoir of Ada Leverson by her Daughter*; Deutsch, 1963.

Index

Àāḥ-Teḥuti, 567
Abercrombie, Lascelles, 86, 113
Abergavenny, Marquess of, 188
Abraham, 472, 560
Academy, The, 194, 205, 260, 332
Achilles, 284, 302
Acton, Harold, 98, 150
Adam, 361
Adam, 179
Agnes, Sister, 541
Aïda, 285
Alexander, Lady, 336
Alexandra, Queen, 78, 142
Allan, Maud, 294, 303
Allen, George, 342
Alpers, Antony, 149
Altamisal, Princess, 559
Altam.ssal family, 559
Amba¹sadress, English (*Artificial Princess*), 157s
Ambassadress, English (*Flower* . . .), see Something, Lady (R.)
Amoucha, 501, 503, 504
Andersen, Hans (*Thumbelina*), 451
Andrew, 155, 360, 455
Angelo, 193, 329, 330
Annesley, Countess, 141
Anthony, Saint, 275
d'Antrevernes, Odette, see Odette d'Antrevernes
Aphrodite, 443, 445, 446, 447, 448, 560. See also Venus
Apollo, 330
Appledore, Lady, 208, 215, 225, 227, 234, 235, 342, 352, 353, 388, 477, 516. See also Lady Appledore's Mésalliance
Apuleius, L., 21
Arbanel, Mrs, 465, 466
Archer, William, 304
Aristotle, 555
Arlen, Michael, 103, 122, 138, 149
Arne, Mary, 465, 466, 469, 470, 471, 473, 488
Arnold, Sir Edwin, 444
'Arrow, Simon', 381, 382
Art and Letters, 129, 433

Artificial Princess, The, 86, 90, 105, 115, 118, 119, 124, 147, 154, 157, 158, 167, 168, 179, 184, 193, 194, 199, 207, 209, 213, 214, 218, 219, 221, 227, 233, 234, 235, 277, 281, 282, 285-99, 301-3, 307, 312, 313, 315, 316, 317, 319, 320, 321, 323, 324, 329, 339, 342, 350, 365, 374, 376, 377, 380, 389, 409, 413, 418, 419, 420-31, 433, 435, 438, 445, 449, 450, 453, 492, 510, 512, 513, 520, 529, 530, 531, 532, 554, 564. See also Salome
Ashringford, Bishop of, see Pantry, Dr
Ashringford Chronicle, 461
Asp, Mrs (R.), 83, 161, 171, 208, 308, 338, 348, 353, 388, 442, 443, 448, 463, 567
Athenaeum, 166
Atthis, 555
Auden, W. H., 104
Austen, Cassandra, 18
Austen, Francis, 86
Austen, Jane, 17, 18, 19, 23, 31-3, 37, 40, 41, 46, 47, 50, 51, 56, 61, 66, 69, 72, 80, 81, 82, 83, 218, 233, 235, 236, 317, 431, 452, 453, 462, 468, 479, 481, 497, 552, 553, 559; Miss Bates, 453; Mrs Bates, 47, 453; Elizabeth Bennet, 82, 453; Mr Bennet, 468; Bennet family, 468; Lady Catherine de Bourgh, 82, 87, 453; Mr Collins, 453, 463; *Emma*, 51, 233; Jane Fairfax, 233; Charlotte Lucas, 453; Catherine Morland, 82; *Northanger Abbey*, 2, 17, 18, 23, 87; *Pride and Prejudice*, 87, 453, 463, 468; *Sense and Sensibility*, 72; Henry Tilney, 82, 87; Emma Woodhouse, 47
Austen-Leigh, J. E., 50, 51, 72, 86; *Memoir of Jane Austen*, 50, 86
Aylesford Review, 162

Babcock, Dr Cunliffe, 344, 523, 535, 543, 544, 545
Bach, J. S., 76
Bachir, 527
Bakst, Léon, 400
Balsan, Consuelo, 118
Bamboo, 556, 557
Bara, Theda, 509
Baring, Maurice, 325

Barker, Harley Granville, 274, 352, 498
Barney, N. C., 366
Barrow, Mrs (later Lady), 346, 348, 378, 384, 385, 451, 453, 459
Barrow, Sir Sartorious, 453
Bartholomew, 336
Bartholomew, Saint, 336
Bathild, Saint, 337
Bathilde, Saint Elizabeth, 337, 340, 371
Baudelaire, Charles, 32, 97, 153, 177, 245, 249
Beard Throughout the Ages, The, 543
Beardsley, Aubrey, 25, 34, 68, 76, 98, 112, 116, 117, 119, 136, 164, 171, 172, 179, 210, 213, 214, 227, 245, 249, 256, 257, 258, 260, 264, 265, 275, 276, 282, 284, 290, 305, 328, 338, 382, 411, 431; *Letters*, 25, 34, 68, 76, 164, 210, 260, 276, 284, 411, 431; Sporion, 382; *Under the Hill*, 98, 282, 382, 390
Beardsley, Mabel, 256
Beauchamp, Katherine, 137. *See also* Mansfield, Katherine
Beaufort, Duke of, 126
Beaumont, C. W., 153, 177, 382, 390
Bedley, Mrs A., 392, 398, 401, 537, 538, 543, 545
Beerbohm, Mary, 227
Beerbohm, Sir Max (*Works*), 404
Beethoven, Ludwig van, 49, 50, 449, 450
Beetle, 26
Belfast Whig, 101
Bellini, G., 196
Benedict, Saint, 275, 278
Benkovitz, Miriam J., 18, 25, 34, 86, 87, 95, 101, 106, 107, 115-17, 118, 177, 196, 234, 236, 252, 290, 338, 443, 493. *See also Bibliography of Ronald Firbank; Ronald Firbank, A Biography*
Bennett, Arnold, 102
Benson, A. C., 164
Benson, E. F. ('Dodo'), 164, 279, 335; *Dodo*, 164
Benson, R. H., 139, 164-6, 169, 170, 179, 212, 216, 235, 279, 334, 374, 389, 460, 562; Chris Dell, 216; *Necromancers*, 165; *Sentimentalists*, 216, 235, 334
Berg, Alban, 152
Berg Collection, 357
Bernadette, Saint, 414, 419, 420
Berners, Lord (G. H. Tyrwhitt; from 1919 Tyrwhitt-Wilson), 93-6, 106, 117, 118, 122-125, 130, 144, 147, 148, 159, 161, 163, 178, 187, 205, 287, 372, 373, 412, 431, 504, 558
Bernhardt, Sarah, 192, 193, 205, 246, 254, 294, 295, 304, 307, 308, 328, 370, 471
Bernini, G. L., 24, 34
Betjeman, Sir John, 103
Bibliography of Ronald Firbank, A (Benkovitz), 105, 106, 115, 119, 149, 178, 180, 192, 206, 209, 212, 234, 236, 237, 270, 271, 276, 277, 278, 283, 286, 294, 324, 334, 338, 340, 342, 351, 356, 381, 390, 416, 431, 433, 442, 463, 471, 474, 475, 479, 487, 517, 522, 546, 549, 551, 567
Blake, Robert, 185
Blake, William, 477, 555
Bloater, Adrian, 344
Bloater, Lilian, 344, 425
Blossome, Mrs, 348, 375
Blueharnis, Atalanta, 434-6, 444
Blueharnis, Lady Georgia, 192, 205, 209, 313, 339, 354, 435, 436, 440, 448, 453, 456, 458, 460
Blueharnis, Lord, 209, 234
Blumenghast, Olga, 368, 505, 529, 536, 542, 543, 545
Boldini, G., 153
Boone, A. M., 222
Booth, 'General', 311
'Bosie', *see* Douglas, Lord Alfred
Botticelli, Sandro, 193, 205, 217, 546
Bottom, Ann, 348
Bottom, Zillah, 348
Bourbon, Isabel de, 78, 142, 217
Bowden, Captain Henry, 212, 220
Brahma, 403, 409
Brassknocker, Lord, 374
Brentano's 73, 74, 143, 144, 236, 258, 346, 387, 406, 497, 506, 507, 511, 513-15, 522, 547, 558, 566
Bricogne, Mme, 223, 224
Bricogne, M., 225, 235
Brill, A. A., 341
Brock, Clutton, 336
Broken Orchid, A, 349, 557
Brooke, Jocelyn, 103-5, 163, 164, 178, 179, 183, 204, 227, 236, 252, 253, 255, 484, 493, 504
Brooke, Rupert, 73, 86, 99, 109, 110-14, 119, 129, 183, 325, 362, 421, 447, 448
Brookes, Winsome, 99, 108, 109, 112-14, 118, 119, 129, 142, 145, 155, 160, 173, 190, 311, 315, 339, 342, 348, 349, 360, 362, 370, 386-8, 429, 432, 433, 437, 445, 447, 448, 455, 553
Brookfield, Charles (*Poet and the Puppets*), 254
Brophy, Brigid: *Black and White*, 119; *Black Ship to Hell*, 18, 179; *Don't Never Forget*, 18, 50, 149; *Finishing Touch*, 49, 100, 346; *In Transit*, xv, 49
Brown, Father, 275
Brown, F. M., 193
Browne, Mrs Culling, 384
Brownjohn, Thisbe, 348
Brown-Potter, Cora, 256
Brueghel the Elder, 194
Buddha, 476
Bunyan, John, 545
Burgon, J. W., 452

INDEX 581

Butcher, S. H., 444
Byron, George Gordon, Lord, 25

Cabinet, Count, 155, 368, 540–3
Calderon, George, 498
Caligula, 185, 205
Calvally, George, 200, 311, 447, 449, 451, 457, 478
Calvally, Mrs, 132, 148, 183, 201, 204, 439, 442, 443, 451, 457
Campbell, Mrs Patrick (B. S.), 370, 371, 389, 456, 465, 472, 473
Caprice, 102, 107, 118, 141, 157, 160, 174, 179, 180, 185, 193, 198, 205, 271, 287, 343, 347, 375, 381, 382, 387, 412, 463, 471–6, 479, 483, 485, 489, 490, 498, 504, 539, 547, 548, 558, 566, 567
Carew, Helen, 161, 268–71, 273, 277, 293, 313, 372, 373, 389, 502
Carew, J. L., 268
Carey, Agnes, 220, 221, 235, 496; *Empress Eugénie in Exile*, 235, 496
Carpaccio, Vittorio, 194, 288, 290, 298
Carroll, Lewis (C. L. Dodgson), 104
Cartaret-Brown, Mrs (L.), 348
Castleyard, Lady, 164, 222, 227, 232, 359, 457, 459-61
Catullus, G. Valerius, 364, 441, 443
Cavaljos, Duchess of, *see* Mistress of the Robes
Centenarians of Glennyfurry, The, 479. See also *Valmouth*
Cervantes Saavedra, Miguel de, 20, 23, 24, 26, 31, 34, 77, 100, 356; *Don Quixote*, xiv, 21, 23, 24, 26, 31, 34
Cézanne, Paul, 355
Chameleon, The, 340
Chansons de Bilitis, Les, 365, 389
Charles V, Emperor (Charles-Quint), 194, 196, 197, 200, 202, 204, 221, 226, 326, 332, 362
Charlus, Baron de, 247
Charmias, 460
Charpentier, 342
Charpon, 460
Charteris, Lady Agnes, 232
Charters, Lady Agnes, 232, 323, 356, 413–15, 419
Chatterton, Thomas, 454
Chavannes, Puvis de, 411, 412, 431
Chedorlahomor, 536
Chekov, *see* Tchekov, Anton
Cherif, 158, 178, 399, 484, 501–8, 528, 541, 547
Chevallier, Gabriel (*Clochemerle*), 525
Chiclet, 156, 562, 565
Chilleywater, Hon. Harold, 343, 538
Chilleywater, Mrs, 108, 119. *See also* Gellybore-Frinton, Victoria
Chimney, Miss, 346
Chrétien de Troyes (*Erec et Enide*), 496

Christie Manson & Woods Ltd, 189
Churchill, Maj.-Gen. George, 190
Churchill, Lady Randolph, 190, 370
Churchill, Sir Winston, 114, 119, 141, 142, 145, 190, 213, 362
Churchill family, 190
Clare, Saint, 462
Claude Lorraine, 85, 351
Clemenza di Tito, La, 193, 205
Cleopatra, 307, 338, 339, 354, 454, 509
Cobb, I. S. (*Laugh a Day*), 338
Cockduck, Elizabeth, 203
Cocteau, Jean, 103, 246, 254, 295, 303
Cohen, J. M., 34
Coleman, Terry, 315
Coleridge, S. T., 25
Colette (S. G.), 137, 138, 149, 366, 502; *Ces Plaisirs*, 366; *Chéri*, 502; *Pur et l'Impur*, 366
Collins, Daisy, 230, 236, 474
Collins, Mabel, 203, 230, 363, 366, 368, 380, 389, 463–70, 471, 483, 553
Collins, Mrs, 470, 553
Colnaghi, P. & D., 189–92
Common Prayer, Book of, 484
Complete Ronald Firbank, The, 102–4, 106, 107, 118, 443, 539
Compostella, Miss J., 370, 372, 389, 432, 437, 438, 440, 444, 447, 454–6, 465, 471, 488, 489, 498, 514
Compton-Burnett, Dame Ivy, 347
Concerning the Eccentricities of Cardinal Pirelli, 34, 69, 74, 86, 123, 125, 154, 171, 179, 203, 208, 215, 228, 234, 285, 297, 300, 326, 341, 351, 361, 364, 387, 400, 408, 507, 540, 548, 549, 552, 557–68
Conder, Charles, 194
Congreve, William, 20, 97, 493, 494, 545; *Incognita*, 20; *Way of the World*, 493, 494; Lady Wishfort, 494
Connolly, Cyril, 83, 87, 103, 104, 118, 122; *Condemned Playground*, 87, 118
Conrad, Joseph, 8
Corba, Lobelia, 152, 176, 348, 413, 420
Corba, Mrs, 413
Corelli, Marie, 52, 248
Cornwallis-West, George, 370
Corvo, Baron (Fr Rolfe), 98, 165, 168; *Hadrian the Seventh*, 165
Cotton, Mrs van, 208, 234
Cotton, Mrs O. Van, 128, 234, 245, 264, 369
Count Fanny's Nuptials, 381, 382, 390. See also Fanny, Count
Coward, Sir Noel, 103
Cowsend, Mr or Prof., 466
Cowsend, Mrs, 466, 467
Crack, 559
Craig, Gordon, 97
Creamway, Mrs, 157, 316, 317, 375

Creamway, Stella, 375, 389
Cresswell, Madam, 281
Cresswell, Mrs, 158, 178, 281, 287, 369, 374, 389, 453, 455, 456, 458, 459, 461, 462, 464, 478
Cresswell, Reggie, 455
Crockodile, Lady Kitty, 464
Crosland, Margaret (*Madame Colette*), 502
Crowley, Aleister, 166-9, 179, 309, 362, 424, 519
Cuenca, Count, 125
Cuna, Archbishop of, 378, 390, 417
Cunard, Nancy, 148, 177
Custance, Olive, see Douglas, Lady Alfred

Dateland, King of, see Jotifa, King
Dateland, Queen of, see Thleeanouhee of Dateland, Queen
Daudet, Alphonse (*Sapho*), 68, 86, 363, 559
Dawkins, Miss, 466, 469, 470
Deane, Peter, 86
Debussy, Claude, 312, 314, 339, 342, 343, 371, 386; Mélisande, 312, 350, 370, 371, 389; Pelléas, 370; *Pelléas et Mélisande*, 343, 370, 389
Defoe, Daniel (*Journal of the Plague Year*), 29
Deirdre, 169, 179, 436, 466, 472, 560
de la Mare, Walter, 86
Delitsiosa, 343
Dell, E. M., 12
Demitraki, Lazari, 527, 530
Dent, Alan, 370, 389, 456, 473
Dent, E. J., 82, 83, 87, 146, 269
Deslys, Gaby, 383, 390
Diaghilev, Serge, 295
Diana, 338, 408
Dickens, Charles, 9, 10, 37, 38, 52
Dionysius of Halicarnassus, 443
Disney, Walt, 414
Disraeli, Benjamin, 7, 185; *Contarini Fleming*, 7
Dolci, Carlo, 194
Donatello, 194
Doppio-Mignoni, Cardinal, 155, 483
Dostoevsky, Fyodor, 54, 56, 65; *Crime and Punishment*, 54; *Idiot*, 54; Karamazov brothers, 54
Dou, Gerard, 194
Douglas, Lady Alfred (Olive Custance), 259-261, 269
Douglas, Lord Alfred ('Bosie'), 179, 256, 257, 259-61, 264, 269, 271, 276, 279, 300, 302, 305, 327-33, 335, 346, 362, 431, 496, 500
Downman, John, 189-91
Dowson, Ernest, 260, 267; *Pierrot of the Minute*, 260
Drama in Sunlight, (A), 487, 546
Dreyfus, Alfred, 248

Duckworth & Co. Ltd, Gerald, 96, 105, 106, 118
Duffy, Maureen, 168, 435
Dukas, Paul, 343
Dulau, 25
Duncan, Isadora, 370
DunEden, Duquesa, 364, 559, 560, 561
Dürer, Albrecht, 194
Duveen of Millbank, Lord (J.), 195, 205, 364, 491

Early Flemish Painter, An, 81, 87, 196, 197, 226, 227
East is Whispering, The, 401
Eastlake, Sir Charles, 195
Eastlake, Lady, 194, 195; *Five Great Painters*, 195
Ebbing, Violet, 348
Ecclesia, Sister, 357, 482, 483
Echo de Paris, 246
Edmonds, J. M., 442
Edna, 452, 454
Edward VII, 71, 86, 219, 315, 318
'Effendi darling', 527
Elder Miss Blossom, The, 348
Elephant-bag, King, 533
Elgar, Sir Edward, 78
Eliot, George (Mary Ann Evans), 9, 10, 24, 25, 32-5; Dorothea Brooke (Casaubon), 24; *Middlemarch*, 24, 33, 34
Ellmann, Richard, 254, 340
Elsassar, Baroness, 221, 235, 536
Elsie, Princess, 539, 541
Embarka, 503, 504
Epstein, Jacob, 271, 277, 293
Ernest, Père, 320, 482
Eros, 565
Escanglon, M. A., 223
Essais, Les, 225
d'Este, Isabella, 192
Eugénie, Empress, 219-22, 275, 325, 326, 340, 417, 496
Evans, Dame Edith, 491
Evans, Montgomery, 148, 153, 177, 504
Evening News, 268, 277
Evening Standard, 29, 96, 177
Eysoldt, Gertrud, 311, 339, 370

Facile-Manners, Hon. Edward, 347, 387
Fanny, Count, 382. See also Count Fanny's Nuptials
Fanny, Lord, 382, 383
Fantasia for Orchestra in F Sharp Minor, 129, 148, 433, 434
Fantin-Latour, Ignace, 355
Farquhar, George, 469
Farquhar, the, 469
Farrar, Geraldine, 311, 312, 339, 350

INDEX

Fawley (or Franley), Mrs, 234, 358
Felicitas, Father, 563
Février, Henri, 344
ffines, 347, 348, 363, 388
ffoliott, 347, 387
Fielding, Fenella, 105
Fielding, Henry (*Amelia*), 22
Firbank (A. A.) Ronald, passim. *For works see under individual titles*
Firbank, Lady (H. J. or J. H.), 106, 117, 139–141, 149, 183, 184, 186, 189–91 195, 204, 209, 216, 218, 219, 223, 224, 228, 232, 263, 268, 286, 318, 379, 416, 417 431, 471, 472, 501, 502, 506, 507, 509, 511, 520, 528, 534, 543, 545, 549–51, 557, 566
Firbank, Heather, 93, 94, 116, 122, 147, 148, 173, 185, 186, 201, 205, 225, 228, 232, 236, 312, 341, 356, 388, 520, 534, 556
Firbank, H. S., 116, 123, 201, 341
Firbank, Joseph, 73, 95, 126–8, 131, 139, 182, 183, 188, 204, 351
Firbank, J. S., 116, 123, 324, 341
Firbank, Sir (J.) T., 95, 131, 139–41, 148, 170, 181–9, 195, 204, 212, 219, 232, 304, 352, 467
Fish, Arthur, 338
Flaubert, Gustave, 58, 65, 294; Emma Bovary, 58; *Madame Bovary*, 58, 65
Fletcher, Mrs C. K., 96
Fletcher, I. K., 18, 25, 81, 86, 87, 94, 96, 97, 110, 116–18, 127, 135, 153, 159–61, 169, 177, 178, 217, 252, 253, 255, 269, 276, 285, 373, 379, 431, 450, 476, 493. *See also Ronald Firbank, A Memoir*
Flower Beneath the Foot, The, 67, 81, 99, 100, 107, 109, 118, 119, 134, 135, 144, 148, 152, 154, 155, 160, 163, 173, 174, 177, 189, 193, 203, 205, 208, 209, 214, 219, 222, 229, 231, 233, 282, 302, 308, 310, 328, 336, 339, 340, 343, 344, 346, 354, 364, 368, 380, 381, 383, 387, 389, 392, 398, 400–2, 407, 420, 427, 497, 505–7, 509–52, 556, 557, 559, 562, 563
Flowerman, Miss, 348, 387
Flowers, April, 541
Folkestone, Lord, 268
Ford, John ('*Tis Pity She's a Whore*), 320
Forrester, Wildred, 335, 336, 342, 350, 352–4, 362, 377, 388, 477, 516
Forster, E. M., 73, 86, 101, 118, 425; *Abinger Harvest*, 118; *Celestial Omnibus*, 425
Fortnightly Review, 302
Foster, J. H. (*Sex Variant Women*), 366, 371
France, Anatole (*Thaïs*), 421, 448
Franley (or Fawley), Mrs, 234, 358
Fräulein, 228, 229, 435
Frechtman, B., 254
Freeman, Gillian (*Undergrowth of Literature*), 378
Freud, Sigmund, 7, 13, 15, 16, 18, 45, 46, 51, 52–65, 70, 130, 148, 339, 341, 390; *Collected Papers*, 18, 65, 148, 339, 390; *Group Psychology*, 58, 65; *Interpretation of Dreams*, 6, 18, 339, 341; *Totem and Taboo*, 51
Fritz, 120
Furbank, P. N. (*Reflections on the Word 'Image'*), 67, 83–6
Furiel, 460

Gallet, Louis (*Thaïs*), 448
Garden, Edward, 371, 389
Garden, Mary, 311, 312, 339, 350, 371, 383, 389
Garnier-Pagès, D. and Mme M., 517
Garrett, Annesley, 141
Garrett, Mrs Annesley, 141, 269
Garrett, J. P., 117
Garrett, William, 263, 276
Gauguin, Paul, 203, 204, 206, 411, 412, 476, 551, 552, 557
Gautier, Théophile, 177, 516; *Émaux et Camées* 516
Geismar, Maxwell, 39, 40, 46, 55; *Henry James* 39, 50
Gello, 442, 462
Gellybore-Frinton, Victoria, 108, 343, 344, 347 386, 538, 540. *See also* Chilleywater
Genders, Roy, 515
Genesis, 221, 361, 536
Geo, King, 533, 539
George V, 533
Georgina, 473
Gerhardi (now Gerhardie), William, 98
Gershwin, George, 105
Ghirlandaio, Domenico, 384
Gibbon, Edward, 172, 225, 406
Gibbons, Stella (*Cold Comfort Farm*), 484, 485
Gibson, Wilfred, 86
Gide, André, 246, 254
Gilbert, W. S. (*Patience*), 254
Giotto, 84
Gladstone, W. E., 185
Glasgow Herald, 102
Glassco, John, 390
Glenmouth, 479. *See also Valmouth*
Glory, Queen, 533, 539
Gluck, C. W. (*Iphigénie en Tauride*), 310
Glyda, 330
Goahead, King, 527, 535
Goatpath, Almeria, 348
Goethe, J. W. von, 76
Goncourt, Edmond de, 338
Gone With the Wind, 41
Goodland, Joshua, 265, 266
Goring, Lord, 7, 18, 297, 303, 346
Gossaert (Gossart), Jan, 194, 196, 199, 200, 202, 362
Governess (*Artificial Princess*), 320, 340

Goya y Lucientes, F. J., 78, 107, 194, 297
Gozzoli, Benozzo, 193, 194, 198, 329
Grandmother of the Artificial Princess, 423
Granta, 194, 205, 302, 375
Gray, John, 274, 275, 278, 284, 308, 462; *Silverpoints*, 274
Greco, El (Domenico Theotocopouli), 194
Greene, Graham, 401
Greuze, J. B., 194
Gripper, 347, 387, 458
Guevara, Alvaro, 153, 176, 340
Guinevere, 136, 155, 177

Hachette, 25
Haggard, Rider, 248
Hammerton, Stephen, 471
Hancock, H. (D.), 364, 365, 389
Handel, G. F., 352, 387, 432, 537; *Acis and Galatea*, 352, 387
Hannah, 461
Hanway, Sir Valerian, 355
Harcourt-Smith, Simon, 154, 177
Hare, Augustus (*Story of My Life*), 336
Harland, Henry, 165, 172, 213, 215; *Cardinal's Snuff-Box*, 215; *Mademoiselle Miss*, 165
Harmonie, 266
Harris, Alan, 118, 128, 176, 388
Harris, Emma, 355
Harris, Frank (*My Life and Loves*), 268, 277
Harrogate Herald, 102
Harvester, Claud, 188, 308, 323, 339, 344, 350, 351, 353, 354, 358, 359, 370, 372, 373, 383, 387-90, 413, 432, 433, 438, 439, 444, 446, 454-6, 464, 471, 472, 486, 487, 492, 509
Harvester, Cleopatra, 454, 509
Hassall, Christopher (*Edward Marsh*), 119, 278, 340
Hastings, Lord Reggie, 327, 346, 362
Heath, Sir James, 188
Heinemann, William, 258, 276, 546, 551
Hemingway, Ernest, 98
Henedge, Mrs, 68, 108, 113, 122, 155, 169, 170, 275, 310, 342, 346, 349, 353, 354, 358, 360, 369, 375, 387-9, 403, 432-7, 439, 440, 445-9, 453-6, 457-9, 495
Henry III, 155
Henry VII, 107
Henry VIII, 483
Her Dearest Friend, 313, 315, 339
Herod, 306, 309, 312, 317, 318, 321, 339, 423, 431, 513
Herodias, 305, 306, 309, 311, 313, 318, 338, 339, 349, 510
Herbert of Cherbury, Lord (*De Veritate*), 95, 118
Hervey, Lord, 382
Hichens, Robert, 164, 179, 279, 327, 335, 336, 340, 346, 350, 401, 421, 431, 448, 517; *Garden of Allah*, 401; *Green Carnation*, 164, 279, 327, 335, 336, 346; *Yesterday*, 164, 179, 340, 350, 431
Hitchinson, Robert, 401
Hitler, Adolf, 50
Hoffman, Heinrich (*Struwwelpeter*), 34
Holland, Cyril, 261
Holland, V. (O.) B., 96, 115, 123, 124, 127, 128, 147, 148, 160, 178, 186, 198, 199, 205, 228, 261-8, 276, 277, 280, 299-301, 313, 332, 336, 404, 409, 421, 427, 451, 455; *Son of Oscar Wilde*, 205, 265, 269, 276, 277, 280, 336
Home Life of Lucretia Borgia, The, 307, 338, 435, 463
Home Life of the Queen of Sheba, The, 307, 338, 428
Homer, 52, 444
Hopkins, Miss, 392
Hospice, Miss, 25, 347, 454, 458
Hudson, Stephen, 271
Hume, David, 22
Huneker, J. G. (*Painted Veils*), 371
Hurstpierpoint, Mrs E., 120, 170, 191, 205, 221, 320, 337, 357, 358, 363, 365, 371, 377, 390, 402, 478, 479, 481-3, 485, 541, 554
Huxley, Aldous, 144, 145, 149, 166, 176, 179, 180, 401, 552; *Crome Yellow*, 179; *Limbo*, 179
Huxley, Maria, 144
Huysmans, J.-K., 102, 459; *À Rebours*, 459
Hyde, H. M., 87, 148, 258, 302, 390

Ibn Ibrahim, 502, 528
Ibsen, Henrik, 304, 455, 456; *Hedda Gabler*, 456; *Little Eyolf*, 456; *Rosmersholm*, 455
Ideas and Fancies, 357
Impression d'Automne, 282, 302, 342
Inclinations, 101, 141, 149, 159, 170, 178, 179, 190, 203, 208, 231, 234, 261, 269, 273, 287, 292, 346, 347, 363, 364, 366, 368, 380, 396, 397, 400, 409, 412, 416, 446, 463-71, 476, 485, 489, 492, 495, 496, 499, 527, 535, 538, 547, 548, 553, 559, 567
Infanta Eulalia-Irene, 564
Infanta Isabella, *see* Bourbon, Isabel de
Inglepin, Professor, 344, 353, 404, 435, 439, 441-4, 446
Ingres, J. A. D., 84, 357, 358, 388, 479
Intriguer, Lord, 162, 327, 362, 544
Iphigenia, 310, 466, 472, 560
Iris, 343
Irving, Sir Henry, 352
Isis, 357
Isolde, 227, 436
Iss'y, 460
Ives, George, 275

Jamaica, Marchioness of, 203
James, Henry, 39, 40, 44, 46, 55, 72, 197, 205,

269, 346, 362, 488–91, 505, 522; *Ambassadors*, 488; Peter Quint, 362; Lambert Strether, 488; *Turn of the Screw*, 197; *Wings of the Dove*, 488
James the Elder, Saint, 370, 438
'Joey', *see* Firbank, J. S.
John, Augustus, 96, 112, 121, 122, 147, 150, 153, 154, 160, 177, 178, 184, 185, 202, 204, 206, 269, 473, 479, 549
John the Baptist, 200, 290, 304, 306, 317, 321, 326, 327, 374, 420, 422, 423, 428, 449, 457, 474
Jones, Ernest, 18, 339
Jones, E., 104, 118
Jordaens, Jakob, 194
Josephus, 306
Jotifa, King, 527, 533, 535
Jourdain, E., 165
Joyce, James, 72, 363
Judas Iscariot, 560
Julian of Norwich, 281
Jullian, Philippe, 254
Juno, 472
Justinian, 113, 447
Juvenal (D. Junius Juvenalis), 539

Keats, John, 9
Kempe, Margery, 281
Kendall, Mrs, 348
Kennard, Sir C. A. R., 69, 86, 105, 106, 115, 209, 268–70, 272, 277, 286–8, 313, 376
Kennard, C. J., 268
Kennard, H. C. D., 268
Kennard, Helen, *see* Carew, Helen
Kenner, Hugh, 441
Kermode, Frank, 28, 35
Kettler, Mrs K., 464
Kiechler, J. A., 100, 132, 174, 227; *Butterfly's Freckled Wings*, 132
King and His Navy and Army, 302
King (*Artificial Princess*), 157, 177, 307, 309, 310, 423, 425, 430, 513
Kipling, Rudyard (*Stalky*), 26, 34
Knopf, Alfred, 12
Kouyoumdjian, Dikran, 149. *See also* Arlen, Michael
Krishna, 477

Lachmann, Hedwig, 310, 311
Lady Appledore's Mésalliance, 208, 213–17, 227, 230, 234, 287, 314, 323, 334–6, 339, 341–343, 349, 353, 400, 407, 408, 417, 472, 491, 492, 516. *See also* Appledore, Lady
La Fayette, Mme de (*Princess de Clèves*), 20, 21
Lamont, Frances, 166, 179; *Adventure*, 179
Lampito, 466
Land and Water, 102
Landsberg, A. C., 153, 308

Lane, John, 257, 258, 274, 276
Lang, Andrew, 444
Langtry, Lily, 308
Largillière, N. de, 194, 298
Laughter, Peggy, 348
Laura L. C. E. de Nazianzi, 282, 345, 357, 369, 381, 388, 510, 514–19, 521, 528, 533, 535–8, 540–2, 544, 545, 549, 558, 563, 568
Lavender of Bromley, 181
Lawrence, Sir Thomas, 203
Lay of the Last Nurserymaid, The, 379, 380, 385, 386, 467, 538
Lear, Edward, 104
Leda, 561
Legend of Saint Gabrielle, The, 230, 236
Lely, Sir Peter, 77
Leonardo da Vinci, 217
Lesbia, or Would He Understand?, 204, 364
Leslie, Sir Shane, 125
Leverson, Ada, 264–6, 271–3, 276, 277, 284, 285, 298–303, 431, 474, 529; *Minx*, 285, 298
Levey, Michael, 217, 516
Lewis, C. T., 563
Lewis, M. G., 171, 561; *Monk*, 561
Lewis, Percy Wyndham, 77, 80, 87, 120, 151, 152, 156, 160, 176, 441, 549
Liddell, H. G., 555
Lifar, Serge (*Russian Ballet*), 119
Life & Letters, 98, 118
Life and Times of Gaby Deslys, The, 383
Lila, 230
Lila, 230, 236, 532
Limousine, Jean, 194
Limpness, Hon. Lionel, 380, 538
Lippincott's Monthly, 254
Liss, Sir George, 213
Listener, The, 35, 103
Listless, Lady, 456
Liverpool Post, 102
Lizzie (Elizabeth), Archduchess of Pisuerga, 520–2, 524–6, 529–31, 533, 536, 539, 540
LM, 179
Longford, Elizabeth (*Victoria*), 338
Longus (*Daphnis and Chloe*), 21, 32, 282
Lostwaters, Countess of, 171, 208, 221
Lostwaters, Melissa Lady, 208, 221, 234
Louÿs, Pierre, 365
Love at all Hazards, 382
Lovelace, Geoffrey, 144
Lucas, E. V., 336
Lucas, F. L., 444
Lucile, 356, 358, 388, 457
Lucretius, T. Carus (*De Rerum Natura*), 446
Ludwig of Bavaria, 530
Luini, Bernardino, 217
Lydell, Miss, 464
Lyra Graeca, 442
Lysistrata, 465, 466, 473

Mabuse, 194
Mabrouka, 501, 503
McAlmon, Robert, 121, 147, 152, 154, 177, 224, 235, 254, 386, 390; *Being Geniuses Together*, 147, 176, 177, 235, 254, 390
Macbean, Alexander, 291
McCarthy, Lillah, 491, 498
McDermott, Frederick, 86, 126, 131, 139, 148; *Joseph Firbank*, 148
Madama Butterfly, 260
Maeterlinck, Maurice, 290, 311, 312, 342-4, 370, 371, 411, 413, 415; *Ariane et Barbe-Bleue*, 342, 343; *Blue Bird*, 342; Mélisande, 312, 350, 370, 371, 389; *Monna Vanna*, 344; Pelléas, 370; *Pelléas et Mélisande*, 343, 370, 389
Magdalen, Saint Mary, 317, 339, 374
Magnasco, Alessandro, 171
Magritte, René, 250, 437
Mahler, Gustav, 305, 441; *Das Lied von der Erde*, 442
Mahoney (Colley-Mahoney), Father, 320, 481, 482
Mais, S. P. B., 102
Malaprop, Mrs, 556
Malleus Maleficarum, 338
Malory, Sir Thomas (*Morte Darthur*), 136
Mandarin-Dove, Senator, 384
Mandarin Dove, Mrs, 208, 234, 312, 559
Manet, Édouard, 183
Mangrove, Mrs, 204
Mann, Thomas (*Holy Sinner*), 472
Mann, William (*Richard Strauss*), 303, 338, 339
Mansfield, Katherine, 137, 138, 149, 166-8, 179, 378, 390; *In a German Pension*, 168
Mant, May, 141, 474
Marcanudo, Marchioness of, 351
Marcus, Frank (*Killing of Sister George*), 130
Mars, 22
Marsh, Sir E. H., 86, 110-14, 122, 129, 162, 274; 325, 340
Martin, Mrs, 17, 19
Martindale, C. C., 165, 179, 235, 389
Mary, Mrs, 343, 499
Mary, Queen (wife of George V), 533
Massenet, J. E. F., 447, 448, 510; *Hérodiade*, 510; *Sappho*, 448; *Thaïs*, 447, 448
Mathews, Elkin, 257-9, 261, 274, 546
Matthew, Gospel of Saint, 338, 450
Matisse, Henri, 411
Maud, Queen of Cassiopia, 481
Maugham, W. Somerset, 285
Mauve Tower, The, 25, 174, 219, 290, 302, 304, 486
Max, Édouard de, 295, 303
Max (lover of Baroness Rudlieb), 377, 386, 424-6, 530
Memoir, see Ronald Firbank, A Memoir

Menard, M., 225, 235
Mencken, H. L., 226, 236; *American Language*, 226
Mengs, A. R., 298
Meris, Saint Automona (de), 371, 384, 478, 481
Methuen & Co. Ltd, 342
Michelangelo Buonarroti, 227
Mills, I. H., 178
Milton, John, 83, 85, 346, 511; *Paradise Lost*, 85
Missingham, Miss, 165, 179, 460
Mistress of the Robes (*Artificial Princess*), 345, 424, 425, 435, 445, 512
Mistress of the Robes (Duchess of Cavaljos), 513, 525, 526
Mr White-Morgan the Diamond King, 127, 351, 387
Moberly, A., 165, 166
Moeller, Philip, 147, 150, 157, 373, 389, 520
Monaco, Princess of, 254
Monet, C. O., 183
Monteith, Hon. 'Eddy', 162, 163, 189, 229, 236, 307, 338, 346, 348, 364, 376, 380, 387, 389, 390, 443, 486, 536, 538, 539, 544, 546, 556
Monteverdi, Claudio, 76
Montgomery, Mrs, 344, 349, 387, 514, 523, 524, 530, 537, 543-5
Moreau, Gustave, 284
Morgan, Hon. Evan, 144, 149, 161-4, 189, 486, 490, 491, 500, 504, 538, 564, 566
Morison, E., 166, 179; *Adventure*, 179
Morley, Countess of, 50
Morning Post, 160
Mountjulian, Mrs (Emma Harris; Duchess of Overcares), 355, 388
Mouth, Charlie, 133, 134, 149, 358, 553-6, 565
Mouth, Edna, 554-7
Mouth, Miami, 347, 552, 554, 556, 557
Mouth, Mr, 349, 553
Mouth, Mrs, 401, 551-5
Mouth family, 132, 204, 412, 503, 552, 554-6, 562
Mozart, (J. C.) W. A., 44, 51, 82, 83, 168, 215, 289; Belmonte, 83; Constanze, 83; *Così Fan Tutte*, 41; *Don Giovanni*, 168; *Die Entführung aus dem Serail*, 83; *Die Zauberflöte*, 83
Muley, 560
Murchison, Lord, 285, 299, 301
Murray, Gilbert, 443
Murray, John, 25
Murry, John Middleton, 166, 167, 179
Musical Times, 205, 339
Mussolini, Benito, 469
Mustapha, 477
Mynx, *see* Mengs, A. R.

Napoleon III, 219, 220

INDEX 587

Nashe, Thomas, 21
Nation, 118
Nattier, J.-M., 194
Neffal, V., 364, 388
Negress, Blanche, 204, 206, 327, 364, 388, 496
New Age, 168
Newman, Ernest, 305, 310, 314, 315, 338, 339
Newman, J. H., 172, 179; *Apologia*, 179
New Rythum and Other Pieces, The, 25, 86, 94, 106, 115, 118, 119, 128, 133, 148, 149, 151, 157, 174, 176–8, 181, 195, 201, 204, 206, 208, 209, 217, 227, 232, 234, 235, 283, 302, 311–313, 315, 334, 339, 342, 433, 443, 459, 486, 528, 536, 548, 549, 558
New Statesman, 101
Nevinson, C. R. W., 109, 135, 136, 149, 515, 521, 549
Nichols, R., 179
Nicholson, Sir William, 355
Nicolson, Harold, 106–9, 114, 118, 129, 144, 146, 202, 278, 449; *King George the Fifth*, 278; *Some People*, 107, 109, 118, 146
Nijinsky, Romola (*Nijinsky*), 119, 303
Nijinsky, Vaslav, 295, 349, 387
Nils, 436
Nineteenth Century, 276
Niri-Esther, 346, 402, 409, 478, 483
Nit, 347, 387
Norfolk, Duke of, 125
Nostradamus, Father, 542

O'Beirne, T. P., 212, 235
O'Brien, Edna, 255
O'Brookomore, Gerald, 159, 203, 208, 363, 366, 368, 380, 388, 412, 463–70, 476, 492, 495
Observer, 101
Ode to Swinburne, 443, 538
Odette, 25, 107, 118, 142, 174, 228, 416–19, 479, 501, 502, 506, 507, 510, 566
Odette d'Antrevernes, 174, 203, 243, 253, 400, 403, 414–22, 426, 501, 512
Odette d'Antrevernes, 97, 106, 107, 174, 184, 211, 214, 224, 281, 282, 292, 376, 414–22, 427, 436, 448, 510, 519
Offenbach, Jacques (*Tales of Hoffmann*), 370
Olaf, Prince, 513, 514, 523, 524, 537, 543
Oliver, Sir, 474
Orangeman, Mrs, 170, 179
Orion, 442
Orkish, Lady, 198
Orkish, Lord, 198, 205, 326–33, 335, 340, 345, 368, 420, 492, 493, 497, 500, 564
Orme, Lambert, 107–9, 209
O'Sullivan, Vincent, 308
Otter, Gwen, 167, 179
Ouardi, 527
Ouida (Louise de la Ramée), 52

Overcares, Duchess of, *see* Mountjulian, Mrs

Pall Mall Gazette, 101
Palmer, 465
Pan, 425
Pantry, Lady Anne, 347, 454, 457–61, 478, 488
Pantry, Aurelia, 186, 459, 460
Pantry, Dr (Bishop of Ashringford), 348, 369, 374–6, 387, 389, 403, 409, 454, 455, 458, 461, 488
Pappenheim, Fräulein, 560
Park, Bertram, 143, 151, 176, 201
Parr, Monsignor, 275, 278, 296, 303, 404, 441 446
Partridge, Eric, 496
Parvula de Panzoust, Lady, 221, 231, 247, 371, 377, 379, 384, 385, 389, 399, 477, 478, 480, 482, 484, 487
Passer, Peter, 155, 540–2, 544, 546
Passing of the Rose, The, 349, 387
Pastorelli, Count, 363, 368, 388, 466, 467, 469, 470
Pater, Walter, 202
Patrick, Saint, 170, 181, 201
Patroclus, 284
Pavlova, Anna, 133, 148, 214, 370
Payen-Payne, de V., 276
Peake, Mervyn (*Gormenghast*), 368
Pearson, Hesketh (*Oscar Wilde*), 149, 179, 254, 269, 271, 277, 305, 340, 431
Peat & Co., W. B., 518
Pedro, 358
Pegeen Mike, 456
Pellegrin, St John, 374, 421
Pen and Brush, 357, 388
Pennisflores, Dowager-Marchioness of, 341, 560
Perugino, Pietro, 217
Pet, Peter, 347, 457
Peters, Whipsina, 381, 390
Phelps, Robert, xv, 86, 303
Picasso, Pablo, 227
Pierrefonds, Comtesse de, 222
Pinero, A. W., 472–4, 489, 490; *Mrs Ebbsmith*, 472, 474; *Notorious Mrs Ebbsmith*, 472; *Trelawny of the 'Wells'*, 473, 474, 489
Pinturicchio, 198, 326, 327, 340
Pirelli, Cardinal Don A. N. H., 25, 156, 165, 172, 177, 203, 206, 227, 368, 369, 374, 379, 383, 390, 408–10, 549, 557–67
Pisanello, N., 196
Pisuerga, Archduchess of, *see* Lizzie
Pisuerga, King of, *see* William of Pisuerga, King
Pisuerga, Queen of, 505, 510, 512, 513, 515, 516, 521, 522, 524, 527, 530, 532, 534–6, 539, 542, 544
Plea for the Separation of the Sexes, A, 383, 459

Poco, Madame, 347, 387, 560, 561, 565
Pontypool, Mrs, 374
'Poor pale Pierrot', 454
Pope, Alexander, 382, 383, 473; 'bug with gilded wings', 382, 390, 473; *Epistle to Arbuthnot*, 382; *Second Satire of the Second Book of Horace*, 382; Sporus, 382, 383
Pope, the, *see* Tertius III, Pope
Porter, A. M. or Porter, J., 172
Potter, Beatrix, 104
Pound, Ezra, 67, 441; *Papyrus*, 441
Poussin, Nicolas, 351
Powell, Anthony, 104, 118
Prancing Nigger, 73, 100, 105, 132, 133, 142, 143, 145, 149, 174–6, 180, 204, 230, 258, 259, 271, 326, 343, 347, 349, 378, 386, 398–400, 412, 503, 546–9, 551–9, 562
Praxiteles, 364
Prince Imperial, 220, 222
Princess, Artificial, 168, 219, 295–7, 304, 307–310, 320–2, 324–6, 335, 337–40, 374, 376, 378, 389, 420–7, 513, 516, 517, 519, 560
Princess (*Mauve Tower*), 290, 304
Princess Zoubaroff, The, 97, 101, 105, 125, 153, 160, 162, 163, 166, 167, 185, 193, 195–7, 204, 205, 225, 228, 229, 231, 236, 259, 287, 326–334, 340, 357, 360, 363, 364, 367, 373, 383, 396, 400, 486, 491–502, 505, 539, 547, 564. See also Zoubaroff, Princess
Princesse aux Soleils, La, 184, 204, 219, 225
Private Eye, 347
Professor, *see* Inglepin, Professor
Proudie, Mrs, 454
Proust, Marcel, 70, 72, 246, 247, 251; *À la Recherche du Temps Perdu*, 32
Psyche, 144, 145, 149, 558
Ptah, 161, 178
Punch, 298, 302

Quarterly Review, 50
Queen (*Artificial Princess*), 219, 307, 309, 310, 320, 322, 338, 340, 424, 428, 429, 453
Queensberry, Marquess of, 87
Queens of the Rod and Birch, 383
Quickstep, Lily, 348
Quint, Charles, *see* Charles V, Emperor
Quintus, Reggie, 197–200, 204–6, 326–33, 353, 362, 368, 374, 389, 452, 497, 500, 564

Ra, 308
Rabelais, François, 21
Racine, Jean, 193, 225
Radcliffe, Mrs Ann, 172
Raffalovich, (M.) A., 275, 284
Rainbow Edition, 96, 102, 443
Rameses, 161, 163, 178, 500
Raphael Sanzio, 217, 369, 389

Rappa, Countess Medusa, 533
Reade, Brian, 179, 305
Redfern, 496
Red Rose of Martyrdom, The, 281, 374
Reginald, 197, 205
Reid, Forrest, 121, 147, 149, 157, 262, 295; *Private Road*, 147, 149, 157, 262, 295
Reinhardt, Max, 311
Réjane, 68, 364
Reviewer, 557
Ricci, Sebastiano, 193, 195, 326
Rice, A. E., 179
Richards, Grant, 134, 149, 166, 167, 231, 236, 258, 259, 273, 276, 277, 397, 471, 476, 479, 489, 490, 498, 500, 501, 506, 507, 511, 515, 517, 518, 521, 522, 546, 549, 551, 557, 567, 568
Richardson, Aubrey, 274
Richardson, Samuel, 21
Richmond, Sir William, 269, 277
Ricketts, Charles, 269, 274, 284, 421, 431
Rienzi-Smith, Mrs, 227, 435
Robinson, Garrett, 268
Robinson, Mrs, 179, 279
Robson & Co. Ltd, 275
Rocktower, Lady, 225, 368, 383, 390, 494
Rolland, Romain, 339
Romuald, 138
Ronald, 138, 141, 205
Ronald Firbank, A Biography (Benkovitz), 18, 25, 34, 86, 87, 95, 101, 115–17, 118, 119, 124, 125, 128, 137, 139, 140, 141, 144, 147–50, 152, 155, 158, 159, 173, 176–8, 181, 182, 184, 187–9, 191, 194, 195, 201, 204, 205, 209, 211, 212, 213, 215–17, 223, 224, 228–30, 232, 234–237, 252, 261, 262, 270, 271, 276, 277, 283, 286, 299, 302, 313–16, 339, 342, 370, 373, 379, 380, 386, 388–90, 409, 410, 431, 443, 452, 454, 461, 471, 485, 487, 489–91, 493, 498, 500, 501, 504, 506, 507, 510, 517, 520, 522, 528, 529, 534, 543, 546, 548–50, 551, 553, 556–9, 563, 567
Ronald Firbank, A Memoir (Fletcher), 18, 25, 81, 86, 87, 94, 96–8, 108–10, 115–17, 119–23, 125, 132, 136, 137, 140, 143, 147–53, 155, 157–9, 163, 167, 168, 174, 176–80, 184, 185, 189, 191, 192, 199, 201, 204–6, 217, 223, 224, 226, 234, 235, 252, 253, 255, 261, 262, 264, 269, 272, 276, 285, 370, 373, 389, 390, 401, 409, 416, 426, 427, 431–4, 436, 449, 450, 476, 493, 500, 516, 520, 548, 551
Rops, Félicien, 190–2, 194, 210, 234, 377, 378, 390
Rose, Stuart, 87, 558
Rose of Lima, Saint, 282
Rosemerchant, Mr, 365
Rosemerchant, Mrs, 133, 148, 283, 312, 348, 364, 365, 384, 387, 389, 568

INDEX

Ross, Robert, 264, 269, 271, 272, 277, 280, 302, 305, 310, 338
Rossetti, D. G., 100
Rostand, Maurice, 295, 303
Rothenstein (Rutherston), Albert, 273
Rothenstein, William, 269, 273
Rubens, Sir P. P., 194, 230, 236
Rubinstein, Artur, 315
Rudlieb, Baroness (T.), 168, 282, 286, 288–90, 298, 309, 323, 335, 339, 366, 369, 376, 377, 386, 389, 390, 413, 420–6, 430, 431, 438, 519, 530
Ruiz, Madame, 555, 559
Ruiz, Vittorio, 555, 557
Runyon, Damon, 175
Ruskin, John, 196, 326
Rutherston, Albert, *see* Rothenstein, Albert

Sacerdotalism and Satanism, 165, 460
Sacher-Masoch, Leopold von (*Venus in Pelz*), 384, 390
Sackville-West, Victoria, 108, 144, 209
St Andrews, Duchess of, 214
St James Gazette, 254
Salome, 200, 218, 283, 288, 290, 296, 304–22, 327, 332, 333, 337, 339, 350, 418–20, 423, 425, 426, 428, 430, 450, 451, 459, 474, 513, 517, 560, 561
Salome (Salome) Or 'Tis A Pity That She Would, 105, 286, 290, 306, 313, 320, 418. See also *Artificial Princess, The*
Sanders, F. J. A., 275
Santal, 178, 218, 226, 233, 235, 236, 270, 280, 281, 302, 398, 400, 403, 432, 484, 486, 491, 493, 501–9, 528, 547, 548, 558, 566
Sappho, 68, 80, 229, 281, 284, 353, 358, 364–6, 384, 388, 404, 419, 427, 439, 441–8, 450, 456–460, 463, 466, 471, 493, 495, 496, 526, 542;
'Ode to Aphrodite', 443–6, 450, 455
Sargent, J. S., 364, 388
Sarmento, Duchess of, 561
Sarraute, Nathalie (*Fruits d'Or*), 250
Sassoon, Siegfried, 133, 145, 148, 149, 173, 177, 180, 397, 407, 409; *Siegfried's Journey*, 148, 149, 177, 180, 409
Satan, 28
Saunter, Lady Lucy, 347
Savoy, 382
Schiff, Sydney, 271
Schiller, J. C. F. von ('Ode to Joy'), 450
Schöne Mama, Die, 506, 529
Schweidler, A., 168, 179, 530
Scotsman, 102
Scott, Sir Oliver, 366, 389
Scott, R., 555
Scott, Sir Walter, 50
Scriabin, Alexander, 93
Seafairer, Lady, 209

Seafairer, Lord, 108, 209
Sebastian, Saint, 376
Secker, Martin, 258, 273, 389, 462
Seligman, Gerald, 265
Seth, 485
Seth, Emperor, 485
Sevenoaks, Lord, 108, 413, 414
Sevier, Michel, 500
Shakespeare, William, 8, 18, 33, 36, 50, 163, 304, 382, 534; Antony, 231, 308; *Antony and Cleopatra*, 308, 339; Bottom, 465; Claudius, 318, 561; *Hamlet*, 36, 50, 296, 317, 318, 339, 370, 561; Hermia, 465; Hermione, 351, 387, 498; Juliet, 474, 490; *Julius Caesar*, 434; *King Lear*, 371; Leontes, 352; Lysander, 465; *Macbeth*, 473; Mercutio, 102; *Midsummer Night's Dream*, 41, 50, 362, 382, 390, 465, 480; Moth, 383; Mustardseed, 383; Oberon, 465; Puck, 480; Peter Quince, 362; *Romeo and Juliet*, 471; Theseus, 36, 50; Titania, 465, 473; Tybalt, 483; *Winter's Tale*, 274, 351, 352, 362, 369, 370, 465, 498
Shamefoot, Mrs, 112, 127, 146, 148, 153, 161, 164, 165, 169, 176, 178, 222, 235, 247, 254, 281, 293, 303, 321, 326, 344, 347, 351, 354–6, 358, 359, 369, 374–6, 378, 379, 387–9, 403, 404, 409, 412, 433, 436, 437, 447, 449, 451–6, 458–61, 464, 478, 518
Shannon, Charles, 269
Shaw, George Bernard, 9, 32, 35, 73, 81, 192, 196, 205, 232, 249, 254, 304, 338, 370, 406, 465, 487, 497–500, 505, *Androcles*, 499; *Doctor's Dilemma*, 499; *Heartbreak House*, 491, 498, 499; *Irrational Knot*, 35; Lavinia, 499; *Man and Superman*, 254, 499; *Our Theatre in the Nineties*, 465; *Letters to Granville Barker*, 498; *Sixteen Self Sketches*, 254; Ann Whitefield, 499
Sheba (Saba), Queen of, 307, 338, 423, 428
Sheil-Meyer, Adrian, 231, 360, 361, 491, 492, 494, 496, 497
Sheil-Meyer, Nadine, 185, 231, 236, 322, 360, 381, 492, 494, 496, 497, 532
Shelley, Edward, 257
Shelley, Percy Bysshe, xiii, xv, 102, 249, 374; *Cenci*, 102
Shutter, E. A., 188
Siddons, Sarah, 471
Sidney, Sir Philip, xiii, xv
Siegfried, 466
Silex, Monsignor, 563
Simnel, Lambert, 107
Simmonds, Harvey, 388
Simon, 374
Sinquier, Canon, 170, 472, 474, 476
Sinquier, S., 170, 174, 179, 180, 471–5, 483, 490, 539
Sitwell, Dame Edith, 144

Sitwell, Sir Osbert, 12, 18, 94–8, 107, 108, 115, 116, 118, 119, 121, 129–32, 145–50, 152, 153, 159, 160, 163, 169, 173, 176–80, 184, 187, 190, 191, 205, 216, 235, 273, 278, 370, 372, 389, 416, 433, 434, 449, 478; *Laughter in the Next Room*, 118, 148, 176; *Noble Essences*, 132
Sitwell, Sacheverell, 99, 104, 129, 141, 144, 145, 148, 164, 169, 173, 273, 278, 362, 372, 389
Sixsmith, Mrs, 160, 472–4, 539
Smee, Mrs, 498
Smith, P. J. (*Tenth Muse*), 343, 344, 448
Smithers, Leonard, 210, 258, 260, 308, 382
Smollett, Tobias, 22
Snob, 559
Snowball, 555
Society for Theatre Research, 118
Society of Authors, 74, 96, 518, 557, 567
Socrates, xiii, xiv, 280, 283
Sodbury, Abbess of, 483
Somerset, Ragland, 276
Something, Lady (R.) (English Ambassadress at the court of Pisuerga), 134, 307, 308, 339, 348, 380, 387, 510–12, 521, 528, 534, 537, 538
Sontag, Susan, 21
Sophax, Mr, 347, 500
Sophocles (*Oedipus Rex*), 40
Sorrow in Sunlight, 73, 144, 175, 487, 546. See also *Drama in Sunlight, (A)*; *Prancing Nigger*
Sotheby & Co. Ltd, 86, 94, 117, 119, 128, 173, 184, 195, 204, 225, 312, 433
Southam, B. C., 235, 236
Souvenir d'Automne, 282, 302, 342
Spectre de la Rose, La, 349
Sphinx, 283–6, 288, 298–302, 308, 319, 347, 511, 512
Spirit Lamp, 302
Squire, Sir J. C., 12, 18, 82, 142, 245, 373, 378
Stagg, Hunter, 128, 148, 153, 177, 504
Steegmuller, Francis, 65
Steeple, Mrs, 221, 346, 370, 443–6, 455, 471
Stein, Gertrude (*Look at Me Now* . . .), 81
Stevenson, R. L., 8
Strauss, Richard, 283, 290, 294, 295, 305, 310–317, 326, 338, 339, 372, 429, 529, 553; *Elektra*, 294, 310, 315, 316, 339; *Feuersnot*, 310, 314; *Guntram*, 310, 314; *Strauss-Rolland Correspondence*, 339; *Der Rosenkavalier*, 310, 529; *Salome*, 290, 294, 305, 310, 311, 313–16, 326, 338, 339, 343, 429
Stravinsky, Igor, 442
Stokes, Sewell, 122, 147, 155, 177
Study in Opal, A, 282, 302, 375
Study in Temperament, A, 106, 108, 152, 176, 291, 292, 303, 323, 348, 356, 413, 414, 416, 418, 420

Stulik, Monsieur, 178
Sudermann, Hermann (*Magda*), 456
Sullivan, Sir Arthur (*Patience*), 254
Summer-Leyton, Lady Cleobulina, 348
Summer-Leyton, Sir Wroth, 348
Summers, Montague, 338
Sunday Times, 118
Surin, Father, 545
Sweet, Rosa, 348
Swinburne, A. C., 364, 443, 444; *Atalanta*, 444, 450
Synge, J. M., 456
Szladits, Lola L., 388

Tagor, Rabindranath, 477
Tail, H. Q., 323, 413, 415
Talboys, R. St. C, 232, 269, 290–3, 295, 296, 302, 303, 318, 334, 335, 349, 358, 374, 414, 452, 482, 526
Tales from Casanova, 307
Tanoski, Xavier, 348
Tarn, Pauline, 366. *See also* Vivien, Renée
Tatler, The, 469
Taylor, Elizabeth, 61
Tchekov, Anton, 498, 499
Teazle, Lady, 465
Teleny, 382, 390
Teresa of Ávila, Saint (T. de Cepeda y Ahumada), 19, 20, 23–6, 34, 69, 368, 369, 371, 376, 389, 562: *Way of Perfection*, 25, 369
Terrasson, Jean (*Life of Sethos*), 22
Tertius III, Pope, 123, 125, 171, 208, 563
Teyte, Maggie, 371
Thackeray, W. M., 10, 33, 545, 546; Crawley family, 21, 22, 545; Becky Sharp, 546; *Vanity Fair*, 22, 32, 33, 53, 545, 557
Thelma, Saint, 222, 383
Thérèse of Lisieux, Saint (M. F. T. Martin), 78
Thleeanouhee, ex-Princess, 208, 527
Thleeanouhee of Dateland, Queen, 208, 527, 528, 533, 535–7
Thompson, Flora (*Lark Rise*), 244
Thoroughfare, Dick, 191, 248, 302, 482, 483
Thoroughfare, Mrs E., 155, 177, 347, 348, 365, 366, 377, 379, 387, 389, 402, 479, 481–3
Thoroughfare, Marigold, 483
Thorpe, Isabella, 82, 87
Those Gonzagas, 463
Thumbler, Mira, 152, 176, 200, 311, 339, 448, 449, 451, 457, 475, 478
Thumbler, Mrs, 83, 353, 388, 440, 448
Thurber, James, 61
Tiepolo, G. B., 192, 193, 195, 205, 210, 308, 439, 459
Times, The, 101, 102, 125, 160, 178, 257, 389
Tintoretto, 196, 198, 326, 327, 340
Tiredstock, Lord, 538

INDEX

Titian (T. Vecelli), 84, 461
Tito, see Clemenza di Tito, La
Tivoli, Rose de, 114, 348, 362, 455. *See also* Brookes, Winsome
Tolga, Count of, 527
Tolga, Countess of (V.), 210, 368, 505, 527, 528, 531, 533, 536, 542, 543, 545
Tolstoy, Leo, 133, 148, 214; *War and Peace*, 41
Tonks, William, 162
Tooke, Dairyman, 480, 484
Tooke, Mrs, 476, 477, 484
Tooke, Thetis, 350, 374, 389, 483, 484, 541
Tooke family, 483, 484
Topolobampa, 203
Town Topics, 102
Tragedy in Green, A, 209, 270, 313, 339
Tredegar, Lord, 162, 189, 327, 362
Tree, Iris, 553
Tree, Tircis, 348
Tresilian, Enid, 185, 322, 326, 361, 492, 493, 496, 497, 539, 540
Tresilian, Eric, 231, 357, 494, 496, 497, 540
Trials of Oscar Wilde, The, 87, 258, 302
Trollope, Anthony, 452, 454
True Love, 25, 232
Tschaikovsky, P. I., 93
Turner, J. M. W., 194, 259
Turner, Reggie, 146, 258, 269
Twyford, Lady, 346
Tyrwhitt (Tyrwhitt-Wilson), G., 149. *See also* Berners, Lord

Ursula, Saint, 288
Ursula, Sister (of the Flaming-Hood), 537, 541, 545

Vaindreams, 231, 250, 309, 323, 372, 419, 432, 446, 456, 459
Vainglory, 25, 46, 68, 74, 82, 87, 99, 101, 108, 109, 112–14, 118, 119, 122, 124, 127, 132, 136, 138, 141, 142, 144–6, 148–50, 153–5, 158, 161, 164, 165, 167, 171, 173, 177, 183, 186, 188, 190–2, 200, 202, 205, 206, 208–10, 214, 217, 221, 226–8, 234–6, 247, 250, 254, 258, 259, 271, 273, 275, 276, 281, 287, 288, 291, 293, 296, 303, 308, 309, 311, 315, 317, 321, 323, 339, 342, 344, 346–50, 352–4, 361, 364, 369, 372, 374–6, 378–80, 384, 387, 399, 403, 404, 411, 412, 416, 419, 430, 432–66, 469, 471, 472, 475, 478, 485, 486, 488–90, 492, 498, 500, 509, 518, 526, 532, 534, 547, 548, 553, 554, 566
Valley, Miss, 25, 287, 346, 455, 459
Valmouth, Mayor of, 348
Valmouth, M.P. for, 469
Valmouth, 93, 94, 102, 105, 118, 120, 129, 133, 155, 166, 167, 170, 179, 191, 203, 206, 221, 284, 307, 326, 345, 348, 350, 357, 358, 362, 365, 366, 371, 374, 377–9, 381, 383, 387, 392, 399, 400, 433, 434, 469, 476–85, 490, 495, 501, 538, 543, 549. *See also Centenarians of Glennyfurry, The*; *Glenmouth*
Value of Smiles, The, 383
Vanbrugh, Sir John, 437
Vanloo, C., 492
Varna, Duchess of, 209, 234, 310, 328, 344, 354, 358, 359, 361, 387, 388, 526, 528, 530, 535–7, 543, 544
Varna, Duke of, 525
Vasari, Giorgio, 42, 77
Vatt, Sir Victor, 94, 348
Vauvilliers, Saint Aurora, 282, 369, 425
Vechten, Carl Van, 18, 73, 81, 82, 86, 87, 98, 103, 105, 128, 133, 142–7, 149, 173, 175, 176, 180, 187, 209, 224, 230, 236, 286, 287, 350, 358, 373, 383, 389, 414, 416, 467, 487, 497, 506, 517, 518, 520, 548–51, 557, 558, 564; *Nigger Heaven*, 175, 176
Velasquez, Don Diego, 107, 297, 548, 564
Venus, 22, 382, 408, 446–8, 450
Venus in Furs, see Sacher-Masoch, Leopold von
Verlaine, Paul, 267
Vermeer, Jan, 194
Veronese, Paolo, 374, 389
Verrocchio, Andrea del, 194, 423
Victoria, Queen, 171, 179, 180, 208, 221, 222, 268, 307, 308, 338, 428, 436, 496
Vie Parisienne, 503
Villon, François, 441
Vision of Salome, The, 294
Vivien, Renée (Pauline Tarn), 366, 367
Vizeu, Duchess-Dowager of, 561
Voltaire (F. M. Arouet), 406

Wagner, Richard, 227, 249, 435; *Tristan und Isolde*, 227
Waldorf, Bertie, 312, 355, 383, 388, 390, 459, 536
Waley, Arthur, 442
Walpole, H. (?), 364, 388, 440
Walton, Sir William, 93, 144, 153, 154, 157, 158, 177; *Belshazzar's Feast*, 93
Wardle, Miss, 453
Watson, Sabine, 440
Watteau, J. A., 76, 77, 531
Waugh, Evelyn, 98–101, 118, 208, 320, 321, 340, 351, 379, 430, 442, 485, 527; *Black Mischief*, 527; *Brideshead Revisited*, 340, 351; *Decline and Fall*, 100; *Handful of Dust*, 98
Wavering Disciple, The, 194, 200, 205, 339
Webster, John, 320, 321, 340, 428; *Duchess of Malfi*, 158, 320, 328, 340; *White Devil*, 340
West-Wind, Hon. Viola, 347, 369
West-Wind, M.P., Sir William, 347, 369

Wetme, Madame, 529, 535, 537, 539, 544, 545, 565
Whately, R., 50
When Widows Love, 234, 358
Whistler, J. M., 217
White, C. J., 189
White, Mrs, 204, 206
White-Morgan, Mr, 351, 352, 355. See also *Mr White Morgan, The Diamond-King*
Whooper, Mrs, 347
Whorwood, Jack, 483
Whorwood, Lieutenant, 483
Widow's Love, The, 234, 358
Wierus, 460
Wilde, Constance, 340
Wilde, Oscar, xiv, xv, 7, 8, 48, 76, 80–2, 87, 120, 132–4, 148, 149, 169, 171, 172, 179, 196, 201, 203, 213, 235, 240, 243–340, 342, 346, 347, 349, 365, 367, 371, 372, 375, 381, 385, 386, 401–3, 406, 411–15, 418–20, 425–31, 436, 437, 448, 449, 453, 455, 459, 474, 482, 487, 492, 494–6, 499, 509, 510, 512, 546, 554, 564–566, 568; *Artist as Critic*, 340; *Birthday of the Infanta*, 297, 425, 564; Lady Bracknell, 82, 87, 182, 262, 482, 494; Cecily Cardew, 82, 407; Mabel Chiltern, 407; Sir Robert Chiltern, 7, 18, 54, 303, 346; *Decay of Lying*, 262, 265, 276; *De Profundis*, 18, 148, 253, 261, 269, 302, 431; Gwendolen Fairfax, 82, 87, 111; *Happy Prince*, 256; *Ideal Husband*, 18, 303; *Importance of Being Earnest*, 18, 82, 87, 257, 271; *Intentions*, 258, 276; Jokanaan, 306, 326, 327, 340; *Lady Windermere's Fan*, 302; Lane, 257; *Letters*, 18, 81, 148, 179, 254, 256, 258, 275–8, 280, 301–3, 338–40, 386, 431, 459; *Lord Arthur Savile's Crime*, 302; *Model Millionaire*, 329, 420; Algernon Moncrief, 7, 18, 82, 87; *Phrases and Philosophies*, 335, 340; *Picture of Dorian Gray*, 244, 254, 256, 275, 414, 459; *Portrait of Mr W. H.*, 18, 257; *Sainte Courtisane*, 421, 431, 448; *Salome*, 246, 254, 290, 304, 305, 311, 324, 326–8, 337, 338, 340, 428, 429, 448, 474; *Salome* (trans. Douglas), 257, 276, 300, 327, 328, 338; *Sphinx* 283–5, 298, 319; *Sphinx Without a Secret*, 285, 288, 299, 301, 329; Lady Windermere, 283, 302, 346; *Woman of No Importance*, 18; Jack (Ernest) Worthing, 7, 182, 346, 482
Willy (H. Gauthier-Villars), 137
William of Pisuerga, King, 67, 68, 231
Wilmington, Lady Violet, 287, 352
Wilson, A. E., 77
Wilson, Colin (*Bernard Shaw*), 35
Wilson, Edmund, 102
Wilson, Sandy, 105
Wilson-Philipson, Lady, 345
Wind and the Roses, The, 433
Winnie, 342
Whipsdom, 381
Wodehouse, P. G., 494
Woman's World, 171
Women Queens of England, 171
Wookie, Brigadier, 361
Wookie, K., 186, 346, 349, 387, 453, 462
Wookie, Mrs, 186, 205, 361, 388, 453, 457, 462
Woolf, Leonard, 118, 344; *Beginning Again*, 118
Woolf, Virginia, 96, 344, 425, 435; *Between the Acts*, 425; Miss La Trobe, 425, 435; *Mrs Dalloway*, 435; Rezia Smith, 435
Worthing, Lady Henrietta, 282, 375, 389
Wyllie, Helen, see Carew, Helen
Wyllie, James, 269
Wyndham, Horace (*Speranza*), 203
Wyndham, Violet (*Sphinx and Her Circle*), 256, 271, 273, 278, 431

Yajñavalkya, Mrs, 231, 345, 401, 476–84, 489, 528, 555, 560
Yellow Book, 213, 258
Yousef of Pisuerga, Prince, 349, 387, 505, 513, 516, 517, 519, 520, 531–3, 535–7, 540–2, 545
Yvorra, Countess, 541, 542

Zeno, 360, 368
Zenobius, 442
Zeus, 442
Zoubaroff, Princess Z., 198, 205, 212, 219, 228, 259, 322, 326, 327, 341, 343, 345, 354, 357, 358, 360, 361, 368, 369, 374, 381, 387–90, 492–500. See also *Princess Zoubaroff, The*